WORLD OF KNOWLEDGE

Sandcastle Books

This edition published in 2008 by Sandcastle Books Ltd
The Stables
Sheriffs Lench Court
Sheriffs Lench
Worcs WR11 4SN
UK

From material originally produced for Grolier U.S.

ISBN 978-1-906020-17-0

Printed in Thailand

The Brown Reference Group plc
First Floor
9-17 St. Albans Place
London
N1 0NX
www.brownreference.com

TABLE OF CONTENTS

Aborigine	6
Addams, Jane	7
Africa	7
Aircraft	11
Alphabet	13
Amazon	14
America, Central	15
America, North	19
America, South	22
Amphibian	26
Ancient Civilizations	28
Animal	31
Arachnid	33
Archaeology	35
Argentina	36
Aristotle	37
Artists, World	38
Asia	42
Astronaut	46
Astronomy	48
Austria	51
Aztecs	52
Beethoven, Ludwig van	53
Bicycle and Motorcycle	53
Biology	54
Biome	56
Bird	58
Book	61
Botany	62
Brain and Nervous System	64
Brazil	65
Buddhism	67
Burr, Aaron	68
Caesar, Julius	69
Camouflage	69
Canada	70
Car	74
Caribbean Sea and Islands	76
Carnivore	78
Carson, Rachel	80
Cartoon and Animation	80
Castle	82
Chemistry	83
Chief Joseph	84
Chile	85
China	86
Circulatory System	88
City	90
Cleopatra	91
Climate and Weather	92
Colombia	94
Colombus, Christopher	95
Comet, Meteor, and Asteroid	96
Composers	98
Conquistadors	100
Constellation	101
Crazy Horse	102
Crime and Law Enforcement	102
Crusades	104
Crustacean	105
Cuba	106
Curie, Marie	107
Desert	108
Design	109
Dinosaur	110
Disaster	113
Dog	115
Earth	117
Earthquake	119
Easter Island	120
Ecology	121
Ecuador	122
Edison, Thomas Alva	123
Education	123
Egypt, Ancient	124
Einstein, Albert	126
Electricity	127
Element, Chemical	128
Ellington, Duke	130
Energy	130
Engine	131
Environment	134
Europe	135
Evolution	139
Extinction	141
Fish	142
Flag	144
Flood	146
Flower	147
Food Chain	149
Force and Motion	150
Fossil	152
France	153
Frank, Anne	155
Franklin, Rosalind	155
Fruit	156

Galaxy	157	Mammal, Hoofed	233
Gandhi	158	Manufacturing	236
Geography	160	Mao Zedong	238
Geology	162	Map	239
Germany	164	Mars	241
Goodall, Jane	166	Math and Numbers	242
Government	166	Matter	244
Grammar	168	Maya	246
Gravity	170	Medicine	247
Greece	171	Mercury	251
Greece, Ancient	172	Metals	252
Habitat	174	Mexico	254
Health	175	Michelangelo	256
Hearing	177	Microscope	257
Heat	178	Middle Ages	258
Hemingway, Ernest	179	Middle East	260
Hinduism	179	Mississippi	262
History	180	Mollusk	263
Hitler, Adolf	182	Money	264
Holocaust	183	Mongols	265
Incas	191	Moon	266
Index	192	Movies	267
Indian Subcontinent	192	Mozart, Wolfgang Amadeus	269
Indonesia	194	Museum and Gallery	270
Industrial Revolution	195	Music	272
Insect	197	Musical Instruments	274
Inuit	201	Musicians, World	276
Inventors and Inventions	202	Music, Popular	278
Ireland, Republic of	204	Napoleon	280
Islam	205	Natural Resources	281
Island	206	Navigation	283
Israel	208	Neptune	285
Italy	209	Netherlands, Belgium,	
Japan	211	and Luxembourg	286
Judaism	213	Newspaper and Magazine	288
Jupiter	214	Newton, Isaac	289
Korea	215	New Zealand	290
Korean War	216	Nightingale, Florence	291
Lake	217	Nixon, Richard Milhous	291
Language	218	Nobel Prize	292
Laser	220	Northwest Territories	293
Lens	221	Nursing	295
Leonardo da Vinci	222	Nutrition	296
Levers	222	Ocean and Sea	298
Library	223	Olmec and Toltec	299
Light	225	Olympic Games	300
Literature	226	Pacific Islands	302
Madison, Dolley	228	Pacific Ocean	304
Madison, James	228	Palestine	305
Magnetism	229	Panama	306
Malaysia	230	Peru	308
Mammal	231	Philippines	309

Philosophy	310	Taste and Smell	386
Photography	312	Technology	387
Physics	314	Telecommunications	389
Pilgrims, The	316	Thailand	391
Plant	317	Theater	392
Platypus	319	Tools	394
Pocahontas	319	Trade	396
Poland	320	Transportation	398
Pollution	321	Tubman, Harriet	400
Portugal	323	Turkey and the Caucasus	401
Prehistoric People	324	United Kingdom	403
Primates	326	United Nations	405
Printing	328	United States of America	406
Radar and Sonar	330	Uranus	410
Radio	331	Uruguay	411
Rainforest	333	Vegetables	412
Religion	334	Venezuela	413
Rembrandt	337	Venus	414
Renaissance	337	Victoria	415
Reproduction	339	Vietnam War	415
Reptile	341	Vikings	416
Revolution	344	Volcano	417
Ride, Sally	345	Warfare	419
River	345	Warhol, Andy	421
Road	346	Water	422
Robot	347	Waterfall	423
Rocket	348	Weights and Measures	424
Rodent	349	Wetlands	426
Roman Empire	351	Wilder, Laura Ingalls	427
Roosevelt, Eleanor	353	Wind	427
Roosevelt, Franklin Delano	354	Women's Rights Movement	428
Rowling, J.K.	355	Women's Suffrage	430
Russia and the Baltic States	355	World Trade Center	431
Satellites	357	World War I	432
Science	358	World War II	434
Scientist	360	Worm	436
Sea Mammal	362	Wright, Frank Lloyd	437
Seasons	364	Wright, Orville and Wilbur	438
Ship and Boat	365	Writers, American	439
Sight	367	Writers, World	441
Sitting Bull	368	X-ray	443
Skyscraper	369	Yukon Territory	444
Solar System	370	Zoology	445
Sound Recording	371		
Space Exploration	373		
Space Shuttle	375		
Spain	376		
Sports	378		
Stanton, Elizabeth Cady	382		
Star	383		
Sun	384		
Switzerland and Liechtenstein	385		

* ABORIGINE

The word *aborigine* describes the earliest known
people to live in a land. It is mostly used to
describe the first inhabitants of Australia.

The Aborigines of Australia left Southeast
Asia more than 40,000 years ago. They
probably crossed the ocean to Australia
by raft or dugout canoe.

Life in Australia
The Aborigines formed about 500 tribal
groups, each with its own language. Each
tribe claimed a territory (an area of land)
and wandered within that area to hunt,
fish, and gather food.

Each tribe was like a large family made
up of several clans, or groups, of 30 to
40 people. Each clan had an emblem,
or totem—usually an animal or a plant.
The Aborigines believed that all things on
Earth—people, animals, plants, and even
rocks—were important parts of nature
and of the unseen spirit world.

The Aborigines adapted to Australia's
often harsh conditions. They used spears
and several types of curved throwing
sticks called boomerangs—
some for sport, others for
hunting or fighting.
They also
created rock
carvings
and painted

pictures on cave walls and strips of
tree bark.

In 1788, when the first European
settlers came to Australia, there were
perhaps more than 300,000 Aborigines.
As the Europeans spread out, they drove
Aborigines from their lands into remote
areas. Many died from foreign diseases.

Modern Aborigines
Today there are about 352,000 Aboriginal
people in Australia, about 1.5 percent of
the national population. About one-third of
them are wholly Aborigine. The rest have
some European ancestry.

Most Aborigines live in cities and towns.
Their standard of living is generally much
lower than that of other Australians. In
the past few decades the government has
run programs to help the Aborigines get
jobs and houses.

The Aborigines want once more to live
freely on their ancestral lands. In 1992 the
Australian High Court ruled that the
Aborigines owned Australia before
Europeans arrived. From 1993
the Aborigines were allowed
to claim land as "natives,"
and they now own parts of
the Northern Territory, South
Australia, and Western
Australia.

*An Aboriginal
elder paints
sacred patterns
on the chest of
a young boy.*

✻ ADDAMS, JANE (1860–1935)

Jane Addams worked to make life better for women and for poor people. She founded Hull House, a center that could be used to help others.

Born in Cedarville, Illinois, on September 6, 1860, Jane Addams came from a wealthy family. She attended Rockford College and then went to medical school, but poor health forced her to drop out.

While traveling in England, Addams became impressed with Toynbee Hall. Founded in 1884, it was a settlement house—a place offering help to the poor.

In 1889, with the help of Ellen Gates Starr, Addams founded Hull House in Chicago. She opened its doors to the city folk from poor neighborhoods. Many of them had come from other countries to seek a better life. Some had not been to school and spoke no English.

By 1907 Hull House had grown to 13 buildings. It offered help with childcare, adult education, and other services. Meanwhile, Addams fought for new labor laws to protect children from having to work for money, and women from working more than eight hours a day. She tried hard to win women the right to vote. She also published books and articles, including *Twenty Years at Hull House*.

SEE ALSO: Nobel Prize; Women's Rights Movement

Jane Addams worked hard for world peace. In 1931 she was awarded a Nobel Peace Prize.

✻ AFRICA

Africa is the world's second largest continent in area after Asia. It is also the second most populous after Asia.

Africa is made up of 53 countries, six of which are islands. It lies across the equator, and much of it is extremely hot. In the north is the world's largest desert, the Sahara, which is almost the same size as the United States. Smaller deserts, the Namib and Kalahari, lie in Southern Africa.

Across Central Africa, near the equator, rainfall is high, and tropical rainforests grow. Between the forests and the deserts lie savannas—grassy plains dotted with trees.

Much of Africa is made up of plateaus (flat areas of land high above sea level). In the east the plateau is broken by the Great Rift Valley, a crack in Earth's crust created by volcanic activity. Some of Africa's largest lakes have formed in the Rift's long valleys.

The Nile River in Egypt is the world's longest river. Africa's rivers are generally full of rapids and waterfalls as they near the coast, making navigation difficult.

(continued on page 10)

KEY FACTS

AREA
11,667,000 sq. mi.
(30,316,000 sq. km)

POPULATION
784,445,000

COUNTRIES
53

RELIGIONS
Islam, Christianity, folk religions, animism

LANGUAGES
Over 1,000, including Arabic, Fulani, Hausa, Swahili, Xhosa

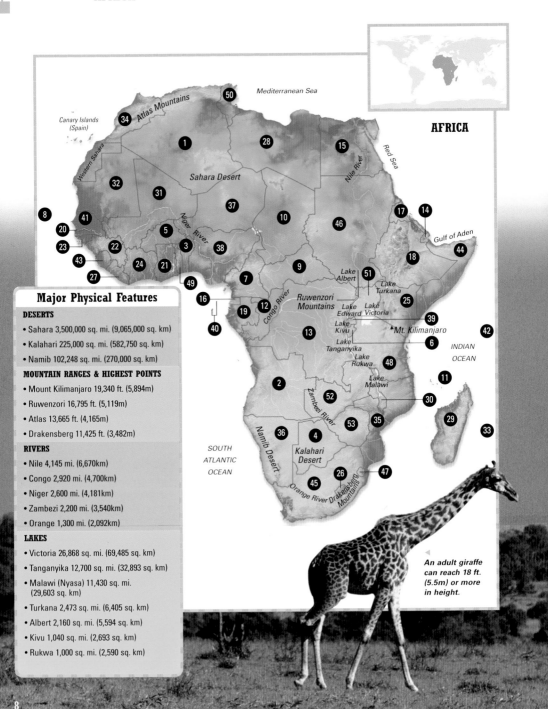

AFRICA

Mediterranean Sea

Canary Islands
(Spain)

Atlas Mountains

Western Sahara

Sahara Desert

Niger River

Nile River

Red Sea

Gulf of Aden

Congo River

Lake
Albert

Ruwenzori
Mountains

Lake
Turkana

Lake
Edward

Lake
Victoria

Lake
Kivu

Mt. Kilimanjaro

Lake
Tanganyika

INDIAN
OCEAN

Lake
Rukwa

Zambezi River

Lake
Malawi

SOUTH
ATLANTIC
OCEAN

Namib Desert

Kalahari
Desert

Orange River

Drakensberg
Mountains

Major Physical Features

DESERTS

- Sahara 3,500,000 sq. mi. (9,065,000 sq. km)
- Kalahari 225,000 sq. mi. (582,750 sq. km)
- Namib 102,248 sq. mi. (270,000 sq. km)

MOUNTAIN RANGES & HIGHEST POINTS

- Mount Kilimanjaro 19,340 ft. (5,894m)
- Ruwenzori 16,795 ft. (5,119m)
- Atlas 13,665 ft. (4,165m)
- Drakensberg 11,425 ft. (3,482m)

RIVERS

- Nile 4,145 mi. (6,670km)
- Congo 2,920 mi. (4,700km)
- Niger 2,600 mi. (4,181km)
- Zambezi 2,200 mi. (3,540km)
- Orange 1,300 mi. (2,092km)

LAKES

- Victoria 26,868 sq. mi. (69,485 sq. km)
- Tanganyika 12,700 sq. mi. (32,893 sq. km)
- Malawi (Nyasa) 11,430 sq. mi.
  (29,603 sq. km)
- Turkana 2,473 sq. mi. (6,405 sq. km)
- Albert 2,160 sq. mi. (5,594 sq. km)
- Kivu 1,040 sq. mi. (2,693 sq. km)
- Rukwa 1,000 sq. mi. (2,590 sq. km)

*An adult giraffe
can reach 18 ft.
(5.5m) or more
in height.*

COUNTRIES OF AFRICA

	Country	Flag	Population	Capital
1	Algeria		31,471,000	Algiers
2	Angola		12,878,000	Luanda
3	Benin		6,097,000	Porto-Novo
4	Botswana		1,622,000	Gaborone
5	Burkina Faso		11,937,000	Ouagadougou
6	Burundi		6,695,000	Bujumbura
7	Cameroon		15,085,000	Yaoundé
8	Cape Verde		428,000	Praia
9	Central African Rep.		3,615,000	Bangui
10	Chad		7,651,000	N'Djamena
11	Comoros		694,000	Moroni
12	Congo, Rep. of		2,943,000	Brazzaville
13	Congo, Dem. Rep. of		51,654,000	Kinshasa
14	Djibouti		638,000	Djibouti
15	Egypt		68,470,000	Cairo
16	Equatorial Guinea		453,000	Malabo
17	Eritrea		3,850,000	Asmara
18	Ethiopia		62,565,000	Addis Ababa
19	Gabon		1,226,000	Libreville
20	Gambia, The		1,305,000	Banjul
21	Ghana		20,212,000	Accra
22	Guinea		7,430,000	Conakry
23	Guinea-Bissau		1,213,000	Bissau
24	Ivory Coast		14,786,000	Yamoussoukro
25	Kenya		30,080,000	Nairobi
26	Lesotho		2,153,000	Maseru
27	Liberia		3,154,000	Monrovia
28	Libya		5,605,000	Tripoli
29	Madagascar		15,942,000	Antananarivo
30	Malawi		10,925,000	Lilongwe
31	Mali		11,234,000	Bamako
32	Mauritania		2,670,000	Nouakchott
33	Mauritius		1,158,000	Port Louis
34	Morocco		28,351,000	Rabat
35	Mozambique		19,680,000	Maputo
36	Namibia		1,726,000	Windhoek
37	Niger		10,730,000	Niamey
38	Nigeria		111,506,000	Abuja
39	Rwanda		7,733,000	Kigali
40	São Tomé & Príncipe		147,000	São Tomé
41	Senegal		9,481,000	Dakar
42	Seychelles		77,000	Victoria
43	Sierra Leone		4,854,000	Freetown
44	Somalia		10,097,000	Mogadishu
45	South Africa		40,377,000	Pretoria (administrative); Cape Town (legislative)
46	Sudan		29,490,000	Khartoum
47	Swaziland		1,008,000	Mbabane
48	Tanzania		33,517,000	Dar es Salaam
49	Togo		4,629,000	Lomé
50	Tunisia		9,586,000	Tunis
51	Uganda		21,778,000	Kampala
52	Zambia		9,169,000	Lusaka
53	Zimbabwe		11,669,000	Harare

Craftsmen in the West African kingdom of Benin created many beautiful bronze statues.

Plant and animal life

The plants, animals, reptiles, and birds of the deserts have had to adapt to the harsh, dry conditions. The equatorial rainforests are home to many animals, including gorillas, forest elephants, and tropical birds. On the savannas lion, cheetah, and hyena prey on antelope, zebra, and other grazing mammals. Across Africa, expanding human settlements are steadily invading wildlife habitats.

The people

Africa is home to many races and tribes. More than 1,000 languages are spoken south of the Sahara alone. The people of northern Africa are mostly Arabs and Berbers, who speak Arabic and follow the Islamic religion. The countries in Southern Africa are largely populated by black Africans. Most Africans are Muslim or Christian, although more than a quarter still follow ancient local beliefs.

Nomadic peoples, such as the Tuareg, wander the Sahara on camels, trading goods such as salt and dates as they have done for centuries. Elsewhere, most Africans live in villages and farm the land. Minerals, such as diamonds, gold, iron ore, and copper, are mined for export. Algeria, Libya, Nigeria, Angola, and Gabon are among Africa's chief oil producers. However, war, disease, and drought mean that Africa is home to two-thirds of the world's poorest countries.

Early civilizations

Fossils indicate that Africa is the continent where humans first evolved as long as seven million years ago.

Nearly 5,000 years ago ancient Egypt, one of the world's greatest early civilizations, arose in northern Africa. In 30 B.C. it became part of the Roman Empire, but continued to thrive. From about 1000 B.C. black peoples who spoke Bantu languages began to spread from their home in West Africa, displacing other peoples, and gradually dominating Central and Southern Africa. In the seventh century the Arabs conquered northern Africa and converted its peoples to Islam.

From colonization to today

For centuries people outside Africa knew little about the continent's interior. Between 1100 and 1500 Arabs trading gold, ivory, and slaves brought news of great empires in West Africa, such as Ghana, Mali, Songhai, Ife, Benin, and Kanem. News of Africa's great wealth attracted the curiosity of Europeans.

The Portuguese began mapping coasts of Africa in the 15th century. They were the first to export slaves from West Africa, a trade that continued into the 19th century. In 1652 the Dutch founded a settlement at Cape Town, later part of South Africa. By the late 19th century almost all of Africa was ruled by Europe.

Between the 1950s and 1970s most of the African colonies gained their independence from European rule. In 1994 South Africa became a democracy under Nelson Mandela. This ended the system of apartheid, in which black people had been separated from white people.

The cheetah is the fastest land animal. It can reach speeds of almost 70 mph (113km/h) as it hunts prey such as zebra and antelope on the savannas.

SEE ALSO: Egypt, Ancient

✳ AIRCRAFT

Airplanes have had a great impact on our lives. They are a convenient, speedy method of travel and transport. They have also changed the nature of war.

Before the beginning of the last century people had only flown in balloons and gliders. However, the development of the gasoline engine and a propeller system enabled Orville and Wilbur Wright to make the first powered, controlled flight in December 1903.

Forces in action

An airplane is heavier than air, so it can fly only if air flows over its wings fast enough to produce an upward force called lift. This force must be stronger than the force of gravity, the force that pulls objects toward the ground. A third force, called thrust, produced by a plane's engines, moves the plane forward through the air. Thrust must be stronger than another force, called drag. Drag is the resistance of the air to anything moving through it.

The force of lift can be explained by looking at the pressure of air particles on the wings. A wing has a curved top surface and a relatively flat lower surface. As the wing moves through the air, the air particles flow either over or under the wing and meet again behind it. The air passing over the top of the wing has a longer distance to travel than the air passing under the wing, so it has to move faster. This means that there is less pressure acting on the top of the wing than on the underside, and that pulls the wing up. This upward force is lift. As

▲ *The B-2 Spirit is a multirole bomber that can deliver both conventional and nuclear bombs. It has a crew of two pilots.*

FORCES ON AIRPLANES

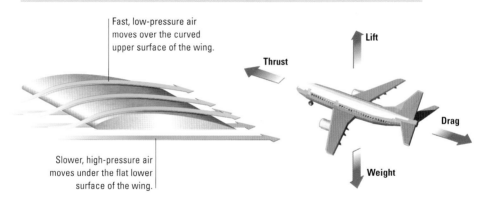

Fast, low-pressure air moves over the curved upper surface of the wing.

Thrust

Lift

Drag

Slower, high-pressure air moves under the flat lower surface of the wing.

Weight

an airplane moves faster along a runway, the lift increases until it is strong enough to overcome the force of gravity and lift the airplane's weight.

More lift is created as the result of the air pushing up on the underside of the wing. In normal flight the wing is tilted, so the front is slightly higher than the back. When the air strikes the underside of the wing, it is deflected, or turned, downward. The force of this deflected air exerts an equal force in the opposite direction, upward against the bottom of the wing. This force provides as much as a quarter of the lift on a wing.

Thrust

At first planes had engines that drove propellers, which scooped their way through the air to provide thrust. Modern planes have jet engines, which work on a similar principle, but have fans inside the engine to suck the air through them. As the air is forced out of the back of the engine, it pushes the aircraft forward.

The fastest planes travel faster than sound. When an aircraft reaches the speed of sound (roughly 750 mph), it breaks the sound barrier. Because the plane is traveling faster than the sound waves in the air, it creates shock waves behind the plane. They explode in a loud sonic boom. It is mainly military aircraft that travel this fast, but there is one supersonic passenger jet, the Concorde.

AMAZING FACTS !

The first powered flight lasted only 12 seconds over a distance of 120 ft. (36.5m), which is less than the wingspan of today's jumbo jets.

The fastest jet is the Lockheed SR-71A Blackbird. It has reached a top speed of 2,193.167 mph (3,537.366km/h), three times the speed of sound, and has held this record since 1976. It is painted black to reduce the effects of heating due to friction with the air.

Helicopters

A helicopter can fly in any direction—forward, backward, to the side, or straight up—as well as hover in one place. The first design for a helicopter dates from the late 1400s, but the first practical helicopter was not developed until the 1930s. The rotor blades of a helicopter are powered by an engine. They provide the lift to hold the helicopter up in the air, as well as the propelling force to move it in all directions. Helicopters can land in small areas, such as a roof, or hover while they lower supplies or rescue disaster victims.

A Coast Guard Jayhawk HH-60J helicopter patrols over New York City. It can stay airborne for about six hours.

SEE ALSO: Engine; Wright, Orville & Wilbur

✳ ALPHABET

An alphabet is a list of signs that are used to write down a language. The signs, called letters, usually represent the sounds of the language.

The earliest writing was made up of simple pictures that represented words. The first writing systems were developed about 3000 B.C. by the Sumerians, who lived in Mesopotamia (modern Iraq), and the Egyptians. The Sumerian writing was called cuneiform, and the Egyptian writing was called hieroglyphs.

Having a picture for every word meant that a huge number of signs were needed. The Egyptians and Sumerians soon simplified their writing by choosing a symbol for each syllable (part of a word) and combining symbols to write words.

The first alphabet

The Phoenicians, who were based on the coast of modern Syria and Lebanon, developed the first alphabet in about 1100 B.C. It had 22 symbols for consonant sounds—you had to guess the vowel sounds. Each symbol had a name. The first two symbols, or letters, were *aleph*, the Phoenician word for bull, and *beth*, the word for house. From these names came our word "alphabet."

About the eighth century B.C. the Greeks took over the Phoenician alphabet, but used some of the symbols as vowel signs. For the first time each sound in their language had its own sign.

Later the Etruscans of northern Italy introduced more changes to the alphabet. The Romans adapted the Etruscan alphabet, and by the third century they used much the same alphabet we know today, but without J, U, W, Y, or Z. By the first century B.C. Y and Z had been added. The remaining letters came much later.

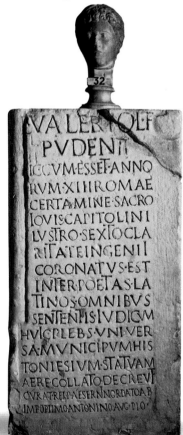

◄
The Romans used capital letters because they were easier to carve onto stone monuments.

AMAZING FACTS !

J was not introduced into the alphabet used in most of Europe and English-speaking countries until the 17th century.

The Romans only used capital letters (which were easier to carve in stone). Small letters were introduced when people started to use pens and brushes and wanted to write more speedily.

👀
SEE ALSO:
Ancient Civilizations;
Egypt, Ancient

✳ AMAZON

The Amazon is South America's most important river and the second-longest river in the world. Only the Nile River, in Africa, is longer.

The Amazon is about 4,007 miles (6,449km) long, and it carries more water than the Nile, the Mississippi, and the Chang Jiang (Yangtze) of China put together. Its source is a glacier high in the Andes Mountains of southern Peru. On its journey to the Atlantic Ocean the Amazon gathers water from hundreds of tributaries, some of which are over 1,240 miles (2,000km) long. The tributaries are fed by heavy tropical rains and melting

(1,609km) to Manaus, Brazil. Smaller vessels travel as far as Iquitos, Peru.

The eight countries of the Amazon basin—Bolivia, Brazil, Colombia, Ecuador, Guyana, Peru, Suriname, and Venezuela—have a written agreement to develop and share the wealth of the region. However, because the Amazon Basin is home to unique varieties of plants and animals, many scientists have opposed large-scale development of the area.

The Amazon winds through dense rainforests in Brazil.

snow from the Andes Mountains. In some places the Amazon is so wide that it is impossible to see the opposite shore.

The Amazon's huge drainage basin—the world's largest—occupies more than one-third of the South American continent. Much of it is covered with some of the world's thickest rainforests, a source of valuable timber. There are rich deposits of gold, bauxite (aluminum ore), copper, tin, and iron ore. Several highways cross the region, but the river is still a major form of transportation. Oceangoing ships can travel upstream about 1,000 miles

AMAZING FACTS !

In a single second the Amazon pours more than 55 million gallons (200,000 cubic meters) of water into the Atlantic Ocean.

SEE ALSO: America, South; River

✳ AMERICA, CENTRAL

Central America is an isthmus (a narrow bridge of land) that connects North and South America. It has coasts on both the Pacific Ocean and the Caribbean Sea.

The term "Central America" generally refers to Guatemala, Honduras, El Salvador, Nicaragua, Costa Rica, and Panama, republics that share a common history. Geographically, Belize is included, although it has a very different history.

Land and climate
Four-fifths of Central America is either hilly or mountainous. There are many volcanoes, some of which are still active. Earthquakes are common and have destroyed some cities more than once.

There are two main breaks in the mountains—one in Nicaragua and one in Panama. These two countries are mostly low lying and have areas of dense jungle. Northern Guatemala and much of Belize are also jungle lowland. Most of the people of Guatemala, Costa Rica, Honduras, and El Salvador live in the highlands.

The Central American climate is tropical, and temperatures are generally high. The highland regions experience wet and dry seasons, but the low-lying regions get heavy rainfall throughout the year.

Plant and animal life
Eastern lowland Central America is covered by rainforest. At an altitude of 6,500 ft. (1,980m) in southwestern Costa Rica is a rare habitat called cloud forest, which is dripping wet throughout the year. Native mammals include jaguars, ocelots, peccaries, howler monkeys, and spider monkeys. North American animals such as pumas and coyotes have migrated south to the region. There are many reptiles, birds, and insects. Central American wildlife is threatened by the growing human population.

Shoppers and traders in the market in Chichicastenango, Guatemala.
▼

Economy

Central America is mainly an agricultural region. The chief export crops are coffee, bananas, and cotton. Sugarcane and rice flourish along the coast. Hemp (used in making rope) and chicle (used in chewing gum) are important products of the jungle regions. Forested areas provide valuable hardwoods, such as mahogany. Fishing is important along the coasts.

Central America has limited resources and one of the highest population growth rates in the world. Industry cannot provide enough jobs for the landless, and falling prices for many exports make it harder for governments to meet the needs of their peoples. In 1998 Hurricane Mitch killed more than 10,000 people and left three million homeless, mostly in Honduras and Nicaragua.

People

Guatemala is a largely Indian nation. Its citizens are descendants of the Maya, an advanced civilization whose empire flourished in the region before the coming of the Europeans. Honduras, El Salvador, and Nicaragua also have a strong Indian heritage, although the people today are mainly mestizo—of mixed Indian and European (chiefly Spanish) ancestry. The population of Costa Rica is largely Spanish in origin. Many people in Belize are descended from black African slaves brought there from the West Indies. Panama contains a mixture of all these different groups.

The populations of most Central American countries have long been divided into wealthy landowners and poor campesinos (peasants). Land ownership is the chief form of wealth in Central America and the main source of political power. Most of the people depend on the big landowners for their living. Some campesinos can only find work in busy seasons of the year. Others work on the big estates in return for the right to grow food for themselves on a small patch of ground. Landless peasants who have moved to the cities often return at harvest time to work on the large estates.

History

Maya-speaking peoples have lived in the northern part of Central America for about 3,000 years. Mayan civilization reached its height from about A.D. 325 to 975.

Christopher Columbus sailed along the coast of Central America in 1502. A decade later, in 1513, Spanish explorer Vasco Núñez de Balboa arrived. The Spanish conquered the region and controlled it for 300 years.

(continued on page 18)

◄ *Central America was once home to the Maya people, who were talented artists and sculptors. This figure is an incense burner.*

Volcán Poás is an active volcano in Costa Rica. It stands in a national park full of forest wildlife. ▼

COUNTRIES OF CENTRAL AMERICA

	Country	Flag	Population	Capital
1	Belize		241,000	Belmopan
2	Costa Rica		4,023,000	San José
3	El Salvador		6,276,000	San Salvador
4	Guatemala		11,385,000	Guatemala City
5	Honduras		6,485,000	Tegucigalpa
6	Nicaragua		5,074,000	Managua
7	Panama		2,856,000	Panama City

The white-throated capuchin is a small monkey that lives in the forests of Central America.

Divers swim with manta rays off the coast of Central America. Ecotourism— which encourages conservation of the environment while allowing visitors to enjoy its wildlife and natural beauty— is an increasingly important industry in the region.

CENTRAL AMERICA

Belmopan
Caribbean Sea
Gulf of Honduras
Sierra Madre
Motagua River
Mosquito Coast
Guatemala City
San Salvador
Tegucigalpa
Coco River
Gulf of Fonseca
Rio Grande de Matagalpa
Managua
Lake Nicaragua
PACIFIC OCEAN
San José
Cordillera de Talamanca
Panama Canal
Coronado Bay
Panama City
Gulf of Panama

In 1821 what are now Guatemala, El Salvador, Honduras, Nicaragua, and Costa Rica became independent from Spain. Panama gained independence from Colombia in 1903. Belize was a British colony until 1981.

During the 1800s much of Central America was torn by political struggles between liberal and conservative groups.

The disputes often led to civil wars and sometimes to military invasions of neighboring countries. By the early 1900s some leaders had become dictators who stayed in office for long periods of time, often using threats and violence to remain in power against the wishes of the people. Armies also grew powerful and usually supported the interests of the wealthy landowners.

Since World War II (1939–45) there have been revolutions led by people seeking social and economic change. In 1948 a new civilian government was elected in Costa Rica, followed by Guatemala, Honduras, and El Salvador in the 1980s and Nicaragua in 1990.

Cars, bicycles, and pedestrians crowd a busy street in downtown San Salvador, the capital city of El Salvador.

KEY FACTS

AREA
Area: 202,000 sq. mi. (523,000 sq. km)

LARGEST COUNTRY
Nicaragua

SMALLEST COUNTRY
El Salvador

POPULATION
36,340,000

COUNTRIES
7

RELIGIONS
Roman Catholic, Evangelical Protestant, Church of England (Belize)

LANGUAGES
Spanish, English (Belize), Indian languages

SEE ALSO: America, South; Columbus, Christopher; Maya; Panama

✳ AMERICA, NORTH

The continent of North America is made up
of three large countries—Canada, the United
States, and Mexico.

North America is the world's third largest
continent in area, after Asia and Africa.
Its greatest length from north to south is
about 5,300 miles (8,500km). Its greatest
width from east to west is about 4,000
miles (6,400km). Along with Canada, the
United States, and Mexico, North America
is sometimes said to include Central
America and numerous islands, including
Greenland (a vast territory of Denmark)
and the islands of the Caribbean Sea,
most of which are independent countries.
North America's climate ranges from polar
in the north to tropical in the south.

The major regions of North America
are the North American Cordillera, the
Appalachian Highlands, the Great Central
Plain, and the Canadian Shield.

The North American Cordillera is an
extensive mountain system that stretches
from north to south across western North
America. It includes the Rocky Mountains,
the Alaska Range, the Coast Mountains,
the Cascade Range, the Sierra Nevada,
and the mountains of the Sierra Madre.

*The Bow River
flows through
Banff National
Park in the
Canadian
Rockies.*

Major Physical Features

MOUNTAIN RANGES & HIGHEST POINTS
- Alaska Range: Mt. McKinley 20,320 ft. (6,194m)
- Sierra Madre: Citlaltepetl (Pico de Orizaba)
  18,405 ft. (5,610m)
- Rocky Mountains: Mt. Elbert 14,433 ft. (4,399m)

RIVERS
- Mississippi 3,741 mi. (6,020km)
- Mackenzie 2,635 mi. (4,241km)
- Missouri 2,315 mi. (3,725km)
- Yukon 1,979 mi. (3,185km)

LAKES
- Lake Superior 31,820 sq. mi. (82,414 sq. km)
- Lake Huron 23,010 sq. mi. (59,596 sq. km)
- Lake Michigan 22,400 sq. mi. (58,016 sq. km)
- Great Bear Lake 12,275 sq. mi. (31,800 sq. km)

DESERTS
- Chihuahuan 196,700 sq. mi. (509,500 sq. km)
- Sonoran 120,000 sq. mi. (310,800 sq. km)

COUNTRIES OF NORTH AMERICA

	Country	Flag	Population	Capital
❶	Canada		31,081,900	Ottawa
❷	Mexico		98,881,000	Mexico City
❸	United States		281,421,906	Washington, D.C.

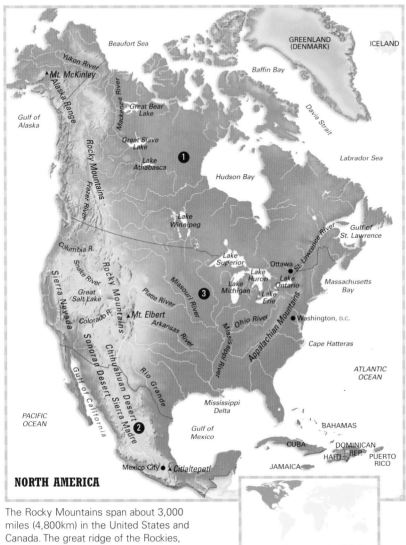

NORTH AMERICA

Beaufort Sea
GREENLAND (DENMARK)
ICELAND
Yukon River
Mt. McKinley
Baffin Bay
Alaska Range
Mackenzie River
Great Bear Lake
Gulf of Alaska
Davis Strait
Great Slave Lake
Rocky Mountains
Lake Athabasca
Labrador Sea
Hudson Bay
Frazer River
Lake Winnipeg
Gulf of St. Lawrence
Columbia R.
Lake Superior
Ottawa
St. Lawrence River
Snake River
Missouri River
Lake Huron
Lake Ontario
Massachusetts Bay
Sierra Nevada
Great Salt Lake
Rocky Mountains
Platte River
Lake Michigan
Lake Erie
Colorado R.
Mt. Elbert
Arkansas River
Ohio River
Washington, D.C.
Mississippi River
Appalachian Mountains
Cape Hatteras
Sonoran Desert
Chihuahuan Desert
Rio Grande
ATLANTIC OCEAN
PACIFIC OCEAN
Gulf of California
Sierra Madre
Mississippi Delta
Gulf of Mexico
BAHAMAS
CUBA
DOMINICAN REP.
HAITI
PUERTO RICO
Mexico City
Citlaltepetl
JAMAICA

The Rocky Mountains span about 3,000 miles (4,800km) in the United States and Canada. The great ridge of the Rockies, called the Continental Divide, separates river systems that flow to opposite sides of the continent. The Sierra Madre is the chief mountain range of Mexico. Its highest peak is the volcano Citlaltepetl (Pico de Orizaba), at 18,405 ft. (5,610m).

The Appalachian Highlands consist of a broad plateau with several mountain ranges, including the Green Mountains in Vermont, the White Mountains in Maine and New Hampshire, and the Blue Ridge Mountains, which run from Pennsylvania to Georgia. The highest point in the Appalachians is Mount Mitchell, at 6,684 ft. (2,037m). The Great Central Plain lies between the Cordillera and the Appalachians. A low ridge that extends from Newfoundland to the Rocky Mountains divides it into northern and southern sections. The Canadian Shield extends over much of eastern and northern Canada. It contains the oldest and hardest rocks in North America. The action of glaciers pockmarked the region with a large number of lakes. It also has many bogs and swamps.

Rivers and lakes

North America has five major river systems named for the bodies of water they drain into. The Arctic system includes the Mackenzie, the Saskatchewan, and the Nelson. In the Atlantic system the major river is the St. Lawrence. The Gulf system includes the great Mississippi and all its tributaries. In the Pacific system the Columbia and the Frazer are the most important. The inland system is made up of streams that do not drain into the sea.

North America has more lakes than any other continent. The five Great Lakes, four of which are shared by the United States and Canada, are some of the largest bodies of water in North America. Lake Superior is the world's largest freshwater lake. Other major lakes, all in Canada, are Great Bear Lake, Great Slave Lake, Lake Athabasca, and Lake Winnipeg. Lake Chapala is the largest lake in Mexico.

Plant and animal life

The far north has no trees; the only vegetation is reindeer moss and a few hardy plants that grow during the brief Arctic summer. The Great Central Plain has large areas of prairie. The dry environment of the southwestern United States and northern Mexico is ideal for cacti. The coastal areas of central and southern California are home to chaparral and other scrub vegetation. Although many of the forests that once covered North America have been cut down, more than 1,000 varieties of trees remain.

The northern tundra is home to muskox, caribou, and polar bears. Wolves, coyotes, moose, bears, and a great variety of birds and fish inhabit the great forest region to the south. Deer and pronghorn roam the western mountain valleys, while bighorn sheep and Rocky Mountain goats live in the northern ranges.

Vast herds of bison once covered the Great Plains, but they were nearly wiped out by hunters. Today only gophers and prairie dogs remain on most of the plains. The eastern forests contain many kinds of birds, as well as deer, squirrels, porcupines, beavers, and foxes. Alligators and opossums live in the southern wetlands. Tropical Mexico has a wide variety of animal life, including parrots and other birds, jaguars, tapirs, and monkeys.

North America's coastal waters are rich in commercial food fish and valuable shellfish. Seals, walruses, and whales are found in the Arctic waters.

American bison were hunted almost to extinction in the 19th century, but today they are returning to roam the Great Plains.
▼

SEE ALSO: America, Central; Canada; Caribbean Sea & Islands; Mexico; United States of America

✷ AMERICA, SOUTH

The continent of South America contains
12 countries and some of the world's most
amazing natural features, including the longest
mountain range and the largest river basin.

KEY FACTS

AREA
6,883,000 sq. mi.
(17,827,000 sq. km)

COUNTRIES
12

LARGEST COUNTRY
Brazil

SMALLEST COUNTRY
Suriname

POPULATION
345,782,000

RELIGIONS
Roman Catholicism, traditional African beliefs

LANGUAGES
Spanish, Portuguese, Indian languages, English, Dutch, French

South America ranks fourth in area and fifth in population among the world's continents. It makes up most of the larger cultural region known as Latin America, which also includes Mexico, Central America, and many of the islands of the Caribbean Sea. These three regions, although geographically part of North America, share a common heritage and historical experience with South America. South America also includes two territories that belong to European countries: French Guiana, an overseas department of France, and the Falkland Islands, a British crown colony.

Land and climate

South America has three main geographical regions. In the west the Andes, the longest mountain range on any continent, run down the entire length of South America. The Eastern Highlands include the Brazilian and Guiana highlands. A vast interior lowland contains the Amazon Basin and a cool, dry, windswept area, called Patagonia, in the southern part of the continent. The interior lowland is drained by three great river systems: the Amazon, the Paraná-Río de la Plata (consisting of the Paraguay, Paraná, Uruguay, and Río de la Plata rivers), and the Orinoco.

South America does not have the extremes of temperature found in North America. Its northern bulge lies on or near the equator, giving the area a hot, humid climate, with heavy rain and temperatures averaging 80°F (27°C). The coldest regions are Tierra del Fuego and the Andes, where temperatures can fall below 32°F (0°C). The highest temperatures occur in the Gran Chaco, with readings above 100°F (38°C) common in summer.

Plant and animal life

More than 40 percent of South America is forested. About 30 percent is grassland, which is ideal for raising cattle. Animal life includes jaguars, mountain lions, capybaras (the world's largest rodent), vampire bats, giant armadillos, and many snakes and insects. The llama, alpaca, guanaco, and vicuña—all related to the camel—are used as pack animals and are prized for their wool. South America is home to many species of fish, including the meat-eating piranha. It also has more species of birds than any other continent.

(continued on page 24)

A Quechua woman tends her alpacas in the mountains of Peru. Alpacas are raised mainly for their soft wool.

ATLANTIC OCEAN

SOUTH AMERICA

Caracas
Port-of-Spain
Lake Maracaibo
Orinoco River
Georgetown
Paramaribo
Cayenne
FRENCH GUIANA (FRANCE)
Magdalena River
Bogotá
Llanos
Guiana Highlands
Mt. Roraima
Mouths of the Amazon
Quito
Negro River
Amazon River
Selvas
Madeira River
Mt. Huascarán
Araguaia River
Tocantins River
São Francisco River
Lima
Brasília
Lake Titicaca
La Paz
Sucre
Paraná River
Brazilian Highlands
Pico da Bandeira
Atacama Desert
Andes
Gran Chaco
Paraguay River
Asunción
Salado River
Paraná River
Uruguay River
PACIFIC OCEAN
Mt. Aconcagua
Santiago
Pampas
Buenos Aires
Montevideo
Río de la Plata
Colorado River
ATLANTIC OCEAN
Patagonia
Tierra del Fuego
FALKLAND ISLANDS (GREAT BRITAIN)
Cape Horn

Major Physical Features

DESERTS

• Atacama 70,000 sq. mi. (180,000 sq. km)

MOUNTAIN RANGES & HIGHEST POINTS

• Andes: Mt. Aconcagua 22,834 ft. (6,960m); Huascarán 22,205 ft. (6,768m)

• Brazilian Highlands: Pico da Bandeira 9,482 ft. (2,890m)

• Guiana Highlands: Mount Roraima 9,094 ft. (2,771m)

RIVERS

• Amazon 4,007 miles (6,449km)

• Paraná-Río de la Plata 3,032 miles (4,879km)

• São Francisco 1,811 miles (2,914km)

• Orinoco 1,700 miles (2,740km)

• Araguaia 1,632 miles (2,627km)

•LAKES

• Maracaibo 5,100 sq. mi. (13,210 sq. km)

• Titicaca 3,205 sq. mi. (8,300 sq. km)

• Poopó 977 sq. mi. (2,530 sq. km)

COUNTRIES OF SOUTH AMERICA

	Country	Flag	Population	Capital
❶	Argentina		37,032,000	Buenos Aires
❷	Bolivia		8,329,000	La Paz (administrative); Sucre (constitutional)
❸	Brazil		170,115,000	Brasília
❹	Chile		15,211,000	Santiago
❺	Colombia		42,321,000	Bogotá
❻	Ecuador		12,646,000	Quito
❼	Guyana		861,000	Georgetown
❽	Paraguay		5,496,000	Asunción
❾	Peru		25,662,000	Lima
❿	Suriname		417,000	Paramaribo
⓫	Uruguay		3,337,000	Montevideo
⓬	Venezuela		24,170,000	Caracas

The toucan, known for its large beak, is one of many colorful birds that live in South American rainforests.

People

South America covers about 12 percent of the world's land surface but contains fewer than 6 percent of its people, though the population is increasing rapidly—more quickly than that of any continent except Africa. About 75 percent of the population live in or near cities. Many parts of South America are too densely forested, too mountainous, or too barren for human settlement.

The people are chiefly of Indian, Spanish, and Portuguese descent, but there are significant numbers with other European, African, and Asian origins. Spanish and Portuguese are the continent's dominant languages.

Economy

South America is rich in natural resources. Brazil is one of the world's largest producers of iron ore and a major producer of manganese and bauxite (aluminum ore). Chile is one of the world's

Chungara Lake in Lauca National Park, Chile, is one of the world's highest lakes.

Maracana Stadium in Rio de Janeiro, Brazil, is the world's largest soccer stadium. When it was built in 1950 it could hold more than 199,000 fans, but now it can only hold 88,000 safely.

two leading copper-mining countries. Bolivia is among the world's top tin producers. Venezuela has South America's largest petroleum deposits and is a major oil exporter. Colombia is one of the world's chief sources of emeralds.

Agriculture has always played the most important role in South America's economy. Corn is the most widely grown food crop. Major commercial crops include coffee, bananas, sugarcane, wheat, and cacao (or cocoa beans). Brazil and Argentina are the continent's major cattle-raising countries. Fish are important both as a source of food and as an export.

The tropical rainforests are a source of valuable hardwoods, chiefly mahogany and rosewood, which are used to make fine furniture. Other important forest products include rubber, nuts, tannin (used to tan leather), palm oil, waxes, and chicle (the base for chewing gum).

History

The first people to live in South America, the ancestors of the Indians, probably came from North America. The most sophisticated Indian civilization that emerged was that of the Incas, who lived in the Andean highlands of what are now Peru, Bolivia, and Ecuador.

The first European known to have reached South America was Christopher Columbus, who landed at the mouth of the Orinoco River in 1498. Spanish adventurers known as conquistadors, drawn to the region by the lure of gold and silver, overcame the native peoples. Although relatively few in number, the Europeans were better armed, and the Indians were weakened by new European diseases and by disputes. Roman Catholic priests arrived with the first colonists to convert the Indians to Christianity. The Catholic church is still a powerful force.

In the late 1700s and early 1800s South Americans began to feel unhappy about being ruled by European countries. The leaders in the struggle for independence suffered early defeats against Spanish troops before victory was finally achieved in 1824. Only Brazil had no major war of liberation, winning independence from Portugal peacefully in 1822. By 1830, 10 of the 12 modern South American nations had formed. Guyana gained independence in 1966 and Suriname in 1975.

Unlike Brazil, which was a monarchy until 1889 and was relatively stable, the 19th-century Spanish-speaking republics were frequently torn by political conflict. Unstable governments led to the rise of military rulers. Uneasy relations between countries led to several long and bloody wars. During the 1950s and 1960s ineffective governments were often overthrown by the military. A pattern of military regimes alternating with civilian rule lasted until the early 1990s, when democratically elected governments were restored throughout the continent. South America's continuing problems include the growing population, poverty, a shortage of schools, and a huge foreign debt.

SEE ALSO: Amazon; Argentina; Brazil; Chile; Colombia; Columbus, Christopher; Conquistadors; Ecuador; Incas; Peru; Uruguay; Venezuela

✳ AMPHIBIAN

Amphibians are vertebrates (animals with a
backbone) that are adapted to live on both
land and water. Frogs and toads are the most
widespread amphibians.

The three groups of amphibians are easy
to tell apart in the adult stage of their
life cycle. Frogs and toads lack tails, but
they have long back legs for leaping and
swimming. Newts and salamanders look
more like lizards, with long tails. Caecilians
look like worms and burrow in the ground.

All amphibians have smooth skins and
are cold blooded. They keep cool by losing
heat through their skins. Amphibians are
found in all parts of the world except
Greenland and Antarctica.

Life cycle of a frog

The life cycle of a frog is typical of most
amphibians. The female lays eggs in a
coating of jelly in a pond or slow-moving
stream, where they are fertilized by
the male. When the baby frogs (called
tadpoles) hatch, they have tails, no legs,
and breathe through gills (feathery
"stalks" on either side of the head that
water passes through so the amphibian
can get oxygen).

Over the next few weeks the small
tadpoles, which scientists call the
frog's larvae, gradually develop into

adults. They grow legs, lose their tails,
and develop lungs to replace their gills.
When they are adults, frogs can move
freely between water and land. Not all
frogs live in damp places, however; some
are found in desert regions.

Not all frogs and toads breed in quite
the same way. The male midwife toad,
for example, carries his mate's eggs on
his back, dipping into water occasionally
to keep them moist. The mouth-brooding
frog keeps her eggs in her mouth,
allowing the babies to hop out when they
hatch. Tree frogs in the rainforest lay their
eggs in tiny pools of water caught in
the leaves of trees.

Newts, salamanders, and caecilians

Newts have a life cycle very similar to
frogs, but the larvae have legs and look
more like adults. Some species of
salamander never develop lungs.
Instead, they keep their gills and also
take in oxygen through their skin.

Axolotls are a rare type of salamander
found only in Mexico. They seldom
develop into adults. They remain in water
and breathe through three pairs of
feathery gills that stick out
around their necks.
They are able to

*A red-eyed tree frog from the
rainforests of Costa Rica hides
on a leaf and waits to catch
insects for food.*

The marbled salamander gets its name from its striking black-and-white markings. It is found in many parts of the United States.

breed without developing adult features. Caecilians, which are only found in the tropics, also have a larval stage with a tail, but the larvae never develop legs.

Food and predators

Frogs and toads are expert hunters. The bulging eyes at the top of their heads can swivel around to watch out for fast-moving prey. They feed on insects, small fish, and larvae. Large toads even catch young birds or small mammals, such as shrews and baby mice. Many types of frog and salamander have a long, sticky tongue attached to the front of their mouth, which they can flick out to catch insects. Frogs and toads have to avoid predators such as snakes, large birds, and mammals.

Newts are well hidden in the water, where they feed on small fish and insect larvae. Many salamanders are poisonous, which helps defend them against even the hungriest predators. Some have tails that break off. Caecilians eat both plants and animals, foraging in their burrows and sometimes coming out at night.

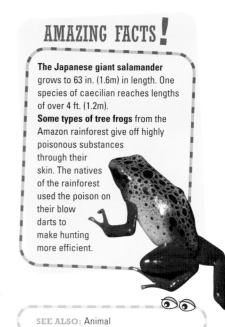

AMAZING FACTS!

The Japanese giant salamander grows to 63 in. (1.6m) in length. One species of caecilian reaches lengths of over 4 ft. (1.2m).

Some types of tree frogs from the Amazon rainforest give off highly poisonous substances through their skin. The natives of the rainforest used the poison on their blow darts to make hunting more efficient.

SEE ALSO: Animal

✱ ANCIENT CIVILIZATIONS

From about 8000 B.C. people created societies
based on farming. These societies gradually
became more organized, and out of them grew
what we call civilization.

Historians use the name ancient
civilization to describe those that
developed before A.D. 500. The world's
oldest civilization developed about 6,500
years ago, before 4500 B.C., when people
in Mesopotamia (modern Iraq) formed a
highly organized society, with cities, laws,
and a shared culture and religion.

*The ruins of the
Indus Valley city
of Mohenjo-Daro
in Pakistan as
they are today.*

The Sumerians and Babylonians
The southern plain of Mesopotamia
between the
Tigris and
Euphrates
rivers was

named Sumer. Its earliest people were
called Sumerians. Another people called
Semites also settled along the rivers.
From 4500 B.C. onward both peoples
began to build cities.

Each city had its own ruler, who tried
to obtain more land. Around 1890 B.C.
Babylon, one of the Semite cities,
conquered and ruled the entire plain,
which became known as Babylonia.

The Sumerians learned how to
make bronze for weapons, tools, and
ornaments. They invented the potter's
wheel and the world's first wheeled
carts, drawn by oxen. They also invented
a form of writing called cuneiform, which
means "wedge-shaped."

People living in cities need laws. The
most famous collection was issued by
Hammurabi, king of Babylon, in about
1750 B.C. There were different laws
for free people and slaves. Most
ancient civilizations allowed slavery.
Prisoners of war were often kept as
slaves rather than killed.

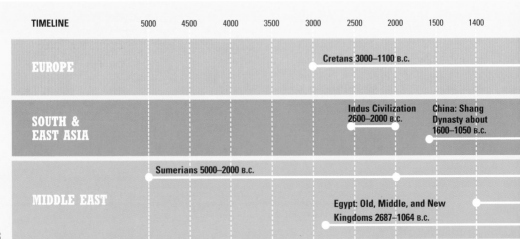

TIMELINE		5000	4500	4000	3500	3000	2500	2000	1500	1400
EUROPE						Cretans 3000–1100 B.C.				
SOUTH & EAST ASIA							Indus Civilization 2600–2000 B.C.		China: Shang Dynasty about 1600–1050 B.C.	
MIDDLE EAST		Sumerians 5000–2000 B.C.						Egypt: Old, Middle, and New Kingdoms 2687–1064 B.C.		

Ancient Egypt

About 3200 B.C. a king named Menes (or Narmer) brought the land along the Nile River in Egypt under his rule. The civilization he founded flourished for over 3,000 years. Egypt was one of the richest and most civilized lands in the world.

Indus civilization

In 1922 scholars unearthed the ruins of cities built about 4,000 years ago in the Indus Valley of India. Mohenjo-Daro and Harappa each had between 20,000 and 50,000 inhabitants and a system of sewers that would only be equaled in modern times. How could such cities disappear and be forgotten? Scholars know only that about 2000 B.C. some disaster struck the Indus cities. Perhaps invaders conquered them, or maybe the climate changed and people moved away. After a time walls fell down, and the winds blew dust over the ruins.

Assyrian and Persian civilizations

A thousand years after Hammurabi Babylon was no longer a great power. In 710 B.C. the Assyrians, who lived in the hills to the north, conquered the city. The Assyrian army was feared for its fierceness. The Assyrians had swift battle chariots and iron weapons that were stronger than any bronze sword.

The Assyrian king Ashurbanipal, who ruled from 669 to 626 B.C., conquered an empire that included Egypt and Babylonia.

A few years after Ashurbanipal's death Babylonia revolted, and in 612 B.C. the Babylonians destroyed Nineveh, the Assyrian capital. In 539 B.C. Babylon was conquered by an Iranian people called the Persians. The Persian Empire became the largest empire the world had seen. In addition to Iran it included modern Turkey, Egypt, Israel, Jordan, Lebanon, Syria, Iraq, Afghanistan, and part of Pakistan.

▲
An artist's impression of how the royal palace at Knossos in Crete might have looked. It covered 5 acres (2ha) and had 1,200 rooms.

1300	1200	1100	1000	900	800	700	600	500	400	300	200	100	A.D.1	100	200	300	400	500

Greece 800 B.C.–A.D. 31

Roman Republic 509–27 B.C.   Roman Empire 27 B.C.–A.D. 476

China: Chou Dynasty about 1050–221 B.C.   China: Han Dynasty 202 B.C.– A.D. 220

Huang Ti 221–210 B.C.

Babylonian Empire 2000–500 B.C.

Assyrian Empire about 1400–612 B.C.   Persian Empire 550–331 B.C.   Parthian Empire 247 B.C.–A.D. 224

Egypt: Ptolemies 305–30 B.C.   Roman Egypt 30 B.C.–A.D. 395

Cretan civilization

Crete is an island in the Mediterranean Sea. About 5,000 years ago the Cretans traded with Egypt, Syria, Italy, and lands even farther away. Knossos was the greatest city in Crete. About 1400 B.C. disaster struck Knossos, but just what happened is not clear. People continued to live there for another 300 years, but its great days were over.

Greek civilization

In 447 B.C. one of the most brilliant societies of the ancient world arose in Athens, the modern capital of Greece. Athenians created beautiful buildings, wrote books and plays, and made important advances in adminstration, law, politics, math, science, and philosophy (the meaning of life). People still study their work today.

In 336 B.C. a 20-year old became king of Macedonia (now part of northern Greece). Alexander attacked and defeated the Persian Empire, and within 10 years he ruled an empire that extended from Greece east to the Indus River. He established cities throughout his realm that became centers of Greek culture. He was known as Alexander the Great.

Roman Empire

When Alexander was conquering his empire in the east, Rome was fighting to control Italy in the west. For hundreds of years Rome then ruled a great empire, which came to include Egypt and Greece. The Romans were excellent engineers and built a vast network of roads and bridges. They brought peace and prosperity to the peoples they ruled.

China

China was isolated from the rest of the world by mountains and deserts. It was governed by great ruling families called dynasties. In 221 B.C. Huang Ti became the first emperor of China. The civilization that developed was the most advanced of its time. The Chinese invented many things such as paper, gunpowder and the compass centuries before the West.

◄
This carved stone column shows Hammurabi, king of Babylon (standing), receiving a set of laws from Shamash, the god of justice (sitting).

SEE ALSO: China; Egypt, Ancient; Greece, Ancient; Roman Empire

✳ ANIMAL

The term "animal" is used to describe a vast
number of different species that live on Earth,
from worms to human beings.

An animal is a living creature that is made
up of many cells. It can move, eats
food rather than makes it (as a plant
does), senses its surroundings, and
reproduces. Animals can be found almost
everywhere on Earth, from the depths of
the ocean to the highest mountain and
the coldest part of Antarctica.

There are two main groups of animals:
vertebrates and invertebrates. Members
of the first group all have vertebrae, or
backbones. Invertebrates do not have a
backbone. Many wear their skeleton
outside their body like a protective coat.
As an invertebrate grows, it sheds the old
coat and grows a new, larger one. The
best-known vertebrate groups are
mammals, birds, reptiles, amphibians, and
fish. The most familiar invertebrate groups
are arthropods, such as spiders, crabs,
millipedes, and insects; sponges;
mollusks, such as slugs, snails, and
octopuses; cnidarians, such as jellyfish;
and worms.

Habitats, niches, and adaptations
Each kind of animal is suited to living in a
particular kind of home, or habitat. An
animal fits into a niche within its habitat.
This means that it has a specific role in its

THE ANIMAL KINGDOM

Scientists group living things into five kingdoms according
to their similarities. The most familiar kingdoms are animals
and plants. Each kingdom is made up of groups, or phyla
(singular phylum). Animals in a phylum are split into classes.
Classes are divided into orders, orders into families, families
into genera (singular genus), and genera into species.

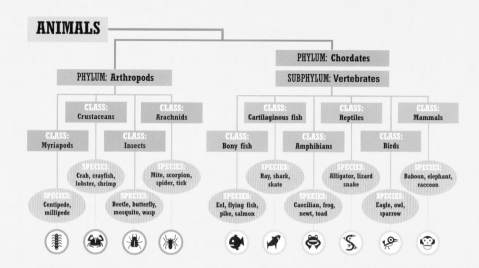

ANIMALS

PHYLUM: **Chordates**

PHYLUM: **Arthropods**

SUBPHYLUM: **Vertebrates**

CLASS: **Crustaceans**

CLASS: **Arachnids**

CLASS: **Cartilaginous fish**

CLASS: **Reptiles**

CLASS: **Mammals**

CLASS: **Myriapods**

CLASS: **Insects**

CLASS: **Bony fish**

CLASS: **Amphibians**

CLASS: **Birds**

SPECIES: Crab, crayfish, lobster, shrimp

SPECIES: Mite, scorpion, spider, tick

SPECIES: Ray, shark, skate

SPECIES: Alligator, lizard, snake

SPECIES: Baboon, elephant, raccoon

SPECIES: Centipede, millipede

SPECIES: Beetle, butterfly, mosquito, wasp

SPECIES: Eel, flying fish, pike, salmon

SPECIES: Caecilian, frog, newt, toad

SPECIES: Eagle, owl, sparrow

community. For example, a heron's habitat includes marshes and riverbanks, while its niche is that of a bird that wades to catch small water animals. The heron's long legs and its hunting behavior—it remains totally still while looking for prey and then seizes it without warning—improve its chances of survival. These characteristics developed over millions of years as species changed, or adapted, to a particular way of life. These adaptations create the remarkable variety of color, shape, and behavior that can be seen in the animal kingdom.

Animal lifestyles

All animals, from the snail to the cheetah, are able to move. Some animals, such as corals and sponges, move when young but remain in one place when they become adults.

Unlike plants, animals cannot make their own food, so they spend much of their time looking for it. Some species eat almost anything, some feed only on plants, and some eat other animals. All animals sense their surroundings through nerves and organs adapted to the way they live. Senses enable animals to hunt, avoid attack, and find mates.

A species must reproduce to survive. Simple animals, such as sponges, need only one parent to produce offspring. Most animals need two parents, a male

The male peacock displays its amazing multi-colored tail feathers in an effort to attract mates (female peahens).

The cheetah is a carnivorous predator (a meat-eating animal that kills its own prey).

and a female. Many fish and insects do not protect their eggs or babies. Birds and mammals generally care for their young until they have learned to find food and protect themselves.

The growing human population has pushed animals out of their habitats and reduced their numbers. Some species, such as the dodo, have died out completely, or become extinct.

AMAZING FACTS !

The great blue whale is 100 ft. (30.4m) long and may weigh more than 130 tons—that is more than the combined weight of 30 elephants.
The ostrich, the largest bird, can tower 8 ft. (2.5m) high and weigh almost 300 lb. (136kg).
The insect-eating shrew, which is the smallest mammal on land, weighs about the same as a dime.

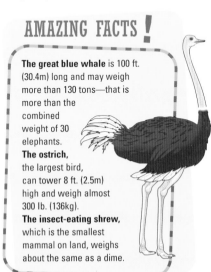

SEE ALSO: Amphibian; Arachnid; Bird; Carnivore; Crustacean; Evolution; Fish; Habitat; Herbivore; Insect; Mammal; Mollusk; Reptile; Reproduction

✳ ARACHNID

There are 74,000 kinds of arachnids in the world, including spiders, scorpions, mites, ticks, and daddy-longlegs. Arachnids look a little like insects, but there are important differences. Unlike insects arachnids do not have wings or antennas on their heads; their bodies are divided into two parts, not three; and they have eight legs, not six. Most arachnids live on land.

Spiders

There are more than 30,000 known kinds of spider. Most range from ⅕ in. (5mm) to 3¹⁄₂ in. (8.9cm) in size. The largest ever found was a tarantula measuring 10 in. (25cm) across with its legs outstretched.

Most spiders eat insects, although some feed on larger prey, such as fish, frogs, and mice. Some spiders lie in wait for their prey. Others chase their prey and, once they have caught it, use their fangs to inject it with poison.

Almost all spiders have glands that produce silk, which is used to trap prey in

The black and yellow garden spider is sometimes known as the writing spider because it weaves a line of white X's down the center of its web.

webs, to create sacs for eggs, or as a kind of safety rope. The silk comes out of the glands as a liquid but hardens into a fiber on contact with the air.

Different species of spider make different kinds of web: For example, grass spiders make big web funnels in tall grass or on the ground; the purseweb spider spins tubes under stones or on the sides of trees; and the common garden spider creates an easily recognizable web that resembles a spoked wheel. One of the cleverest web-builders is the trapdoor spider, which lines its burrow with silk and

The dew-covered webs of common garden spiders often stand out in the early morning sunshine.

makes a hinged door behind which it hides to await the arrival of its unsuspecting prey.

All these webs are a mixture of dry silk, for construction, and sticky material, to catch insects. The spider itself does not get caught in the web because it knows to stay on the dry threads, and because it has oily feet that keep it from sticking.

When threatened, spiders use their silk thread as a safety rope that they can climb up or swing down from to escape their attackers.

▶
Daddy-longlegs have small rounded bodies and very thin, long legs.

Scorpions

Scorpions are usually 1½ in. (4–7cm) in length, although some can be almost 7 in. (18cm) long. There are more than 1,200 different kinds in the world. Scorpions catch prey with special pincers alongside their jaws. They inject poison with stingers on the tips of their tails. Unlike spiders, they do not lay eggs, but give birth to live young. Scorpion poison can be painful to humans but is not usually fatal. In the United States the only scorpion that can kill people is the species *Centruroides sculpturatus*, which is found in parts of Arizona.

Mites and ticks

Mites and ticks are the smallest arachnids—some mites are only $\frac{1}{250}$ in. (0.1mm) long. Mites are parasites (they live off and harm other creatures) and can damage plants and animals. Ticks are also parasites and can spread serious diseases to humans.

Daddy-longlegs

Daddy-longlegs are named for their thin limbs. They can shed their legs to escape enemies and later grow new ones. They can also produce chemicals that taste bad to any creature that tries to eat them. Most daddy-longlegs live on dead insects and fallen fruit.

A scorpion with its young on its back in the tropical dry forest of Costa Rica.
▼

SEE ALSO: Animal; Insect

AMAZING FACTS!

A spider's silk thread can carry 4,000 times the spider's own weight.

Young scorpions ride on their mother's back until they are old enough to survive on their own.

During an experiment spiders taken on a space mission were able to build their webs in zero gravity.

✳ ARCHAEOLOGY

Archaeologists investigate the past: They search the sites of ancient cities and houses for clues about the people who used to live there.

Archaeologists excavating Anasazi ruins near Sand Canyon Pueblo, Cortez, Colorado.

The word *archaeology* comes from two Greek words—*archaios* (ancient) and *logos* (study or talk). So "archaeology" means the study of the past. Archaeologists base their study on the objects that people leave behind. Foundations of buildings, tools, weapons, and even the remains of meals that people ate all give archaeologists information about how ancient people lived. They can learn about their trade, how they found their food, whether they worshiped gods, and so on.

Uncovering the past

Over thousands of years artifacts (things made by people in the past) become buried under layers of building rubble and earth that pile up over ancient towns and other settlements. Archaeologists study history and legends to find a likely place

to dig. Sometimes it may be on a remote hillside that local people believe was the site of an ancient city. At other times it may be in the middle of a modern city, perhaps where builders are excavating a site for a new building. Wherever they start to dig, archaeologists keep a careful record of everything they find.

Archaeologists have various ways of dating artifacts. Sometimes they assess an object's age by the depth beneath the surface that it was found. For more accurate dating they use a method known as carbon dating. All living things receive a set amount of radioactive carbon (carbon-14, or C-14) from the outer atmosphere. When a plant or animal dies, C-14 begins to leave it at a set rate. Scientists measure the amount of radioactive carbon left in material that was once alive and figure out when the artifact was made.

SEE ALSO:
Ancient
Civilizations;
History

✱ ARGENTINA

Argentina is a large country in South America. It is bordered by the Atlantic Ocean, Bolivia, Brazil, Chile, Paraguay, and Uruguay.

KEY FACTS

OFFICIAL NAME
República Argentina

AREA
1,068,297 sq. mi.
(2,766,889 sq. km)

POPULATION
37,032,000

CAPITAL & LARGEST CITY
Buenos Aires

MAJOR RELIGION
Roman Catholicism

MAJOR LANGUAGE
Spanish

CURRENCY
Peso

Argentina's national flag

Puna, a high plateau. The southern Andes are lower. The Gran Chaco, in the far north, is a great lowland covered by areas of thick rainforest and swamp. Its rivers often overflow in the wet season, causing floods. The Gran Chaco is the hottest part of the country.

Mesopotamia, to the east of the Gran Chaco, is a fertile plain lying between the Paraná and Uruguay Rivers. Rainfall is heavy here. The pampas are the center of Argentina's agriculture. Here, too, are the big cities and industrial plants.

Patagonia is a region of dry, windswept plateaus. It is the coldest part of the country. Sheep graze its thin soil. The area includes the southernmost part of South America, Tierra del Fuego. Here penguins live on islands off Cape Horn. Argentina claims several islands in the Atlantic Ocean, including the Islas Malvinas (Falkland Islands).

Argentina is the second largest country in South America, next in size to Brazil. It is a land of contrasts. There are vast prairies stocked with cattle, steamy swamps, icy islands lashed by storms, and towering mountains. A great farming nation, Argentina also has many cities, busy ports, and factories.

Land and climate

Argentina is divided into five main land zones. The Andes Mountains form most of Argentina's western border with Chile. In the north high peaks rise from the

▷

Although most Argentine cattle farming takes place on the pampas, there are also ranches in Patagonia, where this picture was taken. Cowhands in Argentina are called gauchos.

36

People

Argentina has a small native Indian population, but most Argentines are descended from Europeans. Some are mestizos—a mixture of European and Indian. The Spanish started arriving in the 1500s. Between the mid-1800s and the early 1900s a rush of settlers came from all over western Europe.

Today more than 85 percent of the population live in cities and towns. Buenos Aires, the capital, lies on the Río de la Plata (River Plate). It is Argentina's chief port and a center of commerce and industry.

Economy

The pampas soil is fertile and ideal for farming. Forests cover about one-fifth of Argentina. There are deposits of petroleum and natural gas, and of minerals such as coal, iron ore, and tin.

Argentina has traditionally been a farming country and still produces wheat, corn, and soybeans, as well as cotton, sugar cane, and grapes. Cattle and sheep are raised in large numbers; beef and wool are major exports. Today the country also has many industrial plants making leather products, iron, chemicals, and autos.

History

Argentina won independence from Spain in 1816. Over the next century wealthy landowners farmed more and more of the pampas, raising wheat and beef cattle on great ranches. New settlers came from Europe, but life was hard for poor people.

The army seized power in 1943. Working people liked Colonel Juan Perón, and he was elected president in 1946. But he was a harsh ruler. Perón was thrown out in 1955. Since then there have been many changes of government.

SEE ALSO: America, South

✳ ARISTOTLE (384–322 B.C.)

Aristotle was one of the greatest philosophers who ever lived. We still use his way of investigating and observing to explain how and why things happen.

Aristotle was born in northeastern Greece. When he was 17, he went to Athens, where he studied at Plato's Academy for 20 years. Plato was the greatest teacher of the time. Aristotle studied all the sciences, as well as history and politics, but is best remembered today for his work on philosophy. He thought about questions such as: What is happiness? What is the point of life? How do our minds work?

After leaving the Academy, Aristotle became tutor to the young ruler Alexander the Great. Aristotle founded a school, the Lyceum, that contained a museum, a zoo, and the earliest known library.

Although no one knows what Aristotle really looked like, many artists have tried to imagine him. This marble bust is housed in the Louvre Museum, Paris, France.
▶

Aristotle wrote more than 400 books on astronomy, biology, physics, and poetry, as well as politics and ethics. Today, using modern methods, scientists have confirmed that many of the observations Aristotle made were correct. He taught us that every statement should be supported by evidence to show that it is true.

SEE ALSO: Greece, Ancient; Philosophy

✳ ARTISTS, WORLD

World art is a series of movements. New styles develop, become popular, and stay in fashion until another style emerges, and the process starts over.

Art has changed through history. The earliest paintings, by Stone Age people, depicted the animals they hunted for food, such as bison, reindeer, and ibex.

Egyptian art
In the great civilization of ancient Egypt, which arose about 5,000 years ago, artists created images and statues to celebrate their rulers, who were believed to be gods. When kings died, they were buried in huge tombs, called pyramids, inside which were rooms decorated with carvings and paintings of their deeds.

Egyptian art was not very realistic. The artists did not try to make their images look like real people. Later civilizations,

▲
This wall painting from the tomb of an Egyptian official dates from the 14th century B.C.

The Wave is a color woodcut of the sea and Mount Fuji by the Japanese artist Hokusai (1760–1849).
▼

such as those of the Cretans and the Greeks, created statues that looked more human. Most tended to be unnaturally perfect, though; there were no fat people, for example. The Romans based their culture on that of Greece, but brought more realism and character to their art.

The Roman emperor Constantine (ruled A.D. 312–337) converted his empire to

The Creation of Adam *(1508–12)* by Michelangelo. This painting forms part of the roof of the Sistine Chapel in the Vatican City, Rome.

Christianity. When the empire ended in the fifth century, the Germanic people who overran it took up Christianity. They turned their artistic skills to religious art.

Medieval Christian art

For nearly a thousand years most European art was related to the church. Medieval paintings and sculptures showed saints, martyrs, and scenes from the Bible. Many were placed in churches or in vast new cathedrals, which were also decorated with stained glass, mosaics, and carvings. This rich decoration reminded people of the glory of God. It was only in the early 1400s that artists became

concerned with individual human beings. Creators tried to make people in their paintings or sculptures look as they did in real life. For the first time, too, people began to think that the people who created art were not just craftsmen, like carpenters or weavers. They were special people: artists. These changes were part

This autumn river landscape is the work of French Impressionist Claude Monet (1840–1926).

Claude Monet in his famous garden at Giverny, France.

39

of the process sometimes called the Renaissance. The word means "rebirth," and it was used because artists and scholars believed that they were returning to the art produced in the past.

In the centuries after the Renaissance artists continued to try to capture what was most important and truthful about people and the world around them. They included the Italian painter Michelangelo and the Dutchman Rembrandt. Many artists tried to create "rules" about how to make a good picture and what sort of scene it should portray.

Spanish painter and sculptor Pablo Picasso (1881–1973) was one of the founders of the Cubist movement.
▼

Impressionism

The next big change in the way people made art came in the mid-1800s, with a group of French artists called the Impressionists. They thought that the subjects of their pictures were less important than the fresh, free way they applied their paint to the canvas.

The French artist Auguste Rodin is sometimes called an Impressionist even though he was a sculptor, not a painter. However, he also wanted to create surfaces that seemed alive. He transformed the art of sculpture.

At the beginning of the 20th century artists became interested in shapes and patterns for their own sake. They painted pictures as a series of angular shapes, a style called Cubism. Later artists created abstract art, which did not try to represent anything real, but instead used shape and color to arouse a reaction from the viewer.

Surrealism and pop art

In the mid-1920s a new art movement called Surrealism became popular. The Surrealists based their images on dreams and fantasy. In the 1960s many new kinds of art emerged. Pop artists made art fun and had a sharp sense of the absurd. They drew subjects from American popular culture, creating images of giant hamburgers, movie stars, and comic strip characters. Op art arranged colors and forms to create flickering effects called optical illusions. Photorealism imitates photography with detailed images. Minimal art is a kind of abstract art that uses simplified geometric forms.

Artists today experiment with all sorts of influences, materials, and techniques. There are fresh ideas in art all the time.

Other cultures

Art in the East has a separate tradition. As in the West, art has always been a record of what is most important to

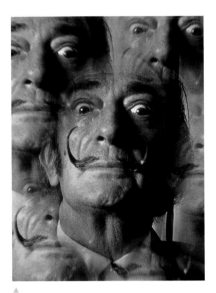

Salvador Dali (1904–89) was a Spanish Surrealist painter and experimental filmmaker.

people. Art in Japan often reflects an appreciation for the beauty of nature. In the 1700s and 1800s Japanese artists began creating woodcuts by carving designs into pieces of wood. The designs could be covered with ink and printed many times. This cheap way of making pictures meant that even quite poor people could buy art.

In India art has almost always been religious. Artists were also interested in what the real world looked like, however. Sculptors, in particular, often portrayed the gods as if they were living human beings.

China's art dates back to 5,000 B.C. It shows respect for tradition and reverence for nature. As well as paintings and drawings the Chinese thought that calligraphy, the art of beautiful writing, was one of the most important visual arts.

SEE ALSO: Leonardo da Vinci; Michelangelo; Rembrandt; Renaissance

GREAT ARTISTS

This is a short list of some of the world's most famous artists. There are many, many more.

Praxiteles (4th century B.C.)
Athenian sculptor considered to be the greatest of his time.

Giotto (di Bondone, Giotto) (about 1267–1337)
Italian painter who began to develop realistic ways of painting.

Leonardo da Vinci (1452–1519)
Italian artist, sculptor, architect, and inventor who painted the *Mona Lisa.*

Michelangelo (Buonarroti, Michelangelo di Lodovico) (1475–1564)
Italian artist, sculptor, and architect who painted the ceiling of the Sistine Chapel in the Vatican, Rome.

Raphael (Sanzio, Raffaello) (1483–1520)
Italian painter famous for his set of wall paintings in the Vatican, the palace of the popes, in Rome.

Titian (Vecelli, Tiziano) (about 1488–1576)
Italian painter from Venice famous for his use of color and depiction of human character.

Rembrandt (van Rijn, Rembrandt Harmensz) (1606–69)
Dutch painter and printmaker who painted many revealing self-portraits.

Goya (Goya y Lucientes, Francisco José de) (1746–1828)
Spanish artist with a vast, varied output.

Hokusai (Katsushika, Hokusai) (1760–1849)
Outstanding Japanese printmaker.

Turner, J.M.W. (Joseph Mallord William) (1775–1851)
English painter whose work experimented with capturing the effects of light.

Cézanne, Paul (1839–1906)
French painter whose nonrealistic way of painting influenced modern art.

Monet, Claude (1840–1926)
French painter who was a leader of the Impressionists.

Rodin, Auguste (1840–1917)
French sculptor famous for his portrayal of the human body.

Van Gogh, Vincent (Willem) (1853–90)
Dutch painter known for his bold use of color.

Kandinsky, Wassily (1866–1944)
Russian painter and the first abstract artist.

Klee, Paul (1879–1940)
Swiss painter who drew simple, childlike figures.

Picasso, Pablo (Ruiz y) (1881–1973)
Spanish painter who developed Cubism.

Dali, Salvador (Filipe Jacinto) (1904–89)
Spanish artist who painted in a style called Surrealism.

✳ ASIA

This heavily populated landmass has a vast range of natural resources. Long exploited by Europeans, its peoples now govern themselves.

Asia is the largest and most heavily populated of the world's continents. It occupies nearly one-third of the Earth's total land surface and is home to about 60 percent of its people. Asia has the world's highest peak—Mount Everest—and its lowest point—the shoreline of the Dead Sea—1,300 ft. (400m) below sea level.

Asia forms the larger, eastern portion of an enormous landmass known as Eurasia (Europe and Asia). Many islands, including those making up the nations of Japan, Indonesia, and the Philippines, ring the continent and form part of it. Politically Russia forms part of Europe, but much of its territory is in Asia.

KEY FACTS

AREA
about 17,297,000
sq. mi. (44,780,000
sq. km).

POPULATION
3,682,550,000

COUNTRIES
48

**LARGEST
COUNTRY**
China

**SMALLEST
COUNTRY**
Singapore

RELIGIONS
Islam, Hinduism,
Buddhism, Taoism,
Shinto, animism,
Sikhism,
Confucianism,
Judaism,
Christianity

LANGUAGES
Many, including
Urdu, Hindi, Tamil,
Persian, Chinese,
Japanese, Korean,
Hebrew, Turkish

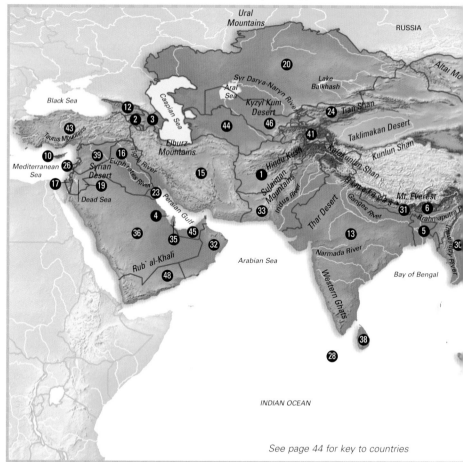

See page 44 for key to countries

A busy street in downtown Kolkata (Calcutta), India. Traffic drives on the left—this is a legacy of British colonial rule.

In the heart of Asia is the great chain of the Himalayas, of which Everest is a part. The Himalayas are themselves part of an even larger mountain system that stretches from Turkey to China. Asia has some of the world's most forbidding deserts, including the Gobi of Mongolia and China, the Syrian, and the Rub' al-

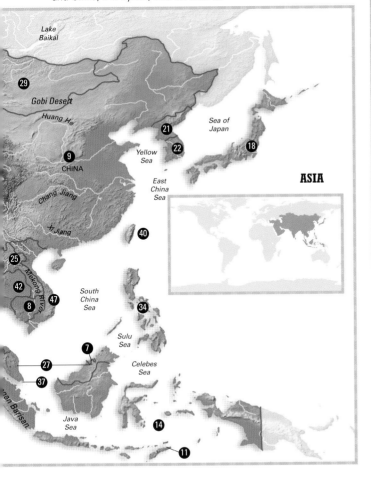

Major Physical Features

DESERTS
- Arabian 500,000 sq. mi. (1,300,000 sq. km)
- Gobi 400,000 sq. mi. (1,040,000 sq. km)
- Turkestan 220,000 sq. mi. (569,800 sq. km)
- Taklimakan 125,000 sq. mi. (320,000 sq. km)
- Thar 100,000 sq. mi. (259,000 sq. km)

MOUNTAIN RANGES & HIGHEST POINTS
- Himalayas: Mt. Everest, 29,078 ft. (8,863m); total of 30 peaks above 24,000 ft. (7,300m)
- Kalakunlun Shan (Karakoram): 4 peaks above 26,000 ft. (7,900m)
- Kunlun Shan: 25,338 ft. (7,723m)
- Tian Shan: 24,406 ft. (7,439m)
- Hindu Kush: 24 peaks above 23,000 ft. (7,000m)
- Elburz: 18,510ft. (5,642m)
- Altai: 14,783 ft. (4,506m)
- Pegunungan Barisan: 12,484 ft. (3,805m)
- Sulaiman: 11,295 ft. (3,443m)
- Ural Mountains: 6,217 ft. (1,895m)

RIVERS
- Chang Jiang (Yangtze) 3,915 mi. (6,300km)
- Yenisey-Angara 3,442 mi. (5,540km)
- Huang He (Yellow River) 3,395 mi. (5,464km)
- Ob 3,230 mi. (5,200km)
- Lena 2,734 mi. (4,400km)
- Mekong 2,702 mi. (4,350km)
- Heilong Jiang (Amur) 2,700 mi. (4,350km)
- Syr Darya-Naryn 1,876 mi. (3,019km)
- Brahmaputra 1,800 mi. (2,900km)
- Indus 1,790 mi. (2,880km)
- Salween 1,750 mi. (2,820km)
- Euphrates 1,740 mi. (2,800km)
- Xi Jiang (Si-Kiang) 1,650 mi. (2,650km)
- Ganges 1,553 mi. (2,500km)
- Irrawaddy 1,300 mi. (2,100km)
- Tigris 1,150 mi. (1,850 km)

LAKES
- Caspian Sea 143,550 sq. mi. (371,800 sq. km)
- Lake Baikal 11,780 sq. mi. (30,500 sq. km)
- Aral Sea 11,600 sq. mi. (30,000 sq. km)

COUNTRIES OF ASIA

	Country	Flag	Population	Capital		Country	Flag	Population	Capital
1	Afghanistan		22,720,000	Kabul	25	Laos		5,433,000	Vientiane
2	Armenia		3,520,000	Yerevan	26	Lebanon		3,282,000	Beirut
3	Azerbaijan		7,734,000	Baku	27	Malaysia		22,244,000	Kuala Lumpur
4	Bahrain		617,000	Manama	28	Maldives		286,000	Male
5	Bangladesh		129,155,000	Dhaka	29	Mongolia		2,662,000	Ulaanbaatar
6	Bhutan		2,124,000	Thimphu	30	Myanmar		45,611,000	Yangon
7	Brunei		328,000	Bandar Seri Begawan	31	Nepal		23,930,000	Kathmandu
8	Cambodia		11,168,000	Phnom Penh	32	Oman		2,542,000	Muscat
9	China, People's Republic of		1,284,958,000	Beijing	33	Pakistan		156,483,000	Islamabad
10	Cyprus		786,000	Nicosia	34	Philippines		75,967,000	Manila
11	East Timor		885,000	Dili	35	Qatar		599,000	Doha
12	Georgia		4,968,000	Tbilisi	36	Saudi Arabia		21,607,000	Riyadh
13	India		1,013,662,000	New Delhi	37	Singapore		3,567,000	Singapore
14	Indonesia		212,107,000	Jakarta	38	Sri Lanka		18,827,000	Colombo
15	Iran		67,702,000	Tehran	39	Syria		16,125,000	Damascus
16	Iraq		23,115,000	Baghdad	40	Taiwan (Republic of China)		22,100,000	Taipei
17	Israel		6,217,000	Jerusalem	41	Tajikistan		6,188,000	Dushanbe
18	Japan		126,714,000	Tokyo	42	Thailand		61,399,000	Bangkok
19	Jordan		6,669,000	Amman	43	Turkey		66,591,000	Ankara
20	Kazakhstan		16,223,000	Astana	44	Turkmenistan		4,459,000	Ashgabat
21	Korea, North		24,039,000	Pyongyang	45	United Arab Emirates		2,441,000	Abu Dhabi
22	Korea, South		46,844,000	Seoul	46	Uzbekistan		24,318,000	Tashkent
23	Kuwait		1,972,000	Kuwait	47	Vietnam		79,832,000	Hanoi
24	Kyrgyzstan		4,699,000	Bishkek	48	Yemen		18,112,000	Sanaa

Khali (Empty Quarter) of Saudi Arabia. Vast treeless plains, or steppes, cover much of Central Asia. Farther north is a broad belt of forest known as taiga.

Asia has almost all the world's varieties of climates. Much of the continent is cold and dry in the winter and warm and dry in the summer. The high mountain ranges that cross Asia act as a huge wall. They keep the cold winds of the Arctic from blowing to the south and the hot winds of the south from blowing north. Winters in Siberia are among the coldest on Earth—the average January temperature is about −60°F (−51°C). In contrast, land temperatures around the Persian Gulf can reach 120°F (49°C). Parts of Southwest Asia receive as little as 4 in. (100mm) of rain a year, while northeast India is one of the wettest regions on Earth.

Plants and animals

Much of Asia has poor soils, particularly in the interior, which is too high, dry, or cold to farm. The most fertile places, where crops can readily be grown, are along the river valleys and in some coastal areas, and it is here that the densest populations are found. Southeast Asia's tropical rainforests include valuable hardwoods such as teak and mahogany.

Polar and brown bears, Arctic foxes, reindeer, elk, and fur-bearing animals such as ermine and sable are found in North Asia. The orang-utan lives in the tropical forests of Sumatra and Borneo. India has many large mammals, including the Bengal tiger, the Indian rhinoceros, and the Asian elephant.

People

Asia's population, already very large, is still growing rapidly. Most of the people live in three regions—South, Southeast, and East Asia. Asia is home to many different peoples speaking a great variety of languages.

About two-thirds of Asia's people earn their livelihood from the land. Major crops are rice, wheat, corn, rubber, tea, sugar cane, cotton, soybeans, silk, and jute. Nomadic herders in Southwest and Central Asia depend largely on their livestock. Although most Asian people live in rural areas, the continent has some of the world's largest cities, including Tokyo (Japan), Seoul (South Korea), Shanghai (China), and Mumbai (Bombay, India).

Natural wealth

Asia is rich in mineral resources. The Persian Gulf area is the world's single largest source of petroleum, with one-half of the total supply. Japan is the most industrialized nation in Asia and ranks among the world's top industrial powers. China and India are a distant second and third to Japan in industrial output.

History

The earliest human settlements in Asia date from around 3500 B.C. in three great river valleys—those of the Tigris-Euphrates in Southwest Asia, the Indus in South

The tiger is one of many rare and beautiful species that are found in the wild only in Asia.
▼

Asia, and the Huang He (Yellow River) in East Asia. These civilizations developed the world's first writing and legal codes, as well as inventing the wheel.

The first great Asian empire, the Maurya, was established in the fourth century B.C. and created unity in India. Under its greatest ruler, Asoka, Buddhism and great monumental art flourished.

In China the Han dynasty, or ruling family (202 B.C.–A.D. 220), established an empire and adopted Confucianism, a system of ethical teachings founded by Confucius. During this period Christianity appeared in Southwest Asia, and Buddhism began to spread to East Asia.

In the seventh century A.D. Muslims (followers of Islam) took over most of North Africa, Southwest Asia, and northern India. In East Asia China flourished under the Tang and Sung dynasties from about 600 to 1200. In the 13th century Genghis Khan, a Mongol warrior, conquered much of Asia, from China to Russia.

After the arrival in India of the Portuguese explorer Vasco da Gama in 1498 many other Europeans came to Asia and carved out empires. In the 20th century the desire for self-rule and unity—called nationalism—became a powerful force in Asia. From World War II onward all countries gained their independence.

> **SEE ALSO:** Ancient Civilizations; Buddhism; China; Indian subcontinent; Indonesia; Islam; Israel; Japan; Korea; Malaysia; Middle East; Mongols; Philippines; Russia & the Baltic States; Thailand; Turkey & the Caucasus

✳ ASTRONAUT

Men and women who travel in space are called astronauts, a modern word that comes from ancient Greek and means "sailors of the stars."

The United States began its manned space travel program in the late 1950s. Although for some years its space agency, the National Aeronautics and Space Administration (NASA), lagged behind the Soviet Union, in 1969 the United States won the race to put a man on the moon.

Soviet pioneers
The first person in space was Soviet cosmonaut Yuri Gagarin, who made a single orbit of the Earth in 1961. (Cosmonaut is the Russian equivalent of astronaut; the word means "sailor of the universe.")

The first NASA manned space flight program was Project Mercury. Its objectives were to orbit the Earth, investigate man's ability to function in space, and recover both man and spacecraft safely. The seven astronauts hired for Project Mercury were all Air Force test pilots with at least 1,500 hours of flight time who had flown 50 miles

Astronauts prepare to board Apollo 11 for the first manned moon landing in July 1969.

An astronaut takes a walk in space outside the International Space Station in July 2001.

(80km) above the Earth. Because of the small size of the Mercury capsule, the astronauts could not be over 5 ft. 11 in. (180cm) tall.

Toward the moon

The second U.S. manned space program, begun in 1962, was named Gemini because its capsules had a two-man crew ("gemini" is the Latin for "twins"). Gemini capsules were larger than the Mercury craft, so the nine men chosen could be up to 6 ft. (183cm) tall. The maximum age was reduced to 35 years old, and civilian test-pilot experience was now acceptable.

Astronauts in weightless conditions aboard the Space Shuttle Endeavour in 1992.

The third series of missions was the

FAMOUS ASTRONAUTS

Gagarin, Yuri (1934–68)
On April 12, 1961, the Soviet Union became the first nation to put a human into space when Gagarin orbited the Earth in Vostok 1.

Glenn, John (above) (1921–)
In February 1962 Glenn became the first American to orbit Earth.

Tereshkova, Valentina (1937–)
This Soviet cosmonaut was the first woman in space. She orbited Earth in June 1963.

Leonov, Alexei (1934–)
In March 1965 cosmonaut Leonov became the first person to leave a spacecraft on a "spacewalk," or extravehicular activity (EVA).

Armstrong, Neil (left) (1930–), and **Aldrin, Edwin "Buzz"** (1930–)
On July 20, 1969, these U.S. astronauts became the first humans to step on the moon. The third crew member was Michael Collins.

Young, John (1930–), and **Crippen, Robert** (1937–)
These U.S. astronauts were the first to fly in the Space Shuttle, in April 1981.

Ride, Sally (1951–)
Orbiting Earth in the shuttle in June 1983, Ride was the first American woman in space.

Apollo Program (1963–72), which aimed to land humans on the moon and bring them safely back to Earth. Of the 14 men originally selected, six were not test pilots but scientists.

The age of the space shuttle
In 1978 NASA named 35 new candidates for positions as astronauts aboard the space shuttle. Six were women—the first ever U.S. female astronauts. Since then candidates have been recruited annually, and astronauts from other nations also take part in shuttle flights.

The first Soviet cosmonauts were also experienced jet pilots, but some later missions were carried out by men without a military or piloting background. The Russians led the way for women in space—in 1963 Valentina Tereshkova became the first female in space.

Astronauts are fully prepared for space-flight conditions, such as weightlessness, and on-board emergencies. There are full-scale spacecraft models at NASA's Lyndon B. Johnson Space Center in Houston, Texas, and elsewhere.

SEE ALSO: Ride, Sally; Space Exploration; Space Shuttle

✱ ASTRONOMY

Astronomy is older than recorded history. It was first used to figure out when the seasons would change. Today it is used to calculate the age of the universe.

Astronomy is the study of everything in the universe beyond Earth. It is one of the oldest sciences. For thousands of years people have gazed at the sky to try to learn about the stars, the planets, and everything else in the universe.

The night sky changes as the year passes. Starting about 10,000 years ago, people studied the changing positions of the sun and the stars to decide when to plant and harvest crops. The earliest astronomers lived before recorded history. Our first knowledge of ancient astronomy dates from about 2,500 years ago, when Greek astronomers carefully recorded what they had learned. They believed that the Earth was at the center of the universe and that the stars and other planets circled the Earth.

Beginning of modern astronomy
The Polish scientist Nicolaus Copernicus (1473–1543) was the first person to suggest correctly that the Earth revolved

Stonehenge in southern England. Built in about 3000 B.C., its exact purpose is unknown, but some historians believe it may have been used by early astronomers to help determine midsummer's day.
▼

An early astronomer observing the stars through a telescope, an instrument first used and possibly invented by Galileo Galilei.

The light-year

Gradually astronomers realized that the universe is much larger than our solar system and that the sun is actually a star just like the others in the night sky. Stars beyond our solar system are so far away that astronomers invented a new unit to measure the vast distances. That unit, known as the light-year, is the distance a beam of light travels in a year.

Although light seems to travel instantly from place to place, it actually moves at a speed of about 186,000 miles (300,000km) per second. A light-year is about 6 trillion miles (9.6 trillion km). A star's distance from Earth in light-years indicates how long ago the light we see now left that star. Most stars are millions of light-years away, and the light we see today left them millions of years ago.

Moving galaxies

In the early 1900s astronomers realized that the distant, glowing clouds they could see in the universe, were great clouds of stars, or galaxies. Our sun is part of the Milky Way galaxy. There are billions of galaxies in the universe, and each galaxy contains billions of stars. Most galaxies are clustered together in groups.

By the 1920s, as telescopes became more powerful, astronomers had noticed that these outer galaxies were moving away from our galaxy. They realized that if the universe is expanding, there must have been a time when all the galaxies were closer together. They now think that between about 10 and 15 billion years ago the expansion of the universe began with a tremendous explosion, which is called the Big Bang.

around the sun, not the other way around. The Italian astronomer Galileo Galilei (1564–1642) was the first to use a telescope to study the sky, and he saw things no one else had seen. Although Galileo believed, like Copernicus, that the planets orbited the sun, he could not explain why.

The person who answered that question was the English mathematician Isaac Newton (1642–1727). Newton discovered that all objects possess a force called gravity that attracts other objects. A large object such as the sun produces enough gravity to hold the planets in orbit around it. Moons orbit planets for the same reason. Because of Newton's discoveries scientists came to accept the idea that the Earth and other planets revolve around the sun.

SEE ALSO: Astronaut; Comet, Meteor, & Asteroid; Constellation; Earth; Galaxy; Gravity; Jupiter; Mars; Mercury; Moon; Neptune; Rocket; Satellite; Solar System; Space Exploration; Star; Sun; Uranus; Venus

✳ AUSTRALIA

Australia is an island country lying between the Pacific and Indian oceans. It is about the same size as the United States, excluding Alaska and Hawaii.

Australia has a low-lying landscape, except for a mountain range in the east. Most of the people live to the east of this range. The hot, dry interior is called the outback.

The tropical north of the country receives heavy rains in summer, but the south has rainy winters. January and February are the hottest months; July is the coolest. In the outback summer temperatures often exceed 100°F (38°C).

Plants and animals

In dry areas there are eucalyptus trees with oily leaves that conserve water. In the northeast tropical rainforests flourish. Native animals include kangaroos, koalas, emus (large, flightless birds), and parrots. There are also many venomous snakes, spiders, and jellyfish.

Economy

Australia is a major producer and exporter of agricultural products. The country's mineral resources include gold, bauxite (aluminum ore), uranium, and oil. Service industries are the fastest-growing sector.

People

Australia's native people, the Aborigines, have lived there for some 40,000 years. Their ancestors came on boats from lands in Asia. Most Australians live in the cities of the fertile southeast.

History

In 1642 the Dutch navigator Abel Tasman visited Australia. In 1770 the British explorer James Cook visited Botany Bay, near what is now Sydney, and it was here that the first British settlers landed in 1788. More British settlers followed. Australia became a nation in 1901. In more recent years Asian settlers have added to Australia's population.

KEY FACTS

OFFICIAL NAME
Commonwealth of Australia

AREA
2,967,895 sq. miles
(7,686,848 sq. km)

POPULATION
18,886,000

CAPITAL
Canberra

LARGEST CITY
Sydney

MAJOR RELIGION
Christianity

MAJOR LANGUAGE
English

CURRENCY
Australian dollar

Australia's national flag

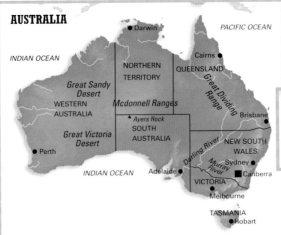

AUSTRALIA

PACIFIC OCEAN
INDIAN OCEAN
• Darwin
NORTHERN TERRITORY
Cairns •
QUEENSLAND
Great Sandy Desert
WESTERN AUSTRALIA
Mcdonnell Ranges
Great Dividing Range
▲ Ayers Rock
SOUTH AUSTRALIA
Brisbane •
Great Victoria Desert
Darling River
NEW SOUTH WALES
• Perth
Murray River
Sydney •
INDIAN OCEAN
Adelaide •
■ Canberra
VICTORIA
Melbourne •
TASMANIA
• Hobart

Ayers Rock, called Uluru by the Aborigines, is the largest outcrop of its type in the world.
▼

SEE ALSO: Aborigine

✳ AUSTRIA

Austria is a small country lying in the heart of Europe. It has a rich history and was once the center of a vast European empire.

Austria's national flag

Austria is dominated by mountains: The Alps, the highest mountains in Europe, extend across the western part of the country and are cut by deep valleys. The Danube River forms a wide valley running across the eastern part of the country. North of the Danube there are forested uplands.

Northern Austria has an Atlantic climate, with mild, rainy winters and cool, moist summers. Southern Austria has a more Mediterranean climate, with hot, dry summers and mild, rainy winters. Eastern Austria has the hot summers and cold winters of a continental climate.

People

The people of Austria speak German, but in some areas they feel more closely linked to neighboring states, such as Slovenia and Slovakia.

Economy

The Austrian economy is based mainly on industry. Most factories are in the Danube valley. The leading manufactured goods include metal products, machinery, textiles, and chemicals. The forested hillsides provide raw material for lumber-based industries. Tourists come to see the mountains and the historic capital, Vienna.

History

In 1278 the Hapsburg family took control of Austria. At one time their empire spread across Europe from Spain north to the Netherlands and beyond Hungary to the east. The empire (known as the Holy Roman Empire) was eventually destroyed in 1806 by the French general Napoleon Bonaparte. The Hapsburg family stayed in power until the end of World War I (1914–18), when Charles I, the last Hapsburg emperor, was forced to step down. The nation then became a republic.

In 1938 Austria was swallowed up by Nazi Germany. When World War II ended in 1945, Austria was divided among the Allies. It became independent in 1955.

SEE ALSO: Europe; Napoleon; World War I; World War II

✳ AZTECS

The Aztecs were an American Indian people based in Central America. Their empire was conquered by the Spanish in the early 16th century.

The Aztec Empire was based in a city called Tenochtitlán built on islands in a lake that was in the valley where Mexico City now stands. The city was founded by a people called the Mexica in 1325. Other peoples founded cities nearby. In 1430, after many battles, the tribes formed an alliance that was the basis of the Aztec Empire. The empire extended from Mexico to what is now Guatemala.

Government and gods

Aztec cities were ruled by kings who tried to gain control over other cities. Any city controlled by a neighboring king had to pay taxes in the form of jewels, gold, food, feathers, fabrics, or building materials. The Aztecs tried to please their many gods by capturing prisoners and sacrificing them. The victims were taken to temples on top of huge stepped pyramids, where a priest cut their chests open and tore their hearts out.

Food and trade

The Aztecs grew corn, beans, squash, and other crops in gardens on islands in the lake. They built the islands by piling up rich soil from the lake bottom. Merchants from the lowlands brought other food to

AZTEC EMPIRE

the city's markets, including cacao, pineapples, and vanilla. Cacao beans, which are the source of chocolate, were sometimes used as money. All the goods were carried by porters—the Aztecs had no wheeled vehicles or pack animals.

Fall of the empire

Hernán Cortés, a Spanish conquistador, came to Tenochtitlán in 1519. The emperor, Montezuma II, welcomed Cortés, thinking that he was the legendary priest-king Quetzalcóatl (pronounced keh-tsahl-koh-áhtl), who had disappeared over the sea long ago but promised to return. But Cortés killed Montezuma and joined forces with other Aztec cities to destroy Tenochtitlán in 1521, ending Aztec rule. Kings, now called governors, served under Spanish authority before completely losing their powers at the end of the 1500s. Today over a million Nahua people, descended from the Aztecs, live in central Mexico.

This turquoise serpent once decorated an Aztec high priest's clothing. It was probably one of many treasures given to Cortés by Montezuma.
▼

SEE ALSO:
Conquistadors;
Incas; Maya;
Mexico; Olmec
& Toltec

✳ BEETHOVEN, LUDWIG VAN (1770–1827)

Beethoven was one of the greatest composers of classical music. His achievement is even more amazing because for much of his life he was deaf.

▲
Ludwig van Beethoven in his late thirties.

SEE ALSO:
Composers;
Music

Beethoven was born in 1770 in Bonn, Germany. His father was an alcoholic and wanted his son to earn money by performing. Young Ludwig was often dragged out of bed at night and made to practice the piano. By the age of 13 he was already working as an organist. After his mother died, when he was 18, Beethoven had to take charge of the family. He played for many princes in and around Vienna, Austria.

Then, about 1799, Beethoven discovered that he was going deaf. After this he developed a new musical style that reflected his violent emotions. At about this time Beethoven composed the Fifth Symphony, one of the most popular and influential of all his works. By 1820 he was so deaf that he could communicate with other people only in writing. But this was his most creative period, during which he wrote his greatest works: the last five piano sonatas, the Mass in D (*Missa solemnis*), the Ninth Symphony, and the last five string quartets.

In 1826 his nephew Karl tried to commit suicide. This badly affected Beethoven's health. He died on March 26, 1827.

✳ BICYCLE AND MOTORCYCLE

All bicycles and motorcycles have two wheels. Bicycles are propelled by their riders; motorcycles have engines.

A German inventor, Karl von Drais, was the first person to build a bicycle. It was made of wood and named a running machine (*Laufmaschine*) because the rider had to stride along to make the cycle work. It was only really useful for downhill runs. It was followed in the 1870s by the Ordinary, or penny-farthing (named for the largest and smallest British coins of the time). This cycle had a tiny rear wheel and a huge front wheel, with pedals attached to the hub. Finally, in 1885 John Kemp Starley came up with the Rover Safety, a bicycle with a chain that linked the pedals to the rear wheel. The design has since been modified and improved to produce the bicycles we know today.

There are modern bicycles for many different purposes: touring bikes, mountain or trail bikes, and racing bikes. The most advanced racing bikes have lightweight, carbon-fiber frames and wheel spokes that are enclosed to reduce drag from the air.

◄
A typical modern bicycle. The rider's gloves, helmet, and sunglasses are for protection.

Very narrow, high pressure tires reduce friction as the cyclist races along; even the helmet and clothes the cyclist wears are designed to reduce wind resistance. The recumbent bike is a relatively new idea: The rider lies back in a seat, with his or her feet on pedals in front that drive a long chain attached to the rear wheels.

Motorcycles

The first motorcycle to appear in public had a gasoline engine attached to a wooden-framed bicycle. It was built in 1885 by Gottlieb Daimler, a German who later became famous as a manufacturer of cars. Today's motorcycles are often as powerful as cars. Usually, riders control the throttle and the front-wheel brake through controls on the handlebars. A foot pedal controls the rear-wheel brake.

SEE ALSO: Leonardo da Vinci; Transportation

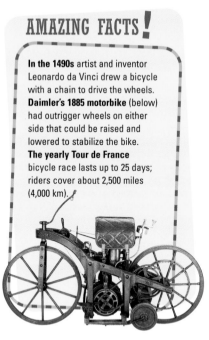

AMAZING FACTS !

In the 1490s artist and inventor Leonardo da Vinci drew a bicycle with a chain to drive the wheels. **Daimler's 1885 motorbike** (below) had outrigger wheels on either side that could be raised and lowered to stabilize the bike. **The yearly Tour de France** bicycle race lasts up to 25 days; riders cover about 2,500 miles (4,000 km).

✳ BIOLOGY

Biology is the scientific study of organisms, or living things—the way they work, their structure, and their interrelationships.

Ecology is a branch of biology. Here ecologists test the biological health of Thighman Lake, Mississippi, by taking samples of bottom sediments. ▶

It is easy to say that biology is the scientific study of living things, but how do we know what is living and what is not? To answer this question, biologists have figured out a set of characteristics that are shared by all organisms.

All living things are made of cells. Most cells are so small that they can be seen only under a microscope. Some organisms, such as bacteria, consist of just one cell. Others might have billions.

All organisms need energy to stay alive. Animals get energy from food. Green plants and some small organisms get energy from the sun through a process called photosynthesis.

Organisms grow as they get older. They become larger and change shape. Organisms create new individuals of the same type to replace those that die. This

The following are some of the most influential biologists in history.

Hippocrates
(about 460–377 B.C.)
Ancient Greek physician who introduced scientific methods to medicine.

Harvey, William (right)
(1578–1657)
English physician who described the circulation of blood in the body.

Van Leeuwenhoek, Antonie
(below right) (1632–1723)
Dutch naturalist who made many discoveries with a microscope.

Carolus Linnaeus (von Linné, Carl) (1707–78)
Swedish botanist who classified the living world, giving each plant and animal its own scientific name.

Schleiden, Matthias (Jakob) (1804–81), and **Schwann, Theodor (Ambrose Hubert)** (1810–82) German scientists who developed cell theory.

Darwin, Charles (Robert)
(1809–82)
English naturalist whose theory of evolution changed people's view of the world.

Mendel, Gregor (Johann) (1822–84)
Austrian monk and botanist who developed the theory of heredity and genetics.

is called reproduction. Life is self-perpetuating—in other words, it can come only from other living things.

Evolution
Organisms can sense and respond to changes in their world. In order to survive, an organism must adjust, or adapt, to such changes. As winter sets in, for example, the fur of an arctic fox turns white and thick to keep it warm and make it less noticeable against the snow. The organisms that adapt best to changes in the environment are most likely to survive and reproduce. This process explains why organisms change, or evolve, over time.

Biologists at work
Biology is divided into many different fields. People who specialize in studying plants are called botanists. Those who concentrate on animals are zoologists. Some zoologists specialize in specific animals. Ornithologists study birds, and marine biologists study animals that live in the oceans and seas. Some biologists study particular parts of organisms. Biochemists study chemical reactions in organisms; geneticists study genes, which determine the qualities organisms inherit from their parents. Ecologists study how living organisms relate to each other within their environment.

In the post-September 11, 2001, war against terrorism a biologist analyzes samples taken from a suspect letter for traces of the deadly anthrax bacteria.

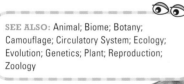

SEE ALSO: Animal; Biome; Botany; Camouflage; Circulatory System; Ecology; Evolution; Genetics; Plant; Reproduction; Zoology

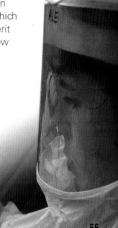

55

✳ BIOME

Biome is the scientific term for a community of specific types of plants and animals that covers a large area of the earth's surface.

The type of biome is usually determined by the type of climate in that region. The major land biomes are grasslands (known as prairies in North America, savannas in Africa, steppes in Asia, and pampas in South America), deserts, chaparral, deciduous forests, coniferous forests, tundra, and tropical rainforests. Aquatic biomes exist in rivers, lakes, and oceans.

Most of the different kinds of biomes can be found on every continent except Antarctica. Each place has unique species of plants and animals, yet the plants and animals of a particular biome tend to be similar regardless of where they are in the world. For example, spine-covered cacti are common in the southwestern deserts of the United States. In African deserts similar prickly plants called euphorbs grow in abundance. Both have adapted similarly to living in the hot, dry desert biome.

In many parts of the world nature's biomes have been altered by people. In the dry grasslands of the Sahel, in western Africa, for example, domestic goats and sheep have overgrazed the land. The thin layer of topsoil has been blown away, and the Sahel is becoming a desert. This process, called desertification, also threatens other parts of the world.

People in Central America, South America, and Southeast Asia have been burning down the tropical rainforests to make farmland and cutting down the trees for lumber. Each year millions of acres of rainforest are destroyed. Their loss may seriously change the world's climate. Environmental groups and government agencies are working to protect the world's biomes. In this way the earth's precious natural resources can be preserved for future life.

One of the biggest threats to biomes is the action of humans. Here a part of the Amazon rainforest in Brazil is burned down to create space for an enlarged cattle ranch.
▼

A prairie in Wyoming. Land such as this is part of the earth's grassland biome.
◄

Grasslands

Grasslands are a biome in which the average annual rainfall is 10–40 in. (254–1,016mm). Animals include large herds of grazing animals, such as zebras and gazelles, and predators, such as lions, leopards, and hyenas.

Deserts

A desert is a biome in which there is less than 10 in. (254mm) of annual rain. The days are very hot, and the nights are cold. Succulents, plants that store water in their leaves or stems, are among the major plants. Many animals stay underground during the day and come out at night. Some can survive with very little water.

Chaparral

Chaparrals are dense growths of shrubs and trees. They are found on the coasts of the Mediterranean Sea, southern California, central Chile, the southern tip of Africa, and southern Australia. Some areas average as little as 10 in. (254mm) of rain a year, all of which falls in winter. Warm, moist air from the oceans prevents conditions from being as severe as those in the desert. The main plants are tough evergreen shrubs with small leathery leaves. Most of the animals there are adapted to a dry climate.

Deciduous forests

The forests of eastern North America, Central Europe, eastern China, and the southeast coast of Australia are made up of deciduous trees, or trees that grow and shed their leaves in a seasonal pattern. Rain falls year-round, averaging about 40 in. (1,016mm). Many plants and animals flourish, including ferns, mosses, fungi, insects, songbirds, amphibians, deer, and small mammals.

Coniferous forests

Temperate coniferous forest is found in moist, coastal environments, including the northern Pacific coast of North America and the east coast of Australia. In California these forests contain giant sequoia (also called redwoods); in Australia they feature towering eucalyptus trees. Boreal forests stretch across the northern reaches of North America, Europe, and Asia. Pine, spruce, and firs are the most common trees. Many different types of animal live there, especially in the summer. They include moose, elk, deer, migratory birds, and bears.

▲
The beautiful fall colors of a deciduous forest in Maine.

Tundra

North of the boreal forest lies the treeless tundra. Beneath it is a layer of frozen ground called permafrost, which may be

For a few short weeks in the summer in Alaska even the Arctic is green.

over 1,000 ft. (305m) thick. The soil on top of the permafrost thaws for only eight weeks during the short Arctic summer. The small flowering plants and dwarf trees that live here have to grow, bloom, and set seed quickly to survive. In summer the tundra teems with life— there are herds of caribou and reindeer, and flocks of migrating birds feeding on the numerous insects. As summer fades, many mammals travel to the forests, and the birds fly south.

Tropical rainforests
In these biomes around the equator annual rainfall averages between 80 and 200 in. (2,000–5,000mm), and falls evenly year-round. Temperatures hardly vary, hovering just below 80°F (27°C) day and night. This steady environment has the greatest variety of plant, animal, and insect species of all the biomes, ranging from parrots to monkeys and jaguars.

SEE ALSO: Arctic; Desert; Ecology; Habitat; Rainforest; Ocean & Sea

✱ BIRD

Birds are found in every area of the world—there are more than 9,000 species. Although most birds can fly, a few have evolved into flightless creatures.

The fossilized remains of an Archaeopteryx, thought to be the earliest species of bird. ▼

Other animals have wings and can fly, but no other creature is covered with feathers. Feathers are formed in special skin cells from a protein called keratin. Feathers smooth and streamline the bird's body, enabling it to move easily through the air or water; they also protect its skin and help it maintain its body temperature.

There are three basic types of flight: flapping, gliding, and soaring. Most birds use flapping flight—that is, after they take off, they continue to fly by moving their wings up and down. When gliding, birds keep their wings extended and coast downward. During soaring flight birds use the energy of rising columns of warm air, called thermals, to fly without having to flap their wings.

Skeleton and muscles
The body systems of birds are all adapted to flight. Over time the skeleton of the bird has developed into an airy, lightweight, yet strong frame. Birds have a large breastbone, or sternum, that protects their internal organs and provides them with strong support for the attached muscles that power flight.

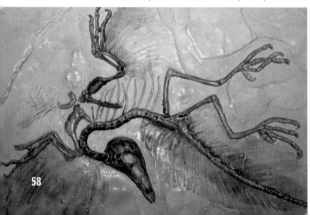

Like all birds of prey, the red-tailed hawk has a powerful, hooked bill and sharp talons for seizing its victims and tearing them to pieces.

The largest muscles in a bird are the pectoral (breast) muscles. They may account for as much as one-fifth of a bird's entire weight. They are attached to the long bone of the wing. When they contract during flight, the bird's wings are pulled down. Other, smaller muscles contract during flight to pull the wings up.

Feeding

Birds feed on a wide variety of food— from fruit and seeds to dead animals. Their beaks are adapted to suit their diet. An eagle, for example, has a powerful, hooked bill to tear its prey to bits.

Because birds have no teeth, their digestive systems must grind up food so that the energy stored in it can be used. Some birds have a gullet storage pouch called a crop. It allows a bird to feed quickly and digest its meal later in safety.

Nearly all birds have a stomach made up of two parts. The first part secretes strong digestive juices. The second part, called the gizzard, has muscular walls that grind and pulverize food. Birds often swallow small pebbles and grit to aid the grinding.

Birds have a higher body temperature, a faster heart rate, and a greater need for oxygen than mammals, so they must eat a great deal of food to get the energy they need to fuel their bodies.

When flying, birds require 10 to 20 times more oxygen than they need when they are at rest. To get the extra oxygen, birds increase their rate of breathing.

Senses

As a group, birds have the best vision of all animals. Their large eyes, which sometimes weigh more than their brains, provide keen sight and often excellent color perception. Hearing is also well developed in birds, with some night birds having especially acute awareness of sound. Only a few birds, such as the kiwi, have a highly developed sense of smell. The kiwi is nearly blind and relies on its sense of smell to find food.

Communicating

Bird songs may sound beautiful, but birds do not sing to make music. They sing to attract mates and to tell other birds to stay off their territory (an area they consider theirs). Birds generally have between 5 and 14 songs, but some species have many more. Subtle differences in the pitch and timing of the songs distinguish individual birds.

Reproduction

All birds lay eggs and care for them in one way or another. The place where birds lay their eggs is called a nest. Some birds lay eggs on bare cliff ledges; others build elaborate structures to hold the eggs.

Eight or nine out of every ten birds die during their first year. For

The great horned owl has large eyes that enable it to see well in the dark and detect even the slightest movement at great distances.

Ducks are birds that live on and near water.

SEE ALSO:
Animal;
Dinosaur

The bald eagle hunts for fish along the rivers and lakes of North America.

most species the greatest threats are bad weather and predators. Regardless of their regular diet, the adults feed their young foods rich in proteins. Before long the nest becomes overcrowded. It is time for the baby birds to leave the nest; this is called fledging.

The migration cycle

Some birds remain in the same area all their lives and are known as residents. Billions of birds travel to distant places: They are called migrants. In the Northern Hemisphere resident birds face long, cold winters and scarce food supplies. It is easier for them to survive in warmer southern countries, even though many migrating birds are killed by storms and other hazards. Birds return north to breed because there are fewer predators there, as well as an extremely large supply of insects to feed growing young.

History of birds

Most scientists now believe that birds evolved from small two-legged dinosaurs called theropods.

The earliest known bird is *Archaeopteryx*, which lived about 150 million years ago. It was about the size of a blue jay and had wings and feathers. Unlike modern birds, it also had a long, bony tail and teeth. The bone structure of its legs suggests that it was a good runner, and scientists believe *Archaeopteryx* could fly, but not very well.

Bird populations have been drastically reduced by people who have hunted them for their meat and feathers. Another threat is the popularity of birds, especially parrots, as pets. This has led to many birds being caught and caged. Many birds have also died when their habitats were destroyed, as woods and forests were cut down, marshes drained, and swamps filled to provide land for farming, development, and grazing. Birds have also suffered from the introduction into new lands of predators, such as cats and rats.

AMAZING FACTS!

The Cuban bee hummingbird is the smallest living **bird**. It weighs about 1/20 oz. (1.6g) and is about 2 in. (5cm) long. It moves its wings 70 times a second when flying and hovering in front of flowers.

The ostrich lays a gigantic egg that can weigh up to 4 lb. (1kg). The tiny Cuban bee hummingbird's egg is only 1/4 in. (5mm) long and weighs 1/100 oz. (.25g). More than 5,000 hummingbird eggs would fit inside an ostrich egg.

The nest built by the male dusky scrub fowl of Australia is a gigantic mound of rotting leaves, sticks, and grass that can sometimes measure 36 ft. (11m) across and over 16ft. (5m) high.

The feather cloak of the Hawaiian King Kamehameha I took at least a hundred years to make and used about 450,000 feathers from more than 80,000 birds.

✳ BOOK

It is hard to imagine civilization without books. They are the most important way of recording and passing on information and knowledge.

of parchment and decorate the pages with colored inks and paints. Parchment codexes soon replaced scrolls.

Invention of paper

The earliest Chinese books appeared about 5,000 years ago and were made from palm leaf or bamboo strips that were joined together at one corner and could be opened out like a fan.

◄
Dating from A.D. 868, this Chinese woodblock is the oldest surviving printed book.

Today we think of a book as a collection of paper pages with words or pictures or both printed on them, bound together in hard or soft (paperback) covers. Many copies of a book can be printed at one time to sell to bookstores and libraries.

History of books

The first books were made not from paper but from reeds called papyrus. The Egyptians were the first people to do this, from about 3500 B.C. The papyrus was rolled into scrolls, which could be sent to all parts of the Egyptian Empire. The ancient Greeks later took bookmaking a stage further by using scribes to make handwritten copies of existing scrolls.

The ancient Romans bound together thin sheets of board that had been specially treated with wax. The writing was then scratched across the surface. The Romans called a bound book a codex (from the Latin word for tree). By A.D. 400 they had found a better material—parchment. Parchment was a thin sheet of leather specially made from the skin of sheep or goats. Scribes could write on both sides

◄
An ancient Egyptian statue of a scribe reading a papyrus scroll.

In the first century A.D. the Chinese produced the world's first paper from wood chips, silk and cotton rags, hemp rope, and even old fishing nets that were made into a pulp and then molded into sheets. To start with, the Chinese wrote with special brushes, copying books by hand. From the sixth century A.D. they used carved wooden blocks to print characters on the pages.

The Chinese jealously guarded their secret method of making paper. It was not until the eighth century, when some Chinese craftsmen were taken prisoner by Arabs, that anyone else discovered how to make it. The craft did not reach Europe until the 12th century.

Books were still copied by hand until the 1400s. The invention of the printing press resulted in a huge increase in the number of books that could be made. Books also became much cheaper. Today, although methods of printing are far more advanced, the basic shape of books, bound down the left-hand side, with printing on both sides of the pages, is still the same.

SEE ALSO:
Egypt,
Ancient;
Greece,
Ancient;
Printing;
Roman
Empire

DID YOU KNOW?

Book production may be about to change. Soon you may no longer need to go to a bookstore or library to get a book. Some titles are already published electronically, so that you can download them onto a computer. You will have to pay a fee, and you will need special software (a computer program) to read it. Manufacturers have developed the eBook reader (below), a small hand-held computer onto which books can be downloaded and read anywhere. You can also listen to music on some readers and store other information, such as a diary or an address book.

✳ BOTANY

Botany is the branch of biology that studies plants, including their classification, structure, physical composition, and ecology.

Plants are essential to all life on earth. Only plants can capture the energy of the sun and use it—in a process called photosynthesis—to make food. Animals cannot do this and so depend on plants for food, as well as for the oxygen plants create during photosynthesis. Botanists have identified about 300,000 different varieties of plant, ranging in size from mosses as small as ½ in. (1cm) to redwood trees, which often are more than 295 ft. (90m) in height.

Branches of botany
There are many specialists within botany. Some botanists study plants in relation to the environment, investigating how soil and water affect their growth and development. Others study the history of plants on earth. This might involve investigating fossils and other evidence of species that became extinct thousands of years ago. This is called paleobotany.

Some botanists concentrate on particular varieties of plant. The study of

▲
Widely known as Linnaeus, the Swedish botanist and naturalist Carl von Linné created the modern system of plant classification.

fungi is called mycology; the study of ferns is called pteridology. Bacteriology, the study of bacteria, is a branch of botany that is important in medicine because many diseases are caused by bacteria.

Other botanists study different kinds of crops or investigate extracting materials such as rubber or drugs from plants.

Plant classification

Every known variety of plant has a unique botanical name. This follows the system originally devised by the Swedish naturalist Linnaeus (1707–78) in his book *Species Plantarum*, published in 1753. Under Linnaeus's method the white pine belongs to the genus, or group, *Pinus*, and its species, or kind, is *strobus*. So the scientific name for the white pine, wherever you are in the world, is *Pinus strobus*. This method of naming botanical species is called plant taxonomy.

AMAZING FACTS !

The biggest ever redwood weighed more than 3,000 tons, the same as about 20 blue whales.
Apples and peaches are in the same family as roses— Rosaceae. And tomatoes are related to tobacco; they are both in the Solanum, or nightshade, family.

SEE ALSO: Biology; Ecology; Flower; Plant

A botanist inspects a giant senecio plant in Tanzania.

✳ BRAIN AND NERVOUS SYSTEM

The brain controls the nerves, the spinal cord, and the sense organs (such as eyes and ears): Together, these body parts are known as the nervous system.

The brain is divided into different parts. The cerebellum controls body movement. The biggest part of the brain, the cerebrum, controls thinking, learning, memory, and imagination. The brain stem connects these parts to the spinal cord and contains the medulla, which keeps the blood flowing and the lungs breathing.

An average adult brain weighs about 3.1 lb. (1.4kg). It consists of two kinds of cell: neurons (nerve cells) and glia. Neurons send information through the body; glia clean, feed, protect, and support the neurons.

There are three main types of neuron: Sensory neurons respond to light, temperature, sound, smell, taste, and touch; motor neurons control muscles and movement; and interneurons relay information between the other two types. Most nerves are invisible to the naked eye, but some can be up to 3 ft. (1m) long.

Nervous system

The nervous system is divided into the central nervous system and the peripheral nervous system. The spinal

This magnetic resonance image (MRI) shows clearly the link between the brain and the spine. The body shape has been altered by an artist.
◀

AREAS OF THE BRAIN

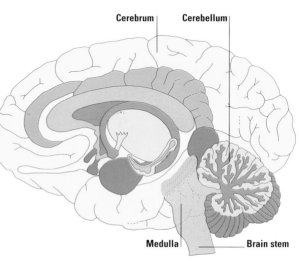

Cerebrum | Cerebellum |

Medulla | Brain stem

▲
Diagram showing the main areas of the human brain. The largest part is the cerebrum.

cord and the brain form the central nervous system. The spinal cord consists of nerves that run through the neck and back. These nerves are protected by the spinal column. The brain and spinal cord process incoming messages and send out messages to the organs and body parts on the periphery, or outside, of the body. The messages are carried by the branching network of nerves that make up the peripheral nervous system.

The spinal cord responds to some messages without involving the brain. If you touch something hot, for example, your hand recoils automatically without thinking. This is called a reflex action.

There are two main types of peripheral nerves: Sensory nerves carry messages to the central nervous system; motor nerves carry messages from the central nervous system to all parts of the body.

SEE ALSO:
Human Body

The autonomous nervous system is part of the peripheral nervous system. It controls vital organs such as the heart, stomach, and lungs. These nerves operate automatically, without your having to think about them.

Brain disorders

The brain is so important to the body that any damage to it can have added effects on the rest of the organism. The brain can be damaged by accident, such as a blow to the head, or by illnesses, such as epilepsy, which causes major electrical discharges within the brain.

Some people also suffer from mental illnesses, which affect their moods and thought patterns. Mental illness is not fully understood, but it can often be controlled through drugs.

AMAZING FACTS !

The human brain accounts for just 2 percent of the body's weight, but uses up to 20 percent of the body's oxygen supply.
Scientists estimate that the human brain contains more than 100 billion neurons (nerve cells).

Other animals

In most larger animals brains and nervous systems operate in a way similar to those of humans. But single-celled organisms do not have nervous systems, and other simple animals, such as jellyfish, have a collection of nerve cells called a nerve net, but no brain.

✳ BRAZIL

Brazil is the largest country in South America. It occupies almost half the continent's area and is home to more than half its population.

Brazil has a mixture of hilly and low-lying areas. It is divided into five regions: the northeast, the east, the south, the central west, and the Amazon Basin. Each region contains several states.

The Amazon Basin is a vast area of rainforest, jungle, and swamp formed by the Amazon River and its tributaries. The world's largest tropical rainforest, the region is home to many rare animals.

Climate

Most of Brazil has a tropical climate—the air is moist and sticky. In parts of the Amazon Basin temperatures stay near

◄

Typically colorful and riotous carnival celebrations in Rio de Janeiro to mark the start of Lent.

VENEZUELA GUYANA
COLOMBIA
SURINAME
FRENCH GUIANA (FRANCE)
Mouths of the Amazon
Amazon River
Belém
ECUADOR
Manaus
Fortaleza
Amazon Basin
Madeira River
PERU
Recife
São Francisco River
Tocantins River
Salvador
BOLIVIA
Goiânia
Brasília
PACIFIC OCEAN
Belo Horizonte
PARAGUAY
São Paulo
Rio de Janeiro
CHILE
Curitiba
ATLANTIC OCEAN
ARGENTINA
Pôrto Alegre
URUGUAY

Brazil's national flag

KEY FACTS

OFFICIAL NAME
Républica
Federativa do Brasil

AREA
3,286,478 sq. mi.
(8,511,965 sq. km)

POPULATION
170,115,000

CAPITAL
Brasília

LARGEST CITY
São Paulo

MAJOR RELIGIONS
Roman Catholicism,
Evangelical
Protestantism

MAJOR LANGUAGE
Portuguese

CURRENCY
Real

95°F (35°C) all the time. Ocean breezes bring cooler weather to the Atlantic coast, and south-central Brazil has mild winters. In the far south snow occasionally falls.

Economy
Brazil is an important producer of soybeans, coffee, cacao (the source of cocoa and chocolate), sugar, corn, fruits, tobacco, and cotton. Farmers raise great herds of cattle, horses, and hogs.

Brazil is also a leading industrial nation. Many of its factories, which turn out textiles, autos, chemicals, and other products, run on hydroelectric or nuclear power. Minerals, gemstones, ores, and wood products are important exports. Tourism and other services, such as education and business, are also important to the national economy.

Major cities
Brasília is the chief city and national capital. It is a modern city laid out in the rough shape of an airplane.

São Paulo, in the state of São Paulo, is the chief industrial city of Latin America and the largest city in Brazil. It is the center of the nation's textile industry.

Rio de Janeiro, in the state of Rio de Janeiro, is one of the world's most beautiful cities, with a fine harbor, steep mountains, and wide, tree-lined avenues. Rio is host to the largest and most exciting of the carnivals (street parties)

The great statue of Christ the Redeemer overlooking Rio de Janeiro.
▼

that take place before Lent every year.

Belo Horizonte, in the state of Minas Gerais, is Brazil's third largest city. It is a major commercial and industrial area. Belém, in the state of Pará, is the main port for Amazon River shipping.

People

Most Brazilians are mestizos (people of mixed European, African, and Indian ancestry). Others have come from Japan, the Middle East, and Europe, especially Portugal. A few Indians still live in remote areas of the tropical rainforest.

Brazil has a rich cultural heritage. Its contemporary music and dance are popular all over the world. The nation's favorite sport is soccer: The national team has won the World Cup more often than any other country.

History

Brazil's earliest inhabitants were Indians. More than 100 native tribal groups inhabited the land. They did not plant crops, but hunted animals and gathered fruits and berries.

Portuguese explorers came in search of gold in 1500. Portugal then ruled Brazil for more than 300 years. Settlers brought slaves from Africa to work on plantations. Brazil became independent in 1822. In 1888 slavery was abolished. In 1889 Brazil became a republic.

Throughout the 20th century Brazil faced problems such as rebellions and falling coffee prices. The government is hard-pressed to build enough schools and hospitals for the soaring population. The rainforest is being destroyed by industry.

SEE ALSO:
Amazon;
America,
South

✳ BUDDHISM

One of the oldest religions, Buddhism is based on the teachings of a man who said he had found the cause of unhappiness and its cure.

Buddha is believed to have been an Indian prince named Siddhartha Gautama who lived 2,500 years ago. When Siddhartha was a boy, his father tried to keep him from knowing how unhappy the world really was, but he discovered sickness and death on trips outside the palace. Filled with love and pity, Siddhartha gave up his wealth, sure that this would help him understand life. After six years of failure he sat beneath a tree and vowed not to move until understanding came to him. When it did, he became known as a buddha (Sanskrit for "enlightened one"). He spent the next 45 years teaching until his death in about 483 B.C. at 80.

Beliefs

There are no gods in Buddhism. Instead, Buddhists respect and worship the Buddha and his teachings. The most important Buddhist teachings are the Four Noble Truths, which are: All is suffering; the origin of suffering is desire; suffering comes to an end in nirvana; there is a way to reach nirvana.

Buddhists believe that nirvana is a state of inner peace and understanding. Misery and suffering are caused because we desire things, people, or life itself. It is possible, however, to find inner peace (nirvana) by following Buddhism and losing our desires.

Buddhists believe that people die and are reborn

▷ *A modern Buddhist monk sounding a bell at a monastery in Bangkok, Thailand.*

over and over again. Those who lead a good life are reborn into a better life, while bad people suffer more the next time around. Those who lose all desire will eventually reach nirvana.

The Buddhist life

The qualities needed to lead a good life include morality, compassion, and respect for others, as well as self-discipline and wisdom. Not all Buddhists follow exactly the same rules; some are stricter than others. Some enter monasteries to escape the world's desires; many visit holy sites or public shrines to make offerings of food or flowers. In every Buddhist's life much time is spent sitting quietly and peacefully.

Today Buddhism is a major religion in Asia, but there are many Buddhists in other countries, including the United States. The best-known form of Buddhism in the West is Zen, which began in China and is now practiced mainly in Japan.

SEE ALSO: Asia; Indian Subcontinent

✳ BURR, AARON (1756–1836)

Aaron Burr was a hero of the American Revolution and vice president, but he later stood trial for betraying his country.

When the American Revolution started, Burr joined the army, but quit in 1779. He served in the Senate and ran for the presidency in 1800. He and Thomas Jefferson each got 73 electoral votes, but the House of Representatives chose Jefferson to be the third president, with Burr as his vice president.

Alexander Hamilton, who became secretary of the treasury, had been one of Burr's leading opponents during the campaign.

Aaron Burr at the height of his career as vice president. He was later disgraced after being arrested for treason.

The bad feeling between the men finally led to a duel on July 11, 1804. A duel is a fight (arranged in advance) with deadly weapons between two people.

Burr killed Hamilton and fled to escape a murder charge. Some people believed that Burr was planning to set up his own empire in the southwestern United States and part of Mexico. In 1807 he was arrested for treason, but a judge ruled that there was no clear proof of the crime.

After his trial Burr went to Europe, but returned to the United States in 1812. He died on Staten Island, New York, on September 14, 1836.

✷ CAESAR, JULIUS (ABOUT 100–44 B.C.)

Julius Caesar was a politician, soldier, writer, and leader of the Roman republic. His name, Caesar, became the title of the Roman emperors.

Gaius Julius Caesar was born into a noble family and began his political career in 78 B.C. In 59 B.C. he formed an alliance with Pompey, a famous general, and Crassus, a rich nobleman. This three-man pact was called the First Triumvirate. Caesar was elected as a consul, became governor of three provinces, and successfully fought the Gauls in France and the Britons in England. Pompey later became jealous of him, and a civil war broke out between them, which Caesar won at the battle of Pharsalus in 48 B.C.

Caesar returned to Rome in 45 B.C. and was named dictator. He began many worthwhile reforms, and the following year he was appointed dictator for life. Other important Romans, such as Brutus and Cassius, thought this was too much power for one man, and they stabbed him to death in the Senate on March 15, 44 B.C.

SEE ALSO: Cleopatra; Roman Empire

▲
Julius Caesar ruled ancient Rome from 49 B.C. until his murder five years later.

✷ CAMOUFLAGE

Camouflage is a disguise that enables animals to blend in with their surroundings. It can help them hide from enemies or get near their prey.

Some camouflage is simply a matter of color. Polar bears have white coats that make them difficult to spot in the snow and ice of their Arctic habitat. Other species have coats that change with the seasons. Some varieties of weasel have brown coats in summer, then grow white coats when the winter snows come.

Some fish, such as tuna and herring, are darker on the tops of their bodies than on their undersides. When they are viewed from above, their dark backs blend in with the dark water below. When they are viewed from below, the light color of their undersides blends with the brighter water nearer the surface.

Patterned coats can also act as camouflage. The stripes of zebras break up the outline of their bodies and make them difficult for predators to spot. The

patterned coats of big cats such as tigers and jaguars make them difficult to see in dappled sunlight and allow them to stalk their prey more easily.

Protective camouflage

Some creatures take on a shape that resembles natural features around them. Some caterpillars and walking stick insects resemble leaves or twigs, and that enables them to hide from

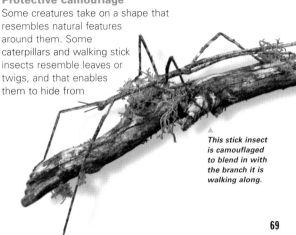

▲
This stick insect is camouflaged to blend in with the branch it is walking along.

predators. Other animals protect themselves by imitating more dangerous
species. The hornet fly, for example,
has no sting; but because it resembles a
hornet, which does sting, birds avoid it.

Camouflage helps animals survive. If
they are killed by predators or starve
because they cannot catch prey, they
will not breed and will not pass on their
genes, or unique characteristics. If they
live long enough to give birth, they will
pass on to their offspring the genes that
carry information about camouflage.

▲
*The cheetah's spotted
fur enables it to blend
into its surroundings,
giving it an advantage
when stalking prey.*

SEE ALSO: Evolution; Genetics; Habitat

✳ CANADA

**Canada, in northern North America, is the
second largest country in the world, after Russia.
Most of its land is very sparsely populated.**

Canada has coastlines on three oceans,
the Atlantic, the Pacific, and the Arctic. Its
border with the United States crosses
four of the five Great Lakes and Niagara
Falls. Canada contains one-third of all the
frozen fresh water on Earth.

The landscape includes the Interior
Plains, or prairies, part of the North
American Great Plains, and the northern
part of the Rocky Mountains. Other areas
include the Pacific Ranges and Lowlands,
and the Arctic Islands, which cover more
than 500,000 sq. mi. (1.3 million sq. km).

Canada tends to have cold winters and
moderately warm summers. In the far
north temperatures
fall below 0°F
(–18°C) for five

*Sea lions resting
on a rock in the
Pacific Ocean off
the coast of
British Columbia,
Canada.*
▶

months of the year. Snowfall can reach
118 in. (300cm) a year. On the east and
west coasts there is more rain—as much
as 265 in. (6,700cm) on Vancouver Island,
British Columbia.

Plant and animal life
Canada's most important plants are trees.
There are about 150 native species,
including maple, Douglas fir, Sitka spruce,
ponderosa pine, and aspen. One-quarter
of Canada is covered by Arctic tundra,
where no trees grow. The most common
plants here are lichen and moss. About 15
percent of the country is covered by
wetland—bogs, swamps, and marshes.

The earliest industry in Canada was the
animal fur and skin trade. Hunted animals
included beavers, lynxes, mink, polar
bears, seals, and walruses. Bison were
hunted so much that they are now
protected and live on reserves in Alberta
and the Northwest Territories.

(Continued on page 72)

Canada's national flag

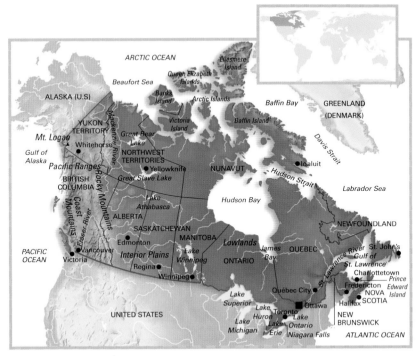

ARCTIC OCEAN

Ellesmere Island

Queen Elizabeth Islands

Beaufort Sea

ALASKA (U.S.)

Banks Island

Arctic Islands

Baffin Bay

GREENLAND (DENMARK)

YUKON TERRITORY

Victoria Island

Baffin Island

Mt. Logan

Whitehorse

Great Bear Lake

Mackenzie River

Gulf of Alaska

Pacific Ranges

NORTHWEST TERRITORIES

Yellowknife

NUNAVUT

Iqaluit

Davis Strait

BRITISH COLUMBIA

Rocky Mountains

Great Slave Lake

Hudson Strait

Labrador Sea

Coast Mountains

Lake Athabasca

ALBERTA

Hudson Bay

Fraser River

SASKATCHEWAN

MANITOBA

NEWFOUNDLAND

PACIFIC OCEAN

Vancouver

Victoria

Edmonton

Interior Plains

Lake Winnipeg

Lowlands

James Bay

QUEBEC

St. Lawrence River

St. John's

Gulf of St. Lawrence

Regina

Winnipeg

ONTARIO

Charlottetown

Fredericton

Prince Edward Island

Québec City

NOVA SCOTIA

Lake Superior

Lake Huron

Toronto

Ottawa

Halifax

UNITED STATES

Lake Michigan

Lake Erie

Lake Ontario

Niagara Falls

NEW BRUNSWICK

ATLANTIC OCEAN

The largest and most populous city in Canada, Toronto is the country's financial and commercial center. It stands on the shore of Lake Ontario.

KEY FACTS

OFFICIAL NAME
Dominion of Canada

AREA
3,851,809 sq. mi.
(9,976,185 sq. km)

POPULATION
31,081,900
(2001 census)

CAPITAL
Ottawa

LARGEST CITY
Toronto

MAJOR RELIGION
Christianity
(Roman Catholic, Protestant)

MAJOR LANGUAGES
English, French

CURRENCY
Canadian dollar

Other native animals include grizzly and black bears, cougars, and coyotes. Caribou and reindeer graze on the northern tundra. Fish include walleye, salmon, lake trout, pike, bass, and sturgeon; birds include mallard, American black duck, osprey, bald eagle, red-winged blackbird, and the Canada goose.

People
The largest group of Canadians is of British ancestry (about 28 percent of the population). The next largest group is French-speaking people (about 23 percent). Recently, large numbers of

Europeans trading with native Canadians during the 1700s.

immigrants have come from Asia, especially Hong Kong, India, China, Taiwan, and the Philippines, and from the Caribbean. Today native peoples make up only about 4 percent of the population.

Much of Canada's vast land area is unsuitable for human habitation, and 85 percent of the population lives within 180 miles (300km) of the U.S. border. More than one-quarter of the population lives in Toronto, Montreal, or Vancouver, the three biggest cities.

Economy
Service industries, including tourism, make up the largest segment of Canada's economy. Other major industries include manufacturing, especially in Ontario and Quebec provinces. Agriculture and fishing are concentrated in the Great Lakes–St.

Lawrence Lowlands and the Prairie Provinces. There are rich mineral resources throughout the country.

History
The earliest inhabitants of Canada were Inuits, who arrived from Asia about 25,000 years ago. Leif Eriksson, a Viking explorer, probably landed in northern Newfoundland in about 1000 B.C., but it was another 500 years before there was any permanent European settlement.

In 1497 the Italian Giovanni Caboto (John Cabot) reached Newfoundland. Many fishermen followed, attracted by the massive stocks of fish in the northwestern Atlantic Ocean. In 1534 Jacques Cartier claimed the Gulf of St. Lawrence for France and named the area Kanata, from the Huron-Iroquois word for "village" or "settlement."

By the end of the 1500s French and English settlers were competing for the fur trade. Humphrey Gilbert claimed Newfoundland for England in 1583, and Samuel de Champlain founded Quebec, a French settlement, in 1608. By 1689 the French, assisted by the Hurons, were in open conflict with the English and their Iroquois allies. Peace returned in 1713 when France surrendered Acadia (now Nova Scotia), Newfoundland, and Hudson Bay. The 1750s brought further disagreements that ended only when the French forces surrendered at Montreal in 1760. Canada was now British.

French people in a British state
There was still a large minority of French-speaking settlers in Canada, and the Quebec Act of 1774 gave them legal and religious rights. American colonists were angry that land they planned to settle was now subject to French law. The act became one of the causes of the American Revolution. Americans tried to invade Canada in 1775 and again in 1812.

The Act of Union in 1840 united the two territories of Upper and Lower Canada (now Ontario and Quebec). In 1867 the British North America Act created the Canadian Confederation, comprising Ontario, Quebec, New Brunswick, and Nova Scotia. The first prime minister of Canada was John A. Macdonald.

In the 1880s a métis (part-French, part-Native American) called Louis Riel led the Northwest Rebellion of prairie settlers unhappy at the pace of westward confederation. Riel was executed in 1885, but he became a figurehead for French-speakers who were unhappy at the increasing power of the Canadian state.

In 1905 the new provinces of Alberta and Saskatchewan were created.

Postwar Canada

After World War II (1939–45) Canadian French-speakers campaigned to make Quebec independent from Canada. The separatist Parti Québécois took control of the province in 1976, but gave up calls for full independence in 1995.

In 1982 the Constitution Act finally granted Canada the right to amend its own constitution without permission from Britain.

◄
The western red cedar is one of many magnificent species of tree native to Canada.

Niagara Falls forms part of the border between the United States and Canada.
▼

An aerial view of Long Beach in the Pacific Rim National Park, British Columbia, Canada.

In 1994 Canada signed the North American Free Trade Agreement (NAFTA) with the United States and Mexico.

In 1999 Nunavut was created as Canada's newest territory, a homeland for the Inuit people. Located in the high Arctic part of the Northwest Territories, the capital of Nunavut is Iqaluit.

SEE ALSO: Inuit; Viking

✳ CAR

Cars are self-propelled vehicles that travel on land without rails. They are a form of automobile, a term that also covers trucks and buses.

The first self-powered road vehicle was built by a Frenchman, Nicolas Cugnot, in 1769. It was a three-wheeled steam engine designed to pull cannons. It was never fully tested because it crashed during a trial run.

Later efforts by the Englishman Richard Trevithick and the American Oliver Evans had little success. It was not until the late 1800s that the car as we now know it began to take shape.

The German engineers Gottlieb Daimler and Karl Benz both created working, engine-driven automobiles in 1886. In the 1890s French engineer Emile Levassor built a car with spring suspension and clutch-and-gear transmission. The next big idea was the brainchild of the Americans Ransom E. Olds and Henry M. Leland, who found it profitable to build all their vehicles from standardized parts.

The greatest advances in car manufacture, however, were made by Henry Ford, who developed the assembly line that made mass production possible. In the Ford plant cars under construction were moved down the line on a conveyor belt, and each worker had a few simple tasks to perform, over and over, many times a day.

Henry Ford and his son, Edsel, in the 1905 Model F Ford outside their home in Detroit, Michigan.

Cars for the masses

Before the assembly line it took 728 minutes to build a complete chassis. Afterward it took 93 minutes. Between

INSIDE A CAR

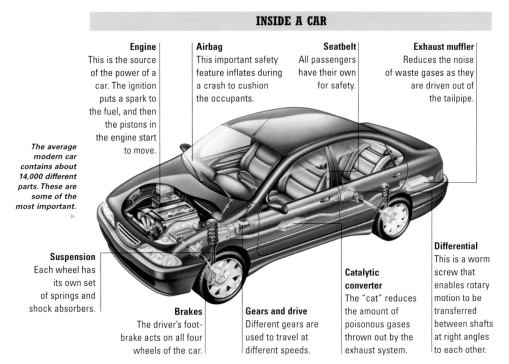

Engine
This is the source of the power of a car. The ignition puts a spark to the fuel, and then the pistons in the engine start to move.

Airbag
This important safety feature inflates during a crash to cushion the occupants.

Seatbelt
All passengers have their own for safety.

Exhaust muffler
Reduces the noise of waste gases as they are driven out of the tailpipe.

The average modern car contains about 14,000 different parts. These are some of the most important. ▶

Suspension
Each wheel has its own set of springs and shock absorbers.

Brakes
The driver's foot-brake acts on all four wheels of the car.

Gears and drive
Different gears are used to travel at different speeds.

Catalytic converter
The "cat" reduces the amount of poisonous gases thrown out by the exhaust system.

Differential
This is a worm screw that enables rotary motion to be transferred between shafts at right angles to each other.

Although cars provide many benefits to society, they have several disadvantages, including congestion and pollution.

1908 and 1925 the cost of a Model T fell from $850 to $290. Cars were now affordable by ordinary people.

In the next few decades developments such as hydraulic brakes, safety glass, and car radios made driving safer and more enjoyable. Large numbers of trucks were built to carry goods.

By the 1960s the massive increase in car use was causing pollution problems. Laws were passed to control the chemicals that cars pumped into the air. In the 1970s there were gasoline shortages,

and manufacturers made cars smaller and more efficient. More recently, battery-powered cars have been developed to protect the Earth's resources, but they are still not generally used.

How a car works

Most cars are powered by internal combustion engines. They are started up by an electrical system that makes a spark and powered by liquid fuel—either gasoline or diesel. When mixed with air and burned, the fuel generates expanding

AMAZING FACTS !

In the United States there are about two people per car; in China there are more than 1,300 people per car.
In a year American motorists travel about 2 trillion miles.
The longest car ever built is a 26-wheel limousine, 100 ft. (30.5m) long.

gases. The gases are a form of energy that is used to turn a shaft. The torque, or twisting force, of this shaft is used to turn the car's driving wheels.

The transmission, or gearbox, of a car uses coupling devices and sets of gears to match the engine's rotating speed to the desired road speed. The device that controls the transmission is called the

clutch. Transmissions may be automatic or manual, with the shifting of gears and pressing of the clutch pedal being carried out by the driver.

Oil protects the various engine parts from rubbing against each other, and a cooling system prevents overheating. The exhaust removes waste gases.

The suspension is a set of springs and shock absorbers that soften unevenness in the road and help the car take corners smoothly and safely.

Today most cars are built with safety features, such as airbags. Yet thousands of people are still killed and injured on the road each year. The car provides many benefits, but it must be used with care.

SEE ALSO: Engine; Pollution; Transportation

✳ CARIBBEAN SEA AND ISLANDS

The Caribbean Sea is a part of the Atlantic Ocean between Mexico, Central and South America, and the islands of the West Indies.

Named for the Carib Indians, who once inhabited some of the islands, the Caribbean Sea covers an area of about 750,000 sq. mi. (about 2 million sq. km). The Panama Canal links the Caribbean with the Pacific Ocean, making the sea one of the world's major waterways.

Island groups
The islands of the Caribbean consist of two main groups: the Greater Antilles and the Lesser Antilles. The Greater Antilles include the four largest islands—Cuba, Hispaniola (shared by the nations of Haiti and the Dominican Republic), Jamaica, and Puerto Rico. The Lesser Antilles include Barbados, the Leeward Islands, and the Windward Islands. The Virgin Islands and the northern islands of the Netherlands Antilles are usually classified as parts of the Lesser Antilles. To the

north the Bahamas and the Turks and Caicos Islands are outside the Caribbean area.

Land and climate
The islands are part of two partly submerged mountain chains that reach their highest point in Hispaniola. The mountains have been worn away on many of the Lesser Antilles, but some of the other islands still have active volcanoes.

The Caribbean region has a moderate climate, cooled by the breezes of the trade

▶
Downtown Kingston, the capital of Jamaica and the home of reggae music.

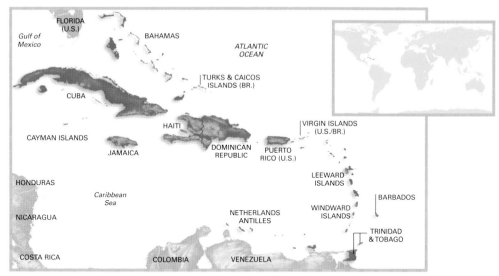

winds. Temperatures range from about 70 to 85°F (21–29°C). Rainfall is heaviest in summer. Hurricanes often develop in the late summer or early fall and may cause widespread damage.

People

St. John, one of the three main U.S. Virgin Islands, which lie about 40 miles (64km) east of Puerto Rico.

The original Indian inhabitants of the islands died out soon after the arrival of European settlers. Most Caribbean peoples today are descended from Africans brought to the region to work as slaves on fruit and sugar plantations. The varied languages of the islands include English, Spanish, French, and Dutch.

KEY FACTS

GREATER ANTILLES
Cuba, Hispaniola (Haiti and the Dominican Republic), Jamaica, Puerto Rico (U.S.)

LESSER ANTILLES
Anguilla (Br.), Antigua and Barbuda, Aruba (Neth.), Barbados, Bonaire (Neth.), Curaçao (Neth.), Dominica, Grenada, Guadeloupe (Fr.), Martinique (Fr.), Montserrat (Br.), Saba (Neth.), St. Eustatius (Neth.), St. Kitts and Nevis, St. Lucia, St. Martin (Fr.-Neth.), St. Vincent and the Grenadines, Trinidad and Tobago, British Virgin Islands, U.S. Virgin Islands (St. Croix, St. John, St. Thomas)

OTHER ISLANDS
Cayman Islands (Br.), Margarita (Venez.), Tortuga (Venez.)

STATUS
All Caribbean islands are independent except where noted:
Br. = Britain
Fr. = France
Neth. = Netherlands
U.S. = United States
Venez. = Venezuela

Economy

For centuries the chief products of the Caribbean have been sugar, coffee, tropical fruits, and spices. However, industry is now Puerto Rico's main source of income. Curaçao and Trinidad have petroleum refineries. Cuba has one of the world's largest deposits of nickel, and Jamaica produces bauxite, the chief source of aluminum. Tourism is an important industry for all the islands.

History

Christopher Columbus reached the Caribbean in 1492. The Spanish then colonized the Greater Antilles. For the next 300 years Spain vied with other European nations for dominance in the region. The Caribbean was also a profitable hunting ground for pirates.

As a result of the Spanish-American War (1898), Cuba won its independence, and Puerto Rico became a territory of the United States. In 1917 the United States bought St. Croix, St. John, and St. Thomas (the U.S. Virgin Islands) from Denmark.

Haiti was the first Caribbean state to gain independence, following a revolt against the French in the late 1700s. The Dominican Republic gained independence from Spain in the mid-1800s, and Cuba became a republic in 1902. Most of the British-owned islands became independent between 1960 and 1980.

SEE ALSO:
Columbus, Christopher;
Cuba;
Music, Popular;
Panama

✳ CARNIVORE

Scientists divide animals into groups called orders. The order Carnivora is made up of the mammals that eat meat.

Ten families make up the Carnivora: dogs, wolves, foxes, and jackals; bears; racoons and pandas; weasels, skunks, otters, and badgers; genets, civets, and mongooses; hyenas; cats; sea lions; seals; and walrus.

Hunting

Meat-eating animals spend much of their time seeking the food they need to survive. A few meat-eating animals do not hunt for themselves; instead, they clean up the remains of animals killed by other creatures. Such animals are called scavengers and include hyenas.

The hunting styles of carnivores are related to the type of prey on which they feed. Wolves and cheetahs hunt fast-running, four-legged herbivores (plant eaters). In a matter of three seconds the cheetah can reach speeds of almost 70

After they have killed their prey, gray wolves fight among themselves as they struggle for dominance within the pack. The strongest eat first. ▶

mph (113km/h), but only for a brief time. If the cheetah does not catch its prey within about 600 ft. (185m), it gives up and looks for another victim. Wolves hunt in packs. Members take turns chasing their victims and can keep up pursuit for miles. The prey becomes exhausted and an easy target for the hungry pack.

Meat eaters have long, sharp teeth for tearing and chewing flesh, and strong jaws. The curved, sharp claws of cats are used to grab and hold prey. They can withdraw, or retract, their claws when they are not needed for this purpose. That enables them to step softly when stalking prey. Cats—from house cats to lions—like to creep up close to their intended victims before they pounce.

Bears are the largest land carnivores. They live mainly on insects, seeds, nuts, plants, and berries; some also eat fish. Only the polar bear lives mainly on meat, principally seals. Pandas are carnivores, but they live mostly on bamboo shoots, while racoons are carnivores that eat

AMAZING FACTS !

The elephant seal, the largest carnivore, can weigh 4 tons (3,600kg). **The least weasel**, the smallest carnivore, weighs only 1–2½ oz. (30–70g).

almost anything. The sea otter eats abalone and other shellfish, which it opens by cracking them on a rock held on its chest as it floats in the water.

Reproduction

Most carnivores have between three and six young. Bears usually have two cubs. The Asiatic polecat may have up to 18 young. Most young are cared for by one or both parents until they have learned to hunt and so can fend for themselves.

SEE ALSO:
Dog

Sea otters are carnivorous mammals that feed mainly on shellfish.

✱ CARSON, RACHEL (1907–64)

American marine biologist Rachel Carson is widely regarded as the founder of the modern environmental movement.

Rachel Louise Carson was born in Springdale, Pennsylvania. Her interest in nature began in early childhood. She graduated from Pennsylvania College for Women in 1929 and received a masters degree from Johns Hopkins University in 1932. From 1936 she worked for the Fish and Wildlife Service.

Author of *Silent Spring*
Carson began to write books about marine life. *The Sea around Us* (1951) became a bestseller and won the National Book Award for nonfiction. In *Silent Spring* (1962), her most famous book, Carson warned that the chemical sprays used by

farmers were poisoning the environment. The spring was silent, she explained, because pesticides had killed the birds and other living things. Her book was publicly attacked by industrial firms, but further research supported many of her findings and led to restrictions on pesticide use. Carson died in 1964. The Rachel Carson National Wildlife Refuge in Maine was named for her in 1970.

SEE ALSO: Ecology; Environment; Pollution

▲
Rachel Carson at work in a government research laboratory.

✱ CARTOON AND ANIMATION

A cartoon was originally a rough drawing done to prepare for a painting. Today the word refers to a drawing, or a series of drawings, with a message.

Cartoons can tell a simple joke or a long story. They can be funny and zany or serious and political. They can appear on a printed page or on a TV or movie screen as animation (moving pictures).

Cartoons as we know them began in the 1700s, when printed books and pictures became cheaply available. Artists such as the Englishman James Gillray (1756–1815) and the Frenchman Honoré Daumier (1808–79) used their skills to attack politicians. Cartoons became common in European newspapers and magazines. The first important American cartoonist was Thomas Nast (1840–1902), who attacked political corruption in *Harper's Weekly* magazine.

In the 1900s one-panel cartoons—

cartoons with a single picture—were very popular in magazines like *The Saturday Evening Post*, but gradually comic strips took their place. The only magazine in the United States that still features large numbers of one-panel cartoons is *The New Yorker*, which has published great cartoonists such as James Thurber and Charles Addams. One-panel cartoons, especially on political subjects, are still popular in other countries.

Animation
Cartoons that are filmed to give

This 1798 cartoon by James Gillray satirizes the struggle between Britain and France for military supremacy in Europe.
▼

AMAZING FACTS!

The first cartoon with a soundtrack was *Steamboat Willie*, made in 1928. It starred Mickey Mouse.
Mickey Mouse was the first nonhuman to win an Academy Award (or Oscar).
Walt Disney has won more Academy Awards than anybody else, with 26 Oscars over 37 years.
The Simpsons is the longest running animated series on television.

the illusion of movement are called animation. There are three main kinds of animation: flat pictures, three-dimensional models, and computer-generated animation.

Primitive animation existed well before the movies. Devices called magic lanterns contained simple drawings that appeared to move when the machine was rotated. The idea behind two-dimensional animation is the same. Each drawing is photographed one at a time. There are very slight differences between the drawings, so that when the frames are run together at speed, the figures appear to be moving. Some animation is drawn directly onto paper, which is photographed, but most cartoons of this type are now created on transparent sheets called cels. Most of the famous movies of the Walt Disney studios, such as *Snow White*, *The Jungle Book*, and *Beauty and the Beast,* were made this way. It is also the most usual technique

▲
Walt Disney (1901–66) drawing a sketch of his first great cartoon character, Mickey Mouse.

The dinosaurs in Jurassic Park were created by combining full-size and small-scale models with computer-generated images.
▼

done in a similar way. Models are moved a tiny fraction at a time, and each move is photographed. An early example of this technique was the 1933 movie *King Kong*. More recently filmmakers have used clay models. In Nick Park's *Chicken Run*, for example, simple actions such as a character scratching his head involved hundreds of tiny movements and took many hours to shoot.

The first big success of computer animation was *Jurassic Park*, an action movie released in 1993 and directed by Steven Spielberg. Computer-generated dinosaurs were used to menace the human characters. Later movies, such as *Toy Story*, *Antz*, and *Monsters, Inc.*, were made entirely with computer technology.

▲
A publicity still from the 1933 film King Kong.

for TV cartoons like *The Flintstones*, *The Simpsons*, and *Rugrats*. Some movies combine animated pictures and live action—examples include *Mary Poppins* and *Who Killed Roger Rabbit?*

Three-dimensional model animation is

SEE ALSO: Movies

✳ CASTLE

A castle is a building or group of buildings with fortifications to protect it from outside attack. It may be a garrison for soldiers or a home for nobles.

Many castles were built in Europe between the 900s and the 1400s. During this period, known as the Middle Ages, kings often granted land to wealthy nobles. In return, nobles swore loyalty to the monarchs and promised to supply them with armed fighting men called knights. The noblemen built castles from which their knights could control and defend the surrounding countryside.

Construction

Castle design changed greatly over the centuries. Early castles were built of earth and timber, but from about 1000 onward most were made almost entirely of stone. A large stone castle was very expensive

to build. Materials often had to be transported over long distances. Construction could take 20 years and employ more than 2,000 workers. Castles were symbols of power and status.

▶
Harlech Castle in Wales has two thick walls, circular towers, and a strong central gatehouse.

✳ CHEMISTRY

Chemistry is the science that deals with the structure and properties of substances and the changes that these substances undergo.

Atomic theory is one of the most fundamental parts of the science of chemistry. This theory states that all substances are made up of tiny particles far too small to be seen even with the strongest microscopes. These tiny particles are called atoms. Everything—glass, brick, iron, water, the stars, and your own body—is made up of atoms.

There are many kinds of atoms. So far scientists know of at least 114 different kinds. Most of them are quite rare. Only about a dozen kinds of atoms are common on Earth.

Then how can there be so many different things on Earth? The answer is that atoms are like the letters of the alphabet—all English words are built out of only 26 letters. Even just a few kinds of atoms can combine into many different arrangements. Each arrangement makes up a different substance.

Chemical and physical changes

Understanding how substances can change is essential to understanding chemistry. But not all changes are chemical changes.

For example, you can break up a bar of iron into tiny pieces. Each piece is still iron because the arrangement of atoms has not been changed. This is a physical change. You can magnetize a piece of iron, or let an electric current pass through it. These, too, are physical changes.

If you heat a mixture of powdered iron and sulfur, a blackish material forms in which you can no longer see separate little bits of grayish iron or yellow sulfur. The new material has a new set of properties unlike those of either iron or sulfur. It is a substance called ferrous sulfide. When the iron and sulfur were heated, each sulfur atom combined with

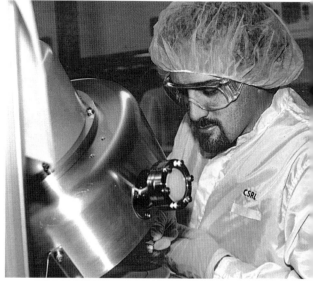

an iron atom, forming molecules of ferrous sulfide. A new arrangement of atoms was formed, and it made up a new substance with new properties. This is an example of a chemical change, which is also called a chemical reaction.

Chemical changes go on all around us. Whenever coal or oil burns, that is a chemical change. The rusting of iron is a chemical change. When food is cooked, it goes through many chemical changes. Chemical changes also go on inside the body at all times. These are the many kinds of changes that interest a chemist.

Branches of chemistry

Chemistry overlaps many other sciences. For example, some chemists might want to know how fast reactions go and what can be done to change their speed. They might want to know how a salt solution can carry an electric current. Questions

▲
A researcher using a device that can detect and analyze tiny amounts of chemicals.

like these are answered by using methods similar to those used by scientists called physicists. This branch of chemistry is called physical chemistry.

Chemists also study the many chemical processes that take place inside living organisms. They might want to know how foods are broken down and digested in the body, for example. Their field of study is called biochemistry.

The study of compounds containing carbon is called organic chemistry because because carbon comes from living or once-living organisms. The study of other compounds is called inorganic chemistry. Analytical chemistry identifies and studies the different chemical substances that make up mixtures.

Specialized branches of chemistry include astrochemistry, the study of the origin and interaction of chemicals in space. Geochemistry is related to the science of geology and is applied in areas such as mineral-ore processing. Nuclear chemistry is concerned with the use of nuclear power and the safe disposal of nuclear wastes. Environmental chemistry focuses on the effect of chemicals on the environment.

Chemistry is put to use in the search for new energy sources, in efforts to fight disease, to improve agricultural yields, and to increase the world's food supply. Chemistry in fact touches many parts of our lives and has been put to use since human history began.

SEE ALSO:
Atom &
Molecule;
Physics;
Science;
Scientist

✳ CHIEF JOSEPH (1840–1904)

Joseph, born In-mut-too-yah-lat-lat ("Thunder Rolling in the Heights"), was chief of the Nez Percé people and a brilliant military leader.

In 1863 the government ordered the Nez Percé to move from their traditional lands in Oregon to a reservation in Idaho. For 13 years the Nez Percé ignored the orders, but the situation became worse when gold was discovered in the area. In 1877 the government sent agents to enforce the removal. Chief Joseph decided to escape with his people into Canada. For more than three months he led them on a 1,000-mile (1,600km) journey across the Rockies. On the way, despite being outnumbered ten to one, he

fought and won more than a dozen battles against some of the Army's best officers. About 30 miles (50km) from the Canadian border troops commanded by General Nelson A. Miles attacked the Nez Percé. Chief Joseph surrendered on October 5, and Miles promised that his people could return to their native lands.

A broken promise
Miles' promise was broken, however. Despite Joseph's efforts, the Nez Percé were sent to a reservation in Oklahoma. Joseph died in Washington in 1904.

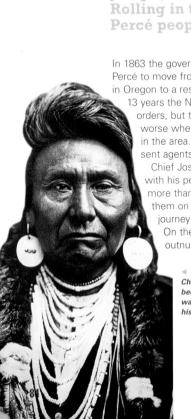

Chief Joseph, aged about 50. He became chief in 1871, when he was 31, after the previous chief, his father, died.

✱ CHILE

Chile lies along the southwestern coast of South America, separated from Argentina by the Andes, one of the world's highest mountain chains.

Chile stretches more than 2,600 miles (4,120km) from north to south but averages only 100 miles (160km) in width. It is generally cold and rainy in the south and hot and dry in the north.

In parts of the Atacama Desert no rainfall has ever been recorded. Although harsh, this region attracts settlers because of its rich mineral deposits.

The Central Valley lies between the Andes and a range of coastal mountains. The soil is fertile, and the climate is mild. Over two-thirds of the population live in this region, mainly in the cities of Santiago and Valparaíso. Three-fourths of Chile's industry is also located here, as are most of the rich farms.

Chile claims parts of Antarctica but this is not recognized internationally. The official boundary stops at Cape Horn. Chile and Argentina share the island of Tierra del Fuego (Land of Fire). Chile owns other islands off its west coast, including the Juan Fernández Islands and Easter Island, which is known for the great stone heads that people there carved long ago.

People

The Chilean people are mainly of mixed Indian, Spanish, and other European descent. The remaining true Indians number only about 500,000.

About 85 percent of the population live in cities and urban areas. A huge gap still separates the few rich people from the many poor. Wealthy Chileans own the factories, banks, and large farms and ranches. In the cities there is a growing middle class of doctors, teachers, clerks, and soldiers. Poor Chileans live in rural shacks or city slums. They try to earn a living as farmhands, miners, factory workers, and laborers. But one in four of all Chileans has no job.

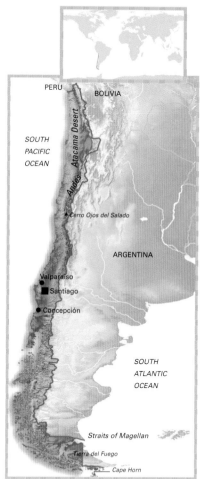

Chile's national flag

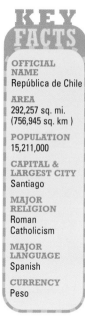

KEY FACTS

OFFICIAL NAME
República de Chile

AREA
292,257 sq. mi.
(756,945 sq. km)

POPULATION
15,211,000

CAPITAL & LARGEST CITY
Santiago

MAJOR RELIGION
Roman Catholicism

MAJOR LANGUAGE
Spanish

CURRENCY
Peso

▶
A view of Constitution Plaza, the main square in the center of Santiago, Chile's capital city.

Economy

Farming employs about 20 percent of the Chilean workforce. Fruits, wines, and vegetables are among Chile's leading

General Pinochet Ugarte, who led a military coup that toppled President Allende in 1973.

agricultural exports. Chile is the world's largest producer of copper. Other important metals are molybdenum, iron ore, gold, and silver. Iodine and boron are valuable by-products of nitrate mining.

Processed foods, wood and wood products (including paper), textiles, and transportation equipment and machinery are some of the chief manufactured products. Commercial fishing is also a major industry.

History

Indians lived in Chile for thousands of years before the Spanish arrived in the 16th century. The first Spaniards came to Chile from Peru, looking for riches. The Indians struggled against Spanish conquest for two centuries, although after 100 years fighting and disease had reduced their number by two-thirds.

When the French invaded Spain in 1808, they removed the Spanish king. Chileans founded their own government in 1810. After a number of battles with the Spanish Chile achieved independence in 1818.

Chileans then fought one another for control. Periods of stability alternated with war. In 1925 Chile adopted a new constitution with a strong presidency.

In 1973 the Chilean military overthrew President Allende, who had given much of the country's property to the poor. The succeeding Pinochet government reversed Allende's policies. In 1988 Pinochet was rejected as president, paving the way for a democratic election.

SEE ALSO: Easter Island; Incas

✳ CHINA

The People's Republic of China is home to one-fifth of the world's population and is also the world's third largest country in area.

Chinese pilots in 1969 holding up Mao Zedong's "Little Red Book" of his thoughts.

Because of China's size its geography is varied. The north, where the Huang He (Yellow River) flows, is cold and dry. The south, which includes Guangzhou (Canton) and Hong Kong, is much warmer. The two areas are divided by the Chang Jiang (Yangtze), the third longest river in the world, which flows to Shanghai, the largest city in China.

History

From ancient times Chinese rulers have passed power to brothers or sons, forming dynasties, or ruling families. China's name comes from the Ch'in (Qin) Dynasty, founded in 221 B.C. The first emperor was Huang Ti.

For many centuries China was far ahead of any European state in terms of prosperity, technical and scientific knowledge, art, and culture. The Chinese

invented many things, such as gunpowder, paper, and printing, long before they were known in the West.

In the 13th century the Venetian explorer Marco Polo visited the court of the Chinese Emperor Kublai Khan, and the Portuguese reached China by sea in the the 1500s. But it was not until the 19th century, during the Manchu Dynasty, that China began to trade widely with Europe.

Weakened by foreign wars, the last emperor was forced out in 1912, and a republic was formed. The first president was Sun Yat-sen, who led the Kuomintang, or Nationalists. In 1949, after a civil war, the Communists, under Mao Zedong, took control. The Kuomintang leader Chiang Kai-shek retreated to the island of Taiwan. In 1950 China invaded and occupied Tibet. However, many people still do not recognize Chinese authority there.

China's national flag

In the 1960s Mao Zedong launched the Cultural Revolution, aimed at keeping the revolutionary spirit alive in China. He made young people join the Red Guards and encouraged them to criticize their teachers and parents if they were not committed to the Communist Party.

For many years the United States did not recognize the People's Republic, but in 1972 President Richard M. Nixon became the first president to visit the country. The United States officially recognized China in 1979.

After Mao Zedong's death in 1976 the government began to introduce capitalism to China. However, that did not mean the people were free to do what they liked. When students demonstrated for political reforms in Beijing's Tianamen Square in 1989, the government sent in soldiers and tanks to crush the demonstrations. Hundreds of people were killed.

Taiwan

The People's Republic still sees Taiwan as part of China. However, Taiwan has its own government and economy, and refers to itself as the Republic of China. Taiwan has a population of about 22 million. Its capital is Taipei.

Part of the Great Wall of China, which was built in ancient times to keep out invaders from the north.

A decorated dragon boat on the water in Beijing, China's capital city.

Hong Kong and Macau

Hong Kong and Macau are both in south China. Macau was ruled by Portugal from 1557, and Hong Kong became a British colony in 1842. Both were returned to China in the 1990s, but have separate economic and political structures from the rest of the country.

Economy

Most Chinese in the past were farmers, and that is still true today. In the 1950s many farms were merged to form communes, and prices were set by the government. Today, however, people are allowed to work their own plots of land.

China produces one-third of the world's rice and 40 percent of the world's pigs. Wheat, cotton, tea, and fish are also important products.

The Chinese government is aiming to modernize its economy and to expand industries such as mining, chemicals, textiles, and tourism.

SEE ALSO: Ancient Civilizations; Mao Zedong

✷ CIRCULATORY SYSTEM

The circulatory system is the network that carries blood around the body of mammals and other animals, including humans.

Blood is the remarkable fluid that keeps us alive. It contains millions of cells that, among other things, transport oxygen and help fight infection. Red blood cells carry oxygen to all parts of the body and remove waste carbon dioxide. It is these cells that give blood its color. White blood cells combat infection, clear away worn-out cells, and attack cells that have become malignant (cancer-causing).

The blood also carries nutrition from digested food in the intestines and takes waste to the kidneys, from where it is excreted in urine. Chemicals called hormones and enzymes, which control various activities and reactions in the body, are also in the bloodstream. The water in blood helps keep body temperature even.

Blood even contains its own repair kit—when a blood vessel is damaged the cells form a clot to prevent leaking.

Blood vessels

The human circulatory system consists of three kinds of blood vessel—arteries, veins, and capillaries.

Arteries carry blood away from the heart. They have thick, muscular walls and, in the human body, can be up to 1 in. (2.5cm) in diameter. As arteries branch out, carrying blood to every part

A magnified picture of the wall of an artery. It is flexible to help the heart pump blood around the body in waves.

CIRCULATORY SYSTEM

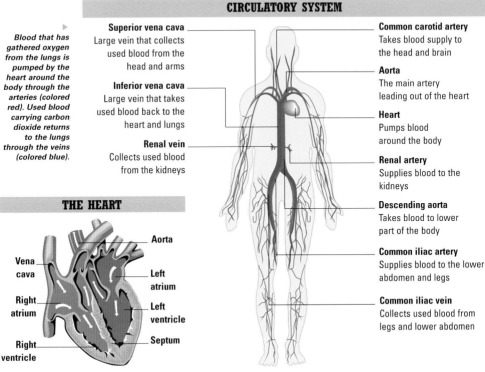

▶
Blood that has gathered oxygen from the lungs is pumped by the heart around the body through the arteries (colored red). Used blood carrying carbon dioxide returns to the lungs through the veins (colored blue).

Superior vena cava
Large vein that collects used blood from the head and arms

Inferior vena cava
Large vein that takes used blood back to the heart and lungs

Renal vein
Collects used blood from the kidneys

Common carotid artery
Takes blood supply to the head and brain

Aorta
The main artery leading out of the heart

Heart
Pumps blood around the body

Renal artery
Supplies blood to the kidneys

Descending aorta
Takes blood to lower part of the body

Common iliac artery
Supplies blood to the lower abdomen and legs

Common iliac vein
Collects used blood from legs and lower abdomen

THE HEART

Aorta

Vena cava

Right atrium

Right ventricle

Left atrium

Left ventricle

Septum

▲
The heart is the driving force of the circulatory system. A thick wall, called the septum, divides the heart into left and right halfs. Valves, which open and close, divide each half into upper and lower parts.

of the body, they split into tiny vessels called capillaries. Some are so small that they can only be seen with a microscope.

As the blood returns to the heart, the capillaries link up to form veins. Veins contain valves—flaps that keep blood from flowing backward. Without valves blood would be pulled back by gravity into the lower part of the body.

The blood vessels are organized into two closed loops, each beginning and ending at the heart. The smaller loop links the heart and the lungs, and is called pulmonary circulation. The larger loop, systemic circulation, leads to all parts of the body, supplying all the organs.

There is a third circulatory system, the lymphatic system. Lymph consists of the watery part of blood, white blood cells, and some chemicals. It helps the body fight infection.

The heart
The most important single organ in the circulatory system is the heart. It is a pump made of muscle, containing four chambers. There are flaps, called valves, between the chambers and also at the outlets to the arteries that carry blood away from the heart. These valves snap shut to keep the blood from flowing backward. The sound of the valves closing is what a doctor hears when listening to the heart through a stethoscope.

Blood flows into the right atrium from veins all over the body. It streams into the right ventricle, which is one of the pumping chambers, then out toward the lungs, where it picks up a fresh supply of oxygen and unloads its carbon dioxide. The oxygen-rich blood then moves to the left atrium, down to the left ventricle, and through the aorta to the rest of the body.

The heart fills and empties in a rhythmic cycle called the heartbeat. The heartbeat rate is controlled by special cells in the heart. Although the heartbeat is usually very regular, it can change. An adult usually has a rate of about 70 beats a minute, but exercise, fear, or sleep can speed up or slow down the rate.

Circulatory disorders

Like any part of the body, the circulatory system can go wrong. Cardiovascular disease—disorders of the heart and blood vessels—is the most common cause of death in developed countries such as the United States. Problems include heart attacks—a blockage of the arteries to the heart, causing the heart muscle to die—and strokes, which are caused by blockages in the arteries to the brain.

Drugs and surgery can help combat these disorders, but people can also protect themselves by exercising and eating a balanced diet low in salt and fat. That can help keep the arteries clear, the blood pressure low, and the heart strong and healthy.

SEE ALSO:
Human Body;
Nutrition

✳ CITY

Cities are the largest communities in which people live and work. People live in cities because they find something there that they want or need.

Cities originally developed on sites where people could obtain regular supplies of food from the surrounding area. Some were on hills, which made them easy to defend. Some were near a source of water. Others grew up where trade routes crossed or around shrines built to gods. The earliest cities formed in Mesopotamia (modern Iraq) about 4500 B.C. The greatest city of ancient times was Rome (the capital of present-day Italy), which ruled much of Europe from 50 B.C to A.D. 476.

Cities today

Cities usually house the headquarters of major business and government organizations, and form the centers of transportation networks. Universities, museums, and places of worship are often based there. People move to cities from smaller towns in search of work. Because cities are so crowded, land is expensive, and people often live in apartment blocks rather than houses.

Transportation is often a problem in cities, with traffic jams, pollution, and noise, especially at rush hour. But despite all this, many people choose to live in cities because there is more entertainment and excitement there, and often jobs are easier to find than in smaller communities.

A night-time view of Seoul, South Korea, which has grown from a population of one million in 1945 to over 10 million.
▼

LARGEST U.S.CITIES		THE WORLD'S LARGEST CITIES	
	Population		Population
1. New York City, New York	21,199,865	**1.** Tokyo, Japan	26,500,000
2. Los Angeles, California	16,373,645	**2.** New York City, U.S.	21,199,865
3. Chicago, Illinois	9,157,540	**3.** São Paolo, Brazil	18,300,000
4. San Francisco, California	7,039,362	**4.** Mexico City, Mexico	18,300,000
5. Philadelphia, Pennsylvania	6,188,463	**5.** Mumbai (Bombay), India	16,500,000
6. Boston, Massachusetts	5,819,100	**6.** Los Angeles, U.S.	16,373,645
7. Detroit, Michigan	5,456,428	**7.** Kolkata (Calcutta), India	13,300,000
8. Dallas, Texas	5,221,801	**8.** Dhaka, Bangladesh	13,200,000
9. Washington, D.C.	4,923,153	**9.** Delhi, India	13,000,000
10. Houston, Texas	4,669,571	**10.** Shanghai, China	12,800,000
The U.S. method of calculating populations makes U.S. cities seem relatively large.		According to United Nations' calculations Mexico City is the largest city in North America.	

SEE ALSO:
Ancient
Civilizations;
Roman
Empire

✳ CLEOPATRA (60–30 B.C.)

Cleopatra VII, queen of Egypt, was the last of the
Macedonian family that ruled Egypt from 323 B.C.
After she died, Egypt came under Roman rule.

A sculpture of Queen Cleopatra, who captivated two powerful Romans.
▼

When her father died in 51 B.C., Cleopatra became joint ruler with her brother Ptolemy XIII, but he drove her out of Egypt three years later. With the assistance of the Roman general Julius Caesar, she returned to Egypt in 47 B.C. and ruled with another brother, Ptolemy XIV. He was later killed, and Cleopatra's son Caesarion (whose father was, she claimed, Julius Caesar) became the new coruler.

After Caesar's death Cleopatra supported Mark Antony in his conflict with Octavian for supremacy in Rome. She married him and had three children with him. After Octavian's victory at Actium in 31 B.C. Antony and Cleopatra both committed suicide, and Egypt fell under Roman domination. According to legend, Cleopatra used an asp—a poisonous snake—to kill herself.

Cleopatra was not beautiful, but her intelligence, charm, vitality, and self-confidence made her attractive to powerful men. Her story has inspired authors and film directors, from William Shakespeare's play *Antony and Cleopatra* to the 1963 movie *Cleopatra*.

SEE ALSO: Caesar, Julius; Egypt, Ancient; Roman Empire; Shakespeare, William

✳ CLIMATE AND WEATHER
Climate and weather are not the same. Climate is the overall state of weather in a specific place over a long period of time.

Weather comes from the changing conditions of the atmosphere (or air). It may be raining or snowing where you are right now. But if it is usually warm and sunny the climate is said to be warm and sunny despite today's wet weather.

The two most important measures of climate are temperature and precipitation. Precipitation is the amount of water that falls to earth, such as rain, snow, or hail.

Why is climate important?
People need to know what the weather conditions will be in a certain place for many reasons. A developer would not want to build a ski resort somewhere that is very warm all year round. A farmer needs to know what crops would grow best on his or her farm.

Why are climates different?
The main reason for differences in climate is distance from the equator. It is called latitude. At 0° latitude, on the equator, the climate is very warm all year around. The broad zone that circles the earth near the equator is known as the tropics. The climate gets cooler as you go toward the poles and farther away from the equator.

Other important factors in climate are altitude and how close a place is to water, such as rivers and oceans. Temperatures usually fall as altitude increases. Water temperature changes more slowly than land temperature, so coastal areas tend to have milder winters and cooler summers than places inland. Winds affect climate because they carry heat and moisture.

Climate change
Scientists who study climate are called climatologists. In recent years they have discovered that climates are changing. Temperatures are rising, and droughts are becoming more severe. Many climatologists believe global warming is caused by people using too much oil, coal, and gasoline, which create harmful gases. Others think it is because of changes in the sun or more dust in the atmosphere. It is important to understand how climate changes because it affects our environment and way of life.

Weather
Weather can take many forms, including wind, rain, and snow. Sometimes weather can be dangerous—hurricanes and tornadoes are destructive.

Changes in the weather affect how we live from day to day. Our choice of clothes reflects the weather—people do not usually wear snow boots when it is hot or swimsuits when it is snowing. Storms can damage property or take people's lives. No one can change the weather, but scientists can try to predict it. The study of weather is called meteorology.

A scientist in Idaho measures the depth of the snow. It is important to figure out the amount of water that will be available for farming and other uses.

This satellite image of the earth shows land and sea temperatures, as well as cloud formations.

Meteorologists try to understand the causes of weather and how to predict weather conditions.

What causes weather changes?

Heat, air, and water act together to affect weather. Variations in the heat of the earth's surface make air rise to different levels. That causes changes in air pressure. Scientists measure air pressure in millibars (mb) or kilopascals (kPa). They use an instrument called a barometer. An area of high or rising pressure usually means that the weather will be fair. Low or falling pressure tends to mean bad weather.

Movement of air between high- and low-pressure areas causes wind. Because of the earth's rotation wind tends to move in a circular direction around it. If the difference between pressure is very great, that can cause powerful storms such as hurricanes and tornadoes.

Clouds, rain, and snow

Meteorologists can also find out a great deal about the weather from studying clouds. The shapes of the clouds are a clue to predicting the weather. Clouds consist of millions of water droplets, ice crystals, or both floating in the air together. The droplets and crystals move and grow inside the cloud until some break away and fall to the ground.

Clouds begin on the surface of the earth. The moisture comes from oceans, rivers, and lakes. When it evaporates, the water changes from being a liquid and

Greenpeace is one of the many environmental groups that are concerned about climate change. Their 1999 expedition to the Arctic proved that the ice pack is melting fast, and that wildlife, such as this walrus, is suffering as a result.

becomes a gas, water vapor. Water vapor is what causes clouds to form. There are three main forms of cloud: cumulus, stratus, and cirrus. Cumulus clouds are puffy. They usually mean that cold weather is approaching. Stratus clouds are in flat layers and usually mean warm and possibly wet weather. Cirrus are high clouds made from ice crystals. They are also associated with rainy weather.

If the air below a cloud is warm, any crystals will melt and reach the ground as rain. If the air is colder, they will fall as snow. If water droplets are carried up into a thunderstorm cloud and freeze, they become balls of ice called hailstones. If rain refreezes before it reaches the ground, it is called sleet. If strong winds and snow combine, the result is a blizzard.

AMAZING FACTS!

The United States experiences more severe storms and flooding than any other country in the world. In a typical year there are some 10,000 thunderstorms, 5,000 floods, 1,000 tornadoes, and several hurricanes.

SEE ALSO: Environment; Hurricane, Tornado, & Typhoon

✴ COLOMBIA

Colombia is in the northwestern part of South America. It is the fourth largest country on the continent and has the second largest population.

Colombia's national flag

KEY FACTS

OFFICIAL NAME
República de Colombia

AREA
439,735 sq. mi.
(1,138,914 sq. km)

POPULATION
42,321,000

CAPITAL & LARGEST CITY
Bogotá

MAJOR RELIGION
Roman Catholicism

MAJOR LANGUAGE
Spanish

CURRENCY
Peso

Laborers weeding the corn crop on an estate in the valley of the Magdalena River.

Colombia has coasts on the Pacific Ocean and the Caribbean Sea. Three great ranges of the Andes Mountains divide Colombia into regions: the highlands, the eastern plains, and the coastal lowlands. Most of the major cities and farmland are in the highlands. Most people live on the coastal plain leading to the Caribbean.

The lowlands have two wet and two dry seasons in a year. The Pacific coastal lowlands are one of the wettest areas in the world. Temperatures depend on altitude. The Caribbean coastal plain has an average temperature of 82°F (28°C), but temperatures in the Andes are lower.

The main river is the Magdalena, which runs for 1,000 miles (1,600km) between the central and eastern Andes and flows into the Caribbean.

People
About 58 percent of Colombia's people are mestizos, that is, of mixed European and Indian ancestry, 20 percent are European, and 14 percent are mulatto—of European and African ancestry. There are smaller groups of African and Indian Colombians.

The official language is Spanish. Roman Catholicism is the religion of 90 percent of the people.

Famous Colombians of recent years include the novelist Gabriel García Márquez and many soccer players, such as Carlos Valderrama and Rene Higuita.

Economy
Service industries such as banking and retail make up 55 percent of Colombia's economy. Manufacturing accounts for 26 percent, and 19 percent comes from agriculture. Coffee is the most important

crop, followed by bananas, sugar, flowers, and tobacco. In the 1990s oil production became a major part of the country's economy. Colombia is also the world's biggest producer of emeralds. Cultivation of coca and the illegal cocaine trade are estimated to bring in $300 million a year.

The mountains make transportation difficult. Much long-distance travel is by river or air. Tourism has been badly affected by recent violence.

History

When Europeans first visited the area, in 1499, Indian tribes were living there. Colombia was named for the explorer Christopher Columbus. In 1549 the Spanish created the colony of New Granada, which included what we now know as Ecuador, Panama, and Venezuela.

In 1810 an independent government was set up, and in 1819 Venezuelan Simón Bolívar became president of the Republic of Gran (Greater) Colombia. In 1830 Venezuela and Ecuador became separate countries.

From 1899 to 1902 a civil war, called the War of a Thousand Days, took place. In 1903 the United States attempted to lease (rent) part of Panama from Colombia to build a canal. When Colombia refused, the Panamanians announced their independence.

There was more unrest after 1948, when Jorge Eliér Gaitán, an important political leader, was assassinated. The following nine years were known as La Violencia (the violence). Antigovernment rebels and drug-trade gangs have been the cause of more recent violence.

SEE ALSO:
America, South;
Columbus, Christopher;
Panama

✳ COLUMBUS, CHRISTOPHER (1451–1506)

Christopher Columbus (Cristoforo Colombo in Italian) was born in Genoa, Italy. He became a sailor and studied mapmaking and navigation.

Christopher Columbus was born in 1451 and worked as a sailor and a fisherman. Between voyages he studied mapmaking and geography. In the 1480s Columbus decided that it would be possible to travel westward to Asia from Europe, and that it would be an easier route for sailing ships. However, he needed money to finance an expedition. In 1492 the Spanish rulers Ferdinand and Isabella financed a voyage. Columbus set off with three ships, the *Niña*, the *Pinta*, and the *Santa Maria*.

After 70 days they reached the islands now called the Bahamas. Columbus thought that he was in the East Indies and called the inhabitants "Indians." In the next 12 years he made three more expeditions to the area. Diseases carried by his men began to kill the native peoples, and many of the sailors treated the Native Americans cruelly.

Columbus never found a route to Asia or the gold and jewels he dreamed about. He never even reached the mainland of the Americas. He died a disappointed man, but his voyages were important steps in the European settlement of the Americas.

▶
Christopher Columbus in 1519, painted by Sebastiano del Piombo.

✱ COMET, METEOR, AND ASTEROID

Comets, meteors, and asteroids are all pieces of matter left over from billions of years ago when the solar system was first formed.

A comet is a mass of ice, rocks, and dust. Comets are usually found in the outer regions of the solar system. Sometimes, however, a comet is pulled closer to the sun. As the comet gets hotter, the outer layers turn to gas and form a long "tail." The tail can be 100 million miles (160 million km) long.

Some comets can be seen from earth, but only when they are near the sun. Halley's comet comes into view every 76 years; the last time it was visible from earth was 1986. A new comet, Hale-Bopp, was discovered on July 23, 1995. It is a lot brighter and larger than Halley's comet.

Asteroids

An asteroid is a small planet made of rock and metal. Most asteroids in the solar system orbit, or circle, the sun between Mars and Jupiter. This area is known as the asteroid belt. In 1996 the NEAR (Near Earth Asteroid Rendezvous) probe was launched. It orbited an asteroid named 433 Eros and sent back pictures of the surface. Scientists hope to discover more about how asteroids were formed, because the same processes may have helped form the solar system.

Meteors

Sometimes tiny pieces of comets or asteroids reach the earth's atmosphere and burn up, leaving a bright trail. They are called meteors, or shooting stars. Sometimes there is a meteor shower, when several meteors appear at once.

Meteorites

Meteorites are pieces of asteroids or comets that strike the earth. They are usually very small and do little damage. However, some meteorites have left large dents, or craters, in the Earth's surface. One crater, in the Yucatan Peninsula, Mexico, is 110 miles (180km) across.

Before people went into space, meteorites were the only extraterrestrial (outside earth) material that scientists could examine. They can learn a great deal about the solar system by studying the substances contained in meteorites.

▲
Comet Hale-Bopp, a very bright comet, was discovered by Alan Hale in New Mexico and Thomas Bopp in Arizona at the same time.

A meteorite crater in Arizona. It is about 50,000 years old and about 656 ft. (200m) deep.
▼

AMAZING FACTS !

Based on the size of a meteorite crater in Mexico, many scientists believe that about 65 million years ago a meteorite caused the extinction of the dinosaurs and many other species of animal.

SEE ALSO:
Dinosaur;
Solar System;
Space Exploration

✳ COMMUNICATION

Communication means sending and receiving information. The word "communicate" comes from the Latin *communicare*, which means "to share."

COMMUNICATION TIMELINE

About 3000 B.C.
Pictorial writing systems in ancient Egypt and symbols used in Sumeria.

A.D. 700s
Chinese and Koreans invent block printing.

About 1100 B.C.
Phoenicians develop first alphabet.

1840
Great Britain issues first postage stamp.

1839
Louis Daguerre develops first practical photographic system.

1890s
Invention of motion picture camera.

1877
Thomas Edison invents phonograph.

1860s–70s
Invention of telephone.

1950s
Invention of videotape; launch of first communications satellites.

1960s Computer chips make computers smaller, cheaper, and faster.

1940s
First practical tape recorder.

1981
IBM produces first personal computer (PC).

1990s
Digital cameras, digital video disks (DVDs), digital TV, World Wide Web.

3000 BC   1100 BC   AD 100   AD 700   AD 1100   AD 1400   AD 1800   AD 1900   AD 2000

Before 3000 B.C.
Spoken stories and songs, paintings in caves.

About A.D.100
Chinese invent paper.

1100s
Paper brought into Europe.

1400s
Johannes Gutenberg develops a printing press.

1861
Telegraph wires connect New York and California.

1895
Gugliemo Marconi sends first radio wave signal.

1920s
Radio broadcasting begins, first televisions appear.

1980s Compact disks (CDs) popular, beginnings of Internet, videocassette recorder (VCR) invented.

Communication requires a sender; a recipient, that is, someone to receive it; a message, or the idea you want to communicate; and a medium, that is, the method of carrying the message. Originally, people sent and received messages by sound or by gesture. This direct communication took place only at one time and over a short distance.

When people began writing their ideas in words and pictures, messages could be seen at a later time and in a different place from when and where they were first written. As a result, knowledge was no longer limited to what a person could see directly or find out from others.

Today modern communication systems carry messages over long distances. They turn spoken words into signals, such as the electrical signals of telephones. These signals are then turned back or converted into messages at the receiving end. Often the sender or recipient of information is no longer a person. Computer systems collect weather data, for example, and can convey a forecast to someone who calls on a telephone.

The tools for communicating with many people are often called the mass media. Printing was the first such tool. Today it is possible to bring news, ideas, and entertainment to millions of people through television, radio, or the Internet.

▲ *This timeline shows some of the key inventions in the history of communication.*

SEE ALSO: Alphabet; Book; Inventors & Inventions; Language; Movies; Newspaper & Magazine; Photography; Printing; Sound Recording; Space Exploration; Telecommunications

✷ COMPOSERS

Composers are people who create pieces of music and then record them in written form. Writing down music preserves it for later generations.

For a very long time music was not written down but was sung or played from memory. This meant that a piece of music might change over time. Gradually, composers developed a way to write down their music so that it would be sung or played exactly as they had composed it. The method that they developed for writing music is called notation.

Western music

The structured music of Western tradition, called classical music, is the artistic expression of an individual composer, who uses notation to show how his or her music should be performed.

The earliest Western musical form was chant, or plainsong, which was used in church music in the Middle Ages. It consisted of a single line of sung melody without instrumental accompaniment. When a simple form of notation developed from about the ninth century, plainsong became more elaborate. Composers began to write poly-

phonic music, in which two or more melodies were sung at the same time, creating harmonies.

Secular music

Church music continued to be important in the 15th and 16th centuries, but composers also began writing secular (nonchurch) music. Demand for it was fueled by the development of music printing. Wealthy people now wanted to play music at home, and so composers wrote songs and short instrumental pieces for amateurs.

The 17th and 18th centuries saw many new musical forms, including the sonata, symphony, concerto, opera, and oratorio. Composers writing for orchestras had to be familiar with the range and sound of all the instruments and be skilled in writing harmony.

In the 19th century composers tried to use their music to express intense emotions. Short pieces for the piano expressed the composer's feelings, while orchestral music became more dramatic.

Modern developments

Until the beginning of the 20th century most music was tonal music, or music for which the composer uses notes from a recognized scale. Some 20th-century composers began to use a new system called the 12-tone system, which

▲
The German composer George Frideric Handel, who lived and worked in England during the reign of King George I. He wrote many successful operas and oratorios, and well-known orchestral pieces such as the Water Music and Music for the Royal Fireworks.

◄
Medieval monks singing plainsong, the church music of the Middle Ages. It was a single melody sung without harmony or any instrumental accompaniment.

FAMOUS COMPOSERS

This is a list of some famous classical composers. There are many more.

Vivaldi, Antonio Lucio (1678–1741)
Italian composer and violinist who wrote over 500 concertos.

Bach, Johann Sebastian (1685–1750)
German composer and organist with a vast output of church, instrumental, and keyboard music.

Haydn, Franz Joseph (1732–1809)
Austrian composer who developed the string quartet and the symphony, earning him the title "father of the symphony."

Mozart, Wolfgang Amadeus (1756–91)
Austrian composer whose operas, symphonies, and concertos are some of the greatest ever written.

Beethoven, Ludwig van (1770–1827)
German composer of symphonies, concertos, and piano sonatas that expressed passionate feelings in masterly musical language.

Chopin, Frédéric-François (1810–49)
Polish composer of beautiful and deeply expressive piano pieces.

Brahms, Johannes (1833–97)
German composer who wrote chamber music, numerous works for piano, four symphonies, and over 100 songs.

Beach, Amy Marcy (1867–1944)
Wrote songs, choral, and instrumental works, including the first symphony to be composed by an American woman.

Ives, Charles Edward (1874–1954)
Composer of American music who used new, experimental techniques.

Stravinsky, Igor Fyodorovich (1882–1971)
Naturalized American composer of Russian origin whose revolutionary rhythms and harmonies greatly influenced 20th-century music.

sounded very strange to people accustomed to tonal music. Others used clashing harmonies and irregular rhythms or turned to electronic music, which used taped sounds either alone or combined with other music.

Classical music often overlaps with popular music, such as jazz and rock, which is written to appeal to a wide audience.

◄
American composer Aaron Copland (1900–90), who wrote popular ballets, including **Rodeo** *and* **Appalachian Spring.**

George Gershwin (1898–1937), an American composer who mixed jazz rhythms and harmonies with traditional orchestral music.
▼

SEE ALSO: Mozart, Wolfgang Amadeus; Music; Musical Instruments; Musicians, World; Music, Popular

✳ CONQUISTADORS

Conquistador **is the Spanish word for "conqueror."**
It is used to describe the Spanish leaders who took
over parts of America in the 1500s.

The two best-known conquistadors are Hernán Cortés, who conquered Aztec Mexico, and Francisco Pizarro, who conquered Inca Peru. The conquistadors were only seeking personal wealth and adventure, but in the process they created a vast and wealthy empire for Spain in the Americas.

Cortés and the Aztecs

In 1504, eager to gain fame and fortune, Hernán Cortés (1485–1547) sailed from Spain to the West Indies, where he became a planter on the island of Hispaniola. In 1519 he set off for Mexico with 11 ships, 600 men, and 16 horses.

At that time Mexico was ruled by the Aztec Emperor Montezuma (or Moctezuma) II. His empire stretched from the Pacific Ocean to the Gulf of Mexico and south to the modern border of Guatemala. Yet within two years Cortés had overthrown the Aztec Empire.

There were many reasons for his victory. The Aztecs thought the Spaniards were gods. They feared the Spanish guns and horses, which were new to them. The Aztecs were resented by other Indian peoples, who helped Cortés. The soldiers brought new diseases, such as smallpox, which killed thousands of native people.

Pizarro and the Incas

Francisco Pizarro (about 1475–1541) sailed from Spain to America in 1502. In 1513 he joined Spanish explorer Vasco Núñez de Balboa. They were the first Europeans to cross the narrow strip of land in Central America known as Panama and reach the Pacific Ocean. Pizarro settled in Panama, where he heard of a wealthy land to the south—Peru, the heart of the Inca Empire.

In 1531 he set off for Peru with about 180 men, a few cannons, and 37 horses.

The Inca Empire was one of the greatest ever known, but it had been weakened by civil war. Pizarro laid a trap for the much larger force of the Inca ruler, Atahuallpa. The Spaniards killed the emperor's guards, took him prisoner, and demanded money to release him. After

the ransom was paid, Pizarro had Atahuallpa put to death. With news of Atahuallpa's death the Inca armies retreated, and Pizarro captured the Inca capital, Cuzco, in 1533. In 1535 he founded Lima, now the capital of Peru.

▲
Aztecs give Cortés a neckband to welcome him to their lands. They believed that he was the great god Quetzalcoatl, who had returned to them from over the seas.

AMAZING FACTS ❗

Atahuallpa, the last Inca emperor, offered to fill a room with gold as a ransom for his release. The Incas brought gold and silver objects from every corner of the empire. Pizarro and his men melted them all down. The final amount came to 24 tons of gold and silver—the richest ransom ever paid.

SEE ALSO:
Aztecs;
Incas; Spain

✳ CONSTELLATION

A constellation is any of the 88 groups of stars that can be seen from the Earth. The name comes from a Latin word meaning "cluster of stars."

The constellation of Sagittarius is at the center of the Milky Way galaxy.

In ancient times people observing the night sky noticed that groups of stars seemed to form patterns that did not change, even though the stars themselves moved across the sky from east to west. Some of these patterns seemed to form specific shapes. One group looked like a crab, another like a great hunter, another like a fish, and so on. Because people then believed that gods and spirits lived in the sky, they named many of the constellations after gods and heroes. They named others after sacred animals and familiar objects.

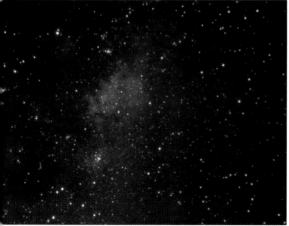

One group of 12 constellations became known as the zodiac. People began to use the movements of the sun, moon, and planets within these constellations to predict the future. This practice is called astrology. It has no scientific basis, but it has been popular for more than 2,000 years.

Today astronomers know that bright groups of stars are not gods or spirits. They know that stars appear to move from east to west because of the way the Earth rotates on its axis. They also know that the stars in constellations are not connected, and that their relative positions change over long periods.

Ancient and modern constellations
In addition to the 12 constellations of the zodiac 36 other constellations were familiar to ancient peoples in the Northern Hemisphere. In the 1500s Europeans sailed to the Southern Hemisphere, where they observed thousands of stars that were unknown to northerners. Later astronomers grouped these stars, as well as many fainter stars in the northern sky, into new constellations.

In 1931 astronomers recognized a total of 88 constellations. In addition to these constellations there are many unofficial groupings of stars. Most of them are part of larger constellations. For example, the Big Dipper, a group of seven stars resembling a pot with a handle, is part of a larger constellation called Ursa Major, the Great Bear.

SEE ALSO:
Astronomy;
Galaxy;
Moon; Solar
System;
Star; Sun

DID YOU KNOW?

Ancient peoples foretold the future by studying the night skies. In particular, they studied the movements of the sun, moon, and planets in relation to 12 constellations. The constellations became known as the zodiac, meaning "circle of animals," because most of them were named for animals. Today we know the constellations as Aries, the Ram; Taurus, the Bull; Gemini, the Twins; Cancer, the Crab; Leo, the Lion; Virgo, the Virgin; Libra, the Pair of Scales; Scorpius, the Scorpion; Sagittarius, the Archer; Capricornus, the Goat; Aquarius, the Water Carrier; and Pisces, the Fish.

CRAZY HORSE (ABOUT 1849–77)

Tashunca-Uitco, or Crazy Horse, was a chief of the Oglala Sioux who firmly resisted white occupation of the northern Plains.

In 1854 Crazy Horse was present at the first clash between U.S. troops and the Sioux near Fort Laramie, Wyoming. All the soldiers were killed. In the 1870s Crazy Horse fought to keep white gold miners out of the Black Hills, a region his people held sacred. In 1873 he took part in two skirmishes with Lieutenant Colonel George Custer's troops on the Yellowstone River.

Followers of Crazy Horse formed the Sioux Confederation that later defeated Custer at the Battle of the Little Bighorn in 1876. In the battle Crazy Horse served as a field leader. He surrendered in 1877, but was fatally stabbed by a guard while resisting imprisonment.

In 1948 work began on a memorial to Crazy Horse. His portrait is being carved from the solid rock of Thunderhead Mountain, five miles north of Custer, South Dakota. When completed, the statue will be 563 ft. (171.6m) tall, making it the world's largest mountain carving.

A memorial to the Sioux chief Crazy Horse. Started in 1948, it is still being carved.

CRIME AND LAW ENFORCEMENT

A crime is an act that is against the law. At different times and in different places there have been various ideas about what defines a crime.

In the United States crimes are classified according to their seriousness. Major crimes are called felonies: They include murder, kidnapping, and assault. Less serious crimes—such as vandalism and public drunkenness—are misdemeanors. In other countries crimes may be classified differently, but the principles usually remain similar. Crimes that involve harm done to people are usually treated more seriously than those in which property is damaged or stolen.

Reasons for crime
There are various reasons why people commit crime. Sometimes the motive is financial—criminals see theft as a quick way to make money. Experts believe that some people's personalities make them more likely to take drugs or commit acts of violence. Poverty, unemployment, poor living conditions, and lack of education may contribute to crime. People may also commit serious crimes for political reasons. When this involves violence, it is called terrorism.

Crime prevention
Society has to try to prevent crime or find a way to deal with criminals after a crime has been committed. If someone wants to rob a bank but sees security guards, he might change his mind. If he is going to rob someone on the street, then sees a police car pull up, fear of being caught might stop him.

These are both examples of crime prevention. But many people feel that crime prevention should begin earlier. If children are taught in the home and at school why crime is wrong, they might not grow up to be criminals.

The criminal justice system

Sometimes, though, prevention does not work. People commit crimes, and society has to do something about it.

The first line of defense is the police. The police solve criminal cases and arrest suspects. They call on experts, such as scientists and psychologists, to help.

The police cannot decide whether someone is guilty of a crime. After a person is arrested and charged, he or she goes to court. In court the charged person is known as a defendant and has a defense attorney to argue his or her case. The state provides a prosecuting attorney to argue that the defendant is guilty. The court is led by a judge, but it is often a jury, a group of ordinary men and women, who make the final decision.

If a defendant is found not guilty, he or she is allowed to go free. If the defendant is found guilty, however, the court must decide on a punishment. It will

DID YOU KNOW?

Fingerprints are the impressions of the ridges of the fingertips. They are used as a means of identification. No two people in the world, not even identical twins, have the same fingerprints. Only ink and paper are required, making fingerprinting simple and inexpensive. The Federal Bureau of Investigation (FBI) has nearly 170,000,000 prints on file. An average of over 25,000 sets of prints arrive at the bureau every day.

be related to how serious the crime is, and how often the defendant has been in trouble before. For minor offenses the court might recommend probation. This

◄ *Police on a drug raid arrest a suspected dealer. The police arrest and charge suspects, but it is the task of the courts to examine the evidence and decide whether they are guilty or innocent.*

means the guilty person must attend regular meetings with officials and care workers. Alternatively there may be a fine, a fixed amount that he or she has to pay.

For more serious crimes the court might recommend a prison sentence. The length of the prison sentence depends on the severity of the crime. In the case of a very serious crime, such as a planned murder, the court may have the power to recommend capital punishment—this is where the criminal is executed or killed by a lethal injection or an electric shock.

Punishment has several purposes. The court might want to make a criminal pay for his or her crime. This is called retribution. It might want a criminal out of the way, so he or she cannot harm other people. It might want to educate a criminal, to make him or her a better citizen. This is called rehabilitation. Or the purpose might be deterrence—using the case as an example, to warn other people against committing a similar crime. In all cases the purpose of law enforcement is to make society a safer place.

✳ CRUSADES

The Crusades were wars undertaken by Christians to defeat people they believed were the enemies of their religion and protect Christianity's holy sites.

The best-known crusades were launched between 1096 and 1291 to conquer Palestine (modern Israel, Lebanon, and Syria). This area, known as the Holy Land, was sacred to Christians because Jesus Christ lived and died there.

The area had been ruled by Muslims (followers of Islam) for over 300 years. They believed that Christ was a holy

man and allowed Christians to visit the places where Jesus had walked the earth. Journeys to such holy sites are called pilgrimages.

In the 11th century it became more difficult and dangerous for pilgrims to visit the Holy Land. Pope Urban II (pope 1088–99) called on Christian men to unite to drive the Muslims out of Palestine.

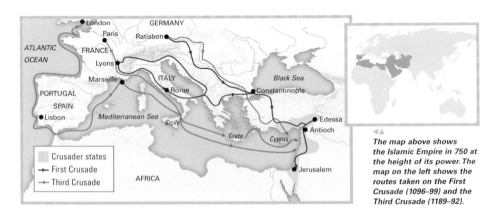

◄▲

The map above shows the Islamic Empire in 750 at the height of its power. The map on the left shows the routes taken on the First Crusade (1096–99) and the Third Crusade (1189–92).

Many people responded. Some went for religious reasons, others to win glory, land, and money, and some for adventure.

The First Crusade
The First Crusade, begun in 1096, was a success. Although the Crusaders were outnumbered by the Muslims, they won because the Muslims were badly divided. In 1099 the Crusaders captured Jerusalem. They killed many of the people there and looted, or stole, their valuables.

The Crusader states
The Crusade leaders divided the lands into states for themselves, one of the most important being the Kingdom of Jerusalem. The Crusaders ruled only a narrow strip of land, mostly along the Mediterranean coast. Muslim rulers waged war occasionally, trying to win back some territory, and the strip grew narrower. In 1187 a powerful Muslim leader, Saladin, recaptured Jerusalem.

The West continued to send Crusades to the East. Some were more successful than others. The Fourth Crusade (1202–04) never reached the Holy Land. Instead, it conquered and plundered the Christian city of Constantinople.

In 1291 Muslims conquered the last of the Crusader states; Christian forces did not threaten to conquer Palestine again until the 20th century.

Christians also went on crusades in other lands, such as southern France and eastern Europe, against peoples they claimed were enemies of Christ.

SEE ALSO:
Islam;
Middle
Ages

✴ CRUSTACEAN
Crustaceans are invertebrates, or animals without a backbone. They have an exoskeleton (hard outer covering), jointed legs, and a body.

There are about 25,000 different species of crustaceans. They can be found in all the oceans of the world. Many live along ocean shorelines. Some species are found in freshwater rivers, lakes, or ponds. A few kinds live on land. Crustaceans range in size from the water flea, which is difficult to see without a magnifying glass, to the giant spider crab, which may be 12 ft. (3.7m) from the tip of one outstretched claw to the other.

Kinds of crustaceans
Decapods are crustaceans with 10 legs. This group includes shrimps, lobsters, crabs, prawns, and crayfish.

Copepods are just barely visible to the eye—about one-eighth of an inch (0.25cm) in length. They are found in very large numbers—as many as 100,000 tiny animals in 10 sq. ft. (about 1sq. m) of water. They include plankton, the drifting and floating animals that provide food for larger marine life. These small animals are a major source of protein for many of the other animals in the ocean. Isopods are also mostly tiny. This group includes sow bugs and pill bugs.

Body
The exoskeleton, or outer shell, of crustaceans is made of a hard material called chitin. A growing crustacean sheds its exoskeleton in a process called molting. Underneath there is a new body covering that then hardens into an exoskeleton.

Crustaceans, such as this Sally Lightfoot crab, are animals without a backbone. They have bodies made up of segments.
▼

A crustacean's three main body parts are the head, thorax, and abdomen. Each of these parts is made up of several segments, and each includes at least one pair of jointed limbs, or appendages. Depending on where they are on the body, a crustacean's limbs can be used for sensing the environment, catching or chewing food, breathing, walking, swimming, or carrying eggs.

SEE ALSO:
Animal;
Ocean & Sea

Lifestyle

Crustaceans lay eggs. The eggs may be shed directly into the water or carried by the female in a special sac called a brood pouch. Crustaceans such as crayfish hatch

AMAZING FACTS!

The heaviest crustacean
ever caught was an American lobster. It weighed more than 44 lb. (20kg) and measured 3.5 ft. (1m) from the end of its tail to the tip of its largest claw.

from their eggs looking much like the adults. Most hatch as a tiny larva called a nauplius. It will molt several times before it finally looks like the adults.

✷ CUBA

Cuba is the largest and most populous country in the Caribbean Sea. It lies only 90 miles (145km) from the southern tip of Florida.

KEY FACTS

OFFICIAL NAME
República de Cuba

AREA
44,218 sq. mi. (114,524 sq. km)

POPULATION
11,201,000

CAPITAL & LARGEST CITY
Havana

MAJOR RELIGION
Roman Catholicism

MAJOR LANGUAGE
Spanish

CURRENCY
Cuban peso

Cuba consists of one large island and more than 1,600 little islands. About 40 percent of the country is mountainous. The coast has many natural harbors. The climate is semitropical, with a dry season and a rainy season. Rainfall averages 54 in. (1,370mm) a year.

People

Most of the original Native American population of Cuba died within 100 years of the Spanish conquest. Today most Cubans are of Spanish and African ancestry.

Economy

Important products are sugar, nickel, coffee, citrus fruits, and cigars. Since the collapse of the Soviet Union in the 1990s

Cuba's revolutionary leader Fidel Castro in about 1970.

Cuba's economy has suffered. In recent years tourism has become an important source of income.

History

Cuba was claimed for Spain in 1492 by Christopher Columbus and remained a Spanish colony until 1898. The United States became involved in Cuba's war against Spain. It then occupied Cuba from 1899 to 1901 and from 1906 to 1909, and continued to be a powerful economic influence in the independent country. In 1958 revolutionaries led by Fidel Castro overthrew President Fulgencio Batista.

Because Castro received support from the Soviet Union, the U.S. cut off relations with Cuba in 1961. Cuban exiles, trained in the U.S., landed at the Bay of Pigs but failed to overthrow Castro. In 1962 the U.S. found Soviet missiles in Cuba, which led to a confrontation between the Americans and the Soviets. The missiles were eventually removed. The U.S. still maintains trade restrictions against Cuba, although it has a naval base there.

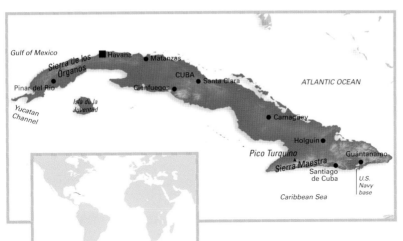

Cuba's national flag

SEE ALSO:
Caribbean
Sea & Islands;
Columbus,
Christopher;
Kennedy, John F.

✳ CURIE, MARIE (1867–1934) & PIERRE (1859–1906)

Marja Sklodowska was born in Warsaw, Poland. In 1891
she went to college in Paris, France, and changed her
name to Marie. In 1895 she married Pierre Curie.

The couple worked together studying the invisible radiation given off by the element uranium. They discovered that the atoms of some elements are constantly breaking down. This gives off radiation that can pass through other materials. These elements are described as radioactive.

In 1903 the Curies and another scientist, Antoine Henri Becquerel, won the Nobel Prize in physics. Pierre Curie died in a street accident in 1906.

Marie continued her research and was awarded a second Nobel Prize in chemistry in 1911 for discovering the elements radium and polonium. She was the first person to receive two Nobel awards in science. When she died, in 1934, it was found that she had been poisoned by exposure to too much radioactivity.

In 1935 the Curies' eldest daughter Irène and her husband, Frédéric Joliot-Curie, were awarded the Nobel Prize in chemistry.

SEE ALSO: Atom & Molecule; Nobel Prize

Marie and Pierre Curie in their laboratory in 1898. Together they discovered radium.

✳ DESERT

A desert is an area where there is very little water. Deserts are not necessarily hot, dry, and sandy— they may equally be cool or even ice covered.

Most dry deserts receive less than 8 in. (200mm) of rainfall in a year. There may be months or even years between storms. Most of the water evaporates in the dry air before it soaks into the ground.

Desert plants must be able to store water in their roots or stems. Cacti are the best flora of this type. Animals must also be able to live with little water. Reptiles, such as snakes, obtain water from food. Mammals, such as gazelles and kangaroos, often travel long distances to isolated water holes or springs. A place in the desert with enough water for dense plant growth is called an oasis. The water comes from underground layers of rock.

The background photograph shows extensive salt flats in the Atacama Desert, Chile.

In tropical deserts the summers are extremely hot, although winters might be cool, sometimes with frost. Examples of tropical deserts include the Sahara in northern Africa and the Atacama in northern Chile.

Some dry deserts can be bitterly cold in the winter. They include the Gobi, in Central Asia, and the deserts of the south-western United States. The ground is often frozen, and water cannot sink deep into the soil. This causes the formation of temporary swamps.

Cold deserts

Cold deserts form in areas where there are constantly low temperatures. They have little plant life and few inhabitants. Most of the high plateaus of the world are cold deserts. Ice deserts occur in the Antarctic and Arctic.

Reclaiming deserts

People have tried hard to make deserts habitable. Some peoples, such as the nomadic, or wandering, Bedouin of the Sahara, have lifestyles adapted to desert life. Water pipelines and irrigation have made it possible to build cities, such as Las Vegas, Nevada, in arid zones.

Deserts often contain great mineral wealth. People live there to extract gold, diamonds, natural gas, and oil. New deserts may be formed by human activity, especially by using too much water or by overgrazing grassland. This process is called desertification.

THE WORLD'S LARGEST DRY DESERTS

Sahara, Africa	3,500,000 sq. miles (9,065,000 sq. km)
Australian	600,000 sq. miles (1,554,000 sq. km)
Arabian, Middle East	500,000 sq. miles (1,300,000 sq. km)
Gobi, Asia	400,000 sq. miles (1,040,000 sq. km)
Kalahari, Africa	225,000 sq. miles (582,750 sq. km)
Turkestan, Asia	220,000 sq. miles (569,800 sq. km)
Taklimakan, China	125,000 sq. miles (320,000 sq. km.)
Sonoran, North America	120,000 sq. miles (310,800 sq. km)
Namib, Africa	102,248 sq. miles (270,000 sq. km)
Thar, Asia	100,000 sq. miles (259,000 sq. km)
Somali, Africa	100,000 sq. miles (259,000 sq. km)

The thorny devil is a lizard specially adapted for life in the arid deserts of Australia.

✳ DESIGN

Design is the plan by which the parts of any human-made object are put together to function well, look good, and make use of available materials.

An industrial designer may want to plan a new car or a crane, a product designer can make a teapot that is easy to use, and every fashion designer wants to create popular clothes to wear. These are just some of the many uses of design.

Principles and elements

There are many rules, or principles, to follow in design. All the different parts of a design must add up to a balanced whole. Nothing should look too big or too small. The design should also have what is called rhythm, which leads the eyes over its features. You can see rhythm in the outline of a sports coupé or the ceiling of a cathedral.

The elements or building blocks of design can include line, color, texture, solids, and space. They are used in different combinations.

Line has been the designer's favorite tool since the earliest cave drawings. Fashion designers use loose and expressive lines, while architects and industrial

designers make very accurate lines, often with the help of computers.

Color adds mood to a design: Reds and oranges are warm and lively, while blues and greens are cool and calm. Changing the lightness or darkness of a color can dramatically alter a design's mood.

Texture is the way an object feels. Silk or stone, satin or steel, the surface of every material has its own characteristic and often unique texture.

Solids are the basis of three-dimensional designs. Sculptors, furniture designers, and potters all work with solids. Architects design solids to form buildings, complex systems of planes that enclose space.

Design is influenced by fashion and culture, so it changes continually. However, the basic elements and principles of design remain the same regardless of time and place.

In many industries today designs are drawn on computers.

English architect Sir Norman Foster designed this spectacular building for the Reichstag (parliament) in Berlin, Germany.

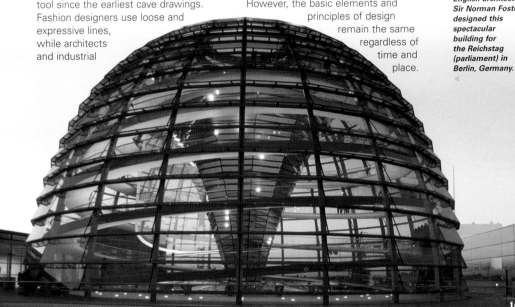

✱ DINOSAUR

Dinosaurs are reptiles that first appeared on Earth about 230 million years ago. They became extinct (died out) about 65 million years ago.

No human has ever seen a living dinosaur. We have known about them only since the 1800s, when paleontologists—scientists who study fossils—pieced together remains such as bones, footprints in rock, and eggs to discover what dinosaurs looked like. In 1841 Richard Owen, an English scientist, created the name "dinosaur" (from the Greek for "fearfully great lizard").

Two main groups
Sometimes paleontologists make mistakes when trying to identify dinosaurs. That is because it is very rare to find a complete skeleton. They have therefore had to make guesses about the parts that are missing. But they now

generally agree that dinosaurs can be divided into two main groups, saurischians and ornithischians.

"Saurischian" means "lizardlike hip." Dinosaurs of this type had hipbones similar to those of modern crocodiles. They are subdivided into two further groups. Theropods, or "beast feet," were carnivores (meat eaters) that walked upright on their back legs. They had huge feet, usually with three or more toes. Their front limbs were very small.

The first theropods appeared in the Triassic period about 225 million years ago. They included *Coelophysis*, which was about 9 ft. (2.7m) long. In the next geological period, the Jurassic, which began about 200 million

Pterosaurs fly above two dinosaurs: Apatosaurus (on all fours) and Tyrannosaurus (foreground).

years ago, lived *Allosaurus*, which was 30 ft. (9m) long. It had sharp teeth and curving claws to slash its prey to shreds.

The most famous dinosaur of all lived during the Cretaceous period (about 144 million to 65 million years ago): *Tyrannosaurus* ("tyrant lizard") was about 50 ft. (15m) long and weighed about 7 tons. Its head alone was almost 6 ft. (2m) long.

The other saurischians were the sauropods, or "lizard feet." They were usually herbivores (plant eaters), and they walked on all four legs. The earliest sauropod was *Plateosaurus*. Later the massive *Apatosaurus* (also called *Brontosaurus*, meaning "thunder lizard"), with its huge legs, slender head, and long neck and tail, emerged. These dinosaurs weighed more than 30 tons.

Ornithischians

The other major group of dinosaurs is the Ornithischia ("birdlike hip"). Ornithischians were plant eaters. Despite their name, they were land-dwelling creatures.

Ornithischians are subdivided into two smaller groups, Ornithopoda and Stegosauria. Ornithopods ("bird feet") resemble modern birds, but many were much bigger than any bird we have ever seen. *Iguanodon*, for example, measured about 30 ft. (9m) in length and weighed more than 4 tons. It walked on its back feet and carried its head more than 14ft. (4m) from the ground.

Many later Ornithopods, such as the hadrosaurs, had strange bumps or crests on their heads. Scientists believe they might have been used to sniff or make sounds.

Stegosauria were dinosaurs with plates, armor, or horns. They first appeared during the Jurassic period. *Stegosaurus* ("plated lizard") had a small head and a brain the size of a walnut, although its body was up to 30 ft. (9m) in length. It had one or two rows of upright, bony plates along its backbone.

The greatest variety of stegosaurs existed during the Cretaceous period. They included *Scolosaurus*, which had a flexible body covering of bone plates separated by softer skin, and the horned dinosaurs, *Protoceratops* and *Triceratops*, which resembled modern rhinoceroses.

Other extinct reptiles

Among the other animals that lived during the age of the dinosaurs were pterosaurs, which could fly, and ichthyosaurs, which lived in the oceans. They also became extinct many millions of years ago, but left behind fossilized remains.

This dinosaur fossil was found in the Gobi Desert, Mongolia. It belongs to a new species that has not yet been named.

Timeline showing the main events during the evolution and decline of the dinosaurs.

248–213 million years ago
The Triassic period, during which the first dinosaurs appeared on earth.

213–144 million years ago
The Jurassic period, during which stegosaurs became widespread.

Timeline continued on page 112

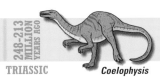

248–213 MILLION YEARS AGO

TRIASSIC *Coelophysis*

Stegosaurus

213–144 MILLION YEARS AGO

JURASSIC

AMAZING FACTS !

Many dinosaurs were watchful parents that carefully tended their young. Some dinosaurs even set up a kind of daycare center. Groups of duck-billed dinosaurs called maiasaurs built their nests in clusters. With the nests close together, it was possible for some of the parents to baby-sit the nestbound young while other parents gathered food for the group.

The end of the dinosaurs

No one knows for certain why the dinosaurs died out. The climate of the Earth may have changed, killing off the plants and animals that made up the dinosaurs' diet. The shape of the land and the seas shifted, and that may have destroyed the dinosaurs' habitats.

Another theory is that the Earth was struck by a meteorite (a large lump of rock from space). It caused a massive cloud of dust that blocked out the sunlight and killed the plants that the dinosaurs ate. Some people now think a nearby star exploded and showered the Earth with deadly radiation.

The problem with these theories is that they do not clearly explain why many other species did not die out. The ancestors of modern animals—including humans—survived whatever killed off the dinosaurs. Scientists can make guesses, but they may never know for certain.

Although dinosaurs died out about 65 million years before human beings appeared, we know a great deal about them through the work of archaeologists and other scientists. There are many books and movies about people encountering dinosaurs, but they are pure fantasy—in reality the two species never met. Among the most famous works of this type are the novel *The Lost World* by Sir Arthur Conan Doyle and the Jurassic Park movies directed by Steven Spielberg. Today you can see the fossilized remains of dinosaurs in natural history museums around the world.

This backbone was dug up in Big Bend National Park, Texas, in 1999. Scientists believe that it is from an Alamosaurus.

SEE ALSO:
Cartoon & Animation;
Comet, Meteor, & Asteroid

144–65 million years ago
The Cretaceous period, at the end of which dinosaurs became extinct.

Triceratops

144–65 MILLION YEARS AGO

Apatosaurus

CRETACEOUS

Tyrannosaurus rex

✳ DISASTER

A disaster is an event that causes destruction. There are two main types: natural disasters, such as floods, and disasters caused accidentally by human error.

Records of natural disasters date back to the earliest civilizations. The great flood described in the Biblical book of Genesis and referred to in the folklore of other cultures is probably based on a real event.

Noah's flood is only one of many such disasters that have struck the Earth. Much of the modern state of Bangladesh, for example, is so close to sea level that large areas of its territory are often flooded, causing destruction and death.

Earthquakes occur on land that lies above underground geological activity. Their effects can be catastrophic. The ancient city of Knossos in the Aegean Sea was flattened by an earthquake in about 1720 B.C. Today some of the most violent tremors occur along the Pacific Rim (the west coast of North and South America and the east coast of Asia). California and Japan are particularly high-risk areas.

Fire is another cause of natural disaster. Knossos was rebuilt after the earthquake, only to be burned down again less than four centuries later. London, England, was destroyed by fire in 1666.

Areas around active volcanoes are in constant danger of being buried beneath eruptions of lava (molten rock) and ash. In A.D. 79 tens of thousands were burned to death or buried alive when Mount Vesuvius erupted and covered the towns of Pompeii and Herculaneum in Italy.

Every year storms called hurricanes and tornadoes wreak havoc with everything in their path. In the Northern Hemisphere the worst time for these winds is June through November. When Hurricane Mitch hit Central America in October 1998, with wind speeds of up to 180 mph (290km/h), it left about 10,000 dead and nearly three million homeless.

Transportation accidents

Of the disasters caused by human error, the most costly in terms of lives lost have always been accidents to mass transportation vehicles. One of the worst crashes in railroad history occurred near Modane, France, on December 12, 1917, when more than 500 soldiers died after their train was derailed.

Throughout maritime history there have been many disastrous shipwrecks. Perhaps the most famous of them took place on the night of April 14, 1912, when the British liner *Titanic* struck an iceberg in the North Atlantic Ocean on its first voyage, from Southampton, England, to New York. The supposedly "unsinkable" ship went down in less than three hours, with the loss of over 1,500 of its 2,200 passengers and crew.

In May 1999 a tornado killed 38 people and destroyed more than 1,500 houses in Oklahoma.
▶

D

The aftermath of the explosion at the nuclear power plant near Chernobyl, Ukraine, in April 1986.

WORST DISASTERS

Air crash	**March 27, 1977** Canary Islands. Pan Am and KLM Boeing 747s collided on runway, killing 582.
Earthquake	**July 1976** Tangshan, China. About 242,000 dead and 164,000 injured.
Flood	**November 1970** Bangladesh. Cyclone winds brought flooding that killed 500,000 people.
Industrial accident	**December 3, 1984** India. Poisonous gas leaked from the Union Carbide chemical plant at Bhopal, killing more than 3,500 and injuring more than half a million people.
Maritime disaster	**December 20, 1987** Philippines. Ferry *Dona Paz* collided with an oil tanker, killing 4,341.
Tornado	**March 18, 1925** U.S. Twister killed 689 people as it tore through Missouri, Illinois, and Indiana.
Train crash	**August 2, 1999** India. Over 500 killed when two passenger trains collided in West Bengal.
Volcano	**August 27, 1883** Krakatoa Island, Indonesia. The explosions were heard over 2,000 miles (3,200km) away, and 30,000 people died.

Air crashes are nearly always fatal. A huge fireball was all that remained of the giant airship *Hindenburg* when it exploded on May 6, 1937, after electricity ignited its hydrogen-gas-filled balloon. Thirty-six of the 97 passengers died, and the accident put an end to mass travel by airship.

Since then there have been many fatal airplane crashes. Most happen when the pilot makes a mistake, although some are caused by mechanical failure. Other causes include objects left lying on the runway, ice or snow on the aircraft's wings, and running out of fuel in midair. A small fault on a booster rocket may have caused the explosion of the Space Shuttle *Challenger* on January 28, 1986. The rocket blew up just seconds after launch, killing all seven crew members.

Industrial disasters
Working below ground is very hazardous. In coal mines the coal reacts with air if it is not kept wet and produces gases that explode at the smallest spark. Hundreds of workers have died in mine explosions, as well as in tunnel collapses and floods. There have also been many disasters caused by fires on oil-drilling rigs.

Some of the most frightening industrial disasters are nuclear accidents. On April 25, 1986, the atomic plant at Chernobyl, Ukraine, blew up. Thirty-two people died instantly, and countless others later became sick or died after exposure to fallout—radioactive dust that drifted on the air across many parts of Europe, poisoning the air, soil, and water.

SEE ALSO: Ancient Civilizations; Balloon & Airship; Earthquake; Flood; Hurricane, Indian Subcontinent; Tornado, & Typhoon; Space Shuttle; Volcano

✳ DOG

Dogs are members of the Canidae family of mammals. There are about 35 different species, including coyotes, foxes, jackals, and wolves.

Most members of the dog family, or canids, are good runners, with muscular, deep-chested bodies and slender legs. They have four toes on each paw, plus a thumblike toe on each forepaw and sometimes on the rear feet as well. They walk on their toes, which are well padded. Dogs have 42 teeth—some for gripping and tearing flesh, some for cutting, and others for grinding food.

Senses

Dogs have superb hearing and fairly good eyesight, but their keenest sense is smell, which can detect the faintest scent days or even weeks after its source has gone.

Dogs use their voices regularly. Domestic dogs bark to raise an alarm, to show aggression or fear, or as a cry for help. Growling usually means "Stay away" or "I'm going to bite." Dogs may also howl, whimper, or whine to show their feelings.

▲
Bloodhounds are often used as tracker dogs.

Wild canids

The largest wild canid is the gray wolf. It was once common; but human

▶
A North American gray wolf rests on a rock.

settlers, fearful of wolves, killed so many of them that today they are found only in remote parts of northern North America and on rugged mountains in Europe and Asia. Wolves live in family groups called packs. The pack works together to hunt prey. With their deep chests and long legs, wolves can trot for hours without tiring.

Coyotes and jackals are wild canids that look like small, rangy wolves. They may form packs or pairs, though some coyotes live alone. Coyotes are found from Alaska to Central America. Jackals live in Africa and south-central Asia. The African wild dog and the Asian dhole are similar animals. They also hunt in packs.

Foxes are small canids that live mostly alone or in pairs. There are more than 20 fox species around the world, from the snowy Arctic to the hottest deserts. The red fox is often seen in towns, eating garbage that has been left lying around by humans.

Other wild canids include the rare bush dog of the Amazon jungles, the Australian dingo, the bushy little raccoon dog of Asia, and the maned wolf of the South American grasslands.

Dogs and people

The dogs we know as pets are descended from wolves. They were domesticated, or tamed and raised by people, more than 12,000 years ago. Today dogs depend on people for food, shelter, and safety. They give a great deal in return. Some are trained to guard property. Others herd farm animals, work with hunters, sniff out bombs or drugs at airports, or search for survivors at disaster scenes. Specially trained dogs assist people who cannot see or hear, or who use a wheelchair.

Breeds of domestic dog

It is because of these special tasks that there are so many different breeds of dog. Over the centuries a new kind of dog was created to perform each task. A hunter who needed dogs to sniff out game would breed together dogs that had a good sense of smell. A farmer who wanted to keep sheep safe from wolves or coyotes would breed together dogs that were brave and easy to train.

The American Kennel Club classifies purebred dogs in seven groups: working, sporting, hound, terrier, herding, toy, and nonsporting dogs.

The working breeds are dogs that are most often used by the police or on guard duty. This group includes Doberman pinschers, German shepherds, and Rottweilers. Dogs that pull sleds, such as the Siberian husky and the Alaskan malamute, are also working dogs.

The sporting breeds are widely used as hunting dogs. German shorthaired pointers, English setters, and Brittany spaniels are among the dogs trained to locate game birds and point them out to the hunters. English springer spaniels and cocker spaniels chase game birds into flight so that the hunters can fire their guns at them.

Some breeds of dog are trained to go and fetch animals and birds after they have been shot down. Golden retrievers, Labrador retrievers, and Chesapeake Bay retrievers recover birds from water and bring them to the hunters.

One of the best-known hounds is the beagle, an excellent rabbit hunter. The black-and-tan coonhound is used to track raccoons and chase them up trees.

▲
A woman combs a Yorkshire terrier, a toy breed, at a dog show in Moscow, Russia.

Dachshunds were originally bred in Germany to chase badgers. Hunters on horseback often follow a pack of foxhounds as they trail a fox. Bloodhounds are "human hunters" that are sometimes used by police to follow the scent of criminals or missing persons.

Terriers were bred and trained to hunt rodents and other small mammals. Breeds such as the Manchester terrier and the Cairn terrier could catch mice and rats and shake them to death. Today these breeds are kept mostly as pets.

Herding breeds chase and direct farm animals. They round up stray sheep and cattle, move herds from one field to another, and guard livestock from danger. Herding breeds include the collie, the Shetland sheepdog, and two types of Welsh corgi, the longtailed Cardigan and the tailless Pembrokeshire.

Most tiny dogs fall into a category called toy breeds. This group includes the Chihuahua, the toy poodle, and the Shih Tzu. These breeds have been kept as house pets for hundreds, and in some cases thousands, of years. These breeds are especially popular as show dogs,

The nonsporting breeds are also widely admired as house pets and show dogs. The many breeds in this group include bulldogs, Lhasa apsos, and chow chows.

SEE ALSO:
Animal;
Carnivore;
Mammal

✳ EARTH
The planet Earth is a vast mass of rock surrounded by layers of air, circling the sun. About 71 percent of the Earth's surface is covered by water.

Scientists believe the Earth was formed about 4.6 billion years ago, probably from tiny pieces of dust and gases that were produced when the sun was created. For the first billion years there was little or no life on the planet. Its atmosphere was probably made of carbon dioxide and steam.

No one knows when life began. The earliest traces suggest that it first appeared in the oceans about 3.8 billion years ago. These early life forms were simple organisms with only one cell each. Very slowly life developed into more complex organisms. Between 600 and 240 million years ago life began to develop on land. The first humans appeared about 6 million years ago.

The Earth in space
All the light, heat, and energy on Earth comes from the sun. The Earth orbits (revolves around) the sun at a distance of about 93 million miles (150 million km). On a complete orbit it travels about 590 million miles (950 million km). Each orbit lasts about 365 days—one year. The moon, about 240,000 miles (386,400km) away, is the planet's only natural satellite. The moon completes an orbit of the Earth once every 29 days—a lunar month.

The Earth itself is spinning, and each complete rotation lasts about 24 hours—one day. The most northerly point on the Earth is the North Pole, and the most southerly spot is the South Pole. Imagine a line connecting the North and South poles through the center of the Earth. This imaginary line is the axis on which the Earth spins.

The Earth's structure
The Earth is basically spherical, but is slightly flattened at the poles. Its diameter is about 7,923 miles (12,751km) at its widest point, called the equator, where its circumference (the distance all the way around the surface) is 24,902 miles (40,076km).

Beneath the surface the Earth is made up of three layers. The topmost layer is called the crust. Its thickness varies from about 22 miles (35km) on land to only 3 miles (5km) beneath the oceans. The crust is made mainly of granite and basalt rocks.

Below the crust is the mantle, which accounts for about four-fifths of the Earth's volume. The core—the center of the Earth—is made mostly of iron, which is molten because it is under great heat and pressure.

Probably because of the iron at its center, the Earth is a massive magnet. It has two magnetic poles, one at the north of the planet, the other at the

◄ *Earth 200 million years ago. Laurasia and Gondwanaland split to form the continents we know today.*

► *This photograph of the Earth was taken from the moon in 1994 by the space mission Clementine.*

EARTH'S INTERIOR

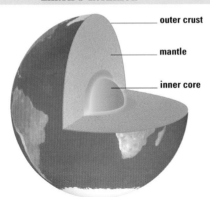

— outer crust

— mantle

— inner core

▲
The three main layers of the Earth—the outer crust, the mantle, and the inner core.

POSITION IN THE SOLAR SYSTEM
Third planet from the sun

AVERAGE DISTANCE FROM THE SUN
93,000,000 miles (150,000,000km)

SOLAR ORBIT
365.25 Earth days

MASS
6.6. sextillion tons

ATMOSPHERE
Mainly nitrogen (79 percent) and oxygen (20 percent). Also small amounts of other gases (argon, carbon dioxide, helium, hydrogen, krypton, neon, and xenon) and dust

AXIAL ROTATION
23 hours 56 minutes

south. The magnetic poles are close to, but not exactly at, the geographic North and South poles.

The ever-changing Earth
The map of the Earth has not always looked the way it does today. Over 150 million years ago Africa and Europe were joined to North and South America, and the Atlantic Ocean did not exist. Australia and Antarctica formed a single continent, and India was a large island.

Since then, however, vast sections, or plates, of the Earth's crust and upper mantle have gradually shifted position, splitting the land apart to form the map we know today. This process is called continental drift.

Today the Earth consists of seven large plates and several smaller ones. Sometimes plates rub against each other, and the rocks they are made of are driven up to form massive mountain ranges. The longest mountain ranges are about 30,000 miles (50,000km) long, but they are largely invisible because they lie submerged beneath the Atlantic, Indian, and Pacific oceans.

The surface of the Earth is still constantly changing, but the process is usually so slow that we cannot see it happening. Many changes are caused by air, water, and wind, which wear away rocks and mountains over millions of years. This process is called erosion.

Other changes are caused by geological forces that originate deep inside the planet. They can be much more sudden and violent than erosion. Strains between the Earth's plates can produce shock waves that result in earthquakes. Molten rock-forming material (lava) from the mantle can escape onto the surface through gaps in the crust called volcanoes. Almost all earthquakes and volcanic activity take place where the edges of plates meet.

Geologists examine a lava stream near an active volcano in Hawaii.
▼

👀 SEE ALSO: Climate & Weather; Earthquake; Geology; Magnetism; Ocean & Sea; Prehistoric People; Solar System; Volcano

✳ EARTHQUAKE

An earthquake is a sudden release onto the surface of the Earth of energy generated by the movement of rocks deep underground.

The shaking movements sent out by earthquakes are called seismic waves. Scientists who study these movements are called seismologists. They used to believe that all earthquakes were caused by slippages, called faulting, in rocks in the lowest reaches of the Earth's outermost layer, or crust. But they now think that faulting is only a secondary cause of earthquakes, and that most shock waves originate in the mantle, the layer below the crust. Here masses of steam are produced. As the steam moves slowly upward, it heats rocks in its path, eventually dislodging them and producing added effects that may eventually be felt on the surface.

Measuring and describing quakes
There are thousands of earthquakes every year, but most are so small that they can be detected only by the most sensitive scientific equipment. One or two are huge: They may cause vast destruction and alter the appearance of the Earth.

During an earthquake the point at which the greatest amount of seismic movement takes place is called the focus. The point on the Earth's surface directly above the focus is called the epicenter. The effects of the earthquake are usually strongest near the epicenter. The magnitude, or total amount of energy, released by an earthquake is usually measured on the Richter scale. The strongest earthquakes measure about 8.6 on this scale.

People can neither prevent earthquakes nor predict when they will happen. However, seismologists know that they are more likely to happen in certain areas, such as along the San Andreas Fault in California and in parts of Japan. In these areas houses and other structures are built to survive shocks.

Earthquakes beneath the ocean floor can produce huge waves called tsunamis that move very rapidly across the ocean. They can cause great damage if they reach land.

▲
This great crack in the sidewalk was caused by an earthquake that hit Taiwan in 1999.

AMAZING FACTS❗

An earthquake in Shanxi, China, in 1556 is thought to have killed at least 830,000 people and measured 8.0 to 8.3 on the Richter scale.
A cat survived for 80 days under a collapsed building after being buried by an earthquake in Taiwan in 1999.

SEE ALSO: Disaster; Earth; Geology

✳ EASTER ISLAND

This small volcanic island lies in the Pacific Ocean 2,200 miles (3,500km) west of Chile. It is famous for its gigantic stone carvings.

The remaining moai statues on Easter Island attract visitors from all over the world. ▼

The island was given its present name because it was discovered by the Dutch explorer Jakob Roggeveen on Easter Sunday 1722. The locals call it Rapa Nui.

Easter Island is just 14 miles (22.5km) long and 7 miles (11km) wide. Its grassy, mountainous landscape is dotted with craters, and high cliffs tower above stony beaches. All along the shores stand huge statues called *moai*. Carved from volcanic rock, some of them are as tall as a house.

People lived on Easter Island before recorded history, but little is known about them.

Settlers from Polynesia (a Pacific island group) arrived in the third or fourth century A.D. They carved the *moai*, perhaps for use in sun worship, and performed religious rituals on great stone platforms called *ahus*. The *moai* were set up around the *ahus*, facing inland.

A thriving culture grew on Easter Island. The locals had their own written language (although no one knows how to read it today). Eventually, however, the

▶ *Easter Island is in the Pacific Ocean. It is administered by Chile, which is 2,200 miles (3,500km) away.*

population grew too large for the island. Food became scarce, and war broke out. During one battle the workers killed all the island's leaders and toppled most of the *moai* to the ground.

In 1862 slave traders came to Easter Island from Peru, and a couple of years later missionaries brought Christianity. The visitors also brought diseases such as smallpox, and many islanders died. After 1888, when Chile took control of the island, its population recovered. Today most of the magnificent statues have been set upright and have become a popular tourist attraction.

SEE ALSO: Chile

✳ ECOLOGY

Ecology is the study of the complex, changing relationships between organisms, or living things, and their surroundings, or environment.

Each organism is suited to a particular habitat that is based on factors such as soil type, temperature, moisture, and light. The plants and animals of a particular habitat form groups called communities. The invertebrates, bacteria, and fungi living in a rotting log form a small community. A large area with a particular

Ecologists have discovered that the number of lodgepole pine seedlings in Yellowstone National Park, Wyoming, has increased tenfold since the forest fires in 1988.

climate and specific types of plants and animals is called a biome. A biome contains a number of different habitats. Biomes include deserts and grasslands.

The role of ecologists
Ecologists try to understand how the relationships between organisms and their environment change and why.

The population of a community varies depending on factors such as supplies of food and water, disease, and weather. Population ecologists try to identify and understand these factors.

Community ecologists try to understand how and why a specific environment is able to support its particular variety of plants and animals. Variety of species is called biodiversity. Ecologists also study food webs and chains. In a simple food chain clover is eaten by rabbits, which are eaten by coyotes. Many interlinking food chains form a complex web.

Ecosystems ecologists study the flow of nutrients, chemicals, and energy in an environment. For example, a tree uses energy from the sun to produce new growth in spring. Its roots draw nutrients and water from the soil. When the leaves fall off or the tree dies, the plant material decomposes on the forest floor, returning nutrients to the soil.

Changes
Ecological systems change constantly. Some changes are caused by natural disturbances such as fires, hurricanes, and floods. If an environment is functioning well, it can survive and even benefit from natural changes. However, human activities, such as clearing a forest, can cause sudden, dramatic change that may lead to the extinction of some species and the loss of biodiversity.

Ecology shows that people are as much a part of nature as animals and plants. Any changes we make in the environment affect all the organisms in it.

SEE ALSO: Biome; Botany; Carson, Rachel; Environment; Food Chain; Habitat; Invertebrate; Lake; Ocean & Sea; Plant; Pollution; Rainforest; River; Wetlands

✳ ECUADOR

Ecuador is on the Pacific coast of South America. The equator crosses the country just north of the capital, Quito. Ecuador is the Spanish word for equator.

The coastal lowlands (*costa*) include tropical forests and rich agricultural land. In the center of the country are the Andean highlands (*sierra*), which include Cotopaxi, the world's highest active volcano, at 19,347 ft. (5,897m). The *Oriente* (eastern region) includes tropical forests and important oil deposits. Ecuador owns the Galápagos Islands, about 600 miles (965km) off the coast. They are famous for their wildlife.

The higher peaks of the Andes Mountains are snow-covered all year. Rainfall is heaviest in the *Oriente*, with 100 in. (2,500mm) or more of rain a year.

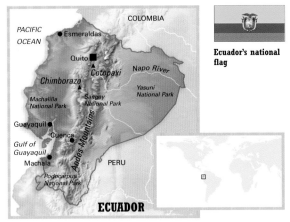

ECUADOR

Ecuador's national flag

People

About 80 percent of Ecuador's population are Indians or mestizos—people of mixed Indian and European ancestry. The remainder are of Spanish, black, or mixed black ancestry. The blacks are descendants of slaves brought from Africa during the period of Spanish rule.

Just over half the population lives in rural areas. The remainder live in cities and towns. Most people live either in the *sierra* (Andes) or *costa* (lowlands).

Economy

Petroleum is Ecuador's biggest industry. One-third of the workforce is employed in agriculture. Bananas, coffee, cacao, and sugarcane are the main crops. Shrimp, tuna, and balsa wood are major exports.

In 1999 the Ecuadorean economy collapsed, and the government adopted U.S. currency to bring stability.

History

In the late 1400s the area that is now Ecuador became part of the Inca Empire. Spain defeated the Incas in the 1530s, founding a new city at Quito in 1534.

In the 1800s Ecuadoreans rose up against Spanish rule, winning their freedom in 1822. In 1830 Ecuador became an independent republic. For much of the 20th century the country suffered from unrest and frequent changes of government.

KEY FACTS

OFFICIAL NAME
República del
Ecuador

AREA
103,930 sq. mi.
(269,180 sq. km)

POPULATION
12,646,000

CAPITAL
Quito

LARGEST CITY
Guayaquil

MAJOR RELIGION
Roman
Catholicism

MAJOR LANGUAGES
Spanish,
Quechua,
other Indian
languages

CURRENCY
U.S. dollar

SEE ALSO: America, South; Incas

✳ EDISON, THOMAS ALVA (1847–1931)

Thomas Edison was one of the most important
inventors ever, making discoveries in electric light,
sound recording, telegraphy, and telephones.

*Thomas Edison
pictured with his
phonograph, or
"talking machine,"
which he invented
in 1877. It was the
first machine that
reproduced sound
from a recording.* ▼

Edison was born in Milan, Ohio, on
February 11, 1847. He was a clever boy
but he did not do well at school, and his
mother educated him at home. When he
was 12, he got a job selling newspapers
on the Grand Trunk Railroad and
later became a telegrapher. That
made him want to improve the
way telegraphs worked.

In 1876 Edison set up an
"invention factory" at Menlo
Park, New Jersey. He built
the first phonograph, an early
version of the record player.
He was also the first person to
build a workable electric light
system. He set up a movie
studio, and his company
produced the first movie that

told a story, *The Great Train Robbery*, in
1903. It was eight minutes long. Next he
developed the first storage battery that
could be used over and over again.

A thousand inventions
By the time Edison died in 1931 he had
received 1,093 patents in the United
States—more than anyone before or
since. A patent gives an inventor the
exclusive right to make, use, and sell a
new invention for a period of time.

SEE ALSO: Communication; Electricity;
Inventors & Inventions; Movies; Sound
Recording

✳ EDUCATION

Education is the gaining of knowledge and skills.
People start learning almost as soon as they are
born, and the process carries on throughout life.

▲
*A stone relief
carving showing
a schoolmaster in
ancient Rome
instructing a pupil.*

Most ancient cultures made
education available for boys
only. Girls did not go to
school. This was common
for many centuries.

In ancient Greece
education was intended
to prepare young men for
playing a part in society.
They were taught reading,
writing, math, singing, and sports. The
greatest teacher was Socrates (about
470–399 B.C.). His followers, including
Plato and Aristotle, set up schools
that instructed the young in philosophy
(the art of thinking).

The Romans took many ideas about
education from the Greeks and spread
them through their empire. When the
western Roman Empire collapsed in
the fifth century, education in Europe
declined. For many years even kings were
unable to read. Only boys intending to be
priests got a good education.

Renaissance and the modern era
The great expansion in learning that began
in the 1400s was called the Renaissance.
After 1455 the development of the
printing press made books cheaper and
widely available. The Reformation, when
many people broke away from the Roman

Catholic Church in the 1500s, also had an effect on education. The Bible was translated from Latin into local languages, so people could read it for themselves. However, churches and religious bodies still controlled most schools.

In the 1700s thinkers such as Jean-Jacques Rousseau (1712–78) argued that education should give more freedom to children and less discipline. Governments began to pay for education, and girls got better access to learning. From the 1900s most Western countries began providing state-funded education to all children, usually for about 10 years from age five.

Education in the United States
In colonial America children learned to read and write by memorizing religious passages. By the end of the 1800s state-funded schools were providing basic education in all states. Many schools remained segregated until 1954.

Today states still have control over the public schools within their borders. Each state is divided into school districts, run by school boards. Most districts organize their schools on a "ladder" system. Children begin with preschool and elementary schools, moving on to middle or junior high schools, and then high schools. After graduating from high school, many students go on to colleges and universities.

SEE ALSO: Ancient Civilizations; Aristotle; Greece, Ancient; Renaissance; Roman Empire

✳ EGYPT, ANCIENT
The civilization of Egypt was one of the most important of ancient times. It was based in the valley of the Nile River.

Although the Nile River was surrounded by desert, the yearly flooding of the river covered nearby fields with water and rich soil, enabling farmers to plant crops when the water retreated.

In about 3200 B.C. a ruler named Menes, or Narmer, united the cities of northern and southern Egypt on the Nile River, founding one of the first great empires of the ancient world. Menes was the first

◄ *The Great Sphinx at Giza, which was carved about 2500 B.C. It has the body of a lion and the head of a man—the face is a portrait of King Khafre of Egypt's Old Kingdom.*

This map shows the area influenced by Egyptian culture. All the great cities of ancient Egypt were near the banks of the Nile River, where the land was fertile enough to grow crops. ▶

Mediterranean Sea
LEBANON
ISRAEL
Nile Delta
Giza ● ■ Cairo
Memphis ● Saqqara
JORDAN
Akhetaten ●
Nile River
Red Sea
● Thebes
SUDAN

where people went when they died, was Osiris, and his wife was Isis. Many gods were depicted as having the heads of animals. For example, Anubis, god of the dead, had the head of a jackal.

In 1379 B.C. Amenhotep IV (also called Akhenaten) became king and introduced worship of a single god. After his death Egyptians went back to their old gods.

Egyptians believed in life after death. The bodies of rulers and other important people were mummified, or preserved, and placed in lavish tombs, along with food, drink, tools, and valued possessions for use in the underworld.

Pyramids

Dead pharaohs were often placed in massive tombs called pyramids. The most famous pyramids are the three great pyramids at Giza, on the west bank of the Nile River. Labor was brought from all over Egypt to build them, probably during the season when the Nile flooded and farmers were unable to work on the land.

king or pharaoh (pronounced fair-oe) of the first dynasty (ruling family). Thirty-one dynasties ruled Egypt until it was conquered by Alexander the Great in 332 B.C. The dynasties are grouped into periods of stability (called the Old, Middle, and New Kingdom) and periods of confusion and unrest when several people claimed the throne.

One of Alexander's generals ruled Egypt as Ptolemy I. The last of Ptolemy's descendants was Cleopatra VII. After her death Egypt became a Roman province.

Egyptian religion

The ancient Egyptians worshiped many gods and goddesses. The most important was Re, the sun god. The pharaohs were believed to be descendants of Re. The king of the underworld,

A painted limestone bust of Queen Nefertiti, the wife of King Akhenaten, who ruled Egypt from 1353 to 1336 B.C. Nefertiti bore six daughters, two of whom were later to become queens of Egypt. ▼

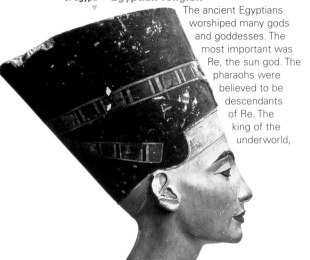

AMAZING FACTS !

The Great Pyramid at Giza, built for Khufu, or Cheops, in about 2600 B.C., is so large that it could easily contain the Capitol building in Washington, D.C. The pyramid is made of about 2,300,000 blocks of finely cut limestone. They have an average weight of 2.5 tons each. The largest stones were cut and floated almost 700 miles (1,125km) down the Nile River to the pyramid site. With only the simplest of tools, the stones were dragged up earth ramps and set in place to build the pyramid.

Egypt not only had rich farming land, it also had other valuable natural resources, such as gold. Gold was so abundant that the king of a neighboring state wrote enviously to the pharaoh, "In your country gold is like dirt." Craftsmen made elaborate gold jewelry for the pharaohs.

Queen Nefertiti and King Akhenaten shown in an Egyptian wall painting.

The gold coffin that contained the remains of King Tutankhamun (reigned 1332–22 B.C.).

When they died, gold masks covered their faces, gold breastplates were laid over their chests, and golden tips were added to their fingers and toes. All these items were inlaid with semiprecious stones.

Egypt's dry climate means that many artifacts have survived to be discovered by archaeologists. They include writings on papyrus (paper made from reeds) and some of the earliest board games.

SEE ALSO: Cleopatra; Roman Empire

✳ EINSTEIN, ALBERT (1879–1955)

Albert Einstein was one of the most important scientists in history. He developed ideas that changed people's view of the universe.

Einstein was born in Ulm, Germany, and grew up in Munich, where his father ran a small factory making electrical equipment. At college he studied mathematics and physics and later worked in an office in Switzerland, checking applications for patents (official documents that protected new inventions). In his spare time he worked on his theory of relativity—the idea that things such as gravity, light, and time are all related. He published his ideas in 1905. At first very few people understood his ideas, but they began to change the thinking of scientists in many different subjects.

International recognition
In 1914 Einstein went to work at the university in Berlin and continued to publish his theories. After World War I (1914–18) he became known to a wider

public and was recognized internationally. In 1921 Einstein was awarded the Nobel Prize in physics.

In 1933, when the Nazis took power in Germany, Einstein accepted a position at Princeton University. Although he hated war, he persuaded President Roosevelt to promote the development of the atomic bomb. Einstein died on April 18, 1955. His ideas influenced many areas, including art, science, and philosophy.

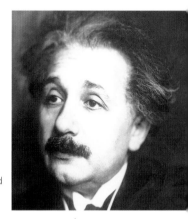

▲ *Albert Einstein in 1920, the year before he received the Nobel Prize in physics.*

SEE ALSO: Nobel Prize; World War II

✳ ELECTRICITY

Electricity provides lighting, heat for cooking, cooling for refrigeration, and power for many things such as computers, televisions, trains, and subways.

A bolt of lightning is an electrical current caused by a buildup of static electricity.

People observed electricity long before they understood it or could make it useful. The ancient Greek scientist Thales (about 625–547 B.C.) rubbed amber (fossilized tree resin) with a woolen cloth. Afterward the amber attracted small, light materials, such as lint. Thales believed that there was an unknown force in the amber. The Greek word for amber is *elektron*, and this gives us the word "electricity."

Atoms and static electricity

Scientists now know that all matter is made of tiny atoms. The nucleus—the center of the atom—contains one or more protons, particles with a positive charge, and neutrons, particles with no charge. Electrons, particles with a negative charge, circle the nucleus.

An atom usually has the same number of protons and electrons. That makes it electrically neutral—neither positive nor negative. In some kinds of atoms electrons furthest from the nucleus are loosely held and can easily be set free.

When two substances, such as amber and wool, are rubbed together, the loose electrons are pulled off the atoms in one of the materials and stick to the atoms in the other. Materials that lose electrons are positively charged, and materials that gain electrons are negatively charged. Opposite charges attract each other; like charges repel. The charge attracting the lint is called static electricity.

More discoveries

The Italian Alessandro Volta (1745–1827) discovered that he could generate electricity from a chemical reaction between metals and salt water. His invention was called the voltaic pile. It was the first manufactured source of electric current, which is what happens

▶

A girl touches a Van de Graaff generator. The generator creates a negative charge of static electricity. The charge passes from the dome through her hands to her hair. As her hairs become charged, they repel each other and stand on end.

when electrical charges move from one place to another. Volta also found that some materials carry electricity better than others. They are called conductors.

Later, the English scientist Humphrey Davy (1778–1829) joined voltaic piles together to produce an even stronger current. His invention is called a battery.

The English scientist Michael Faraday (1791–1867) found that a moving magnet inside a coil of wire generates an electrical charge. This is the basis for electrical generators and motors.

Until about 1830 electricity was of little use. Inventors worked with scientists and found so many uses for it that they greatly changed the way people live.

SEE ALSO: Inventors & Inventions; Magnetism; Matter

✳ ELEMENT, CHEMICAL

Chemical elements are the basic substances out of which everything in the universe is made. Iron, aluminum, and sulfur are common elements.

A chemical element is a piece of matter that cannot be broken down into anything simpler by chemical or physical means (excluding nuclear reactions).

Every atom of an element is identical and unlike that of any other element. Each element has its own chemical symbol. Usually the symbol is the first letter of the element's name or the first letter and one other. For instance, the chemical symbol for carbon is C, and the symbol for aluminum is Al. Sometimes the symbol is taken from the Latin name. For instance, the Latin word for iron is *ferrum*, and the chemical symbol for iron is Fe.

Atomic number

The most important property that distinguishes one element from another is the internal structure of its atoms. Each atom contains three types of particle: protons, which carry a positive electrical charge; negatively charged particles called electrons; and neutrons, which have no charge at all.

The defining characteristic of any element is the number of protons it contains. For example, carbon atoms have six protons, hydrogen atoms have one each, and oxygen atoms have eight protons. The number of electrons in an atom is always the same as the number of protons.

From the way the electrons are arranged, scientists can predict—even if they have not seen for themselves—how an atom will react chemically. They can tell properties such as stability (the ease with which an element will change when exposed to other elements). They can also predict the boiling point (the temperature

A high school student in a chemistry laboratory. Behind him is a poster showing the periodic table, which lists all the chemical elements.

DID YOU KNOW?

Some elements are radioactive, and as a result, they break down naturally to form a more stable element. For example, uranium decomposes over millions of years into lead.
By the mid-1990s 112 elements were known. Of them 90 are found in nature, and the others are produced in laboratories. All synthetic elements are radioactive.
There are 269 stable isotopes that occur naturally and over 900 radioactive isotopes.
Two elements, bromine and mercury, are liquid at room temperature, 77° F (25° C).
The most abundant elements in the Earth's crust are oxygen and silicon.

ISOTOPES OF HYDROGEN

Ordinary hydrogen   Deuterium   Tritium

○ **Electron**   ○ **Proton**   ○ **Neutron**

The three different forms, or isotopes, of hydrogen have their own names. Deuterium and tritium are heavier than ordinary hydrogen.

at which an element will turn from liquid to gas) and conductivity (the ease with which electricity or heat can pass through an element).

Atomic mass
Chemical elements also differ from each other in weight, or atomic mass. Atoms are too small to weigh on scales, so their atomic mass is expressed in relation to the supposed mass of a carbon atom. It is taken to be 12 atomic mass units, or amus. Although all atoms of the same element have the same number of protons and electrons, the number of neutrons they contain may vary. These different forms of the same element are called isotopes. The atomic mass of an element that may contain varying numbers of neutrons is taken as the average weight of its isotopes.

Although every atom of every element is identical, some elements can take more than one physical form; the different forms are called allotropes. Carbon, for example, may take the form of diamond, the hardest natural substance, or graphite, the soft so-called "lead" in pencils.

The periodic table
In 1869 the Russian chemist Dmitri I. Mendeleev published a periodic table of the elements. He ordered them by their atomic mass and chemical properties. He also showed several gaps in the 60-odd elements known at that time and boldly predicted the properties of three as yet undiscovered elements. Gallium, germanium, and scandium were discovered within the next 15 years, and their properties closely matched Mendeleev's descriptions.

Seventy-five of the first 103 chemical elements in the periodic table are metals. Metals are characterized by their conductivity, luster (sheen), and ductility (capacity to be drawn into threads).

Seventeen elements are nonmetals. Examples include carbon and sulfur. Between the metals and the nonmetals are elements called semimetals or metalloids, such as boron and silicon.

The periodic table is still the most important chemistry reference there is. An element's position on the table enables students to figure out a lot of information about its properties, even if they have never heard of it.

A crystal of sulfur. Sulfur has the atomic number 16. It is a yellow nonmetallic element that occurs naturally.

SEE ALSO: Chemistry

✳ ELLINGTON, DUKE (1899–1974)

Edward Kennedy Ellington, known as "Duke," was one of the most important orchestra leaders and composers in the history of jazz music.

Ellington played over 20,000 performances.

Ellington began studying piano at age seven, and at age 17 he began to play professionally. He formed an orchestra in New York City in 1923 and soon became nationally famous. For four years he and his orchestra were stars at the Cotton Club, Harlem's best-known nightspot.

Ellington wrote over 1,000 jazz and nonjazz works. With the help of his highly talented band members Ellington grouped instruments together in unexpected and very effective new ways. His most popular numbers are songs like "Mood Indigo," "Sophisticated Lady," and "Satin Doll." The works that best demonstrate his genius as a composer and arranger are instrumental pieces, such as "Ko-ko" and "Concerto for Cootie."

Important members of his orchestra included drummer Sonny Greer, saxophonists Ben Webster and Johnny Hodges, trumpeter Cootie Williams, and composer and arranger Billy Strayhorn.

SEE ALSO:
Music

✳ ENERGY

Energy is everywhere in many different forms, from sunlight to motion. Energy can be converted from one form to another, but it can never be destroyed.

Scientists define energy as the ability to do work. In physics work is done when a force applied to an object moves it in the direction of the force. If a woman hammers a nail into wood, she exerts a force to drive the nail into the wood. If she stands without moving, holding a heavy weight, she is not doing any work because the position of the weight remains unchanged. The weight has not been moved any distance by force.

Different forms of energy
Work can be done in various ways. Each way represents a different kind of energy. The two most basic kinds of energy are potential energy and kinetic energy. When the hammer is raised but not moving, it has potential energy—it is capable of doing work. When the head hits the nail, it has kinetic energy. The word *kinetic* comes from a Greek word meaning motion. Together kinetic energy and

Wind turbines gather kinetic energy from the wind and convert it to electricity.

potential energy are known as mechanical energy. Kinetic energy is also closely related to heat energy. An object is hot because its atoms (the tiny particles that make up all matter) are constantly in motion. The faster its atoms move, the hotter the object becomes.

Most of the time that energy is used to do work, part of it is wasted as heat. Most of the energy of the hammer, for example, goes to heating up the nail and the head of the hammer. Only a small part of the energy actually moves the nail.

Sources of energy
Ancient peoples used only the energy their bodies obtained from food. When they learned to use fire, they changed the chemical energy of wood into heat and light. The chemical energy in wood comes from the energy of the sun. Plants absorb energy from the sun and change it into chemical energy through a process called photosynthesis. The energy in coal, oil, and natural gas also comes from the sun. Most scientists believe that these fossil fuels were formed from the remains of ancient plants and animals.

Other sources of energy include nuclear energy, which releases the energy in the nucleus of an atom. Fears about the safety of nuclear power plants have prompted scientists to turn to natural forms of energy such as the sun, wind, and water. However, at the moment it is difficult to produce large amounts of electricity from natural energy.

▲
When wood is burned, its chemical energy is turned into heat energy and light energy.

SEE ALSO: Chemistry; Electricity; Engine; Food Chain; Heat; Matter; Natural Resources; Plant

✳ ENGINE
Engines are machines that turn energy into movement, which is then used to do work. Windmills and waterwheels were some of the earliest engines.

Windmills and waterwheels harness the energy of wind and moving water, and are still used to pump water and make electricity. Most other engines turn heat energy into movement. Heat engines almost always burn a chemical fuel, such as wood, coal, oil, or gasoline, to produce the heat. Heat engines include steam, gasoline, diesel, jet, and rocket engines.

Steam engines
The first true heat engines ran on steam, which is produced when water is boiled. Steam occupies much more space than the water from which it is made. So when steam is produced in an enclosed space, it pushes parts of the steam engine to create movement.

Fuel to heat the water is burned outside the engine. For this reason steam engines are called external-combustion engines. External means outside, and combustion means burning. The water is heated in a boiler, and the steam is then piped into the engine.

In 1712 Thomas Newcomen, an English blacksmith, built the first successful piston-operated steam engine. A piston is like a stopper that slides back and forth inside a cylinder (a tube closed at one end). A rod on one end of the piston connects to a wheel. Steam enters the cylinder and pushes the piston, which turns the wheel.

Newcomen's engine was used to pump water out of flooded coal mines. In later years steam engines

This racing car is powered by an internal-combustion engine with a lot of cylinders.
▼

ENGINE TYPES

STEAM ENGINE

Steam is produced when water is boiled. This happens outside the engine. When steam is piped in, it pushes parts of the engine so that they move.

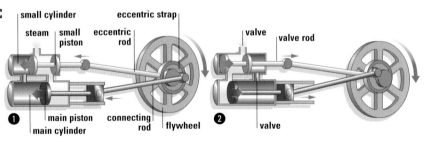

(1) Steam presses on the main piston, pushing it toward the end of the cylinder. That pulls the connecting rod toward the engine, making the wheel turn. As the flywheel turns, so does the eccentric strap, pushing the eccentric rod left.

(2) The valve rod links the eccentric rod to the smaller piston, which is pushed to the end of the cylinder. That makes steam in the main cylinder switch to the left-hand side. The larger piston moves to the right, restarting the whole process.

FOUR-STROKE INTERNAL-COMBUSTION ENGINE

The internal-combustion engine has many advantages over the steam engine. Its design led to the invention of the automobile.

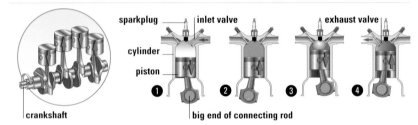

Fuel is burned inside the cylinder in the internal-combustion engine. The piston is connected by a crankshaft and connecting rod to a wheel that drives the machine. The sparkplug lights the fuel. When the piston moves down, it sucks fuel and

air into the cylinder through the inlet valve (1). The piston moves up, compressing the fuel and air (2). The fuel and air expand as they burn and push the piston down (3). The piston moves up, pushing burned gases out of an exhaust valve (4).

JET ENGINE

The need for faster military aircraft led to the development of the jet engine. In the 1950s jet engines came into widespread use for air travel.

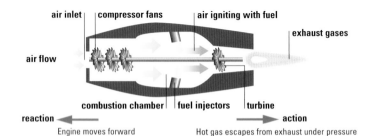

Jet engines draw in air at the front of the engine. The air is squeezed and put under pressure by a device called a compressor. Fuel is added to the compressed air, and it is ignited in the combustion chamber. The temperature quickly rises to around

370°F (700°C). As the mixture burns, hot exhaust gases are forced out the back of the engine. First, they go through a turbine. The turbine drives the fuel pumps, electricity generators, and the compressor at the front of the engine.

were built to power manufacturing plants or to pull trains. Steam trains are still used in many parts of the world, such as India and Africa.

Today the steam turbine has replaced the piston engine. A turbine is a set of metal blades attached to a central rotor. It looks like a pinwheel or a fan, and it fits inside a tube. A fluid or gas rushing through the turbine pushes the blades, making the rotor spin. The spinning rotor provides the power to do work.

Steam turbines power electric generators and large ships. On some ships and submarines the turbine steam is made by the heat from a nuclear reactor on board the vessel.

Internal-combustion engines

An internal-combustion engine is a heat engine that burns fuel and air inside the engine itself. Most internal-combustion engines are gasoline or diesel engines. Others are gas-turbine engines, in which gases drive a turbine rotor.

The gasoline engine, or spark-ignition engine, consists of one or more cylinders that contain pistons. The fuel is a spray of gasoline and air. It is sucked into each cylinder. A spark-producing device, called a sparkplug, ignites the fuel. The explosion of the burning fuel pushes down the piston, which turns a crankshaft, causing it to work.

Gottlieb Daimler, Wilhelm Maybach, and Carl Benz designed the first practical gas engines in Germany at the end of the 19th century. Today, gas engines have countless uses, from simple one-cylinder units in lawn mowers to powerful, multi-cylinder engines in racing cars.

The diesel engine, or compression-ignition engine, works very much like the gasoline engine, except that there are no sparkplugs. The piston compresses—forces into a smaller space—the air in the cylinder. As it is compressed, the air becomes hot—hot enough to ignite the

▲
A steam train is powered by an external-combustion engine. The first engines invented were powered by steam.

diesel fuel. Diesel engines power most heavy trucks, buses, and locomotives.

A gas turbine works in a similar way as the steam turbine, except for two major differences. First, a hot gas other than steam turns the turbine blades. Second, the fuel is burned within, not outside, the engine. Gas turbines are used in some boats and airplanes, and in industry.

Jet engines

During the 1930s engineers worked on jet engine designs. The first jet plane, a German Heinkel, flew in 1939, but the jet plane was not widely used until after 1945. Today it is in widespread use in military and other aircraft.

A jet engine, like a turbine, is contained in a tube. As the plane flies, air rushes through the front of the engine, passing a compressor. It reaches the burner, where it is mixed with fuel and ignited. The hot, expanding gases rush out the back of the engine, spinning a turbine that turns the compressor.

Today, some manfacturers are working on the design of cleaner engines that run on hydrogen or electricity instead of fuel.

SEE ALSO: Aircraft; Car; Energy; Force & Motion; Natural Resources; Rocket; Ship & Boat

✳ ENVIRONMENT

The environment is the surroundings in which animals and plants live, and which tend to influence their development and behavior.

All living things, or organisms, interact with and influence their surroundings. Organisms form a network of interconnected environmental systems called biomes. A rainforest is a biome, as is a desert. The branch of science that studies the way organisms relate to their environment is called ecology.

Natural events such as droughts or fires may damage the environment, but they are temporary disturbances. Given time, the environment will come back into balance.

Farmers in Sumatra need land for houses and crops, but by using it they have destroyed the forests.
▼

SEE ALSO: Biome; Carson, Rachel; Ecology; Energy; Extinction; Food Chain; Habitat; Natural Resources; Pollution

People and the environment
Humans, however, have had a greater effect on the environment than any other species, and not everything they have done has been good for it.

Since the 1950s the number of people in the world has more than doubled, and they all need food, water, and shelter. The increased demand on natural resources can unbalance the environment, causing problems for other species. Many have become extinct (died out completely) or are endangered.

It is only recently that people have begun to worry about the effect they are having on the environment and have started to think about halting various damaging practices. Should people cut down fewer trees to preserve the rainforests, have fewer children to keep population numbers down, stop driving cars, which pollute the atmosphere, and be prepared to pay more for electricity?

There are no easy answers to these questions. If logging is banned, people who live by harvesting timber will have no income. What gives one person the right to tell another not to start a family or to stop driving a car?

Today most people agree that something needs to be done about environmental problems. But they do not agree on the solutions.

☀ EUROPE

Europe is the world's second smallest continent after Australia, but its long history as a world power makes it important out of all relation to its size.

Although Europe and Asia occupy the same land mass, they are always classified as two separate continents. The boundary between them runs north to south from the Ural Mountains to the Caspian Sea. Although Russia is part of Europe politically, much of its land lies in Asia.

Much of the northwest coast of Europe is mountainous. Farther south the great North European Plain spreads from southwest France into Russia. This area has good farmland, valuable minerals, and easy transportation. It is drained by broad, deep rivers, busy with boats carrying goods to Europe's seaports. South of the plain are the Central Uplands, a belt of higher ground from Spain to Poland.

In southern Europe there are many mountain chains, including the Sierra Nevada, the Pyrenees, the Apennines, the Alps, the Carpathians, and the Caucasus.

Sea air brings mild, wet weather to western Europe. Deep in central Europe, the winters are cooler and the summers hotter. The highest rainfall is in the mountains. The Mediterranean region is very hot and dry in the summer.

In the far north lies the tundra, a region of treeless, rolling plains. The soil is frozen for much of the year and cannot be farmed. Farther south is the taiga, a huge expanse of evergreen trees, which are an abundant source of lumber and paper. Over much of lowland Europe most trees have been cleared for human settlement. Only in the uplands are parts of the forest still standing, protected for their timber.

Natural resources
There are large coal deposits in many parts of Europe. The North Sea floor is drilled for petroleum and natural gas, though Europe still imports much of its oil.

Austria, France, Russia, Sweden, and Switzerland use hydroelectric power (electricity generated by the flow of rivers). Nuclear power is an important energy source in western Europe.

People
Europe is the most densely populated of the continents. It is home to one-seventh of the world's population, and more than 40 of its cities have over 1 million inhabitants. Some of these people immigrated in the late 1900s from parts of other continents that were formerly ruled by European nations: Algerians to France; Indonesians to the Netherlands; Asian Indians and West Indians to Britain.

Early history
Throughout Europe's long and complex history its countries have regularly changed their boundaries. One of the earliest great European civilizations arose 3,000 years ago in Greece. The ancient Greeks were the first people to adopt democracy, and they started rich traditions in arts and science.

▲ *The flags of the European Union (EU) and its 15 member nations fly outside the European parliament building in Strasbourg, France. Ten more nations are scheduled to join the EU in 2004.*

(continued on page 138)

EUROPE

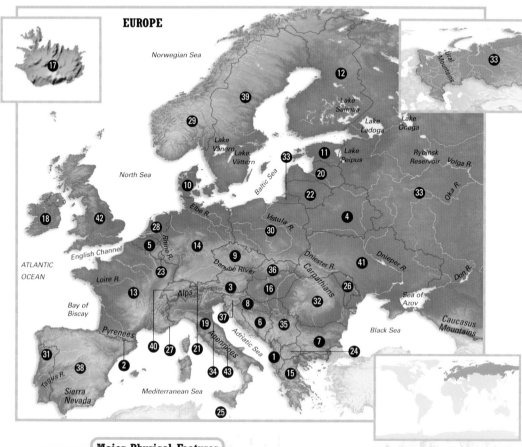

Norwegian Sea

Lake Saimaa

Lake Ladoga

Lake Onega

Lake Vänern

Lake Vättern

Lake Peipus

Rybinsk Reservoir

Volga R.

North Sea

Baltic Sea

Elbe R.

Oka R.

Vistula R.

Dniester R.

Carpathians

Dnieper R.

Don R.

ATLANTIC OCEAN

English Channel

Rhine R.

Danube River

Loire R.

Alps

Bay of Biscay

Pyrenees

Apennines

Adriatic Sea

Sea of Azov

Black Sea

Caucasus Mountains

Tagus R.

Sierra Nevada

Mediterranean Sea

Ural Mountains

The background picture shows the city of Cadiz, the capital of Adalusia, Spain. It was founded in about 1100 B.C.

Major Physical Features

MOUNTAIN RANGES & HIGHEST POINTS

• Caucasus, 18,510 ft. (5,642m) at Mt. Elbrus

• Alps, 15,780 ft. (4,810m) at Mt. Blanc

• Pyrenees, 11,169 ft. (3,404m) at Pico de Aneto

• Sierra Nevada, 11,411 ft. (3,478m) at Mulhacén

RIVERS

• Volga, 2,193 mi. (3,530km)

• Danube, 1,770 mi. (2,850km)

• Ural, 1,588 mi. (2,540km)

• Dnieper, 1,424 mi. (1,958km)

• Don, 1,220 mi. (1,900km)

• Pechora, 1,124 mi. (1,809km)

• Kama, 1,128 mi. (1,805km)

• Dniester, 840 mi. (1,352km)

• Oka 930 mi. 1,488km

• Belaya 889 mi. (1,422 km)

• Rhine, 820 mi. (1,320km)

• Elbe, 725 mi. (1,165km)

• Vistula, 668 mi. (1,069km)

• Loire, 634 mi. (1,120km)

• Tagus, 626 mi. (1,007km)

LAKES

• Ladoga, 6,826 sq mi. (17,678 sq km)

• Onega, 3,753 sq mi. (9,720 sq km)

• Vänern, 2,156 sq mi. (5,585 sq km)

• Rybinsk, 1,757sq mi. (4,550sq km)

• Saimaa, 1,690 sq mi. (4,377 sq km)

• Peipus, 1,373 (3,555)

• Vättern, 738 sq mi. (1,912 sq km)

COUNTRIES OF EUROPE

	Country	Flag	Population	Capital city
1	Albania		3,113,000	Tirana
2	Andorra		78,000	Andorra
3	Austria		8,211,000	Vienna
4	Belarus		10,236,000	Minsk
5	Belgium		10,161,506	Brussels
6	Bosnia-Herzegovina		3,972,000	Sarajevo
7	Bulgaria		8,225,000	Sofia
8	Croatia		4,473,000	Zagreb
9	Czech Republic		10,244,000	Prague
10	Denmark		5,293,000	Copenhagen
11	Estonia		1,396,000	Tallinn
12	Finland		5,176,000	Helsinki
13	France		59,080,000	Paris
14	Germany		82,220,000	Berlin
15	Greece		10,645,000	Athens
16	Hungary		10,036,000	Budapest
17	Iceland		281,000	Reykjavik
18	Ireland, Rep. of		3,730,000	Dublin
19	Italy		57,298,000	Rome
20	Latvia		2,357,000	Riga
21	Liechtenstein		33,000	Vaduz
22	Lithuania		3,670,000	Vilnius

	Country	Flag	Population	Capital city
23	Luxembourg		431,000	Luxembourg
24	Macedonia		2,024,000	Skopje
25	Malta		389,000	Valletta
26	Moldova		4,380,000	Chisinau
27	Monaco		34,000	Monaco
28	Netherlands		15,786,000	Amsterdam
				The Hague
29	Norway		4,465,000	Oslo
30	Poland		38,765,000	Warsaw
31	Portugal		9,875,000	Lisbon
32	Romania		22,327,000	Bucharest
33	Russia		146,934,000	Moscow
34	San Marino		27,000	San Marino
35	Serbia & Montenegro		10,640,000	Belgrade
36	Slovakia		5,387,000	Bratislava
37	Slovenia		1,986,000	Ljubljana
38	Spain		39,630,000	Madrid
39	Sweden		8,910,000	Stockholm
40	Switzerland		7,386,000	Bern
41	Ukraine		50,456,000	Kiev
42	United Kingdom		58,830,000	London
43	Vatican City		1,000	Vatican City

KEY FACTS

AREA
4,066,000 sq mi.
(10,531,000 sq km).

**LARGEST
COUNTRY** Russia

**SMALLEST
COUNTRY**
Vatican City

POPULATION
728,887,000

COUNTRIES
43

RELIGIONS
Christianity, Judaism,
Islam, Hinduism

LANGUAGES
More than 70, including
English, French, German,
Spanish, Italian, Polish,
Russian, Romanian

Greece was later conquered by Rome as the Italian city built up a European empire that, at its height, covered most of Europe and the countries bordering the Mediterranean Sea.

The western Roman Empire was invaded and destroyed in 476 A.D. The eastern Roman Empire survived until 1453, when it fell to the Ottoman Turks.

From the fifth to the ninth centuries A.D., the Franks, a Germanic tribe, ruled much of Europe from France to the Balkans. They helped establish the power of the Roman Catholic church, whose monasteries became centers of learning.

From the Renaissance to the EU
During the 1400s there was great artistic and cultural activity in Europe. This was the start of a period known as the Renaissance. The word means "rebirth" and describes how classical (Greek and Roman) ideas and values became popular again. The rebirth, which started in Italy, can be seen in painting, sculpture, architecture, and writing.

By the 1500s Spain and Portugal had become rich from their gold mines in the newly discovered Americas. England and the Netherlands sent trading ships west to the Americas and east to Asia.

In Europe great changes were taking place. The Protestant church broke with the Roman Catholic church in northwest Europe. The Industrial Revolution began in Britain in the mid-1700s and transformed Europe. Goods that had once been made individually by hand were now mass-produced by machines. Cities grew as country folk moved to work in factories.

In 1789 a revolution turned France from a monarchy, ruled by a king, into a republic. Ten years later Napoleon Bonaparte seized power in France. His armies conquered most of Europe before his final defeat in 1815.

Britain lost many of its American territories as the result of the American Revolution, but in the 1800s it and other European nations claimed new lands in Africa and Asia. In 1870 Italy became a single nation for the first time; Germany was united in the following year.

Power struggles between the nations of Europe led to World War I (1914–18), in which 10 million people died. After the war new countries were formed—Czechoslovakia, Hungary, and Yugoslavia.

Meanwhile, in Russia a revolution in 1917 had overthrown the czar (emperor) and led to the creation of the Soviet Union, the world's first communist state.

Germany then led Europe into World War II (1939–45). The conflict brought another terrible death toll. After the defeat of Germany the Soviet Union became a superpower and spread communism throughout Eastern Europe. The Soviet Union broke up in 1991.

In 1957 six European nations formed the European Economic Community (EEC) to make trade easier among themselves. In 1993 the EEC was renamed the European Union (EU). In 2002, 12 EU states adopted a new currency, the euro.

The green woodpecker is a shy bird that is seldom seen. The subspecies shown is only found in Spain.

French Emperor Napoleon Bonaparte (1769–1821) at the head of his army in 1814.

SEE ALSO: Ancient Civilizations; Austria; France; Germany; Greece; Greece, Ancient; Industrial Revolution; Ireland, Republic of; Italy; Middle Ages; Napoleon; Netherlands, Belgium, & Luxembourg; Poland; Portugal; Renaissance; Revolution; Roman Empire; Russia & the Baltic States; Spain; Switzerland & Liechtenstein; United Kingdom; World War I; World War II

✳ EVOLUTION

Evolution is the slow, gradual change or development of the characteristics of animals or plants from one generation to the next.

Some people, especially those who believe the literal truth of the Bible, question whether evolution exists. Most scientists, however, believe that evolution explains how all living things descend from common ancestors in a pattern that resembles a family tree.

Evidence of evolution

Large changes in life forms take place over thousands or millions of years. Because we cannot watch evolution taking place, scientists look for evidence that it has occurred.

Fossils, which are the remains of ancient life, provide the most important evidence. Different fossils are found in rocks of different ages. This shows that life on Earth has changed over time. Fossils also show that certain groups of animals or plants have evolved from other groups. For example, fossils indicate that amphibians, such as frogs, evolved from fish that were capable of breathing air and moving on land.

Different modern species often share similar features. This suggests that they inherited them from a common ancestor. For example, the front limbs of lizards, birds, bats, whales, and people all have the same basic structure, even though they are used very differently.

DID YOU KNOW?

Charles Robert Darwin (1809–82) changed people's understanding of their relation to all other living things when he published his great work *On the Origin of Species by Means of Natural Selection* in 1859.

Darwin was born in Shrewsbury, England. He always had a strong interest in nature, and in 1831 he was appointed geologist for a five-year voyage around the world on board the ship H.M.S. *Beagle*. Wherever he went, Darwin studied the geology, searched for fossils, and observed plant and animal life. He thought hard about the relationships between living creatures and fossilized animals. In 1836 Darwin returned to London, where he wrote his account of the voyage.

By now he was sure that all forms of life had evolved from earlier forms. The question was: How did such evolution occur? *On the Origin of Species* set out both the theory of evolution and the evidence for it.

Charles Darwin
circ-1854

The humpback whale is a mammal that breathes air but is specially adapted to live in the sea.

DARWIN'S FINCHES

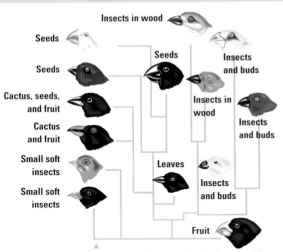

Insects in wood

Seeds

Seeds

Seeds

Insects
and buds

Cactus, seeds,
and fruit

Insects in
wood

Cactus
and fruit

Insects
and buds

Small soft
insects

Leaves

Small soft
insects

Insects
and buds

Fruit

▲ *Darwin found from studying finches that different species had different types of beak depending on what types of food they ate.*

Giraffes can feed from leaves that cannot be reached by other animals. ▼

So it seems likely that a common ancestor of these animals had this bone arrangement.

Pythons have the remains of hind leg bones, even though snakes do not have legs. Again, the most likely explanation is that the ancestor of snakes had legs.

How evolution takes place

The theory that explains why organisms, or living things, change over time is called natural selection. It is based on three basic facts about animals and plants.

First, individuals within a species vary slightly from one another. They inherit these differences from their parents. Second, plants and animals produce more offspring than can survive to adulthood. This causes competition for limited resources such as food. Third, some individuals are better (or worse) competitors for these resources based on their individual traits. Organisms with traits that are helpful in a certain environment will, on average, survive and reproduce better than those with less favorable

traits. The favorable traits will be passed on to more offspring and will become more common in the overall population.

Traits are determined by combinations of genes—biological instructions that control how every living creature generally appears, how it functions, how it reproduces, and even partly how it behaves. Sometimes when genes are passed from the parents to the offspring, bits are accidentally changed. These changes are called mutations. Most are harmful, but some produce slight variations without causing harm. Without these variations there would be no evolution because there would be no possibility of change.

Adaptation

Traits that enable a species to fit into its environment are called adaptations. They result from natural selection. For example, the long neck of the giraffe is an adaptation for eating leaves from the tops of trees. Ancestors of the giraffe did not have long necks. But those individuals that had slightly longer necks than others could find more food simply because they could feed on leaves that others could not reach. Longer-necked giraffe ancestors therefore had more offspring than shorter-necked giraffes. The result, over many generations, is the modern giraffe, the world's tallest land animal.

Rates of change

Sometimes evolution happens very quickly. For example, in just a few decades many species of insects have evolved the ability to survive insecticides, the poisons farmers use to kill them. However, fossils show that in some kinds of organisms small evolutionary changes occurred little by little over long periods, perhaps millions of years.

SEE ALSO: Dinosaur; Fossil; Geology; Genetics; Prehistoric People

✳ EXTINCTION

A species of plant or animal becomes extinct when its last living member dies. Once this happens, that species will never be found alive on Earth again.

Most species that have ever lived on Earth are now extinct. Extinction is thus a very common occurrence, but it usually happens at a very slow rate. That is, only a small number of species become extinct at any one time.

However, there have been five times during the Earth's history when at least three-quarters of all species alive at that time have gone extinct within a short period (a few million years at most, which is short in comparison to the age of the Earth). These episodes of rapid dying off of many species are known as mass extinctions. The dinosaurs are the best-known examples.

Extinction today
One of the greatest mass extinctions in the Earth's history is happening right now. Scientists estimate that between 18,000 and 55,000 species go extinct each year because of the activities of humans. Many

Park rangers in the Central African Republic with illegally hunted ivory. Trade in ivory was banned worldwide in 1989 in an attempt to protect elephants. However, hunting continued, and elephants are still endangered.

of them are insects and other small creatures that may not yet have been discovered by scientists. Species that are in immediate danger of dying out are known as endangered.

By converting forests to farms and building roads and houses, humans destroy the habitats of many plants and animals. This process, which is called deforestation, drives out native species. If its habitat disappears completely, a species may become extinct.

Hunting also causes extinction. The dodo and passenger pigeon were both hunted to extinction. Some whale species came close to the same fate. Today animals like elephants, black rhinoceroses, and some parrots are hunted or captured illegally, so their survival is threatened.

Extinctions may also occur when humans introduce new species to areas where they do not live naturally. For example, cats and rats introduced to islands have caused the extinction of many species of ground-nesting birds that had no defense against these predators. Environmental damage caused by pollution, such as oil spills, can also pose a serious threat to many species.

DID YOU KNOW?

The passenger pigeon was once the most abundant bird in North America. A single flock could have two billion birds or more. In 1813 artist John J. Audubon reported that a flock migrating over Kentucky made the sky "black with birds" for three days. European settlers hunted the birds for their meat. By 1850 several thousand people were employed in the passenger pigeon industry. In one year in Michigan alone a billion birds were slaughtered. By 1900 the passenger pigeon was extinct in the wild. The last captive bird died in 1914.

SEE ALSO:
Environment;
Evolution;
Habitat;
Pollution

141

✳ FISH

Fish live in water. They are vertebrates, that is, animals with a backbone and an internal skeleton. There are over 21,000 different species of fish.

▲ *Salmon can leap tall waterfalls in a single bound, soaring 6 ft. (1.8m) in the air.*

Not all animals that live in water are fish. Some, such as whales, are mammals, others, such as frogs, are amphibians. The characteristics that set fish apart from other animals include breathing oxygen from the water, having fins, and being cold-blooded (dependent on their surroundings for body temperature).

Fish have forms that are contoured, or shaped, to help them swim smoothly through water. All have mucus-coated skins. Most have movable fins, and many have scales. Fish use their respiratory organs, usually gills, to get oxygen from the water.

▶ *The background picture shows double-saddle butterfly fish near a coral reef.*

Most bony fish have an organ called a swim bladder that fills with gas like a balloon. The swim bladder enables fish to float, to hover, and to sink. Many bottom-dwelling fish do not have swim bladders. Sharks and rays also lack one. To keep from sinking to the bottom, they must swim constantly.

The eyes of most fish are placed on either side of the head. In many species each eye moves independently. This gives fish a wide view of what is in front of, behind, below, and above them. Many fish have a keen sense of hearing. They also depend heavily on their sense of smell. They use it to help locate prey, detect predators, and communicate.

The life of fish

Fish come together to spawn, or produce young, sometimes in pairs or in schools, which are large, teeming groups. In most fish the female lays its eggs in the water, and they are fertilized there by sperm released into the water by the male. The fertilized eggs then develop and hatch in the water.

Young fish, or fry, emerge from the eggs. Some are cared for by the parent fish; however, most fend for themselves.

Some fish feed mainly on plants, such as algae and seaweed. Most fish eat other fish, as well as worms, insects, and shellfish.

Early in their lives about 80 percent of fish live in schools. However, only about 20 percent of adult fish live in schools. Fish form schools because there is safety in numbers, mates are readily available, and it is easier for a fish to travel through water in the wake of the fish in front of it.

Where fish are found

Although 97 percent of the world's water is found in the oceans, only 58 percent of all fish are marine, or saltwater, species. Less than 1 percent of the world's water

is fresh, and yet it contains 41 percent of the fish species alive today. The remaining 1 percent can go back and forth between fresh and salt water.

In the oceans most fish live within the top 600 ft. (183m) of coastal waters. However, deep-sea fish have been collected from a depth of more than 27,000 ft. (8,200m). Some fish live only in certain places, such as the Arctic Ocean or the Amazon River. Others are found all over the world. Migrating fish, like salmon and eels, move from one body of water to another, sometimes over great distances. Warmer seas have more species of fish, but cooler seas are home to huge numbers of certain kinds of fish, such as cod, herring, and haddock.

Fish and humans

Over time the harvesting of the seas has seriously reduced the fish populations in nearly three-quarters of the world's marine fisheries. Another major problem is habitat loss. For example, building dams or diverting the course of rivers affects the populations of river fish and may prevent

KINDS OF FISH

Ichthyologists, scientists who study fish, have divided fish into two main groups: jawless fish and jawed fish. Jawed fish are further divided into cartilaginous fish and bony fish.

Jawless fish include lampreys and hagfish.

Cartilaginous fish, or Chondrichthyes, include sharks, skates and rays, and ratfish. They have skeletons made of cartilage, the same material that forms people's outer ears and nose. About 800 species roam the world's oceans and fresh waters.

Bony fish, or Osteichthyes, are the largest group of fish by far. Bony fish, which have true jaws and skeletons made of bone, are divided into four groups of fish species: lungfish, coelacanths, bichirs, and rayfinned fish. Rayfinned fish are the largest group of fish alive today.

migrating fish, such as salmon, from traveling upriver to breed. Pollution of rivers and seas has also contributed to reduced fish stocks. Regulations and strict catch limits are needed to preserve fish populations, but many countries disagree on the best course of action.

AMAZING FACTS!

The dwarf goby of the central Indian Ocean is no bigger than a pencil eraser, reaching only about 1/3 in. (0.8cm) in length.
The whale shark, found in the warm areas of the Atlantic, Pacific, and Indian oceans, can grow to lengths of 42 ft. (13m) and weigh 16 tons.
Cod lay as many as 100 million eggs in a season.

SEE ALSO: Animal; Habitat; Pollution

✻ FLAG

A flag is a piece of cloth, often attached to a pole or staff. It is decorated with a design and used as an emblem, a symbol, or as a means of signaling.

There are special flags for nations, states and provinces, counties and cities, and for international organizations like the United Nations. Thousands of different military flags are also in use, as well as personal rank flags—including the banners used by kings, queens, and presidents.

The design of each nation's flag has special meaning to its citizens. Many flags have symbols such as stripes, stars, animals, crosses, and so on. The symbol of an eagle might represent strength or a famous ruler from the past. Even the colors chosen for a flag usually have meaning. For example, blue might represent the waters surrounding an island nation.

The earliest forerunners of modern flags were made about 5,000 years ago in ancient India, China, and Egypt. Known as standards, they were not cloth, but carved figures secured on the tops of poles. They were used for signaling to and from ships and during battles because they could be seen from a long distance. Today the eagle at the top of flagpoles carrying the American flag and the spearhead on an army banner are reminders of the standards of the past.

In the Roman Empire troops carried a red or purple flag hung from a crossbar attached to a pole. This kind of flag was called a *vexillum*. This is the source of the English word "vexillology," which means "the study of flags."

The Chinese may have been the first to invent cloth flags. By about A.D. 1000 most flags in Europe were made of cloth, although carved standards were still used.

The U.S. flag

Over the years the U.S. flag, the Stars and Stripes, has been changed 27 times, mostly by the addition of stars to represent new states. The very first American flag, however, had no stars on it at all: It showed the Union Jack, the symbol of Great Britain. After the Declaration of Independence Americans wanted to show that they were no longer loyal to the mother country but to the "new constellation" of American states. The 13-star flag was designed by Francis Hopkinson, a member of the naval board, and, according to tradition, sewn by Betsy Ross.

▲ A Union cavalry flag from the Civil War (1861–65).

When the original 13 states increased to 15, two more stars were added to the flag, along with two stripes. In 1818 Congress realized that the flag would look like mattress ticking if stripes continued to be added. A new law said there should be 13 stripes for the original 13 colonies and one star for each state. For a long time the stars were arranged in various ways. In 1912 President Taft established an official pattern.

Signal flags

The crews of ships at sea communicate by using a special group of flags and pennants known as the International

TYPES OF FLAGS

STARS & STRIPES

▶

The U.S. flag through the ages, from the late colonial period to the present.

1776   **1777–95**   **1795–1818**   **1912–59**   **Present day**

On the earliest U.S. flag the 13 stripes represented the original states, and the Union Jack showed that they belonged to Britain. After independence the British inset was replaced with 13 stars. After Vermont and Kentucky joined the Union, the flag acquired another two stars and two stripes. In 1912 the number of stripes reverted to 13, and each state had its own star.

UNION JACK

▶

The design of the Union Jack is a combination of the flags of the three countries that make up the United Kingdom.

St. George's Cross (England)

St. Andrew's Cross (Scotland)

St. Patrick's Cross (Ireland)

The flag of the United Kingdom, often known as the Union Jack, is an overlay of the flags of St. George (for England), St. Andrew (for Scotland), and St. Patrick (for Ireland). The overlay is quite intricate and is often drawn incorrectly. The flag is twice as wide as it is high.

INTERNATIONAL CODE FLAGS

▶

Used on ships, each flag can represent either a single letter or a message.

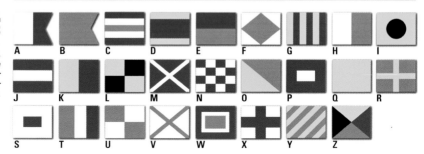

One of the best known ship's flags is that standing for P—it is the Blue Peter, which is flown when a ship is about to sail. Other meanings include C: Yes; H: Pilot on board; N: No; O: Man overboard; Q: *Request pratique* (permission to use a foreign port); V: Require assistance.

Code of Signals. They are colorful and simple in design so that they can be seen from far away. The code consists of a flag for each of the 26 letters of the English alphabet, 10 flags for the numbers zero through 9, a code pennant to indicate the use of a scrambled message, and three repeater pennants that are used to restate the messages on previously hoisted flags.

Another group of message flags is plain-colored with specific meanings. The most familiar are the white flag meaning "truce" and the red flag meaning "danger."

SEE ALSO: Communication; Roman Empire

145

✴ FLOOD
Floods occur when the level of a body of water rises too high for its banks and pours onto the surrounding land. They may cause severe damage and loss of life.

Floods have many possible causes. Heavy rainstorms can increase the amount of water in a river, making it overflow. If the surrounding land is hard or waterlogged, it cannot absorb the extra water, which stays above ground. If farms or buildings are near the river, they may be invaded or even completely submerged by water.

Tropical storms can also cause flooding. Hurricanes and typhoons can bring destructive winds and rain to coastal areas. Underwater earthquakes can cause tsunamis—huge, fast-moving waves that can flood coasts.

Another cause of floods, especially in mountain areas, is melting snow. If snow melts too quickly, and the ground is too frozen to let the water soak in, great torrents can pour down the sides of mountains, flooding the valleys below.

Flood protection
Scientists can figure out where and when floods are likely to occur. The shape of land near a river can make the area more

▲
In the wake of Hurricane Floyd the Tar River floods part of Greenville, North Carolina, in 1999.

or less likely to flood. Meteorologists—weather scientists—can predict when heavy rain is going to occur. In North America the major tributaries of the Mississippi River often flood. Elsewhere the basins of the following rivers are particularly at risk: the Huang He (Yellow River) in China, the Indus River in Asia, and the Danube River in Europe.

Although floods cannot be completely prevented, steps can be taken to protect people and property. Drainage systems can be built to keep floodwater off the surface of the land. Dams can control the flow of rivers and ensure that they do not burst their banks. Levees are high riverbanks that allow the river to carry more water without overflowing. Reservoirs are huge artificial lakes that can hold excess water.

AMAZING FACTS !

A cyclone hit Bangladesh in 1970 causing widespread floods. Over 500,000 people died. Another cyclone in 1991 killed over 138,000 people.
Flooding in China along the Yangtse River valley in 1931 caused the deaths of over three million people from disease, drowning, or starvation.
The worst floods in the United States occurred in 1993, when the waters of the Mississippi and Missouri rivers flooded 16 million acres in nine states, causing dozens of deaths and $10 billion worth of damage.

SEE ALSO: Disaster; Earthquake; Hurricane, Tornado, & Typhoon; River

*FLOWER

There are approximately 240,000 different kinds of flowering plants, or angiosperms. They live on every land mass except Antarctica.

A typical flower, such as a rose or a lily, has four main parts: sepals, petals, pistils, and stamens. The sepals are the tough, outer leaflike structures that cover the flower bud; petals are the delicate leaves that make up the most noticeable part of the flower when it is in bloom; pistils are the female reproductive structures; and stamens are the male reproductive structures. Together the sepals of a flower form the calyx. The calyx protects the developing bud and, if the sepals are green, produces food for the plant. The flower's petals form the corolla.

The reproductive structures are responsible for producing seeds. The pistil is divided into three parts: The ovary encloses and protects the ovules, which hold the eggs; the stigma is the sticky top of the pistil; the style is the thin tube connecting the stigma and the ovary. Each stamen is made up of two parts: the slender filament that sticks up from the base of the flower and the anther that sits

The flowers of the rafflesias, from the jungles of Southeast Asia, measure up to 3 ft. (0.9m) across and weigh more than 15 lb. (6.8kg).

By taking nectar, bees feed themselves and help plants reproduce.

on top of the filament. Inside the anther are two sacs containing pollen grains. The pollen grains produce sperm.

The life of a flower
All flowers have a similar life cycle. A flower starts as a tightly closed bud. As the petals and other structures inside the bud grow, the bud swells and eventually opens. After the bud bursts, and the sepals or other enclosing structures begin to fold away, the petals begin to unfurl. At this time the reproductive structures and the glands called nectaries begin to grow. The nectaries produce the sweet liquid called nectar.

Pollination, the transfer of pollen from the anther to the stigma, takes place once all the structures are fully developed. If the pollen from a stamen lands on the pistil of the same flower, it is called self-pollination. When the pollen is transferred from the stamens of one flower to the pistil of a flower on another plant of the same kind, it is called cross-pollination.

Cross-pollination happens when bees, butterflies, moths, birds, and other animals visit flowers to drink the nectar. As they gather the nectar, their bodies become covered with sticky pollen grains. When they land on another flower, their bodies brush the sticky surface of the stigma, transferring the pollen. Some flower species rely on the wind to transfer pollen. Instead of showy flowers or nectar, they make huge amounts of pollen, which wafts away on the wind. By the time the seeds are beginning to form, the flower has died. The flower's ovary may ripen into a fleshy fruit, such as an apple, or a dry, hard fruit, such as a nut or a grain of wheat. Animals may collect and eat the fruits and unknowingly scatter the seeds. Other fruits may float away on the wind or water. Once a seed is released from its fruit, and conditions are favorable for it to sprout, it can grow into a mature plant that produces its own flowers.

Some flowers produce flowers and fruits within a single year; then the plants die. These species are called annuals. Biennial species take two years to produce their flowers and fruits, after which time the plants die. Perennial species live for many years. Some perennials produce flowers and seeds one or more times a year; others may go for decades before flowering and producing seeds.

Saving our flowers

Today many species of flowers are endangered or threatened with extinction. Some flowers, including certain orchids and cacti, have been collected by people who sell them to florists. Other flowers are endangered because their habitats have been destroyed. When flower species are endangered, the animal pollinators, such as butterflies, that depend on the species for food can also become threatened.

Many people are working to save endangered flowers. Organizations such as the Nature Conservancy buy land in threatened habitats. Government agencies work to preserve flowers through regulations and laws.

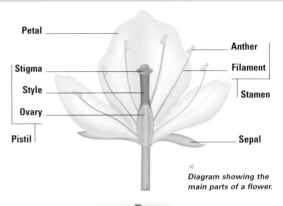

PARTS OF A FLOWER

Petal

Anther

Filament

Stigma

Style

Stamen

Ovary

Pistil

Sepal

Diagram showing the main parts of a flower.

AMAZING FACTS !

The common duckweed has the smallest flowers of any plant. They measure only $1/16$ to $3/16$ in. (1.6 to 4.8mm) in length and weigh just a fraction of an ounce.

The world's largest flowering plant is a Chinese wisteria planted in 1894 in Sierra Madre, California. It spreads its branches over nearly an acre and weighs 25 tons. It is estimated that more than 1.5 million flowers decorate its branches during its five-week flowering period.

Frailejones are only found in the Andes Mountains.

SEE ALSO:
Fruit; Habitat;
Insect; Plant

✳ FOOD CHAIN

A food chain is made up of a series of living creatures, or organisms, each one using the next one in the chain as part of its food supply.

Energy from the food is transferred from one organism to the next. The energy to start the chain comes from the sun. The first organisms in the chain are called the primary producers. They use a process called photosynthesis to obtain energy from the sun. On land the primary producers are green plants. In water the primary producers are tiny, floating organisms called plankton.

Primary consumers eat the primary producers. On land primary consumers are herbivores, or animals that feed on plants. Cows and grasshoppers are both examples of herbivores.

Secondary consumers—carnivores—feed on primary consumers. Some animals are both primary and secondary consumers: Bears, for example, eat berries and fish.

Bacteria and fungi are also primary and secondary consumers. They feed on dead plants and animals, converting them into nutrients that can be reused by other organisms in the food chain. They are called decomposers.

Food webs and the community

A community is made up of all the different species that live and interact with one another in a certain area. Food chains interact when

The osprey—a meat-eating bird of prey—is a secondary consumer.

members of different chains feed on one another. Together they form a food web. Energy is

A FOOD WEB

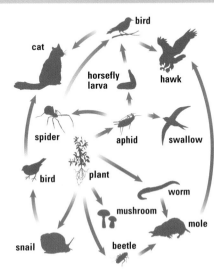

This illustration shows a simplified food web. It is formed from several food chains in which each organism preys (eats) others and is in turn preyed on (eaten). The arrows show the direction of nutrient flow.

transferred though the community in the form of food. At each stage of the food chain energy is lost. The primary consumer only receives 10 percent of the energy produced by the primary producer. The secondary consumer gets 10 percent of the primary consumer's energy (only 1 percent of the original energy). That is why primary producers are such an important part of a community. Without them there would be no energy.

👀

SEE ALSO: Animal; Biome; Carnivore; Ecology; Energy; Environment; Plant

✳ FORCE AND MOTION

A force is an influence that changes the motion of an
object or distorts its shape. The study of forces and
motion forms a branch of physics called dynamics.

Forces act on all objects, from the protons
and neutrons in the center of every atom
to the largest stars in the universe. People
make use of force and motion all the
time. If you stretch a rubber band, the
force you apply changes its shape.
Throwing a ball, walking down the
sidewalk, and riding a bicycle all need a
force to produce the desired motion.

Galileo's breakthrough

The idea of force and motion puzzled
scientists for thousands of years. While
ancient Greek and Roman scientists knew
forces existed, they did not realize how
they influenced the motion of objects.

The first great breakthrough came in the
late 1500s. Italian scientist Galileo Galilei
(1564–1642) was attending a service at
the Duomo Cathedral in Pisa, Italy, when
he noticed a lamp swaying back and forth
on the cathedral's ceiling. Galileo noted
that each complete cycle of the lamp took
about the same time, but the lamp swung
through less distance in each successive
cycle. He realized that some kind of
draining force was reducing the distance
through which the lamp swung in each
cycle. Take away this force, Galileo
thought, and the lamp would swing
through the same distance forever.

While observing the lamp, Galileo also
realized the difference between speed
and velocity. He showed that speed is
the rate of movement, while velocity is
speed in a particular direction.

Velocity and acceleration

The velocity of an object changes if a
force is applied to it. A change in velocity
is known as acceleration. Positive
acceleration is increasing velocity.
Negative acceleration, or deceleration, is
decreasing velocity. Acceleration also
occurs when an object moves in a circular
motion, for example, the motion of the
Earth around the sun. Circular acceleration
constantly changes the direction of the
object, but the speed of the object does
not necessarily have to increase.

Newton's laws of motion

Galileo's ideas about forces and motion
laid the foundations for the three laws
of motion formulated by English scientist
Isaac Newton (1642–1727). Newton's first
law states that an object moving at a
steady speed in a fixed direction will
continue to do so unless a force changes
its speed or direction of motion. In other
words, an object will only accelerate or
decelerate if a force is applied.

Newton's second law states that the
acceleration depends on the size of the
force and the mass of the object. His third
law states that whenever a force acts on
an object, there must be an equal reaction
in the opposite direction. In honor of
Newton's work all forces are measured in
units called newtons (N). One newton (1
N) is the force required to accelerate one
kilogram (1kg) of mass at a rate of one
meter per second per second (1m/s^2).

*Scientists call
all changes
in velocity
acceleration.
However, non-
scientists say
that a car is
accelerating when
it increases its
speed and
decelerating when
it slows down.*
▼

When parachutists jump out of an airplane, they are pulled toward the Earth by gravity.

Different forces

There are many different forces. When you ride a bicycle, for example, your foot applies a mechanical force on the pedal to move it. In the case of Galileo's lamp a mechanical force called air resistance, or drag, slows down the lamp. Mechanical forces occur when objects touch each other. Other forces act on objects without touching them. For example, gravity is a force that pulls objects toward the center of the Earth. Electromagnetism is a force that holds molecules together. Forces called weak and strong nuclear forces act within the nucleus of an atom. All these forces act over a distance and arise from a field of force. Physicists call these four forces—gravity, electromagnetism, the strong and the weak nuclear force—the fundamental forces of the universe.

RESULTANT FORCES

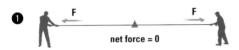

(1) Two people pull against each other on a rope with equal force F. The net force is zero since the two forces act in opposite directions.

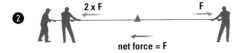

(2) Two people now pull against one person, all with equal force F. The net force is F and will act in the direction of the two-person team.

(3) Two people pull a wagon, one with twice as much force as the other. To figure out the net force, draw a diagram like the one on the right. By drawing the diagram to scale, the blue arrows show the size and direction of the two forces. Draw a parallelogram using the arrows. The red diagonal indicates the net force. To find out the size of this force, measure the length of the diagonal against one of the sides.

Interacting forces

Often more than one force acts on an object at any one time. All the forces combine to produce a net, or resultant, force. If the combined forces move an object, they are called unbalanced forces. If the combined forces do not move the object, they are called balanced forces. An object is said to be in equilibrium if all the forces combine to produce no net force.

SEE ALSO: Energy; Gravity; Matter; Newton, Isaac; Physics

✳ FOSSIL

Fossils are the remains or evidence of life in ancient times. There are many kinds of fossil because plants and animals were preserved in different ways.

Only a small part of the Earth's early life has been fossilized, or preserved as fossils. Usually they are organisms with a skeleton or a shell; the soft parts of animals or plants are seldom preserved.

Kinds of fossil

Sometimes, in very hot dry areas a piece of bone or a tooth of an ancient animal is preserved. In moist areas bone material or woody material is gradually replaced with minerals, creating a fossil.

If an animal had a shell, it may fill with sand after its death. The shell gradually disappears, but the sand inside turns to stone, creating a mold of the inner shape of the shell. The same thing can happen when the body of an animal decays, leaving a hollow mold that gradually fills with minerals, forming a cast of the animal's shape.

The footprint of an ancient animal or the outline of a leaf can be preserved under layers of sand, which harden into rock.

Tree sap, tar, and ice can also preserve organisms. Insects, became trapped in the sticky sap of trees. The resin hardened into amber, and the insect inside became a fossil. Many types of animals accidentally fell into tarpits. Their flesh decayed, but their bones and teeth were preserved.

Entire woolly mammoths, giant elephants that lived over 10,000 years ago, have been found in frozen soil or embedded in the ice of glaciers. Their bodies did not decay or turn into fossils, but were frozen in ice. Once thawed out, their flesh begins to decay.

The fossil record

Scientists who study fossils are called paleontologists. By studying fossils, they can find out about life long ago and the environment that existed then. In some places, such as the Grand Canyon, Arizona, it is possible to see the layers of rock that have built up over millions of years to form the Earth's surface. Each layer contains different types of fossil. The sequence of layers is called the fossil record. By studying it, paleontologists can track how life forms evolved, or changed, through time.

This fossil fish was found in Germany. It dates from 163 to 144 million years ago. ▼

SEE ALSO: Dinosaur; Earth; Evolution; Extinction; Geology

✱ FRANCE

France is the largest country in western Europe. It has borders with Spain, Andorra, Italy, Monaco, Switzerland, Germany, Luxembourg, and Belgium.

France has a varied landscape. Mountains called the French Alps run north from the Mediterranean and include Mont Blanc. At 15,760 ft. (4,810m), Mont Blanc is the highest peak in western Europe. Other ranges include the Jura and Vosges Mountains and the Pyrenees. The Massif Central covers one-sixth of France. It is mostly plateaus (high flatland). The Paris Basin in north central France and the Aquitaine Basin in the southwest have fertile soils and are ideal for farming.

France's climate varies like the landscape. The south has a warm, dry, Mediterranean climate, while the Atlantic and northern coasts are cooler. The high mountains are snow-capped all year.

The dukes of Bourbon and Orléans are captured by English soldiers. The battle of Agincourt in 1415 was one of many battles fought between the English and French during the Hundred Years' War.

The Eiffel Tower, Paris, is a 984-ft. (300-m), iron structure. It was finished in 1889 to commemorate the 100th anniversary of the French Revolution.

People

The French are descended from many ethnic groups. Celts settled in Brittany and Norse people in Normandy. Alsace, Flanders, and Corsica were settled by people of German, Dutch, and Italian ancestry, respectively. Recently there have been immigrants from France's former colonies, mainly in North Africa.

Economy

Before World War II (1939–45) France had a mainly agricultural economy. Today industrial production is more important, especially cars, aircraft, and armaments. The country's cheeses and wines are world-famous, and tourism is one of the largest industries.

History

When the Roman general Julius Caesar led an expedition to the area now called France in 58 B.C., the inhabitants were Gauls, a Celtic people who had lived there for many centuries. By 50 B.C. Caesar had defeated the Gauls. Rome ruled the area for the next 400 years.

After the Romans left, Germanic tribes invaded Gaul. In 481 Clovis founded the first great Frankish kingdom, from which France takes its name. Clovis was France's first Christian ruler. The greatest Frankish king was Charlemagne, who ruled from 768. His empire included Germany and much of Europe.

In the following centuries there was much conflict with England. In the 1300s a series of wars began, now known as the Hundred Years' War. At first England occupied large areas of France. But in the early 1400s a young farm girl called Joan of Arc led the French army to victory against the English, who were eventually driven out of France.

In the 1500s there was bitter conflict between Catholics and Protestants, or Huguenots. Henri IV, a Huguenot, became king in 1589, but he converted to Catholicism. In the early 1600s two high-ranking church officials (cardinals), Richelieu and Mazarin, controlled France. When Mazarin died in 1661, King Louis XIV (1638–1715) announced that he would govern the state by himself. He became an absolute monarch with total control over his people. He built a grand palace at Versailles to show off his power.

France's economy declined after Louis XIV died in 1715. France also lost

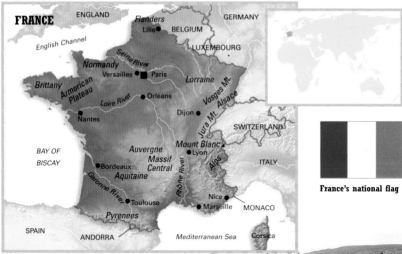

FRANCE

ENGLAND
English Channel
BAY OF BISCAY
SPAIN
ANDORRA
Flanders
Lille
BELGIUM
GERMANY
LUXEMBOURG
Normandy
Seine River
Versailles
Paris
Brittany
Armorican Plateau
Loire River
Orléans
Nantes
Lorraine
Vosges Mt.
Alsace
Dijon
Jura Mt.
SWITZERLAND
Auvergne
Massif Central
Aquitaine
Garonne River
Bordeaux
Mount Blanc
Lyon
Alps
Rhône River
Toulouse
Pyrenees
Nice
Marseille
MONACO
ITALY
Mediterranean Sea
Corsica

France's national flag

KEY FACTS

OFFICIAL NAME
République Française

AREA
211,208 sq. mi.
(547,030 sq. km)

POPULATION
59,080,000

CAPITAL & LARGEST CITY
Paris

MAJOR RELIGION
Roman Catholicism

MAJOR LANGUAGE
French

CURRENCY
Euro

Grape pickers work in the fields of Burgundy, France. The grapes are used to make wine, for which France is famous.

overseas territories such as Canada to Britain between 1756 and 1763. The country was close to bankruptcy, and King Louis XVI had lost the confidence of the people.

On July 14, 1789, a mob stormed the Bastille, a fortress in Paris that was viewed as a symbol of the monarchy. The event marked the start of the French Revolution. July 14 is still celebrated as France's national day. The revolution destroyed the idea that the king had a god-given right to rule. The revolutionaries' slogan was "Liberty, Equality, and Fraternity." However, the fine ideals fell apart as the revolutionaries fought among themselves. Thousands of people died on the guillotine. In 1793 King Louis XVI and Queen Marie Antoinette were executed.

France was soon at war with most of Europe. Napoleon Bonaparte, who made himself emperor in 1804, led the French to many victories and became master of almost all of Europe However, in 1815 Napoleon was defeated by an alliance of European powers and sent into exile.

The French then alternated between a republican government based on the ideals of the revolution and a return to monarchical government. In 1852 Napoleon's nephew became Emperor

Napoleon III. Many people hoped he would recapture the glory of his uncle's rule. However, Napoleon was defeated by the German state of Prussia in 1870. France became a republic again.

Germany occupied much of northeastern France during World War I (1914–18) and the whole country during World War II (1939–45). Many French people fought bravely against the German occupation. The Allies liberated France in 1945. In recent years France has become a leading member of the European Union (EU), an economic and political grouping of European countries.

SEE ALSO: Caesar, Julius; Europe; Europe, Central & Eastern; Joan of Arc; Napoleon; Revolution; Roman Empire; World War I; World War II

✻ FRANK, ANNE (1929–45)

Anne Frank is remembered for her diary. It gives a personal account of Germany's persecution of the Jews during World War II (1939–45).

Anne Frank's diary was found by a woman who helped the family.

Annelies Marie Frank was born in Frankfurt, Germany. In 1933 her family moved to the Netherlands. Germany invaded seven years later. On July 6, 1942, Anne's family and eight other people moved into a secret group of rooms where they hid for two years. Anne received a diary from her parents on her 13th birthday. She wrote in it regularly until the Germans discovered the secret rooms on August 4, 1944.

Anne and her family were taken to Auschwitz, a concentration camp in Poland, where Jews were sent to be killed in gas chambers. In October Anne was moved another camp in Germany. In March 1945 she died of typhus just before the British Army set the camp free.

Anne's diary was found in the secret rooms and given to Anne's father, the only member of the family to survive the war. It was published in 1947 under the title *The Diary of a Young Girl* and has been made into several films, as well as a play.

SEE ALSO: Germany; Holocaust; World War II

✻ FRANKLIN, ROSALIND (1920–58)

Rosalind Franklin was responsible for much of the research and discovery work that led to the understanding of the structure of DNA.

Rosalind Elsie Franklin was born in London, England. She excelled at science and received a doctorate in physical chemistry from Cambridge University in 1945. She spent three years in France, where she learned to use x-rays to study tiny structures such as crystals. At King's College, London, Franklin used this technique to discover crucial keys to DNA's structure. DNA stores all the information needed to create an organism, or living individual. It is the way parents pass on their characteristics to their children.

Without Franklin's knowledge a colleague, Maurice Wilkins, presented her findings to James Watson and Francis Crick, rival scientists at Cambridge University. They used her data to build a description of DNA's structure.

In 1962, four years after Franklin's death at 37 from cancer, Watson, Crick, and Wilkins shared the Nobel Prize in Physiology and Medicine. Many scientists believed that Franklin should have been honored with them.

◄ *The research of Rosalind Franklin enabled scientists to discover the structure of DNA. Even today she has not gained full public recognition for her scientific discoveries.*

SEE ALSO: Genetics; Nobel Prize; X-ray

155

F

*FRUIT
The name fruit is usually given to any fleshy part
of a plant that has developed from a flower and
has seeds, such as apples and strawberries.

Many common vegetables, such as
tomatoes, cucumbers, and squash, are
actually fruits, too. However, most people
do not think of them as fruit because they
are not eaten as dessert.

In nearly all parts of the world where
people live, some kinds of fruit grow wild.
Early people gathered fruits from wild
plants long before they grew crops for
food. When people began to plant crops
instead of gathering their food from the
wild, they probably planted the seeds
from the best wild fruits. Gradually the
fruit from cultivated plants became bigger
and better than the wild varieties.

Spread of fruits
When people began to travel, fruit seeds
traveled with them. In this way many
fruits spread from the places where they
first grew to other parts of the world

where the climate was suitable. Oranges,
for example, are native to Southeast Asia
and have been grown in China for
thousands of years. They reached
southern Europe in the ninth century.
Christopher Columbus is thought to
have introduced citrus fruits to America
when he brought orange seeds on his
second voyage in 1493.

▲
*Cranberries grow
in boggy areas of
North America.
They are picked
with hand rakes or
special machines.
Native Americans
ate these berries,
and the first
settlers used them
in cooking.*

Cultivation of fruit
Today fruits native to many different areas
of the world are grown wherever the
climate is suitable. Apples, peaches,
pears, plums, and grapes are grown in all
lands having temperate climates.

Nearly all fruit is picked by hand. Once
fruit is harvested, it may be shipped at
once to be sold fresh, it may be put into
cold storage, or it may be processed. In
the processing plant it may be canned,
frozen, dried, or squeezed for juice. Fruit
is shipped to markets around the world by
truck, boat, railroad, or air.

DID YOU KNOW?

Before about 1850 very few Americans had
tasted a banana, although Alexander the
Great had reported finding bananas
growing in India in 327 B.C. Scientists
believe the roots of banana plants were
carried to the east coast of Africa by a
people who moved there in ancient times.
From there the banana plant was carried
across the African continent to the Guinea
coast by early Arab traders. When
Portuguese explorers visited West Africa
in 1482, they found bananas growing there
and took them to the Canary Islands. In
1516 a Spanish missionary brought the
banana to the Caribbean island of
Hispaniola. In the late 1800s ships began
to bring bananas to American ports.

SEE ALSO: Columbus, Christopher; Plant

✳GALAXY

A galaxy is an enormous group of stars. All the stars that we see from Earth without a telescope are part of a single galaxy called the Milky Way.

SEE ALSO:
Astronomy;
Gravity; Solar
System; Star

There are billions of galaxies in the universe. They can be elliptical, irregular, or spiral in shape. The most common shape is an ellipsis—roughly like an egg. They usually contain only stars, with little or no dust or clouds of gas.

Galaxies with irregular shapes can be between 9,000 and 32,000 light-years in diameter. (A light-year is the distance light travels in one year: about 6 trillion miles, or 9.6 trillion kilometers.)

The least common shape is the spiral. These galaxies are like pinwheels wound around a nucleus or a bar of stars, gas, and dust at the center. The Milky Way is an example of a spiral galaxy.

The Milky Way

Sometimes it is possible to see a faint band of light arching across the night sky. Ancient peoples believed it was formed from milk that a goddess had spilled across the heavens and called it the Milky Way. That is how the galaxy got its name.

Scientists believe that the Milky Way galaxy is about 10 billion years old. It contains more than 100 billion stars. The nucleus, at the center, is a tremendous source of energy and exerts a powerful gravitational pull on the rest of the galaxy, which rotates around it at great speed. Earth's solar system orbits around it at a speed of about 155 miles (250km) a second. Even at this rate it takes about 250 million years to complete one orbit.

The central bulge revolves around the nucleus. The bulge is about 3,000 light-years across. Extending from it is the galactic disk, containing the spiral's arms. The Earth is on the inner edge of an arm of the Milky Way called Cygnus.

In the 1920s the American astronomer Edwin Hubble figured out that the Milky Way was just one of many galaxies and that the universe was much larger than anyone had realized.

Only the brightest stars in this spiral galaxy can be seen individually. Scientists use the Hubble Space Telescope to observe the galaxy.
▼

*GANDHI, MOHANDAS (1869–1948)

Gandhi was the most important leader in the history of modern India. He is often known as Mahatma, meaning "great soul."

SEE ALSO:
Indian
Subcontinent;

Mohandas Karamchand Gandhi was born in Porbandar, India, on October 2, 1869, to a large Hindu family of merchants. When he was 18, he went to London, England, to study law.

In 1893 Gandhi went to work as a lawyer in South Africa. Indians in that country were treated harshly, and Gandhi led a campaign of nonviolent resistance called civil disobedience against the government. He spent some time in jail in South Africa, but won some reforms.

Return to India

In 1915 Gandhi returned to India, which was then part of the British Empire. He joined the Indian National Congress, a political party working for the independence of the country.

Gandhi's protests were always nonviolent and used a method called passive resistance. He led boycotts—refusing to buy British goods—and fasts, or refusing to eat. The British had put a tax on salt, which led to much hardship for poor people, who could not afford to buy it. Gandhi led a march to the sea, where his followers made salt from seawater, which was against the law. The march forced the British to allow salt to be gathered for personal use.

Gandhi also campaigned for social justice within India. Hindu society was divided into castes—social classes—and Gandhi worked to help the "untouchables," who were the lowest group. He also worked for peace between Hindus and Muslims.

India became independent in 1947. The country was divided on religious lines between Hindus and Muslims, creating the new state of Pakistan. A Hindu who objected to this partition shot and killed Gandhi on January 30, 1948.

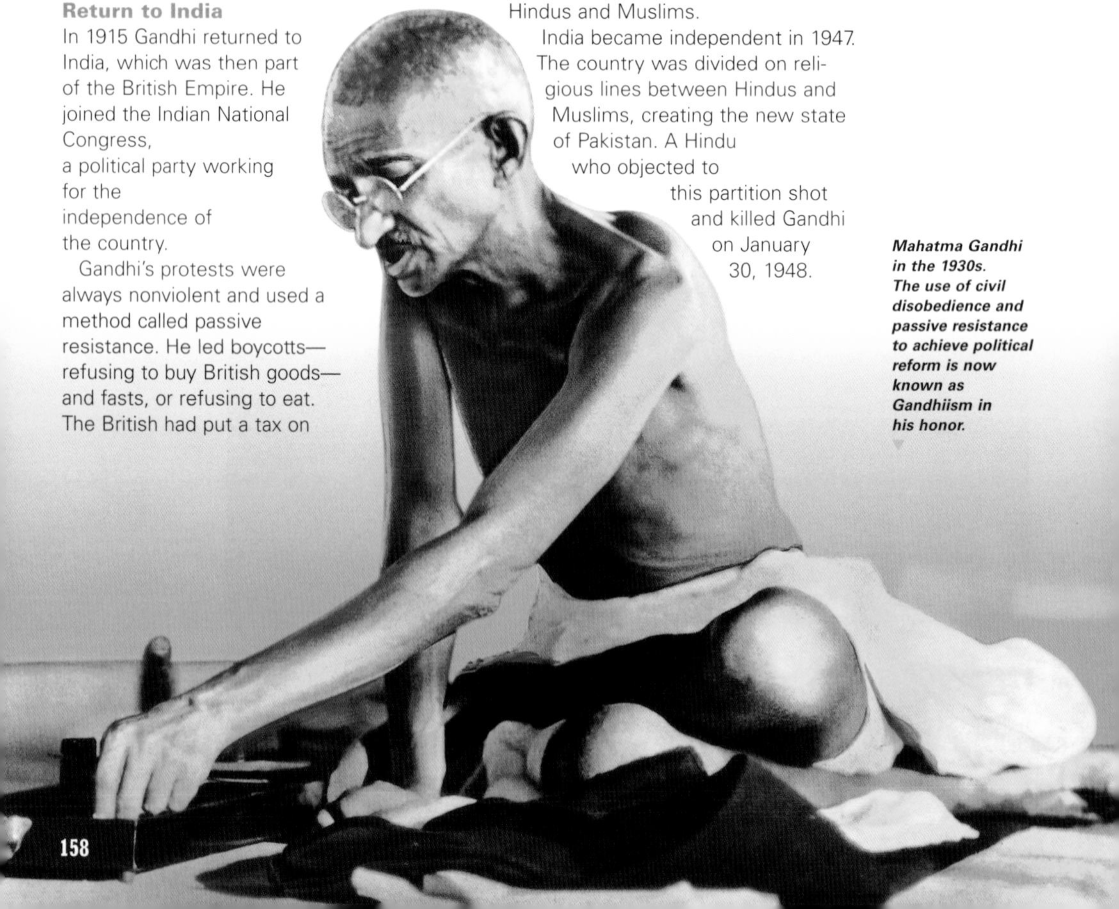

Mahatma Gandhi in the 1930s. The use of civil disobedience and passive resistance to achieve political reform is now known as Gandhiism in his honor.

✳ GENETICS

A branch of biology, genetics is the study of heredity, reproduction, evolution, and the development of all forms of life.

Genes are biological instructions that control how every living creature appears, how it functions, how it reproduces, and even partly how it behaves. They are step-by-step instructions that contain the recipe for the various parts of cells and control the work they do.

Genes are found inside the cells of the body and are inherited, or passed down, from one generation to the next. You may inherit dimples from your mother or the ability to roll your tongue from your father. These features, or traits, are determined by combinations of genes that are different for every child.

While each individual is unique, most genes are common to everyone. In fact, humans share many of the same genes with other kinds, or species, of animals—from the simple fruit fly to our close cousin the chimpanzee.

Although genetics has been studied since the mid-1800s, the greatest advances in the field were made at the end of the 1900s. Modern breakthroughs have enabled doctors to diagnose and treat previously incurable diseases, police to investigate crimes, and agricultural scientists to design better crops.

The complete collection of genes for each organism is called its genome. Each species has its own unique genome.

The genetic code

Genes are "written" in a language called the genetic code, which is contained in deoxyribonucleic acid, or DNA. Every molecule of this chemical is shaped like a twisting ladder, often called a double helix.

DNA molecules can contain thousands of genes and form a long, threadlike part of cells called chromosomes. In humans and other animals chromosomes are found in every cell in the body except red

blood cells. Chromosomes come in pairs that are similar in both size and shape. Half of the chromosomes come from the individual's mother and the other half from the father.

Different species can have different numbers of chromosomes in their cells. The fruit fly has only 4 pairs. Corn has 10 pairs. Humans have 23 pairs of chromosomes, or a total of 46.

Heredity and variation

Genes are the basic units of heredity—the inheritance of traits from one generation to the next. Genes determine physical features, including your sex, height, and hair and eye colors.

When variations in genes are harmful, they result in what are called genetic disorders. These illnesses are inherited by offspring from their parents. Genetic disorders may be caused by mutations, alterations to the normal genetic makeup.

In 1997 Dolly the sheep (left) was the first animal to be cloned using cells from an adult sheep. This process, a form of genetic engineering, has many practical advantages for farmers, but it also raises a difficult moral question: Is it right for humans to create life in this way?
▼

SEE ALSO: Crime & Law Enforcement; Evolution; Franklin, Rosalind; Human Body; Medicine; Reproduction

✳ GEOGRAPHY

Geography is the study of the Earth's various physical features—the land itself, climate, and soils—and humans' relationship to them.

Geography overlaps with many other subjects, but it has two main divisions: physical geography and human geography.

Physical geography

Physical geography is mostly concerned with the physical environment of regions (areas with similar features). The study of landforms, such as mountains, on Earth—where they are, what they are made of, how they developed, and their relationships to people—is called geomorphology. Biogeography is the study of how environmental factors such as soil and temperature affect living things in a region—where these creatures are found, where they move, how they are distributed, and how their populations change over time. Communities of plants and animals that thrive in specific climates are called biomes. Examples of biomes include grasslands and deserts.

No geographical study of a region is complete without an understanding of its climate. Climate is the overall state of weather in a region over a long period. The study of climate is called climatology. Of all the environmental elements, climate has the greatest influence on a region's plant and animal life. Plant and animal life, in turn, affect the activities of people, who depend on them.

Human geography

While physical geography focuses mainly on the importance of landforms, living things, and climate, human geography is concerned with people and how they live.

A people's culture includes their language, literature, art, music, customs, laws, religion, clothing, housing, food, and health practices. When cultural geographers study a group of people, they investigate various cultural aspects, such as how the people obtain food or how they communicate and trade with each other. As geographers compare these traits, large areas of common cultural features often emerge. They are called cultural realms or worlds. All English speakers, for example, share a common linguistic realm.

The study of how groups of people are distributed is called population geography, or demography. This science can be used to produce censuses and to predict population growth.

Economic geographers study why certain economic activities, such as the trading of goods between countries, take place where they do. They may draw maps to show trade routes or the distribution of a region's natural resources, such as forests, mineral deposits, and agricultural land.

Political geographers study how laws and government actions affect landscapes. For example, on the American side of the border between the United States and Mexico there are vast irrigated farm fields, while on the Mexican side the fields are drier and less productive. The land is the same. The difference lies in the political decisions affecting its development.

Urban geographers study how cities and landscapes affect one another. Historical geographers study the changes in landscapes and settlements over time.

History of geography

The first real geographer was Thales, a Greek who lived over 2,600 years ago on the shore of the Aegean Sea. Everywhere Thales traveled, he kept accurate notes and maps of what he had seen. By questioning other travelers, Thales also collected information about places he had not seen himself. Later Greek travelers added to this growing knowledge of geography.

From about A.D. 400 much of the knowledge of the Greeks was forgotten. Some people in Europe even came to believe that the Earth was flat. However, the Arabs of North Africa and Arabia continued the tradition of geography and mapmaking. They also believed in the Greek idea that Earth was round.

The age of exploration

In the 1400s explorers sailed uncharted oceans and discovered new lands. Geographical knowledge grew again. By the late 1700s all of the continents had been sighted. For the first time people had real knowledge of Earth's size and the variety of the world's lands and peoples.

Early geographers gathered information mainly by exploring. Today they can collect data without ever surveying a region on the ground. Since the 1960s math and technology have made geography much more scientific. Statistics (the study of mathematical trends), computers, and satellites help geographers measure and analyze information better and make predictions.

Geographic information systems, or GIS, can be used to create computerized maps, models, and databases—highly organized records of information. These databases can help identify patterns in geographic data. They can also be used to publish geographic information on computer systems such as the Internet, making it readily accessible to geographers around the world.

High-flying planes can take pictures of large areas, such as this aerial photograph of the Rocky Mountains. This helps geographers gather information about an area.

SEE ALSO: Biome; Climate & Weather; Earth; Geology; Map; Math & Numbers; Technology

✳ GEOLOGY

Geology is the scientific study of the origin, history, composition, and structure of the Earth since the planet formed 4.6 billion years ago.

A geologist takes a rock sample on a field trip to Antarctica.

The word *geology* comes from the Greek words for earth science. There are many different branches of geology. They include mineralogy (study of minerals), geomorphology (study of the processes that produce landforms), petrology (study of rocks), paleontology (study of fossils), stratigraphy (study of the rock layers, or strata), and astrogeology (study of the

evolution of planets and their satellites). There are also economic geologists, mining geologists, and petroleum geologists. All these branches interlink with each other and with other fields, such as physics and chemistry.

History of geology

Ancient peoples believed that the Earth and its geological features had been created by magic or by gods. Around 2,500 years ago ancient Greek scholars began to base their explanations of the Earth and its geological features on observations of nature. This was the beginning of modern geology.

In the 1500s Georgius Agricola, a German doctor, wrote the first modern textbook on rocks, minerals, fossils, and metals. In 1795 Scottish geologist James Hutton proposed that the Earth was constantly changing as a result of erosion and mountain-building forces. The first

GEOLOGICAL TIMELINE

Precambrian Era

Earth formed—both its surface and its oceans. Single-celled organisms developed. Soft-bodied plants and animals evolved. Earth's atmosphere gained oxygen.

single-cell algae

4,600 –590 Million Years Ago

Paleozoic Era

Cambrian
Life was restricted to the seas. The first vertebrate, a small fish, appeared.

trilobite

590-248 Million Years Ago

Ordovician
Seas spread across much of North America. Shellfish were plentiful.

ammonite

Silurian
Animals and plants moved onto the land.

Devonian
The Age of Fish. On land large fern trees and other plants developed. The first amphibians appeared.

icthyosaur

Pennsylvanian/ Mississippian (Carboniferous)
The Coal Ages. Plant growth in swampy low-lands laid the foundations of later coal deposits. The first reptiles and giant insects developed.

Permian
Cone-bearin▮ trees appear▮ Climates changed, and glaciers covered ma▮ areas. The Appalachian▮ Mountains formed.

geological map showing the strata of different ages was drawn in 1815 by the English engineer William Smith. Geologists gradually plotted a chart that summarized the changes in rock strata and fossils over time. In the 1900s they proved that the Earth's landforms had originally been a single large continent named Pangaea. Later Pangaea broke up into smaller continents that drifted very slowly apart. This movement is called continental drift.

Geologists also showed that comets or asteroids occasionally collided with the Earth, perhaps causing mass extinctions of animals and plants. Since the advent of space travel, in the last 30 years the field of geology has expanded to include the study of the solar system— the moon, the planets, and their satellites.

Today many geologists look for natural resources that have not yet been discovered, such as oil, minerals, and even fresh water. They also study volcanoes, earthquake faults, and flood plains in an effort to reduce the dangers that these natural hazards pose to people living nearby.

Arches National Park, Utah. This natural feature was formed by wind erosion of surrounding layers of softer rock.
▼

Scientists divide geological time into periods based on the kinds of animals and plants that existed during those times. The names of the periods are mostly taken from the areas where their rocks were studied. Few traces of life have survived for about seven-eighths of the time Earth has existed. This period is called the Precambrian era. The start and end dates of a period sometimes have to be changed if new fossils are discovered.
▼

SEE ALSO: Climate & Weather; Comet, Meteor, & Asteroid; Dinosaur; Earth; Earthquake; Fossil; Volcano

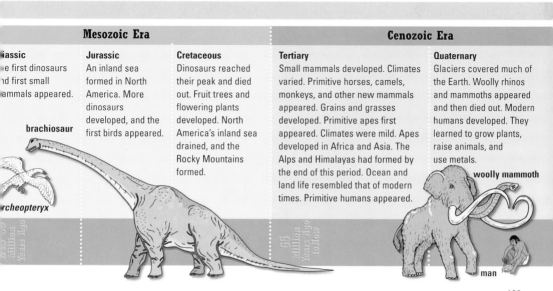

Mesozoic Era

Triassic
The first dinosaurs and first small mammals appeared.

brachiosaur

archeopteryx

230 Million Years Ago

Jurassic
An inland sea formed in North America. More dinosaurs developed, and the first birds appeared.

Cretaceous
Dinosaurs reached their peak and died out. Fruit trees and flowering plants developed. North America's inland sea drained, and the Rocky Mountains formed.

Cenozoic Era

Tertiary
Small mammals developed. Climates varied. Primitive horses, camels, monkeys, and other new mammals appeared. Grains and grasses developed. Primitive apes first appeared. Climates were mild. Apes developed in Africa and Asia. The Alps and Himalayas had formed by the end of this period. Ocean and land life resembled that of modern times. Primitive humans appeared.

65 Million Years Ago to Now

Quaternary
Glaciers covered much of the Earth. Woolly rhinos and mammoths appeared and then died out. Modern humans developed. They learned to grow plants, raise animals, and use metals.

woolly mammoth

man

✳GERMANY

Germany is positioned in the heart of Europe and has few natural barriers to mark its borders. It is the sixth largest nation in Europe.

Germany is divided into three geographical regions: the northern lowlands, the central uplands, and the southern mountains. In the northern lowlands forests alternate with meadows and marshy lakes. In the central uplands deep river valleys alternate with forested hills. Southern Germany contains the Black Forest and the Bavarian Alps. The Zugspitze is the highest peak in Germany at 9,718 ft. (2,962m).

The Rhine River, with a total length of about 820 miles (1,320km), is the chief river of Germany and the most important commercial waterway in western Europe. The Danube, one of eastern Europe's major rivers, rises in the Black Forest.

Most of Germany has a fairly mild climate. Inland regions in the south and east normally have hotter summers and colder winters. There is usually more rain during the summer.

Economy

Nearly 45 percent of the German work force is employed in industry. The rich coal mines of the Ruhr district provide energy for factories. Germany is among the world's chief steel-producing nations and is Europe's leading automobile manufacturer. It is also famous for precision instruments, cameras, and lenses, and makes large quantities of chemicals, medical drugs,

and electronic and scientific equipment. It is the second largest producer of plastics, after the United States.

People and history

Various Germanic peoples arrived in northern and central Europe at least 2,000 years ago. They developed a common language, culture, and customs that distinguished them from other peoples of Europe.

By the 12th century Germany was divided into small states ruled by princes, who were often more powerful than the king. From 962 the king was also crowned Holy Roman emperor by the pope (the head of the Catholic church). In 1701 Frederick I took the title of king of Prussia (one of the German states). Prussia developed a strong army and an efficient government. Under Frederick II (ruled 1740–86) Prussia became a major European power.

In 1871 Otto von Bismarck (1815–98), chancellor to King William I of Prussia, united Germany by force. Germany prospered under Bismarck's leadership. Bismarck expanded its overseas territory and made Germany a leading commercial and naval power. Britain, France, and Russia united against Germany and Austria-Hungary. World War I (1914–18) broke out between the rival

Modern German automobile manufacturers have factories worldwide. This is the Mercedes-Benz assembly plant at Sacramento, California.

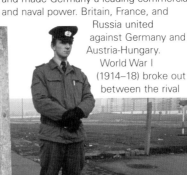

Two soldiers stand on either side of the remains of the Berlin Wall. The wall, built by the East Germans in 1961 to divide the German capital, was destroyed in 1989.

Germany's national flag

KEY FACTS

OFFICIAL NAME
Bundesrepublik Deutschland

AREA
137,803 sq. mi.
(356,910 sq. km)

POPULATION
82,220,000

CAPITAL & LARGEST CITY
Berlin

MAJOR RELIGION
Christianity

MAJOR LANGUAGE
German

CURRENCY
Euro

A great castle in Bavaria in the south of Germany, built between 1869 and 1886.

SEE ALSO:
Hitler, Adolf;
Holocaust;
World War I;
World War II

European powers. When Germany lost the war, it was stripped of some of its territory and had to pay $33 billion to the U.S., Britain, France, and Russia.

The worldwide depression, which began in the United States in 1929, hit Germany especially hard. By 1933 more than six million people were out of work.

In 1932 a right-wing party led by Adolf Hitler came to power. Hitler established himself as dictator, or supreme leader, and by 1934 he had turned Germany into a police state. German Jews were made second-class citizens, and many fled the country.

In 1938 Germany annexed, or occupied, Austria. In 1939 Hitler invaded Poland, and World War II (1939–45) broke out. German victories brought most of Europe under his control. In 1941 he invaded the Soviet Union. This marked the beginning of a change in Hitler's fortunes. In 1945 Germany was forced to surrender, and Hitler committed suicide.

The country was immediately divided into four zones of occupation. In 1949 West Germany was formed from the British, French, and U.S. zones, and East Germany from the Soviet zone. For about 45 years the German people lived in a divided land. West Germany had a democratic form of government. East Germany was a communist state.

In October 1990 the two Germanys were reunited. One of the greatest challenges that faced the new government was to bring the economic level of East Germans up to western standards.

✻GOODALL, JANE (1934–)

Jane Goodall is a British zoologist whose studies of wild chimpanzees have cast new light on the relationship between animals and humans.

Jane Goodall on a visit to Europe in 2001.

Goodall began her research in 1960 in a part of Africa that is now called Gombe National Park, Tanzania. Within less than six months she had made some surprising discoveries about chimpanzees. She found that they are not strictly vegetarians, as had previously been thought, but that they hunted animals and ate their flesh. They also made tools to capture insects such as termites.

Goodall had no formal scientific training. But for her findings to be taken seriously, she needed qualifications. In 1965 she earned a doctorate from Cambridge University, England.

By the 1970s Goodall had gained worldwide recognition for her work on chimpanzees. Her books include *My Friends, the Wild Chimpanzees* (1967) and *In the Shadow of Man* (1971). Since the mid-1980s Goodall has also been working to improve the conditions for chimpanzees used in medical research and to get chimpanzees listed as an endangered species.

SEE ALSO: Primate; Zoology

✻GOVERNMENT

Every one of the world's independent nations has its own form of government, which runs that country's political affairs.

The state opening of Parliament, a ceremonial event at which the king or queen of Great Britain outlines the government's plans for the next year. Britain is a constitutional monarchy.

Since earliest history groups of people living together have needed rules to regulate their daily lives. At first societies were run by chiefs or other leaders who made and enforced the laws by which they lived. As cultures developed, people wanted to be more involved in making the rules or laws that governed them. Gradually they developed the idea of choosing leaders who would draw up laws that the people wanted and thought desirable. People also began to put into operation their own systems for enforcing these laws. They had learned how to create a government.

The power of government

The governments that people establish can influence their lives in many ways. Governments regulate relations with other

countries (foreign policy) and can declare war. Governments decide such matters as what kinds of property should be publicly owned (that is, owned by the state in the name of the people) rather than privately owned, and how much each person must pay in taxes.

Governments can set educational requirements, place limits on immigration, and conscript (draft) citizens into military service. The availability of public libraries, museums, hospitals, and parks depends at least in part on government decisions.

Monarchy

A government run by a king or a queen is called a monarchy. An absolute monarch rules without checks on his or her power. Absolute monarchies exist today only in some of the states of the Arabian Peninsula. A monarch who rules cruelly and selfishly is called a tyrant.

Constitutional monarchy is a democratic government in which the monarch is the ceremonial head of state but has little or no political power. Probably the best-known constitutional monarchy is that of the United Kingdom.

Democracy

The term "democracy" comes from the Greek words *demos*, meaning "people," and *kratos*, "rule." Most modern democratic states are republics in which the people do not take a direct role in legislating or governing but elect representatives to express their views. A democratic government is a government whose representatives are freely chosen, or elected, by the people. The representatives then try to carry out the people's desires.

In addition, democratic governments have other standards by which they can be measured. One is freedom of speech, under which people may criticize the government without fear of persecution, and form political parties in opposition to the government. Another is the peaceful transfer of political power when new leaders are elected to office.

Today there are two main types of democratic government—parliamentary and presidential. Parliamentary government, also known as cabinet government, is modeled on the British parliamentary system. The government is headed by a prime minister (or premier), who is usually the leader of the political party that has won a majority of seats in elections to the parliament. The prime minister and cabinet form the government but are responsible to the parliament, of which they are members. If defeated on an important measure, the government must call new elections. In any event, no government of this type may

In April 2002 East Timor, which had belonged to Indonesia, became an independent republic under President Xanana Gusmao.
▼

167

rule for longer than a certain period without calling an election. In Britain, for example, the maximum length of a parliament—in other words, government without an election—is five years.

Presidential government

Presidential government, such as that of the United States, is based on the separation of powers. Political power is distributed among three branches of government—the executive (the president), the legislative (Congress), and the judiciary (the Supreme Court and other courts). The purpose of these divisions is to provide checks and balances that limit the power of government. In contrast to the British system, the powers of the U.S. government are strictly defined by a written constitution.

Dictatorship

A dictator is a ruler who has complete power and often governs cruelly or unfairly. The term totalitarianism was first used in the 1920s and 1930s to describe regimes such as those of Fascist Italy and Nazi Germany. Later it was applied to the governments of the Soviet Union and the communist states of Eastern Europe.

A totalitarian government has total control over all aspects of its citizens' political and economic activities. It may also have a distinct set of beliefs, such as Fascism, Nazism, or Communism.

SEE ALSO: Dictatorship; United Nations

✱ GRAMMAR

Grammar is a branch of linguistics that deals with the syntax (sentence structure) and the morphology (word structure) of a language.

Three kinds of meaning occur when words are used to express ideas: the meaning of each word by itself; the meaning of a word when it changes its form, as for example when an "s" is added to the word "dog" to express the idea that there is more than one of them; and the meaning of words as they are arranged in a certain order in a sentence. Grammar is the study of these meanings.

Word meanings

Every word has some meaning; most words are symbols for a group of ideas. In English a single word used alone may have very little meaning. If you say to a friend, "Head," she will probably be puzzled. If you say, "My head," she will be less puzzled, and if you say, "My head aches," she will understand you. When you arrange words into a sentence, you have created a pattern that is a basic element of grammar. Adding punctuation will make the meaning even clearer.

Sometimes, however, a single word can convey a complete thought. If someone says to you, "When do you go to camp?" you may answer, "Tomorrow." In this case a single word conveys the sentence: "Tomorrow I will go to camp."

Forms of words

The changing forms of certain words signal their meanings. Early English had many of these changing forms; only a few survive in modern English. Here are some examples still in use: large, larger, largest; go, going, goes, went, gone; I, my, mine, me. English-speaking children learn most of these forms before they go to school. People whose native tongue is not English may find these forms difficult to use correctly. An important part of grammar is knowing the meanings signaled by the changing forms of words like these.

Patterns of words and sentences

A third type of meaning comes from the order in which words are used. Compare these word groups:

1. Dog frightened the cellar hid in the.
2. The frightened dog hid in the cellar.

We know the words in pattern 1, but they make no sense. The same words arranged into pattern 2 give a clear meaning. Why? Because there is an expected pattern, or structure, to English sentences that creates meaning. The order in which the words are arranged creates different meanings.

Although the different combinations of words that make sentences are almost beyond number, they are all based on four patterns. Each pattern contains a subject and a verb. The first two patterns have verbs indicating an action.

Pattern 1. Henry sings. The subject, "Henry," performs an act. He sings. "Sings" is the verb. In grammar this kind of verb is called intransitive because the action is confined to the subject.

Pattern 2. Police captured Capone. The subject, "police," performed an act,

PARTS OF SPEECH

Words are classified into eight parts of speech.

Noun	The name of a person, place, or thing. *Henry; Chicago; automobile*
Pronoun	A word used instead of a noun. *He; she; they; it*
Adjective	A word that qualifies a noun or pronoun. *Mad* Max; *New* England; *red* bus
Verb	A word or words that define an action or a state of being. *Have; go; hit; am; was going; have given*
Adverb	A word that modifies a verb, an adjective, or another adverb. *Slowly; very interesting; slightly unsteadily*
Preposition	A word used before a noun or pronoun to relate it to some other part of the sentence. He went *to* market; they played *at* Shea Stadium
Conjunction	A word that connects one word, phrase or clause to another. *And; while; but*
Interjection	A word that expresses emotion or exclamation. *Wow; gosh; ouch; doh*

"captured," on an object, "Capone." In this sentence the verb is called transitive because the action performed by the subject carries over to a person or thing acted on, which is called the object.

The next two patterns use verbs that show a connection instead of an action.

Pattern 3. Mary is brave. The verb "is" has the name "linking verb" because it connects the subject, "Mary," to an adjective, "brave."

Pattern 4. John is captain. Here the linking verb "is" connects the subject, "John," with another noun, "captain."

No matter how long and complicated an English sentence may be, it is always based on one of these patterns or a combination of two or more.

What is good English?

Good English is English that is acceptable to, and used by, educated people. For example, an educated speaker would say "Where were you?" while an uneducated speaker might say "Where was you?" The form of the language called standard English involves the use of the same words and sentence structures as those adopted by cultivated speakers and writers.

✳GRAVITY

Gravity is a natural force. Every time you drop a ball from your hand or throw it upward or straight ahead, it is pulled back to the Earth by gravity.

Physical events that occur repeatedly, reliably, and invariably are said to conform to a natural law. The force of gravity is one such law—any object on Earth that is dropped or thrown will behave in much the same way, according to the same principle, every time.

Isaac Newton

The first person to figure out the law of gravity was the English scientist Isaac Newton (1642–1727). Newton was puzzled about the motion of the moon. He wondered why the moon did not just fly off into space; what force kept it in its orbit, or curved path, around the Earth?

According to legend, Newton's ideas were influenced by seeing an apple falling from a tree. This and similar events showed him that the Earth is pulling all objects toward itself. The force that pulled the apple to the ground must have been the same as the one that keeps the moon in orbit around the Earth.

Newton showed that every object in the universe must have gravity, and that every object, or body, pulls on every other body. His idea is known as the theory of universal gravitation.

👀

SEE ALSO: Earth; Force & Motion; Newton, Isaac; Solar System; Space Exploration

LAW OF GRAVITY

Tube without air (a vacuum)   *Air-filled tube*

▲
The space shuttle and everything inside it, including astronauts, are weightless because they are not resisting gravity—they are all falling together at the same speed.

◄
In a vacuum (left) any two objects dropped together will reach the ground at the same time. In normal conditions (right) air slows objects down: The larger surface area of the feather will make it fall more slowly than the marble.

✳GREECE

Greece is a small nation in southeastern Europe where one of the world's greatest civilizations flourished more than 2,000 years ago.

Greece's national flag

Nearly one-fifth of the area of Greece is islands. Three-quarters is hilly. Olympus, in northern Greece, is the country's tallest mountain. It rises to 9,570 ft. (2,917m). Greece has hot, dry summers and colder, wet winters. Snow is rare, except in the mountains.

Plant and animal life
Lowland Greece has few trees apart from scattered pines and cypresses. Firs grow in the high mountains. Brown bears, wildcats, and roe deer are found in the north, and porcupines and jackals in the south.

People and economy
About 60 percent of Greeks live in urban areas. Almost one-third of the population lives in or around Athens.

Wheat is the main crop, and tobacco one of the main agricultural exports. Olive

trees and grapevines are also important. Manufacturing now ranks ahead of agriculture as a source of income for Greece. Mining, fishing, and tourism also play key roles.

History
Greece gained independence in 1830. The first half of the 20th century was a time of upheaval, and Greece was invaded by Italy during World War II (1939–1945). Civil war raged from 1946 to 1949. In 1967 the king fled the country, and Greece was ruled by a military government until 1974.

SEE ALSO:
Europe;
Greece, Ancient;
World War II

The island of Thera (Santorini) is the remaining half of a volcano that exploded about 1500 B.C.

✳GREECE, ANCIENT

The civilization of ancient Greece centered
around the Aegean Sea, the region that today
includes Greece and the western part of Turkey.

Ancient Greece was not a single country ruled by one person. Instead, there were a number of independent communities with a common language and culture.

City-state
About 800 B.C. Greeks began to form city-states, or *polis*. Each governed itself. Some only had a few thousand inhabitants, but some, such as Athens, had as many as 250,000. City-states were set up as far from Greece as France and Spain. There were several different forms of government in the city-states. Some were tyrannies, ruled by one person who had absolute power. Some were oligarchies—ruled by a small group of wealthy people. Others were democracies, from the Greek for "people," *demos*. They were not democracies in the modern sense. Women could not take part in political debate, nor could the many slaves.

Religion, philosophy, and literature
Greek thinkers laid the foundations of modern science and philosophy over 2,000 years ago. One of the most important developments in Greek thought was philosophy. Great thinkers and teachers such as Socrates, Plato, and Aristotle considered questions about the purpose of life and morality. Their works still influence modern philosophers today.

Greek literature—poetry, plays, and histories—are also still studied. The most famous poems are the *Illiad* and the *Odyssey*, written by Homer; the most famous playwrights are Aristophanes, Sophocles, and Euripides.

One thing that united the Greeks was

Greek dramatists were writing plays 2,000 years ago that are still performed today. These two models of actors are wearing comic masks and were made from clay about 50 B.C.

their religion. They believed in many gods whose personalities were very human. The gods were believed to inhabit Mount Olympus, and there were ceremonies and sacrifices in their honor. The Olympic Games, dedicated to Zeus, the king of the gods, were held every four years.

Athens and Sparta
From about 500 B.C. the two most important city-states were Athens and Sparta. Athens was the main center for

These are some of the major sites of the ancient Greek world. Greeks traveled far beyond the borders of mainland Greece to Anatolia, Italy, and Sicily.

ANCIENT GREECE

philosophy and literature. The core of public life was the *agora*, or marketplace, which lay below the Acropolis, the hill where the main temples stood. Most political debate took place at the *agora*.

Athens was an important military power and had an especially strong navy. The strongest army in ancient Greece was that of Sparta. Boys entered military school there at age six and did not return to their families until they were 30.

The Spartans became concerned about the power of Athens, and war broke out between the two states in 431 B.C. The Spartans cut off shipments of food to Athens, and the Athenians were starved into defeat in 404 B.C.

Sculptors and builders in ancient Greece created beautiful statues and temples. The Parthenon, Athens, was built to house a statue of the goddess Athena.
▼

The decline of Greece

The last great Greek leader was Alexander of Macedon, known as Alexander the Great, whose conquests stretched as far as India. Greek culture then dominated large parts of Europe, Asia, and Africa. It continued to be very important even after political control passed to the Roman Empire. The last of the Greek states to fall to Rome was Egypt in 30 B.C.

SEE ALSO: Ancient Civilizations; Aristotle; Government; Olympic Games; Philosophy; Roman Empire; Theater

✳HABITAT

A habitat is the natural home of an animal or plant. Since different species have different needs, the habitat of one may not be suitable for another.

All habitats are part of an ecosystem. The whole planet Earth can be described as an ecosystem, but the term is usually used to mean a smaller area, such as a forest or a river. The ecosystem of a forest, for example, is more than just a collection of trees. It also includes the soil, air, water, rocks, and all the plants, animals, and microbes that live there.

The habitat of an animal or plant may include all or part of an ecosystem. A bird might live in the trees, fly in the air, walk on the ground, and swim in the water. These areas together form its habitat. Yet a plant might have a very limited habitat, growing only in a certain kind of soil.

Animals and plants adapt to different habitats through evolution. For example, animals like the arctic fox have developed extra fat for warmth and white fur for camouflage.

Destruction of habitats

Some animals and plants can live in a variety of habitats. Others can survive only in a very specific type of habitat. If a habitat is destroyed, species may no longer be able to find food or shelter, so they die out.

As the human population of the Earth increases, there is a greater need for food, places to live, and fuel. To meet these requirements, tropical forests, wetlands, grasslands, and other natural areas are cleared, settled, and developed, and their resources harvested for human use. In the process many habitats have been destroyed, and their animals and plants have become endangered or, in the worst cases, extinct.

DID YOU KNOW?

Orangutans are in danger of extinction because most of the forests in which these apes once lived have been destroyed. Orangutans are now found on only two islands of Southeast Asia—Borneo and Sumatra. Although orangutans are protected by law, their forests are being destroyed by wildfires and by illegal logging. Poachers hunt them. Baby orangutans are sometimes captured and sold as pets. In one area of northern Sumatra the number of orangutans shrank from 12,000 to 6,500 between 1993 and 1999.

SEE ALSO: Endangered Species; Environment; Evolution; Extinction

✳ HEALTH

Health can simply mean the absence of disease, or it can be a feeling of fitness and well-being. The most important part of health is keeping the body well.

There is plenty that people can do to stay healthy. One of the most important things is to have a healthful, varied diet. In many parts of the world people do not get enough to eat, but in North America and Europe the problem is often the opposite: too much food—and often too much of the wrong kind of food.

Food provides the body's energy. The energy comes from nutrients in certain types of food, such as fruit and vegetables, as well as starchy carbohydrates, such as bread, rice, or pasta. Fiber, which can be found in wholewheat foods, cereals, and vegetables, is important for the digestion. Calcium, which is contained in dairy foods and green vegetables, is important for the growth of bones. A wide variety of foods should ensure that a person gets all the minerals and vitamins he or she requires.

Water is essential to life, so it is important to drink enough of it. Many people drink less water than they should.

Regular exercise helps the body be healthy. Wearing protective equipment to prevent injuries is important.

DID YOU KNOW?

In 1999, 13 percent of American children aged 6 to 11 years were overweight. That was double the percentage 20 years earlier. Fourteen percent of kids aged 12 to 19 years were overweight, triple the percentage in 1979. Children are gaining weight for several reasons, but lifestyle plays a big part, especially lack of exercise and unhealthy eating habits. Overweight children are more likely to be overweight as adults. And being overweight puts people at greater risk of developing diabetes, heart disease, and other illnesses.

Sleep

Getting enough sleep allows the cells of the body to recover from the work of the day and to build up energy. Elementary and high-school students need about 8 to 10 hours of sleep each night. Dreaming during sleep may be important for learning and memory.

Exercise

Exercise tones the muscles, helps keep bones strong, and reduces weight. This does not mean playing sports for hours at a time, but moderate activity every day benefits the heart and lungs and helps the body break down and process food more efficiently.

Avoiding hazards

Tobacco is the main cause of lung cancer and contributes to other cancers. It also contributes to heart disease and a lung disease called emphysema. Alcohol can also be harmful. Heavy drinking can seriously damage the brain, the liver, and the heart. It also plays a large role in accidents—half of all fatal highway

or if they last a long time, the person might have a mental health problem. Mental and physical health are often linked. Stress and unhappiness can worsen conditions such as high blood pressure and ulcers. On the other hand, if someone is physically well, he or she will probably find it easier to achieve mental health.

Public health
Some aspects of a healthful environment are outside the control of the individual, although our actions and choices may influence them. Air that is safe to breathe, water that is free from disease, and food that is not dangerous to eat all depend to a large extent on government and state regulation.

Immunization is used to prevent infectious diseases in adults as well as children.

crashes are related to drinking. Other drugs such as cocaine, marijuana, and tranquillizers can all damage physical and mental health.

Accidents and injuries can be prevented by always wearing a seatbelt when traveling by car and by wearing the right protective equipment, such as a helmet or kneepads, when biking, skating, or playing sports like hockey or football.

Preventing disease
Many infectious diseases can be prevented by immunization with vaccines. Most people in the United States have been immunized against diptheria, whooping cough, polio, and tetanus. People living or traveling in other parts of the world may need vaccines for diseases such as typhoid and yellow fever. Or they may need to take medication to protect themselves against diseases like malaria.

Hand washing and general cleanliness help prevent the spread of colds, flu, and food poisoning. Brushing teeth helps prevent dental cavities and gum disease.

Mental health
Health is not just a question of the body functioning well. Some people can be very well physically, but might feel sad, angry, or confused. These feelings come to everyone; but if they are very severe

In the United States the Food and Drug Administration regulates the safety of foodstuffs, drugs, and cosmetics. It is illegal to use any food additives that have been found to cause cancer in animals. The Environmental Protection Agency sets standards for air and water quality, and can act against companies that create pollution. The Occupational Safety and Health Administration ensures that employers cannot put workers at risk of injury or illness. The Federal Trade Commission requires health warnings on cigarette packages and advertising. These agencies are not able to get rid of all the hazards they are set up to control, but without them the environment would be much less healthful.

SEE ALSO:
Human Body;
Medicine;
Nutrition

✳ HEARING

Hearing is the sense that receives sound. A part of the brain called the cerebrum is the center of sensation for hearing as well as the other senses.

Sound is described by volume—how loud it is—and by frequency—how high or low it is. Volume is measured in decibels. An ordinary conversation is about 65 decibels. Frequency is measured in hertz. Most people can hear frequencies between about 16 and 20,000 hertz.

People hear sounds when something sends out vibrations called sound waves. The waves enter the ear and strike the eardrum, causing a vibration that moves tiny bones inside the skull. This sends an electrical message along the auditory nerves to the brain.

The brain does not just register the volume and frequency of sounds. It also makes sense of them. A loud rock band and a pneumatic drill might sound similar, but the human brain can tell them apart.

Other species have different hearing ranges. Many animals need more sensitive hearing than humans so they

Hearing-impaired children are taught using sign language.

AMAZING FACTS!

The Beatles' album *Sergeant Pepper's Lonely Hearts Club Band* (1967) ends with a sound so high-pitched that humans cannot hear it—but dogs can.

A blue whale can make low-frequency noises with a volume of 188 decibels. A jumbo jet on takeoff only makes a sound of 120 decibels.

can hear their prey and avoid their enemies. Dolphins and bats make sounds that are too high-pitched to be heard by the human ear. They are called ultrasonic sounds, or ultrasound.

Hearing problems

When a person cannot hear the normal range of volume or frequency, he or she has a hearing impairment. If someone cannot hear sounds below 90 decibels, the condition is identified as deafness.

Hearing problems can be hereditary, or they can be caused by illnesses. They can be caused by injury or exposure to loud noises. Loss of hearing often occurs with age. People with hearing impairments can learn to lipread or to use sign language.

INSIDE THE EAR

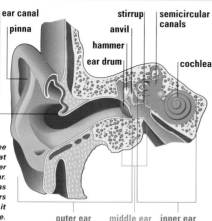

ear canal | pinna | stirrup | anvil | hammer | ear drum | semicircular canals | cochlea

The outer ear is made up of the pinna, which is the part that you can see, and the ear canal. The middle ear contains three tiny bones that connect the inner and the outer ear. The inner ear has sensory receptors for hearing, and it controls balance.

outer ear | middle ear | inner ear

SEE ALSO: Brain & Nervous System; Human Body; Sea Mammal; Sound Recording

✳ HEAT

People use the words "hot" and "cold" to describe things that have high or low temperatures. To a scientist heat is not the same as temperature.

Heat is a form of energy that exists inside matter. Matter is anything that takes up space and has mass. The more matter there is, the more heat energy there is, whether the temperature is high or low. There is more heat energy in a large iceberg than in a cup of hot coffee.

Heat is measured in calories. One calorie of heat will raise the temperature of 1 gram (0.03 ounces) by 1°C. Another measurement is the British thermal unit. A BTU will raise the temperature of 1 lb. (454g) of water by 1°F.

Temperature

Molecules, the tiny particles that make up matter, are always moving and giving off energy. Temperature measures the average kinetic energy, or energy of motion, of a molecule. There is more average energy in the molecules of hot matter than there is in cold matter.

Temperature is measured on a number of scales. Scientists use the Celsius, or centigrade scale, in which water freezes at 0°C—zero degrees—and boils at 100°C. It was developed in 1742 by the Swedish astronomer Anders Celsius.

Most people in the United States use the Fahrenheit scale, named for the

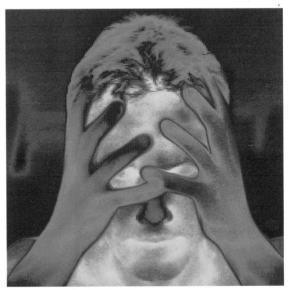

German physicist Gabriel Fahrenheit, in which water freezes at 32°F and boils at 212°F. On the Kelvin scale, named for the British scientist Lord Kelvin, water freezes at 273.16K (kelvins). Absolute zero, the temperature at which no more heat energy can be removed from matter, is known as 0K. Scientists have achieved temperatures very close to absolute zero, but have never reached 0K precisely.

A thermogram records differences in temperature. The scale runs from red as the warmest through to mauve as the coldest. This image is of a man holding his head in his hands.

The laws of thermodynamics

Thermodynamics is the study of heat and its relation to other forms of energy. The three laws of thermodynamics state that: Energy cannot be created or destroyed; heat naturally flows from a warmer body to a cooler body; and it is impossible to reduce temperature to absolute zero.

AMAZING FACTS !

The sun is the source of most of the Earth's energy. The center of the sun is approximately 27,000,000°F (15,000,000°C). Many other stars are even hotter.

SEE ALSO:
Energy;
Matter

✳ HEMINGWAY, ERNEST (1899–1961)
The American author Ernest Hemingway wrote with a distinctive style that strongly influenced later generations of writers.

Ernest Hemingway was born in Oak Park, Illinois. He wrote for his high school newspaper, then worked as a reporter for the *Kansas City Star*. There he developed his trademark writing style of short, simple sentences, made up mainly of nouns and verbs. He tried to avoid descriptions of emotion; instead, he described actions. His dialogue sounded natural and was brief and to the point.

During World War I (1914–18) Hemingway joined the Red Cross. His experiences formed the basis for the novel *A Farewell to Arms* (1929). His other major novels were *The Sun Also Rises* (1926), *For Whom the Bell Tolls*

▲
All his life Ernest Hemingway was a keen angler and hunter.

(1940), and *The Old Man and the Sea* (1952). For this last work Hemingway won the Pulitzer Prize. In 1954, for both his novels and short stories, Hemingway was awarded the Nobel Prize in literature.

Hemingway married four times, indulged his passion for hunting and fishing, and lived in Paris, France; Key West, Florida; Havana, Cuba; and Ketchum, Idaho. By 1960 he was in poor health and suffering from depression. In 1961 he took his life with a shotgun.

SEE ALSO: Nobel Prize; Writers, American

✳ HINDUISM
Hinduism is a major world religion, with about 900 million followers. It began in India and is now practiced in many countries.

Hinduism recognizes several holy books, not just one. The oldest and holiest of the Hindu books are the four Vedas. (*Veda* means "knowledge" or "wisdom.") Second, many Hindus worship more than one god. Some of the best-known gods include Vishnu, Shiva, and Ganesha. Popular goddesses include Durga, Kali, and Lakshmi. All Hindus believe that there is one unifying spirit that runs through everything in the world—plants, animals, and people—called Brahman. The gods represent different sides of Brahman.

Reincarnation
In Hinduism, just as in Buddhism, Jainism, and Sikhism (other religions

from India), followers believe in reincarnation, or being born again. When a person dies, he or she is born again into a new body. The cycle of death and rebirth continues until the person's soul (inner being) understands life so well that he or she is set free from this world.

For the Hindu this means that life must be lived as purely as possible. Hindus try to follow rules of behavior. They must honor their family, go for periods without food, and meditate (spend time in

A Hindu woman bathes in the sacred waters of the Ganges River at Varanasi, India.

179

A statue of the Hindu god Ganesha in Java, Indonesia.

quiet thought). They worship at shrines in their homes and in temples. Some important Hindu festivals include Divali, Navratri, and Holi.

Caste system

One complicated aspect of Hinduism is its caste system. It is the ancient belief that everyone belongs to a level, or caste, in society. The highest caste is that of priests and scholars, or Brahmans. Outside the four main castes are people called untouchables, who traditionally did work that others saw as unclean.

In 1947 laws were passed in India to make discrimination against untouchables illegal, but the caste system remains an important part of family and social life.

SEE ALSO: Buddhism; Indian Subcontinent; Religion

✻ HISTORY

History is the branch of knowledge that records and explains past events. Historical writings are often set out in the order in which things happened.

Many people believe that understanding what has already happened might help humankind avoid making the same mistakes in the future. The philosopher George Santayana (1863–1952) once wrote that "Those who cannot remember the past are condemned to repeat it."

In the past people learned history as if it were a simple record of events. They learned the names of powerful people,

1300s–1500s Renaissance

1492 Christopher Columbus discovers America

1347 Black Death sweeps Europe, killing millions

1455 Johannes Gutenberg unveils his printing press

1430s Rise of Aztec Empire

1517 Protestant Reformation starts in northern Europe

1526 Mogul dynasty founded in India

1530s Inca civilization falls to Spanish conquistadors

1521 Aztec Empire falls to Spaniard Hernán Cortés

1775 American Revolution begins

1759 General James Wolfe wins the battle of Quebec

1712 First steam engine invented

1620 *Mayflower* lands in Massachusetts

1804 Napoleon becomes emperor of France

1789 French Revolution

1807–3 Americ countri indepe from Sp

1815 Napo defea

1300 1400 1500 1600 1700 1800

such as kings and generals, and their great achievements. Children learned long lists of dates, so that they knew when wars happened, or when governments made important laws.

The modern approach

Historians still believe that such records of events are the foundation of history. However, in recent decades they have also begun to explore different types of history. Instead of studying the few privileged and powerful people in a society, they believe it is just as important to learn about the lives of the many millions of ordinary people. What did they eat? What gods did they worship? And in what way?

As well as studying the lives of a wider range of people, modern historians also use a wider range of evidence. They used to concentrate on written accounts. Now they draw on subjects such as biology, economics, geology, psychology, and sociology. They also refer to folklore, myths, and everyday documents, such as household accounts.

Some historians study a tiny part of history in great detail—they try to discover as much as they can about a

History is more than documents. This painting from an ancient Greek vase tells scholars about life when it was made in about 400 B.C.

single village at a particular time, for example. Others study the rise and fall of whole civilizations.

Some historians study politics; others study ideas or the history of families. Some specialize in wars and warfare. There are also historians who study history before the existence of records, which is called prehistory.

A complex subject

Although history seems simple, it is often very complicated. Any event can have many interpretations. For Americans, for example, Christopher Columbus's arrival in the "New World" in 1492 helped lead to the creation of the United States. For Native Americans, however, Columbus's arrival was a disaster. It brought disease

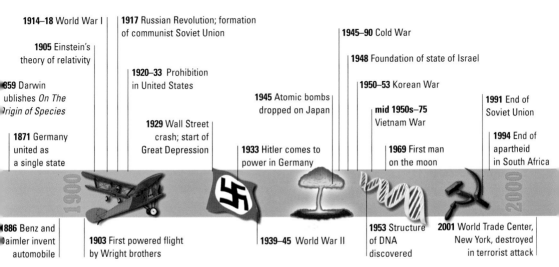

1914–18 World War I

1917 Russian Revolution; formation of communist Soviet Union

1905 Einstein's theory of relativity

1945–90 Cold War

1948 Foundation of state of Israel

1920–33 Prohibition in United States

859 Darwin ublishes *On The rigin of Species*

1945 Atomic bombs dropped on Japan

1950–53 Korean War

1991 End of Soviet Union

mid 1950s–75 Vietnam War

1871 Germany united as a single state

1929 Wall Street crash; start of Great Depression

1933 Hitler comes to power in Germany

1969 First man on the moon

1994 End of apartheid in South Africa

886 Benz and aimler invent automobile

1903 First powered flight by Wright brothers

1939–45 World War II

1953 Structure of DNA discovered

2001 World Trade Center, New York, destroyed in terrorist attack

that killed millions of people. Which view is correct? There are many other examples that show that history is not a single story but many intertwined stories.

The history of history
The Western tradition of history has its origins in the Hebrew Bible and ancient Greek writings. These works have influenced the study of history in Europe, America, and the Islamic world.

The non-Western tradition began in ancient China but spread to Japan, Korea, and elsewhere. Since the time of the Chou dynasty (about 1000 B.C.) Chinese historians have traditionally taken evidence from a wide range of sources, rather like Western historians today.

SEE ALSO: Ancient Civilizations; Archaeology; Philosophy; Renaissance; United States of America

✳ HITLER, ADOLF (1889–1945)

Adolf Hitler was leader of the Nazi Party in Germany. He was the country's dictator (supreme ruler) from 1933 to 1945.

Adolf Hitler at a Nazi rally in Nuremberg, shortly after he was elected chancellor of Germany in 1933.

Adolf Hitler was born in Braunau, Austria. He served in the army during World War I (1914–18). The defeat of Germany at the end of this conflict was a great shock to him, and he decided to devote his life to restoring the country's greatness.

Hitler built up the National Socialist German Workers' Party, or Nazis for short. The Nazis took advantage of the fact that millions of Germans lost their jobs in the Depression of 1929. Many people believed that Hitler was the man to lead them out of crisis and make Germany great again. In 1933 Hitler became chancellor of Germany.

Hitler soon took complete control of the police and the state, his chief opponents were murdered, and he became dictator. In 1938 he made Austria part of Germany. When he invaded Poland in 1939, World War II (1939–45) broke out. By 1941 further victories had made Hitler master of most of Europe. But his invasion of the Soviet Union failed. From that point Germany began to lose the war. On April 30, 1945, Hitler committed suicide.

One of Hitler's worst crimes was the Final Solution, an attempt to kill all Europe's Jews, whom he blamed for Germany's defeat in World War I. Six million Jews died in the resulting Holocaust.

SEE ALSO: Dictatorship; Germany; Holocaust; World War II

HOLOCAUST

Adolf Hitler, Germany's leader from 1933 to 1945, ordered the killing of six million Europeans, mostly Jews. This mass murder is called the Holocaust.

In the early 1930s about nine million Jews lived throughout Europe. The Jews had been persecuted since Roman times for many reasons to do with religion, culture, and tradition.

Hitler's Nazi Party came to power soon after Germany's defeat in World War I (1914–18). It was easy for Hitler to blame Germany's misfortunes on the Jews. He said that the Jews were "unworthy of life," and with them he included Roma (gypsies), communists, intellectuals, Jehovah's Witnesses, the handicapped, and homosexuals. Hitler believed that all these people stood in the way of his vision of a new German empire that would contain only pure-blooded peoples.

Under a Nazi law of 1935 German Jews lost their citizenship. They also had to wear a yellow Star of David on their clothing and were barred from mixing with non-Jews.

DID YOU KNOW?

Institutions across the world honor the memory of the Holocaust victims. They include Yad Vashem in Jerusalem, the Anne Frank House in Amsterdam, the United States Holocaust Memorial Museum in Washington, D.C., the Museum of Jewish Heritage in New York City, and the Simon Wiesenthal Center in Los Angeles. The dead are honored on Holocaust Remembrance Day (usually April 19).

World War II

On September 1, 1939, Hitler's army invaded Poland, marking the beginning of World War II. By the middle of 1940 most of Europe was under Nazi control. The Nazis crowded the Jews into tiny sections of cities, called ghettoes, where they were given almost no food, water, or heat. Many died of cold, illness, or starvation.

From 1942 the Nazis moved the Jews to concentration camps such as Auschwitz, Treblinka, and Dachau. Many of them were gassed to death soon after they arrived.

The Jews made escape attempts. Once other nations realized what the Germans were doing, they tried to save the Jews. Before the end of the war the World Zionist Organization helped 450,000 Jews flee to Palestine, but help came too late for most Jews. In 1945, at the end of World War II, those left in the camps were liberated. After the war Nazi leaders were punished for their crimes.

▲
A Jewish citizen of Warsaw, Poland, in 1940, who was made to wear the Star of David, the symbol of Judaism.

SEE ALSO: Hitler, Adolf; Judaism; World War II

HOPPER, GRACE MURRAY (1906–1992)

Grace Murray Hopper was a pioneer computer scientist. She invented the compiler—a program that translates English into computer language.

Hopper's 1934 doctorate in math was a rare accomplishment for a woman at that time. By 1941 she was associate professor in math at Vassar. In 1943 she joined the Navy. She was assigned to the Bureau of Ordnance Computation Project at Harvard University. After World War II (1939–45) Hopper held a number of jobs in the military, universities, and industry, working well into her 80s. By 1985 she was a rear admiral.

In addition to inventing the compiler, Hopper helped develop and promote high-level computer languages and standardize compilers. Her work in this area led to the development of national and international standards for most programming languages.

Grace Hopper had several successful careers in traditionally male-dominated areas.

In 1969 she was awarded the first ever Computer Science Man-of-the-Year Award from the Data Processing Management Association. In 1971 the Sperry Corporation set up an annual award in her name. In 1973 she became the first American and the first woman to be made a Distinguished Fellow of the British Computer Society. She was buried with full naval honors.

HOSPITAL

Sick or injured people are given medical care in hospitals. Women also give birth there, and they are centers for educational and research programs.

Although a hospital is a building or a number of buildings, the most important part of it is the people who help make patients better. They include doctors and nurses, as well as laboratory technicians, cleaners, cooks, and maintenance and office workers. Each one has a special job that contributes to the care of the patients and the organization of the hospital.

Hospital departments

There are many different kinds of hospitals. Some only treat people with one kind of disease. Others only treat one age group, such as children.

Most hospitals are short-term, general hospitals. They are divided into

▲ *A 15th-century illustration showing patients in a ward at the Hôtel Dieu in Paris. Medical treatment at the time was extremely limited, and lack of space meant that patients had to share beds.*

departments that provide different kinds of care. Sick children under 16 are admitted to the pediatrics department. This department often has play facilities and space for parents to stay overnight with their children. Some pediatric departments have schoolrooms and teachers, so that the children who are patients at the hospital do not miss out on their education.

patients can be seen as quickly as possible. The most seriously ill people go to the trauma room. Radiology (x-ray) departments and laboratories are usually near the emergency department.

Very sick patients go to the intensive care unit (ICU) or coronary care unit (CCU). Here department staff constantly check their blood pressure, pulse, breathing, and other body functions.

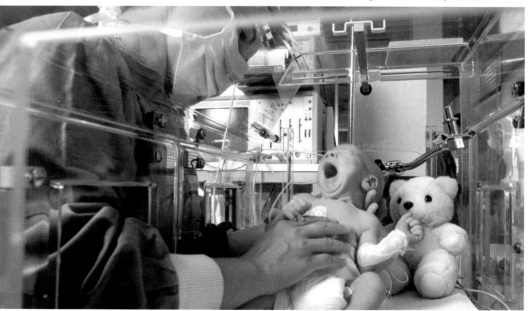

▲
When a baby is born early, he or she is often put in an incubator, which acts like a greenhouse, regulating the surrounding temperature and the amount of oxygen in the air.

In North America most births take place in hospital obstetrics departments. They are usually on a separate floor from other departments to keep mothers and babies free from infection.

Operations are performed in the surgery department. Patients are given anesthetics—substances that make them lose consciousness—before and during the operation. Afterward they go to a recovery room until the effects of the anesthetic wear off.

The busiest department is usually emergency, which is where people go when they suffer an injury or illness that must be treated promptly. The emergency department is usually on the first floor so

People who do not need to stay in the hospital attend as outpatients. Staff may need to perform tests on them or to give them treatment. Outpatients do not stay overnight in the hospital. Inpatients stay for the night or for a longer period.

History of hospitals
In early history places of worship cared for the sick. The first separate medical institutions appeared in Rome, Italy, in the first century A.D. The word *hospital* comes from the Latin *hospitium*, meaning a place to receive guests.

The first American hospitals were built in the 1700s. They were mainly to confine patients with infectious diseases. Later, hospitals were built to provide care and treatment for the poor. Wealthy people were still treated in their homes. The first not-for-profit or voluntary hospital in North America was the Pennsylvania Hospital in Philadelphia, founded in 1751 by Benjamin Franklin and Dr. Thomas Bond. Hospitals became much safer and more effective in the 1800s because of the discovery of antiseptics, which help prevent infection, and anesthetics, which kill pain. In the first half of the 1900s sulfa drugs and antibiotics also helped medical staff treat disease and operate more safely.

In recent years developments such as transplant surgery and laser treatment have greatly increased the range of services that a hospital can offer. Illnesses and injuries that once killed people can now be treated fairly easily by skilled staff.

SEE ALSO: Medicine; Nursing; X-ray

✳ HUDSON, HENRY (UNKNOWN–1611)
The English navigator Henry Hudson was an important explorer of North America who increased Europeans' knowledge of the world.

In 1607 Hudson sailed in a small ship called the *Hopewell* from England to the icy waters around Greenland and Spitsbergen. His aim was to find a route to Asia via the North Pole. Hudson sailed closer to the North Pole than any explorer before him but had to turn back. Next year he tried again but without success.

In 1609 the Dutch East India Company paid him to make another attempt to find a northern passage to Asia. This time his ship, *Half Moon*, reached what is now New York state and sailed up the river now named the Hudson. The crew encountered native peoples and claimed the area for Holland.

The following year, in the English ship *Discovery*, Hudson went past Greenland to the bay now named for him. Winter arrived, and the ship got stuck in the ice in James Bay. In the spring Hudson wanted to carry on westward, but his men wanted to return to England. On June 23, 1611, they forced Hudson, his son John, and a few other loyal men into a little boat and set them adrift without food or water. They were never heard from again.

▲
Henry Hudson has a river, a bay, and a strait in North America named after him.

*HUMAN BODY

People often compare the human body to a machine, but it can do far more than the most complicated machines ever built.

Like all things, the human body is made of elements—chemicals that cannot be broken down into simpler substances. The most common elements in the body are carbon, hydrogen, nitrogen, and oxygen. There are many others, including sodium, calcium, iron, phosphorus, and potassium. Many of the elements in the body are joined together as compounds. The main compounds in the body are water, carbohydrates, proteins, nucleic acids, and lipids, or fats. Carbohydrates provide the energy for the body's activities. Lipids store fuel and build new cells. Some proteins also build cells, while others take part in chemical reactions. Nucleic acids carry genetic instructions from one generation to the next.

Cells and tissues

The basic unit of all living things is the cell. There are more than 100 different kinds of cell in the human body, all doing different tasks. Most cells join together with similar cells to make tissue. Blood cells are the main exception.

There are four main types of tissue: epithelial tissue, which covers the body's surface; connective tissue, which helps support and join together parts of the body; muscle tissue, which makes movement possible; and nervous tissue, which carries nerve signals.

Tissues form together to make organs. They are body parts that perform a specific job. The brain, heart, liver, and lungs are all important organs.

BODY SYSTEMS

SKELETAL SYSTEM
The skeleton provides strength and support for the body and protects soft organs. Bones and muscles allow body parts to move.

CIRCULATORY SYSTEM
The heart pumps blood containing oxygen through arteries. Used blood containing carbon dioxide returns through veins.

RESPIRATORY SYSTEM
The respiratory system provides cells with oxygen so they can produce energy and takes away waste carbon dioxide.

DIGESTIVE SYSTEM
The digestive system breaks down food and converts it into chemicals that the body uses for nourishment; waste is expelled.

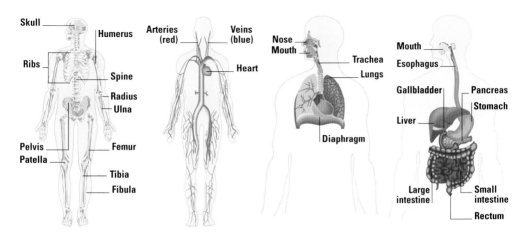

SKELETAL SYSTEM: Skull, Humerus, Ribs, Spine, Radius, Ulna, Pelvis, Femur, Patella, Tibia, Fibula

CIRCULATORY SYSTEM: Arteries (red), Veins (blue), Heart

RESPIRATORY SYSTEM: Nose, Mouth, Trachea, Lungs, Diaphragm

DIGESTIVE SYSTEM: Mouth, Esophagus, Gallbladder, Pancreas, Stomach, Liver, Large intestine, Small intestine, Rectum

Some organs work together as systems. For example, the lungs, throat, and windpipe form the respiratory system, which enables an individual to take in oxygen. The heart works with the veins, arteries, and capillaries to transport blood around the body—this is called the circulatory system.

The skin is also an organ. It protects the body from air, water, dirt, and germs. It holds fluid inside the body and helps maintain body temperature. Fingernails and toenails are made of skin cells. The skin also contains hair roots, which contain cells that form hair.

Skeleton

The skeleton is a framework of bones and ligaments that supports the body. It also protects delicate organs, such as the brain and heart.

Bones cannot move by themselves. They are attached by tissue called tendons to muscles, which make them move. There are other muscles, not connected to the skeleton, that move automatically. They are called smooth muscles and control movements such as changes in the pupils of the eyes. The heart is made of a third kind of muscle, called cardiac muscle.

The digestive system

Muscles need energy to work efficiently. They get it from burning fuel. The fuel comes from food and water; but before they can be used, they need to be converted by digestion. Food passes from the mouth down the esophagus to the stomach, where the body begins to absorb the nutrition it needs. Solid waste passes through the large intestine to the rectum and leaves the body through the anus.

Some liquid waste evaporates from the skin as sweat; most is removed by the urinary system. The urinary system consists of the bladder, two kidneys, and connecting tubes. The bladder stores the urine until it leaves the body.

URINARY SYSTEM
In order to function properly, the body must get rid of its waste. Most of the liquid waste is removed by the urinary system as urine.

REPRODUCTIVE SYSTEM
A male reproductive cell, called a sperm, joins with a female reproductive cell, called an ovum to produce a new human being.

ENDOCRINE SYSTEM
The endocrine system produces powerful chemical messengers called hormones. They keep the body working normally.

MUSCULAR SYSTEM
The body has more than 600 muscles. Muscles move the bones. A simple movment like taking a step requires 200 muscles.

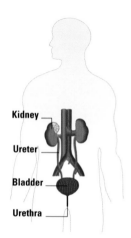

Kidney

Ureter

Bladder

Urethra

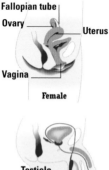

Fallopian tube

Ovary

Uterus

Vagina

Female

Testicle

Penis

Male

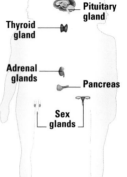

Thyroid gland

Pituitary gland

Adrenal glands

Pancreas

Sex glands

Male   Female

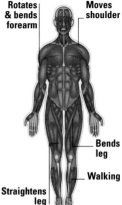

Rotates & bends forearm

Moves shoulder

Bends leg

Walking

Straightens leg

THE SENSES

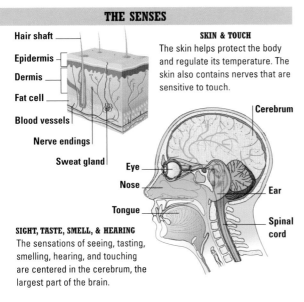

Hair shaft
Epidermis
Dermis
Fat cell
Blood vessels
Nerve endings
Sweat gland

Eye
Nose
Tongue

Cerebrum

Ear

Spinal cord

SKIN & TOUCH
The skin helps protect the body and regulate its temperature. The skin also contains nerves that are sensitive to touch.

SIGHT, TASTE, SMELL, & HEARING
The sensations of seeing, tasting, smelling, hearing, and touching are centered in the cerebrum, the largest part of the brain.

The respiratory system

The digestive system takes in fuel and expels waste. In a similar way the respiratory system takes in oxygen and expels waste carbon dioxide. Oxygen is contained in air, which enters the body through the nose and sometimes through the mouth. It passes through the pharynx, the larynx, and the trachea, or windpipe. The oxygen then enters the lungs, from where it passes into the blood vessels that carry it to the heart.

Breathing is controlled by muscles in the chest wall and by a muscular sheet called the diaphragm that separates the chest from the abdomen.

The heart and blood vessels move blood through the body, carrying oxygen and nutrients to cells. The blood also helps remove waste, cool the body, and fight bacteria and disease.

The reproductive system

Males and females have different reproductive systems—this is the only major difference between the bodies of the two sexes. During puberty and adolescence hormones act on the reproductive system. The male testes produce sperm, and the female ovaries produce ova (eggs). If they are brought together, new life can be created.

The immune system

The immune system is made up of three types of white blood cell. These cells are produced in the bone marrow and defend the body against infection. The body's natural immunity can be boosted by vaccines that protect the individual against diseases such as polio and tetanus.

Communication systems

The various systems perform so well because the body has ways to communicate. The nervous system consists of the brain, nerves, and spinal cord. The endocrine system produces control chemicals called hormones.

Hormones usually come from patches of cells called glands. The thyroid gland in the neck produces hormones that provide energy. Adrenalin, which prepares the body for quick action, comes from the adrenal glands in the kidneys. Hormones from the pituitary gland control other glands. Some hormones come from other organs. For example, insulin, which controls blood sugar, is made in the pancreas.

SEE ALSO: Brain & Nervous System; Circulatory System; Element, Chemical; Health; Hearing; Medicine; Reproduction; Sight; Taste & Smell; Touch

✳HURRICANE, TORNADO, AND TYPHOON

Hurricanes—known as typhoons in Asia—are violent storms, with fast, rain-bearing winds. A tornado is a storm with a twisting column of air.

Hurricanes begin over tropical seas, usually in late summer and early fall along the eastern coast of North America and the Caribbean. They can happen at any time of year in the Pacific Ocean.

Hurricanes need two "fuels" to start them and keep them going: moist air and heat. As the surface of the ocean heats up, water evaporates into the air and turns into water vapor. The air above the ocean becomes moist.

In certain conditions the warm, moist air begins to form a column. Surrounding air starts to rush toward the column, forming a spiral around it. The whole system of air—the column of rising air surrounded by spiraling air—is called a cyclone.

As the column of air becomes warmer, the winds pick up speed. If they reach more than 74 mph (119 km/h), the storm is called a hurricane.

Hurricanes often extend up to 500 miles (800km) in width. Some last a few hours; some as long as two weeks. They often cause massive damage. In 1998 Hurricane Mitch killed an estimated 10,000 people in Central America.

DID YOU KNOW?

In 1950 meteorologists, who study weather, began naming hurricanes. For many years the names were all female; now they use male names as well. The first storm of the season is given a name starting with A. The names continue through the alphabet until the season is over. New names are used every year to avoid confusion.

Tornadoes

A tornado—or twister—is also a type of cyclone. When streams of hot, humid air meet streams of colder, dry air, they form thunderstorms. In certain conditions a rapidly rotating column of air forms within the thunderstorm and begins to extend toward the ground in a funnel shape.

The rotating winds may range from about 40 miles (64km) an hour to over 300 miles (480km) an hour. They may last only a few minutes or up to an hour or so. The high winds can cause severe damage, sometimes picking up people, animals, and vehicles and carrying them long distances. Every year, especially in the Midwest, there are about 1,000 tornadoes in the United States.

▲
A tornado begins to form over Oklahoma. As the tornado picks up soil and debris, it becomes brown, gray, or black in appearance.

SEE ALSO:
Climate & Weather;
Disaster

✳ INCAS

The Incas were an American Indian people who built a vast and powerful empire in the Andes Mountains of Peru in the 1400s.

According to legend, the god-man Manco Capac was sent to earth by his father, the Sun. Manco Capac founded the city Cuzco, and his descendants became Inca emperors. Pachacuti, the ninth emperor, extended Inca territory from the present border of Bolivia to central Ecuador. Pachacuti's son, Tupa Inca Yupanqui, took the empire south to central Chile.

Spanish conquerors broke up the Inca Empire in the 1500s. When the Spanish conquistador (conqueror) Francisco Pizarro arrived in 1532, Inca land spanned a distance of 2,500 miles (4,000km). This huge empire was linked by an impressive network of roads and bridges. The Incas were also famous for their architecture. Individual stones were cut to fit together exactly. Many Inca buildings still stand, although modern buildings have been destroyed by the strong earthquakes that shake the Andes Mountains.

Incas lived in villages grouped together into provinces. All men served as soldiers at some time in their lives. Common foods were corn, potatoes, beans, peppers, and guinea pigs.

Religion was based on worship of the sun and other gods. People also worshiped their ancestors. The emperor was seen as all-powerful because he was descended from the sun. Our knowledge of the Incas comes from explorers and missionaries, and from written accounts kept by two Incas.

INCA EMPIRE

BRAZIL
ECUADOR
● Huanuco Pampa
PERU   BOLIVIA
Lima ●
Andes
Pisac ● ● ● Machu Picchu
Cuzco
PACIFIC OCEAN
Mountains
Inca Empire
ARGENTINA
CHILE

👀
SEE ALSO:
America, South;
Conquistadors;
Peru

The Inca city of Machu Picchu in the Cordillera Blanca Mountains of Peru was discovered in 1911.
▼

The end of the empire

In 1525 the empire was split by a civil war between the brothers Huáscar and Atahuallpa. Atahuallpa had Huáscar executed. Pizarro took advantage of the confusion and captured Atahuallpa. He agreed to free Atahuallpa for a huge ransom; instead, he had Atahuallpa killed.

This was not the end of the Incas. Two leaders, both called Tupac Amaru, led revolts against the Spanish in the 1500s and the 1700s. The Inca language, Quechua (pronounced ketch-wah), is still spoken by half the Peruvian people.

✻ INDEX

The index is the key to finding the contents
of a book. It guides the reader to the exact
page on which particular information is found.

Many indexes give directions on how to use them. Always read these instructions. All indexes are arranged alphabetically. They may list entries either letter by letter or word by word.

Letter by letter	Word by word
Newark	New Jersey
New Jersey	New York
Newspapers	Newark
Newsweek	Newspapers
New York	Newsweek

Each entry is followed by the number of the page or pages in the text on which the information about it is found. If the book contains a lot of information about a subject, subheadings help the reader find particular areas of interest. Subheadings are usually placed in alphabetical order below the main heading.

Advertising, 306–13
    magazines, 309
    marketing, 308
    newspapers, 310

Cross-references
There are two types of guideposts, called cross-references, that make all indexes easier to use. The first is the "see" reference. It directs the reader away from a term not used as an entry and to the entry where the information can be found.

Ping-pong *see* Table Tennis

The other is the "see also" reference. It directs the reader to related information.

Games, 222–26
    See also Athletics; Sports

SEE ALSO:
Book

✻ INDIAN SUBCONTINENT

India is the seventh largest country in the world.
Along with Sri Lanka, Pakistan, Nepal, Bhutan, and
Bangladesh, it makes up the Indian subcontinent.

The subcontinent has three main land divisions—the Himalaya Mountains of the north; the lowland plains of the Indus, Ganges, and Brahmaputra rivers; and the Deccan plateau of southern India. Pakistan contains much of the Indus River. Bangladesh is a low-lying land dominated by the delta (mouth) of the Ganges and Brahmaputra rivers. Nepal and Bhutan lie along the southern slopes of the Himalaya Mountains. Sri Lanka lies off India's southern tip. The Maldives, a small island nation in the Indian Ocean, is sometimes considered to be part of the subcontinent.

Forests cover one-fifth of India and much of Bangladesh and Sri Lanka.

Temperatures vary widely from north to south. Intense summer

▶
*The Taj Mahal,
India, was built in
the 1600s by
an emperor as a
tomb for his wife.*

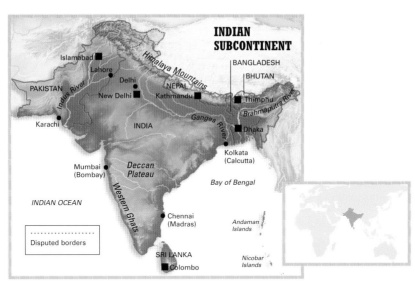

INDIAN SUBCONTINENT

- Islamabad
- Lahore
- PAKISTAN
- Indus River
- Delhi
- New Delhi
- NEPAL
- Kathmandu
- Himalaya Mountains
- BANGLADESH
- BHUTAN
- Thimphu
- Brahmaputra River
- Karachi
- INDIA
- Ganges River
- Dhaka
- Kolkata (Calcutta)
- Mumbai (Bombay)
- Deccan Plateau
- Bay of Bengal
- INDIAN OCEAN
- Western Ghats
- Chennai (Madras)
- Andaman Islands
- Disputed borders
- SRI LANKA
- Colombo
- Nicobar Islands

KEY FACTS

AREA
1,722,145 sq. mi.
(4,452,268 sq. km)

POPULATION
1,334,201,000

COUNTRIES
6

LARGEST COUNTRY
India

SMALLEST COUNTRY
Bhutan

RELIGIONS
Hinduism,
Buddhism, Islam,
Christianity,
Sikhism, Jainism

LANGUAGES
Many, including
Hindi, Urdu,
Bengali, Sinhala,
Tamil, Dzongkha;
Nepali; English

heat brings the monsoon wind, and with it comes heavy rainfall. The monsoon winds move across the subcontinent to the Indian Ocean. Low-lying Bangladesh suffers from tropical storms and flooding, which flatten crops and take many lives. The highlands of Bhutan and Nepal are bitterly cold in winter, with heavy snows.

People and economy

The subcontinent is home to many different peoples and languages. In India over four-fifths of the population follows the Hindu religion. The rest of the population is mainly Muslim. The people of Bangladesh and Pakistan are mostly Muslim. In Sri Lanka the Sinhalese people are Buddhist; the Tamil people are Hindu. The people of Nepal are mainly Hindu. In

Bhutan the majority follow Buddhism, and the remainder are Hindu.

Across the subcontinent nearly three-quarters of the people make their living from the land. Rice, wheat, sugarcane, cotton, tea, rubber, coffee, coconuts, and spices are important crops and are still largely grown by hand. Industry is expanding rapidly, especially in textiles, food products, and modern machinery. Tourism is an important part of the economy, especially for India and Nepal,

Many of the subcontinent's people are poor. Though most of the people live in villages, large cities such as Delhi, Kolkata (Calcutta), Chennai (Madras), and Dhaka are growing rapidly.

Plantation workers pick tea in Sri Lanka. Tea is also an important crop in Bangladesh and India.

History

One of the world's earliest civilizations developed in the valley of the Indus River more than 4,500 years ago. The area is now part of Pakistan. The remains of two large cities have been found there.

As the centuries passed, invaders settled in the north and west of India, and generations of rulers came and went. For much of its history India was a collection of small kingdoms and states.

In the 1600s there was a strong Muslim influence under the Mogul emperors. By the 1700s Portuguese, Dutch, French, and British traders had settled on India's west coast, and in 1877 India became part of the British Empire. The Indians rebelled against British rule—first with weapons and then with politics.

Indians won independence under the leadership of Mohandas Gandhi. In 1947 the British withdrew. At the same time, they created the state of Pakistan as a new home for India's Muslims. Ever since, India and Pakistan have fought for ownership of Kashmir, a valley on their border. In 1972 India helped turn the eastern part of Pakistan into what is now Bangladesh.

Sri Lanka has also been torn by years of conflict between the Tamils and the Sinhalese. The Tamils want to have their own state or at least to have more say in the way they are governed.

SEE ALSO:
Ancient Civilizations;
Buddhism;
Flood;
Gandhi, Mohandas;
Hinduism;
Islam

✷ INDONESIA

Indonesia is a nation made up of thousands of islands that form a long, curving line between the mainland of Southeast Asia and Australia.

Indonesia's 13,700 islands stretch for about 3,500 miles (5,640km) from Sumatra in the west to Irian Jaya, the western part of the island of New Guinea. The equator runs through Indonesia. The climate is hot and humid, with high seasonal rainfall. Thick rainforests blanket some islands, though many have been cut for lumber or burned to clear land.

Between Sulawesi and New Guinea are the Moluccas, or Spice Islands—famous for their cloves, nutmeg, and other spices. Indonesia's other resources include petroleum, natural gas, tin, and gems. The fertile soil is used to grow crops such as coconut, rubber, palms (for oil), and rice.

More than half of Indonesia's huge population lives on Java. Nearly half of all Indonesians work on small farms. About 90 percent follow the religion of Islam, though most people on Bali are Hindus.

History

Some of the earliest human beings lived in Indonesia, but little is known of their history. Indian traders and priests from Asia came to Sumatra and Java around A.D.100. They brought Buddhism and Hinduism. Islam reached the area in 1100.

From the 1500s European traders came to the islands. Most important were the Dutch, who by the 1800s were in control of all Indonesia. In 1945, at the end of World War II, Indonesia claimed its independence. A bitter war followed; the Dutch did not hand over power until 1949. Indonesia's modern history has been troubled by revolts against the government and economic problems.

Dance in Bali has a strong Indian influence. Dances are performed in temples during religious festivals.

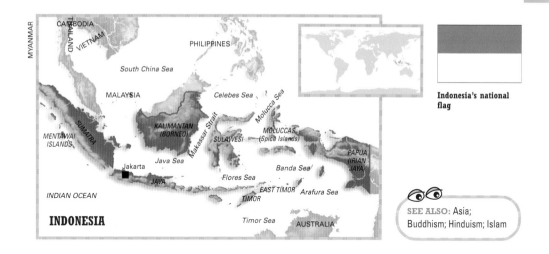

INDONESIA

Indonesia's national flag

SEE ALSO: Asia;
Buddhism; Hinduism; Islam

✳ INDUSTRIAL REVOLUTION

The invention of many new machines in the 1700s changed the way that goods were produced. The changes were great and seemed to happen suddenly.

▲

The Coalbrookdale foundry, England, was founded in 1709. It pioneered the technique of melting iron with coke, a modified type of coal.

The Industrial Revolution began in England in the 1760s. Until that time all kinds of goods, from yarn and clothing to furniture and tools, were made by hand by workers in their own homes. England, a mainly farming and shipbuilding nation, did not produce enough goods of its own and had to buy them from other lands. England's leaders hoped to make their country a stronger producer.

The first leap forward came in about 1764, when James Hargreaves invented the spinning jenny. It was a machine that spun eight threads of yarn at once, doing as much work as eight people. However, the cloth had then to be woven on a hand-operated loom—a slow process. So in about 1785 Edmund Cartwright built a fast automatic loom.

New power

Meanwhile, in about 1769 Richard Arkwright had the idea of harnessing the new spinning jenny to a waterwheel to draw power from the energy of a river's flow. He built textile plants, called mills, beside rivers. The mills brought machines and workers together under one roof; they were the first manufacturing plants.

The next breakthrough was in steam. Coal was in high demand in order to make

iron, but the coal mines kept flooding. Thomas Newcomen designed a steam engine that pumped water out of the mines. Soon inventors, such as James Watt and Matthew Boulton, produced better engines that were cheaper to run.

Rush to the cities

The new steam engines meant that textile mills no longer needed water power and could be built anywhere. Cities and new plants grew rapidly. The textile machines were easy to operate, and untrained farm laborers flocked to the cities to work. Even young children were employed. The laborers worked long hours for very little money and lived in crowded apartments.

American developments

The new plants turned England into a powerful nation, and other European countries took notice. So, too, did the United States. In 1789 an English textile worker named Samuel Slater came to

New York and set up textile plants. In 1793 American Eli Whitney invented the cotton gin, a machine that could rapidly comb cotton fibers and prepare them for the textile mills. People eagerly took to planting cotton across the South.

Further developments

The Industrial Revolution turned industry and society upside down. Europe and Japan became industrialized during the 1800s, and the Soviet Union, China, and India followed in the 1900s.

Rapid change continues today, with the growth of electronics and Internet business. None of today's technology would have happened, however, without the dawn of the machine age in England.

Cotton being made in a mill near Preston, England, in 1834. Children often worked long hours doing dangerous work in the mills.

SEE ALSO: Inventors & Inventions; Manufacturing

✳ INSECT

Insects are the largest group of animals in the world. There are about 1,000,000 known species, and more are discovered every year.

There are more species of insect on Earth than all other species of living creature put together. Insects live almost everywhere, from the hot, dry continental deserts to the cold of Antarctica. Some insects live in underground caves, others on high mountain tops. Insects have been on Earth for over 350 million years. The scientific study of insects is called entomology.

The praying mantis is a carnivorous (meat-eating) insect that catches and chews its prey.
▶

Identification

The one sure way to tell that an animal is an insect is to count its legs. Adult insects always have six legs, three on each side of the body.

An insect's body is made up of three parts—a head, a thorax, and an abdomen. The thorax is the middle part of the body enclosed by the ribcage; it is equivalent to the chest in humans. The abdomen is the lowest part of the body; in humans it is the area between the bottom of the ribcage and the top of the legs.

All insects have a pair of antennae (singular antenna), or feelers, at the front of the head. Most insects have one or two pairs of wings. The wings and the legs are attached to the thorax.

Most insects have a tough outer shell covering the body. This shell is called an exoskeleton. It protects and supports the body—just like our skeleton, but from the outside, not the inside. The shell is waterproof and also prevents the insect from drying out in extreme heat.

Metamorphosis

Most insects lay eggs, although a few give birth to live young. Some insects lay one egg at a time. Others, like termites, can lay more than 10,000 eggs in a day.

Most insects go through several forms as they become adult. This is called metamorphosis, from the Greek meaning "change in shape." Ants, bees, beetles, butterflies, moths, and wasps all undergo this process.

The young creature that hatches from an insect egg is called a larva. The plural is larvae. Larvae look somewhat like worms. Some larvae, such as the caterpillars of butterflies, have more than six legs.

As soon as a larva hatches, it begins to eat and grow. As it grows bigger, it sheds its outer skin and grows a new one. This process is called molting.

When larvae reach full size, they stop eating. Some hide underground, and others attach themselves to trees or other safe places. This stage of development is called the pupa. Many insects form a protective covering during this period. The pupa stage can last several weeks. Some

197

The giant swallowtail is the largest butterfly in North America.
▶

insects pupate over the winter. During this time the insect grows into an adult. Its body becomes ready for reproduction. Many insects grow wings.

When the insect is ready, the case splits, and the adult crawls out. It may take a few hours to dry out. If it is a winged insect, it is now ready to fly.

Some insects, including cicadas, crickets, dragonflies, grasshoppers, and lice, do not go through a full metamorphosis. When the young hatch from the eggs, they look like smaller versions of the adults, but with no wings. These small insects are called nymphs. As they grow, they molt when their skin becomes too tight, and those that are going to fly develop wings. This is called incomplete metamorphosis.

Senses

Insects have special organs for sensing the world around them. But an insect's sense organs are not the same as a human's. Insects feel, smell, and taste with their antennae. Some, like the male mosquito, can use their antennae to hear. Antennae are also used to test for humidity or temperature.

AMAZING FACTS!

When a bombardier beetle is disturbed, it lets out a puff of gas from the rear of its body to scare its enemy.
Adult mayflies only live for a few hours. However, some queen termites can live for up to 50 years.
The female Queen Alexandra's birdwing of New Guinea is the world's largest butterfly, with a wingspan of up to 12 ½ in. (32cm)
Some beetles can lift 300 times their own weight.

Using their antennae, insects can smell food and identify the right plants on which to lay their eggs. Female insects produce hormones, called pheromones. The antennae of male insects can detect this scent, sometimes at a distance of more than a mile.

Insects taste with tiny hairs on the antennae and mouth. Many insects can also taste with their feet. Hairs on the antennae, skeleton, and feet enable insects to feel. Some insects, such as flies, can feel with their wings.

Insects have compound eyes. Each eye has several different lenses, called facets. Some insect's eyes have only nine facets; some dragonflies' eyes have 28,000. Each facet sees an image of part of an object. Nerves carry these images to the brain, where they are put together as one complete image. Insects cannot see an object clearly if it is more than 3 ft. (about 1m) away.

Most insects have an eye on each side of the head. This helps them see in all directions. Insects, especially plant-eating species, can see some colors.

Most insects also have additional simple eyes, called ocelli. They are probably for sensing light and dark.

Insects' "ears" are on different parts of their bodies. A grasshopper's ears are on its abdomen, beneath the wings. Other insects have simple ears near the

BUTTERFLY LIFE CYCLE

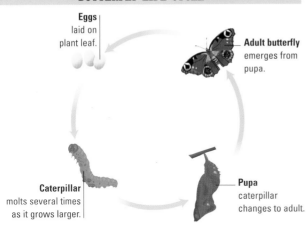

Eggs laid on plant leaf.

Adult butterfly emerges from pupa.

Caterpillar molts several times as it grows larger.

Pupa caterpillar changes to adult.

Butterflies and moths go through four stages of development in their life cycles.

antennae. Some butterflies and moths are deaf. The insects with the best hearing are those that make sounds, such as cicadas, crickets, and katydids. Some of the sounds are so high-pitched that they cannot be heard by humans.

Eating

Insects eat many different things in many different ways. Some insects eat other insects. The ladybug beetle feeds on aphids (insects that live by sucking the juice from plants) and is therefore welcomed by humans into their gardens. The praying mantis also eats garden pests and is sometimes a cannibal—after mating, the female eats the male. Dragonflies feed mainly on gnats and mosquitoes, but may also eat small fish and frogs.

Mosquitoes suck blood from other animals, including humans. They can pass on diseases, such as malaria. Other insects lay eggs inside animals' bodies. Sometimes, when the eggs hatch, the larvae eat the animal from the inside.

Bees and most butterflies and moths take nectar and pollen from plants. The caterpillars of some butterflies and moths only live on one plant. The caterpillar of the monarch butterfly, for example, will die if it cannot find milkweed. On the other hand, some insects, such as cockroaches, will eat anything.

The eating habits of some insects cause problems for humans. Termites can destroy wooden buildings. Locusts and Colorado beetles destroy crops.

The shape of an insect's mouth depends on its diet. Some insects' mouths are long tubes that can drink nectar from flowers or suck blood from animals. Other insects, such as ants and cockroaches, have powerful jaws. An insect's mouth will often change during its lifetime. A butterfly will have jaws when it is a caterpillar, then a tube when it is an adult.

Like most animals, insects must digest their food. Saliva pours into the mouth and begins to digest the food with chemicals called enzymes. More chemicals break the food down as it passes through the body.

The Colorado beetle is a serious pest of potatoes.

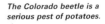

The eyes of a fly have thousands of lenses that enable it to detect the slightest movement.

Defense and societies

Insects use color for defense. Some disguise themselves so that they blend into their surroundings. That is called camouflage. Some moths and butterflies fool their enemies by looking like an insect that is bad tasting or has a poisonous sting. That is called mimicry. Many stinging insects are brightly colored to warn their enemies that they are poisonous and to stay away.

Many insects live in large groups called societies. Examples include ants, termites, and some bees. They help each other by dividing labor. In that way they achieve more collectively than they could if they all worked alone.

Movement

When an insect walks it moves three legs forward at the same time. They are the front and hind legs on one side, and the middle leg on the other. This way, the insect is always resting on at least three of its legs. Most insect legs end in a pair of claws and a sticky pad. They allow the insect to grip slippery surfaces or even to walk upside down on ceilings.

Flying insects have very thin wings that look like cellophane. Many insects can move their wings at great speed. A housefly's wings beat about 345 times a second. Hawkmoths and dragonflies can fly at over 30 mph (48km/h).

SEE ALSO: Camouflage; Flower

Ladybug beetles on a fava bean leaf search for aphids, their staple diet.

✳ INUIT

The Inuit are the native people who live in the Arctic areas of Greenland, Canada, Alaska, and Siberia. Today there are almost 100,000 Inuit.

The Inuit first came to North America and Greenland from Asia about 5,500 years ago. They are descended from an ancient people in Siberia, now part of Russia. The word *Inuit* means "the people."

The first Europeans to encounter the Inuit were a Scandinavian people called the Vikings who settled in Greenland in about A.D. 1200. After 1850 whalers and fur traders began to settle in the Arctic. They brought diseases, such as smallpox and diphtheria, that killed many Inuit people. They also killed animals in huge numbers, threatening the Inuit way of life.

An Inuit man wearing caribou furs checks the sealskin line on his harpoon at Grise Fiord, Ellesmere Island, northern Canada.
▼

From the 1960s the Inuit began a campaign to preserve their own language and culture. On April 1, 1999, the Canadian government created a new territory, Nunavut, meaning "our land," which is administered by the Inuit people.

Way of life

Before the 1800s the Inuit usually lived in small groups of fewer than 50 people. They spent winter near the coast, hunting seals and fish. In summer they moved inland to hunt caribou. They traveled on dog sleds and in open boats called *umiaks*. They lived in tents made of animal skins or, sometimes, in shelters, called *igloos*, made of snow and ice.

Today only about 10 percent of the Inuit still live off the land all the year around. Most live in wood-frame houses, with modern conveniences such as heating, telephones, and televisions. Most people wear modern, Western clothes. Inuit children attend modern schools. However, most Inuit are still aware of the customs and culture of their people. On the weekends many go hunting and fishing, much as their ancestors did centuries ago.

Traditionally the Inuit believe in a supernatural power called Sila and a number of powerful spirits. Today many Inuit have adopted Christianity.

The Inuit language has been spoken for thousands of years but has only recently been written down. In Greenland Inuit is an official language equal in status to Danish. Inuit is taught in school in Alaska and Canada.

SEE ALSO: Canada; Vikings

✳ INVENTORS AND INVENTIONS

An invention is a new and unique technical or scientific solution to a specific problem. Without inventions there would be no progress.

An invention is different from a discovery. Finding a new metal is a discovery; making a new machine is an invention.

Until the invention of paper and printing knowledge of new technology spread very slowly, and things were often invented or reinvented in different places and at different times. Often historians have no way of knowing who invented a particular thing, or when it was invented.

Although today we think of inventors as specific individuals, in the past it was often impossible to say who invented something. Many people made small improvements in the objects they used, and gradually new objects developed.

Earliest inventions

Some of the earliest inventions were wood or stone tools for cutting down trees and killing animals to eat. Later, metal tools were invented.

The wheel was invented in about 3500–3000 B.C., and people or animals no longer had to carry loads. At about the same time, writing was invented, enabling people to make permanent records.

Another great advance was made when people learned to use the energy of natural forces such as running water and wind. The waterwheel, invented about 2,000 years ago, was the first source of energy that did not rely on muscle power.

Printing using woodblocks was invented by the Chinese around A.D 700. The invention of movable type—a more flexible system using metal blocks—in Germany in the 15th century meant that books and knowledge became much more widely available.

Patents

To safeguard an invention, many inventors file a patent. A patent is the rights given by a government to an inventor. They

▲
The invention of wheeled vehicles revolutionized transportation— people no longer had to drag or carry loads. This panel, showing a horse-drawn cart, dates from about 2500 B.C.

◄
This painting shows a steam engine pumping water from a coal mine in England during the 1700s.

FAMOUS INVENTORS

These are just a few of the people who have become known for their inventions. There are many, many more.

Archimedes (about 287–212 B.C.)
Ancient Greek mathematician who invented many things, including a device, called the Archimedes' screw, for raising water.

Galilei, Galileo (1564–1642)
Italian mathematician and physicist who invented the telescope. He used it to discover the four moons of Jupiter, sunspots, and many new stars.

Harrison, John (1693–1776)
English clockmaker who perfected the marine chronometer, a clock so accurate that sailors could calculate their position correctly.

Watt, James (1736–1819)
Scottish instrument maker whose steam engine (patented 1769) was used throughout the mills and factories of the Industrial Revolution.

Daguerre, Louis (Louis-Jacques-Mandé) (1789–1851)
French painter who perfected permanent photographs on silver-coated copper plates—daguerreotypes—in 1839.

Faraday, Michael (1791–1867)
British scientist who discovered that electricity was present in a wire moving near a magnet, leading to the invention of the electric generator.

Morse, Samuel (Finley Breese) (1791–1872)
American inventor of the electric telegraph for sending long-distance messages and an alphabet system of dots and dashes called the Morse code.

Bell, Alexander Graham (1847–1922)
Scottish American teacher who specialized in teaching the deaf to speak. He filed a patent for the telephone in 1876.

Edison, Thomas Alva (1847–1931)
American technological genius who invented hundreds of devices, including the phonograph (early record player) and the first workable electric lighting system.

include the right to make and sell the invention or discovery, or to profit from it by allowing another person or company to sell or use it. The first recorded patent dates from 1421 in Florence, Italy.

Scientific inventions

The 17th and 18th centuries saw many scientific inventions. The telescope enabled astronomers to study the stars and planets, while the microscope was important for the study of biology. The invention of the steam engine made large quantities of power available wherever and whenever needed.

Michael Faraday was a chemist and a physicist. He conducted pioneering experiments in electricity and magnetism. ▼

Some of the most important discoveries of the early 19th century had to do with electricity. In 1800 an Italian scientist, Alessandro Volta, invented the electric battery, from which an electric current could be obtained. The battery was followed by the electric generator and the light bulb.

Increased technical knowledge brought many new inventions: the electric telegraph in 1837, the telephone in 1876, and the wireless telegraph (forerunner of the radio) in 1896. The invention of the internal-combustion engine led to automobiles and airplanes. From 1957 communications satellites began to relay telephone calls and television signals worldwide. Engineers and scientists continue to develop more advanced devices, such as robotic space probes.

SEE ALSO: Aircraft; Ancient Civilizations; Astronomy; Bicycle & Motorcycle; Car; Communication; Edison, Thomas Alva; Electricity; Engine; Industrial Revolution; Magnetism; Microscope; Photography; Printing; Radar & Sonar; Radio; Robot; Sound Recording; Technology; Telecommunications; Television; Wright, Orville & Wilbur; X-ray

* IRELAND, REPUBLIC OF

An island in the North Atlantic Ocean, most of
Ireland is occupied by the Republic of Ireland.
Northern Ireland is part of the United Kingdom.

Ireland's national flag

The center of Ireland is a plain covered with farm fields and peat bogs. Around this area is a ring of hills and low mountains. There are many lakes and rivers. Ireland's climate is greatly affected by the surrounding seas. Winters are mild, summers are cool, and even in the driest months it often rains.

People
Most Irish people are descended from the ancient Celts, who came from what is now France. Almost everyone speaks English, and Gaelic (Irish) is spoken in some areas. Irish authors, most of whom write in English, have won fame as novelists, poets, and dramatists. Irish music is popular around the world. The Irish are also sports lovers who enjoy Gaelic football and horse racing.

Economy
In the past Ireland's economy was based on agriculture because its climate is ideal for raising cattle and growing oats and potatoes. Today service industries—especially businesses related to tourism—bring in more than half of the country's annual income. Irish companies make and export a wide range of goods, including cloth, whiskey, beer, crystal, chemicals, pharmaceuticals, machinery, and transportation equipment.

History
In the fifth century A.D. Saint Patrick brought Christianity to Ireland. As a result many monasteries were built, Irish monks brought Christianity to Europe, and Ireland became a center of learning.

The English first invaded in 1171. From the late 17th century Protestant English and Scottish settlers governed a Roman Catholic majority. That led to long-running conflict. After a war of independence (1919–21) the island was split into the Irish Free State (now the Republic of Ireland) and Northern Ireland, which is still part of the United Kingdom.

IRELAND

North Channel
NORTHERN IRELAND (U.K.)
Donegal Bay
Belfast ●
IRELAND
Irish Sea
Dublin ■
Galway
Galway Bay
ATLANTIC OCEAN
Shannon River
Limerick
Waterford
Dingle Peninsula
Cork ●
River Lee
Celtic Sea

The Dingle Peninsula—the large amount of rainfall in Ireland makes the countryside very green and has given rise to the nickname "The Emerald Isle."

SEE ALSO:
United Kingdom

✳ ISLAM

Islam is one of the world's major religions. More than one billion people, called Muslims, follow the teachings of Islam. Muslims believe in Allah.

The Muslim religion is based on statements, or revelations, that Muslims believe came from Allah through prophets. Those prophets include Abraham, Moses, and Jesus. The most important of all the prophets, however, was Muhammad (about A.D. 570–632).

Muhammad was born in Mecca, in modern Saudi Arabia. Muslims believe that the angel Gabriel appeared to him and passed on the teachings of Allah. Muhammad began to preach and attracted many followers. Opponents forced him to flee from Mecca in 622. He went to the city of Medina. His flight is called the *hegira* (migration). It is the starting point of the Islamic calendar.

By the time Muhammad died, Islam had become the main religion in Arabia. It soon spread, and today it is the religion of one-fifth of the world's population.

Islamic beliefs

The word Islam means "submission." Muslims submit to the will of Allah, an all-powerful, loving God. The teachings and laws of Islam are contained in a holy book called the Koran. Other teachings are in the *Hadith*, a collection of stories about the life and sayings of Muhammad.

Islamic law, or *shari'a*, forbids killing, stealing, lying, eating pork, and drinking alcohol. The Muslim also has five key duties, called the five pillars of Islam. *Shahadah* is the profession of faith. Every Muslim believes that there is one God, and that Muhammad is his messenger and prophet. *Salat* is prayer. Muslims must pray five times a day. At noon on Friday they attend the mosque, the main place of worship. *Zakat* is charity. Muslims must give part of their income to the poor. *Sawm* is fasting. No adult Muslim, apart from pregnant women and the sick, may eat during daylight in the sacred month of Ramadan. The fifth pillar of Islam is *Hajj*, or pilgrimage. All Muslims who can afford to do so must travel to the holy city of Mecca at least once during their life.

▲
A mosque in Washington, D.C. The mosque is the place where Muslims gather for prayer. It also acts as a community center.

SEE ALSO: Religion

✳ ISLAND

An island is a landmass smaller than a continent that is completely surrounded by water. Islands vary enormously in size and origin.

Geographers divide islands into two main groups—continental and oceanic. Continental islands were once connected to the mainland. Changes in the Earth's crust or sea level mean that sections of land became separated from the main part of a continent. Great Britain is an example of a continental island—it was once part of the mainland of Europe.

Most of the world's islands are oceanic—they were never joined to a continent. Oceanic islands can be volcanic or coral. Volcanic islands are created when lava—liquid rock—erupts beneath the surface of the ocean. The lava cools and becomes solid, and builds up until it rises above sea level. The Hawaiian islands and Iceland are volcanic islands. Coral islands are created by accumulations of tiny sea animals called polyps. Many islands in the South Pacific are made of coral.

There are other, less common kinds of island that differ in size and origin. A tidal island is part of the mainland. When the tide is high, it is cut off and cannot be reached on foot. Floating islands are made from matted vegetation and soil. They are found in rivers such as the Nile, Africa, and along coasts such as in Southeast Asia. Barrier islands are made from fine soil deposited by offshore waters.

Isolation

An island is surrounded by water, and so it can be difficult to reach. That means some islands have a unique plant and animal life found nowhere else. When settlers bring new plants and animals

Keas are the world's only mountain parrot and live only on the South Island of New Zealand. Because thousands were killed in the past, they are now protected.
▼

with them, they often destroy the island's native plants and creatures. Isolation also makes islands easier to defend. In World War II (1939–45), for example, Germany captured much of continental Europe but could not invade the island of Great Britain. Some islands, such as Alcatraz, California, were used as prisons. Some small islands are so remote that they have problems with communication. They may not receive food supplies or mail for months because airplanes and large boats are unable to land there.

Coral reef around Vava'u, one of the islands that form the Pacific nation of Tonga.

SOME IMPORTANT ISLANDS AND ISLAND GROUPS

Aleutian Islands (U.S.)
A group of about 150 volcanic islands that extends about 1,200 miles (1,900km) southwest from the Alaska Peninsula.

Alexander Archipelago (U.S.)
A chain of more than 1,000 islands off the southeastern coast of Alaska made up of the summits of submerged mountain ranges.

Borneo
The world's third largest island, located in the western section of the Pacific Ocean, includes parts of Malaysia and Indonesia, and the whole of Brunei.

Canary Islands (Spain)
A group of seven major islands in the North Atlantic Ocean off the northwestern coast of Africa.

Cape Breton Island (Canada)
The island was a separate British colony until 1820, when it was united with Nova Scotia.

Faroe (or Faeroe) Islands (Denmark)
A group of 18 volcanic islands in the North Atlantic Ocean.

Greenland, or Kalaallit Nunaat (Denmark)
The world's largest island is set in the North Atlantic Ocean.

Iceland
An island nation in the North Atlantic Ocean.

New Guinea
The second largest island in the world, in the Pacific Ocean, it is divided between Irian Jaya (Papua), part of Indonesia, in the west, and the nation of Papua New Guinea in the east.

Sicily (Italy)
The largest island in the Mediterranean Sea, it lies just off the southwestern tip of Italy.

SEE ALSO: Caribbean Sea & Islands; Cuba; Easter Island; Indonesia; Ireland, Republic of; Japan; New Zealand; Ocean & Sea; Pacific Islands; Philippines; Prince Edward Island; United Kingdom; Volcano

✱ ISRAEL

Israel is a small nation on the eastern shore of the Mediterranean Sea in an area known as Palestine. The modern state was formed in 1948.

Israel's national flag

The center of Israel is a range of hills running north to south. To the east is the valley of the Jordan River. To the west is a coastal plain of varying width. To the south is the Negev Desert.

People

About 80 percent of Israel's population is Jewish. Many are immigrants from the United States, Eastern Europe, and other areas. The remainder are mostly Arabs.

History

The earliest records of the Jewish people in the area now called Israel date from about 2000 B.C. Over the years the region was ruled by many other powers.

From 1920 to 1948 Palestine was controlled by Britain. During World War II (1939–45) the Nazi Party of Germany killed over six million Jews. Many survivors wanted to join the Jews living in Palestine, and Britain supported the idea of a Jewish homeland. On May 14, 1948, David Ben-Gurion (1886–1973) declared

the independence of the State of Israel. Within hours neighboring Arab countries attacked Israel. Thousands of Arab Muslims were forced from their homes and land and fled to the Gaza Strip and the West Bank. Israel has remained in conflict with its Arab neighbors ever since.

After a war in 1967 Israel occupied the Gaza Strip, the West Bank, and the Golan Heights. The main issue facing Israel today is whether the Palestinians, who make up the majority of the population in the Gaza Strip and the West Bank, should be allowed to form their own state.

Jerusalem, the capital of Israel, is a holy city for three faiths—Christianity, Judaism, and Islam.

ISRAEL

Mediterranean Sea

LEBANON
SYRIA
GOLAN HEIGHTS
Haifa
Tiberius
Nazareth
Jordan River
WEST BANK
Tel Aviv–Jaffa
Jerusalem
Bethlehem
Dead Sea
GAZA STRIP
Beersheba
JORDAN
NEGEV
EGYPT
Occupied Territories
Gulf of Aqaba
Elat

👀 SEE ALSO: Holocaust; Islam; Judaism; Middle East; Palestine; Religion; United Nations; World War II

✳ ITALY

A country in southern Europe, Italy consists mainly of a long, narrow peninsula shaped like a boot and many islands, including Sardinia and Sicily.

Italy is dominated by mountains. In the north are the Alps. They rise to heights of between 14,800 and nearly 15,800 ft. (4,500–4,800m). Another mountain chain, the Apennines, runs from the northwest south to the tip of the "boot." San Marino, one of the world's smallest countries, is located on their eastern slopes.

South of the Alps is the valley of the Po River. It is Italy's largest and most fertile plain, and the site of major cities such as Milan and Turin. The cities of Rome and Florence lie on the central plains.

The south is dominated by the great port of Naples. Sardinia and most of Sicily, the more heavily populated of the two islands, are mountainous. The south often has severe earthquakes. The active volcano of Vesuvius can be seen from Naples. Sicily has the highest active volcano in Europe—Mount Etna.

Climate
Italy has a generally moderate climate, with regional variations. The Po Valley has damp, warm summers, fairly cold winters with occasional snowfall, and considerable rainfall. In the south and on the islands winters are cool and rainy, and summers hot and dry. The mountainous regions on the mainland have the severest winters. Rainfall is heaviest in the north and lightest in the south and on the islands.

Plant and animal life
Most of Italy's remaining forests are in the north. Trees include fir, larch, oak, beech, and chestnut. Poplars are common in Tuscany (around Florence), and olive trees thrive on the lower Apennines. Bears, wild goats, deer, and chamois (a kind of antelope) still live in the mountains.

Religion
Roman Catholicism is the main religion. Vatican City, the world's smallest country, lies within the city of Rome. It is ruled by the pope, who is the bishop of Rome and head of the Roman Catholic Church.

Economy
Before World War II (1939–45) more than half of Italy's workers were employed in agriculture. Today only about 6 percent of the labor force works on the land. In the 1950s Italy became one of the founding members of the European Community (or Common Market), an economic union of several western European nations. By the 1970s Italy had become one of the most powerful industrial nations in Europe. Most industries are located in the north, especially in the triangle bounded by the cities of Turin, Milan, and Genoa.

History
Many myths and legends surround the origins of civilization in Italy, particularly the founding of Rome, but little is actually known about early settlement. The Romans established a republic in about 500 B.C. and eventually built an empire that included much of Europe, northern Africa, and western Asia. The western half of the Roman Empire collapsed in the fifth century A.D., and power passed to the

According to legend, the city of Rome was founded by Romulus. He and his twin brother, Remus, were abandoned by their parents and brought up by a she-wolf.

◄

KEY FACTS

Italy's national flag

OFFICIAL NAME
Repubblica Italiana

AREA
116,320 sq. mi.
(301,268 sq. km)

POPULATION
57,298,000

CAPITAL
Rome

LARGEST CITY
Milan

MAJOR RELIGION
Roman Catholicism

MAJOR LANGUAGE
Italian

CURRENCY
Euro

eastern half of the empire, later called the Byzantine Empire.

The peninsula was broken up into many competing states. The Renaissance, the great rebirth of European culture, began in Italy in the early 1300s and lasted into the 1600s.

The areas of land that make up Italy were finally unified between 1859 and 1870. Economic progress was interrupted in 1915, when Italy entered World War I (1914–18). In 1926 Benito Mussolini, leader of the Fascist Party, became dictator (supreme ruler). His alliance with Nazi Germany in World War II (1938–45) left Italy's economy in ruins. Defeat in the war brought an end to fascism and the monarchy. In 1946 Italy became a republic.

SEE ALSO: Caesar, Julius; Renaissance; Roman Empire; World War I; World War II

The port of Venice in northeast Italy is built on mud flats and more than 100 islands. Its main thoroughfares are canals.

✳ JAPAN

Japan is a nation in the North Pacific Ocean. Its
many islands form an arc about 1,500 miles
(2,400km) long off the eastern coast of Asia.

The four main islands of Japan are
Hokkaido, Honshu, Shikoku, and Kyushu.
Honshu, containing the main
farming regions, has about
three-fifths of Japan's land area
and is home to four-fifths of its
people. Hokkaido, to the north, is
rugged and cold. Southerly Kyushu is
densely populated. Shikoku, between
Kyushu and Honshu, has fewer
inhabitants.

*The white-naped
crane is one of
Japan's most
beautiful and rare
native birds.*

   Almost three-quarters of
Japan is mountainous, and
about two-thirds is heavily forested. There
are many volcanoes, and earthquakes are
very common.

   Japan gets about 40–100 in. (1,000–
2,500mm) of rainfall each year. Pleasant
springtimes and hot, humid summers give
way to clear, bright falls and cool to cold
winters. Snow is heavy in the north.
Steep hills and rushing rivers provide
Japan with hydroelectric power
(electricity created from flowing water).

*Dancers wear
traditional kimono
costumes at a
cherry blossom
festival in Kyoto.*

People
Japan is one of the world's most densely
populated countries, and more than 80
percent of the Japanese live in cities.
Tokyo, the capital, is the world's largest
city. Yokohama, Kobe, and Osaka are
major seaports. Other big cities are Kyoto,
Nagoya, Sapporo, and Kitakyushu.
Most Japanese follow
both Shinto and
Buddhism.
Shinto
involves
the worship
of ancestors and the
spirits of nature. There
are many festivals through
the year, and New Year's Day
is an especially important date.

Economy
Because Japan has little flat land for
farming, much of the nation's food is
imported. The main locally produced
food is rice, which is grown on tiny, flat
paddies—or flooded fields—on hillsides.
Fishing is also very important.

   Since the late 1800s Japan has grown
into an industrial giant known especially
for its high-quality cars and electronic
goods, such as televisions.

History
The earliest settlers of Japan came from
the Asian mainland in about 8000 B.C. By
A.D. 400 Japan was a network of small
states ruled by powerful clans. Japan was
greatly influenced by China. The Japanese
adopted the Chinese writing system and
calendar, and borrowed their techniques
for weaving silk.

   The Japanese believed that the emperor
was divine, but from about the ninth
century he had little real power. Warring
clans grew increasingly powerful. Each lord

211

had his own army of samurai. They were skilled warriors who believed that honor was more important than death. By 1185 the Minamoto clan was the most powerful. In 1192 the emperor gave their chief, Yoritomo, the title of *shogun*, great general. This was the start of a new style of military government that ruled Japan for the next 700 years.

During the 1600s Japan shut itself off from the outside world. No one could leave or enter except for a few traders. In 1868 a group of young samurai overthrew the shogun in favor of the Emperor Meiji. They were determined to make Japan a strong, modern nation that would be the military and economic equal of Western nations.

Japan began to increase its international trade and developed its industry. It won wars against China in 1894–95 and Russia in 1904–5, and invaded Manchuria in China in the 1930s. During World War II (1939–45) Japan sided with Germany and attacked the U.S. fleet at Pearl Harbor, Hawaii, on December 7, 1941. That brought the United States into the war. In August 1945 the United States dropped two atomic bombs on the cities of Hiroshima and Nagasaki, and Japan surrendered. Helped at first by the United States, Japan quickly rebuilt its economy to become one of the world's richest and strongest nations.

JAPAN (map)

CHINA
RUSSIA
Sea of Okhotsk
HOKKAIDO
Sapporo
NORTH KOREA
Sea of Japan
HONSHU
NORTH PACIFIC OCEAN
SOUTH KOREA
Korea Strait
Toyama Bay
Wakasa Bay
Kyoto
Mt. Fuji
Nagoya
Tokyo
Yokohama
Kobe
Osaka
Hiroshima
Kitakyushu
SHIKOKU
Nagasaki
KYUSHU
East China Sea
Ryukyu Islands
Naha

KEY FACTS

OFFICIAL NAME
Japan

AREA
145,887 sq. mi.
(377,819 sq. km)

POPULATION
126,714,000

CAPITAL & LARGEST CITY
Tokyo

MAJOR RELIGIONS
Shinto, Buddhism

MAJOR LANGUAGE
Japanese

CURRENCY
Yen

Japan's national flag

The sacred Mount Fuji, or Fujiyama, is an extinct volcano on Honshu island. It is 12,388 ft. (3,776m) high.

SEE ALSO:
Buddhism;
Religion;
World War II

✳ JUDAISM

Judaism is the religion of the Jewish people, a cultural and ethnic group that came originally from the Middle East but spread across the world.

The Jews believe that their ancient leader Moses presented his people with a set of laws. Most of these laws are included in the Torah (also called the Pentateuch), the first five books of the Jewish bible. The Jewish bible is the original Hebrew text of what Christians know as the Old Testament.

The Jews entered into a covenant—an agreement—with God. They would keep to his laws, and he would protect them and make their land fertile. The Jews see themselves as a chosen people of God.

Jewish life

The history of the Jews has been marked by long periods of exile and suffering. Jewish people have settled all over the world, especially in Europe and North America. Over thousands of years Jews have interpreted their laws and faith in different ways. Some are very orthodox and believe that anything that goes against the Torah is sinful; others are more relaxed and liberal.

The main Jewish place of worship is the synagogue, or *shul*. The leader of each community is the rabbi, which means "teacher" in Hebrew.

The Jewish sabbath runs from sunset on Friday to sunset on Saturday. No work is done during this period. On Friday evening the whole family gathers for a special meal. On Saturday morning people attend the synagogue for a service.

The main Jewish festivals are Passover, which celebrates the escape of the Jews from Egypt, and Yom Kippur, or Day of Atonement, when Jews pray for forgiveness for their sins.

▲ *A rabbi serves food during Seder, a religious meal shared in the first two days of Passover.*

When a boy reaches the age of 13, he becomes Bar Mitzvah— son of the commandment—and is allowed to read from the Torah in the synagogue. Recently some branches of Judaism have allowed girls to become Bat Mitzvah—daughter of the commandment.

SEE ALSO: Holocaust; Israel; Religion

✳ JUPITER

Jupiter is the largest planet in the solar system. It is so vast that more than one thousand Earths could fit inside it.

The surface of Jupiter. The black spot in the lower left of the photograph is the shadow of Europa, one of the 28 moons that are known to orbit the planet.

KEY FACTS

POSITION IN SOLAR SYSTEM
Fifth planet from sun

AVERAGE DISTANCE FROM THE SUN
483,000,000 mi.
(778,000,000 km)

SOLAR ORBIT
11.9 Earth years

DIAMETER
89,000 mi.
(143,000 km)

MASS
1,900 quintillion tons

ATMOSPHERE
Hydrogen, helium

AXIAL ROTATION
9 hrs 55 mins

Unlike the Earth, Jupiter does not have a solid surface. It is a huge ball of gases, including 82 percent hydrogen, 14 percent helium, and 4 percent other elements. It is referred to as a gas giant.

If you were to travel toward the center of this ball, you would find the gases getting hotter and denser, and the pressure increasing. The pressure of the gases, or atmosphere, is so strong at the center that hydrogen becomes a hot, molten metal. Astronomers believe that the deepest layers of Jupiter have a temperature of about 36,000°F (20,000°C).

Jupiter has a magnetic field that is 10 times stronger than the field around the Earth. The circulation of molten metal at the center creates an electric current, which generates the magnetic field.

Moons and clouds

In 1610 the Italian scientist Galileo discovered four moons circling, or orbiting, Jupiter. They were named Ganymede, Io, Callisto, and Europa. Later, astronomers found more moons. Scientists now know of 28 moons around the planet. The largest, Ganymede, has a diameter of 3,270 miles (5,270km), slightly larger than the planet Mercury.

Clouds of ammonia and water, some of which are brightly colored with other elements, surround Jupiter. These clouds are blown around the planet, some of them at speeds of up to 350 mph (560km/h). The most amazing feature of Jupiter's clouds is a huge orange-red, oval-shaped area over twice the width of the Earth, called the Great Red Spot. It is made up of violently swirling gases rising from deep inside the planet. In the 1970s the Voyager space probe found that the Great Red Spot has a continuing source of energy and is something like an everlasting tornado.

The Voyager probe also discovered that Jupiter is surrounded by three thin, delicate rings of very small rocks. Previously astronomers had believed that Saturn was the only planet with rings.

A closeup of Jupiter's Great Red Spot.

SEE ALSO: Astronomy; Solar System; Space Exploration

*KOREA

The divided country of Korea lies on a peninsula in East Asia situated between China and Japan.

Korea was freed from 35 years of Japanese rule in 1945. Three years later the country was divided into two states—the Republic of Korea (South Korea) and the Democratic People's Republic of Korea (North Korea).

Land and climate
Although Korea has wide, fertile valleys in the south and west that produce rice and other crops, the rest of the countryside is mountainous. Only about one-fifth of the land is suitable for farming. The highest of the Korean mountains is Paektu-san (Changpai), an extinct volcano that rises to 9,003 ft. (2,744m).

In the northern inland areas winter temperatures remain below freezing for five months. Along the southern coasts warm ocean currents moderate temperatures so that they rarely fall below freezing. All of Korea has hot summers.

People
Although North Korea is the larger of the two states in area, South Korea has nearly twice as many people. Most of the population is concentrated in lowland areas in the west and south.

The main religions are Buddhism, Christianity, and a native Korean religion called Chondokyo, or "religion of the heavenly way." In North Korea, where a communist government holds power, all forms of religion are strongly discouraged.

Economy
The economy of North Korea is controlled by the state. North Korea aims to meet all its own needs for food and other goods. It has little foreign trade, and most of that is with neighboring China. South Korea, by contrast, has concentrated on producing goods for export and is now the world's 11th largest trading country.

History
Korea's history dates back thousands of years. China and Japan have been a strong influence on Korea throughout its history. Both North and South Korea were admitted to the United Nations in 1991. Later that year they signed a treaty of reconciliation and nonaggression.

KOREA

North Korea's national flag

South Korea's national flag

SEE ALSO: Buddhism; China; Japan; Korean War

KEY FACTS

OFFICIAL NAME
Democratic People's Republic of Korea (North Korea)

AREA
46,540 sq. mi. (120,538 sq. km)

POPULATION
24,039,000

CAPITAL & LARGEST CITY
Pyongyang

MAJOR RELIGION
None

MAJOR LANGUAGE
Korean

CURRENCY
Won

OFFICIAL NAME
Republic of Korea (South Korea)

AREA
38,025 sq. mi. (98,484 sq. km)

POPULATION
46,844,000

CAPITAL & LARGEST CITY
Seoul

MAJOR RELIGIONS
Buddhism, Christianity, Chondokyo

MAJOR LANGUAGE
Korean

CURRENCY
Won

✴ KOREAN WAR

The Korean War lasted from 1950 until 1953. It began when the armed forces of the Democratic People's Republic of Korea invaded the Republic of Korea.

On June 25, 1950, the military forces of communist North Korea crossed the 38th parallel, the line dividing Korea into two parts. The attack was aimed at reuniting the country under communist rule. Two days later the United Nations approved a resolution, introduced by the United States, asking member nations to provide assistance to South Korea.

United Nations forces patrol through a ruined South Korean village in 1950.
▼

United Nations defense

Sixteen countries, under the flag of the United Nations, sent military forces to South Korea's defense. Most troops came from the United States. Many others contributed equipment and supplies. North Korea's main allies were the Soviet Union, which supplied it with arms, and China, which later poured masses of troops into the conflict. Within the first two days of war the well-equipped and well-trained North Korean forces had pushed aside the outnumbered and poorly trained Republic of Korea army and captured Seoul, the South Korean capital. On September 15, 1950, the United Nations forces launched a combined naval, marine, and army attack on the North Korean-occupied port of Inchon, on South Korea's west coast. It was hazardous and daring but successful. Seoul was recaptured in late September, and in October North Korean troops retreated back across the 38th parallel.

Peaceful conclusion

By June 1951 a stalemate had developed, with both sides entrenched along the 38th parallel. The war became one of brutal fighting, as each side fought for a small advantage over the other.

The war raged across the Korean peninsula, causing enormous destruction and loss of life before an armistice was signed in 1953. Military casualties on both sides exceeded 1.5 million. More than 54,000 Americans had died in action or from injuries and disease. Millions of Koreans had died, and many more were left homeless or had become refugees.

The Soviet Union proposed negotiations for a ceasefire at the United Nations on June 23, 1951, but the talks continued for two years until the armistice was finally signed on July 27, 1953. Militarily, the war ended with a victory for neither side; but the aggression against South Korea had been repulsed, and the right of states to be free from the threat or use of force had been preserved.

👀
SEE ALSO:
Korea;
United
Nations

✳ LAKE

A lake is an inland body of water in a depression in the surface of the land called a basin. The water in a lake can be fresh or salty.

Lake basins can form in several ways. Some are made by movements of the Earth's crust; others are carved out by ice in glaciers or by waves of water. Some lakes form in the craters of extinct volcanoes. Other lakes are artificial, created as reservoirs or behind dams.

Lakes are formed when water flows into these depressions. It might enter across the surface, from rivers or streams, or from underground, flowing out of springs or groundwater.

When the climate is humid, more water flows into a basin than escapes through evaporation. The level of water in the basin rises, forming a lake. If the climate is dry, water is lost through evaporation, leaving crusty deposits of salty minerals on the bed and sides of the lake. Saline, or saltwater, lakes include the Great Salt Lake in the United States and the Dead Sea in the Middle East.

Many lakes disappear over the years. Rivers can form, and they drain water away. Sometimes the basin fills with mud, silt, and vegetation, until the lake becomes a swamp. Changes in climate can cause a lake's water to evaporate.

THE WORLD'S LARGEST LAKES

1. Caspian Sea, Asia	143,550 sq. mi.	(371,800 sq. km)
2. Superior, North America	31,820 sq. mi.	(82,414 sq. km)
3. Victoria, Africa	26,868 sq. mi.	(69,485 sq. km)
4. Huron, North America	23,010 sq. mi.	(59,596 sq. km)
5. Michigan, North America	22,400 sq. mi.	(58,016 sq. km)
6. Tanganyika, Africa	12,700 sq. mi.	(32,893 sq. km)
7. Great Bear, North America	12,275 sq. mi.	(31,800 sq. km)
8. Baikal, Russia	11,780 sq. mi.	(30,500 sq. km)
9. Malawi (Nyasa), Africa	11,430 sq. mi.	(29,603 sq. km)
10. Aral Sea, Asia	11,600 sq. mi.	(30,000 sq. km)

People and lakes

Lakes act as reservoirs, storing fresh water. People use lakes for fishing, boating, swimming, and when they freeze, ice-skating.

But people can also damage lakes. Companies and communities use them to dump sewage and other waste. Chemicals can cause weeds and algae to grow too fast. That uses up oxygen in the water and kills off other life in the lake.

Crater Lake, Oregon, stands on the site of a mountain that exploded in a volcanic eruption more than 6,000 years ago.
▼

SEE ALSO: Earth; Volcano; Wetlands

✳ LANGUAGE

Language is a set of sounds or symbols that a group of people use to communicate. Without language much human activity would be impossible.

The word *language* comes from the Latin *lingua*, meaning "tongue." The tongue is the most important organ in human speech. Most languages are spoken first, then written down later. Many animals can communicate with each other, but only humans can communicate complex ideas with speech.

No one knows exactly how languages developed. Some people think that the first words came from attempts by humans to copy natural sounds, such as running water or animal calls.

Over many centuries different cultures used different sounds to communicate. That is why people from various countries use languages that others might not understand. There are nearly 3,000 separate languages in the world today. They range from Chinese, English, and Spanish, which are spoken by billions of people, to tribal languages that are spoken by only a few thousand people. Sometimes it is hard to draw a clear line between a language and a dialect, which is a local variation of a language. Some languages, known as dead languages, stop being used. The most famous example is Latin, the language of the ancient Romans.

Written language

When all language was spoken, ideas, history, and many other forms of knowledge were passed from generation to generation because people memorized stories they were told. This is called oral tradition. From about 3500 B.C. the ancient Sumerians, who lived in what is now Iraq, developed the earliest known writing. Each word had a separate, unique picture, a system called pictograms. The Chinese still use this method of writing.

In about 1100 B.C. the Phoenicians, a Mediterranean people, began to use symbols that stood for sounds rather than words. They arranged these sound symbols to make parts of words. This was the first alphabet. Before this development people had to learn a new symbol for each word. Now that there was an alphabet, people only needed to learn a fixed number of symbols to make a written language.

How languages change

If you speak English, you are speaking the same language that George Washington spoke over 200 years ago. But the way you speak and the words you use would

▲
This clay cylinder from Sumer, dating from about 1800 B.C., is inscribed with cuneiform writing.

In World War II (1939–45) the U.S. army sent top-secret messages in Navajo, a language that was understood by very few people because it had not been written down.
▶

sound very strange to the first U.S. president. That is because languages change over time. People create new words for new things and ideas. Washington would not have known the words "television" or "airplane."

New words are coined, and existing words change their meaning, partly because of need and partly because of fashion. Some people think that new technological developments, such as e-mail, will make spoken and written English more informal.

Travel also affects language. When the Pilgrim Fathers came to North America, they spoke the same kind of English as

▲
Chinese children take part in a calligraphy (handwriting) class. Written Chinese contains more than 40,000 characters.

DID YOU KNOW?

Some languages are invented for a particular reason. Sign language was invented so that deaf people can communicate more easily. In 1887 a European professor invented Esperanto because he thought that if everybody spoke the same language, the world would be a more peaceful place. More recently scientists have created Lingua Cosmica. It is a language for communicating with creatures from other planets.

their neighbors in England. But over the years American English and British English have become different. Americans and Britons have different accents and use different words for the same things. For example an "elevator" is called a "lift" in Britain. There are similar differences between the Spanish used in Spain and the Spanish spoken in South America.

Learning language

Whatever their nationality, most children learn their language from listening to people around them and copying the sounds they make. The first voice they hear is usually that of their mothers, so

people's first language is called their mother tongue. Some children are brought up in places where more than one language is spoken, and they become bilingual—able to speak two languages.

After they have mastered their mother tongue, many people learn new languages. They do this in different ways. Some spend time in classes in which a foreign language is the only one spoken. This is called the immersion technique. It is similar to the way they learned their first language as babies. Others prefer to learn a new language from textbooks and teachers who use their own language. In either case the best way to learn a language is through regular practice, ideally talking with someone who speaks the language well.

SEE ALSO: Alphabet; Ancient Civilizations; Communication; Hearing; Shakespeare, William

✴ LASER
A laser is an instrument that produces a special kind of light. Laser light can be used to slice through steel—or to play your favorite CD.

Rays of light are swarms of photons (light particles) that travel in waves. The distance between the crest, or top, of one wave and the crest of the next wave is called a wavelength. Different colors of light have different wavelengths.

Ordinary light, such as sunlight or the light from a light bulb, is called "white light," but it is really a mixture of different colors. Rays of white light travel in many different directions and weaken as they go farther from their source.

The word laser is formed from the first letters of "light amplification by stimulated emission of radiation." Unlike ordinary light, laser light is only one color. Its rays all have exactly the same wavelength, and they all move together in the same direction without spreading. Because rays

of laser light do not spread, they can be focused by a lens or curved mirror into an intense beam on a very small spot.

Most laser machines have three parts: a light-emitting medium, an energy source to stimulate the medium to emit light, and a device to control the direction of the resulting beam.

A laser can aim an immensely powerful beam of light onto a very small spot, heating it to thousands of degrees. That makes the laser useful for welding small components such as battery cases for heart pacemakers.

Widespread use
Lasers are now common in everyday life. Supermarket checkouts use laser scanners to "read" the price of an item from a pattern of lines, called a universal product code (UPC), printed on the package. A compact disk (CD) player bounces laser light off tiny pits in the disk's surface and converts the reflected light into sound. Doctors use beams of laser light to correct vision defects and to remove tumors, skin blemishes, and tattoos.

▶
Lasers can cure vision defects without having to cut the eye.

SEE ALSO:
Lens; Light

INSIDE A LASER

▶
In a ruby laser the light-emitting medium is an artificial gemstone shaped like a rod with two reflective ends, one heavily silvered, the other partially. These ends act as mirrors that control the direction of the laser beam. The energy source is a tube-shaped lamp wrapped around the ruby rod.

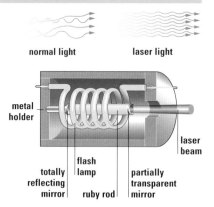

normal light   laser light

metal holder

totally reflecting mirror

flash lamp

ruby rod

partially transparent mirror

laser beam

✴ LENS
A lens is a curved piece of glass or other transparent material used to bring rays of light closer together or to spread them further apart.

Lenses are used in optical instruments such as eyeglasses and telescopes. The word *optical* means "making use of light or sight." Optical instruments use combinations of lenses and mirrors to magnify—make small objects look bigger.

There are two common types of lens. A convex, or converging, lens has a center that is thicker than the outer edge. A concave, or diverging, lens has a center that is thinner than the outer edge.

Light and lenses
Light travels in a straight line as it passes through the air. When it hits a transparent material with a different density (such as glass), it bends, or refracts, at the point where the two surfaces meet. Lenses use refraction of light to form an image. A convex lens bends the light rays together so that they meet at a single point, or focus, behind the lens. The distance between the focus and the center of the lens is the focal distance. If a sheet of paper is placed behind the focus, an upside down and reversed image of the object in front of the lens can be seen.

A concave lens bends the light rays so that they diverge and cannot form a focus behind the lens. An image produced by a

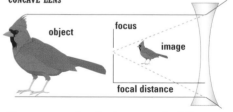

A high-powered zoom lens helps this nun get a closeup picture of the pope during his visit to Turin, Italy, in 1998.

CONVEX AND CONCAVE LENSES

CONVEX LENS

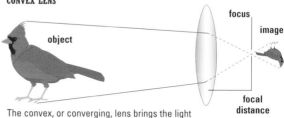

The convex, or converging, lens brings the light rays together at a point called the focus. The image of the object formed behind the lens is upside down and reversed.

CONCAVE LENS

The concave, or diverging, lens causes the light rays to spread apart. The light rays appear to come from the focus. The image of the object appears small and upright.

concave lens is upright, but it can only be seen by looking through the lens.

Several parts of the human eye together form a converging lens. An upside down image forms on the retina, the inner back surface of the eye. The brain flips the image so that we see things the right way up.

SEE ALSO:
Astronomy;
Light;
Microscope;
Photography;
Sight;
Telescope

* LEONARDO DA VINCI (1452–1519)

The most versatile talent of his age, Leonardo da Vinci was a painter, sculptor, architect, military engineer, inventor, musician, and scientist.

▲
This is thought to be a self-portrait of Leonardo da Vinci sketched in about 1512.

Leonardo was born in Vinci, Italy, which is why he is called Leonardo da (from) Vinci. In 1469 he became apprenticed to the artist Andrea del Verrocchio in Florence. In 1482 Leonardo went to work for the duke of Milan. He supervised court entertainments, built military equipment, installed central heating in the duke's palace, and painted *The Last Supper*. Leonardo filled notebooks with ideas for inventions. By studying his drawings of machines, 20th-century engineers have been able to build models of them that work perfectly. Leonardo used mirror (backward) writing to protect his ideas.

Leonardo studied the human body, dissecting (cutting up) dead bodies to see what they looked like inside. He also found time to examine the structure of plants, making many discoveries about plant growth.

In 1503 Leonardo returned to Florence, where he painted his most famous picture, the *Mona Lisa*. He died in France on May 2, 1519.

SEE ALSO: Artists, World

* LEVERS

A lever is a simple machine that magnifies force or a movement, making it easier to move a load. A lever moves around a fixed point called a fulcrum.

This wheelbarrow is a lever that enables a street trader in Laos to carry lots of produce. The wheel is the fulcrum.
▼

In scientific terms work is done only if a push or a pull on an object makes it move in the direction of the push or the pull; work is not the effort required to push or pull. The work needed to lift any given weight is always the same no matter how it is lifted, but the effort can be reduced by increasing the distance over which it is carried out. For example, a rock that is

too heavy to lift by hand can be raised by placing one end of a plank of wood under it, and then putting another object under the middle of the plank. That object is the fulcrum. If a downward force is applied to the upper end of the plank, the rock will rise. The plank is acting as a lever.

The force put on the free end is the applied force. The weight of the rock is the resisting force, or load. The ratio between the applied force and the load is the mechanical advantage. If a person pushes with a force of 10 lb. (4.5kg) to lift a rock weighing 100 lb. (45kg), the mechanical advantage will be 10 because the resisting force is 10 times greater than the applied force.

Three types of lever

First-class levers are those in which the fulcrum lies between the applied force and the resisting force. An example is a claw hammer being used to remove a nail. In second-class levers the resisting force lies between the fulcrum and the applied force. A wheelbarrow is a second-class lever.

In a third-class lever, such as tweezers, the applied force lies between the fulcrum and the resisting force. The human forearm is another third-class lever: The elbow is the fulcrum, the forearm the load, and the biceps muscle above the elbow is the input force to lift the arm.

SEE ALSO: Force & Motion; Physics

LEVER TYPES

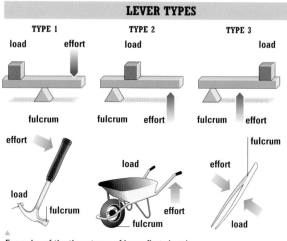

Examples of the three types of lever: first class (a claw hammer); second class (a wheelbarrow); and third class (tweezers).

✻ LIBRARY

A library is a room or a building with a collection of books, and often computers, periodicals, and audio and video material.

The first libraries were set up thousands of years ago in ancient Egypt and Babylon. Most early libraries were in religious temples. Today many important libraries are attached to schools, colleges, and government organizations. The largest library in the world is the Library of Congress in Washington, D.C. Other important libraries include the British Library in London, England, and the Bibliothéque Nationale in France.

Using the library

Most libraries work the same way and have the same rules. Users are expected to be quiet and to take good care of the books, periodicals, and other materials.

The most important part of any library—apart from the books and other resources themselves—is the librarian. He or she is there to help visitors find the books they need and to guide them through the library system and the catalog.

Catalog

The titles of all the books in a library are contained in a catalog. It used to be a system of cards arranged alphabetically in drawers, but many libraries now have computerized catalogs. School libraries and many public libraries use a system called the *Sears List of Subject Headings*. Large public libraries and most colleges use the Library of Congress subject

Founded in 1800, the Library of Congress in Washington, D.C., contains more than 118 million books and documents on over 500 miles (805km) of shelves.

headings. A standard list of categories enables all librarians to classify books in the same way.

On the shelves

Books are organized under one of two systems: the Dewey Decimal System or the Library of Congress System. Both systems use combinations of letters and numbers to help users find the books they want. The classification numbers, called class numbers, are marked on the spine of the book. Underneath these numbers the library may add the first few letters of the author's last name. The combination of the class number and the letters is known as the call number. This system makes it possible to pinpoint quickly the whereabouts of any particular book, even in the largest library.

SEE ALSO: Book

LIBRARY CLASSIFICATION SYSTEMS

Dewey Decimal Classification System

000	General works	600	Technology
100	Philosophy		(applied sciences)
200	Religion	700	Arts
300	Social sciences	800	Literature
400	Language	900	History
500	Pure science		

Library of Congress Classification System

A	General Works	L	Education
B	Philosophy and religion	M	Music
C	History—	N	Fine arts
	auxiliary sciences	P	Language and literature
D	History and topography	Q	Science
	(except America)	R	Medicine
E-F	American history	S	Agriculture
G	Geography and	T	Technology
	anthropology	U	Military science
H	Social sciences	V	Naval science
J	Political sciences	Z	Bibliography and
K	Law of the United		library science
	States		

✳ LIGHT

Light is the source of all life on Earth. Without light plants would not grow, and without plants to provide oxygen, animals would not be able to live.

The aurora borealis, or northern lights, is a great curtain of light that appears in the night sky in polar regions.

For many centuries scientists argued about whether light was made of particles or of waves. Today most scientists agree that both ideas are true. Light is made up of electrical and magnetic forces traveling through space at high speed in waves, and it is also a stream of energy particles called photons.

Any object that produces light, such as a flashlight or the sun, is called a light source. Other objects do not produce light of their own but reflect some or all of the light of other objects that do. For example, the moon is not a source of light. It appears to shine because it reflects light from the sun.

The colors of light

The English scientist Isaac Newton discovered that "white" light is made up of several different colors. When sunlight passes through a three-sided pyramid of glass called a prism, it splits into bands of red, orange, yellow, green, blue, indigo, and violet: They are the visible colors of the spectrum. That effect—known as refraction—happens because light changes direction whenever it moves from one material into another. There are also colors of light, that we cannot see, called infrared and ultraviolet.

The color of an object depends on the way it reflects and absorbs light. Many objects absorb six colors of the spectrum and reflect the seventh. A red ball appears red because the material of which it is made (or the paint with which it is covered) reflects only that one color.

REFLECTED LIGHT

| light from sun | reflected light | light from sun | reflected light | light from sun |

White   **Red**   **Black**

The surface on the left reflects all seven colors of the spectrum and therefore appears white. The surface in the center absorbs six colors and reflects the seventh, red. The surface on the right absorbs all seven colors and therefore appears black.

SEE ALSO: Laser; Lens; Newton, Isaac; Physics; Plant; Sight

✱ LITERATURE

Literature is written material that has lasting value or interest. It includes imaginative works and factual accounts.

Literature is divided into fiction and nonfiction. Fiction is work that the writer invents or imagines. It aims to stir the reader's feelings by describing moods of joy or sadness, by telling exciting stories, and by introducing characters whose emotions can be understood and shared by the reader. Fiction can be in the form of novels, plays, poems, or short stories.

Nonfiction is writing that tells readers the facts about a certain subject, such as science or history. This kind of writing may be regarded as literature when the ideas are beautifully expressed in language that gives added pleasure.

Autobiographies, biographies, diaries, and essays are works of nonfiction. An autobiography is the author's own account of his or her life. A biography is the life of someone other than the author. An essay is a short piece of prose that discusses a subject from a personal point of view.

Drama

A drama is a story meant to be acted out on stage. Serious plays are often called tragedies, especially if they end with the death of the leading character. Comic plays, or comedies, emphasize the ridiculous aspects of human behavior.

The ancient Greeks invented drama, but the great age of dramatic writing was during the reign (1558–1603) of England's Queen Elizabeth I. Playwrights of the time included William Shakespeare, Christopher Marlowe, and Ben Jonson. Like the Greek playwrights, the Elizabethans wrote their dramas in poetic form. In more recent times most playwrights have written in prose.

Poetry

Poetry differs from prose in having a regular rhythm, sometimes using rhyme. The ancient Greeks wrote epic poems. They were long story-poems about heroic events. Homer's *Iliad* describes the 10-year siege of Troy, and the *Odyssey* recounts the adventures of Ulysses on his voyage home from Troy. Lyric poetry is short, very personal, and songlike. The ode, a form of lyric poetry, is dignified in style. Narrative poetry tells a story.

In the early 1800s poetry was an important literary form. Percy Bysshe Shelley, William Wordsworth, and John Keats are remembered for their lyrics and odes. Samuel Taylor Coleridge's "The Rime of the Ancient Mariner" is a ghostly tale of magic and mystery. These four poets brought new subjects and a new richness of language into poetry. They had a great influence on the poets of later generations, including Alfred Tennyson, Robert Browning, Matthew Arnold, and Walt Whitman.

Novels and short stories

A novel is a long story, often with many characters and an involved plot. The earliest known novel comes from Japan.

A performance of William Shakespeare's comedy play A Midsummer Night's Dream.
▼

The Tale of Genji was written by Lady Murasaki Shikibu in the early 11th century. One of the earliest European novels was *Don Quixote* by the Spaniard Miguel de Cervantes, completed in 1615.

By the middle of the 1800s prose fiction had replaced poetry as the most popular literary form in both England and the United States. Great novels of the period include *David Copperfield* by Charles Dickens, *Jane Eyre* by Charlotte Brontë, *Moby Dick* by Herman Melville, and *Huckleberry Finn* by Mark Twain. In the 20th century James Joyce, Ernest Hemingway, and William Faulkner expanded the scope of the novel.

This illustration is taken from a 1919 edition of Edgar Allan Poe's 1843 short story "The Tell-Tale Heart."

Short stories

Short stories are generally between 1,000 and 20,000 words. They usually have only a few characters and focus on a single incident. Among the world's greatest short-story writers have been the Russian Anton Chekhov and the Frenchman Guy de Maupassant. In the United States the leading short-story writers have included Nathaniel Hawthorne, Edgar Allan Poe, O. Henry, Flannery O'Connor, and Katherine Anne Porter.

SEE ALSO Elizabeth I; Hemingway, Ernest; Language; Literature, Children's; Shakespeare, William; Theater; Writers, American; Writers, World

✳ MADISON, DOLLEY (1768–1849)

Dorothea (Dolley) Payne Todd Madison was the wife of the fourth president, James Madison, and one of the most famous of all the First Ladies.

Dorothea (Dolley) Payne was brought up in Virginia and later Philadelphia. In 1790 she married John Todd, Jr., a lawyer, and the couple had a son, Payne. Todd died three years later from fever, and Dolley married again in 1794. Her new husband was James Madison, a member of the House of Representatives.

Dolley loved to dress finely and give parties. From 1801 she acted as White House hostess for President Thomas Jefferson, who was a widower. Her social duties continued when Madison became president in 1809.

During the War of 1812 the United States fought Britain, whose navy had been blocking American trade with Europe. When the British invaded Washington, D.C., in 1814, Dolley was one of the last people to leave the White House. Before she fled to safety, she packed trunks containing important state papers and rescued the famous Gilbert Stuart painting of George Washington that hung in the White House.

In 1817 the Madisons retired to Virginia. After James died in 1836, Dolley spent her last years back in the U.S. capital.

SEE ALSO: Madison, James; United States of America

▲
This portrait of Dolley Madison is a print of a painting by Gilbert Stuart, whose picture of George Washington she saved from a fire in the White House in 1814.

✳ MADISON, JAMES (1751–1836)

James Madison was the fourth president of the United States from 1809 to 1817. He was one of the founders of the nation and helped write the Constitution.

James Madison was born into a family of wealthy Virginia tobacco farmers. He graduated from the College of New Jersey (now Princeton University) in 1771 and trained as a lawyer.

In 1776, during the American Revolution, Madison helped pass a resolution asking the Continental Congress to issue the Declaration of Independence. In 1780 he was elected to the Continental Congress.

Many of Madison's ideas were written into the Constitution in 1787. For that reason he is sometimes called "the Father of the Constitution."

James Madison was one of the founders of the United States. This portrait was painted in about 1810, during his first term as president.
▶

KEY FACTS

BIRTHPLACE
Port Conway, Virginia

OCCUPATION
Lawyer

MARRIED
Dolley Payne Todd

PARTY
Democratic–Republican

AGE WHEN PRESIDENT
57

TERM
1809–17

AGE AT DEATH
85

In 1789 Madison was elected to the House of Representatives, where he helped pass the first 10 amendments to the Constitution, known collectively as the Bill of Rights.

In 1801 Madison became President Thomas Jefferson's secretary of state. In that role he helped the country buy the Louisiana Territory from France in 1803.

At the time, Britain and France were at war. Both countries interfered with American ships bound for Europe.

President

With Jefferson's support Madison easily won election as president in 1808. He declared war on Britain in 1812 and soon after was reelected president.

The war started and ended well for the United States, although Washington itself came under attack. When the war ended in 1814, neither side could really claim victory. But the new peace cheered Americans, and in the following years much was achieved. The nation's wealth grew, and settlers pushed farther west.

When Madison left the presidency in 1817 he and his wife, Dolley, returned to Virginia, where he spent his final years studying new methods of farming. Madison died on June 28, 1836.

SEE ALSO: Bill of Rights; Constitution; Madison, Dolley

✳ MAGNETISM

Magnetism is an invisible force that enables certain objects to pull other things toward them or to push them away.

Every magnet has two ends, or poles: a north pole and south pole. If two magnets are placed close together, the two north poles or two south poles push each other away (repel). A north and a south pole pull toward each other (attract). This push or pull is called a magnetic field.

A magnetic compass works because the Earth has a magnetic field, with a north pole and a south pole. The north and south magnetic poles are not in exactly the same places as the geographic north

AMAZING FACTS!

Telephones contain electromagnets that are made to move by electricity as it passes through them. The movements create the sounds we hear.

and south poles. Some animals, such as whales and birds, can feel the Earth's magnetic field. They use it to find their way when they travel.

Magnetism and electricity

Electricity also has positive and negative charges. Like charges repel, and opposite charges attract. In the early 1800s scientists found that when they ran an electric current through wire, it made a magnet that could be switched on and off. It is called an electromagnet.

Electromagnets are used in many devices, including electric motors and generators, computer disks, and video

A maglev train is tested at the Railway Technical Research Institute in Japan.

records. In medicine magnetic resonance imaging (MRI) machines produce views of the body's inner organs to show possible illnesses.

Magnet-driven trains

During the 1950s scientists started to experiment with trains which float above their rails, lifted by the force between electromagnets in the train and electromagnets below the tracks. They can travel smoothly at speeds up to 300 mph (480km/h). They are called maglevs, short for magnetic levitation.

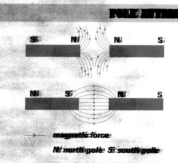

POLE ATTRACTION

If the like poles of two magnets are placed within range of each other, they will repel (upper diagram). If a south pole is placed within range of a north pole (lower diagram), they will attract each other.

magnetic force

N: north pole S: south pole

SEE ALSO: Earth; Electricity; Medicine; Migration; Radar & Sonar; Radio; Sound Recording; Television; Train & Railroad; Video Recording.

✳ MALAYSIA

Malaysia is the only country of Southeast Asia situated on both the mainland of Asia and on one of the islands that also make up part of the region.

Modern Malaysia was created in two stages. In 1957 what was then Malaya won independence from Britain. The addition of Sabah, Sarawak, and Singapore in 1963 brought Malaysia into being. Singapore formed its own

A Buddhist temple in the city of Penang (formerly known as George Town under British rule).

independent nation in 1965.

Malaysia is divided into two distinct regions: Peninsular Malaysia and East Malaysia. In the west Malaysia occupies part of the Malay Peninsula on the Asian mainland. East Malaysia includes Sabah and Sarawak on the island of Borneo. Mainland Malaysia is separated from the islands by more than 400 mi. (650km) of the South China Sea.

A mountain chain, rising to over 7,000 ft. (2,100m), runs down the middle of the Malay Peninsula. Between the hills and the sea are low-level plains with many large freshwater and saltwater swamps. Most of the peninsula's cities and towns are located on the western coastal plain. A new administrative capital, Putrajaya, is being built to the south of Kuala Lumpur.

People

Malaysia has a rich and diverse mixture of races and cultures. Native Malays are the largest single group, followed by Chinese. There are also people from India,

Malaysia's national flag

Pakistan, Sri Lanka, and Bangladesh. Most people live on the peninsula.

Economy

Malaysia leads the world in the production of tin, palm oil, and rubber. It also has large deposits of natural gas, petroleum, bauxite (the main source of aluminum), copper, and iron. Its chief industries are manufacturing, especially electrical and electronic products, fishing, and mining.

History

The modern history of Malaysia began around 1400 when a Malay ruler founded Malacca, which became the strongest trading power in Southeast Asia. However, by 1511 Malacca was in Portuguese hands, and by 1824 it was controlled by Britain. During World War II (1939–45) Japan seized Malaya, but Britain reoccupied it in 1945. In 1948 nine Malay states became the Federation of Malaya. Between 1948 and 1960 there was a state of emergency as the government fought communist rebels. In 1957 two more states joined the federation. Malaysia came into existence on September 16, 1963. Brunei did not join, and Singapore withdrew in 1965.

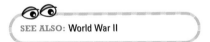

SEE ALSO: World War II

✲ MAMMAL

Mammals are the only animals that nurse their young with milk. Mammals are also the only animals that have hair.

There are more than 4,000 species of mammals. They all have a diaphragm, a muscle that aids breathing by expanding and contracting the chest cavity. The jaws of other vertebrates (animals with backbones) are made up of several bones, but a mammal only has one bone on each side of its lower jaw. Most mammals have seven neckbones, although the number of bones in their spines varies. Unlike most animals, mammals are warm-blooded, which means they are able to maintain a constant body temperature.

Movement

Mammals are found on land, in the trees, in the air, and in the water. Nearly all land mammals use four limbs for walking. Dogs and cats are among the many mammals that walk on the tips of their toes. In horses, deer, and some mammals these toes are protected by hard "toenails" called hooves.

Most mammals can swim. Seals, sea lions, and walruses spend most of their lives in the water, and their four limbs are short, flat flippers. Sirenians and whales live in the water from birth until death. Instead of hind limbs they have a broad, flat tail.

Tree-living mammals, such as squirrels and monkeys, have sharp claws to grip tree trunks when they climb. Bats are the only mammals that can fly. This is because their long, slender forelimbs have become wings.

Lifestyle

Solitary mammals, such as bears and jaguars, live alone except when breeding. Many mammals, such as monkeys, whales, and deer, live in groups. That helps them find food, look after each other, and escape predators (hunters).

At certain times of year some mammals migrate (travel from one area to another) in search of warmth or food. Other mammals feed heavily and then hibernate (sleep through the winter).

Mammals make babies by sexual reproduction. The male's sperm (sex cell) enters the female's body to fertilize her sex cell, the egg. Each fertilized egg, or embryo, grows into a baby. In most mammals the young grow within the mother, or gestate, for a period before birth. A few mammals, such as the duckbilled platypus in Australia, lay eggs from which the young hatch. Marsupials, such as koalas and opossums, give birth to offspring that are not fully formed. After birth the young feed and grow inside a pouch on the female's belly.

Food and feeding

Most mammals are herbivores (plant eaters). Cattle and deer, for example, graze on leaves and shoots; monkeys like fruit. Some mammals, such as lions and weasels, are carnivores (meat eaters). Mammals that eat both plants and meat are called omnivores. The black bear, for instance, eats berries and buds as well as insects and fish.

Most mammals are prey for carnivores. They can escape in different ways. Most hoofed mammals can run swiftly to avoid being caught and eaten. Porcupines rely on their coat of spines to deter enemies, and armadillos have a coat of scaly armor. Plain-colored, spotty, or striped coats may

Beluga or white whales swim off the coast of northern Canada.

Cats have sharp teeth and claws to hunt with and also to defend themselves.

▶ *The armadillo is a mammal of South America and southern North America. Most of its body is covered with horny plates for protection.*

also help mammals disguise themselves and hide in undergrowth. This form of protection is called camouflage. Whether for defense or attack, mammals have plenty of weapons. Cats attack with sharp teeth and claws, while hoofed mammals slash with hooves, horns, or antlers. Skunks spray a strong-smelling chemical.

The first mammals

Fossilized remains show that the earliest mammals lived at the time of the dinosaurs. They were small creatures that looked like rats or shrews. After the dinosaurs disappeared about 65 million years ago, the mammal population steadily grew, changed (evolved), and spread all over the world. They began to vary in shape, size, and living habits. Today mammals, especially humans, are the dominant animals on Earth.

AMAZING FACTS !

Largest mammal: Blue whale, weight over 120 tons
Smallest mammal: Kitti's hognosed bat, length 1.2 in. (3cm), wingspan 6 in. (15cm)
Largest land mammal: African elephant, up to 16,500 lb. (7,550kg)
Tallest mammal: Giraffe, 18 ft. (5.5m) or over
Fastest mammal: Cheetah, 70 mph (113 km/h)
Slowest mammal: Sloth, 0.5 mph (0.8 km/h)
Longest gestation: Elephant, 20–22 months
Shortest gestation: Opossum, about 12 days

SEE ALSO: Animal; Carnivore; Dog; Fossil; Mammal, Hoofed; Platypus; Primate; Rodent; Sea Mammal

✳ MAMMAL, HOOFED

Some mammals have toes that are encased in hard cases, or hooves. Hoofed mammals are also known as ungulates.

Scientists classify the ungulates in two groups according to whether the animals' feet have an odd or an even number of toes. Horses, rhinoceroses, and tapirs are the best-known of the odd-toed ungulates. Mammals of this type carry their body weight either on one large, central toe on each of their four feet or on three toes.

The even-toed ungulates are a very large group that includes deer, cattle, giraffes, camels, and others. These animals usually carry their weight on two large, hoofed middle toes.

Several hoofless animals are related to the ungulates and are sometimes classed with them. Among them are elephants, hyraxes, aardvarks, whales, and sirenians.

Odd-toed hoofed mammals

The horse family is well known for its domesticated, or tamed, forms, the horse and the donkey. The best-known wild horses are probably the black-and-white-striped zebras of the African plains. Rare wild horses include the kiang of Tibet and the kulan of Central Asia.

Rhinoceroses are large, heavyset animals with one or two nose horns and thick, grayish skin. There are five species of rhinoceros, found from Africa to India and Southeast Asia.

Tapirs look like large pigs with long snouts. Three species live in Central and South America, and a fourth in Southeast Asia. Surefooted animals, they live in forests and feed on leaves, fruit, and other vegetation.

Even-toed hoofed mammals

Hoofed mammals that have an even number of toes are divided into three subgroups: ruminants, piglike animals, and camels.

Ruminants have four-chambered stomachs that allow them to get the most nutrients possible from the tough plant food they eat. Food is swallowed and then partially digested in the first stomach, the rumen. It is later brought back up into the mouth to be chewed a second time. This is called "chewing the cud." The food is then swallowed again and fully digested. There are five families of ruminants: chevrotains, giraffes, deer, the pronghorn, and cattlelike animals.

Chevrotains are secretive, rabbit-sized animals of Asia and Africa. Giraffes, the tallest animals in the world, are found in Africa south of the Sahara Desert. Their cousins, the okapi, are shy, forest-dwelling ungulates with shorter necks.

Deer make up a large family of ungulates. They are widely distributed across the world. The males, and some females too, have bony antlers that are lost and regrown each year. Moose are the largest deer. In Europe they are called elk. In the United States the animal known as elk is also called the wapiti.

The pronghorn of North America is one of the world's fastest-running mammals. Its forked, hollow horns are shed and regrown each year.

▲
The Malayan tapir lives in dense rainforest and is mainly active at night. Its black-and-white coloring makes it nearly invisible in the moonlit jungle.

Kulans are rare wild asses of the Russian steppes.
▼

A wild mountain goat. Many goats have been domesticated by humans and are used for their milk and meat.

Cattlelike animals

There are more than 150 types of cattlelike animal, or bovid. They make up the family Bovidae and include cattle, antelope, sheep, and goats. Bovids have hollow horns that are not shed but kept for life. Wild cattle include buffalo and bison, as well as the rare gaur and banteng of Asia.

Antelope are fast-moving, alert animals. Most live on areas of savanna—grassland and open woodland—in Africa and Asia.

Wild sheep and goats are surefooted animals that live on mountains. They include the bighorn sheep of North America. Many have majestic curving horns.

Piglike animals

Three families of mammals are classified as piglike—pigs, peccaries, and hippopotamuses.

Pigs use their flexible, flattened snouts—and sometimes their tusks too— to root in the ground for roots, fruits, mushrooms, and other foods. Intelligent and courageous, wild pigs usually live in groups led by sows (females). The adult

A one-humped Arabian camel, or dromedary, in Australia. They were taken to that country for use as pack animals in the desert.

males live alone. The wild boar of Europe and Asia is the ancestor of the domestic hog. A number of pig species, including the warthog, live in Africa. The babirusa of Southeast Asia is a hairless pig that looks like a deer.

Peccaries are closely related to pigs. They, too, have snouts, bristly coats, and small tusks in their upper jaws. They are native to North, Central, and South America.

The hippopotamus, or hippo, is a huge, heavyset animal with a large head and mouth. It is found in the wild only in Africa. The river hippo lives in water by day and feeds on grass at night. A smaller species, the pygmy hippo, lives in forests.

The camel family

The one-humped Arabian camel, or dromedary, lives in the hot deserts of the Middle East. The two-humped Bactrian camel lives in the cold deserts of Asia. By turning some of the fat in their humps

into water, camels can survive long periods without drinking. People have domesticated both types of camel for use as hardy pack animals. Camels chew the cud, but in scientific terms they are not true ruminants because their stomachs have only three chambers rather than four.

Other members of the camel family live in South America. The vicuña and the guanaco are small, humpless camels that roam grasslands high in the Andes Mountains. The llama is raised as a pack animal, the alpaca for its soft wool.

For many years people have used hoofed mammals as sources of milk, meat, clothing, and transportation. Sheep and goats were the first hoofed mammals to be domesticated, about 10,000 years ago. Cattle, pigs, and horses followed. More recently, deer have been domesticated and farmed.

SEE ALSO: Animal; Mammal

✳ MANUFACTURING

Manufacturing is the process of making new products from raw materials, usually on a large scale with the aid of machinery.

Until 250 years ago almost all goods were made at home by skilled craftspeople. Many goods were so costly that few people could buy them. The development of modern manufacturing was based on new sources of power and machines.

For centuries the only sources of power were human and animal strength and waterwheels. That changed in the 1700s. Machines, such as weaving looms, were invented. Later, steam engines provided the power to drive them. Even later, other sources of power, such as electricity, were developed. Steel, a strong, workable combination of iron and carbon, replaced brittle iron in the making of machines and tools. This exciting period of change and growth started in Europe in about 1760 and spread to America. It is called the Industrial Revolution.

Mass production
During that revolution industries began using large machines to produce goods. Factories were built to house the machinery. In a system known as mass production hundreds of factory workers could produce great quantities of an item. Manufactured items cost less to produce than handmade goods and could be made far quicker. Thus they were cheaper to buy, and more people than ever before could afford them.

Standardization
For successful mass production parts are standardized—they are all made in the same way and look the same. This means, for example, that a clock manufacturer will make all the hour hands of the same type of clock the same, all the minute hands

◀

This production line completes thousands of pairs of rubber gloves every day.

the same, and so on. As a result, the parts can be put together quickly to make lots of clocks. It is also cheaper for workers to make parts in large quantities than to make a few at a time.

Two Americans came up with the idea of standardization during the early 1800s. Simeon North and Eli Whitney each ran workshops making guns, and each had the idea of using standardized parts. After all the parts were made, a gun was passed from one worker to another, with each worker adding a new part. Soon other products, such as clocks, watches, sewing machines, and farm machinery, were made in this way.

Assembly lines

Standardization works even better when an assembly line is used. It is like a long, moving workbench. In 1908 Henry Ford (1863–1947) used an assembly line to build his famous Model T Ford. The bare frame of the car started at one end of the line. As the frame moved along, each worker added a new part. Ford improved the system until the time needed to build a car fell from over 12 hours to only 1½ hours. Soon cars were being mass-produced in their thousands.

Automation

Automation is a short way of saying "automatic mechanization." It describes the way in which many factory machines today are run. Some factory machines are robots. They have "arms" and "hands" moved by motors that perform tasks on the assembly line. Bottles, cans, and paper are just some of the products made by automated machinery.

The industrial world

In 1820 more than two-thirds of Americans worked on the land. As industry grew, people left the farms to

◀

The original spinning jenny—a machine for spinning wool and cotton yarn—was built in the 1760s by the English inventor James Hargreaves (died 1778).

work in factories. By 1990 fewer than 3 percent of Americans worked on the land. The number of people working in factories also dropped, mostly because of automation. Today the United States is the world's leading industrial nation—no other country produces a greater quantity of manufactured goods.

SEE ALSO: Car; Electricity; Energy; Engine; Industrial Revolution; Inventors & Inventions; Metal; Natural Resources; Robot; Technology; Tools; Trade

✳ MAO ZEDONG (1893–1976)
Mao Zedong led the communist revolution in China in 1949. He then founded the People's Republic of China and ruled it until his death.

Mao Zedong was born on December 26, 1893, the son of a farmer in a small village in Hunan province, south China. He was a brilliant pupil at school, with a great love of books.

In 1911 the Chinese rose against their weak and corrupt rulers, the Manchu Dynasty. Mao joined the revolt, but he was disappointed with the new Chinese Republic it created. He felt that the revolution had failed to bring reforms. In 1921 Mao became a founding member of the Chinese Communist Party.

Along with the founders of the Han and Ming dynasties, Mao Zedong was one of only three peasants who rose to rule all of China. He restored China's independence and distributed land to the small farmers, but millions of people died during the civil war or were executed for disagreeing with his policies.

The long march
At first the Communists worked with the Kuomintang, a nationalist republican political party. But in 1927 the Kuomintang turned on the Communists and attacked them. Mao took control of the Communist armies and led them to the safety of the mountains. Then in 1934 he took them on a 6,000-mile (9,700km) march to a new base in a far-off valley in south China.

In 1937 the Japanese invaded China. For a short time the Kuomintang and the Communists fought together against Japan. After Japan's defeat in 1945 the two parties battled each other again in a bloody civil war (1946–49). The Communists won, and the nationalists went into exile on the island of Taiwan.

On October 1, 1949, Mao proclaimed the People's Republic of China, and the Communist Party seized control of the whole country. The Communists' rule became so strict, however, that Mao feared the revolutionary spirit would die out. At various times he tried to weaken the power of the Communist Party workers, but without much success.

In 1966 Mao and his wife Jiang Qing started the "Cultural Revolution." They gave power to young revolutionaries, called Red Guards, who fought against the party, plunging the country into years of violence and unrest.

Mao's health began to fail in the late 1960s. He died aged 82 on September 9, 1976.

SEE ALSO: China; Revolution

✳ MAP

A map is a representation, or a type of picture, of an area. Maps contain useful information and can show city streets, a state or country, or the entire world.

Maps help people find their way from one place to another. They can show information about the land, population, or economic activities. There are also weather, undersea, and star maps. Because the Earth is round, a globe gives the most accurate picture of the shapes and sizes of the land and water areas of the Earth. Flat maps are easier to handle, however, and they can show small areas in greater detail than a globe.

A history of map-making

People have made and used maps throughout history. The oldest surviving maps date back to Babylonian times, more than 4,000 years ago. Geographers in ancient Greece were the founders of scientific cartography (mapmaking).

The Romans used maps to help them wage wars, build roads and aqueducts, and administer their conquered provinces. The Polynesians sailed the Pacific using maps made of palm fiber and shells. The Chinese also made many maps. The oldest printed Chinese map (1155) was made about 300 years before the first map was printed in Europe.

Between 1470 and 1700 information gathered by explorers led to great

advances in cartography. The oldest existing globe (1492) was the work of the German merchant and navigator Martin Behaim. The first map to use the name America was made 15 years later by another German, Martin Waldseemüller. In 1570 the Flemish publisher Abraham Ortelius reproduced many maps of the same size and bound them into the first modern atlas. However, the term atlas was not used for a bound volume of maps until Gerhard Mercator published his book of maps entitled *Atlas* in 1595.

In the 17th century new techniques enabled cartographers to construct much

▲
This 17th-century illustration shows the world as it was known to the Greek historian Herodotus in about 450 B.C. The ancient Greeks created scientific maps, but with less detail than is shown here.

◀
To find a specific place on a map, you need to know its latitude and longitude. The east–west lines are parallels of latitude. The north–south lines are meridians of longitude. New Orleans, for example, is located at 30°N and 90°W.

more accurate maps of the world. Today cartographers, assisted by computers, remote sensing devices, and satellite photographs, can make maps of the moon, the planets, and the ocean depths.

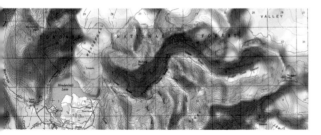

A relief map shows hills and valleys by shading and coloring instead of by contours (lines). This image shows the Juneau Mountain Range, Alaska, and was generated by a computer.

Geographic grids

One basic use of maps is to locate specific places or features. To do this, the ancient Greeks invented a geographic grid that is still used today. It is made up of two sets of imaginary lines. One set is a series of circles, called parallels of latitude, that run east and west around the Earth. The other set, called meridians of longitude, are north–south lines stretching between the poles. All latitude and longitude grid lines are circles or parts of circles and are shown in degrees (°). Any place on Earth can be located exactly if you know its latitude and its longitude.

There are other kinds of map grids that help you locate places. Many maps have a series of letters beginning with "A" running across the top and bottom of the map, and a series of numbers beginning with "1" running up or down the right and left edges. To find a place located at A-3 in the map index (the list of place names on the map), look in the box formed where sections A and 3 cross each other.

Direction and distance

Maps tell you direction. On most modern maps north is at the top of the map. If you face north, east is to the right, west is to the left, and south is behind you.

To find the distance between two cities on a map, mark the distance between the two places on the edge of a piece of paper. Place the paper along the graphic scale, or bar scale, and read the distance. Use a piece of string to measure curved features, such as waterways.

Flat maps

"Flattening" a picture of the Earth's surface to make a map stretches and distorts the image. Cartographers get around this problem either by showing the planet's surface as a series of slices or, more commonly, by stretching or shrinking some areas. That is why Greenland, for example, looks much larger on many maps than it really is in relation to other countries.

Understanding map symbols

Relief or physical maps show natural features, such as mountains, oceans, and rivers. Cultural maps include human-made features, such as political boundaries, highways, and towns. Cartographers often use symbols and colors to stand for various features. The outline of an airplane may indicate an airport, for example. Symbols and other information are usually placed in a box called the legend, or key. Maps use different symbols, so always look at the key to see what they mean.

Physical relief features, such as hills, and valleys, are hard to depict on a map because they must be shown from above rather than from ground level. To deal with this problem, contour lines mark elevation above sea level. The contour lines link points of the same height. Color and shading are also used to show altitude.

SEE ALSO: Geography; Navigation

✳ MARS

Mars is the fourth planet of the solar system. Its surface features sandy deserts, canyons, volcanoes, and ice caps.

The red color of parts of the surface of Mars is caused by the sands of its many deserts.
▶

KEY FACTS

POSITION IN THE SOLAR SYSTEM
Fourth planet from the sun

AVERAGE DISTANCE FROM THE SUN
142,000,000 mi. (228,000,000km)

SOLAR ORBIT
687 Earth days

DIAMETER
4,200 mi. (6,760km)

MASS
642 quintillion tons

ATMOSPHERE
Carbon dioxide

AXIAL ROTATION
24 hours 37 minutes

The orbit, or path around the sun, of Mars is more elliptical (oval-shaped) than that of most other planets. So, the distance from Mars to the sun varies throughout the Martian year. At its closest approach Mars is 128.4 million miles (206.7 million km) from the sun; at its greatest distance from the sun it is 154.8 million miles (249.2 million km) away. A year on Mars (the time the planet takes to complete its path around the sun) is almost twice as long as an Earth year.

The red planet

Mars looks distinctly orange or red. This color, associated with anger, led the ancient Romans to name the planet for Mars, their god of war. The color comes from minerals containing forms of iron. The surface of Mars is covered with dark orange or brown boulders and drifts of fine orange sand. The diameter of Mars is a little over half that of the Earth. Two small satellites, or moons, named Deimos and Phobos, orbit Mars.

Mars has little atmosphere—there is 600 times more air around Earth than there is around Mars. The air on Mars is usually crisp and clear. Even though almost every day is sunny, it is always cold. Even in the middle of the Martian summer day temperatures reach no more than freezing point, 32°F (0°C).

Some scientists believe that Mars once had much more atmosphere, a warmer climate, and running water, but that over a few billion years all of the water evaporated into space.

Voyages

When the Mariner 9 spacecraft arrived at Mars in 1971, a big dust storm was in progress. The probe's cameras showed nothing but dust and four spots. As the storm subsided, scientists saw that the spots were the tops of four giant volcanoes. Mars Rover is the latest expedition to explore the surface of Mars. It landed on Mars in 2003 and will send detailed information back to Earth.

SEE ALSO: Astronomy; Solar System; Space Exploration

✳ MATH AND NUMBERS

Math, or mathematics, is the study of numbers and the relationships among them. Math is also a way of reasoning and analyzing ideas.

An ancient Arabic manuscript on the subject of algebra, a branch of math in which letters are used to represent unknown numbers.

One of the main aims of math is to solve a problem in a systematic way so that similar problems can be solved more easily in the same way. Math is divided into two categories—pure and applied.

Pure, or theoretical, math is concerned with problems and questions within the world of math itself. The four main branches of pure math are arithmetic, algebra, geometry, and calculus. Arithmetic uses four basic operations— addition, subtraction, multiplication, and division.

Algebra uses symbols, generally letters, to take the place of unknown numbers. For example, in the statement $x + 5 = 8$, x represents an unknown number. From this information alone it is possible to figure out the numerical value of x. Statements such as this are known as mathematical equations.

Geometry is the study of shapes and measurement. It can be used to figure out the area of a field, the volume of a box, or the size of the moon.

Calculus is the study of change and motion. It is used to work out numerical values that are inconstant and variable, such as the speed of a car, which may be said to be traveling at a steady 50 mph (80km/h), but whose speed is in fact varying, although only slightly, from moment to moment. It is also used to find the areas and volumes of irregularly shaped figures and the lengths of curves. Calculus is a very important tool of modern physics.

Applied math is concerned with the practical uses of math in the world around us. It uses the principles of pure math to solve problems in such areas as astronomy, business, computer science, economics, navigation, and physics. It is also important in statistics, the science of collecting, organizing, displaying, and analyzing information.

The language of numbers
Math is a language that uses symbols to express size and order. The system used all over the world today for writing numbers came originally from India. In

▲
The father of geometry, Euclid, was a Greek who lived and worked in Alexandria (a city in modern Egypt) in the third century B.C.

about A.D. 700 Indian mathematicians began using nine symbols for the first nine counting numbers and also created a symbol for zero, or nothing. The Arabs adopted that number system, and in about 1200 it reached Europe. There it replaced the Roman system of writing numbers, which was limited by having no symbol for zero. The new numbers became known as digits, from the Latin word for finger, *digitus*.

In the modern system units (one to nine) are written on the far right of any number. The next digit, written to the left of the unit, is a number of tens, the third digit is a number of hundreds, the fourth digit a number of thousands, and so on. Using this system just 10 symbols—1, 2, 3, 4, 5, 6, 7, 8, 9, and 0—can stand for millions, billions, trillions, and more.

SOME IMPORTANT MATHEMATICIANS

A few of the people who made valuable contributions to the science of math.

al-Khwarizmi (about 780–850)
Arab who introduced algebra to the West.

Descartes, René (1596–1650)
Frenchman who developed analytic geometry.

Newton, Isaac (1642–1727)
Englishman who invented calculus at the same time as Gottfried Leibniz (see below).

Leibniz, Gottfried Wilhelm (1646–1716)
German who invented calculus at the same time as Newton.

Euler, Leonhard (1707–83)
Swiss who wrote more than 900 books on math and introduced several important mathematical symbols, such as pi (π).

Von Neumann, John (1903–57)
Hungarian-born American who developed a computer that enabled the United States to complete the calculations necessary for building and testing its hydrogen bomb.

Turing, Alan Mathison (1912–54)
Englishman who made important contributions to mathematical logic and the development of modern computers.

There are different ways of writing or expressing numbers. If 10 is divided by 20, the answer can be written either as a decimal (0.5) or as a fraction (½).

Some numbers cannot be written in normal ways. The number known as pi, or π, is the mathematical definition of the relationship between the diameter, or total width, of any circle and its circumference, or the distance around its edge. Pi cannot be calculated exactly, but it is usually taken as ²²⁄₇, or 3.1416. Special formulas involving pi can be used to calculate the circumference and area of any circle—the circumference of a circle is the diameter multiplied by pi.

SEE ALSO: Einstein, Albert; Newton, Isaac

✳ MATTER

Matter is any substance that has mass and occupies space. That effectively includes everything in the universe.

▲ *A piece of modeling clay can be squeezed into any shape, but it always takes up the same amount of space, and its volume stays the same.*

Everything that we can see and everything that is invisible but that is known to exist, such as air, is a form of matter. The three basic forms, or states, of all matter are solids, liquids, and gases. A solid resists changes in shape and size. A liquid takes the shape of any container into which it is put. A gas expands indefinitely to fill any container.

Changes in state

All substances change their physical form, or state, when they are heated or cooled beyond a certain level. For example, water is liquid at room temperature but turns into a solid (ice) when it freezes. When water is boiled, it turns to steam, which is a vapor or gas. The temperature at which a solid turns to liquid is called its melting point; the temperature at which a liquid turns into a gas is called its boiling point. When a gas cools and turns into a liquid, it is said to condense; when a liquid turns into a solid, it is said to freeze or solidify. The exact temperature at which any of these changes occur is different for different forms of matter. Some forms of matter, such as iodine, change from solids to gases and back again without going through the intermediate, liquid stage. This process is called sublimation.

Volume, mass, and density

The amount of space that any form of matter takes up—in other words, its size—is known scientifically as its volume. There is no link between the size of an object and its weight. The volume of an inflated party balloon, for example, is much greater than that of a cellphone, but the phone is much heavier—in other words, it requires more effort to pick up.

The mass of any form of matter is different from its weight. Weight is the force of gravitational attraction between an object and the Earth (or some other astronomical body). Mass does not change (at least not under ordinary circumstances), but weight does change depending on where the object is. For example, because the moon is less massive than the Earth, the force of attraction between the moon and a person on it is less than the force of attraction between the Earth and the same person on it. In other words, the person weighs less on the moon. An astronaut weighing 154 lb. (70kg) on the

DENSITY

An object can be measured in two ways: by its volume or by its mass. All the objects below have the same volume—they take up the same amount of space and are the same size. They vary in density however. Lead is a very dense metal, and the same volume weighs 13 times more than the wax and 56 times more than the balsa wood.

Lead

Wax

Balsa wood

Earth weighs only about 26 lb. (12kg) on the moon, but the astronaut has the same mass in both places.

The mass of the person is the same in both cases assuming that the person has not grown fatter or thinner during the journey from one body to the other. To take another example, suppose that a body existed entirely alone in space in a universe empty of other objects. That body would then have no weight, but its mass would still be the same.

The amount of mass in a particular volume is its density. Iron, for example, is about three times denser than aluminum. This means that a certain volume of iron weighs about three times as much as the same volume of aluminum.

Atoms and molecules

All matter is made up of tiny particles called atoms. Atoms usually form tight bonds with other atoms of the same type or with one or more different atoms. A group of tightly bonded atoms is called a molecule. Some molecules are small and are made up of only two or three atoms. Other molecules are much larger.

Atoms are made up of smaller parts called subatomic particles. The more massive particles are called protons and neutrons. They form a tiny but very dense atomic nucleus at the center of the atom around which are less massive particles called electrons.

Ordinary chemical changes affect the electrons at the surface of the atom. However, changes can take place in the atomic nucleus. They are nuclear changes. One example of nuclear change is radioactivity. The atomic nuclei of radioactive elements give off subatomic particles, releasing energy in the process. Although nuclear changes can now be caused by scientists in laboratories, they have been happening in nature since the

CHANGES TO MATTER

Matter can be made to change its properties in three main ways.

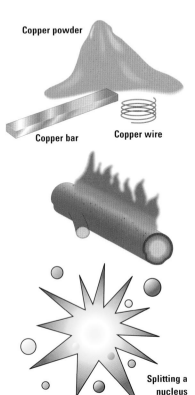

Copper powder

Copper bar   **Copper wire**

Splitting a nucleus

A metal such as copper can be drawn out into wires or heated until it melts, but it is still copper. These changes are called physical changes. In a physical change the substance has the same atomic makeup as before, but its form is altered.

When wood is burned, it produces heat and light (fire) and turns into a new form of matter, charcoal. This is a chemical change in which its atomic makeup is altered.

Changes can take place in the atomic nucleus of a form of matter. In a nuclear change the central core, or nucleus, of an atom is altered. Great amounts of energy are released in the process.

dawn of time. The element uranium, for example, decomposes over millions of years into lead, which is a more stable form of matter.

SEE ALSO: Atom & Molecule; Chemistry; Force & Motion; Gravity

✳ MAYA

The Maya are an American Indian people who have lived in southern Mexico and Central America for more than 3,000 years.

The oldest surviving relics of the Maya date from about 1500 B.C. By about A.D. 200 their ceremonial centers had developed into cities. Every Mayan city—there were 40 of them—had its own king, who ruled with the help of his nobles. The Maya were a warlike people, and each king tried to conquer rival kings. The warriors wore armor of quilted cotton and fought with axes, clubs, and spears.

Religion

Priests were in charge of religious ceremonies, which included making offerings of blood and human sacrifices to the gods of the sun, moon, and rain. The Maya believed that the gods would give them what they wanted in return for food and blood. The victims were often prisoners of war. Many had their hearts cut out with knives made of flint.

The priests also acted as astronomers. By observing the positions of the sun, moon, and stars, they were able to calculate exactly how long it took for the moon to go around the Earth and for the Earth to go around the sun. They used this information to look back into the past and to predict the future.

The Quetzalcoatl pyramid at Chichen Itza, Mexico, is one of the greatest monuments of the Maya civilization. ▼

AMAZING FACTS ❗

The astrological tables developed by the Maya were accurate to within one day over the course of 6,000 years. Astronomers needed computers and modern observatories before they could confirm the accuracy of Mayan figures.

Most Maya were farmers, growing corn, beans, squash, tomatoes, and other food crops. They wove cotton into cloth for clothing. There were no beasts of burden or wheeled vehicles, so porters carried goods from town to town. The Maya were great traders and had a market in every city, selling goods from as far away as central Mexico.

Writing

The Maya developed their own system of writing. It was made up of picture symbols called hieroglyphs. Some of these symbols represented whole words, while others represented sounds. Only priests, nobles, and scribes (writers) could read and write.

In about A.D. 900 many of the Mayan cities were abandoned, and the kings and priests lost their power. Historians think that wars and bad harvests might have caused the decline. By the time the Spaniards arrived in the 1520s, most Maya were living in villages. The Spanish forced them to work on plantations. Today there are nearly five million Maya people who continue to speak Mayan languages and carry on the traditions of their ancestors.

SEE ALSO: Alphabet; America, Central; Astronomy; Conquistadors; Mexico; Olmec & Toltec;

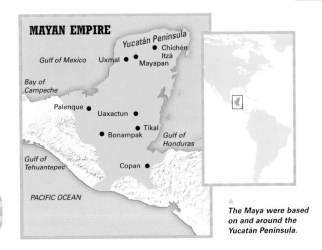

MAYAN EMPIRE

Yucatán Peninsula

Gulf of Mexico

Uxmal ● ● Chichén Itzá
● Mayapan

Bay of Campeche

Palenque ●
Uaxactun ●

● Tikal
● Bonampak

Gulf of Honduras

Gulf of Tehuantepec

Copan ●

PACIFIC OCEAN

The Maya were based on and around the Yucatán Peninsula.

✳ MEDICINE

Medicine is the use of science to cure disease and maintain good health. There are four aspects: prevention, diagnosis, treatment, and rehabilitation.

A doctor uses a sphygmo-manometer to take the blood pressure of a child in his care.

Doctors are men and women who use medicine to treat illnesses. Most people visit them only when they are unwell, but doctors do not only treat the sick: They try to keep people from becoming ill in the first place. They do so by increasing health awareness—teaching people about cleanliness, good food, and immunization (vaccination) against infectious diseases, and encouraging them to seek medical advice at the right times. This is called prevention, or preventive medicine.

Diagnosis
Diagnosis is the identification of illness. When patients visit a doctor, they expect to be told what is wrong with them and to be given the prognosis (the doctor's view of their chance of recovery).

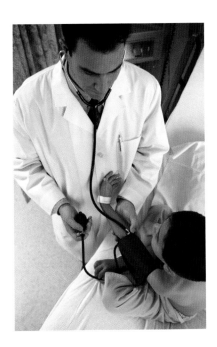

No two illnesses and no two patients are ever exactly alike. When making a diagnosis, the doctor looks at three things—the case history, the symptoms, and the signs. A patient's case history includes his or her pattern of disease, personal details about health habits, family, and job, and how the patient feels at the moment. A symptom is evidence of illness that the patient can detect, such as pain, loss of weight, or unusual tiredness. A sign is evidence of something abnormal, such as a tumor, that the doctor finds during the course of examination.

The doctor's experience and observation are often enough to provide a diagnosis without any special equipment. However, there are many devices that assist in diagnosis. Some are very simple. A stethoscope is two pieces of rubber tubing with earpieces at one end and a flat metal disk at the other. A doctor uses it to hear inside the patient's chest. A thermometer can tell the doctor if the patient has a fever.

More complicated equipment includes the electrocardiograph (ECG), which can reveal whether the heart is behaving normally. The ultrasonoscope uses sound to make a picture of organs inside the body. It is also used to observe the development of unborn babies. X-rays enable doctors to see inside the body without having to cut it open.

Treatment

Treatment, or therapy, is the method used to help the patient recover from his or her illness. It may involve taking prescribed medicines, a course of action, such as physical exercise, or quitting an unhealthy activity, such as cigarette smoking.

Rehabilitation begins after the severe part of the patient's illness is over. Its aim is to help the patient recover completely; but if that is impossible, it tries to keep pain and loss of function to a minimum.

Doctors' qualifications

To become a doctor in the United States, a person must study for at least seven years after graduation from high school

and then serve a year's internship (practical experience) in a hospital. Doctors who start practicing right after that are called general practitioners. They may have to deal with any illness. Other student doctors continue training and eventually become specialists in a particular illness or part of the body.

Surgery

Surgery is a branch of medicine in which specially trained doctors, called surgeons, treat patients by operating on them. The removal of an appendix is a fairly common example of a surgical treatment. Sometimes surgery is combined with other treatments, such as drugs or

Computerized axial tomography (CAT) scans help medical diagnosis by producing stereoscopic (apparently three-dimensional) pictures of the insides of the body.

Surgeons perform an operation with the help of onscreen images produced by a laparoscope inside the patient's body.

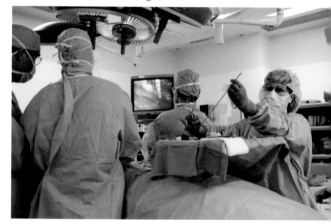

*This sculpture
from the fourth
century B.C. shows
the ancient Greek
Amphiaraos
healing a patient.*

This sculpture from the fourth century B.C. shows the ancient Greek Amphiaraos healing a patient.

chemotherapy (used on tumors). Machines such as a special viewing camera, called a laparoscope, have enabled surgeons to see inside the body as they perform operations. This technique, called keyhole surgery, means that the surgeon only needs to make a small incision, or cut, in the body. The patient recovers much more quickly as a result.

Medical professionals
In addition to doctors there are many other people who work to fight sickness and injury. Nurses have a great deal of medical knowledge and assist doctors and surgeons. Anesthesiologists administer anesthetics, which provide the patient with a safe, pain-free sleep during operations. Researchers and technicians work in laboratories, testing samples of blood and other body products. Technicians with training in mechanics and electronics look after medical equipment.

The science dealing with the properties of drugs and the way they act on particular organs in the body is called pharmacology. People working in the pharmaceutical industry develop new drugs and give out existing drugs to the sick. Clerical and support workers, who do not have medical or scientific training, provide doctors with administrative backup.

History
From the earliest times people have had ways of making themselves and others feel better, but modern medicine began only when people started testing various treatments. Ancient people did not really understand what caused disease, and it was often thought to have been brought about by evil spirits or black magic. Cures involved magic and spells, as well as medicines made from olive oil, honey, many kinds of herbs, and other ingredients. Almost all medicines were made from plants.

India and China have very ancient traditions of medicine, and the Western use of alternative or complementary treatments based on these traditions has grown since the 1960s. The first people in the West to approach medicine as a science were the ancient Greeks, most famously Hippocrates (about 460–377 B.C.).

The Romans made great advances in health care by using money raised from taxes to pay for hospitals, improved drainage, and sewer systems. They were pioneers in public health policy. Claudius Galen (about A.D. 129–199), the greatest of Rome's medical teachers, wrote the first study of anatomy and described many surgical procedures.

After the fall of the western Roman empire in the fifth century A.D. people lost interest in scientific medicine, and superstition took over. When a plague called the Black Death killed millions in Europe in the Middle Ages, many thought it was a punishment from God.

It was not until the 1400s that European scientists rediscovered Greek and Roman medical authors, whose writings had been ignored in the West for so long that they survived only in Arabic translations.

18th century to today
From the mid-1700s, as industry became mechanized, many people moved from the countryside to the cities to work in factories. That caused overcrowding and illness. As scientists began to understand how bacteria spread diseases, social reformers campaigned for improved sanitation and clean water supplies.

In the 1900s new anesthetic techniques meant that surgeons could carry out operations such as the removal

Sir Alexander Fleming holds a bowl containing penicillin, a fungus that cures a wide range of illnesses.

IMPORTANT FIGURES IN MEDICINE
The following are just a few of the people who made important advances in medical knowledge. There have been many others.

Hippocrates (about 460–377 B.C.)
Ancient Greek doctor who provided the basis for modern Western medicine.

Avicenna (Ibn Sina) (A.D. 980–1037)
Persian who wrote two important books on medicine that were used by doctors for centuries after his death.

Vesalius, Andreas (1514–64)
Belgian doctor who wrote a major book on anatomy, correcting many mistaken beliefs about the structure of the body.

Harvey, William (1578–1657)
English doctor who discovered the circulation of the blood.

Pinel, Philippe (1745–1826)
French doctor who reformed the care of the mentally ill.

Jenner, Edward (1749–1823)
English doctor who developed vaccination.

Laënnec, René-Théophile-Hyacinthe (1781–1826)
French doctor who invented the stethoscope.

Long, Crawford Williamson (1815–78)
American surgeon who was the first to use ether as an anesthetic in an operation.

Lister, Joseph (1827–1912)
English doctor who invented antiseptic (germ-free) techniques.

Röntgen, Wilhelm Conrad (1845–1923)
German doctor who discovered the medical uses of x-rays in 1895.

Mayo, William James (1861–1939) and **Charles** (1865–1939)
American brothers who founded the first modern medical clinic.

Landsteiner, Karl (1868–1943)
Austrian-born American doctor who discovered the existence of blood groups.

Fleming, Alexander (1881–1955)
Scottish doctor who discovered penicillin in 1928.

Barnard, Christiaan (1922–2001)
South African surgeon who performed the first successful heart transplant.

of limbs while the patient was unconscious. The average person worldwide now lives to 66 years. In 1950 the average was 46, and in 10,000 B.C. it was only 20 years.

A Malaysian woman in Sarawak picks Tuba aka, a medicinal plant that is used to cure fever.
▶

SEE ALSO: Greece, Ancient; Health; Hospital; Nightingale, Florence; Nursing; Nutrition; Psychology & Psychiatry; Roman Empire; X-ray

✳ MERCURY

Mercury is the second smallest planet in the solar system. Its orbit, or path, around the sun is the shortest and fastest of any planet.

KEY FACTS

POSITION IN THE SOLAR SYSTEM
Closest planet to the sun

AVERAGE DISTANCE FROM THE SUN
35,900,000 mi. (57,800,000 km)

SOLAR ORBIT
88 Earth days

DIAMETER
3,032 mi. (4,880 km)

MASS
330 quintillion tons

ATMOSPHERE
Almost none

AXIAL ROTATION
59 Earth days

Mercury is not easy to see clearly from the Earth even with a telescope. Most of what scientists know about the planet has been gathered from 2,700 photographs sent back by the spacecraft Mariner 10 during its three voyages to the planet in 1974 and 1975.

Structure
Astronomers now believe that the interior of Mercury consists of a core of iron and nickel. It is probably surrounded by a rocky zone about 360 miles (580km) thick and a light crust no more than 40 miles (65km) thick. The core of Mercury may be larger than the Earth's moon. Because of the iron in the core Mercury has a magnetic field, although it is not as strong as that of the Earth.

◀
Mercury is named after the messenger of the gods in ancient Roman mythology. This is a reference to the speed with which the planet orbits the sun.

Surface

Mercury's surface looks a lot like that of the Earth's moon. It has many craters, which were caused by meteorites crashing into the planet. The largest crater is the Caloris Basin, which is over 800 miles (1,280km) in diameter. The surface temperature ranges from −280°F (−170°C) to 800°F (420°C).

The surface of Mercury is covered with many flat, dark plains. They are known as seas because early astronomers thought they might contain water. Scientists now know that there is no water on Mercury, and that these features are made of lava (hot, liquid rock that pours out of a volcano and then turns solid).

Mercury has a series of cliffs, called scarps, hundreds of miles long. They were probably formed early in the planet's history. The interior cooled and expanded, forcing sections of the planet's crust to split, creating the cliffs.

The lack of atmosphere on Mercury means that there are no natural forces to erode (wear away) the surface. Craters and other surface features have remained unchanged for millions of years.

SEE ALSO: Astronomy; Comet, Meteor, & Asteroid; Solar System; Space Exploration

✳ METALS

Metals are a group of chemical elements. Metals such as gold are valued for their beauty, and metals such as iron are mined for use in industry.

At room temperature metals are solid, with the exception of mercury. When they are polished, metals reflect light. This sheen is called luster. Metals can be pulled and stretched into wires—this quality is called ductility. Metals are also malleable—in other words, they can be hammered into sheets. Most metals allow heat and electricity to pass through them, a property called conductivity. Silver and copper are particularly good conductors.

A few metals, such as gold and platinum, occur naturally in a pure form in the earth. Most metals, however, are found combined with other elements and have to be isolated by chemical means.

Metals combined with oxygen are called oxides. Metals combined with sulfur are called sulfides. Any geological material that contains a metal is called an ore. When ores are mined, the metals in them are separated and processed into forms that can be used in industry. The science of separating and processing metals is called metallurgy.

▲
Iron is melted so that it can be combined with carbon and turned into steel.

Alloys

Sometimes a metal does not have all the properties needed for a particular purpose. Metallurgists fill the gap by combining two metals or combining a metal with a nonmetal to form an alloy.

Molten gold is poured into a mold. When the metal cools, it will resolidify into a bullion bar.

Iron, for example, is a cheap and useful metal, but it tends to rust. If iron is combined with carbon (a nonmetallic element), the result is steel. Steel does not rust and withstands heat better than pure iron.

Extraction processes

Once an ore has been mined, the metal has to be extracted from it. The ore is first crushed and then passed through filter screens to remove as much waste material, such as sand, soil, and rock, as possible. Strong magnets attract metals such as iron to separate it from nonmagnetic material. Other ores are separated in water. Some metals rise to the top, others sink to the bottom. Early gold prospectors shook pans containing ore under running water. The waste washed away, and the heavier gold sank to the bottom.

Refining metals

When a metal has been extracted from its ore, it still may not be pure. The process of removing impurities is called refining. In a process called smelting the ore is melted in a furnace. The impurities float to the top of the furnace, and the molten (liquid) metal flows out of the base. Zinc,

iron, lead, and copper are the main metals extracted through smelting. Chemicals or electric current are also used in refining.

Once the metal has been extracted and refined, it can be worked or shaped as required. Metal can be worked cold or hot. The oldest method is hot forging, when the metal is heated until it becomes soft and hammered between two flat surfaces, such as an anvil and a hammer.

Modern methods use machines to form sheets, tubes, or bars. When the metal is cold, it can be worked again to harden and strengthen it or to give it luster. Metals can also be reduced to powder and poured into a mold. The powder is then compressed and heated until it forms the desired shape.

Using metals

The discovery of how to extract and work metal was one of the keys to the development of human civilization. By about 8000 B.C. people in several parts

This figure of the ancient god Ba'al dates from about 2000 B.C. It is made of bronze covered with gold and silver leaf.

of the world had learned to shape nuggets (pure lumps) of copper and gold into ornaments and simple tools.

In about 6000 B.C. people in western Asia and southeastern Europe discovered how to smelt copper and gold in the kilns (ovens) they used for pottery. However, copper and gold are soft metals that are not suitable for making tools or weapons.

When people discovered how to make a hard alloy called bronze from copper and tin, they were able to make tools and weapons. Bronze was first made in the Middle East in about 3500 B.C. and gradually spread across Europe and Asia. In about 2000 B.C. people discovered how to smelt iron. One of the first peoples to do this were the Hittites, who lived in Anatolia (part of modern Turkey). Iron weapons were more effective than bronze, so the Hittites were able to win more battles and enlarge their empire. Iron replaced bronze for most uses, and it is still one of our most important metals. Silver was not mined until about 600 B.C. because its smelting and refining processes are quite complex.

This comb from about 1000 B.C. is made of bronze, an alloy of copper and tin.

SEE ALSO: Ancient Civilizations; Chemistry; Electricity; Natural Resources; Warfare

✳ MEXICO

Mexico is bordered by the United States to the north, Guatemala and Belize to the south, the Pacific Ocean to the west, and the Gulf of Mexico to the east.

The Zócalo is the main square in the center of the Mexican capital, Mexico City. On the left is the Metropolitan Cathedral and on the right the National Palace.

The United States of Mexico is the northernmost country of Latin America. It is the third most populous country in the Western Hemisphere after the United States and Brazil.

Land and climate
The central upland region, known as the Mexican plateau, contains most of the population and most of the important cities. The plateau is roughly triangular, with its base along the U.S. border and its tip extending south to Mexico City.

High, rugged mountain ranges border the plateau. On the west is the Sierra Madre Occidental, which has several spectacular volcanoes. A second range, the Sierra Madre Oriental, lies along the plateau's eastern edge. Near Mexico City the two mountain ranges meet at the country's highest peak—the snowcapped volcano of Citlaltepetl, or Pico de Orizaba, 18,405 feet. (5,610 m) high.

The climate varies from tropical and wet to temperate and dry. The coastal plains are hot and humid, with heavy

UNITED STATES OF AMERICA

Tijuana

Gulf of California

Baja California

PACIFIC OCEAN

Ciudad Juárez

Sierra Madre Occidental

Sierra Madre Oriental

Monterrey

Guadalajara

Gulf of Mexico

Veracruz

Mexico City

Puebla

Yucatán

Acapulco

BELIZE

MEXICO

Gulf of Tehuantepec

GUATEMALA

Mexico's national flag

KEY FACTS

OFFICIAL NAME
Estados Unidos Mexicanos

AREA
756,066 sq. mi.
(1,958,201 sq. km)

POPULATION
98,881,000

CAPITAL & LARGEST CITY
Mexico City

MAJOR RELIGION
Roman Catholicism

MAJOR LANGUAGES
Spanish (official), various Indian languages

CURRENCY
Peso

rainfall. The north is dry, with extremes of temperature, while the region around Mexico City has a pleasant, temperate climate. Only the coast and parts of the central region get enough rainfall for farming.

Plant and animal life
Forests cover nearly a quarter of Mexico's land. Animal life throughout the country is enormously varied and includes wolves, jaguars, tapirs, monkeys, and colorful birds such as parrots and macaws.

People
Most Mexicans are mestizos—that is, people of mixed Indian and European (mainly Spanish) ancestry. About 30 percent of the population is of pure Indian ancestry, and about 15 percent is of exclusively European origin.

Economy
Only about 13 percent of the land is suitable for farming, and only about half of that is cultivated. Mexico has rich mineral resources. It is the world's largest producer of silver, and its land contains many other valuable metals. Mexico's biggest export is oil, of which the nation has the fifth largest supplies in the world. More than 75 percent of the oil is exported to the United States. After oil tourism is Mexico's largest source of income.

History
The Aztec Indians ruled central Mexico from the 1300s to the 1500s. The Spanish under Hernán Cortés (1485–1547) invaded the country in 1519 and conquered it in under two years. For the next 300 years Mexico, then known as New Spain, was ruled as a Spanish colony.

For many years Indians and mestizos (mixed Indian and European ancestry) fought the Spanish. Spain was forced to sign a treaty in 1821 granting Mexico independence. But the country still had no real government, and its progress to nationhood was slow and difficult. Between 1846 and 1848 Mexico was at war with the United States over disputed territory. In 1848 the United States paid Mexico $15 million for all of California, Utah, and Nevada and most of Arizona and New Mexico.

The beautiful countryside along the Pacific coast of Baja California in northern Mexico.

255

A monarchy was established in 1864, but overthrown in 1867. President Benito Juárez laid the foundation for Mexico's industry, transportation, and communications systems. When he died in 1872, Mexico had finally become a fully fledged nation.

Porfirio Díaz, one of Juárez' generals, seized power in 1876 and ruled Mexico for nearly 35 years. He brought stability, built railroads, improved harbors, and increased agricultural output. However, his iron rule led to rebellion in 1910.

In 1934 Lázaro Cárdenas established the Institutional Revolutionary Party (PRI), which stayed in power until 2000. He nationalized the oil industry and the railroads, gave land to the poor, and increased the number of schools.

In 1942 Mexico joined World War II (1939–45) fighting against Germany. Demand for oil during the war stimulated Mexico's industrial growth. In the 1980s and 1990s the economy suffered. In 2000 Vicente Fox Quesada of the National Action Party (PAN) became president.

SEE ALSO: America, North; Aztecs; Conquistadors

✳ MICHELANGELO (1475–1564)

Painter and sculptor Michelangelo is most famous for his paintings of biblical scenes on the ceiling of the Sistine Chapel in Rome, Italy.

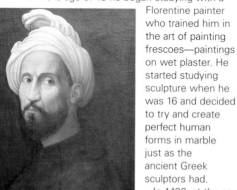

A self-portrait of Michelangelo painted in 1522.

Michelangelo di Lodovico Buonarroti Simoni was born near Florence, Italy. At the age of 13 he began studying with a Florentine painter who trained him in the art of painting frescoes—paintings on wet plaster. He started studying sculpture when he was 16 and decided to try and create perfect human forms in marble just as the ancient Greek sculptors had.

In 1496, at the age of 21, Michelangelo went to Rome, where he carved his first major sculpture, called the *Pietà*. Returning to Florence, he then carved a magnificent marble statue of David that was 14 ft. (4.2m) high. The statue was so popular with the Florentines that he was asked to produce far more work than he could possibly complete. Pope Julius II commissioned Michelangelo to build him an impressive tomb and to paint the ceiling of the Sistine Chapel in the Vatican.

In 1547 Michelangelo became chief architect for the rebuilding of St. Peter's in Rome and designed the famous dome of the church. He continued working until his death at age 89.

SEE ALSO: Artists, World; Rome

✳ MICROSCOPE

Microscopes use lenses to produce enlarged images of small objects, especially details that are too small to be seen by the naked eye.

The most common type of microscope is the light microscope or optical microscope, which uses light and lenses to magnify images. If light waves reflected off an object are passed through a lens in a certain way, they will refract, or bend. The refracted light waves are spread out and appear to be coming from a bigger object. The simplest light microscope is the magnifying glass, a lens that can magnify an image up to 25 times.

Compound light microscopes—the type most often found in schools—contain two magnifying lenses. Visible light reflected from the mirror on the base passes first through a condenser lens, then the specimen and objective lens, and into the eyepiece lens, forming a magnified primary image. The primary image is further magnified as it passes through the ocular lens, or eyepiece. The final image is projected onto the retina of the viewer's eye. Most compound microscopes give a choice of objective lenses mounted on a rotating disk, each lens providing a different magnification of up to 50 times.

Electron microscopes

The most powerful microscopes create magnified images by passing beams of electrons through the specimen to be viewed. The most advanced electron microscopes can magnify objects up to a million times. That has allowed scientists to investigate tiny individual atoms.

Microscopes help scientists study body cells and microorganisms that are too small to view with the unaided eye. In the early 1800s microscopes brought huge advances in medicine by revealing that many diseases were caused by bacteria that had previously been invisible.

Microscopes are also used in other fields. Scientists use them to examine rocks or plastics. Engineers use them to study the surface properties and structure of metals. Microscopes are also used in forensic science to analyze hair, fabric, and other materials found at crime scenes, and in the service, manufacturing, and pharmaceutical industries to check the safety and quality of products.

◄
The world's smallest published alphabet book, with a millipede for comparison, seen through an electron microscope. Each page of the book measures ⅒ in. (less than 3mm) in height and can be read only with the aid of a magnifying glass, which comes free with every copy.

INSIDE A COMPOUND MICROSCOPE

This diagram shows the path of light (red lines) past an adjustable mirror, through a condenser lens, then through the specimen (which is placed on a glass slide), and up the lens tube to the eyepiece lens and the eyepiece itself.

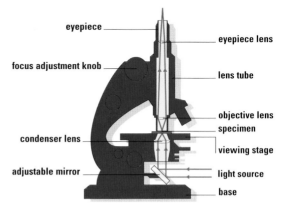

eyepiece · eyepiece lens · focus adjustment knob · lens tube · objective lens · specimen · condenser lens · viewing stage · adjustable mirror · light source · base

SEE ALSO: Biology; Human Body; Lens; Medicine; Sight

✳ MIDDLE AGES

The Middle Ages were the period of European history
from the fall of the Roman Empire in 476 to 1453,
when the Ottoman Turks captured Constantinople.

At its height the Roman Empire controlled most of western Europe. In 395, however, the empire finally split in two—the western empire ruled from Rome, and the eastern empire ruled from Constantinople (modern Istanbul, Turkey).

Germanic tribes, whom the Romans called barbarians, were settling in western Europe. In 476 they removed the last western Roman emperor from the throne.

The Middle Ages were once known as the Dark Ages. People thought of them as a time of ignorance, but in fact artists, craftsmen, and scholars thrived. During the 13th and 14th centuries there was increasing prosperity, towns and cities grew, and trade networks reached India and China.

A French book illustration by the Limburg brothers, dating from about 1416, of the grape harvest in September. In the background is the Château de Saumur. The castle was rebuilt throughout the 1200s and 1300s and is typical of medieval architecture.

Kings and nobles
The barbarian tribes that overran the Roman Empire were led by chiefs or kings. Their power was based on their ability to win battles and reward their followers with goods. Each area had its own ruler.

For three centuries after 476 there were only small states and kingdoms. Then Charlemagne (742–814) became king of the Franks in 771. He built an empire that extended across western and central Europe and set up Christian schools to encourage learning. Nobles were given land in exchange for military support.

Charlemagne's empire crumbled after his death in 814, but the memory of his Christian empire was important.

In the early Middle Ages kings struggled to control their nobles. In many cases the nobles were more powerful than the king. In France and England the power of the king slowly increased until the king was the most powerful of the princes. In some areas, like Germany, a single dominant king did not emerge. It was not until the end of the 14th century that the modern idea took shape of a state governed by a ruler whose authority came from the community.

Between the ninth and 12th centuries in England and northwestern Europe kings and lords gave grants of land, called fiefs or fiefdoms, to their nobles. In return the nobles owed the lords loyalty and military service. Similarly, nobles granted land to peasants (small farmers) in return for services, such as labor. Historians later gave this complicated system of loyalties and services the name of feudalism.

The church

The Catholic Church grew powerful during the Middle Ages. It was governed by bishops and archbishops under the authority of the pope at Rome. The church was also served by monks and nuns. Monks were men who lived together in a house called a monastery. They devoted their lives to the service of God. Nuns were women who followed a similar life in houses usually called convents.

During the Middle Ages monasteries were the principal centers of learning and education in western Europe. Monks hand-copied books until printing was invented in the 15th century and ran schools that taught reading, writing, and Latin to students who hoped to enter the church or work in government. Bishops, too, established schools, called cathedral schools. In the 12th century some cathedral schools became great centers of learning called universities.

Islam

Shortly after the prophet Muhammad founded the Islamic religion in 610, Muslim armies began to conquer new territory. By 750 the Islamic Empire stretched from India in the east to Spain and Morocco in the west. Islam was usually tolerant of other religions, and Muslim scholars preserved and transmitted the learning of ancient Greece and Rome to western Europe.

Christianity and Islam clashed between 1096 and 1291 in a series of wars called the Crusades, or "wars for the cross." The Crusaders' aim was to protect the holy sites of Christianity and recapture Palestine (modern Israel, Lebanon, and Syria) from the Muslims. Christians also fought to regain the Iberian Peninsula (modern Spain and Portugal) from the Muslims. They finally succeeded in 1492.

The late Middle Ages

Great changes swept Europe during the late Middle Ages. Between 1337 and 1453 France and England fought a series of campaigns called the Hundred Years' War. In the late 1340s the Black Death, a terrible plague, killed about one-third of Europe's population. Farmland stood idle, with few laborers to work it. The peasants who survived the plague were able to demand more freedom from their noble lords as well as payment in wages.

The church's power started to fade, and in its place came a new spirit of freedom in art, science, and learning. This new spirit would become known as the Renaissance, meaning "rebirth," because people drew their ideas from the art and learning of ancient Greece and Rome.

In 1453 France and England made peace. That same year Constantinople, the capital of the Byzantine Empire, fell to the Muslim Ottoman Turks. Its fall was a tremendous shock to Christendom and gave the Ottoman Empire control of the main trade route between the Mediterranean Sea and Asia.

An illumination (illustration) from a French manuscript showing Louis VI founding an abbey. The king—nicknamed "Louis the Fat"—ruled France from 1108 until his death in 1137.

SEE ALSO: Black Death; Castle; Crusades; Europe; France; Germany; Islam; Italy; Printing; Renaissance; Roman Empire; United Kingdom

✳ MIDDLE EAST

The Middle East is the cradle of some of the world's earliest civilizations and of three great religions— Judaism, Christianity, and Islam.

The Middle East is a geographical area that includes the nations of southwest Asia, the Arabian Peninsula, and eastern North Africa. High mountains rise to the north of the region. Others extend along the eastern Mediterranean coast and along the west and south of the Arabian Peninsula. Huge deserts stretch across the inland regions.

Important rivers in the Middle East include the Nile, the world's longest river, which flows through Egypt. The Tigris and Euphrates rivers rise in Turkey, flow through Syria, join in Iraq, and empty into the Persian Gulf.

The Middle East is hot and dry for much of the year except in the highest mountains. In the deserts the daytime temperature often rises above 125°F (52°C), yet at night the deserts are cool or even cold. There is little rainfall, and fresh water is scarce. Although little of the land is suitable for farming, agriculture is important. More than half of the world's known oil reserves are found in the Middle East, bringing great wealth to parts of the region.

Cities
The largest city of the Middle East is Cairo, Egypt. Founded by Arab conquerors in 641, it was originally known as al-Fustat. The older Egyptian port of Alexandria was rebuilt by the Macedonian leader Alexander the Great in the fourth century B.C. Damascus,

Middle Eastern oil wells. The wealth and political importance of the region result from its vast reserves of this important fuel.
▼

Syria, was founded about 5,000 years ago. Baghdad, Iraq, was founded in 762 A.D. Jerusalem, Israel, contains places holy to Jews, Christians, and Muslims.

People
The fertile regions of the Middle East are densely settled, while others, especially in the deserts, are empty of human life. There are three main ethnic groups: Arabs, Turks, and Iranians. Smaller groups include Armenians, Kurds, Pakistanis, Jews, Indians, and Greeks, who live mainly on the island of Cyprus. The major languages are Arabic, Turkish, and Persian (or Farsi). Most Middle Easterners are Muslims—followers of Islam. At one time most people lived in villages, but now about half the population live in cities.

History
Wandering tribes first settled and grew crops beside the Tigris and Euphrates rivers more than 8,000 years ago. The world's first-known civilizations, notably Sumer, arose in the fertile valleys.

Before the Christian era began 2,000 years ago, the Middle East had seen the rise and fall of many powerful peoples. Among them were the Egyptians, Hittites, Babylonians, Assyrians, and Persians.

Alexander the Great brought Greek culture to the region when he invaded it in the fourth century B.C. The Romans invaded in the first century B.C. While the western Roman empire fell in the fifth century A.D., the eastern, or Byzantine, empire, centered in Constantinople (modern Istanbul in Turkey), lasted another thousand years.

In the 600s the Arabs, newly converted to Islam by the prophet Muhammad, swept out of the Arabian Peninsula and created a vast empire that stretched from

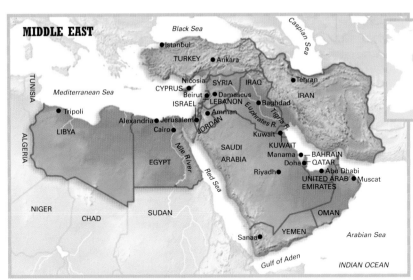

MIDDLE EAST

Black Sea

Caspian Sea

Istanbul

TURKEY • Ankara

TUNISIA

Mediterranean Sea

Nicosia   SYRIA   IRAQ   • Tehran

CYPRUS

Beirut • • Damascus   IRAN

LEBANON   • Baghdad

ISRAEL

Amman   Euphrates R.   Tigris R.

Tripoli

Alexandria • • Jerusalem   JORDAN

LIBYA   Cairo •

Kuwait •

KUWAIT

SAUDI   • Manama — BAHRAIN

ARABIA   Doha • QATAR

EGYPT   • Abu Dhabi

Riyadh •   UNITED ARAB • Muscat

Nile River   EMIRATES

Red Sea

ALGERIA

NIGER   OMAN

CHAD   SUDAN

Arabian Sea

Sanaa •   YEMEN

INDIAN OCEAN

Gulf of Aden

India in the east to Spain in the west. The last great empire of the region was that of the Ottoman Turks, who by the 1500s ruled most of the Middle East. Their empire crumbled after their defeat in World War I (1914–18).

After the war Britain and France governed large areas of the Middle East. Saudi Arabia and Iraq were created in 1932, and other nations won their independence during or after World War II (1939–45). The state of Israel was created in 1948 as a homeland for the Jews. This caused resentment among the Palestinian Arabs, who lost their land as a result, and led to five Arab-Israeli wars between 1948 and 1982, as well as continuing terrorist attacks. Between 1980 and 1988 there was a war between Iran and Iraq. Iraq invaded Kuwait in 1990 but was driven out in 1991 by the United States and its allies.

SEE ALSO: Ancient Civilizations; Islam; Israel; Judaism; Palestine; Turkey & the Caucasus

KEY FACTS

AREA
3,500,000 sq. mi.
(9,000,000 sq. km)

COUNTRIES
17

LARGEST COUNTRY
Saudi Arabia

SMALLEST COUNTRY
Bahrain

POPULATION
246,000,000

RELIGIONS
Islam, Christianity, Judaism

LANGUAGES
Arabic, Turkish, Persian (Farsi), Kurdish, Hebrew, English, French

A panoramic view across the rooftops of Damascus, the capital of Syria.

✶ MISSISSIPPI RIVER

The Mississippi River is the most important inland waterway of the United States and one of the longest rivers in the world.

From its source near Lake Itasca in northern Minnesota the Mississippi River flows through a broad, shallow valley until it reaches the Falls of St. Anthony in Minneapolis. From this point to Cairo, Illinois, it varies in width from ½ mile to 3½ miles (0.8–5.6km). Below Cairo it is joined by its main tributary, the Ohio River.

South of Illinois the Mississippi flows through a broad plain and winds its way past Memphis, Tennessee, Vicksburg and Natchez in the state of Mississippi, then Baton Rouge and New Orleans, Louisiana. Finally, it fans out through the Mississippi Delta into the Gulf of Mexico. The river twists and turns so much that the author Mark Twain, who piloted a steamboat on the Mississippi in the 1800s, called it "the crookedest river in the world."

History
In 1682 the French claimed all the land east of the river to the Appalachian Mountains and west of the river to the Rocky Mountains. When the United States gained independence from England in 1783, the Mississippi became the western boundary of the new nation.

In 1803 the Americans purchased the western lands from France. The river became the center of a vast territory stretching from the Atlantic Ocean to the Rocky Mountains.

The invention of the steamboat made it possible to transport goods and passengers upriver against the strong currents faster than with rafts and barges.

In the years of slavery before the Civil War (1861–65) the expression "sold downriver" meant the harshest of conditions to African American slaves because the most back-breaking work took place on the sugar and cotton plantations in the Deep South. On the other hand, the expression "going upriver" meant escape.

DID YOU KNOW?

The most devastating flood in U.S. history occurred in the summer of 1993. The Mississippi River at St. Louis, Missouri, was above flood level for 144 days. Around 3.9 billion cubic yards of water overflowed from the river channel onto the floodplain downstream from St. Louis. About 17,000 sq. mi. (44,030 sq. km) of land were covered by floodwaters in nine states (North Dakota, South Dakota, Nebraska, Kansas, Missouri, Iowa, Wisconsin, Minnesota, and Illinois).

A busy stretch of the Mississippi River at Baton Rouge, Louisiana.
▼

SEE ALSO:
Flood; River;

✳ MOLLUSK

Mollusks are invertebrates (animals without backbones). Some live on land or in fresh water, but most make their home in the ocean.

▶ *The zebra mussel is a common freshwater mollusk from Europe that has spread to North America.*

There are at least 100,000 different species of mollusk. Their bodies consist of a boneless structure called the visceral mass. The animals' internal organs are protected by a skinlike structure called the mantle. In many species the mantle produces material that forms a shell. Snails, oysters, and scallops have hard external shells. In other mollusks, such as cuttlefish, the shell forms an internal skeleton. Mollusks like slugs and octopuses have no shell.

All mollusks have some kind of muscular foot. In many species, such as clams, mussels, whelks, and snails, the foot is easily recognizable. But in others, like octopuses and cuttlefish, the foot has evolved into arms or tentacles.

Lifestyle

Some mollusks feed by drawing in water through a tube called a siphon and filtering the food the liquid contains. Others, such as limpets, graze on algae, using a toothed, tonguelike organ called a radula. Cephalopods, such as octopuses, grab prey with tentacles and tear it apart with beaks.

Most mollusks are either male or female. However, some snails, slugs, and other species are hermaphrodites—they have both male and female organs.

Reproduction usually takes place outside the parents' bodies. Eggs and sperm are released into water at the same time. In some species the male deposits sperm inside the female's body. Predators often eat the eggs and larvae of mollusks.

As they grow, many mollusks develop defense mechanisms. Snails have hard shells to protect them from birds and other enemies. Octopuses and squid produce thick, dark ink to hide themselves.

AMAZING FACTS !

There are more species of mollusk in the oceans than any other kind of animal, including fish.
Mollusks are some of the oldest animals, appearing on Earth more than 500 million years ago.
The largest known mollusk is the giant squid, which can measure 57 ft. (17m) in length including its tentacles and weigh more than 2 tons.

SEE ALSO: Animal

✳ MONEY

Money can be anything that is generally accepted as payment for goods or services. Today's money is bills and coins, but other materials have also been used.

Before the invention of coins people exchanged one thing for another, a practice called barter. For example, one person might offer some grain to another in return for a fish. Barter still takes place in some societies today, but it is not a perfect system. People may not agree on how much grain equals a herring, for example.

Many ancient civilizations used grain or metal in exchange for other goods. In ancient China and Africa seashells were used as currency. Native Americans used shell beads, called wampum, as trading counters. Each bead had a certain value.

Coins and notes
The first coins were made at about the same time, around 600 B.C., in three different parts of the world—India, Lydia (part of modern Turkey), and China. In about A.D. 1024 the Chinese issued the world's first paper money. Early Roman coins were made in the temple of the goddess Juno, or Moneta. That is the origin of the English word *money*.

It took hundreds of years for coins to replace barter and other forms of money. In the 13th century, as trade routes expanded, coins became more widespread. They were usually made of metal, especially gold or silver, and their value was determined by their weight. Governments controlled the supply of coins, and people who counterfeited—copied coins illegally—were punished.

Paper money and credit cards
Paper money was cheaper to make and easier to carry around than coins. Coins could be minted only if there was enough gold and silver available, but paper could be produced in almost unlimited quantities. At first governments tried to limit the creation of paper money by insisting that it be backed by gold or silver. In the United States, for example, people were once entitled to exchange a dollar bill for a set amount of gold. However, governments eventually found this requirement too limiting. In 1972 the nations of the world abandoned the system known as the Gold Standard.

Today many people use credit cards instead of money. When they buy goods, they sign a slip. The card provider (a firm such as Mastercard or Visa) pays the retailer, and the customer later pays back the card provider. Credit cards can now be used to buy almost anything in nearly all parts of the world.

◄
A moneychanger in Nigeria uses the shells of cowrie (marine mollusks) as currency.

DID YOU KNOW?

The earliest bankers were moneylenders. They had strong-boxes in which to keep money, and people left money with them for safekeeping in exchange for a receipt. People also borrowed money in exchange for a fee. The first banks appeared in northern Italy in the 1400s. The first bank in the United States was the Bank of North America, Philadelphia, which was given a charter, or license to operate, in 1781.

✳ MONGOLS

The Mongols were horse-mounted warrior nomads (people who wandered from place to place) who created a vast empire in Central Asia in the 1200s.

This Persian illustration of the 1300s shows Genghis Khan (seated on throne) with some of his vassals (lords).
▶

Genghis Khan imposed strict laws on the Mongol people. He led a strongly disciplined army, and that enabled him to control a vast area of land. This map shows the extent of the Mongol Empire in 1227, the year of Genghis Khan's death.

The earliest Mongol tribes herded sheep and horses on the vast plains of Central Asia. They lived in felt tents called yurts, which they took with them as they moved to new pastures. In 1206 the Mongols were united by a tribal leader called Temüjin (about 1162–1227). He became known as Genghis Khan (universal leader).

Genghis Khan created a highly organized and mobile army of cavalry (mounted troops) whose main weapons were powerful bows. Through warfare the Mongols created a huge empire that stretched 8,000 miles (13,000km) from China in the east to Hungary in the west, including much of modern Iran and Russia. The Mongols treated the people they conquered harshly. They sometimes killed all the inhabitants of towns they captured. Stories of such cruelty terrified people into surrendering without a fight.

When Genghis Khan died, his four sons extended the empire even farther. One of Genghis Khan's grandsons, Batu, conquered much of eastern Europe. Another of his grandsons, Kublai Khan, became ruler of China.

Modern Mongolia

In the late 1300s the Mongol Empire began to fall apart, although parts of it remained powerful for centuries longer. The Manchu rulers, from Manchuria in northeastern China, took over what is now Mongolia in the 1600s. The Mongols overthrew the Manchus in 1911. In 1921 Mongolia became a Communist state. When the Soviet Union broke up in the 1990s, Mongolia became a democracy. Today Mongolia occupies the northern half of the Mongolian plateau. It is sometimes called Outer Mongolia to distinguish it from Inner Mongolia, a region of China.

MONGOL EMPIRE

RUSSIA

● Moscow   SIBERIA

Black Sea   Aral Sea   ● Karakorum
Caspian Sea   MONGOLIA
TURKEY   IRAN   Beijing ●
● Baghdad   Yellow Sea
ARABIA   TIBET   CHINA
INDIA
Arabian Sea   Bay of Bengal   THAILAND   South China Sea

SEE ALSO: China

✳ MOON

A moon is any natural object that orbits, or circles, a planet. However, the word is most often used for the only natural satellite of the Earth.

Scientists have a number of theories about how the moon came into being. One idea is that it originally orbited the sun but was captured by the Earth's gravitational pull. Another is that the Earth and the moon were once a single mass of material. As the mass grew, it formed a bulge that broke away into space and became the moon. A more recent theory is that the moon formed when a giant object crashed into the Earth. Some of the debris that broke off became a satellite orbiting the planet.

Size and structure

The moon has a diameter of 2,160 miles (3,478km), about one-quarter the size of the Earth. It travels at an average speed of 2,237mph (3,600km/h). It speeds up when it gets closer to the Earth because of gravitational pull.

Like the Earth, the moon's surface is not smooth. It has mountainous areas, with some peaks as high as Mount Everest. There are also millions of depressions called craters. Dark patches are called seas because early astronomers thought they contained water. However, they are areas of lava (solidified molten rock). There is no water on the moon.

Scientists know a little about the interior of the moon thanks to instruments placed by astronauts who landed there in the 1960s and 1970s. The moon has a crust, with an average thickness of 40 miles (64km). Beneath is a mantle of about 435 miles (700 km), but no one knows what is under the mantle.

There is almost no atmosphere on the moon. There is no air to breathe and nothing to filter out radiation. The

This view of the moon was taken from the spacecraft Galileo as it flew by in December 1992. The photograph is made up of 18 images. It helps scientists study the surface of the moon.
▶

> ## DID YOU KNOW?
>
> The moon has no light of its own—moonlight is sunlight that is reflected off the moon's surface. Sometimes we can see the entire lighted side of the moon. At other times we see only a portion of it lit, so the moon appears to change its shape from night to night. These changes occur because the Earth's shadow blocks sunlight from reaching the moon.

temperature varies between 250°F (120°C) and –255°F (–160°F). People can only survive on the moon wearing special suits and using breathing equipment.

SEE ALSO: Astronaut; Astronomy; Earth; Gravity; Satellite; Solar System; Space Exploration

✳ MOVIES

Movies—also called motion pictures, films, or cinema—are one of the most popular forms of entertainment today.

◄
Children view a magic lantern slide after a Christmas party. This picture was made in about 1870. Magic lantern shows were a very popular form of entertainment during the 1800s.

The forerunner of movies was the magic lantern, a popular form of entertainment in the 1800s. It consisted of a box with a series of images that spun very quickly in front of a light source. The still images changed so fast that they appeared to the audience to be moving.

Inventors such as the Lumière brothers in France and the Englishman William Friese-Greene worked on systems that made photographic images appear to move. In the United States Thomas Edison and William Dickson invented the kinetoscope, a machine that allowed one viewer at a time to peep into a viewfinder to see about 20 seconds of full motion.

Modern films consist of long reels of flexible plastic. The plastic is divided into frames, each one containing an image

that is very slightly different from the next. These reels are run through a projector to produce an image on a white screen. To the audience the images seem to be moving because the reels run through the projector so quickly.

Early movies

The first movies were very short and simple. Audiences were happy to see images of everyday scenes, such as workers leaving a factory, because the illusion of movement was exciting on its own. However, moviemakers were soon telling stories on film.

In the early 1900s several studios set up in the Hollywood area of California. People such as Charlie Chaplin and D.W. Griffith produced movies that were popular

Now in 70 mm. wide screen and full stereophonic sound!

DAVID O. SELZNICK'S PRODUCTION OF MARGARET MITCHELL'S

"GONE WITH THE WIND"

Winner of Ten Academy Awards

CLARK GABLE
VIVIEN LEIGH
LESLIE HOWARD
OLIVIA de HAVILLAND

A SELZNICK INTERNATIONAL PICTURE · VICTOR FLEMING · SIDNEY HOWARD · METRO-GOLDWYN MAYER INC.
IN 70mm. WIDE SCREEN · STEREOPHONIC SOUND · METROCOLOR

Gone With the Wind (1939) opened a few months after the outbreak of World War II (1939–45) in Europe. It is based on a novel about the American Civil War (1861–65) by Margaret Mitchell.
▶

Anthony Minghella films The Talented Mr. Ripley (1999). Minghella wrote the screenplay and also directed the movie.
▶

around the world. In 1927 *The Jazz Singer* was the first movie with a built-in soundtrack. Now moviegoers could hear their favorite stars speak and sing. The 1920s also saw the first Academy Award ceremony. These prizes, also known as Oscars, go to the best directors, actors, and other contributors to movies.

The 1930s and 1940s are known as the Golden Age of Hollywood. Actors such as Clark Gable and Joan Crawford provided glamour and escapism during the dark days of the Great Depression and World War II.

In the 1960s movies became more realistic and dealt with difficult political and

social issues. More recently, special effects have become very important. Movies like *Jurassic Park* and *Toy Story* set new standards for what can be done through the medium of film.

How a movie is made
Moviemaking today is a mixture of technology, art, and business. Almost all movies begin with a script—a document that tells the story and lays out what the characters say and do. Sometimes the writer produces a script and then tries to find someone to make the movie. On other occasions a studio executive, or a producer, has an idea and gets a writer to create a script. Sometimes the story can be based on a book, a TV show, or another work that already exists.

Once the script is written, the most important people are the producer and the director. The producer finds money to finance the project and keeps overall control. The director interprets what is in the script and helps the actors give their best performances.

For many moviegoers the actors are the key people in a movie. Some fans will go to any movie that features their favorite performer. Sometimes producers persuade big stars to take roles in their movies by offering huge amounts of money, but most actors have to audition—they perform a section from the script in front of the director and the producer. If they seem right for the part, then they get the job. Once the action has been recorded on film, the editor and the director work together to choose the best scenes. They combine them to make a film that entertains and makes sense as a story. Other technicians may add sound effects or special visual effects. Nowadays these effects are often created with computers.

Often the producers will show a finished version of the movie to a test audience to see how they react. The movie may be changed before it is released. Sometimes a director changes a movie years after it has been released. George Lucas, the director of *Star Wars*, for example, has remade movies he created in the 1970s using new technology.

SEE ALSO: Cartoon & Animation; Communication; Edison, Thomas Alva; Photography

✳ MOZART, WOLFGANG AMADEUS (1756–91)

Many people believe that Mozart is the greatest composer of all time. His operas, symphonies, and other pieces are still performed all over the world.

This portrait of Mozart was painted in 1766–67.
▼

Mozart was born in Salzburg, Austria, the son of a composer. He was composing (writing music) by the age of five, and at eight years old he wrote his first symphony. He became concert master to the archbishop of Salzburg when he was just 13. In 1781 he quarreled with the archbishop and was dismissed. Mozart decided to settle in Vienna.

In 1782 Mozart married Constanze Weber. Although he had many troubles, including the deaths of four of his children and his wife's ill health, his greatest works were written during his years in Vienna. They included the operas *The Marriage of Figaro* and *Cosi fan tutte*, and his last three symphonies, which he wrote in less than seven weeks.

In 1791 Mozart began to suffer from fevers and headaches. One rumor is that another composer, who was jealous of his genius, poisoned him. Mozart's final opera, *The Magic Flute*, had its first performance in September. When Mozart died, on December 5, 1791, his last great work, the *Requiem*, was unfinished. Mozart died penniless, and because he had no money, his body was buried in an unmarked grave. To this day no one knows where this great composer lies buried.

SEE ALSO: Composers; Music

✳ MUSEUM AND GALLERY

Museums are places where collections of objects are preserved and displayed. Galleries display works of art, such as paintings and sculpture.

◄ *Sculptures of the Roman emperors in the Capitoline Museum, Rome, Italy. Sculptures depicting the head, shoulders, and upper chest of a human subject are called busts.*

The English word "museum" comes from the Greek *mouseion*, meaning "temple of the Muses." The Muses were goddesses of the arts and knowledge. Early museums in ancient Greece and Egypt were places where scholars could study and research. Sometimes they also contained old objects or works of art.

From about the 11th century A.D. the Christian church collected beautiful and valuable objects in cathedrals and monasteries. Ordinary people only saw them on special holy days. From the 1400s the noble families of Europe began collecting great works of art, but only scholars, artists, and important persons were able to visit them.

The first collections

The Ashmolean Museum at Oxford University, England, opened in 1683. The United Kingdom's first science library, it was based on the collection of Elias Ashmole, an English collector. The British Museum in London, England, was founded in the middle of the 18th century, but only scholars were allowed entry. Even they had to wait about two weeks before they could get tickets. It was not until the 1800s that museums and galleries opened to the general public.

The first museum in the United States was established in 1773 by the Charleston Library Society in Charleston, South Carolina. In the 19th century buildings were specially designed as museums to hold national collections. Before that, museums were based in churches, monasteries, palaces, or government buildings that no longer served their original purposes.

Art galleries

A museum that contains mainly paintings, sculptures, and other works of art is usually called a gallery. Almost every country in the world has at least one art museum that is a source of national pride. Some galleries have a general collection with works by many artists from different periods. Others are devoted to a specific

This 1796 painting shows one of the galleries in The Louvre, the great art museum in Paris, France.

period or style, such as the Museum of Modern Art in New York City, or to works by a single artist.

Types of museum

Some museums have very specific collections. For example, in Barcelona, Spain, there is a museum devoted to sewers. Bangkok, Thailand, has a museum of pathology, the study of dead bodies. Local museums have collections concerning their local area. Most museums, however, can be divided into a few general types.

History museums contain documents and objects that show how people lived in the past. Some museums are based in houses where famous people used to live. Experts maintain the buildings so that they look as much as possible as they did during the life of the original owner. To add to the authentic atmosphere, sometimes even the museum attendants are dressed in period costumes.

There are several types of science museum. Museums of natural history are concerned with all living things, from plants to humans, and also with minerals. Some house the remains of extinct animals, such as dinosaurs. Experts create models of animals and plants, and place them in surroundings that look like their natural habitat.

Other museums are devoted to industry and technology. People can see early machines, such as printing presses, cars, and steam engines. Because technology advances so quickly, equipment that was in the stores only a few years ago may soon turn up in a museum. Many museum collections include computers, game consoles, and mobile telephones that were produced commercially within the last 20 years.

A planetarium is a museum of astronomy. Images of stars and planets are projected onto the inner surface of a large dome.

The first children's museum was organized by the Brooklyn Museum in New York in 1899. The idea of having special museums or departments and exhibition space in museums set aside for young people soon caught on. Today there are children's museums in many countries around the world.

For some people it is enough just to look at beautiful or interesting objects on a visit to a museum or gallery. However, many museums offer talks by experts, guided tours of the highlights in a collection, and videos giving more detailed background information about the exhibits. There are also sections where visitors can perform experiments or play games that help them learn more about subjects relating to the collection.

Behind the scenes

The person in overall charge of all a museum's activities is the director. The registrar keeps records of all the objects in a museum. A museum's archive of books and documents is staffed by librarians. Large museums are divided into departments. Each department is under the care of a curator, who is an expert in a particular field, such as ancient art, modern painting, reptiles, or fossils. Large art galleries employ specialists who clean the works of art and keep them from deteriorating. Many museums have their own printing plants, where bulletins, announcements, and catalogs are printed.

SEE ALSO:
Archaeology;
Art; History;
Science

✳ MUSIC

From ancient times people have sung and played music. Each culture developed its own style of singing and its own instruments.

Music contains certain basic elements, such as melody, rhythm, harmony, and form. A single musical sound is called a tone. When music is written, tones are represented by symbols called notes. Most music is a combination of tones chosen from a set of tones called a scale.

In Western music most scales consist of seven tones. If you have a keyboard you can play a scale by starting at C (which is always a white key immediately to the left of two black keys) and playing each of the next seven white keys up to C again (see diagram below).

The interval between two notes of the same letter (C to C, D to D, and so on) is called an octave. The distance between adjacent tones can be either a whole step or a half step. A whole step is called a tone; a half step is called a semitone. There is no black key above (to the right of) E because the distance between it and F is a semitone. Similarly, the notes B and C are as close together as they can be: There is no note between them, so they are one semitone apart.

Sharps and flats

The black note to the right of—in musical terms above and therefore higher than—C is called C sharp. It can also be called D flat in reference to its position relative to the next white note above it. Thus all the black notes on a keyboard have two names—for example, the black note in the center of the keyboard diagram (above)

may be called either G sharp or A flat. In the same way some white notes also have two names.

Major and minor

Major scales are those in which full tones predominate. Music written in major keys sounds cheerful and positive. Minor scales, in which there are more semitones, produce sad and mysterious music.

The chromatic scale is a slightly different form of scale in which all 12 notes within an octave are played, all in half steps.

Oriental music uses different scales. Chinese and Japanese music is often based on a pentatonic scale—that is, a scale with only five notes, all spaced in whole tones.

Melody is a tune that can be whistled or sung. Beat is the underlying pulse of the music, while the way notes are played or grouped in patterns gives music its rhythm. Two or more tones played at the same time make up the harmony.

Harmony is a simultaneous sounding of two or more notes to make chords that give each piece of music its particular mood and texture. Form is the way rhythm, melody, and harmony are put together to make a piece of music.

Written music

Music is written in a special way called notation. Notation tells musicians which notes to play, how long they should last, and whether the music should be played quickly or slowly, loudly or softly.

stave

Notes are written on a stave—five parallel lines and the spaces between them (see diagram above).

Different shapes are used to indicate how long a note should last, as shown in the diagrams below.

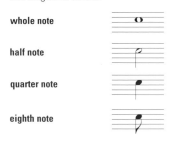

whole note

half note

quarter note

eighth note

The position of a note on the stave tells the musician its pitch—how high or low it is. A sharp sign (#) placed in front of a note raises the pitch of the note half a tone; a flat sign (♭) in front of a note lowers it by half a tone.

At the beginning of the stave is a clef sign. The most common clef signs are the treble clef and the bass clef (see below).

treble clef   **bass clef**

The treble clef is used to indicate that the notes are in the higher range. The bass clef shows that the music should be played in the lower range. Most instruments use written music that starts with a treble clef, but the music for some bass instruments, such as the tuba, is preceded by a bass clef. If the music is written for piano, the treble clef indicates use of the right hand, the bass clef the left hand.

The sharp signs or flat signs shown at the beginning of a piece of music form the key signature. They look like this:

sharps   **flats**

The key signature tells the musician the key (or scale) in which the music is written. If the key changes, another signature appears in the appropriate place.

Vertical lines on the stave divide it into measures, or bars, which each contain a certain number of beats. They look like this:

bars

The number of beats in each measure is indicated by the time signature. For example, 3/4 indicates three quarter-notes in each bar, 6/8 indicates six eighth-notes in each bar, and 4/4 indicates there are four quarter-notes in each measure (see below).

time signature

Western composers of structured music, usually called classical music, often write in established forms, such as sonata, concerto, symphony, opera, and oratorio.

The sonata is usually written for a solo instrument or a very small group of instruments and consists of three or four movements. The concerto is a piece for solo instrument (generally piano or violin) and orchestra, and has three movements. The symphony is a longer work for orchestra, usually with four movements.

An opera is a dramatic piece for solo singers, chorus, and orchestra. It is staged in a theater with costumes and scenery. An oratorio, performed in a concert hall without costumes or scenery, is a musical setting of a dramatic, usually religious, text.

Jazz and popular music are not always written down and are generally played without music, although they may be published later as sheet music. Folk music is learned primarily "by ear," without written music. Folk songs are usually passed on from person to person, a process called oral tradition.

SEE ALSO: Composers; Musical Instruments; Musicians, World; Music Popular

✷ MUSICAL INSTRUMENTS

Musical instruments are devices used to make musical sounds. Most musical instruments fall into three great sections: strings, winds, and percussion.

A traditional band playing in a park in Beijing, China.

When a musical instrument is played, it quivers with vibrations that produce sound waves in the air. Every instrument gives off its own distinct pattern of sound waves.

Stringed instruments

Stringed instruments consist of one or more strings stretched over a sound box or soundboard, which amplifies the sound. The strings are made to vibrate by plucking, striking, or bowing.

One of the oldest instruments is the harp, which is played by plucking the many strings with the fingers of both hands. Other plucked instruments are the lute, the guitar, the banjo, and the Indian sitar. For all of them the player's left-hand fingers press the strings to alter their length and therefore their pitch, while the fingers of the right hand pluck the strings.

Instruments of the violin family (violin, viola, cello, and double bass) are usually played with a bow, although they can also be plucked, in which case the sound is called "pizzicato." They produce a rich, mellow tone and are the basis of the modern symphony orchestra.

Some stringed instruments are operated from a keyboard. The strings of a harpsichord are plucked by a quill when the keys are pressed. In the piano a felt-covered hammer strikes a string when a key is pressed.

Wind instruments

In wind instruments the player blows into a hole at the end of a tube, making a column of air vibrate and so producing sound. The length of the tube and the amount of air pressure determine the pitch of the note.

Wind instruments fall into two groups—woodwind and brass. Bassoons, clarinets, flutes, and oboes are woodwind. They were once all made from wood, but some are now made from metal or plastic. Cornets, horns, trombones, trumpets, and tubas are brass instruments. They are all made from metal.

DID YOU KNOW?

The organ is like a collection of many different wind instruments linked by machinery so that one performer can play them all from a keyboard.

THE ORCHESTRA

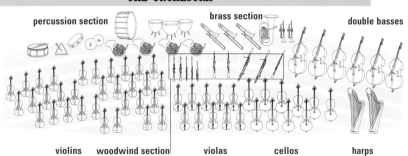

percussion section

brass section

double basses

violins   woodwind section

violas

cellos

harps

Woodwind instruments have three different kinds of mouthpiece. The clarinet has a single reed attached to the mouthpiece, while the oboe and bassoon both have a double reed. When the player blows across a reed, it vibrates and moves the air inside the instrument. Flutes simply have a hole across which the player blows a thin stream of air that vibrates inside the flute. To produce different notes in woodwind instruments, the player's fingers cover and uncover holes along the length of the tube.

Brass instruments
Brass instruments have a mouthpiece shaped like a funnel. The player puts his or her mouth against the mouthpiece and blows into the tube. Most brass instruments have valves that can be opened and closed to alter the length of the tube and so change the note. Trombones use a slide mechanism to achieve the same effect.

Percussion instruments
Percussion instruments are struck with the hands, fingers, or sticks to produce a musical sound. The best known are drums, cymbals, triangles, xylophones, and glockenspiels.

Drums are found all over the world. They are usually made by stretching a membrane, such as skin or vellum, across one or both ends of an open cylinder. The membrane is struck with the hand or a drumstick to make it vibrate and produce a sound. The pitch of the note produced can be changed by altering the tension of the membrane across the cylinder—the tighter the membrane, the higher the note.

Cymbals are brass plates that are clashed together to make an exciting sound. The triangle is a bent rod of steel that is hit with another rod. The xylophone is a row of wooden bars that produce a dry, eerie sound when played. The glockenspiel has metal bars that give a ringing, magical sound. Xylophones and glockenspiels are played with hammers.

SEE ALSO: Composers; Hearing; Music; Sound Recording

✳ MUSICIANS, WORLD

There are many rich and contrasting traditions of music around the world, some of which have blended to produce vibrant new forms.

◄
In Havana, Cuba, a woman rumbas to the music of a street band.

In Africa south of the Sahara Desert music is a vital part of everyday life, and there are special songs for many different occasions. African music is often based on a call-and-response format, in which a soloist sings a phrase that is answered by a group of singers. However, it is rhythm that is most important. Interacting layers of rhythm are sounded by a variety of instruments, including drums, gongs, xylophones, rattles, and bells. One of the most distinctive African instruments is the mbira, or thumb piano (also called kalimba), which consists of metal tongues attached to a solid or hollow piece of wood. The tongues are stroked or plucked with the thumbs to produce soft tones.

African music has had a strong influence on the music of other regions of the world, particularly North America, Latin America, and the Caribbean.

In the Caribbean, African rhythms combine with melodies from Europe to produce new forms such as calypso, mambo, merengue, ragga, rumba, and son. In Latin America, African and European styles have combined with traditional Indian music to produce dance forms such as the tango, samba, bossa nova, cumbia, and lambada.

Asian music

A common thread in the music of Asia is the dominance of melody. In south China folk songs have smooth, flowing melodies, while the northern style favors angular melodies with large leaps between tones. Instruments commonly used in Chinese music include stringed instruments such as the pipa (a lute) and the ch'in (a type of zither). Flutes and percussion instruments are also used.

WORLD MUSICIANS

These are some famous musicians from around the world. There are many more.

Gardel, Carlos (1887–1935)
Argentinian singer who was celebrated for popularizing the music, song, and dance of tango, earning the title "King of Tango."

Shankar, Ravi (1920–)
Indian sitar player who has been largely responsible for introducing Indian music to Western audiences.

Cruz, Celia (1924–)
Cuban singer who has performed worldwide, earning herself the title "Queen of Salsa."

Kussudiardjo, Bagong (1928–)
Indonesian composer of music and dances for gamelan orchestras and dancers.

Sosa, Mercedes (1935–)
Argentine singer whose songs of love, poverty, and politics have brought her a passionate following.

Jara, Victor (1932–73)
Chilean singer-songwriter whose *nueva canción* ("new song") political lyrics led to his murder by Chile's military regime.

Kuti, Fela (1938–97)
Nigerian musician whose powerful "afro-beat" music was consistently critical of his country's military regimes.

Blades, Ruben (1948–)
Panamanian singer who introduced a political element into his salsa songs.

Guerra, Juan Luis (1956–)
Singer-songwriter from the Dominican Republic whose songs, with a social and political message, are set to merengue music— the traditional folk music of his country.

Estefan, Gloria (1957–)
Singer who helped popularize salsa (a brass-based form of jazz developed by Cubans living in the U.S.) before moving on to pop.

N'Dour, Youssou (1959–)
Singer from Senegal, West Africa, who has toured the world with his songs and modern arrangements of traditional Senegalese melodies.

Diabaté, Tourmani (1965–)
Musician from Mali, West Africa, whose brilliant playing of the kora (a kind of African guitar) has made it a well-known solo instrument worldwide.

The traditional music of Japan is based primarily on pentatonic (five-tone) scales, sometimes supplemented with two additional tones. The most common style of Japanese music is a single melody played with slight variations on several different instruments at the same time. Typical instruments include various flutes, the koto (a type of zither), and the shamisen (a lute). Japanese music is closely linked with other forms of artistic expression, such as dance, drama, and song.

The music of India is based on melodic formulas called ragas. Drone harmonies that sustain (hold) certain notes accompany these melodies. In many performances the musician makes up some of the music as it is played. A popular instrument is the sitar, a stringed instrument, which can play microtones— intervals smaller than the half steps of Western scales.

Among the other regions of Asia with a distinctive musical tradition is the Middle East, where the melodic formulas on which the music is based are called magams. In Indonesia large orchestras called gamelans use gongs and metal bars to create shimmering sounds.

SEE ALSO: Music; Music, Popular

An originator of the style known as afro-beat, the Nigerian Fela Kuti (1938–97) was one of the most influential African musicians of the late 20th century.

◄

✳ MUSIC, POPULAR

Since the 1950s popular, or pop, music has expressed the thoughts of young people. It is one of the major entertainment forms of modern times.

In the 1940s many blues performers from the Southern states moved to Chicago, Illinois, where they developed a new form of the music using electric guitars. In 1949 a Cleveland, Ohio, disk jockey named Alan Freed began playing rhythm and blues records that soon became popular with both white and black teenagers. It was Freed who popularized the phrase "rock-'n'-roll." In 1953 Bill Haley and His Comets became the first rock-'n'-roll group to enter the Billboard pop chart with the single "Crazy Man Crazy." In the mid-1950s Elvis Presley, a white man from Memphis, Tennessee, began to record rhythm and blues songs with country influences, and rock-'n'-roll soon became a worldwide phenomenon.

The 1960s

The next major influence came from England. The Beatles, four young men from Liverpool, were influenced by rock-'n'-roll, but brought their own style, energy, and wit to the music. When they first visited the United States in 1964, they influenced a generation of musicians.

Another important musician of the time was Bob Dylan, who used folk music to express his political and social ideas. The Beatles, Dylan, and others led a movement of young people who questioned contemporary society's ideas about sex, drugs, minorities, and the war in Vietnam.

At the same time, soul music was at its height. Performers on record labels such as Tamla Motown, in Detroit, Michigan, and Stax, in Memphis, Tennessee, combined gospel, rhythm and blues, and pop influences. By the 1970s soul had developed into the intense rhythms of funk and then disco.

Reggae was a style of popular music that originated in Jamaica in the late 1960s. Jamaican singer and composer Bob Marley and his band The Wailers introduced reggae music to a worldwide audience.

The 1970s and later

In the early 1970s rock music became louder and more complex, leading to heavy metal and progressive rock. After

Elvis Presley's first U.S. No. 1 single was "Heartbreak Hotel" in 1956.

The Beatles, from left to right: John Lennon, George Harrison, Paul McCartney, and Ringo Starr.

IMPORTANT MODERN MUSICIANS

These are some of the popular musicians who have established a lasting reputation. There are many others.

Berry, Chuck (1926–)
U.S. guitarist who wrote some of the earliest rock-'n'-roll songs.

Presley, Elvis (1935–77)
One of the first white rock-'n'-roll singers.

The Beatles
The best-selling and most influential pop group of all time.

Dylan, Bob (1941–)
U.S. songwriter who began as a political protest singer, then brought folk and country elements to rock music.

The Beach Boys
U.S. band whose complex harmonies and songs of surfing, cars, and girls presented a classic image of California to the world.

Franklin, Aretha (1942–)
U.S. singer who brought the gospel music of the African American churches to a mainstream pop and soul audience.

Hendrix, Jimi (1942–70)
U.S. guitarist, singer, and songwriters whose astonishing guitar work influenced heavy rock and funk musicians.

The Rolling Stones
Long-lasting English band with an outrageous stage act.

Marley, Bob (1945–81)
Jamaican singer-songwriter of reggae—songs of social protest with a throbbing beat—who became an international superstar.

Springsteen, Bruce (1949–)
U.S. guitarist/singer who writes songs about the working classes.

Wonder, Stevie (1950–)
U.S. singer, songwriter, producer, and multi-instrumentalist who had his first hits at the age of 12.

Madonna (1958–)
U.S. singer/songwriter. The best-selling female musician of all time.

Eminem (1973–)
Controversial white U.S. rap singer who had his first hit in 1999.

Jones, Nora (1979–)
U.S. singer who won eight awards at the 45th Grammy Awards in 2003. She is the daughter of Indian sitar player Ravi Shankar.

a few years a simpler, more aggressive form developed. Punk rock, led in Britain by bands such as the Sex Pistols and in the United States by The Ramones, developed into new wave and alternative music. In the early 1990s grunge became popular. The most successful exponents of this style of music were Nirvana, a U.S. band fronted by Kurt Cobain.

In the late 1970s black New York musicians created a new form of dance music called hip-hop, or rap. Rap contains two main elements: Rhymed lyrics spoken over rhythm tracks, and pieces of recorded music and sounds, called samples, taken from older records. Rap and other dance styles such as house and techno have remained popular and influential into the 21st century.

By the end of the 20th century many of these styles had melded together: Some of the most successful groups and singers were influenced not by a single genre but by many different types of pop music. This form of pop is called fusion.

Madonna performs live on stage in Tokyo, Japan, during her 1990 "Blonde Ambition" world tour. Her first hit single was "Holiday," in 1983.
▼

 SEE ALSO: Music; Musicians, World

✳ NAPOLEON (1769–1821)

Napoleon Bonaparte ruled as emperor of France
from 1804 to 1814. A military genius, he also wrote
a new code of laws that protected people's rights.

Napoleon was born on the French island of Corsica. He attended a military school and joined the French army in 1785. At the time France was at war with much of Europe. In 1796 Napoleon was given command of the French army in Italy. He won victories there and in Austria. In 1798 he invaded Egypt.

In 1799 Napoleon returned to Paris. On November 9, with the aid of his followers, he overthrew the unpopular French government. A consulate of three men was established to govern France, but Napoleon, named First Consul, held all the power.

Napoleon brought stability to France. In 1804 he helped write the Napoleonic Code, a set of laws that is still widely used today. That year he crowned himself emperor. His next aim was to conquer Europe. A series of brilliant campaigns, known as the Napoleonic Wars, followed. By 1807 his armies held Europe from Spain to the borders of Russia.

In 1812 Napoleon tried to conquer Russia, but the long marches and cold weather were too much for his troops. Also, a British-led campaign in Spain was driving back French forces. In 1814 Paris fell. Napoleon was forced to abdicate (give up) his throne and was exiled to the island of Elba near Corsica. On March 1, 1815, he returned to lead France again, but his troops were finally crushed at Waterloo on June 18, 1815. Napoleon was imprisoned on the South Atlantic island of St. Helena until his death on May 5, 1821.

As well as being an outstanding military leader, Napoleon Bonaparte modernized the French government, giving more power to the citizens. This sketch was drawn by Jacques-Louis David in 1799.

SEE ALSO: Europe; France

✳ NATURAL RESOURCES

Anything that occurs naturally on the Earth becomes
a natural resource when people use it to supply their
needs or serve their wants.

◂
*The Dalles Dam
in Oregon makes
use of an
important natural
resource by
harnessing the
water of the
Columbia River
to generate
electricity.*

Air and water are two important natural
resources—people need them to live.
Land is a natural resource if people can
use it to grow crops for food or dig useful
minerals out of it. Wildlife is another
resource. Wild animals are used for
food, skin, and fur. Forests are natural
resources. The wood from trees is used
to build houses and make paper.

Usefulness to people is very important
in determining whether or not a material
is thought of as a natural resource. For
example, the mineral bauxite has been in
the ground for millions of years, but it did
not become a resource until the 1880s,
when scientists found a cheap way to
extract the aluminum it contains.

There are two main types of natural
resource—renewable and nonrenewable.
Most of the Earth's mineral resources are
nonrenewable. Once they are used, they
will be gone forever. In contrast, sunlight
is constantly renewed. No amount of use

will make it less available. Our modern
way of life is based on nonrenewable
mineral resources, mainly coal, natural
gas, and petroleum. They are all fossil
fuels—sources of energy that have
formed over millions of years through the
accumulation and compression of organic
material—the decayed remains of dead
animals and plants.

Coal
Coal is made mainly of solid carbon, an
element that burns well. Coal is carved
out of the ground in a process called
mining. Originally the main use of coal
was to heat homes. Today it is used to
generate electricity, refine steel, and in
the production of fertilizers.

Natural gas
Like coal, natural gas—which is mainly
methane—forms from the remains of
plants and animals. It is found in rocks

▶
Petroleum industry workers drill for oil, a nonrenewable natural resource.

on the ocean floors. It is excavated by drilling, an expensive and dangerous process. The main use of natural gas is in heating, but it is also used to make some fertilizers, plastics, paints, and other materials.

Petroleum
Petroleum, or crude oil, is a liquid fossil fuel that forms in the same way and from the same raw materials as coal and natural gas. Scientists can pinpoint places where oil is likely to be, but deposits can be reached only by drilling on land or under the oceans. Once crude oil has been removed from the ground, the impurities it contains are removed by a process called refining.

People use refined petroleum for hundreds of purposes. It is the raw material for the gasoline that powers cars and other vehicles; it heats buildings and provides electricity; and it is used to make plastics, synthetic fibers, asphalt, and many other substances.

Renewable resources and recycling
Mineral resources are nonrenewable. They took millions of years to form, and people are using them up increasingly quickly. If we carry on using petroleum, coal, and natural gas in the same quantities, there will be none left in a few hundred years.

People also damage and destroy other natural resources. They dump wastes into streams, killing fish or making the water unfit to drink. Factories and cars release smoke into the air, making the air unfit to breathe. These are examples of pollution.

If we want to carry on heating and lighting our homes, wearing new clothes, and traveling in cars and other vehicles, we need to increase our use of renewable resources. Solar power—using the energy from the sun—is one possibility. Solar panels catch sunlight and use it for heating and other purposes.

Scientists are also investigating the use of wind and water power. Wind farms in open spaces have rotating arms that move in the wind to generate energy. Hydroelectric power uses the energy produced by sea tides and the flow of rivers to generate electricity.

Wood is another renewable resource. If we manage forests sensibly, we can grow trees as quickly as we use them.

Already people are making more use of recycling. We can use old aluminum cans to make new metal products. We can pulp waste paper to make newspapers. Garden and kitchen waste can be composted to make natural fertilizer.

Natural resources have made a great contribution to human civilization. But if we want to survive, we must all use them more sensibly.

SEE ALSO: Energy; Geology; Metals; Pollution

✳ NAVIGATION

Navigation is the science of finding your way. Many birds and animals have a built-in sense of direction, but people have to learn skills to navigate.

The English word *navigation* comes from the Latin words meaning "ship" and "move." Today the word means finding your way on or under the sea, on land, in the air, or even in space.

The first navigators were sea travelers. They stayed close to familiar coasts and used landmarks, such as islands, to figure out where they were. This technique, called piloting, is very useful when a ship is close to shore because the navigator can tell the distance between the craft and rocks or other dangers. Buoys and lighthouses help navigators guide their ships safely.

Navigators also use charts—maps of sea areas—to help them. Compasses, with metal needles that always point to the magnetic North Pole, help the navigator figure out the right direction to steer.

When people began to explore farther out to sea, where there are no landmarks, they first used the positions of the sun and stars to find their way.

By about the second century B.C. mapmakers had devised a system of imaginary lines that covered the Earth and helped sailors plot their position more accurately than ever before.

The first and longest of these imaginary lines is the equator, which circles Earth midway between the North and South poles, where its circumference is about 25,000 miles (40,000km). Its name comes from the Latin word *aequare*, meaning "to make equal." The equator divides the Earth into two equal halves, the Northern and the Southern Hemispheres.

Latitude and longitude

Lines of latitude are shown on maps and globes as lines or circles parallel to the equator. Latitude is measured in degrees, with the equator at zero degrees (0°). Any point north of the equator is said to be in north latitude; any point south of the equator is said to be in south latitude. For example, Miami, Florida, has a latitude of 26 degrees north, or 26°N; Buenos Aires, Argentina, has a latitude of about 35 degrees south, or 35°S. The farther a place is from the equator, the higher the number of degrees in its latitude—the North and South poles are at 90°.

Longitude indicates the number of degrees any place is to the east or west of an imaginary straight line drawn from the North Pole to the South Pole through Greenwich, London, England. This line is called the prime meridian. Thus New York City's longitude is 74 degrees west (of Greenwich), or 74°W. The longitude of Tokyo, Japan, is 140 degrees east (of Greenwich), or 140°E.

◄ *A compass is an instrument for finding direction. The magnetized needle swings freely on a pivot to point toward magnetic north.*

Celestial navigation

When a ship is on the equator, certain stars will seem to be overhead. If the ship sails north, these stars appear to move

Conservationists in Sumatra, Indonesia, use the global positioning system (GPS) to determine whether illegal logging is being carried out within a restricted area in which tree felling is banned.
▶

lower in the sky. By measuring the distance between the stars and the horizon, a navigator can judge the ship's latitude. For centuries navigators used a device called a sextant, a telescope fixed on a metal scale, to measure the distance between the sun and the horizon.

To judge longitude, navigators needed a clock to tell them the exact time in Greenwich. In 1735 John Harrison, an Englishman, made the first accurate clock, or chronometer, for use at sea. By observing the sun, a navigator found the time it was aboard the ship. Then, by comparing the ship's time with Greenwich time, the navigator could figure out the ship's longitude. If the ship's time was earlier than Greenwich time, its longitude had to be west of Greenwich. If the ship's time was later than Greenwich time, the ship's longitude had to be east. It is 15 degrees east or west for each hour's difference in time.

Using these two systems for latitude and longitude, skilled navigators were able to figure out their exact position anywhere in the world. This method is called celestial navigation.

Electronic navigation

Today navigators can use electronic equipment to find their positions. Radar provides a "picture" of the surrounding area and can also identify other ships, airplanes, or other craft.

A recent development in navigation is the global positioning system, or GPS. It is a group of 24 satellites around the Earth that send signals to receivers giving them their precise location. As well as ships and airplanes, many cars are now equipped with GPS receivers. Even people on foot can find their way by using handheld receivers of this type.

Electronic navigation is also vital to space travel. But because of the danger of computer error, astronauts still need to be aware of celestial navigation to figure out where they are and the direction in which they are traveling.

SEE ALSO: Geography; Map; Radar & Sonar; Satellite

✳ NEPTUNE

The planet Neptune is so far away from Earth that very little was known about it until recently. It cannot be seen from Earth without a telescope.

Neptune is about four times larger than Earth. The planet revolves around the sun in a huge elliptical (oval-shaped) orbit about 30 times greater than that of the Earth. Since its discovery in 1846 Neptune has not yet completed a single revolution of the sun.

In 1989 the planetary space probe Voyager 2 flew past Neptune and revealed some remarkable facts about the planet and its moons.

This picture of Neptune was taken by the Voyager 2 space probe in 1990 when it was 4.4 million miles (7 million km) away from the planet.

▶

Blue gas giant

Unlike Earth, which has a rocky crust with an interior of molten rock, Neptune has a deep, thick atmosphere of hydrogen and helium gases, together with traces of methane gas, surrounding an ocean of water, methane, and ammonia.

About 10 percent of Neptune's mass is made up of hydrogen and helium. The other 90 percent of its mass consists mostly of heavier elements, such as carbon, nitrogen, and oxygen. In contrast, Jupiter's mass is about 96 percent hydrogen and helium.

All white light is made up of a spectrum of seven colors—red, orange, yellow, green, blue, indigo, and violet. Objects appear to be one color or another because their surfaces absorb the other colors. Methane absorbs six spectral colors but reflects blue, which is why Neptune appears that color when it is hit by light from the sun. Thin wispy clouds floating in the upper atmosphere are above most of

the methane, so they appear to be white. The upper atmosphere of Neptune is very cold, but temperatures increase closer to the center of the planet. Within Neptune astronomers think there may be a rocky core about the size of Earth. The temperature at the core may reach 15,000°F (8,000°C).

SEE ALSO: Astronomy; Light; Solar System; Space Exploration

KEY FACTS

POSITION IN THE SOLAR SYSTEM
Eighth planet from the sun

AVERAGE DISTANCE FROM THE SUN
2,800,000,000 mi. (4,500,000,000km)

SOLAR ORBIT
165 Earth years

DIAMETER
30,800 miles (49,600km)

MASS
103 sextillion tons

ATMOSPHERE
Hydrogen, helium, methane

AXIAL ROTATION
16 hours 5 minutes

✳ NETHERLANDS, BELGIUM, AND LUXEMBOURG

The Netherlands, Belgium, and Luxembourg are small countries in northwest Europe. Together they are sometimes known as the Low Countries.

◄ Brouwersgracht and Prinsengracht Canals meet in Amsterdam. The canal network was developed in the 1600s for the nobles and wealthy merchants.

The Netherlands is often called Holland, after the province (now divided in two) that has long been the political and economic center of the country. The people and language are known as Dutch.

The country is very low and flat. More than one-quarter lies below sea level and has been reclaimed from the sea over many years. Dikes were built around flooded areas, and the water was pumped out with windmills. The drained areas are called polders. With its many rivers and canals the Netherlands has the densest network of waterways in the world.

Farming, fishing, shipping, and trade have traditionally been the main economic activities. The country's location on the North Sea has made it a natural trade center, and in the 17th century Dutch merchants and sea captains made this small nation a leading world power, with colonies in Asia, Africa, and the Americas. Today

Rotterdam is the largest port in Europe and one of the largest in the world, the gateway through which much of western Europe's shipping must pass.

The area that is now the Netherlands was ruled by the Romans, the Franks, the French dukes of Burgundy, and the Spanish. In 1648 Spain recognized the independence of the Dutch Republic.

In 1795 the Netherlands was occupied by the French. It regained independence in 1813 as a monarchy and united with Belgium between 1815 and 1830. During World War II (1939–45) the country was occupied by Germany. After the war the Netherlands became one of the first countries to campaign for cooperation among European states.

▲ King Leopold II of Belgium (ruled 1865–1909) claimed a huge expanse of land in Africa's Congo River basin as his own personal colony.

KEY FACTS

OFFICIAL NAME
Kingdom of the Netherlands

AREA
16,033 sq. miles
(41,530 sq. km)

POPULATION
15,786,000

OFFICIAL NAME
Kingdom of Belgium

AREA
11,787 sq. miles
(30,530 sq. km)

POPULATION
10,161,000

OFFICIAL NAME
Grand Duchy of Luxembourg

AREA
999 sq. miles
(2,587 sq. km)

POPULATION
431,000

NETHERLANDS, BELGIUM, AND LUXEMBOURG

Netherlands'
national flag

Belgium's
national flag

Luxembourg's
national flag

Like the Netherlands, Belgium was part of the Roman Empire and later came under Spanish, and then French rule. It was united with the Netherlands for 15 years until 1830.

Germany invaded the country during World War I (1914–18) and World War II (1939–45), causing great devastation. Today Belgium is a highly industrialized nation, and Belgian products are sold all over the world

Luxembourg
Luxembourg is a tiny country, smaller than the state of Rhode Island. It is a very prosperous nation, with one of the highest standards of living in the world. Important industries include iron and steel, banking, and agriculture. The traditional language is Letzeburgish, a dialect of German. French and German are also widely spoken.

Luxembourg was first an independent state in 963, when Count Siegfried of Ardennes took over an old Roman fortress on the Alzette River. In 1443 Duke Philip of Burgundy conquered Luxembourg, and several European powers fought over the area for the next four centuries. It became independent again in 1839, but was invaded by Germany in both world wars.

Belgium
Belgium is divided into three regions with different cultures. Flanders, in the north, is the home of the Flemings, who speak Flemish. They make up about 60 percent of the population. The French-speaking Walloons, who live mostly in Wallonia in the south, form about 30 percent. About 60,000 German speakers live in the east.

European unity
In 1948 Belgium, the Netherlands, and Luxembourg set up an economic union called Benelux. In 1957 they joined with France, Germany, and Italy to form the European Economic Community (now called the European Union). Its administrative center is in Brussels.

The castle at Vianden in Luxembourg dates from the ninth century but has been restored to its 18th-century appearance.
▼

SEE ALSO: Europe; Roman Empire; World War I; World War II

✳ NEWSPAPER AND MAGAZINE

Newspapers and magazines are among the most
important ways of transmitting information and
opinions about current events.

◄
*This newsstand in
Lisbon, Portugal,
sells a range of
newspapers and
magazines.*

In ancient Rome news was broadcast by
handwritten notices posted on walls in
public places. Newspapers as we now
know them first appeared in Europe in
the 1500s and magazines about 150
years later. The first newspaper in America
was published in 1690, but the colonial
authorities soon closed it down. Across
the world governments have often been
frightened by the power of the press.

Many of today's newspapers, including
The New York Times, were first published
in the 1800s. Printing had become
cheaper, and for the first time in history
most people could read. In the 1900s
improved printing techniques made it
easier to produce magazines in color.

By the 1980s computer technology had
made it possible to print the same
newspaper or magazine simultaneously in
different places. *USA Today*, the first
national newspaper in the United States,
was launched in 1982.

Newspapers

Although there are differences between
big, internationally known newspapers and
local publications, they share certain
features. The most important part of any
newspaper is news. Reporters are the
people responsible for getting news
stories. Some reporters may be specialists,
concentrating on sports, politics, or other
subjects. Others may be general reporters,
who can cover any story. Sometimes
newspapers take their stories from a news
agency, such as Reuters, whose reporters
supply many publications.

Editors decide which subjects get
covered, and how much space they
should take up. A large newspaper may
have many editors, covering all the main
areas of importance. On a small paper
one person might make all the decisions.
But there will always be a single person,
often called the editor-in-chief, who will
have the final say about content.

In addition to news, newspapers contain photographs and illustrations that help explain stories and add impact. A really good front-page photo can make a huge difference to sales of a paper. On the inside pages there are articles of serious comment about events, lighter pieces that take an amusing look at life, cartoons, comic strips, and crosswords. There are also reviews of movies, books, and exhibitions. And there is usually space for letters from readers.

Other important jobs on a newspaper include selling space for advertising and distribution—the physical process of getting the paper to the customer.

Magazines

The literal meaning of the word *magazine* is "storehouse" or "treasury." Magazines are sometimes called periodicals because they are published regularly—often once a week or once a month—at specific times. In the United States alone there are 9,000 magazines that are published at least quarterly (four times a year).

Magazines are divided into general- or special-interest magazines, also called consumer magazines, and business magazines, also called trade magazines. There are also scholarly journals, which report on research in various fields.

Many special-interest magazines deal with a single subject, such as baseball or photography. Some are published for a specific readership, such as teenagers or African Americans.

The success of newspapers and magazines depends on their ability to make people want to buy them.

SEE ALSO: Cartoon & Animation; Comic Strip; Communication; Photography; Printing

---

✳ NEWTON, ISAAC (1642–1727)

Isaac Newton was one of the most important scientists in history. His ideas about gravity, motion, and other subjects still influence modern science.

▶ *This portrait of Isaac Newton was made after he had been knighted (become Sir Isaac Newton) by Queen Anne of England in 1705.*

Isaac Newton was born on Christmas Day 1642 in the small English town of Woolsthorpe. A dreamy, impractical boy, he left school to work on his mother's farm, but he was such a failure that she sent him back. At age 18 he went to Cambridge University. Aged only 22, he worked out a basic formula, called the binomial theorem, that has been used by mathematicians ever since. In 1669 he became a professor at Cambridge.

Newton's studies of light and color led him to make the first reflecting telescope. He also developed the theory of gravity. In 1687 he published *The Mathematical Principles of Natural Philosophy*, usually known as the *Principia*, which many people think is the most important scientific book of all time. It included his three laws of motion and his law of universal gravitation. Newton's ideas explain why a ball falls to the ground when it is thrown in the air, and why drivers jerk forward when their cars stop suddenly.

SEE ALSO: Force & Motion; Gravity; Light; Math & Numbers; Physics

✳ NEW ZEALAND

New Zealand lies southeast of Australia in the South Pacific Ocean. It consists mainly of two large islands—North Island and South Island.

On both main islands mountains rise among the green, rolling landscape. Some are active volcanoes. There are geysers and hot springs, and earthquakes are common. Lake Taupo is the largest lake. The Chatham Islands lie about 400 miles (650km) to the east.

Summers are mild; winters are cool and stormy. Over 300 in. (7,600mm) of rain fall in Fiordland, but to the east there are only 15 in. (380mm) of rain a year.

Plants and animals

Bush once covered half of New Zealand, but settlers have cleared much of it for pastures or crops or replaced it with pine plantations. Along the southwest coast there are dense rainforests.

New Zealand is rich in native birds. Many are flightless, including the brown kiwi and the kakapo, a large parrot. The tuatara is a native reptile found today only on small offshore islands.

People

New Zealand's earliest inhabitants, the Maori, came from Polynesia in the 1300s. Today most New Zealanders are descended from British people, who first arrived in the 18th century. New Zealand became independent from Britain in 1907. The majority of the population live on the North Island. Auckland is the most important port.

Economy

New Zealand has many millions of sheep and cattle, which yield meat, dairy, hide, and wool products. There are fruit farms on North Island and vineyards in the South, and the forests are logged for lumber.

Auckland
NORTH ISLAND
Tasman Sea
Lake Taupo
Napier
Cook Strait
Wellington
SOUTH ISLAND
Christchurch
Mount Cook
PACIFIC OCEAN
Fiordland N.P.
Dunedin

KEY FACTS

OFFICIAL NAME
New Zealand

AREA
104,454 sq. mi. (270,534 sq. km)

POPULATION
3,862,000

CAPITAL
Wellington

LARGEST CITY
Auckland

MAJOR RELIGION
Christianity

MAJOR LANGUAGE
English

CURRENCY
New Zealand dollar

New Zealand's national flag

A crater lake in Tongariro National Park, an active volcanic area on the North Island of New Zealand.
▼

SEE ALSO: Island; Pacific Ocean

✳ NIGHTINGALE, FLORENCE (1820–1910)

Florence Nightingale, an Englishwoman, is regarded as the founder of modern nursing and a pioneer in hygiene and sanitation.

▲
Florence Nightingale in about 1845.

Florence Nightingale was born May 12, 1820, in Florence, Italy. Her parents were very wealthy, and she was brought up in great luxury in England. By the age of 24 Nightingale was certain that God was calling her to nurse the sick. Her family was horrified at the prospect, and it was not until 1851 that she was allowed to go to Germany to gain nursing experience. In 1853 she undertook the management of a small hospital in London.

When the Crimean War (1854–56) broke out between Britain and Russia, the British government asked Nightingale to lead a party of nurses to the war area. There she found more than 5,000 sick and wounded men in terrible conditions. Working night and day, she inspected every ward, equipped the hospitals to carry out medical care, and made them clean. The soldiers called her the "Lady of the Lamp."

On returning to England, Nightingale continued her efforts to improve the diet and health of soldiers. In 1858 she published a huge book on army hospitals. She opened the Nightingale Training School for Nurses at St. Thomas's Hospital in London in 1860.

In 1907 Nightingale became the first woman to be awarded the Order of Merit. She died on August 13, 1910, at the age of 90.

SEE ALSO: Hospital; Medicine; Nursing

✳ NIXON, RICHARD MILHOUS (1913–94)

Richard Milhous Nixon was the 37th president of the United States from 1969 to 1974. He is the only president to have resigned from office.

Richard Milhous Nixon was born on January 9, 1913, in California. His parents were poor lemon farmers.

Nixon went to college and law school. In 1942 he joined the Navy and rose to the rank of lieutenant commander. In 1946 he won a seat in the House of Representatives for California. Four years later he became a senator. In 1952 Dwight D. Eisenhower chose him as his vice-presidential running mate.

Nixon served as vice president for eight years. In 1960 he won the Republican nomination for the presidency, but John F. Kennedy defeated him. Two years later he lost the election for governor of California.

He returned to practicing law. In 1968 Nixon again won his party's nomination for the presidency. In the election he defeated the Democrat candidate, Vice President Hubert Humphrey.

Presidency

In his first term Nixon announced the gradual withdrawal of troops from Vietnam, and a ceasefire took place in his second term. He relaxed trade restrictions with the communist powers and signed an arms limitation treaty with the Soviet Union. In 1972 Nixon made a historic visit to China—the first by a U.S. president since the Communists came to power in 1949.

Despite his achievements, the name of Richard Nixon will forever be associated with Watergate.

During the 1972 election campaign five men had been arrested for breaking into the Democratic National Committee headquarters in the Watergate building in Washington, D.C. They were employees of Nixon's reelection committee.

The president claimed to know nothing about the breakin, but he refused to hand over White House tape recordings to the committee investigating the affair. The House of Representatives voted for his impeachment, or formal charges of misconduct. In August 1974 Nixon resigned from office. His successor, President Gerald R. Ford, pardoned him of all offenses against the United States.

SEE ALSO: Middle East; Vietnam War

KEY FACTS

BIRTHPLACE
Yorba Linda, California

OCCUPATION
Lawyer

MARRIED
Thelma Catherine (Pat) Ryan

PARTY
Republican

AGE WHEN PRESIDENT
56

TERM
1969–74

AGE AT DEATH
81

✳ NOBEL PRIZE

Nobel Prizes are awards for major achievements in specific fields. They commemorate Alfred Nobel, the inventor of dynamite.

The Swede Alfred Bernhard Nobel (1833–96) made his fortune from the invention of dynamite and other explosives, as well as artificial fabrics. When he died, he left most of his fortune to fund annual awards to the men and women who had made the greatest contribution to humanity in the fields of physics, chemistry, medicine, literature, and peace. An individual award can be shared or can be given to an organization. Since 1969 experts in economics have also been eligible to receive prizes.

Choosing a winner

Expert committees in Norway and Sweden, Nobel's homeland, decide each year who will win prizes. Sometimes there is controversy over an award. For example, the Russian author Boris

In 2001 the Nobel Peace Prize was won jointly by the United Nations and its secretary-general, Kofi Annan.

SOME FAMOUS NOBEL PRIZE WINNERS

These are just a few of the best-known Nobel Prize winners.

Curie, Marie (France): physics, 1903; chemistry, 1911

Einstein, Albert (Germany): physics, 1921

King, Martin Luther, Jr. (United States): peace, 1964

Mother Teresa (Albania): peace, 1979

Mandela, Nelson and **De Klerk, F. W.** (South Africa): peace, 1993

Morrison, Toni (United States): literature, 1993

Naipaul, V. S. (Britain/Trinidad): literature, 2001

Carter, James E. (Jimmy) (United States): peace, 2002

Pasternak was awarded the literature prize in 1958, but the Soviet authorities would not let him accept it.

Each winner gets an award of about $1 million, a gold medal, and a diploma. The value of the prize is greater than this—Nobel prizewinners have made a huge contribution to the human race.

SEE ALSO: Curie, Marie & Pierre; Einstein, Albert; Explosive; King, Martin Luther, Jr.; United Nations

✳ NORTHWEST TERRITORIES

The Northwest Territories make up over 12 percent of Canada's total area. Despite its vast size, the territory is one of the most thinly populated areas in the world.

The climate of the Northwest Territories is extremely cold. The average daily temperature in July does not exceed 60°F (15°C). Winter temperatures often drop to −40°F (−40°C) and lower for many weeks. The islands in the Arctic Ocean and along the coast of the mainland have an Arctic climate, with extremely long, cold, and dark winters and short summers.

People

The population is split almost equally between native and nonnative Canadians. Native people include Dene and métis, who are of mixed ancestry. Most people live in small towns and villages along the shores of the Great Slave Lake and the banks of the Mackenzie River.

History

Nomadic (wandering) native peoples lived by hunting and fishing. The first known European explorers to visit the Northwest Territories were the Vikings, who sailed to the eastern Arctic about A.D. 1000. From the 1500s onward European explorers came in search of a passage to Asia through the Arctic islands, and fur traders further explored the area in the 1700s.

Until 1870 the Northwest Territories were part of British North America. In that year the British government transferred lands formerly under the control of the Hudson's Bay Company to Canada. Over time the size of the Northwest Territories decreased as some of its lands were given to five other provinces. The most recent division occurred in 1999, when Nunavut was carved out of the eastern part of the Northwest Territories.

Economy

The Northwest Territories is rich in resources, including fresh water, timber, and wildlife. Minerals, such uranium, tungsten, lead, zinc, copper, silver, and gold are plentiful. Huge oil and gas reserves have been discovered in the Beaufort Sea and the Mackenzie Delta, but they have not been developed because of the high cost of production and transportation to southern markets. About 80 percent of the labor force works in service industries, such as government agencies.

SEE ALSO: Canada; Inuit; Vikings

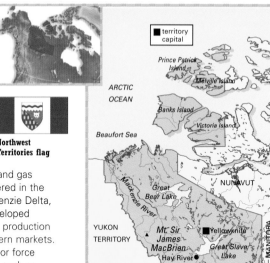

Northwest Territories flag

territory capital

Prince Patrick Island
Melville Island
ARCTIC OCEAN
Banks Island
Beaufort Sea
Victoria Island
Mackenzie River
Great Bear Lake
NUNAVUT
YUKON TERRITORY
Mt. Sir James MacBrien
Yellowknife
Great Slave Lake
Hay River
MANITOBA
BRITISH COLOMBIA
ALBERTA
SASKAT-CHEWAN

KEY FACTS

AREA
481,728 sq. mi. (1,235,200 sq. km); territory rank, 1st

POPULATION
40,900 (2001 census); territory rank, 1st

ELEVATION
Highest—9,062 ft. (2,762m) at Mt. Sir James MacBrien; lowest—sea level

CAPITAL
Yellowknife

TERRITORY ESTABLISHED
1912

ABBREVIATION
NWT

TERRITORY MOTTO
None

TERRITORY FLOWER
Mountain avens

TERRITORY TREE
Tamarack

TERRITORY BIRD
Gyrfalcon

◄ *Dempster Highway runs across the Northwest Territories between Dawson City, Yukon, and Inuvik, Nunavut.*

✳ NURSING

The word *nurse* comes from the Latin meaning "to nourish" or "to cherish." A nurse is someone who cares for the sick, the injured, and the disabled.

Nurses have always worked with physicians in the treatment and care of the sick. Their many duties include changing dressings, dispensing medicine, taking patients' temperatures and blood pressure, giving injections, doing physical examinations, and delivering babies.

Nurses today have to understand the effects of powerful drugs. They must care for patients who have had surgery and must operate machines used in the treatment of illness. They must also know about modern methods of fighting illness and promoting health.

Where nurses work

Nurses are essential members of a team of workers who provide health care to individuals, families, and communities. Many nurses work in hospitals, clinics, and nursing homes, and in patients' own homes. Some nurses work in doctors' offices or in health-maintenance organizations. Others serve in public health departments or community health agencies. Schools, industries, business firms, and governments also employ nurses. Nurses may serve abroad with organizations such as the Peace Corps, the World Health Organization, and the International Red Cross.

History

In Europe and later in North America Christianity had a major influence on the development of nursing. Many hospitals were started by the church, and nursing was carried out by men and women in religious groups. In the 1500s, however, many monasteries in Europe were closed, and nursing declined.

An upturn began in 1633, when Saint Vincent de Paul founded a nonreligious nursing order in Paris. Members of the order worked in many parts of the world. Florence Nightingale, an English nurse, was the founder of modern professional nursing. She established the first school of nursing in London in 1860. Schools based on the Nightingale model were started in the United States and Canada in the early 1870s. Nightingale's ideas about nursing and nursing education are still valid today.

Training

Students usually have to complete a number of years of general schooling before they can move on to take courses in nursing. In the United States student nurses attend nursing schools in universities and colleges. Elsewhere nurses train in hospital schools, but some countries are now starting to adopt the U.S. system.

A hospital nurse prepares to give an injection to a young patient.
▼

SEE ALSO: Hospital; Medicine; Nightingale, Florence

295

✳ NUTRITION

Nutrition is the science that deals with how the body uses food. A nutritious diet is one that keeps the human body healthy and helps it function properly.

If we ate only our favorite foods all the time, we would probably get sick very quickly. We need to eat a wide variety of foods to stay healthy.

Food supplies nutrients, various chemicals that ensure our bodies keep working. Too little or too much of a nutrient can cause illness or even death, so our diets need to be balanced.

Protein

Protein provides energy and is vital to build and repair body tissue. It is especially important for growing bodies. Meats, fish, eggs, dairy, and beans are rich in protein.

Carbohydrate

The body needs two kinds of carbohydrate. Complex carbohydrates provide energy over a long period. The best sources are grains, such as wheat and rice, and potatoes. Simple carbohydrates, such as sugar, provide immediate bursts of energy. They are found in fruits and milk.

Fat

Fats are a source of energy, but they are high in calories and can lead to weight gain and heart disease if eaten in large quantities. Fats are found in meat, fish, dairy, eggs, nuts, and some vegetables.

Vitamins

Vitamins help cells work the right way. There are 13 vitamins in all, each of which has a particular purpose. Important vitamins include ascorbic acid, or vitamin C, found in fruits and green vegetables. It helps the body fight infection and maintain healthy bones and skin. Vitamin

E, found in nuts and seeds, protects cells and prevents the blood disorder anemia. Vitamin B1 assists the conversion of carbohydrates to energy.

Minerals

The human body needs a total of 21 minerals to run correctly. The most important are calcium and phosphorus, which are needed to maintain bones and teeth. Calcium occurs in dairy products, and phosphorus is in meat, fish, and eggs.

Water and fiber

Humans need plenty of water to assist the chemical processes taking place inside their bodies, to cool them down, and to carry away waste as urine. It is important to eat fiber because it helps clear solid wastes from the body. Fiber is present in fruits, vegetables, and grains. Too little fiber can cause constipation and may lead to cancer.

The best way to ensure a nutritious diet is to eat a wide variety of foods. However, some people have diets that avoid certain foods. That may be because of allergies or intolerances—particular foods make them unwell. Other people, such as vegetarians, may choose not to eat some foods for reasons of conscience.

The food pyramid is an easy way to remember the foods you should be eating most. At the base of the pyramid are staple foods, such as bread, rice, pasta, and cereals, of which we should eat 8–20 ounces every day. At the top of the pyramid are butter and sugar, which should be eaten in small quantities not more than once a day.

Fats
Sugar

Proteins

Dairy

Vegetables Fruit

Carbohydrates

👀 **SEE ALSO:** Health; Human Body; Medicine; Nutrition

✳ OCEAN AND SEA

Seawater covers more than 70 percent of the Earth's surface. Oceans and seas contain valuable resources for human life, such as food and energy.

Most scientists today agree that the continents were created when the plates forming the Earth's crust slid apart. The gaps between the continents form the areas of the Earth's oceans. No one knows for certain how these gaps filled with water. One theory is that the Earth was surrounded by a cloud layer that cooled, releasing huge quantities of rain. Another idea is that water vapor was released by hot rocks in the Earth's crust.

Sometimes the word "ocean" is used to refer to all areas of seawater. But geographers generally use the word to define the world's four largest bodies of water—the Arctic, Atlantic, Indian, and Pacific oceans. There is some disagreement about whether the seas around Antarctica should be considered a fifth ocean. Other areas, such as the Caribbean and the Mediterranean, are called seas.

The measure of salt in water is called salinity. Seawater usually has a salinity level of about 35 parts per thousand—in other words, 1,000 ounces of water contain 35 ounces of dissolved salt.

Seawater also contains dissolved carbon dioxide and oxygen, which are necessary to maintain plant and animal life in the sea. Nitrates, phosphates, and many trace elements are also present.

Waves, currents, and tides
The waters in the oceans and seas are constantly moving. Winds cause movements called waves on the surface. Waves can be tiny or can reach heights of 100 ft. (30m). Some movements are continuous and in a single direction—they are called currents.

Currents affect climate because they carry warm water into cold regions and cool water into tropical regions. This mix of temperatures creates many kinds of weather patterns.

Tides are daily rhythmic rises and falls in the level of the sea. They are caused by the gravitational pull of the moon and the sun.

As the world's oceans and seas pound the coasts, they alter the shape of the surrounding land.
▼

THE WORLD'S LARGEST OCEANS AND SEAS

Pacific Ocean	96,658,638 sq. miles (155,557,000 sq. km)
Atlantic Ocean	53,785,890 sq. miles (86,560,000 sq. km)
Indian Ocean	42,598,723 sq. miles (68,556,000 sq. km)
Southern Ocean	12,630,612 sq. miles (20,327,000 sq. km)
Arctic Ocean	8,220,740 sq. miles (13,230,000 sq. km)
South China Sea	1,848,330 sq. miles (2,974,600 sq. km)
Caribbean Sea	1,710,634 sq. miles (2,753,000 sq. km)
Mediterranean Sea	1,555,292 sq. miles (2,503,000 sq. km)
Bering Sea	1,409,394 sq. miles (2,268,200 sq. km)
Gulf of Mexico	958,714 sq. miles (1,542,900 sq. km)

Life in the sea

Thousands of species of plants and animals live in the seas and oceans. Many can survive only at particular depths, temperatures, and levels of salinity. Some fish can live only in the darkness at the bottom of the deepest oceans.

Coral is made from the skeletons of billions of tiny sea animals called polyps. Coral reefs form when polyps anchor themselves to undersea volcanic islands. Over millions of years more polyps attach themselves to the skeletons of dead polyps until they form a structure that resembles a giant rock, called a reef. Reefs can reach lengths of 1,000 miles (1,600km) and are the biggest structures made by nonhuman animals. Coral reefs are very fragile and can easily be destroyed by global warming, pollution, or mining.

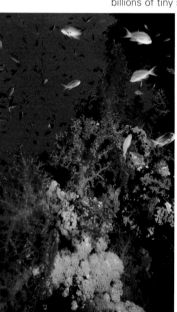

Shoals of fish swim around a tropical coral reef.

People and the oceans

The seas and oceans are an invaluable resource. Fishermen harvest tons of fish and shellfish for food. Engineers drill for oil and natural gas. Ships and boats transport passengers and cargo more cheaply by sea than by land or air. Vacationers enjoy sailing, game fishing, swimming, and diving. However, human activities also harm the oceans, polluting them with wastes from homes, factories, oil and chemical spills, and overfishing.

SEE ALSO: Climate & Weather; Earth; Ecology; Fish; Fishing Industry; Island; Pacific Ocean; Pollution; Sea Mammal; Water

✴ OLMEC AND TOLTEC

The Olmecs formed the earliest civilization in what is now Mexico, between about 1200 and 400 B.C. The Toltecs inhabited Mexico before the Aztecs.

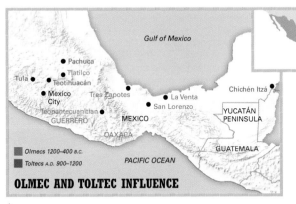

Gulf of Mexico

Pachuca
Tlatilco
Tula
Teotihuacán
Mexico City
Tres Zapotes
Teopantecuanitlan
GUERRERO
MEXICO
OAXACA
Chichén Itzá
La Venta
San Lorenzo
YUCATÁN PENINSULA
GUATEMALA
PACIFIC OCEAN

Olmecs 1200–400 B.C.
Toltecs A.D. 900–1200

OLMEC AND TOLTEC INFLUENCE

The main Olmec centers lay near the Gulf of Mexico, but their trading empire stretched south to Guerrero and Oaxaca. The Toltec's influence was felt as far away as Chichén Itzá.

As far as is known, they had no written language and no pack animals. All transportation was on foot or by canoe. Among the materials they carried was the rock used to carve their massive statues and monuments. Many of these statues are of huge heads. They may represent Olmec rulers. Other carvings show a figure that is half-man, half-jaguar, and there are many carvings of rattlesnakes. Archaeologists believe that they may represent Olmec gods.

The Olmec civilization was based on the religious center of La Venta, in the Isthmus of Tehuantepec (pronounced "tAwantApek"). Historians do not know where the Olmecs came from, or why their civilization died out.

Olmecs built houses and public buildings on platforms. The remains of one of these platform cities have been found in Mississippi, which suggests that Olmecs crossed the Gulf of Mexico into the United States. Olmecs farmed the land around these great buildings, using irrigation to water their crops.

The Toltecs

The Toltecs established an empire in about A.D. 900 just north of the Valley of Mexico. The first ruler was Prince Ce Acatl Topiltzin. Their empire extended as far south as Yucatan and Guatemala. The Toltecs worshiped the god Quetzalcoatl (pronounced keh-tsahl-koh-ahtl), who was represented as a feathered serpent.

The Toltecs were farmers. They grew crops such as corn, squash, and beans. They must have traded with other peoples, because Toltec pottery and sculptures have been found all over Mexico. Artworks found at the Toltec capital of Tula include images of jaguars and of eagles eating human hearts.

The Toltecs were the strongest civilization in Mexico until about 1200, when the Aztecs began to dominate the region. The Aztecs claimed to be descendants of the Toltecs and kept their warlike culture as well as many of their gods and other traditions.

One of the gigantic stone heads found at the Olmec ceremonial center of La Venta. The sculptures are made out of a rock called basalt and are 10 ft. (3m) high.

👀
SEE ALSO: Aztecs; Mexico

✳ OLYMPIC GAMES

The Olympic Games draw athletes from all over the world. The modern Olympics began in 1896, but the idea is much older.

No one knows when the first Olympics took place, but there are records of games honoring the god Zeus in 776 B.C. They were held at Olympia in ancient Greece. For many centuries Greek cities competed against each other in events that included running, wrestling, jumping, discus, and javelin. Warring states even stopped fighting while the games took place. Interest in the games spread, and foreign athletes came to compete.

When Rome conquered Greece in the first century B.C., Olympic standards began to decline. The Roman emperors demanded prizes and cheated to win. The games were stopped in A.D. 394.

The modern Olympics
In the late 1800s Baron Pierre de Coubertin, a Frenchman, became interested in the ancient Olympics. He believed that sports and exercise were a vital part of young people's education. He also believed that people should take part in sports without financial and commercial pressures, so the games were for amateur sportspeople only. The original Olympians were crowned with laurel leaves but received no money prizes. In 1896 Coubertin organized the first modern Olympic Games in Athens, Greece. They have been held in different places around the world every four years since then, except in 1916, 1940, and 1944, when world wars prevented them.

Organization
Coubertin founded the International Olympic Committee (IOC), and this organization continues to run the games. Each country has its own national olympic

Runners compete in the women's 1,500 meter semifinal in the 2000 Olympics in Sydney, Australia.
▼

PORTUGAL

2833

3778

1840

committee, and each sport has an international federation to oversee selection of athletes for the games.

Cities compete for the honor of hosting the games. Every four years thousands of athletes, coaches, officials, and spectators come to one place, and millions more watch on television. A modern Olympic Games requires many different facilities for the various sports, and they are often spread through an entire city and the surrounding area. Track and field events need an open-air arena. Weightlifting, gymnastics, and combat sports such as boxing and judo take place in covered spaces. The swimmers and divers need pools; and other water sports, such as canoeing, are held outdoors. For many spectators the greatest event is the marathon, a running race of 26 miles 385 yards (42.195km), which usually takes place on the streets of the host city, finishing in the main stadium. The race was included in the 1896 Olympics to commemorate the run Pheidippides was said to have made to Athens to tell the citizens of their army's victory at the battle of Marathon in 490 B.C. Women first competed in the marathon at the Los Angeles Olympics in 1984.

Tommy Schwall, ski jumper for the United States, at the 2002 Winter Olympics held in Salt Lake City, Utah. Cold-weather Olympic sports also include cross-country skiing, skating, hockey, and bobsledding.
▶

Ceremonies

The Olympics have changed greatly since their origins, but some aspects remain the same. Most importantly, there is no prize money for competitors. Athletes who claim first, second, or third place win medals—gold, silver, or bronze.

Every games begins when the Olympic torch enters the main stadium. Athletes running in relays carry the torch from Olympia. An athlete from the home nation uses the torch to light a flame that burns for the duration of the games. The games begin and end with elaborate ceremonies celebrating the history and culture of the home nation and the Olympic ideals of fair play. The Olympic symbol of five colored rings is often used in these ceremonies.

Winter Olympics

The first Winter Olympic Games were held at Chamonix, France in 1924. They took place in the same year as the summer games until 1992. Since 1994 the winter games are held two years before and after the summer games. The cold-weather sports of today's Winter Olympic Games could not have developed in the warm climate of Greece.

AMAZING FACTS!

At the 2000 Games in Sydney, Australia, 10,651 athletes from 199 nations competed in 300 events.
The Olympic torch was first lit at the 1928 games in Amsterdam, Netherlands.
At the 1904 games in St. Louis, Missouri, Fred Lorz (USA) was the first marathon runner to cross the line. However, he was disqualified when it turned out that he had covered most of the course in a car.

SEE ALSO: Greece, Ancient; Sports

✳ PACIFIC ISLANDS

There are about 25,000 islands in the Pacific, most of them in the southern ocean. They are often called Oceania and are divided into three main groups— Polynesia, Melanesia, and Micronesia.

◄ The shore of American Samoa, one of the groups of islands that make up Polynesia.

The islands in the Pacific Ocean are of two main types—continental and oceanic. Continental islands rise from the continental shelves, the underwater areas surrounding most continents. These islands are the tips of the long chains of mountains and volcanoes that border the Pacific Basin.

Two processes formed the Pacific's oceanic islands—volcanism and subsidence. Volcanic islands form when lava (molten rock) pours out from the Earth's interior, then cools. Hawaii is the largest Pacific island created in this way.

In subsidence the weight of the volcanic mass forces the crust of the ocean basin to sink, or subside. The older an island is, the more it will have sunk, and therefore the lower it appears in the ocean.

As a volcanic island subsides, colonies of small organisms called corals, living just below the surface of the water, sometimes attach themselves to it. In time the volcanic material may disappear beneath the ocean. But the corals go on building upward, forming reefs. If sand, made by erosion of the coral rock, collects on top of the rock, a low sandy island

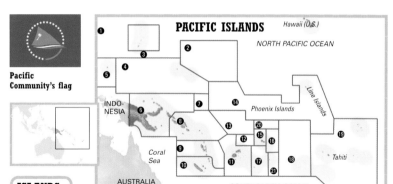

Pacific Community's flag

PACIFIC ISLANDS

Hawaii (U.S.)

NORTH PACIFIC OCEAN

INDO-NESIA

Line Islands

Phoenix Islands

Coral Sea

Tahiti

AUSTRALIA

SOUTH PACIFIC OCEAN

ISLANDS

1. Northern Mariana Islands (U.S)
2. Marshall Islands
3. Guam (U.S.)
4. Federated States of Micronesia
5. Palau
6. Papua New Guinea
7. Nauru
8. Solomon Islands
9. Vanuatu
10. New Caledonia (Fr.)
11. Fiji
12. Wallis & Fortuna (Fr.)
13. Tuvalu
14. Kiribati
15. Samoa
16. American Samoa (U.S.)
17. Tonga
18. Cook Islands (NZ)
19. French Polynesia (Fr.)
20. Tokelau (NZ)
21. Niue (NZ)

AMAZING FACTS!

In 1993 scientists discovered more than 1,000 volcanoes underwater in the South Pacific. It is the largest concentration of active volcanoes in the world.

results. If this sandy island is shaped like a ring, it is called an atoll. The water enclosed by an atoll is a lagoon. Many islands of Tonga formed in this way.

Polynesia and Melanesia

Polynesia—the name means "many islands"—is a large triangle of islands in the central and southeastern ocean. Major island groups in Polynesia include Hawaii, Tonga (the Friendly Islands), Tuvalu (formerly the Ellice Islands), Samoa and American Samoa, and part of Kiribati, including Christmas Island. Also in Polynesia is Easter Island, which is famous for its mysterious, giant carved heads. The Maoris, the original inhabitants of New Zealand, are Polynesians.

Polynesian people share the same basic language, although there are different dialects across the islands. Many Chinese, Japanese, and European people have also settled in Polynesia.

The islands of the southwestern Pacific are called Melanesia. The word means "black islands" and refers to the dark

skins of the original inhabitants. Melanesia includes New Guinea, Fiji, New Caledonia, the Solomon Islands, and Vanuatu (formerly the New Hebrides).

Micronesia

The 2,000 tiny islands of northwestern Oceania are known as Micronesia, meaning small islands. Many of them are coral atolls. Four island chains—the Carolines, the Gilberts, the Marianas, and the Marshalls—dominate the region.

Johnston Atoll and the islands of Nauru and Wake are also in Micronesia. So too is Midway, the scene of a crucial battle in 1942 during World War II (1939–45). Politically, Micronesia is divided into five independent nations, eight U.S. territories, and one U.S. commonwealth.

Economy

Most Pacific islanders are subsistence farmers, growing food for themselves and their families. Some of the higher volcanic islands produce pineapples, sugar, and bananas for export. The lower coral islands have little fertile soil, and copra, the dried flesh of coconuts, is the only cash crop.

There are few mineral resources. Nauru has phosphates, and New Guinea has deposits of oil and gold. Some islands earn money from tourism, but most are too remote for easy access. Many islanders worry that tourism will damage their ecology and culture. They also fear that global warming will melt the ice of Antarctica, raising the level of the oceans and threatening to cover low-lying islands.

SEE ALSO: Climate & Weather; Easter Island; Indonesia; Island; Ocean & Sea; Pacific Ocean; Volcano; World War II

* PACIFIC OCEAN

The Pacific is the largest of the world's oceans, covering just under one-third of the Earth's surface. In parts it is also the deepest.

The Pacific extends from the Arctic to the Antarctic, a distance of over 9,000 miles (14,480km) from north to south. Along the equator it extends about 11,000 miles (17,700km) from the west coast of the Americas to the east coast of Asia and Australia. The equator divides the North and South Pacific.

The Pacific joins the Indian Ocean at the Strait of Malacca between Indonesia and Malaysia and south of Australia. It meets the Arctic Ocean at the Bering Strait and the Atlantic Ocean at Cape Horn, the southern tip of South America.

There are about 25,000 islands in the Pacific Ocean, as well as coral reefs and many underwater mountains.

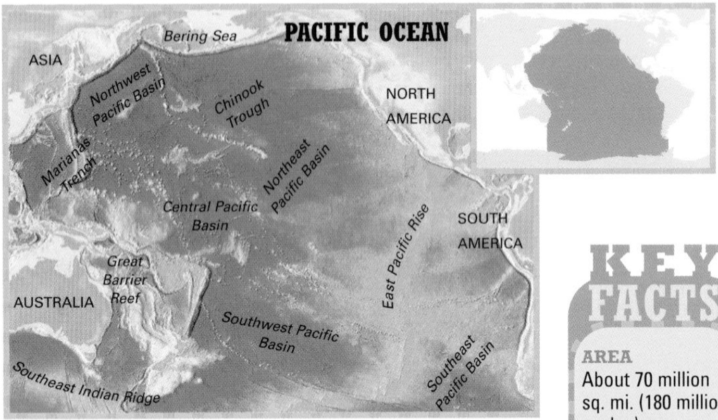

History

The earliest inhabitants of the Pacific islands probably migrated there thousands of years ago, when there was a land bridge from Southeast Asia. The first European to see the ocean was the Spanish explorer Vasco Núñez de Balboa, in 1513. In the 1520s the Portuguese navigator Ferdinand Magellan named the ocean "Pacific," meaning peaceful. In the 1700s the English explorer James Cook discovered many islands, which were later colonized by European powers and the United States.

In World War II (1939–45) the United States and Japan fought many battles in the Pacific. Since the war most Pacific states have become independent.

Map labels: Bering Sea, ASIA, Northwest Pacific Basin, Chinook Trough, NORTH AMERICA, Marianas Trench, Central Pacific Basin, Northeast Pacific Basin, SOUTH AMERICA, East Pacific Rise, Great Barrier Reef, AUSTRALIA, Southwest Pacific Basin, Southeast Pacific Basin, Southeast Indian Ridge, PACIFIC OCEAN

KEY FACTS

AREA
About 70 million sq. mi. (180 million sq. km)

AVERAGE DEPTH
About 14,000 ft. (4,270m)

DEEPEST SPOT
Challenger Deep in the Marianas Trench, the deepest point on Earth, 35,852 ft. (10,924m) deep

WIDTH
About 11,000 mi. (17,700km) along the equator from the west coast of the Americas to the east coast of Asia and Australia

Ice floes floating on the sea in the most northerly stretches of the Pacific Ocean near the Bering Strait between Alaska and Siberia, Russia.

SEE ALSO: Island; Ocean & Sea; Pacific Islands; World War II

✳ PALESTINE

Palestine is a region of southwestern Asia at the eastern end of the Mediterranean Sea. Christians, Jews, and Muslims all consider the area to be holy.

Palestine's flag

▷

In 1917 the area controlled by the British and known as Palestine stretched from the Mediterranean Sea to the east of the Jordan River. In 1923 the British divided the area. In 1948 the state of Israel was established. After the 1967 war Israel occupied the Gaza Strip, the West Bank, Sinai, and the Golan Heights. Sinai was returned to Egypt in 1982, but Syria's Golan Heights remain under Israeli control.

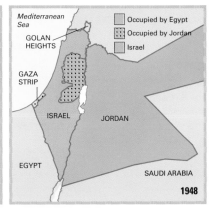

Palestine takes its name from that of the Philistines, one of many ancient peoples who have lived in the area. In about 2000 B.C. the Hebrew people settled in Palestine. The Hebrews, who followed the Jewish religion, controlled the area until the eighth century B.C., when the Assyrians and then the Babylonians forced them into exile. In the following centuries Palestine fell under the control of the Persians and then of Alexander the Great. In 167 B.C. Judah Maccabee led a revolt that reestablished a Jewish kingdom that lasted until 63 B.C.

For the next 700 years Palestine was part of the Roman and then the Byzantine empires. During this time Jesus Christ began his ministry in Palestine and was crucified by the Romans. Shortly after A.D. 630 the Arabs, who followed the new faith of Islam, conquered the area.

305

Muslims, or followers of Islam, believe that their prophet Muhammad went to heaven from Jerusalem, the main city of Palestine. Palestine also contains many places described in the Bible, including Nazareth, Bethlehem, and the sea of Galilee.

Zionism and the Palestinian Arabs
From the 1500s the Turkish Ottoman Empire ruled Palestine. At the end of World War I (1914–18) the area became a British protectorate. Zionism became popular with European Jews. Zionists wanted Palestine to be a homeland for the Jewish people. After World War II (1939–45) many Jewish survivors of persecution in Europe wanted to move to Palestine. Muslim Arabs who lived there did not want the area to become a Jewish state. In 1948 the State of Israel declared independence. It was attacked by its Arab neighbors but defeated them. Thousands of Arabs were forced from their homes.

After another Arab–Israeli war in 1967 Israel occupied more Palestinian land. In 1996 Palestinians living in two of the occupied areas—the Gaza Strip and the West Bank—elected their own National Authority. Palestinian groups continue to use terrorist tactics to try to force Israel to let them govern themselves.

> **SEE ALSO:** Ancient Civilizations; Crusades; Holocaust; Islam; Israel; Judaism; Middle East; Roman Empire

✴ PANAMA
Panama is a small nation in Central America. A canal linking its Pacific and Atlantic coasts makes the country important to world trade.

Panama stands on the Isthmus of Panama, the thinnest part of Central America, which is only about 32 miles (51km) wide at its narrowest point. A long mountain range divides the country into Caribbean and Pacific sides. Dense jungles and rainforests cover much of Panama. The rest is thinly wooded grassland called savanna. The forests provide timber, and Panama is rich in minerals such as copper and coal.

Panama has a tropical climate, with warm, sticky days and cool nights. The annual temperature averages 81°F (26°C) on the coast but lower in the mountains. Rainfall is heavy, especially on the Caribbean coast, which receives about 128 in. (3,250mm) a year.

Animal and plant life
Panama has more than 2,000 kinds of flowering plants. The wildlife of the forests includes jaguars and crocodiles.

◄ *A cargo ship in one of the Gatun locks on the Panama Canal. The locks allow ships to be raised or lowered 85 ft. (26m) between the canal and the surface of Gatun Lake, a vast lake created by the damming of the Chagres River.*

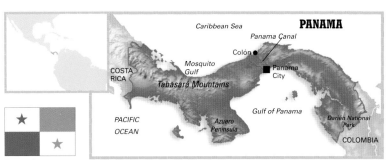

Caribbean Sea

PANAMA

Panama Canal

Colón ●

COSTA RICA

Mosquito Gulf

Panama City

Tabasará Mountains

Gulf of Panama

PACIFIC OCEAN

Azuero Peninsula

Darién National Park

COLOMBIA

Panama's national flag

People

Most Panamanians are mixed-race descendants of early Spanish settlers and American Indians. Immigrants from the Caribbean, the United States, and Africa added to the rich cultural mix.

Economy

Farming, fishing, and logging occupy much of the workforce, but the Panama Canal and its related businesses are the top money earners. Panama's major industry is oil refining and the processing of petroleum products. The Colón Free Zone is one of the world's largest free-trade areas. Raw materials and partly finished goods can be imported and turned into finished products for export without payment of duties (taxes). Financial services are also important.

History

Spanish explorers first came to Panama in 1501 and soon had the Native American Indians under their power. In the 1500s the Spanish established ports on both coasts. By the 1600s they were shipping silver from Peru across the isthmus to send home. This made Panama wealthy for more than a century.

In the 1800s the people of South America fought to end Spanish rule in their countries. At first Panama was loyal to Spain. After Colombia won independence in 1821, however, Panama joined the Colombian union. For the next 82 years Panama was Colombia's most troublesome province. Several times Panama broke away from Colombia, and each time it was brought back by military force.

In 1903 Panama won its independence from Colombia with the help of the United States. By then plans for building the Panama Canal had been made. From 1968 onward there were struggles between the army and the government, but in 1994 Panama became a true democracy for the first time.

The Panama Canal

Until the 20th century ships wanting to travel between the Pacific and Atlantic oceans had to sail around the southern tip of South America. A canal across the narrow Isthmus of Panama would knock over 7,000 miles (11,200km) off the journey. The French tried to build one in the 1880s but failed. The Americans were more successful. In return for protecting Panama's 1903 independence, they were allowed to build and own the canal.

More than 30,000 workers, many of them from the West Indies, labored for 10 years on the canal, which opened in 1914. The canal is 51 miles (82km) long. It contains several locks—chambers of water that work like elevators to lift ships over the hilly sections. The crossing takes about eight hours from coast to coast. An average of 12,000 ships, most of them American, use the canal every year. In 1999 ownership of the canal passed from the United States to Panama.

✳ PERU

Peru is the third-largest country in South America after Brazil and Argentina. It lies on the west coast of the continent and is bounded by the Pacific Ocean.

Peru's national flag

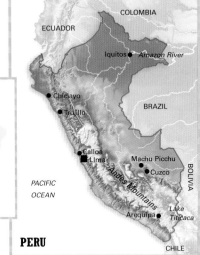

PERU

Much of Peru lies in the Andes, the mountain range that runs the length of South America. Because of the great variations in height between the tallest peaks and the Pacific shore Peru has many different climate zones. The weather is hot and dry in the north, and cool and humid farther south. Most of the cities and farms are in coastal valleys. The densely forested interior plains form part of the Amazon Basin. This region covers more than half the area of Peru, but few people live there.

People

Most Peruvians are descendants of either the Incas and other Indian people or mestizos, people of mixed Indian and Spanish ancestry. About 10 to 15 percent of the people are of pure Spanish origin. The remainder of the population includes the descendants of black African slaves and immigrants from China, Japan, Italy, Germany, and Britain.

Economy

Traditionally a few wealthy families owned most of the land. They grew cotton, sugarcane, and rice in plantations along the coast and crops for export in the highlands. The rest of the people were very poor. That caused 150 years of conflict until in 1969 the government passed a land reform act that broke up the estates, called haciendas, and turned many of them into cooperatives. Mining, fishing, and textile manufacture are important industries.

History

Peru was the center of the vast Inca Empire until the 1500s, when it was conquered by the Spanish, who ruled for 300 years. War with Chile (1879–83) left the country bankrupt. In the 1990s political upheavals forced Peru's military leaders to call elections. In 1998 Peru and Ecuador settled their longstanding border dispute.

KEY FACTS

OFFICIAL NAME
República del Perú

AREA
496,222 sq. mi.
(1,285,216 sq. km)

POPULATION
25,662,000

CAPITAL & LARGEST CITY
Lima

MAJOR RELIGION
Roman Catholicism

MAJOR LANGUAGES
Spanish and Quechua (both official)

CURRENCY
Nuevo sol
(new sol)

El Misti, Peru's best-known volcano, towers above the city of Arequipa. The mountain is still active.

SEE ALSO: America, South; Chile; Conquistadors; Ecuador; Incas

✷ PHILIPPINES

The Philippines is an island nation lying off the southeastern coast of Asia. It is in the Pacific Ocean northeast of Borneo and south of Taiwan (Formosa).

◄
In the Philippines rice has been grown on terraces such as these since before the birth of Christ.

Philippines' national flag

The Philippines is made up of more than 7,000 islands that form a chain, or archipelago, stretching 1,100 miles (1,800 km). The three main groups are Luzon and Mindoro, the central group, and Mindanao and the Sulu Archipelago.

Temperatures average 75–85° F (24–29° C). There are about 80 in. (2,030mm) of rain a year. Violent storms called typhoons occur between July and November. The area is also prone to earthquakes.

People
Most Filipinos (people of the Philippines) are of Malay ancestry and are related to the people of Malaysia and Indonesia. Many Filipinos also have some Spanish, American, or Chinese ancestry.

Most people live on the 11 largest islands. The biggest island is Luzon, where about half the population live. The majority of Filipinos live in rural areas, though recently large numbers have moved to the cities, especially to Manila, the capital.

Economy
The Philippines is still mainly an agricultural nation. Rice is the most important food crop. Corn is also

KEY FACTS

OFFICIAL NAME
Republika ng Pilipinas

AREA
115,600 sq. mi. (299,404 sq. km)

POPULATION
75,967,000

CAPITAL AND LARGEST CITY
Manila

MAJOR RELIGION
Christianity

MAJOR LANGUAGE
Pilipino, English (both official)

CURRENCY
Peso

important. Copra (dried coconut meat), sugarcane, and abaca (a fiber used to make ropes) are the chief cash crops. Recently, by taking advantage of cheap labor, the economy has expanded rapidly. Major industries include textiles, food processing, chemicals, machinery, and electronic products. Money sent home from Filipinos working abroad is an important source of foreign currency.

History

Situated at the crossroads between East and West, the Philippines has been influenced by Asian and Western cultures. The first people to live in the Philippines probably migrated there from Southeast Asia about 50,000 years ago.

The Philippines was ruled by Spain from the 1500s until the Spanish–American War of 1898. It then came under the control of the United States. The people of the Philippines finally gained complete independence in 1946.

President Ferdinand Marcos held power from 1965 to 1986. He was popular at first, but in later years the country suffered unrest and economic problems. In 1986 Marcos was exiled to the United States. A period of unrest ended in 1987 on the election of Corazon Aquino. She was the widow of Benigno Aquino, the chief political opponent of Marcos, who had been killed by government agents in 1983.

SEE ALSO: Hurricane, Tornado, & Typhoon

✳ PHILOSOPHY

Philosophy is the study of truth, wisdom, and the nature of knowledge—why do we think what we think, and how do we know what we think we know?

Philosophy has both a popular and a technical meaning. In the popular sense it is any set of beliefs about human beings, nature, society, and God. Everyone who has wondered about the meaning of life and found an answer that is satisfying has a philosophy. In its technical sense philosophy means a highly disciplined and rational method of criticizing beliefs to make them clearer and more reliable.

Analytical method

The English word *philosophy* comes from the ancient Greek meaning "lover of

◄
Plato (left) and Aristotle as imagined by the Italian artist Raphael (1483–1520) in his painting The School of Athens.

Lao-tzu was the founder of Taoism, a philosophy that advocates a simple life and advises against interference in the course of natural events.

wisdom." A philosopher is thus someone devoted to the pursuit of knowledge for its own sake without regard for its practical uses. The earliest philosophers were ancient Greeks in the sixth century B.C. who studied the underlying causes of natural phenomena such as birth and death, and the fall of heavy objects toward the earth.

Another Greek, Socrates (about 470–399 B.C.), was more concerned with human society. His motto was "Know thyself." He was the first to use the analytical method of reasoning, which tries to define central ideas such as virtue, justice, and knowledge. It also explores the reasons for beliefs that most people accept without question, such as the idea that pleasure, wealth, and power are the best things in life.

Synthetic method

Socrates' pupil Plato (about 427–347 B.C.) founded a school called the Academy. Its most gifted student was Aristotle (384–322 B.C.), who organized every field of human knowledge into a unified view of nature and humankind. This is called synthetic philosophy.

Synthetic philosophy has become more difficult to carry out as human knowledge has increased. Today's philosophers set themselves more limited goals. They connect psychology with biology in explaining the relation between the mind and the body. They relate science to religion in order to try and explain how the world began and how life grew out of inanimate matter.

Philosophy is now divided into smaller areas according to the type of problems

FAMOUS PHILOSOPHERS

The following are just a few of the most world's most influential philosophers. There are many others.

Lao-tzu (sixth century B.C.)
Chinese philosopher who founded Taoism, which had a great influence on the Buddhist religion.

Confucius (K'ung Ch'iu) (551–479 B.C.)
Chinese philosopher who placed great emphasis on society and values.

Socrates (about 470–399 B.C.)
Ancient Greek who believed that understanding ignorance led to wisdom, and that question-and-answer study led to knowledge.

Plato (about 427–347 B.C.)
Ancient Greek who believed that certain ideas could be understood by the use of reason.

Aristotle (384–322 B.C.)
Ancient Greek philosopher. Western culture is based on his broad understanding of the world of humans, nature, and science.

Hobbes, Thomas (1588–1679)
Englishman who claimed that humans are naturally violent and need to be kept under control.

Descartes, René (1596–1650)
Frenchman who believed in two separate worlds—mind and body. He distrusted knowledge and, like Plato, attached great importance to Rationalism—the use of reason.

Locke, John (1632–1704)
Englishman who disputed Hobbes's ideas, believing instead that humankind's natural state is happiness. Supported Empiricism (understanding through experience), not Rationalism.

Kant, Immanuel (1724–1804)
German who separated the world of objects as we see them from the world of objects as they really are. He encouraged people to act as if their behavior were ruled by universal laws.

Hegel, Georg (Wilhelm Friedrich) (1770–1831)
German who claimed that we can understand our continually developing and changing reality only if we see it as one big idea.

Russell, Bertrand (Arthur William) (1872–1970)
Englishman who attacked what he saw as wrong in society and contributed to the understanding of math.

investigated. Ethics is the study of the meaning of terms such as justice, virtue, morality, and responsibility. Epistemology tries to define truth, logic, and perception, and investigates the ways in which knowledge is acquired. Metaphysics deals with the nature of reality. Aesthetics tries to define art and beauty.

In addition, each field of scholarship has to define its own subject matter and methods of procedure. That is why people talk about, for example, the philosophy of physics, the philosophy of religion, and the philosophy of history.

SEE ALSO: Aristotle; Religion

✳ PHOTOGRAPHY

A photograph is a picture made through the action of light. The English word *photography* comes from the Greek words meaning "light" and "writing."

To take a photograph, you need light and a camera. Traditional cameras use film. The film is made of transparent (see-through) plastic coated with a chemical that changes when light shines on it. When you take a picture, light rays reflected from your subject enter the camera and create a hidden image on the film. When the film is treated with chemicals, the image is made visible, and a print can be made from it.

Modern digital cameras do not use film. They have sensors that convert the light into electrical charges so that the image can be stored on a computer.

All cameras are made up of four basic parts—body, lens, shutter, and viewfinder. The body of a camera is a box that keeps

out all light except the light that passes through the lens. The lens is a piece of glass or plastic with curved surfaces.

The lens concentrates the light rays as they enter the camera tomake a sharp image of the photographed object.

It is important that you focus on a subject before shooting the picture. Otherwise, the picture may be blurry. When a picture is in focus, it is sharp and clear. Some cameras have a fixed-focus lens, but others have a lens that you can focus on subjects at almost any distance. With a telephoto lens you can photograph a distant scene or even the moon. With a closeup lens you can photograph a flower or insect.

Ansel Adams photographing the Pacific coast at Big Sur, California.

FAMOUS PHOTOGRAPHERS

A few of the people who have captured the qualities of the natural world or human life in photographs.

Cameron, Julia Margaret (1815–79)
British woman who took portraits of famous people.

Emerson, Peter Henry (1856–1936)
Englishman who was one of the first to turn photography into an art form.

Atget, Eugène (1856–1927)
Frenchman who photographed the buildings and people of Paris.

Stieglitz, Alfred (1864–1946)
American who pioneered artistic photography.

Salomon, Erich (1886–1944)
German photojournalist (telling news stories through photographs) and portraitist.

Ray, Man (Rudnitsky, Emmanuel) (1890–1976)
American photographer, filmmaker, and artist.

Lange, Dorothea (1895–1965)
American who photographed the suffering caused by the Great Depression.

Brassaï (Halász, Gyula) (1899–84)
Hungarian-born Frenchman who photographed Paris by night .

Adams, Ansel (Easton) (1902–84)
American who was famous for photographing landscapes.

Edgerton, Harold E. (1903–90)
American who pioneered high-speed photography.

Siskind, Aaron (1903–91)
Influential American teacher known for his abstract photographs.

Cartier-Bresson, Henri (1908–)
French pioneer of documentary photojournalism.

Karsh, Yousuf (1908–2002)
Armenian-born Canadian who took portraits of famous people.

Capa, Robert (Friedmann, Andrei) (1913–54)
Hungarian-born American war photographer who helped found Magnum Photos Agency in 1947.

Arnold, Eve (1913–)
American photojournalist; the first woman to work for Magnum.

DeCarava, Roy (1919–)
American celebrated for his portraits of black Americans.

The shutter is a mechanical device behind the lens. It opens and closes to let the light into the camera. By releasing a button on the outside of the camera, the photographer opens the shutter. In many cameras you can change the speed at which the shutter opens and closes. If the shutter opens and closes quickly, little light enters the camera. If the shutter is set to stay open longer, more light enters. In bright sunlight the photographer can set the shutter at a fast speed since there is plenty of light to make an image on the film. On gloomy days or in dim light the shutter can be set at a slower speed. That gives time for more light to enter the camera. A fast shutter speed lets you take pictures of moving subjects without blurring.

The viewfinder shows you the scene that the lens will focus on the film. Some viewfinders are glass windows, and some make use of lenses. Others are reflecting prisms that show the actual image coming through the lens.

History

The earliest photographic pictures were produced in the camera obscura (Latin for "dark chamber"), a dark room with a tiny hole in one wall. Light came through the hole and produced an image on the opposite wall of whatever was outside.

For about 500 years the camera obscura was used mostly for watching eclipses of the sun. Over the years artists and mapmakers gradually invented smaller, more handy versions of the device.

In 1727 Johann Schulze, a German doctor, discovered that a chemical, silver nitrate, turned black when he shined light on it. This discovery led to photographic film. The first hand-held camera arrived in the 1880s. Both this and the roll of film that went in it were invented by George Eastman, founder of the Eastman Kodak Company in Rochester, New York. Eastman's company even processed the film. Now anyone could take photographs.

In 1924 the Leica, a German camera, used a film strip 35mm wide. Today the 35mm camera is one of the most popular sizes available.

Digital camera technology dates from the 1960s, when NASA spacecraft sent digital images home from space. The first popular digital, or filmless, cameras were made in the 1970s and 1980s.

SEE ALSO: Astronomy; Lens; Light; Medicine; Microscope

✳ PHYSICS

Physics is the study of matter and energy. Matter is the basic substance of which everything is made; energy is what makes matter move and change.

Physics is the science that studies the structure of matter. Physicists study all aspects of nature. They want to know what forces hold atoms together, how gases change to liquids, why metals conduct electricity, and how stars evolve.

Physics can be loosely divided into two categories: classical physics and modern physics. Classical physics deals with several fields of study that were quite well developed before the 1900s. It includes mechanics, heat, sound, light, and electromagnetism—the relationship between electricity and magnetism.

◄

Accelerators, or atom smashers, increase the kinetic energy of subatomic particles. Physicists use them to study the nature and behavior of materials and to develop nuclear fusion devices.

Mechanics

The science of mechanics looks at the effects of forces on bodies at rest or in motion. For example, Earth's gravity is a force. When you throw a ball, gravity acts on it, pulling it toward the ground. On a larger scale the sun's gravity acts on Earth, holding it in orbit. The English scientist Isaac Newton described such effects in his laws of motion, written in 1687.

Heat

Heat is a form of energy. It can be produced from other forms of energy. You can make heat energy by rubbing your hands together. Heat can also make other forms of energy. It is turned into kinetic (movement) energy in a steam engine. The way one kind of energy changes to another is an important area of study.

Sound

Sound is caused when the atoms that make up a substance are made to vibrate, or move back and forth, very rapidly. Sound travels in waves—through air, water, or other substances—to our ears. Because sound is caused by motion, it can be explained by Newton's laws.

Light

Light is also a wave. James Clerk Maxwell, a Scottish physicist, proved that in 1865. A light wave travels in an electromagnetic field—a force in space that is both electrical and magnetic. The wave radiates (sends out) energy as light. Light is only one form of electromagnetic radiation. Other forms produce radio, microwaves, x-rays, and television.

Electromagnetism

The study of electromagnetism developed in the 1800s. Hans Christian Oersted in Denmark and Michael Faraday in England experimented with electricity and magnetic fields. Maxwell later showed that they were two forms of the same force: electromagnetism. He predicted that the force moved at the speed of light— 186,000 miles (300,000km) per second.

By the late 1800s it seemed that little remained to be discovered in physics. At the start of the 1900s, however, scientists saw things that could not be explained, and so modern physics was born.

Modern physics

In 1911 the British physicist Ernest Rutherford found that the center of every atom contained a tiny object, the nucleus. His discovery led to the science of nuclear physics, which studies the properties of the nucleus, and also to the study of smaller parts of atoms called subatomic particles. Nuclear physics has led to new ways of generating power and treating cancer, as well as nuclear weapons.

From 1905 the German scientist Albert Einstein wrote a series of laws about light speed, energy, mass, space, and time that changed almost everything that physicists believed or understood. His discoveries led to the age of atomic bombs and nuclear power. His ideas also made it possible to explain how the planets move in time through outer space.

Together with another German scientist, Max Planck, Einstein also developed

Danish physicist Hans Christian Oersted (1777–1851) discovered that a compass needle moves when subjected to an electric current. ▼

quantum theory, a complicated area of study that describes how light does not always behave as a smooth wave should. Sometimes it behaves like a stream of tiny, separate "grains" of matter.

Quantum physics is gradually unlocking the world's deepest secrets. It has led to new ideas about atoms, matter, and motion, and paved the way for computers and laser beams. Scientists now know that there are even smaller particles than the nucleus, and that is giving them new ideas about how stars are made.

Modern physics covers the study of everything that exists, from this book to the most distant galaxies. The universe is larger than we can imagine, yet scientists think it is still growing. Will it go on growing forever, or will it shrink back into nothing? The answer to this question will come from future discoveries in physics.

SEE ALSO: Astronomy; Einstein, Albert; Electricity; Element, Chemical; Energy; Force & Motion; Gravity; Laser; Lever; Light; Machine; Magnetism; Matter; Newton, Isaac; Science

✳ PILGRIMS, THE

The Pilgrims were the people who sailed from England to America in the *Mayflower* and founded the Plymouth colony in 1620.

On September 16, 1620, the *Mayflower* set sail from England. Aboard the 90 ft.-(27m-) ship were 102 men, women, and children. Thirty-five travelers were Separatists—members of the Puritan Christian movement. They were fleeing religious persecution in England. Other members of the party had been hired by a company in London, the Merchant Adventurers. The settlers had been granted land in America on condition that they earned money for the company. Also on board were craftsmen, servants, and a crew of 28.

After a rough 66-day crossing, the *Mayflower* landed at Cape Cod on November 21, 1620. After Christmas the colonists moved to the site where they would build the colony of Plymouth.

At first the founders were known as the Old Comers or Forefathers. The term "Pilgrims," or "Pilgrim Fathers," was first used at a celebration in 1820 to mark the 200th anniversary of their landing in the New World.

◄

The Pilgrims leave Plymouth, England, for America in 1620.

SEE ALSO: United States of America

✳ PLANT

There are more than 500,000 plant species. They make oxygen and remove carbon dioxide from the air—without them there would be no life on Earth.

▲ *Ferns have compound, or multipart, leaves called fronds. Here they are in the process of unfurling, when they are known as fiddleheads.*

A plant is a living, growing organism made of many tiny cells. It does not eat food and cannot move around by itself. It usually grows in a medium provided by soil, water, or another plant, such as the branch of a tree.

Parts of a plant
Most plants have roots, a stem, and leaves. The roots grow into the ground, take nutrients from the soil, and support the plant. The stem also supports the plant and carries nutrients. The leaves usually manufacture food. Other plant parts include the flowers, seeds, and fruits, which are used in making new plants.

The cells of plants usually have tough walls made of cellulose. Most plants contain chlorophyll (green pigment) and can make their own food from sunlight during the process of photosynthesis. Sunlight and moisture are most abundant in tropical regions, and that is where the greatest number of plants are found.

Classification
People classify plants in different ways. One way is according to growth: Plants over 8 ft. (2.4m) are trees; low, woody plants are shrubs; and plants with tender stems are herbs. A second classification is according to their life cycles. Annuals sprout, flower, and die within a year. Biennials need two years to complete their life cycle. Perennials live for more than two years.

Scientists arrange the plant kingdom in order from the simplest to the most complex. Algae, which include seaweeds, are the simplest plants. All other plants are either vascular or nonvascular. Vascular plants have special tissues in them, called xylem and phloem, to carry food around the plant. Nonvascular plants, such as mosses, liverworts, and hornworts, lack these food-carrying tissues.

The most successful vascular plants are the seed plants. The first four groups are often called gymnosperms because their seeds lie exposed on the scales of cones. The flowering plants are often called angiosperms because their seeds are enclosed in fruit. The fruit may be soft, like a strawberry, or hard, like a pecan nut.

Reproduction and defense
Plants reproduce either sexually or asexually. In sexual reproduction a male sex cell (sperm) and a female sex cell (egg) join to produce a seed. This union takes place within a flower. The ripe seed eventually parts from the plant and enters the soil, where it puts out roots and a leafy shoot. From this point growth usually continues by photosynthesis.

In asexual reproduction there is no joining of separate sex cells. Instead, a new plant forms from some part of the old plant—the root, for example, or a stem.

Plants have many enemies. They are eaten by all kinds of animals from insects to cattle. They are attacked by diseases and destroyed by frost, fire, and high winds. Plants defend themselves with weapons that include poisons, bad-tasting juices, unpleasant odors, thorns and burrs, deep roots, and thick seed coverings.

Plants live in communities made up of other plants and animals. Often these species rely on each other. Many plants need insects, for example, to help their sex cells mingle and reproduce. Animals use plants for food and shelter. Plant roots also help stop rain and wind from removing topsoil.

Human are totally dependent on plants. They use them for food and fuel, and to make clothing, paper, and medicines. About 20 species of plant supply nearly 90 percent of the world's food. The most important food crops are wheat, rice, and corn, which are specially bred grasses.

SEE ALSO: Biome; Botany; Evolution; Flower; Habitat; Insect; Wetlands

PHOTOSYNTHESIS

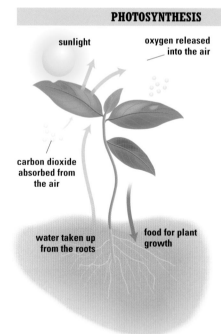

sunlight

oxygen released into the air

carbon dioxide absorbed from the air

water taken up from the roots

food for plant growth

Most plants make their own food by photosynthesis, a process in which energy from sunlight is captured by chlorophyll in their leaves and stems. The plant uses the energy to take carbon dioxide from the air and nutrients and water from the soil. It turns them into sugars that are used for growth. It also releases oxygen back into the air.

THE PLANT KINGDOM

Scientists group all living things into five kingdoms. The plant kingdom is made up of divisions. They can be arranged in four groups based on the structure of the plant. Plants in a division are split into classes. Classes are divided into orders, orders into families, families into genera (singular genus), and genera into species.

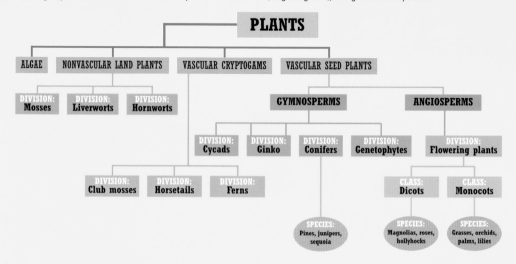

PLANTS

ALGAE   NONVASCULAR LAND PLANTS   VASCULAR CRYPTOGAMS   VASCULAR SEED PLANTS

DIVISION: Mosses   **DIVISION: Liverworts**   **DIVISION: Hornworts**

GYMNOSPERMS   **ANGIOSPERMS**

DIVISION: Cycads   **DIVISION: Ginko**   **DIVISION: Conifers**   **DIVISION: Genetophytes**   **DIVISION: Flowering plants**

DIVISION: Club mosses   **DIVISION: Horsetails**   **DIVISION: Ferns**

CLASS: Dicots   **CLASS: Monocots**

SPECIES: Pines, junipers, sequoia   **SPECIES: Magnolias, roses, hollyhocks**   **SPECIES: Grasses, orchids, palms, lilies**

* PLATYPUS

The platypus is a very unusual animal. It is a mammal; but instead of giving birth to babies, it lays eggs, like birds and reptiles.

The platypus only lives in eastern Australia and Tasmania. It was discovered in 1797. It has fur and milk glands, so it is a mammal, but it also has webbed feet and a flat, leathery bill similar to that of a duck. But it reproduces by laying eggs.

The male platypus grows to 2 ft. (60cm) in length and may weigh 4½ lb. (2kg). The female is smaller. Both sexes have thick coats of soft, dark brown fur.

All four feet of the platypus are webbed. The webs on the front feet extend some distance beyond the claws. These outer portions are folded under when the platypus walks around on land.

Platypuses live in burrows that they dig in the banks of streams, lakes, or ponds. They sleep in their burrows by day but come out at dusk to hunt for food.

Swimming along stream bottoms, they forage in mud and pebbles in search of worms, crayfish, and other freshwater animals. They have huge appetites.

In spring the female makes a nest of leaves and grass inside the burrow where she lays her eggs. The babies hatch out about 10 days later. Newborn platypuses are blind, naked, and little more than 1 in. (2.5cm) long. Young platypuses leave the nest when they are about 17 weeks old.

▼
Platypuses were once hunted for their soft, dark brown fur, but they are now protected by law.

SEE ALSO: Mammal; Reproduction

* POCAHONTAS (ABOUT 1596–1617)

Pocahontas, also known as Matoaka, was a Native American who helped improve relations between her Algonquian people and English colonists.

▲
When Pocahontas married John Rolfe, she converted to Christianity and took the name Rebecca.

Pocahontas was the daughter of Powhatan, who ruled a group of Algonquians. In 1607, when English settlers arrived in Jamestown, Virginia, there was hostility between the two groups, but Pocahontas became friendly with the colonists.

In December 1607 Powhatan's followers captured the leader of Jamestown, Captain John Smith. According to Smith's own account, Pocahontas saved him from execution, although most historians believe this event never happened.

In 1613 Captain Samuel Argall captured Pocahontas. She married the colonist John Rolfe and had a child. In 1616 they sailed to England. Just before she was due to return to Virginia, she died suddenly. She is buried at Gravesend, in southeast England.

✳ POLAND

Poland covers part of a vast plain that extends
across much of east–central Europe and takes its
name from the Slavic word *pole*, meaning "field."

Most of the country consists of a low plain dotted with small lakes and forests. The land rises toward the south, reaching its greatest height in the Carpathian Mountains on the border with Slovakia. In the north Poland borders on the Baltic Sea.

Winters are very cold and frequently snowy. The average January temperature near the German border is about 30°F (–1°C). In the east it is colder. Summers are cool. The average precipitation (rain and snowfall) each year is 24 in. (600mm).

People

Poland suffered heavily during World War II (1939–45). After the war the eastern territory, with a variety of peoples, was given to the Soviet Union. In return Poland received part of Germany. Many Poles from the eastern territory moved westward to settle in these new lands.

Economy

Before World War II Poland's economy was mainly agricultural. Today less than one-third of the workforce is employed in agriculture. The raising of pigs, sheep, and cattle is important, and meat products are a leading export.

One of the main industries is the production of metals, especially iron and steel. Shipbuilding is also important, with shipyards located at Gdansk and other ports on the Baltic Sea. Coal mining provides fuel and coal for export.

History

Poland's recorded history dates from A.D. 966. It was once one of the largest kingdoms in Europe, but in later centuries it was invaded and occupied by other countries. Between the late 1700s and early 1900s Poland disappeared from the map of Europe altogether, after being divided among its neighbors.

The nation regained its independence at the end of World War I (1914–18). It was invaded by German armies at the outbreak of World War II. After the war a communist government, backed by the Soviet Union, seized power.

In 1980 workers, led by Lech Walesa, won the right to form a union. Called Solidarity, it was the first free labor union permitted in a communist country. In 1989 Solidarity won a majority in the new Senate. In 1990 Poland held its first fully democratic elections since World War II, and Lech Walesa became president.

KEY FACTS

OFFICIAL NAME
Rzeczpospolita Polska

AREA
120,725 sq. mi. (312,677 sq. km)

POPULATION
38,765,000

CAPITAL & LARGEST CITY
Warsaw

MAJOR RELIGION
Roman Catholicism

MAJOR LANGUAGE
Polish

CURRENCY
Zloty

Poland's national flag

SEE ALSO:
World War II

✳ POLLUTION

Air and water are essential to life on Earth. Human activity, however, can sometimes damage their purity and make them polluted, or dirty.

Children in Turin, Italy, protest traffic pollution by wearing gas masks. Exhaust fumes from automobiles are a major source of pollution.

Air is considered to be polluted when it contains enough harmful impurities to affect the health, safety, or comfort of living things. Clean air is made up of nitrogen and oxygen, with small amounts of water vapor, carbon dioxide, and other substances. Nature can cause air to carry impurities. Plants release pollen into the air, for example. Forest fires and volcanic activity create smoke and other particles that pollute the atmosphere.

The term pollution, however, usually means damage to the environment caused by human activity. Vehicles such as cars and airplanes give out exhaust fumes. Factories burn fossil fuels, such as coal, and chemicals, and release waste matter into the air.

When people use fossil fuels—such as gasoline, oil, and coal—carbon dioxide and other gases are released into the air. These gases act like the glass in a

greenhouse, trapping heat from the sun. This "greenhouse effect" causes the atmosphere to warm and world temperatures to rise.

Artificial pollutants can sometimes combine with natural weather conditions. Smoke, for example, can combine with fog to create smog. This is especially dangerous to people who suffer from breathing disorders, such as asthma, bronchitis, and emphysema. Sometimes high temperatures above an area can trap pollutants on the Earth's surface. This is called temperature inversion and is a common occurrence in cities such as Los Angeles and Mexico City.

Water pollution
Water, like air, is polluted when it contains harmful impurities that affect living things. Pollution of water can also have natural causes. Storms can cause soil and other

321

debris to dissolve in water. But, as with air pollution, human activity causes the most damage to water supplies. Factories release harmful chemicals into rivers and lakes. Sewage—household waste from toilets, sinks, and bathtubs—pumps into the oceans. If an oil tanker sinks, thousands of tons of oil can cover the surface of the sea and the shore. Fish, birds, and other wildlife die. Even if polluted water is not dangerous, excess chlorine and other chemicals can make it unpleasant to drink. Waste material on land can also pollute groundwater—the water contained in soil and among rocks. Dangerous material can pass into the food cycle through crops or animal feed.

Acid rain

When certain pollutants mix with water vapor, they cause a particular form of pollution called acid rain. Acid rain is mostly the result of industrial processes, but agricultural chemicals and vehicle fumes also have an effect.

When rainwater contains too much hydrochloric or nitric acid, it can change the composition of soil, damaging plants. If the acid reacts with aluminum in the soil, it releases poisonous substances. Acid rain changes the contents of lakes and rivers, killing fish. It also damages metal, stone, and brick constructions.

Stopping pollution

Most scientists agree on the main causes of pollution. However, it is harder to agree on solutions. Harmful emissions from motor vehicles have decreased since the introduction of catalytic converters and unleaded gas. Legislation, such as the 1990 Clean Air Act, requires government and industry to take action to remove pollutants from fuel and other materials. There are now heavy fines for companies that pollute water sources. International restrictions on the use of harmful gases called CFCs (chlorofluorocarbons) have slowed down the loss of the ozone layer—the vital strip in the atmosphere that protects the Earth from harmful rays from the sun.

Some big industrial companies say that too many controls on pollution will harm the economy. In 2001 many nations of the world met in Kyoto, Japan, and agreed to restrict pollution. The United States would not sign the agreement, however, saying that it was bad for industry.

Everyone can take steps to protect the environment from pollution in easy ways such as by making fewer car journeys, using less electricity, and throwing away less garbage. However, major changes do need to come from the big industrial companies and governments.

SEE ALSO:
Atmosphere;
Conservation;
Environment;
Health;
Natural
Resources;
Ozone Layer;
Water

Oil from shipwrecks is a serious cause of pollution. It does not break down and kills many birds and fish.

✳ PORTUGAL

Portugal shares the Iberian peninsula with its larger neighbor, Spain. It directly faces the Atlantic Ocean and is the westernmost country in mainland Europe.

The Tagus River divides the country in half. The north is mountainous. The major mountain range is the Serra da Estrela, whose highest peak, Malhão da Estrela, is 6,532 ft. (1,991m). South of the river the land is flat, with many plateaus. The Atlantic islands of Madeira and the Azores belong to Portugal, but they each have their own elected legislature.

The climate is generally cooler and rainfall heavier in the north than in the south. Winters are mild, except in the mountains, where it is cold and snowy. Summers are warm or hot.

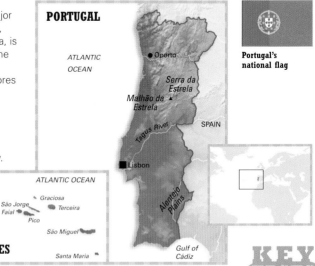

Portugal's national flag

People

The first inhabitants of the peninsula were Iberians. Around 1000 B.C. Celtic peoples settled in the north. At the same time, Phoenicians, a people from the eastern Mediterranean, and later Greeks and Carthaginians founded cities and colonies in the south. The Romans conquered the area in the first century A.D. When the western Roman Empire collapsed in the fifth century, two Germanic tribes fought for control of the region. Muslims, followers of Islam, invaded in the 700s, conquering most of Spain and more than half of Portugal.

Economy

Agriculture and fishing were traditionally the mainstay of the economy. Recently the emphasis has been on developing industry and tourism. Textiles and clothing are the chief manufactured products.

History

In 1179 Portugal became a kingdom under Alfonso Henriques. Later kings conquered more land, and by 1270 the country had its modern boundaries. A son of King John 1 became known as Henry the Navigator (1394–1460). He encouraged voyages of discovery and was responsible for starting the process that led, after his death, to the Portuguese sailing all the way around Africa and the building of an overseas empire. The new trade routes brought wealth to the country.

Portugal held on to its colonies longer than other European powers, but many people disagreed with the costly wars needed to defend them. In 1974 General António de Spínola led a military coup. In 1776 democractic government was restored. In 1999 Portugal returned its last overseas territory, Macao, to China.

👀 **SEE ALSO:** China; Exploration & Explorers; Islam; Spain

KEY FACTS

OFFICIAL NAME
República Portuguesa

AREA
35,553 sq. mi. (92,082 sq. km)

POPULATION
9,875,000

CAPITAL & LARGEST CITY
Lisbon

MAJOR RELIGION
Roman Catholicism

MAJOR LANGUAGE
Portuguese

CURRENCY
Euro

✳ PREHISTORIC PEOPLE

Prehistoric means "before written history." People have lived on Earth for about seven million years. Most of this time was before written history.

Scientists believe that humans developed from early primates, mammals that were also ancestors to apes such as gorillas, chimpanzees, and orangutans. Over many thousands of years primate species changed and adapted to new environments through a process called evolution. Originally scientists saw human evolution as a ladder with simple steps from ape ancestor to modern humans, but now they see it as a branching tree with many unclear connections.

In 2002 scientists discovered a skull in the Central African country of Chad that is almost 7 million years old. They nicknamed this hominid Toumai, which means "hope of life" in the local language. Toumai was like an ape in some ways. Its brain was the size of a chimp's, and the skull had a big ridge over the eyes, like a gorilla. But Toumai's teeth put it in the human family. Also, its face is flatter than a chimp's and more humanlike.

Fossil finds
Scientists have formed their ideas about prehistoric people from finding fossilized bones and teeth. New finds mean that scientists keep having to revise their opinions about the origins of humans. In 1974 scientists found a fossil skull, which they called Lucy, in East Africa. It dated from about 3.2 million years ago. In 1998 they discovered a fossil skeleton in South Africa dating from about 3.5 million years ago. In September 2002 French scientists located a skull in the Central African country of Chad that is almost 7 million years old.

Hominid to human
These early humans are called hominids—primates that walk on two legs. By 2.3 million years ago, at least one form had developed a slightly larger brain and more skillful hands, enabling it to make stone tools. This species is called *Homo habilis*, or "handy person." Scientists consider it to be the first human. *Homo habilis* lived in open grassland and ate wild plants and meat killed by other animals.

About 1.8 million years ago a new human form appeared in Africa. This species had a more upright posture, and scientists call it *Homo erectus*, or "person who stands erect." Over the next 1.5 million years *Homo erectus* spread into Asia and Europe. They still ate wild plants, but they also used wooden spears to kill animals for meat.

Neanderthals and *Homo sapiens*
By 250,000 to 200,000 years ago some hominids had developed larger brains. Scientists called them Neanderthals because they found the first Neanderthal skeleton in the Neander Valley, Germany. Neanderthals lived in caves, wore skins, used fire, hunted animals, made and used stone tools and wooden spears, and buried their dead.

For many years scientists thought that Neanderthals were the direct ancestors of modern humans, but many now believe that, although Neanderthals and modern humans shared a common ancestor, the two lines separated between 550,000 and 690,000 years ago.

Scientists do not agree on the exact origins of modern human beings, known as *Homo sapiens sapiens*, a subspecies of *Homo sapiens*, meaning "people who are wise," or modern humans. Most believe that *Homo sapiens* appeared in Africa between 100,000 and 200,000 years ago, then spread rapidly elsewhere. Others argue that *Homo sapiens sapiens* appeared in Africa, Asia, and Europe all about the same time.

By 32,000 years ago only modern human beings lived in Europe. By this time modern people had also settled in Central Asia and Siberia, China, and Southeast Asia.

The earliest modern Europeans are known as the Cro-Magnons, named after a rock shelter in southwestern France where their skeletons were first found in 1868. They lived between 40,000 and 10,000 years ago and were among the first humans to develop art. Their cave paintings and engravings, which depict animals, are believed to have had deep spiritual meaning.

The first Americans

Some scientists believe that people crossed from Siberia to Alaska as early as 40,000 years ago. Most argue for a much later settlement, about 15,000 years ago. Low sea levels, caused by an Ice Age, meant that people could walk from Asia to America. By 12,500 years ago small groups of hunter-gatherers had spread as far south as Chile in South America.

Farming

From about 15,000 years ago the climate of the Earth began to warm rapidly. People settled by lakes and rivers, and developed fishing techniques. From about 8000 B.C. some groups in Asia planted food crops, such as wild barley and wheat. Instead of hunting animals, they kept herds of cattle.

Civilization

From about 8000 B.C. trade developed between farming communities. Some villages between the Tigris and Euphrates rivers in Mesopotamia (modern Iraq) became small towns, with more than 5,000 inhabitants. Similar communities grew up along the banks of the Nile River

▲
Archaeologists can learn a great deal about prehistoric life by studying cave paintings. These paintings at Tassili n'Ajjer in southern Algeria date from about 4500 B.C. Although today the Sahara is a dry desert, the cave paintings show it as a moist area full of animal life and the home of hunters and herdsmen.

SEE ALSO: Ancient Civilizations; Archaeology; Art; Evolution; History; Primates

✴ PRIMATES

Primates are a group of mammals that includes monkeys, apes, and humans. They are descended from tiny mammals that lived 70 million years ago.

Primates have body hair and give birth to live young. Almost all primates have fingers, and sometimes toes, that can grasp objects. They use them to climb trees, to grasp food, and in some cases to use tools. Most primates have flat nails rather than claws. Primates' vision is the most important of their five senses.

Primates usually live in the tropical and subtropical areas of Africa, Asia, and the Americas. Humans are the only primates to have spread through most of the world.

Most primates are mainly vegetarian. Some lemurs and monkeys eat insects, and pottos will eat young birds. Baboons and chimpanzees eat larger animals, and humans also eat meat.

Primates have fewer offspring than other mammals, and the young stay longer with their mothers. Some larger apes do not let their young become independent for seven years.

There are 233 species of primate. They are divided into two main groups, prosimians and anthropoids.

Prosimians

Prosimians include lemurs, tarsiers, galagos, aye-ayes, lorises, and pottos. They are nocturnal—active at night—and usually have

very large eyes. They tend to be smaller than other primates and are usually not so intelligent.

Prosimians usually live in small groups. Some, such as the indri lemur, live in family units of an adult male and female and their offspring. Weasel lemurs and aye-ayes live alone, only coming together to mate. Many unique varieties of lemur are found only on the island of Madagascar in the Indian Ocean.

Anthropoids

Humans are part of the anthropoid group, which also includes monkeys and our closest relatives. the apes. Anthropoids have color vision and can see in three dimensions. That helps them move around safely in trees. They are diurnal—active during daylight. The main difference between monkeys and apes is that monkeys have tails, and apes do not.

The mountain gorilla lives in the forests of central West Africa.

Anthropoids are divided into several further groups. The largest and most intelligent—apart from humans—are Pongidae, or great apes. They include chimpanzees, gorillas, and orangutans. The lesser apes include the gibbons.

The Amazon squirrel monkey is a small New World monkey that lives in the forests of northern South America.

The most intelligent apes are chimpanzees, who have learned how to use simple tools to get food. Scientists have trained chimpanzees to communicate with humans using sign language. Some have vocabularies of more than 100 words.

Scientists also divide monkeys into two groups—New World and Old World. New World monkeys, from Central and South America, include marmosets, tamarins, douroucoulis, and woolly, howler, spider,

AMAZING FACTS!

The smallest primate is the pygmy mouse lemur, which lives on Madagascar. It weighs about 1 oz. (30g). **The siamang gibbon** has arms that span over 5 ft. (1.5m), more than twice the length of its body.

and squirrel monkeys. Old World monkeys inhabit Africa, Asia, and a very small part of Europe. They include macaques, langurs, baboons, guenons, and colobus monkeys. Old World monkeys have nostrils that are close together and open at the front of the face. The nostrils of New World monkeys are further apart.

Most apes and monkeys live in communities that can consist of hundreds of animals. Baboons and macaques form the largest communities.

Primates in danger

In common with many other wild animals primates today are greatly at risk from human activities. Illegal hunters, or poachers, in Africa shoot gorillas and sell the bodies as souvenirs. Orangutans have their habitats destroyed by forest clearance and logging in their native Borneo.

Naturalists such as Dian Fossey and Jane Goodall have devoted their lives to studying primates and to bringing their plight to the world's attention. But the number of primates in the world is still declining—for example, there are probably fewer than 10,000 mountain gorillas left in the wild. It is quite likely that in just a few years, some of our closest relatives will exist only in zoos, if at all.

SEE ALSO: Goodall, Jane; Habitat; Mammal

✳ PRINTING

Until the invention of printing it could take years to create a book. Now thousands of books, newspapers, and magazines roll off the presses every hour.

The earliest recorded information known is in the form of European cave paintings more than 30,000 years old. About 5,000 years ago people in Mesopotamia (modern Iraq) and Egypt began carving records on stone. The Chinese invented paper about 2,000 years ago. They also used woodblocks to print books. The oldest surviving copy dates from A.D. 868.

Printing press
However, printing as we know it dates from about 1455, when Johannes Gutenberg built the first printing press in Mainz, Germany. He molded individual letters from metal and used them to print a bible.

Until this time books were very rare and expensive. Each one was handwritten by specially trained scribes. Very few people were able to read. Even with Gutenberg's invention only very rich people could afford books. However, within a few decades most families in Europe and North America had bibles, and newspapers and pamphlets became more common. Cheaply printed "primers" made it easier to teach children basic reading and writing.

From the 1800s new industrial developments began to influence printing methods. The process of putting the characters together to make pages is called typesetting. Automatic techniques for using images and color meant that books could be produced more cheaply and quickly, and the finished products looked more interesting than ever before. With the advent of computers books, newspapers, and other publications can be put together, say, in New York, sent to China electronically, and immediately printed. Easy access to photocopiers and cheap printers means that anyone with an idea and a few dollars can put out (publish) a book.

The printing process
Printing has changed a great deal since Gutenberg, but some principles remain the same. Most printed material begins with type. Each type character represents a letter, number, or other mark. The characters can be made of solid material, such as metal or they can be photographic or in digital form on a computer.

Images, such as photographs or diagrams, are added to create a page design. The design is checked, or proofed; once it is corrected, a plate is made. The plates print text and images onto paper or other material, and the sheets are then folded, cut, and bound to make a book, magazine, or other publication.

Letterpress and lithography
The oldest printing method is letterpress, or relief printing. It is the method that Gutenberg used for his bible. The image to be printed is carved or molded so that it is raised from the surface around it. When ink is rolled over, it sticks to the image and not to the surface. Rubber stamps also use this technique. Flexography, a form of letterpress using rubber plates, is increasingly widely used for printing newspapers.

▲ *A reconstruction of the first printing press, originally built by Johannes Gutenberg (about 1390–1468).*

A color press machine in a modern printing factory. From here the pages are taken to a bindery, where they are turned into books.

Lithography, or offset printing, uses photographic negatives on aluminum plates. When the plates are dampened, the unexposed areas reject ink. The ink sticks to the image, which is transferred to a rubber blanket, and then onto paper. Lithography is now the most common method of printing.

Gravure and other methods
Gravure printing uses carved images in a metal plate. Ink sinks into the grooves left by the carving and transfers to the paper. Gravure is used for reproductions of artworks and specialized illustrations.

In screen printing artists place a stencil on a mesh screen to cover nonimage areas, then squeeze ink through the screen onto paper, canvas, or cloth.

Photocopying uses static electricity on a rotating cylinder to transfer black powder onto paper. A photocopier can make hundreds of copies in the time it once took a scribe to write a few characters.

SEE ALSO: Book; Communication; Design; Newspaper & Magazine; Photography

BASIC LITHOGRAPHY

Lithography is based on the principle that grease and water do not mix. The original procedure, first developed in 1798, is shown below. In the 1900s lithography was improved when the flat stone was replaced by a light-sensitive metal plate, and the images were transferred, or offset, onto paper.

First draw a letter on a flat stone with a greasy crayon, then wipe the stone with a damp sponge, leaving water on the areas that are not covered in crayon.

Cover the stone with ink, which does not mix with water, and will therefore stick only to the area that has been marked with crayon.

Press a sheet of paper onto the top of the stone. When the paper is removed, it will be marked with a reversed image of what was originally drawn in crayon.

✳ RADAR AND SONAR

An echo happens when sound waves bounce off an object. Radar and sonar use the echoes of radio signals to locate objects and for navigation.

In 1935 Robert A. Watson-Watt and other British scientists developed a system of radio echoes that could detect approaching aircraft. During World War II (1939–45) U.S. Navy scientists named this system "RAdio Detection And Ranging," or radar. Its first use was to give warning of German air raids against Britain.

A radar system has four main parts: a transmitter, an antenna, a receiver, and an indicator. The transmitter produces short radio pulses. The antenna sends out the pulses and picks up the echoes from the target object. The receiver increases the strength of these echoes and transfers them to the indicator. Here, the echoes appear as bright spots known as blips. They show how far away the object is.

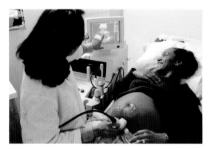

A doctor uses high-frequency sound waves (ultrasonography) to produce an image of an unborn child. It enables the doctor to monitor the baby's growth.

Navigators use radar at sea and in the air to identify other craft and to find buoys and other positioning aids. Radar also has many military uses, especially as an early warning system for approaching missiles and enemy aircraft or ships.

Sonar

SOund NAvigation Ranging, or sonar, uses sound signals. It is very useful underwater, where radio transmission works badly. Submarines use sonar to detect other underwater craft, as well as natural hazards such as rocks and whales. Sonar is also used to measure the depth of water and to locate schools of fish. Sonar also has uses on land, in the search for oil, and in medicine.

AMAZING FACTS!

Radar transmitters send out extremely short radio signals. Each pulse lasts about one one-millionth of a second.

Dolphins produce ultrasonic sounds of about 196,000 vibrations per second. These sounds reflect from underwater objects to give dolphins the ability to "see" when waters are cloudy or dark.

SEE ALSO: Navigation; Radio

✳ RADIO

Radio is an electronic technology used in many areas. It makes communication possible between two points without connecting wires.

▶ *A girl tunes into a radio station and listens using headphones. Radio stations broadcast on different frequencies.*

Radio waves are electromagnetic waves, moving at about 186,000 miles (300,000km) per second—the speed of light. They are created when an electrical current flows through a metal wire or rod—the transmitting antenna. When the waves reach a receiving antenna, they produce a second current that is converted into sound.

Each radio wave has a high point—a crest—and a low point—a trough. The distance between one crest and the next is called the wavelength. The number of complete waves, or cycles, in a second is called the frequency, and it is measured in kilohertz (kHz), or thousands of cycles per second.

A radio station broadcasts on a unique frequency. By setting a radio receiver to the correct frequency, the listener can pick up the radio station that he or she wants. Some frequencies are restricted to specific uses for emergency services, the military, and other organizations.

No one person invented the radio. In 1864 the English scientist James Clerk

Maxwell used mathematics to predict the existence of radio waves. It was a German, Heinrich Hertz, who proved they existed, in 1888. The unit of frequency is named in his honor.

An Englishman, Ernest Rutherford, sent the first radio signal, while another Englishman, Oliver Lodge, figured out the basic principle of the tuner. Guglielmo Marconi (1874–1937), an Italian based in England, created the first practical radio transmitter. In 1901 he sent and received a series of dots and dashes across the Atlantic Ocean. Marconi's wireless was used for signaling to ships at sea.

In 1904 another Englishman, John A. Fleming, created a vacuum tube that

AMAZING FACTS !

The tallest radio tower ever built was 2,120 ft. (646m) tall. It was built in Poland in 1974 and fell down in 1991.

331

made it possible to send sounds—speech and music—by radio. An American, Lee DeForest, improved on this in 1906, adding a grid to the tube. This was the earliest loudspeaker. That same year R.A. Fessenden made the first voice and music broadcast from his home in Massachusetts. Over the next few decades sales of radios increased rapidly, and broadcasting stations began setting up in North America, Europe, and beyond.

An important development came in 1948, when the transistor was invented at Bell Telephone Laboratories. This meant that radios could be smaller and more portable. Young people were becoming wealthier and more independent, and transistor radios allowed them to listen to the new music that they loved.

Frequency modulation—FM—radio, stereo, and digital radio have all added to the quality and variety of radio broadcasts. A big boost for FM radio was stereophonic sound, or the stereo, with two speakers. The principle remains the same, however, as it was when Marconi made his first broadcasts—the transmission of information without the restriction of wires.

Two-way radio

Many radios are both receivers and transmitters, enabling two-way communication. Police officers communicate with each other through two-way radios. Fire departments,

ambulance services, and taxi companies use radio to control and keep track of their vehicles. Security guards and ushers at public events also use radios. Safe airplane travel would be impossible unless pilots could communicate with air traffic control. Radio waves can even travel beyond the atmosphere and back, as astronauts keep in touch with Earth.

Radio waves do not only carry sounds. Radar is a form of radio. Pagers also use radio waves to send alerts or text messages. Radio telescopes can also pick up natural waves from distant galaxies.

◄ *Guglielmo Marconi at Signal Hill, St. John's, Newfoundland, just after receiving the first wireless signal to cross the Atlantic from England on December 12, 1901.*

◄ *A two-way radio is used during rescue work. Two-way radios are used to transmit and receive messages.*

SEE ALSO: Communication; Electricity; Radar & Sonar

R

✳ RAINFOREST

Rainforests are jungles that receive over 59 in. (1,500mm) of rain evenly through each year. The largest rainforests are found in tropical regions.

Tropical rainforests

Rainforest trees usually have tall trunks and grow close to one another. Their leafy crowns form an almost solid canopy, like a ceiling, up to 150 ft. (40m) above ground. The canopy takes nearly all the sunlight. Vines and creepers reach up the tree trunks to the canopy, and branches are covered with plants whose roots absorb water from the humid air. Plants of the lower understory have broad leaves that capture as much light as possible.

On the ground fungi and invertebrates, such as ants and millipedes, break down fallen leaves into nutrients. Tree roots quickly absorb the nutrients.

Most rainforest animals, such as sloths, flying squirrels, and various monkeys, live in the canopy and seldom visit the ground. Colorful birds of the rainforest include toucans, hornbills, and parrots.

The importance of rainforests

Rainforests contain more plant and animal species than any other habitat. People living in rainforests have long depended on the forest for food, shelter, and medicine. Rainforests have given the world rubber, coffee, and chocolate, and they help control temperature and rainfall. That is because the trees form a canopy that keeps in moisture, creating a hot and humid atmosphere in which plants can grow and animals can live. Today the rainforests are destroyed for timber and to make room for mining and farmland.

Many people and organizations are working to protect the rainforests from destruction. One way of achieving this aim is to avoid buying rainforest products that have been harvested and not replaced.

Tropical rainforests are found close to the equator from the Brazilian Amazon and Central America to Southeast Asia, northeast Australia, and Equatorial Africa. In tropical rainforests the average annual temperature is 77°F (25°C). Rainforests farther from the equator are cooler and receive less rain. Known as temperate rainforests, they grow in the Pacific Northwest of the United States, southeast Australia, New Zealand, and Chile.

SEE ALSO: Biome; Botany; Climate & Weather; Environment; Habitat; Natural Resources; Pollution

333

✳ RELIGION

Religion takes many different forms and is found in almost every culture, past and present. It can unite people, but it can also be a cause of wars.

Religion probably started when early humans tried to understand life's mysteries—how and why the world was created, why they were alive, and what would happen to them when they died. Most early religions involved worship of a wide range of gods, each of whom was associated with a particular activity or force of nature. People would pray to sun or rain gods to ensure a good harvest, or make sacrifices to gods of war before an important battle.

Religion today

Today there are thousands of religions throughout the world. Since there are so many of them, it is hard to identify elements common to all faiths. But most definitions of religion point to certain characteristics. They include a set of beliefs about what is important and real; a community of believers; rituals and sacred practices (such as the Christian baptism); sacred texts (such as the Buddhist Lotus Sutra); and authoritative traditions (such as rules about what to wear or eat).

For many people religion involves worshiping one supreme being, or god. Other people worship many gods or may have a more general belief in a higher power or a universal life force. Religions generally include a moral code governing thoughts and actions.

Not everyone who is religious belongs to an identifiable religion. Some people simply believe in a divine power or spirit and do not fit into any recognized faith.

The purpose of religion

Religion serves many purposes. It can unite people with similar beliefs and require them to behave in a way that benefits others. That has traditionally helped people form communities, raise families, and live together more harmoniously, so ensuring survival. This was more true in the past because in many countries there was just one religion. Everyone had the same faith, and the ruler was both a political and a religious leader. In some parts of the world that is still the case.

At a school in Jakarta, Indonesia, Muslim women study the Koran (Qur'an in Arabic), the sacred book of Islam.

On another level religion can provide a sense of fulfillment and inner peace, giving believers a feeling of security. They think a higher power is watching over and protecting them. However, some people are intolerant of those with different beliefs. That has led to many wars and violent clashes between individuals.

Types of religion

There are several ways to classify religions. One is to group them according to their beliefs about a deity. Followers of some religions believe in one god: That is called monotheism. Followers of other religions believe in polytheism—more than one god. Religions can be classified historically. Prehistoric religions existed before people could read or write. Many live on in the form of myth. Those practiced today are called living religions.

Living religions can be subdivided into other groups. The faiths in each group may be related to each other because they all developed in the same part of the world or because they share some authoritative texts or beliefs. They may also be related because they revere some of the same teachers or prophets, or because they have influenced each other.

One large group includes the faiths that started in India and spread throughout Asia. They include Hinduism, Buddhism, and Sikhism.

Confucianism, Taoism, and Shinto are another important group. They originated in China and Japan, and chart a way of life based on time-honored traditions, texts, and revered leaders.

Nearly one-third of the world's population belongs to religions in a third group: Judaism, Christianity, and Islam. These faiths all share a belief in one god.

Judaism

Judaism originated about 1800 B.C. in the Middle East. It is one of the world's oldest faiths. Believers in Judaism are called Jews. They believe in one God who, according to Hebrew scriptures, entered into a covenant (agreement) with a herdsman called Abraham. In return for Abraham's loyalty God promised to give him land and bless his descendants. Today there are about 14 million Jews worldwide.

Christianity

Christianity began in the first century A.D. as a sect within Judaism. It is based on the life and teachings of Jesus Christ, a Jewish preacher. Christ taught that there was one all-powerful God and that people should live according to his laws. Today Christianity is the world's largest religion, with about 2 billion followers.

Islam

Islam began in Arabia in the seventh century A.D. It is based on divine statements, or revelations, made by Allah (God) to Muhammad, the last of a line of prophets that included Abraham and Jesus. The revelations were collected in the Koran, Islam's scripture. Today Islam has over 1 billion followers, called Muslims.

Hinduism

Hinduism is a set of beliefs and practices that originated in India thousands of years ago. It has no founder or prophet, but there are several holy books. Some Hindus worship more than

In the 11th century the Christian church in Europe became divided between east and west. This bishop is a member of the eastern Russian Orthodox church.

A Shinto priest bangs a drum during a religious ceremony in Kyoto, Japan.

one god, and all believe in a unifying spirit called Brahman and in reincarnation, that is, being born again. There are about 900 million Hindus in the world today.

Buddhism
Buddhism was founded in India in the sixth century B.C. by an Indian prince who became the first Buddha, or enlightened one. There are an estimated 325 million Buddhists today. They do not believe in a supreme creator. They try to lead a life based on morality, compassion, and respect for others in the hope of achieving inner peace and enlightenment, or nirvana.

Sikhism
Sikhism began in northwest India in the 1500s as an alternative to Islam and Hinduism. Sikhs have one God who can be known through meditation (quietly focusing the mind on God). They believe that people are reborn again and again until they are finally united with God. There are about 23 million Sikhs worldwide.

Confucianism
Confucianism is more a philosophy than a religion. It was founded in China in the sixth century B.C. by Confucius. He taught that people should live in

harmony with others, behaving with honesty, courage, and courtesy. Many people combine Confucianism with other beliefs. Today there are about 160 million Confucians. Most live in China.

Taoism
Taoism is based on the writings of Lao-tzu, a sixth-century B.C. Chinese philosopher. Taoists believe that the Tao, a form of energy, is the source of everything in the universe and consists of two complementary aspects, yin and yang, that need to be balanced. Today there are about 20 million Taoists, mainly in China and Taiwan.

Shinto
Shinto is the religion of Japan. Its sacred books, dating from 700s A.D., are collections of myths from a time when the world was young, and the gods mingled with Japanese people. At its core is the belief in kami (the sacred power), which is present in many animals and objects and helps connect humans with the natural world. Followers of the kami way show their reverence at home, at shrines, and at festivals. Today there are about 4 million Shintos in Japan.

The Nihang Singhs are warrior Sikhs who live in the Punjab area of India. Five symbols are particularly important to Sikhs: uncut hair, a special comb, "drawers" or trousers, a saber, and a bracelet of steel.

SEE ALSO: Buddhism; Hinduism; Islam; Judaism; Philosophy

✳ REMBRANDT (1606–69)

One of the greatest European painters, the Dutch artist Rembrandt van Rijn is noted for his handling of shade and light, especially in portraits.

Rembrandt Harmensz van Rijn was born in Leiden, Holland, on July 15, 1606. As soon as he was old enough, he set up as a portrait artist. In about 1632 he moved to Amsterdam to paint wealthy patrons. He quickly became successful and lived with his wife Saskia in a grand home.

In 1642 Saskia died, leaving Rembrandt with a son, Titus. By now his portraiture style was out of fashion, but that did not trouble him. Until then he had painted people in the midst of dramatic action, as in *The Night Watch*, which has since been widely acclaimed as his masterpiece. Now he became more interested in their inner feelings. He painted new subjects, such as Bible stories. His last years,

although spent as a poor man, marked the most creative period of his life.

Rembrandt's paintings, drawings, and prints cover many subjects, but his work can often be identified by its contrasts of light and dark or the golden-brown haze surrounding his figures. He painted more self-portraits than any other artist.

The Dutch artist Rembrandt painted Self-Portrait as a Young Man between 1633 and 1634.

SEE ALSO: Art; Artists, World

✳ RENAISSANCE

The Renaissance was a period in European history that saw a rebirth of interest in the learning and arts of ancient Greece and Rome.

It was also a time of discovery and growth. Europeans developed new scientific ideas and inventions, produced new literature and art, and discovered new lands and trade routes. They began to think about the world in new ways.

The word Renaissance literally means "rebirth." The Renaissance began in Italy in the 1300s and gradually

spread to other European countries. At that time Italy was divided into a number of independent city-states, the most powerful of which were Florence, Milan, and Venice. Their rulers supported artists and scholars by commissioning (ordering) new buildings and works of art. This system encouraged new ideas to flourish.

The humanists

The learned scholars who revived interest in ancient Greek and Roman culture were known as humanists. For hundreds of years before the Renaissance art concentrated mainly on religious themes. The new generation, however, studied the history of antiquity and admired its literature, which told of human deeds and

The dome of Florence Cathedral, Italy was designed by Filippo Brunelleschi. Built between 1420 and 1436, the cathedral is considered to be the first building of the Renaissance.

feelings rather than the glory of god. The humanists modeled their own works on those of the ancient authors, concentrating on the joys of this world rather than the rewards of the next.

Humanists wrote mostly in Latin, the scholarly language of the time, but some started writing in the vernacular, the everyday language of the people. The Italian poet Petrarch wrote many poems in Italian and his friend Boccaccio wrote a collection of stories in Italian entitled the *Decameron*. Other writers started writing in their own languages, and the development of printing meant that ideas spread rapidly.

Some scholars felt that the Bible should be translated into European languages rather than being in Latin, which most people could not understand. In the 14th century an English translation was made, and in the early 1500s Martin Luther made a German translation. People could read the Bible in their own languages, and this helped the Protestant Reformation—a religious movement to reform the Catholic church—spread in Germany.

Art and architecture

Renaissance artists also turned for inspiration to the classical (ancient) world. They borrowed classical forms and used them in new ways. Medieval artists had focused on religious subjects; Renaissance artists looked to the world around them.

Painters and sculptors often drew their subject matter from Greek and Roman mythology. Although that subject matter was old, the way of painting it was new. To give the appearance of reality, painters studied the human body, the interplay of light and shade, and perspective (the method of creating the illusion of space on a flat picture surface). They painted worldly subjects, such as the portraits of powerful men and women. When a Renaissance artist painted a religious painting, he made the people in the painting look like real people rather than the stylized characters of medieval art.

Renaissance architects used the domes, round arches, and columns of the buildings of antiquity to create a new Renaissance architecture based on ideas of harmony and geometry. Renaissance architects often based their designs on circles or squares, because they were considered to be perfect shapes.

Exploration and science

The Renaissance was a time when Europeans made many discoveries about the physical world. Explorers found sea routes to Asia and to the Americas—their voyages were made possible by improvements in navigational aids. There were important developments in mining, trade, and commerce. Coinage was standardized to meet the growing needs of bankers, traders, and merchants.

Michelangelo's David, a statue standing about 13 feet (4m) high, has become a symbol of the flourishing art world in Florence during the 1500s.
▶

In scientific matters there was a new emphasis on direct observation and experiment, rather than relying on the traditional knowledge of the past. The Swiss-born physician Paracelsus used chemical remedies rather than the old plant-based remedies, laying the foundations of modern chemistry. The Belgian anatomist Andreas Vesalius dissected human bodies and produced the first authoritative book on human anatomy. The astronomer Nicolaus Copernicus rejected the idea that the sun moved around the Earth, in favor of the Earth and planets moving around the sun.

Europeans had begun to think about the world in new and different ways. By the end of the 1500s the ideas of the Renaissance were being replaced by even newer ideas, but this period marked the beginning of the modern world.

SEE ALSO: Artists, World; Astronomy; Columbus, Christopher; History; Leonardo da Vinci; Literature; Medicine; Michelangelo; Middle Ages; Printing; Science

✴ REPRODUCTION

Reproduction is the process by which a living thing, or organism, copies itself. There are two types of reproduction, asexual and sexual.

The 1.5 million known species of living things have a wide variety of ways to reproduce, but the methods they each use are generally divided into a few broad kinds. The most fundamental difference is whether sex is involved.

Asexual reproduction

Organisms that reproduce asexually do so alone—there is no need for two members of the same species to link cells or share in any way. There are three main types of asexual reproduction—division, budding, and the creation of spores.

Many single-celled creatures, such as amebas and bacteria, reproduce simply by dividing themselves in half. Some worms and other larger creatures do the same. The worm's body slowly pinches in around the middle until the worm splits into two parts.

Rainbow trout hatch on a trout farm in South Africa. The fish reproduce by spawning, or producing eggs that are fertilized in the water by the male sperm.
▼

339

▶

This diagram shows an egg being approached by tadpolelike sperm. Only one sperm can fertilize a single egg.

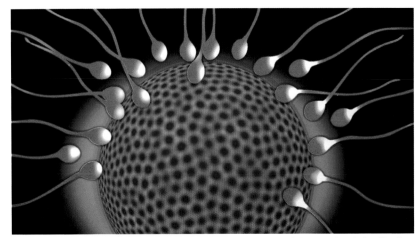

The front end of the worm grows a new rear end, and the rear end develops a new front.

Yeasts, sponges, corals, and grasses reproduce by forming buds. For example, the hydra, a marine creature related to the jellyfish, develops a bulge in its side. The bulge, or bud, slowly grows into a complete new animal just like the parent.

Mosses and a number of other plants reproduce by means of tiny specks of life called spores. When the spores are ripe, they fall. Those that land on moist, cool ground sprout into tiny new plants.

Sexual reproduction

The same basic processes are also at work in sexual reproduction, but here the process begins only when the egg

of the female of the species is fertilized by the sperm of the male. In some species fertilization takes place inside the creatures' bodies; in others it is external. Female frogs, for example, release their eggs into the water, and the male frog deposits his sperm on them.

Adaptation for survival

Sexual reproduction recombines the genes—chemical building blocks that control how organisms appear, grow, and breed—so that offspring have different sets of genes from those of either parent. That makes each organism produced by sexual means unique, except in the case of siblings derived from a single fertilized egg. The advantage of genetic diversity is that it makes species better able to adapt to environmental changes—those that are better equipped for survival will leave more offspring, thus contributing to the survival of the entire species.

There are advantages and disadvantages to both methods. In species in which all individuals arise asexually, there is little or no genetic variation. Thus environmental changes that are unfavorable for one organism will be unfavorable for all and may threaten the survival of the species. On the other hand, because sexual reproduction normally requires that an egg be fertilized by a sperm from the same

AMAZING FACTS !

The only mammals that lay eggs are the duck-billed platypus and the echidna, or spiny anteater. Both animals live in Australia.
The eggs of some animals are huge—the largest, the ostrich egg, may weigh 3 lb. (1.4kg). Others are smaller than the period at the end of this sentence.

species, there is a greater element of luck in the reproduction of the species. Chance plays no role in asexual reproduction since fertilization does not occur. Some organisms, such as the common plumose sea anemone, can reproduce both sexually and asexually. They thus make the most of their chances of continuing the species.

Once animals of many species can no longer reproduce, their work in effect ends, and they die. Nowhere is this more clearly shown than in certain species of mayflies, insects whose adult lives are devoted exclusively to reproducing. Within a few hours of a summer day they hatch, swarm, mate, lay their eggs, and die. Still other species of animals survive reproduction itself but die almost as soon as their young can fend for themselves. Essentially, reproduction—and through it the survival of the species—is the central event in the life of any organism.

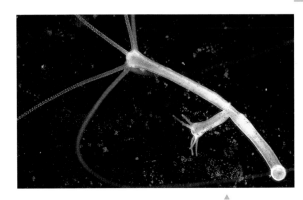

The hydra reproduces asexually by a process known as budding.

SEE ALSO: Animal; Biology; Bird; Evolution; Genetics; Human Body; Insect; Mammal; Plant; Platypus; Reptile

✳ REPTILE

Reptiles form a group of egg-laying vertebrates (animals with backbones) with scaly skin. There are about 6,000 different species of reptile.

Crocodiles, lizards, snakes, and turtles are all reptiles. Reptiles share a variety of characteristics. They all have internal skeletons. Dry scales cover their bodies. They breathe air through their lungs.

All reptiles are ectothermic, or cold-blooded, which means that their temperature depends on the temperature of their environment. Species have various ways to control their temperatures. Some move to shady areas or burrow in sand when it gets too hot. Others change their skin color to reflect more heat away.

Most reptiles, except for snakes and some lizards, have four legs, each ending in a foot with five clawed toes. Most females lay eggs that hatch outside the body, although some lizards give birth to live young. Reptile eggs dry out easily, so females lay them in damp places in the earth or sand or in rotten wood. Newborn reptiles resemble their

The emerald tree boa is found in South America. It gives birth to live young rather than laying eggs. When they are younger, the boas are a dull orange color, but they turn green as they mature.

parents—they do not go through stages of development, like insects or amphibians.

The first reptiles evolved about 300 million years ago. Most scientists believe that reptiles are the ancestors of birds and mammals. The dinosaurs were among the reptilian species that are now extinct. Reptiles exist throughout the temperate and tropical parts of the world, although they are more common in warmer areas.

Crocodiles and alligators

Crocodiles, alligators, caimans, and gavials are called crocodilians. Crocodilians all have long tails and large jaws. They spend their lives in or close to water. Although they are strong swimmers, they are only able to run short distances. They feed mainly on fish and birds, but larger crocodilians can attack animals, including dogs, cattle, and people.

Crocodilians vary in size. American crocodiles can reach lengths of 23 ft. (7m), and one specimen weighed 1,350 lb. (612kg). The South American dwarf cayman, on the other hand, is under 5 ft. (1.5m) long when fully grown.

AMAZING FACTS!

There are no snakes in Ireland. According to legend, St. Patrick, the patron saint of Ireland, banished them.
When a crocodile closes its mouth, it appears to be grinning. Alligators do not have this "grin."
A tortoise named Tui Mala died in 1965 aged at least 188. It belonged to the royal family of the Pacific nation of Tonga.

Crocodiles and the smaller gavial have long, tapering snouts and triangular heads. Crocodiles live in the Americas, Australia, Africa, and Asia. Gavials only live in India and parts of Southeast Asia. Alligators and caymans have broader, rounded heads. They live in the Americas, apart from one species of alligator that is found in eastern China.

Turtles and tortoises

Reptiles with hard, bony shells are called chelonians. Those that live in water are usually called turtles, and those that live on land are called tortoises. There are about 250 species in this group. They range in size from

Like many other reptiles, crocodiles lay eggs. When the mother hears the eggs hatching, she comes back to the nest to guard the young.

tiny bog turtles, about 3 in. (7cm) long to massive leatherbacks that can reach almost 9 ft. (2.5m) in length and weigh 1,500 lb. (680kg).

A chelonian's shell is made of two parts joined by bony bridges. The upper part is called the carapace, and the lower part is called the plastron. The animal uses the shell for protection, drawing its head and legs inside when in danger. Some species, such as mud turtles, can shut up their shells completely. Others squirt out unpleasant fluids or bite and claw their enemies.

Like crocodilians, most turtles can only move slowly on land. However, freshwater turtles can move faster on land than most tortoises.

Snakes

Snakes are long, slender reptiles without legs. They do not have movable eyelids, which gives them a glassy, unblinking stare. Most snakes live in the warmer parts of the world, although some, such as the rattlesnake, are found as far north as the Arctic Circle.

There are more than 2,900 species of snakes. Most snakes belong to the largest family, Colubridae, which has more than 1,700 species, including garter snakes, hognose snakes, and vine snakes. The viper family contains more than 200 species of vipers and pit vipers. Pit vipers have a deep pit between the eye and the nostril on each side of the head. They include rattlesnakes and copperheads.

Snakes have two main methods of killing their prey—constriction and poisoning. Constrictors coil around their prey and suffocate it. They range in size from 30-ft. (9-m) pythons and anacondas to 1-ft. (30-cm) scarlet king snakes. Venomous snakes produce venom in special glands and inject it into the victim through a grooved or hollow fang.

Many people think that snakes have slimy skins. However, a snake, like most reptiles, is dry to the touch. A snake's skin does not grow with the animal and has to be shed at regular intervals.

Snakes are often hunted for their attractively patterned skins, which are made into purses, shoes, and belts. They are also captured for the pet and zoo trade. As a result, some species are becoming seriously endangered.

Lizards and tuataras

Chameleons, iguanas, skinks, monitors, anoles, and geckos are all types of lizard. Most lizards have four legs, although some have two or even none. All lizards have shoulder bones, which snakes lack. The skulls of lizards are also more complex than those of snakes.

Most lizards are less than 16 in. (40cm) long, but the largest, the Komodo dragon, can grow up to 10 ft. (3m) in length and reach weights of 300 lb. (135kg). Some species of gecko are less than ¾ in. (2cm) long, making them the smallest reptiles.

Scientists classify the tuatara, found only on islands off the coast of New Zealand, as a separate group, although it looks similar to lizards. In common with some lizards, it has a third eye. It can also remain active at a colder temperature than most reptiles. It is the last surviving member of a reptilian group that was common in prehistoric times.

▲
The iguana is a member of the lizard family. Like all lizards and snakes, iguanas shed their skins from time to time. Green iguanas use their strong claws for climbing trees.

SEE ALSO: Animal; Dinosaur; Evolution

✳ REVOLUTION

A revolution is the overthrow of a ruler, government, or social class followed by its replacement with another ruling party or class.

▶ *Russian revolutionary Vladimir Ilyich Lenin leads the people in* Long Live the Revolution, *painted by Pavel Kuznetsov.*

Revolutions often take place in countries where the ordinary people have been suffering under cruel laws or an uncaring leadership. Conditions may be so bad that the people have no food, no jobs, and no rights. Eventually they feel that their only choice is to bring down the leadership and replace it with a fairer system.

Famous revolutions

The 1700s and 1800s saw many revolutions in America and Europe. In the American Revolution of 1775–83 the American colonies broke free from British rule and went on to create the United States. A few years later bloody revolution shook France. The French royal family had become unpopular, and the noble ruling class lived in luxury while peasants (laborers) and soldiers starved. In 1789 the mob rioted in Paris, bringing down the government. Over the next few years the people executed thousands of nobles, including King Louis XVI and his wife Queen Marie Antoinette.

Revolution rocked Russia during the First World War (1914–18). The country suffered greatly during the war. In 1917 the government collapsed, and the army turned against the head of state, Czar Nicholas II, who stepped down. Peasant armies seized the land, and civil war broke out. The revolution led to the creation of the communist Union of Soviet Socialist Republics (USSR) in 1922.

After the revolution

During the chaos of a revolution it is not easy to establish a stable government. In France the people tried repeatedly to create a republic. Eventually, in 1799 Napoleon Bonaparte seized power, and in 1804 he made himself emperor. In Russia the revolution replaced czarist rule with a dictatorship, first under Vladimir Lenin (1870–1924) and then under Joseph Stalin (1879–1953).

SEE ALSO: Europe; France; Government; History; Napoleon; Russia & the Baltic States

344

✱ RIDE, SALLY (1951–)

Sally Ride became the first American woman in space aboard the space shuttle Challenger in 1983. She was also the youngest U.S. astronaut to date.

Sally Ride floats on the flight deck during the 1983 space mission.

Sally Kristen Ride was born in Encino, California, on May 26, 1951. Although she was a superb tennis player, she gave up hopes of playing professionally and studied physics at Stanford University.

In 1977 she was selected by NASA to become an astronaut. Ride achieved fame when she flew around the Earth on the seventh space shuttle mission on June 18, 1983. At the age of 32 she was also the youngest U.S. astronaut. During the six-day mission the crew put satellites in space and conducted research.

Ride also flew on the 13th mission in 1984 and later served on the commission that investigated the 1986 Challenger disaster, when the shuttle exploded after takeoff. In 1989 she became head of the Space Institute of the University of California at San Diego. After retiring, Ride spent much of her time encouraging young women to study science and math and to become scientists and engineers.

SEE ALSO: Astronaut; Space Exploration; Space Shuttle

✱ RIVER

A river is a natural stream of water that flows in a definite channel. Rivers range in length from tiny streams to the mighty Nile and Amazon.

When rain falls, some of it flows downhill. Sometimes water that remains on the surface gouges a gully out of the ground as it moves. If there is enough water to provide a constant flow, and if it moves quickly enough to cut a channel, then a river often forms.

Rivers are very different in size, shape, and form, but all rivers have certain things in common. The place where a river begins is called its source. A river always runs through a channel in the ground called a river valley. The place where the river ends is called a mouth—this is usually the place where it flows into a lake, a sea, or an ocean.

The water of most rivers picks up soil and other matter as it flows. If the river ends at a quiet sea or lake, it will deposit

◄
A river estuary in northwestern Madagascar. The soil is not fertile, and salt marshes have formed.

THE WORLD'S LONGEST RIVERS

Nile, Africa	4,145 mi. (6,670km)
Amazon, South America	4,007 mi. (6,449km)
Chang Jiang (Yangtze), Asia	3,915 mi. (6,300km)
Mississippi, North America	3,741 mi. (6,020km)
Yenisey–Angara, Asia	3,442 mi. (5,540km)
Huang He (Yellow River), Asia	3,395 mi. (5,464km)
Ob, Asia	3,230 mi. (5,200 km)
Paraná–Rio de la Plata, South America	3,032 mi. (4,879km)
Congo, Africa	2,920 mi. (4,700km)
Lena, Asia	2,734 mi. (4,400km)

this matter at the mouth. This deposit is called a delta, and it usually includes plenty of fertile soil. The Rhine, in northwest Europe, the Nile, in Egypt, and the Mississippi, in the United States, end in deltas. When sea tides at the mouth of the river are strong, however, they carry away the soil, and there is no fertile delta. Instead, the mouth is called an estuary. Examples of rivers with estuaries include the Hudson, in New York, and the Thames, in England.

The importance of rivers

Like any area of water, a river can be rich in life, especially in fish and plants. Rivers are also valuable areas for recreation and to enjoy water sports, and are very useful for transportation. River barges carry heavy cargoes on the Illinois, Mississippi, Ohio, and Hudson rivers. River deltas often provide rich farming areas. Increasingly, the energy of rivers is harnessed to create electricity.

SEE ALSO: Amazon; Egypt, Ancient; Energy; Flood; Geography; Mississippi River; Water; Waterfall

✳ ROAD

A well-planned, well-built network of roads is vital to modern society. Building a modern road requires planning and many people working together.

Thousands of years ago people found their way through forests by following the tracks of wild animals. Later they filled ruts with soil and laid logs over wet spots. This was the beginning of road construction.

Many of the great ancient civilizations built roads, but the most impressive constructions were those of the Romans. They built over 50,000 miles (80,000km) of roads throughout their empire, some of which still exist today.

After the end of the western Roman Empire in the fifth century the quality of roads declined. It was not until the 1700s that French and English engineers began to construct high-quality, long-lasting roads for the increasing amount of traffic.

In the 1900s, as cars became the most popular form of transportation, good road networks became vital to the world's economies. For many people the interstates and freeways of the United States or Germany's autobahns symbolize progress and freedom.

Modern roads

The first step in building a modern road is to plan the route. Surveyors, engineers, and government representatives consider the amount of traffic that a road might take now and many years into the future. This will determine the road's width, the number of lanes, and the strength of the construction. Builders have to determine how well the soil drains on the proposed routes and must consider what the road will displace. New roads sometimes cut through areas such as forests, and there are environmental considerations such as the destruction of wildlife habitats. If the route runs through private property, the owners will have to be paid compensation.

After all the planning and testing are completed, construction crews can begin their work. Bulldozers clear a path for the foundation, or roadbed. Earth and stones, called fill, are laid down, and large rollers press down the fill to make a level band of dirt. Pipes, called culverts, are laid to drain away water from the roads.

The next step is to put down two or more layers of rocks and stones. The bottom layer consists of large stones, the next layer has slightly smaller stones, and so on. The surface layer of the road must be strong and watertight. Today this pavement layer is made of either concrete or a material such as asphalt.

A Roman road in Petra, Jordan. The Romans built over 50,000 miles (80,000km) of roads.

SEE ALSO: Car; Roman Empire; Transportation

✴ ROBOT

A robot is a machine capable of being set up and programmed to perform a wide variety of tasks for which it must physically move itself or other objects.

For hundreds of years people fantasized about creating artificial forms of life clever enough to perform tasks. The first use of the word "robot" was by the Czech dramatist Karel Capek in 1921 in his play *R.U.R.* (for Rossum's Universal Robots). The play was about a man who creates humanlike machines to work in his factory. Capek coined the word "robot" from the Czech word *robota*, meaning "work" or "slavery."

The first actual robot was developed by American inventors George Devol and Joseph Engelberger in 1958. General Motors purchased the first industrial robot and installed it in a Trenton, New Jersey, automobile factory to lift and stack hot pieces of metal.

Today commercial robots are available in two basic types: manipulator and mobile. A robot manipulator looks like a mechanical arm and may range in length from 12 in. (30cm) to 12 ft. (3.7m) or more. Most robots used today are manipulators. Mobile robots roll on wheels from place to place. So far they have only a few practical applications. However, mobile robots are being extensively developed

"Asimo" the robot has been designed to perform basic tasks, such as walking up and down stairs and greeting people.

in research laboratories. Researchers have built a humanoid (humanlike robot) that can walk slowly, turn, and climb stairs.

Robots have "brains" that are computers programmed for the jobs they do. Some robots have powerful computers, but they cannot think in the way that people can. It is possible to program a robot to perform the exact motions needed to dust a room, for example, but it cannot decide whether or not the room needs dusting.

Many robots today are able to recognize objects using a special computer that translates a television picture into a form the robot's brain can understand. Others can "talk" using a device called a voice synthesizer. Thousands of industrial robots are used in factories to perform tasks that people find difficult, dangerous, or boring, such as pouring hot metal, welding, and spraying paint. Robots are very accurate and precise. They are also important in space exploration. In 1997, for example, a robotic rover explored the surface of Mars, studying its soil and rocks.

Scientists are continually improving robot technology. Some people fear that as robots become more useful, people will not be able to find jobs. Others believe that the use of robots will open up new and more interesting jobs for people.

SEE ALSO: Manufacturing; Space Exploration

✴ ROCKET

A rocket is a device used to propel a vehicle, often a spaceship. However, rockets can also be used to move cars, boats, and aircraft.

In its simplest form a rocket is a tube of fuel that is closed at one end and open at the other. As the fuel burns, it creates hot gases that expand and rush out of the open end. This action is called thrust, and it causes the rocket to move in the opposite direction from the hot gases. The expanding gases are released through a chemical reaction. The chemicals that produce this reaction are called propellants. Rocket propellants can be either liquid or solid.

Most fuels need oxygen from the air to work, which means that they cannot be used in space. Rockets, however, carry their own supply of oxygen. Also, when a rocket moves through air, it creates friction, or drag, which slows down the rocket. Because there is no air in space, there is almost no drag against the rocket to slow it down.

History
The first rockets were invented in the 1200s by the Chinese. These early rockets were produced by stuffing gunpowder into sections of bamboo tubing. They were used as weapons, to send signals, or to create firework displays. It was not until the mid-1900s, however, that the principles of rocket propulsion were understood well enough for them to be used for journeys into space.

Russian inventor Konstantin Tsiolkovsky developed the ideas that made space travel in rockets possible. He published

his theories in 1903. Another important step was in 1917, when German scientist Hermann Oberth proposed using a liquid fuel for rockets. The first liquid-fuel rocket to fly was launched by American scientist Robert Goddard in 1926.

During World War II (1939–45) German scientist Wernher von Braun led a team of scientists in the development of the V-2 rocket, which became the first long-range guided missile. After the war he and other German scientists worked in the United States developing other missiles and rockets, including the Saturn V rocket that launched U.S. astronauts to the moon in 1969. Since then rockets have become more powerful and efficient, and are still an essential part of space travel.

Friendship 7, launched in 1962, was the first crewed U.S. rocket to orbit around the Earth.

SEE ALSO: Space Exploration; Space Shuttle

✳ RODENT

Rodents are mammals that gnaw. About 50 percent of all mammal species are rodents. They include squirrels, rats, mice, and porcupines.

The word *rodent* comes from a Latin word that means "to gnaw," and the easiest way to identify a rodent is to study the animal's teeth. Every rodent has four gnawing teeth, called incisors. They are shaped a little like chisels, and they keep growing throughout the animal's lifetime. In normal circumstances they wear against each other, so they stay the same length.

All rodents eat plant food. Their gnawing teeth help them cut through plant fibers. Some also eat small animals. Scientists divide rodents into three main groups.

Squirrels
Tree squirrels have thick plumed tails that can aid balance and warm the animal as it sleeps. Squirrels live in holes in trees or in leaf nests. Flying squirrels have membranes of skin joining their front and rear legs. They use them to glide from tree to tree, sometimes covering 150 ft. (45m) in one leap.

Chipmunks, marmots, and prairie dogs are members of the same group.

Kangaroo rats and their relatives play an important part in the growth of Indian rice grass, whose seeds provide their food.

▶ *Beavers spend most of their lives near water. They build dams across small streams to form ponds.*

Chipmunks are ground squirrels, common in North America. Marmots, including groundhogs, or woodchucks, are large, heavy-bodied relatives of the squirrels. The slightly smaller prairie dog looks very similar. Marmots and prairie dogs live in burrows that they dig underground.

Rats and mice
Rats and mice are the most abundant of all rodents. The house mouse and the brown rat have populated most areas of the world. Both species breed very quickly throughout the year. The brown rat is one of the most destructive creatures on the planet. It destroys millions of dollars' worth of food every year and spreads serious diseases.

Kangaroo rats and their close relatives, on the other hand, are responsible for the production of the food that they live on. They bury thousands of Indian rice-grass seeds during the brief growing season, but often do not return to dig up and eat the seeds. Many of the seeds sprout and grow the following year.

Field mice, or voles, live in fields and woodlands, and can do great damage to crops. Lemmings, their close relations, live in the far northern areas of the world. In favorable weather conditions lemmings breed very quickly. They migrate, that is, move to new habitats, in great hordes, sometimes numbering many millions. If they come to a sea cliff, they plunge over and drown. This has led to a myth that lemmings commit suicide. Other mice and rats include the muskrat, which lives in ponds and marshes, and the hamster, a popular household pet.

Porcupines and their relatives
The third group of rodents, porcupines, has only a few species. Unlike most rodents, the young of these species are born fully furred with their eyes open.

The porcupine's most obvious characteristic is its dense covering of sharp quills. An adult North American

AMAZING FACTS!

The largest rodent is the South American capybara. Some specimens are more than 4 ft. (1.2m) long and weigh 100 lb. (45kg).
The quills on the neck and back of crested porcupines from Africa and Asia can be as long as 20 in. (50cm).
A beaver can fell trees as thick as 2 ft. (0.6m) in diameter. Their dams can be over 100 ft. (31m) long and up to 10 ft. (3m) high.

porcupine can be 3 ft. (1m) long, weigh 30 lb. (14kg), and have up to 30,000 quills. If an animal attacks a porcupine, the quills come off and stick in the attacker's flesh. Porcupines live in wooded areas and make homes in burrows or trees. Their main food is the bark of trees, and they kill many trees by stripping off the bark.

Beavers are members of the same group of rodents. They are easily recognized by the flat, scaly tails that help them swim. Beavers use their incisors to cut trees to make their homes, or lodges, and dams to stabilize the water level of their habitat.

Guinea pigs, coypus, capybaras, and chinchillas also belong in this group. All these rodents originated in the Americas. Guinea pigs are still eaten in parts of South America, and coypus and chinchillas are bred for their fur.

Some rodents are harmful to people. Many are infested with fleas that carry diseases. Others damage crops or eat stored food. Other species are very useful to people; for example, burrowing rodents help farmers and gardeners by turning over the soil and sowing seeds. Many rodents are bred or trapped for their fur.

SEE ALSO: Animal; Mammal

✳ ROMAN EMPIRE

The ancient city of Rome was the heart of one of the longest-lasting empires in history. It began as a small city-state in about 500 B.C.

At its height the Roman Empire stretched from western Asia to Britain and Spain, and from the Danube River in central Europe to the edge of the Sahara Desert in North Africa. The empire in the west lasted to 476 A.D., while an Eastern Empire endured another thousand years.

In creating their empire, the Romans were often ruthless. They destroyed cities and enslaved whole populations. At the same time, they brought peace, an advanced culture, and the rule of law to the conquered lands. The many different peoples in the far-flung empire were eventually united by common citizenship. They enjoyed free trade and travel over good roads, safe waterways, a high level of public services (including public baths, libraries, and museums), and a uniform law code, government, and system of money. Latin, the Roman language, spread to all parts of the Western Empire. Even after the fall of the empire in the west Latin remained a common language of educated people as well as the language of the Roman Catholic church, the law, medicine, and science. The Latin alphabet was adopted by most European languages. Latin was the ancestor of modern French, Italian, Spanish, Portuguese, and Romanian, which are known as Romance languages.

The republic

According to legend, the city of Rome was founded in 753 B.C. by Romulus, who was its first king. The last king was overthrown in 509 B.C., when a republic was set up. It was ruled by popular assemblies of male citizens, a senate composed of wealthy citizens, and two chief magistrates, called

The ruins of the Colosseum, which was ancient Rome's largest amphitheater, or public arena. On public holidays Romans enjoyed watching men, called gladiators, fight each other.
▼

THE ROMAN EMPIRE

☐ Roman Empire at its
greatest extent

North
Sea

BRITANNIA

ATLANTIC
OCEAN

Cologne
GERMANIA

GAUL

CRIMEA   ASIA

DACIA

Black Sea

ITALIA

CORSICA   MACEDONIA   ● Constantinople
IBERIA   Rome   Athens ●
SARDINIA   ANATOLIA
                         GREECE

Carthage ●   SICILY   CYPRUS   SYRIA
MAURETANIA   CRETE   ● Jerusalem
          Mediterranean Sea   Persian
                                                                Gulf
                         Alexandria ●   ARABIA   Arabian
AFRICA   Sahara   Desert
            Desert   EGYPT   Red Sea

Caspian Sea
Adriatic Sea
Arabian Desert

▶
*The extent of
the Roman
Empire at its
height in A.D. 116.*

consuls. The republic had an efficient and well-trained army, which by the end of the third century B.C. had conquered Italy. It then went on to conquer many of the lands bordering the Mediterranean Sea.

In the first century B.C. a powerful consul and general, Julius Caesar, became dictator (an all-powerful ruler). Many Romans were unhappy at having a single ruler, and Caesar was assassinated in 44 B.C. Seventeen years after his death his adopted son, Octavian, became the first Roman emperor, taking the name Augustus.

The empire

Under Augustus and later emperors the Roman Empire expanded and enjoyed a period of prosperity and peace for 200 years. Roads were built to link all parts of the empire and aqueducts to bring water to the cities. The provinces were well ruled, and many people in the provinces

▶
*This mosaic, or
picture made up
of small pieces of
colored stone,
shows scenes
from Roman
country life at the
end of the fourth
century or the
beginning of the
fifth century A.D.*

rose through the ranks of the army or civil service to become Roman citizens. Wealthy citizens built luxurious homes with central heating, and their households and farms were worked by slaves. However, poorer people lived crowded together in apartment houses.

As the empire grew, the old gods of Greece and Rome no longer seemed appropriate. People started to worship the emperor and to become interested in other religions. Christianity began in the Roman province of Palestine and gradually spread, even though Christians were unpopular with the authorities and were often persecuted. Gradually, however, the new religion spread throughout the empire. Christianity was eventually made legal in A.D. 313 by the Emperor Constantine, who was baptized in 337 on his deathbed, making him the first Christian emperor.

The enormous size of the empire made it increasingly difficult to defend all its borders. In the third century Germanic peoples attacked Roman provinces in the north, and the Sassanid kings of Persia (modern Iran) attacked the empire in the east. The Roman Émpire started to break up. In 330 the Emperor Constantine moved his capital to the old Greek city of Byzantium, which was renamed Constantinople after him. It is now Istanbul in Turkey. In 395 the empire was split into two—the Western Empire, with its capital in Rome, and the Eastern Empire, with its capital in Constantinople.

The Western Empire was increasingly invaded by Huns from Asia and Visigoths and other tribes from Germany, whom the Romans called barbarians. In 476 the last western emperor, Romulus Augustus, was overthrown by the Germanic chieftain Odoacer. The Eastern Empire survived as the Byzantine Empire until 1453, when Constantinople was captured by the Ottoman Turks.

SEE ALSO: Caesar, Julius; Cleopatra; Dictatorship; Italy; Road; Warfare

---

* ROOSEVELT, ELEANOR (1884–1962)
The most politically active first lady the United States has ever known, Anna Eleanor Roosevelt was a tireless crusader for human rights.

The niece of President Theodore Roosevelt, Eleanor was born in New York City on October 11, 1884. In 1905 she married her distant cousin, Franklin Delano Roosevelt. They had six children, one girl and five boys. Eleanor devoted herself to her family while her husband developed his political career. After Franklin was stricken with polio in 1921, Eleanor herself became politically active.

When her husband became president in 1933, Eleanor traveled for him and reported on what she had seen. An enthusiastic supporter of social causes, including civil rights for blacks and women, she held press conferences, had her own radio program, and wrote a daily newspaper column called "My Day."

After Franklin Roosevelt died in 1945, Eleanor was appointed as a delegate to the United Nations, where she helped draft the Declaration of Human Rights. She died in New York on November 7, 1962, and was buried at the Roosevelt estate at Hyde Park, New York.

SEE ALSO: Roosevelt, Franklin D.; United Nations; Women's Rights Movement

Eleanor Roosevelt was a tireless campaigner for social causes. They included opening a furniture shop in New York to provide jobs for the unemployed.

✳ ROOSEVELT, FRANKLIN DELANO (1882–1945)

Franklin D. Roosevelt was the 32nd president of the United States from 1933 to 1945. He led the country through the Great Depression and World War II.

▶ *Franklin D. Roosevelt during one of his "fireside chats," the radio broadcasts to the nation that he made throughout his presidency.*

President Roosevelt quickly brought in measures to implement his New Deal. They included jobs for the unemployed, funds to feed the hungry, the right to join a union, unemployment insurance, and old-age pensions. He set up vast public works projects and established a national standard of minimum wages and maximum working hours.

Franklin D. Roosevelt was the longest-serving president and one of the best loved. He was born into a well-to-do family in Hyde Park, New York, and went to Harvard College and law school. He entered a Wall Street law firm and at age 23 married his distant cousin, Eleanor. Theodore Roosevelt was his fifth cousin.

In 1910 Roosevelt was elected to the state senate and in 1913 became assistant secretary of the Navy. During World War I (1914–18) he gained a reputation as a rising political star.

In 1921 Roosevelt caught polio, which paralyzed him from the waist down. It seemed his political career was finished, but in 1928 he became governor of New York. He was reelected in 1930 and became the Democratic candidate for the presidential election in 1932. That was during the Great Depression, when many people were out of work and without money or food. In his presidential campaign Roosevelt promised the people a "New Deal," and they voted for him in overwhelming numbers.

At the outbreak of World War II (1939–45) Roosevelt wanted to help Britain and its allies without involving the United States in the war. He also wanted to block Japan's advances into China and Southeast Asia. When Japanese planes attacked the U.S. base at Pearl Harbor on December 7, 1941, the United States was forced to enter the conflict.

Roosevelt increased the production of arms, helped plan major offensives in Europe, and gradually pushed back the Japanese in the Pacific. As the war continued, Roosevelt planned to create an international organization that would settle disputes between countries in a peaceful way. It would be called the United Nations. But his health was declining, and he died on April 12, 1945, less than a month before the end of the war in Europe.

KEY FACTS

BIRTHPLACE
Hyde Park, New York

OCCUPATION
Lawyer, public official

MARRIED
Anna Eleanor Roosevelt

PARTY
Democratic

AGE WHEN PRESIDENT
51

TERM
1933–45

AGE AT DEATH
63

SEE ALSO: Depression, Great; Roosevelt, Eleanor; United Nations; World War II

✳ ROWLING. J.K. (1965–)

The British novelist J. K. Rowling is the author of a series of hugely successful books featuring a young wizard named Harry Potter.

J.K Rowling, the author of the widely popular Harry Potter books. Readers of all ages sympathize and identify with Harry as he escapes his grim home life and enters the world of a school for wizards.
▶

Joanne Kathleen Rowling was born near Bristol, England. She began to write stories at age six, but her first job was as a teacher. In 1990 she came up with the idea of writing a series of stories about a young boy at a school for wizards. She later married and gave birth to a daughter, but soon divorced. She was living in Edinburgh, Scotland, when she decided to finish her first book, entitled *Harry Potter and the Sorcerer's Stone*.

Several publishers rejected the book before it was published in 1997. The publisher thought that boys would not want to read a book written by a woman, so they asked Joanne to call herself "J. K. Rowling." She achieved instant fame.

The Harry Potter stories are among the most successful children's books in history, selling millions of copies and being translated into many languages. Adults also enjoy the novels. The first two books have been filmed.

SEE ALSO: Literature, Children's

✳ RUSSIA AND THE BALTIC STATES

Until 1991 Russia was the dominant part of the Soviet Union, which also included the Baltic states of Estonia, Latvia, and Lithuania.

St. Basil's Cathedral, with its distinctive onion-shaped domes, stands in Red Square at the heart of the Russian capital, Moscow.
▽

The Russian Federation is the largest country in the world, comprising more than one-tenth of the Earth's land surface. It also has the seventh largest population of all the world's nations.

Within its borders there are vast plains, called the steppes, and the Ural and Caucasus mountain ranges.

Over many centuries the Goths, Huns, Vikings, Mongols, and others ruled over what is now called Russia. From 1462 the most important ruler was Grand Prince Ivan of Moscow. He was the first Russian leader to call himself "czar," a word derived from the Roman title "caesar." Ivan greatly expanded the territory under Moscow's control.

In 1613 the Russian nobles elected Michael Romanov as czar, and his family ruled for the next 300 years. Nicholas II, the last czar, was forced to abdicate (give up his throne) during the Russian Revolution in 1917. He was later murdered.

Communism
After the revolution Russia adopted communism, a system of government based on the abolition of private property. The first communist leader was Vladimir Lenin. He established the Union of Soviet Socialist Republics, also known as the

355

RUSSIA & THE BALTIC STATES

Russia's national flag

Estonia's national flag

Latvia's national flag

Lithuania's national flag

USSR, or the Soviet Union. After Lenin died in 1924, power went to Joseph Stalin, a harsh ruler who had at least 20 million Russians murdered.

After 1945 the world was divided between the Soviet Union and its allies and the West, especially the United States. This period, known as the Cold War, ended in 1991. Under the last Soviet president, Mikhail Gorbachev, Russia gave up communism. All of the former Soviet republics broke away from Russian domination and declared independence. Since then Russia has suffered many problems, including high prices, racial unrest, and unemployment.

Estonia

Estonia is the smallest of the three Baltic states. The land is mainly rolling plains, broken up by thousands of small rivers and lakes. Manufacturing is the most important economic activity. Farming and fishing are also strong. The capital is Tallinn.

Estonia was ruled by Germans, Danes, and Swedes until it became part of the Russian Empire in the 1700s. After the Russian Revolution Estonia declared independence in 1918, but the Soviet Union invaded in 1940. After that Estonia remained a Soviet republic until 1991.

Latvia

Like Estonia, Latvia was ruled by other European powers until a brief period of independence between 1918 and 1940. It left the Soviet Union in 1991.

Latvia had one of the most effective economies of the Soviet states, and industry and agriculture are still strong. About half the population lives in or around the capital, Riga.

Lithuania

The largest and most populous of the Baltic states, Lithuania is heavily industrialized, with two-thirds of its people living in cities, including the capital, Vilnius.

Unlike Estonia and Latvia, Lithuania was an independent state for many centuries. It united with Poland in 1569 and became part of the Russian Empire in 1795. Like its neighbors, it gained independence in 1918, was annexed by the Soviet Union in 1940, and became independent again in 1991.

SEE ALSO: Catherine the Great; Revolution; World War II

KEY FACTS

AREA
6.7 million sq. mi.
(17.3 million sq. km)

POPULATION
154,357,000

COUNTRIES
4

LARGEST COUNTRY
Russian Federation

SMALLEST COUNTRY
Estonia

RELIGIONS
Russian Orthodoxy, Roman Catholicism, Islam, Judaism

LANGUAGES
Russian, Lithuanian, Latvian, Estonian, Polish, Tatar, Chuvash

✻ SATELLITE

A satellite is an object that revolves around a planet.
Some are natural, like the moon, but thousands of
others are artificial, or made by humans.

Earth's moon is a natural satellite, as are the moons circling other planets in the solar system. The moon is unusual because it is made up of very dry rocks. Most other planets' satellites contain large amounts of water or other liquids.

Artificial satellites are ones that have been designed and built on Earth then launched into space. In 1957 the Soviet Union launched the first artificial satellite, Sputnik 1. Since then the designs have become more sophisticated. Satellites continue to provide information about space and Earth.

Uses of artificial satellites

Many human-made satellites are used for astronomical research. On the ground we can see visible light coming from the stars, galaxies, and other objects in space. We cannot detect other types of radiation, such as x-rays, ultraviolet radiation, and microwaves, because they are absorbed by Earth's atmosphere. Satellites can detect these types of radiation and reveal important information about what is happening in the universe.

Satellites are also used to collect information about Earth. Some, such as the Landsat satellites, take pictures of the Earth's surface and collect data about the oceans, natural resources, and changes in the environment. Others gather information about the weather. They help scientists give advance warning of hurricanes and other severe storms.

Many communication satellites orbit Earth. Since Echo 1 was launched in 1960, satellites have transmitted radio and television programs around the world. In the 1990s satellites were launched to form networks that cover the entire globe and provide almost total worldwide access to telephone lines and computers.

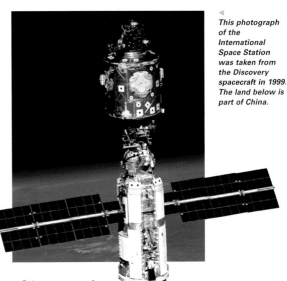

This photograph of the International Space Station was taken from the Discovery spacecraft in 1999. The land below is part of China.

Other uses are for military spying or guiding missiles. Automobiles, ships, and airplanes can also use satellites as navigation aids. A special type of satellite is the orbiting space station, where people live for months conducting research. The United States launched its first space station, Skylab, in 1973. Crew members on the Soviet Mir space station, launched in 1986, set a record by remaining in space for more than a year. In 1998 the United States, in partnership with other countries, began assembling the largest satellite to date, the International Space Station.

DID YOU KNOW?

Of the nine planets in the solar system only Mercury and Venus have no known satellites.

SEE ALSO: Climate & Weather; Communication; Earth; Geography; Moon; Navigation; Planet; Solar System; Space Exploration; X-rays; Warfare

✳ SCIENCE

Science is the systematic study of matter and
the physical universe. It is based on observation,
experiment, and measurement.

*An 18th-century
scientist carries
out an experiment
to measure
the electricity
produced by
lightning.*

People were studying the world around
them at least as long ago as 2500 B.C. The
Babylonians observed the movements of
the stars and planets. The Egyptians made
detailed studies of the human body.

The ancient Greeks' ideas of science
often came from their great philosophers,
or thinkers. Thales of Miletus (about
625–547 B.C.) was one of the first Greeks
to conclude that physical forces caused
occurrences such as weather and tides.
Before then people thought that the gods
controlled everything.

Between A.D. 500 and 1400 the Greek
ideas about science were kept alive by
European monks and Arab scholars. In the
1300s a period known as the Renaissance
began. It brought a new spirit of scientific
inquiry. Scientists such as the Italian
Galileo Galilei (1564–1642) challenged the
thinking of the Roman Catholic church by
stating that the Earth and planets revolved
around the sun, although the church
believed that the Earth was the center of
the universe.

By the 1700s inventors and engineers
were putting new ideas to practical use.
Steam engines and then electricity
revolutionized people's lives. In the 1900s
atomic power, the transistor, and DNA
were among the scientific discoveries
that had a huge effect on society.

Fields of science
Science is such a vast subject that no one
can become an expert in all areas, so
scientists tend to specialize in their work.
The two main areas of specialization are
physical sciences and life sciences.

The physical sciences involve the study
of nonliving things. Astronomy, chemistry,
and physics are all physical sciences.

A laboratory worker examines the patterns in DNA, the genetic code whose structure was established by scientists in 1953.

The life sciences are those that deal with living things. Botany—the study of plants—and zoology—the study of animals—are the main life sciences. Many branches of life sciences are used in medicine. They are called biomedical sciences.

Scientific method

All humans make observations about the world around them. But just making observations is not science. Scientists follow a set of procedures called the scientific method. The English scientist Francis Bacon (1561–1626) was one of the first people to approach problems in this way. The details of the scientific method vary, but it usually involves: stating a problem or question that needs to be studied; gathering and organizing facts about the problem; using logic to form an idea; conducting experiments to test the idea; and using information from these experiments to draw conclusions. These steps apply equally for professional scientists and for students performing experiments in school. It is this process that makes observations scientific.

Kinds of scientific research

The scientific method can be used in many ways. In experimental research scientists begin with a hypothesis—a statement that may or may not be true. They then conduct careful experiments that will prove or disprove the hypothesis.

Some research is based on theory alone. The great scientist Albert Einstein spent most of his time just thinking about problems, but his thoughts led to a revolutionary breakthrough in our understanding of natural forces. Today most scientists use computers to aid their theoretical research. Computers can process information such as mathematical data very quickly. But it still takes a human brain to interpret the data and to make scientific conclusions.

The oldest kind of science is observational research. Many of the great historic discoveries of science have involved observation, from Archimedes discovering in his bath how different materials float to Isaac Newton watching an apple fall to earth and discovering his universal law of gravitation. Charles Darwin developed his theory of evolution after observing plants and animals in different parts of the world.

Many modern scientists still use observational research. Astronomers study the light and radiation from celestial objects. Geologists observe the formations of rocks.

Research can also be basic or applied. Basic research has no immediate practical use, although it can sometimes lead to important scientific discoveries. Applied research seeks knowledge that can be used in a practical way. Its aim might be anything from a candy bar that does not melt in hot weather to a new drug for cancer patients.

SEE ALSO: Astronomy; Biology; Botany; Chemistry; Einstein, Albert; Electricity; Engine; Evolution; Geology; Greece, Ancient; Inventors & Inventions; Matter; Medicine; Newton, Isaac; Physics; Renaissance; Scientist; Zoology

✳ SCIENTIST

Scientists are people who study or practice any of the subjects classified as sciences. Some do research; others find practical uses for new discoveries.

◄
Linus Pauling (1901–94) won the Nobel Prize in chemistry in 1954 and the Nobel Peace Prize in 1962. He is the only person to have won two unshared Nobel Prizes.

A scientist is anyone whose job or area of study concerns the nature or behavior of the material or physical universe. Although the term science includes a vast number of subjects—astronomy, botany, chemistry, geology, medicine, physics, psychology, and zoology, to name but a few—all scientists work in much the same way. They observe, measure, and experiment.

The English word *scientist* comes from the Latin *scientia*, meaning "knowledge." Yet although all science is knowledge, not all knowledge is science. Learning a foreign language, for example, is not a science because it does not involve scientific method—an investigation in which a problem is first identified, and then observations, experiments, and other relevant information are used to form theories that aim to solve the problem. By contrast, linguistics—the study of the development of languages and the ways people learn them—is a science.

Theory and practice

There are two types of research. Basic research tries to uncover new knowledge that has no immediate practical use. Applied research seeks knowledge that can be used to create new products or in other practical ways.

Scientists carrying out new research may be astronomers looking for new bodies in space or doctors trying to find cures for illnesses. The most famous scientists are those who have made big breakthroughs leading to discoveries and inventions.

Yet not all research need be original. For example, school pupils who use litmus paper to tell whether a substance is acid or alkali

◄
Nicolaus Copernicus was an astronomer whose theory of the solar system was published in 1543.

IMPORTANT SCIENTISTS
The following are just a few of the world's greatest scientists.

Archimedes (about A.D. 287–212)
Ancient Greek who discovered many principles still used by scientists, such as how different materials float.

Copernicus, Nicolaus (1473–1543)
Polish astronomer who first figured out that the Earth revolves on an axis and orbits the sun.

Bacon, Francis (1561–1626)
English philosopher who defined the scientific method.

Galilei, Galileo (1564–1642)
Italian who laid the groundwork for modern physics.

Kepler, Johannes (1571–1630)
German astronomer who explained how the planets move.

Newton, Isaac (1642–1727)
English scientist whose ideas about gravity, motion, and other subjects still influence modern science.

Volta, Alessandro (Giuseppe Antonio Anastasio) (1745–1827)
Italian physicist who developed the first electric battery.

Faraday, Michael (1791–1867)
Englishman who showed that magnets can create electricity.

Darwin, Charles (Robert) (1809–82)
Englishman who formulated the theory of evolution.

Lovelace, Ada Byron (1815–52)
English mathematician who wrote the first computer program.

Mendel, Gregor (Johann) (1822–84)
Austrian botanist who discovered the laws of heredity.

Ehrlich, Paul (1854–1915)
German bacteriologist who used chemicals to treat disease.

Hamilton, Alice (1869–1970)
American toxicologist who investigated industrial poisons.

Fermi, Enrico (1901–54)
American physicist who helped create the first atomic reactor.

Hawking, Stephen (William) (1942–)
English astrophysicist and mathematician who developed new theories about black holes and the formation of the universe.

are carrying out a form of research. They are using scientific method to determine facts for themselves through their own observations, rather than taking information on trust.

Many scientists work in industry. They make sure that established products are made in the right way, safely, and according to valid scientific principles. For example, pharmaceutical chemists may prepare thousands of capsules and pills every day. It is their responsibility to ensure that every one of their products contains exactly the same materials in the correct proportions.

English chemist Dorothy Crowfoot Hodgkin (1910–94) at work in her laboratory in 1964, the year she was awarded the Nobel Prize in chemistry.

SEE ALSO: Aristotle; Carson, Rachel; Curie, Marie & Pierre; Einstein, Albert; Evolution; Franklin, Rosalind; Newton, Isaac; Nobel Prize; Science

✴ SEA MAMMAL

Mammals that spend all or most of their lives in the water include whales and dolphins, seals, sea lions, and manatees and dugongs.

◄
The humpback whale produces the longest and most varied songs in the animal world, ranging from high-frequency whistles to low rumbles in long and organized patterns.

Millions of years ago a number of mammals—animals that nourish their young with milk—moved from the land to live in the water. Over time their forelimbs became flippers and their hind legs disappeared. Most developed a layer of fatty tissue, or blubber, beneath the skin to keep them warm in water.

Most sea mammals live in groups. They swim and dive well, but they must return regularly to the surface to breathe air. Seals and sea lions have to leave the water each year to molt (shed their fur), give birth, and mate. In all species one young is usually born each year.

Scientists categorize sea mammals into three orders, or groups—cetaceans (whales and dolphins), pinnipeds (seals, sea lions, and walruses), and sirenians (manatees and dugongs).

Cetaceans
The largest cetacean species are known as whales, while the smaller species are called dolphins or porpoises. Whales make up two groups: toothed whales and baleen whales.

Most toothed whales belong to the family known as delphinids. Most delphinids are dolphins, but a few reach such a large size that they are called whales. The best known are pilot whales and killer whales. Other toothed whales include the sperm whale, white whale, narwhal, and about 12 species of bottlenose whale. The killer whale earned its name because it preys on seals, sea lions, dolphins, and other whales as well as fish and squid, which are its primary diet. Killer whales live and hunt in packs of four to forty.

Baleen whales are named for the curtains of baleen that hang from the roof of their mouths. Baleen, a substance like stiff hair, filters small animals from mouthfuls of seawater. Baleen whales include right whales, fin whales (or rorquals), and gray whales. The blue whale, a fin whale, is the largest animal ever to have lived. It may be up to 100 ft. (30m) long and weigh over 130 tons.

There are about 50 species of dolphins and porpoises. Some live in fresh water, but most are marine. Dolphins have excellent vision and hearing, and a highly developed sense of touch. Like many bats, dolphins use echolocation to navigate and to find prey. They make sounds, then listen to the echoes that bounce back from objects in the water around them.

Pinnipeds

Scientists divide the pinnipeds into eared seals and true (earless) seals. The eared seals have an ear flap and are agile on land. True seals have no ear flaps and are less agile. All pinnipeds are excellent swimmers and divers. They hunt fish, squid, and crab.

Eared seals divide again into two main groups: fur seals and sea lions. The nine fur seal species have thick coats; most live in southern oceans. There are five species of sea lion living off coasts from Alaska to New Zealand. The walrus is related to the eared seals, but has no ear flaps. A large, mustached animal with two long tusks, it lives in Arctic waters, eating clams and seabed shellfish—up to 6,000 each day.

For part of each year certain beaches throng with pinnipeds as females give birth, nurse their young, and then mate soon after the cub is weaned. In polar regions as little time as possible is spent in the freezing air.

Sirenians

The sirenians are three species of manatee and one species of dugong. Their rounded spindle shape comes from their thick blubber. Their tails are paddle-shaped, powering them along. Their upper lips are split, or cleft.

Manatees live in the coastal waters of the American Gulf states, the Caribbean Islands, Central America, northeastern South America, and western Africa. Dugongs live on the coasts of the Indian and Pacific oceans. Sirenians graze on aquatic plants. They are peaceful animals that enjoy lolling in warm waters, though some make long migrations.

Threats and conservation

By the mid-1900s blue whales, right whales, grays, and humpbacks had been hunted almost to extinction. Despite a worldwide agreement to ban whaling, some nations, such as Norway and Japan, continue to hunt them. Manatees are endangered worldwide. They are still hunted illegally, and many are seriously injured or killed by motorboat propellers and by fishing nets. The most serious threat to dolphins is tuna fishing. Dolphins are captured in nets alongside tuna and drowned. New types of net and fishing regulations have reduced the number of dolphins killed. Water pollution affects all sea mammals.

SEE ALSO: Animal; Mammal; Ocean & Sea; Pollution

Elephant seals are found in coastal waters from southeastern Alaska to Baja California and around the islands of southern Argentina. They may be up to 20 ft. (6m) long and weigh as much as 8,000 lb. (3,700kg).

✳ SEASONS

The four periods of the year called seasons—spring, summer, fall, and winter—occur because Earth revolves at a tilt around the sun.

On Christmas Day Greenland (top) is covered in snow, while people in Australia (above) relax on the beach in the midsummer heat. This seasonal contrast between the Northern and Southern hemispheres is caused by the Earth's tilted axis.

Once every 24 hours Earth completes one rotation on its own axis, an imaginary line through the center of the planet between the North and South poles. Earth's rotation on its axis is what causes day and night—at any one time about half the Earth faces the sun and is therefore in daylight; the other half faces away from it and is therefore in darkness.

Once each year Earth completes one revolution in its orbit, or path, around the sun. If it revolved without deviating, the world's weather would be the same throughout the year. But in fact Earth's orbit is tilted at 23.5 degrees away from the perpendicular. As a result, for one half of the year the Northern Hemisphere is closer to the sun than the Southern Hemisphere—then it is spring and summer in North America, fall and winter in Australia. For the other half of the year the situation is reversed.

The Earth's rotation also affects the relative lengths of day and night—there are more hours of daylight in the summer than in the winter in most parts of the world other than at the equator.

In the same way the differences between the seasons are most evident in the temperate regions of the Earth and least evident near the equator. The polar regions are always cold, but temperatures fluctuate on a seasonal basis.

Seasonal datelines

From about March 21 to September 23 more of the Northern than the Southern Hemisphere faces toward and is warmed by the sun. Thus, beginning on March 21 in the Northern Hemisphere, the seasons run approximately as follows: spring, March 21—June 22; summer, June 22—September 23; fall, September 23—December 22; and winter, December 22—March 21. The seasons are reversed in the Southern Hemisphere, with spring beginning about September 23.

SEE ALSO: Earth; Sun

✳ SHIP AND BOAT

For thousands of years people have used ships and boats to trade goods, fight their enemies, and explore the world. They are also used for pleasure.

▲
The U.S. frigate United States (right) does battle with the British warship Macedonian during the War of 1812. The British ship was forced to surrender.

A ship or boat is a watertight, waterborne vessel usually powered by oars, sails, steam turbines, or internal-combustion engines. The back of a ship or boat is called the stern; the front is the bow or bows. The body of the boat is called the hull. Facing forward, the left side is known as port and the right side as starboard.

Different types
Ships are large seagoing craft such as cargo vessels, oil tankers, warships, and cruise liners. The term "boat" is normally used to describe smaller craft, ranging from yachts and motor cruisers to racing dinghies and open rowboats.

Some vessels have unusual designs. Aircraft carriers serve as ocean-going airstrips. Submarines can travel under the water and are used mostly as warships or for exploration. Hydrofoils skim over the water on skilike struts designed so that their hulls can lift clear out of the water at high speeds. Hovercraft sail on a

cushion of air a few inches above the surface of the water. Catamarans have two hulls; trimarans have three hulls.

History
The earliest craft were probably hollowed-out logs, bundles of reeds, and inflated animal skins. By 3000 B.C. ancient Egyptians had built the first boats made of wooden planks. They were propelled by oars and a single square sail.

The Chinese were the first to invent the rudder (a fixed underwater device that steers a ship) in the fourth century B.C., bulkheads (solid planked walls) that divide the hull into separate compartments, and slatted sails. Their ships, called junks, were much more maneuverable than Western boats.

The age of sail
From the 13th century onward larger ships were built to carry more cargo over greater distances. Instead of one mast with a singe sail, ships had numerous sails on two or three masts. Dividing the sails in this way made them easier to handle. Open ships were replaced by decked ships. Many ships had several several decks built on top of each other.

Warships carried oars as well as sails. Their crews used the oars in battle when fighting enemy ships. By the late 1500s warships fought under sail, firing cannons at each other from a distance.

The American colonies built ships for sailing to Europe, ferrying goods, and

AMAZING FACTS !

The world's largest ship is the oil supertanker *Jahre Viking*. It is 1,504 ft. (459m) long and, when laden, displaces more than half a million tons of water. It will be dwarfed, however, by *Freedom*, a megaship planned by Florida engineer Norman L. Nixon. His "floating city," with apartment space for 70,000 people, will measure 4,320 ft. (1,317m) and displace 2.7 million tons.

▲

Launched in Japan in 1979, the world's largest ship was sunk by Iraqi jets in 1986, then salvaged and restored in 1990. Now named Jahre Viking, it carries oil between the Middle East and the United States.

hunting whales. After the American Revolution (1775–83) armed frigates were built to protect American shipping from pirates.

The first scheduled sailing-ship service across the Atlantic began in 1816. The ships were called packet ships because they carried packets of mail as well as passengers and cargo. They took several weeks to cross the ocean.

The greatest of all sailing ships were the clippers. Built from the finest wood, these giants carried more sails than any ships before them. They were sleek, beautiful, and fast. In 1852 the clipper *Challenge* sailed across the Pacific from near the coast of Japan to California in 18 days.

Steam power and metal

In the early 1800s steam power began to take over from sail. The first steamships were propelled by twin paddle wheels. Steam power was more reliable than sail, since it did not depend on the winds. Another important development was iron hulls. Iron is stronger and longer-lasting than wood. In the late 1800s steel replaced iron, screw propellers replaced paddle wheels, and new high-speed turbines were developed. The diesel engine replaced steam power during the early 1900s. This was the dawn of the age

of the luxury liner, huge ships that carried passengers in style across the oceans. Mighty battleships and huge freighters were also launched at this time.

Modern cargo vessels include container ships—large, flat-decked craft that can be stacked high with sealed freight containers. The cargo may be loaded on and off railroad flatcars at the ports, or the containers may be rolled directly on and off the ship by trucks. The largest ships in the world are oil-carrying supertankers.

Fueled by on-board nuclear reactors, modern submarines and aircraft carriers can sail for months without refueling. Hydrofoils and hovercraft are used for fast, short-range passenger services.

Air travel has taken many passengers away from the water—it is much quicker—but cruise liners remain popular as "floating hotels." And ships continue to carry millions of tons of cargo every year.

SEE ALSO: Ancient Civilizations; China; Egypt, Ancient; Engine; Middle Ages; Navigation; Radar & Sonar; Transportation; Warfare

✳ SIGHT

For humans and many other animals sight is the most important sense. We see when light forms images in the eyes. The brain interprets the images.

INSIDE THE EYE

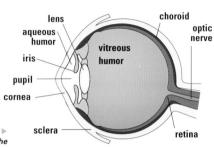

▶
Light enters the eye through the pupil, passes through the lens, and lands on the retina, where it triggers a message that travels down the optic nerve to the brain.

An adult human eye is about the size of a table-tennis ball. Most of its surface is made of a tough layer called the sclera. At the front of the eye is a clear layer called the cornea.

Inside the sclera is the choroid. Part of this layer contains the colored iris. In the center of the iris is the pupil. Behind the iris is a clear, rubbery lens. At the back of the eye is the retina, which contains light-sensitive cells.

DID YOU KNOW?

Color blindness is an inherited disorder caused by the absence of a type of cone cell. Most color-blind people cannot see red and green, but some can see no color at all—only black, white, and shades of gray. Males are about 10 times more likely than females to be color-blind.

Most of the eye is filled with a jellylike substance called vitreous humor. The cavities at the front of the eye contain a thinner substance called aqueous humor.

Light enters the eye through the pupil. Muscles control the size of the pupil—when light is very bright, the pupil automatically becomes smaller. Other muscles control the shape of the lens, which makes focusing possible.

Light passes through the lens and lands on the retina. Here there are two kinds of light-sensitive cells, rods and cones. Rods make it easier to see in dim light. Cones allow us to see fine detail, and together they make color vision possible.

Sight disorders

The most common sight problems are nearsightedness and farsightedness. They occur when the cornea and the lens cannot make a clear image on the retina. It is easy to correct these disorders with eyeglasses or contact lenses. More serious disorders include cataracts—cloudy areas on the lens—and glaucoma—high pressure in the eyeball. Diseases or accidents can damage the eyes, optic nerves, or brain, causing sight impairment or total blindness.

SEE ALSO: Brain & Nervous System; Human Body; Lens

✴ SITTING BULL (ABOUT 1831–90)

Sitting Bull was a great and respected leader of the Sioux tribe. His Native American name was Tatanka Iyotake.

▲
Sitting Bull in 1885, when he joined Buffalo Bill's famous traveling Wild West show for a few months.

Sitting Bull was born on the Grand River in South Dakota. He joined his first war party at the age of 14 and soon gained a reputation for courage. He helped extend Sioux hunting grounds westward. In 1863 he fought his first battle with white soldiers. For the next five years the Sioux clashed with soldiers who invaded Sioux hunting grounds. In 1867 Sitting Bull was made chief of the entire Sioux Nation.

With two other warriors, Crazy Horse and Gall, he fought to prevent the whites from mining gold in the Black Hills of South Dakota in 1873. He was a key figure in planning the defeat of Colonel George Custer and his troops at the Battle of Little Bighorn in 1876.

White settlers killed the bison that provided food for the Sioux. In 1877, to avoid starvation, Sitting Bull led his followers to Canada, but the Canadian government was unable to supply them with food. After four years Sitting Bull was forced to surrender and return to the United States. He was imprisoned and then confined on the Standing Rock Reservation in South Dakota. In 1890 Sitting Bull was shot and killed by U.S. troops while resisting arrest.

SEE ALSO: Crazy Horse

✴ SKYSCRAPER

First built in the United States in the late 1800s, skyscrapers are a practical way of accommodating large numbers of people in limited ground space.

Until the 1870s the maximum possible height for buildings constructed from bricks and stone (masonry) was no more than six stories—about 250 ft. (75m). The first skyscrapers were built in Chicago, Illinois, after the Great Fire of 1871 destroyed most of the city and inspired a radical rethinking of how buildings were constructed.

Elevators
Although the idea of tall buildings was not new, they had never previously been constructed because of the difficulties of getting people up and down hundreds of steps to their offices. That problem was

solved after 1857, when Elisha Graves Otis installed the first passenger elevator. By 1878 Otis's sons had developed a hydraulic elevator with a speed of 800 ft. (245m) per minute. This mechanism was followed by the electric elevator in 1889. What is called the Chicago school of architecture was made possible by this revolutionary development.

Metal framework
Skyscrapers can be built to great heights because their frameworks are made from iron and steel. Those metals are stronger and lighter than bricks and mortar, so they can be used to support the floor,

walls, and roof of each level independently. They also enable the buildings to withstand the high winds that can bend even the strongest structures. The stone exterior of the modern skyscraper is no more than a curtain wall—a wall that supports only its own weight and is not load-bearing. Skyscrapers are thus quite different from conventional masonry structures in which the walls—known as bearing walls—support the beams, which in turn support the floors and roof, restricting the height of the building.

The foundations of a skyscraper must be strong enough to support its vast weight. They are usually made of concrete piers that are sunk deep into the ground. Beds of solid rock are the most desirable base, but ways have been found to build skyscrapers on soft earth.

Onward and upward

The world's first skyscraper was the 10-story Chicago Home Insurance Building, completed in 1885. The first skyscraper to break the 100-story barrier was the Empire State Building in New York City, which was opened in 1931.

Although historically skyscrapers were built as offices, some of the latest structures of this type have been more like minicities, with almost every possible amenity under a single roof.

For example, the John Hancock Center in Chicago, a 100-story building standing 1,127 ft. (344m) high, contains not only the usual offices and parking lots but also apartments, restaurants, banks, theaters, and an observatory.

The windows of the earliest skyscrapers were sealed for safety reasons, and the internal temperature was controlled by air conditioning. Modern concerns with energy conservation have led to the installation of working windows and glass walls that are tinted to reflect the sun's rays.

THE TALLEST SKYSCRAPERS IN THE WORLD

Petronas Towers, Kuala Lumpur, Malaysia (1998)	1,483 ft. (452m)
Sears Tower, Chicago, Illinois (1974)	1,450 ft. (442m)
Jin Miao Building, Shanghai, China (1999)	1,381 ft. (421m)
Citic Plaza, Guangzhou, China (1996)	1,283 ft. (391m)
Shun Hing Square, Shenzen, China (1996)	1,260 ft. (384m)
Empire State Building, New York City (1931)	1,250 ft. (381m)
Central Plaza, Hong Kong, China (1992)	1,227 ft. (374m)
Bank of China Tower, Hong Kong, China (1989)	1,209 ft. (369m)
Emirates Tower One, Dubai, United Arab Emirates (1999)	1,165 ft. (355m)
The Center, Hong Kong, China (1998)	1,148 ft. (350m)

SKYSCRAPER CONSTRUCTION

Rooftop access
Some skyscrapers have helipads on their roofs.

Services
Electricity and water supplies are stored either between floors or on a special service floor.

Steel frame
Long pieces of metal (girders) are bolted together for strength.

Elevator shafts
They are usually deep in the building, where daylight is not needed.

Reinforced concrete foundations
They are built deep in the ground.

Revolving doors
They minimize the effects of high winds.

A typical modern skyscraper.

SEE ALSO: World Trade Center

✳ SOLAR SYSTEM

The solar system consists of the sun and all the planets and other bodies that revolve around it. It is shaped like a disk with the sun at its center.

The largest objects orbiting the sun are the nine planets, Mercury, Venus, Earth, Mars, Jupiter, Saturn, Uranus, Neptune, and Pluto. Some planets have moons—natural bodies that revolve around them. Other bodies orbiting the sun include thousands of tiny objects called asteroids and comets—chunks of ice, rock, and dust. The solar system also contains dust and gases left over from when it was formed.

All the planets and most asteroids revolve around the sun in nearly circular orbits (paths) that are in nearly the same plane. They all move in counterclockwise orbits, as seen from "above." Some moons have clockwise motion.

Theories about the solar system

Five planets—Mercury, Venus, Mars, Jupiter, and Saturn—are regularly visible from Earth and have been known since ancient times. Around 300 B.C. some ancient Greek scientists suggested that the sun was the center of the solar system. Until the mid-1500s, however, most people believed that the Earth was the center of the solar system, and that everything else revolved around it. Then, in 1543 the Polish astronomer Nicolaus Copernicus (1473–1543) figured out that the Earth and the other planets traveled around the sun in circular orbits.

By 1618 further discoveries by the German astronomer Johannes Kepler (1571–1630) led to what became known as Kepler's three laws of planetary motion. The English scientist Isaac Newton (1642–1727) used a form of math called calculus to show that gravity, the force that holds objects to the Earth, also holds the planets in their orbits round the sun.

The German astronomer Johannes Bode (1747–1826) discovered a mathematical relationship in the distances of the planets from the sun. In 1781, when the English astronomer William Herschel (1738–1822) discovered Uranus, it fitted into Bode's pattern, as did many asteroids when they were discovered. Astronomers discovered Neptune in 1846 and Pluto in 1930.

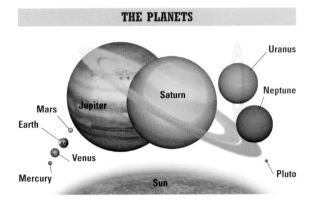

THE PLANETS

Uranus

Neptune

Saturn

Mars   Jupiter

Earth

Venus

Mercury   Sun

Pluto

▲
In this diagram the nine planets of the solar system and part of the sun have been brought closer together to give an idea of their relative sizes.

SEE ALSO: Astronomy; Comet, Meteor, & Asteroid; Earth; Gravity; Jupiter; Mars; Mercury; Moon; Neptune; Newton, Isaac; Sun; Uranus; Venus

✳ SOUND RECORDING

Sound recording is a means of preserving sound in a permanent form so that it can be reproduced at a later time.

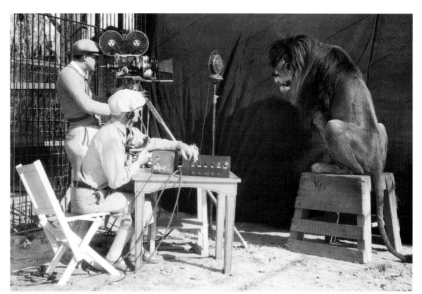

▶ *At the dawn of the talking movie era in 1929 Leo the lion was filmed and recorded for the opening sequence of MGM films. Sound for a motion picture is recorded on magnetic tape and transferred to the edge of the film as a series of light and dark areas. When the film is played, a beam of light from the projector passes through the film. It varies as the light and dark regions pass by, and the variations are converted back into sound.*

Cassettes, compact disks, and vinyl records (the least-used material today) are all methods of storing sound recordings. Special machines such as record players, tape recorders, and CD players turn the recordings back into sound.

Early recording

The oldest method of sound recording, the phonograph record, was invented by Thomas Alva Edison in 1877. Early recordings—in other words, direct from the sound without converting it into any other form. The person making the recording had to speak or sing loudly into a megaphone. Attached to the narrow end of the megaphone was a tightly stretched membrane, or diaphragm, that vibrated when hit by the sound waves made by the person's voice. The vibrations were transferred to a needle, or stylus, that engraved a rotating cylinder with

grooves. The cylinder was later replaced by the flat phonograph disk. Playback was the reverse of the recording process. The playback needle vibrated the diaphragm, and the resulting sound was amplified (made louder) by the megaphone.

From the 1920s megaphones were replaced by microphones that converted sound waves into electric current. The movement of the diaphragm produces variations in the electric output. They form the signals that are recorded.

Playback

Reproduction, or playback, of sound is essentially the reverse of recording. The recorded patterns are converted back to electrical waveforms nearly identical to the originals. These waveforms are amplified and sent to a loudspeaker or headphones, where they produce sounds that are close imitations of the originals.

The term fidelity is used to describe how closely the reproduced sound matches the original. The term high fidelity, or hi-fi, refers to high-quality sound reproduction.

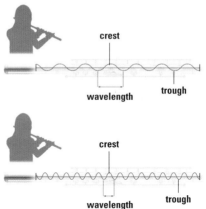

Magnetic recordings

Magnetic recordings are made on thin plastic tape coated on one side with tiny metal particles. The tape passes over an electromagnet—a magnet produced by electricity—called the recording head. The head magnetizes the particles weakly or strongly depending on the electronic signals it receives. These variations form magnetic patterns on the tape. This is known as analog recording.

To play back the recording, the tape is rewound and passed over the playback head—another electromagnet. It reads the magnetic patterns and produces faint signals that are amplified and then changed back into sound by loudspeakers.

One problem with analog recordings is that they can be changed by repeated use. The playback head gradually wears away the magnetic particles on the tape, which means the sound heard becomes less like the sound recorded.

In digital recording, the analog signal from the microphone is converted into binary numbers—a series of 0s and 1s. During playback the digital signal passes through a converter that changes the digital 0s and 1s back to an analog signal.

Because the same series of numbers is used to make up the sound each time the recording is played, it always sounds the same as when it was first recorded.

Compact disks

First released in 1982, compact disks (CDs) produce better sound and are more longlasting than any other form of recording. The signals are recorded as a spiral track containing millions of tiny pits.

Inside a CD player a laser scans the spiral track. The beam is reflected from the pits onto a photo detector that sends out a signal when light hits it and remains off when there is not enough light. These ons and offs produce a digital signal that matches the orginal recorded signal. It is decoded by a converter into the original analog signal, which is converted back to sound by the loudspeakers. CDs can store text, images, and graphics as well as sound.

◄ *A magnetophone was an early reel-to-reel tape recorder, first produced in the 1930s. Reel-to-reel tapes were replaced by cassette tapes, which contain both reels in a plastic housing.*

WAVES OF SOUND

crest

wavelength   trough

crest

wavelength   trough

◄ *Like all waves, waves of sound repeat themselves over and over. Waves have crests (peaks) and troughs (hollows between the peaks), with regular spacing between them. If a sound wave has a long wavelength, as in the upper diagram, a low note is produced. If the crests are closer together, as in the lower diagram, the note is higher.*

SEE ALSO: Edison, Thomas Alva; Electricity; Hearing; Laser; Magnetism; Movies; Music; Radio

*SPACE EXPLORATION

The Earth's atmosphere extends for
hundreds of miles around the planet.
Beyond that is space. Scientists do not
know where space ends, or if it ends at
all. The greatest distance that humans
have traveled in space is the 250,000
miles (400,000km) to the moon. The star
nearest our sun is 25 trillion miles (40
trillion km) away; in space that is a
relatively small distance. There are billions
of galaxies, each containing billions of
stars. Space probes and astronomers
have collected much information from
areas in space many millions of miles
away. But there is still much that we do
not know about the planets and stars.

Travel beyond the atmosphere
Science fiction authors began imagining
journeys into space in the 1800s. For
many years technology did not have the
means to make a spacecraft. To escape
the Earth's gravity, a craft needs to reach
a speed of about 7 miles per second
(11km/s), or 25,000 mph (40,000km/h).
This is called escape velocity.
   Long-range rockets, built for military
use in World War II (1939–45), provided
the answer. By the 1950s scientists in the
United States and the Soviet Union were
developing rockets that could travel
beyond the Earth's atmosphere.

The space race
The Soviet Union began the space age
on October 4, 1957. It launched the first
artificial satellite, Sputnik 1, into orbit.
The first man in space was the Soviet
cosmonaut Yuri Gagarin. He made a single

*Astronaut Buzz Aldrin walks on the moon
during the Apollo 11 space mission in 1969.
This photograph was taken by Neil Armstrong,
the first astronaut to step on the moon's surface.*

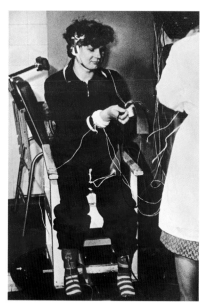

◄

*Valentina
Tereshkova trains
for a space flight.
She became the
first woman in
space on June
16, 1963, in the
Soviet spacecraft
Vostok 6.*

orbit of the Earth on April 12, 1961, in his craft Vostok 1. The Soviet Union also had the first woman in space—Valentina Tereshkova, in 1963—and the first man to walk outside his orbiting craft—Alexei Leonov, in 1965. The first American astronaut in space was Alan Shepard, on May 5, 1961. The first American to orbit the Earth was John Glenn in 1962.

Scientists and politicians in the United States were concerned that their rivals were advancing more quickly. At the time, the two countries were the most powerful states in the world. Many people thought that space exploration could have military advantages.

Moon landing

On July 16, 1969, the Apollo 11 spacecraft took off from Cape Kennedy, Florida. Aboard were Neil Armstrong, Edwin "Buzz" Aldrin, and Michael Collins. Four days later Armstrong and Aldrin descended in the lunar module of the spacecraft. Armstrong was the first human to step onto the surface of the moon. He and Aldrin spent about two and a half hours there. Hundreds of millions of people around the world watched them on television. There were five more successful moon landings up to 1972.

Stations, shuttles, and satellites

In 1971 the Soviet Union launched the first space station, Salyut 1. It was a craft that orbited the Earth permanently, with enough room for astronauts to remain there for many months. The first United States space station was Skylab, launched in 1973. In 1998 the first modules of the International Space Station, or ISS, were joined together in space. Built by 16 nations, it will act as an orbiting laboratory for up to seven astronauts.

In 1981 the United States launched the first space shuttle. It was a reusable spacecraft that returned to Earth by touching down on a runway.

Although humans have not yet traveled further than the moon, satellites have sent back messages from beyond the Earth's solar system. People have not yet achieved all the feats that science fiction writers imagined, but they have made great progress since the first satellite orbited the Earth in 1957.

AMAZING FACTS !

On March 22, 1995, Russian cosmonaut Valery Polyakov returned to Earth after orbiting in the Mir space station for a record-breaking 438 days. During his mission he circled the Earth about 7,000 times. **In 1962** John Glenn was the first American to orbit Earth. In 1998, at the age of 77, he became the oldest person ever to go into space.

SEE ALSO: Astronaut; Astronomy; Atmosphere; Galaxy; Gravity; Moon; Rocket; Satellite; Solar System; Space Shuttle; Star; Sun

✳ SPACE SHUTTLE

A space shuttle is a craft that can travel into space many times. The first working space shuttle, Columbia, was launched in 1981.

▷ The space shuttle Atlantis was launched on March 24, 1992, for its eleventh flight. It had twin solid rocket boosters and three main engines. On board was a crew of seven astronauts.

The space shuttle is launched with its nose pointing to the sky. It is attached to a disposable fuel tank and two solid-fuel rocket boosters.

The boosters provide the main power for the first two minutes of launch. They then separate from the shuttle and fall into the ocean. The fuel tank is discarded after a further six minutes. The space shuttle has 44 tiny engines that control its position while in orbit. Solar panels on the shuttle also provide some power.

The shuttle's cargo bay is 60 ft. (18m) long and 15 ft. (4.6m) wide. It can hold several satellites, which can be launched when the shuttle is in orbit. Since the late 1990s the space shuttle has also carried equipment for the International Space Station. The shuttle takes 90 minutes to orbit the Earth.

To return to Earth, the shuttle travels at about 17,000 mph (27,370km/h). It has special heat-resistant tiles to protect it when it reenters the Earth's atmosphere. Without them it would burn up. As the shuttle returns to Earth, it acts like a glider, using its wings and tail to remain stable. It lands just like a jet airplane. However, it needs a longer runway than an airplane because of its greater speed. Shuttles are designed to launch and return more than 100 times. This has reduced the cost of space travel.

THE SPACE SHUTTLES

Columbia	First launched on April 12, 1981, exactly 20 years after Gagarin's first spaceflight. It made 36 orbits of the Earth on that trip, which took 54 hours. It was destroyed just before landing in 2003.
Challenger	First launched in 1983. It was destroyed shortly after takeoff in 1986.
Atlantis	First launched in 1985. In 1989 it deployed probes to Venus and Jupiter.
Discovery	First launched in 1984. It deployed the Hubble Space Telescope in 1990 and in 1998 brought back NASA's last astronaut to work at the Mir space station.
Endeavour	First launched in 1992. It was used to service the Hubble Space Telescope.

Success and disaster

On October 11, 2000, the space shuttle Discovery made history when it set off on the 100th shuttle flight. However, the shuttle's successful history has been marred by two fatal accidents. In 1986 Challenger exploded shortly after launch, killing all seven astronauts. In 2003 Columbia blew up in the skies over Texas as it returned to Earth. Again, all seven astronauts were killed.

SEE ALSO: Astronaut; Ride, Sally; Rocket; Satellite; Space Exploration

✳ SPAIN

Spain is a country in southwestern Europe. For several centuries it took a leading role in the exploration and colonization of the New World.

Spain is the fourth largest country in Europe. It has rugged mountains, high plateaus, and river valleys. The coastal areas are fertile and densely populated. The country also includes two major island groups, the Balearics in the Mediterranean Sea and the Canaries in the Atlantic Ocean. Tenerife, in the Canary Islands, includes Spain's highest point, Pico de Teide—12,198 ft. (3,718m). Major rivers include the Ebro, the Guadalquivir, and the Tagus. The British colony of Gibraltar is on Spain's southern coast.

The north and west of Spain have a moderate climate, with substantial rainfall. Further south there is a Mediterranean climate, with hot, dry summers and mild winters.

SPAIN

FRANCE
Bilbao
Pyrenees
Duero River
Ebro River
ATLANTIC OCEAN
Madrid
Barcelona
PORTUGAL
Tagus River
Valencia
Balearic Islands
Guadiana River
Guadalquivir River
Mediterranean Sea
Canary Islands
Seville
Granada
MOROCCO
Málaga
WESTERN SAHARA
GIBRALTAR
MOROCCO

People

The Spanish are descendants of many peoples. The oldest group is the Iberians, who also inhabited what is now Portugal. Over the years the Phoenicians, from the eastern Mediterranean, the Greeks, and the Romans all settled in Spain. Muslims and Jews from North Africa and Visigoths from central Europe arrived after the western Roman Empire fell in the fifth century A.D. The Basques of northern Spain have a culture and language unlike any other Europeans. Their origins remain a mystery.

Economy

Service industries provide about half of Spain's total wealth. Tourism is one of the country's main sources of income. Each year more than 30 million people visit Spain's

beaches and historic cities. Manufacturing employs more than one-third of the population. Agriculture is less important than in the past, but Spain is still a major producer of oranges, olives, wine, and cork.

History

In 200s B.C. Spain became a key part of the Roman Empire. The Visigoths then ruled Spain until A.D. 711, when Muslims from North Africa defeated the Visigoth King Roderick. The Muslim Umayyad dynasty ruled until 1031.

Spanish Christians, led by the kingdom of Castile, began to drive the Muslims out of Spain, moving southward. By 1248 the southern area of Granada was the only part of Spain still in Muslim hands. Granada finally fell to the Christians in 1492.

Spain's national flag

This wood carving of King Ferdinand II of Aragón (1452–1516) and Queen Isabella I of Castile (1451–1504) dates from the 17th century. They were both very religious, and Ferdinand II was known as "The Catholic."
◀

Segovia Cathedral took over 50 years to build. Work started on it in the 1520s after the old cathedral was destroyed by fire. It is an example of the gothic style of architecture popular in Europe during the 16th century.

The two largest kingdoms in Spain united in 1479, when Isabella of Castile married Ferdinand of Aragón. They were the monarchs who sent Christopher Columbus on his voyages to the New World and later ruled over vast areas in North and South America, as well as colonies in North Africa and Asia.

Ferdinand and Isabella's daughter married into Austria's Hapsburg dynasty in 1496. Her grandson, Philip II (1527–98), took Spain to its highest level of power. Spain ruled Portugal, the area that is now Belgium and the Netherlands, and much of Italy, as well as its vast overseas empire. Spanish armies were the best in Europe.

Philip II was a devout Catholic who tried hard to stop the spread of the Protestant religion. However, in 1566 the Dutch began a revolt against Spanish rule in Holland, one of its richest lands. The Dutch Revolt proved costly to Spain. That same decade, while attempting to invade the British Isles in 1588, the great Spanish fleet known as the Armada was defeated by British naval forces.

Decline of Spanish power

From the 1700s Spain declined in power. It lost most of its American possessions in the early 1800s and then, in 1898, suffered defeat by U.S. forces in the Spanish–American War.

In the 19th century Spain suffered a series of civil wars and rebellions known as the Carlist Wars. In 1931 King Alfonso XIII was forced to leave the country, and a republic was proclaimed. In 1936 a new government threatened the interests of the Catholic church and landowners. Army units revolted, beginning a civil war that lasted until 1939. One million Spaniards were killed or wounded in the conflict, and a further million fled the country.

The Nationalists, who opposed the republican government, won the Civil War, and General Francisco Franco ruled as a dictator (supreme ruler). After Franco's death in 1975 Alfonso's grandson, Juan Carlos, became king.

Under King Juan Carlos Spain quickly reestablished a democratic government and in 1977 held the first free elections since before the Civil War. Spain became a member of the European Community— now the European Union (EU)—in 1986. In 1999 the Spanish adopted the euro, the EU's common currency, as a further step toward European economic integration.

SEE ALSO: Columbus, Christopher; Europe; Mexico; Napoleon

✳ SPORTS

People have been playing sports for thousands of years. More recently, sports have become organized, with fixed rules and international competitions.

The earliest sports were based on skills that people needed to survive. Hunters and warriors needed to be able to run quickly, to fight, throw stones and spears, and wrestle or box. The earliest known boxing matches in front of spectators took place in Ethiopia, and by about 4000 B.C. the sport had spread to Egypt.

The ancient Greeks organized sporting events to honor their gods. The original Olympic Games began in 776 B.C. The Romans enjoyed watching chariot races and fights to the death between gladiators, fighters who were usually slaves or prisoners of war.

By about A.D. 1200 many people in Europe played games similar to modern soccer and field hockey. There were few rules, and the games were sometimes violent. The Christian church regarded such games as sinful. English kings also discouraged them because they wanted men to concentrate on archery—a skill needed for the army.

When Europeans reached the New World, they found that the inhabitants had sports of their own. The Native Americans played a form of lacrosse, and the Aztecs and Maya played games that were similar to basketball.

Modern sports

Organized sports, with written rules, became common in the 1800s, especially in England. Leagues, championships, and international games were set up for soccer, rugby, cricket, tennis, track and field, rowing, and other sports. At about the same time, new sports

were developed in North America. Among the most popular were football, baseball, and basketball.

The first modern Olympic Games were held in Greece in 1896. Soon most countries of the world competed against each other in many sports every four years. In 1930 the first soccer World Cup was played in Uruguay. Soccer quickly became one of world's most popular team sports.

In recent years television and sponsorship have made great changes in sports. The stars of basketball, boxing, football, soccer, and other sports are professionals who can make millions of dollars in a year. Meanwhile, millions of other people still take part in sports simply for fun and fitness. They are

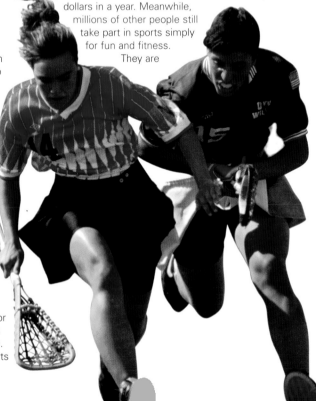

Originally played by Native Americans, lacrosse has since become popular in many countries.
▼

Serena Williams on her way to winning the final of the 2003 Australian Open tennis championship against her older sister, Venus.

amateurs—people who do not make money out of their activities.

Track and field

The early Olympic Games tested athletes' abilities at running, jumping, and throwing. These skills still form the basis of track and field events. The length of races varies between short dashes of 100 meters and the marathon, which is run over a course measuring 26 miles 385 yards (42.12km). In relay races teams of four have to pass a baton to each other. Hurdling events and steeplechases combine running and jumping skills. In competitive walking events athletes must not lift both feet off the ground at the same time. Field events include long jump, triple jump (hop, skip, and jump), pole vault, discus, and javelin.

Most top modern athletes concentrate on one or maybe two events. But the decathlon—10 events, for men—and the heptathlon—seven events, for women—test athletes' skills in many areas.

Ball sports

Players of ball sports are some of the wealthiest and best-known athletes in the world. In some ball sports players use only hands or feet to propel the ball. They include football, basketball, soccer, volleyball, and handball. In others they use implements, such as bats or sticks. Baseball, field hockey, golf, and cricket are stick-and-ball sports. Lacrosse is a team sport in which players use a basket on a stick to move the ball. In racket sports, such as tennis and squash, a player tries

The front crawl is the fastest and most popular stroke in competitive swimming.

to hit the ball so that his or her opponent cannot return it. In bowling a player tries to knock down pins at the end of a long alley. All these sports require fitness, coordination, and accuracy of aim.

Water sports
The simplest water sport is swimming. Competitive swimmers use one of four swimming styles, called strokes—front crawl, backstroke, breaststroke, or butterfly. In individual medley races they use all four.

Competitive divers jump off a high board and have to perform a certain number of movements in the air before hitting the water as straight as possible. Synchronized swimming teams perform dance routines in the water. In water polo players have to get a ball into their opponents' goal.

There are also many forms of racing in boats. Rowing, canoeing, yachting, and motorboat racing pit two or more craft of the same type against each other.

Surfing, which started in the Pacific islands, involves standing on a flat board and riding on waves in the ocean. There are now surfing championships in which competitors are judged on style and endurance.

Combat sports
Some of the earliest sports tested athletes' military skills. Wrestling and boxing are based on unarmed combat. Early boxing matches could last for hours, and boxers fought with bare knuckles. The Queensberry Rules,

written in 1867, made it compulsory for boxers to wear gloves in the ring.

Fencing is based on sword skills, which were important to soldiers until the 1800s. Modern fencing swords have buttons on the tips, so they cannot hurt opponents. Shooting and archery events also test skills that were originally used in warfare.

In recent years martial arts from China, Japan, and Korea have become very popular in the West. They are often based on ancient religious teachings. Sports such as judo, karate, and kung fu teach self-discipline and self-defense, as well as preparation for competitive events.

Winter sports
In some parts of the world snow and cold temperatures make sports such as soccer impossible. Skiing, snowboarding, and tobogganing are very popular in mountainous areas.

Ice sports, such as ice hockey and skating, began on frozen lakes, but they now usually take place on artificial rinks. Skiers can also use artificial slopes. In 1924 the first Winter Olympics were held, bringing together the best winter sportsmen and women in the world.

Judo is a sport based on a traditional Japanese system of unarmed combat. The object of judo is to achieve physical control over another person by using throwing and grappling techniques.

FAMOUS SPORTSPEOPLE

Here are just a few of North America's top sportspeople. There are many, many more.

Ruth, George Herman "Babe" (1895–1948)
American baseball player who hit 714 home runs in 8,399 times at bat.

Zaharias, Mildred (Ella) "Babe" (1914–56)
American all-around athlete, born Mildred Didrikson. An All-American as a high school basketball player; set world records in four different track and field events, and won three Olympic medals; won 55 professional golf tournaments.

Owens, Jesse (1913–80)
American track and field athlete. Set four world records in one day in 1935 and won four Olympic gold medals the next year.

Ali, Muhammad (1942–)
American boxer, born Cassius Clay, who changed his name on joining the Nation of Islam religious group. The first boxer to become world heavyweight champion three times.

Spitz, Mark (1950–)
American swimmer. Won seven gold medals at the 1972 Olympics.

Griffith Joyner, (Dolorez) Florence "Flo-Jo" (1959–98)
American runner. Set new world records for 100 and 200 meters in 1988 that still stand today.

Gretzky, Wayne (1961–)
Canadian hockey player, known as "The Great One." Holds NHL and Stanley Cup career points records.

Jordan, Michael (1963–)
American basketball player. Holds a record average of 31.5 points per NBA game.

Armstrong, Lance (1971–)
American cyclist. Won the Tour de France in four consecutive years (1999–2002) after surviving cancer.

Woods, Eldrick "Tiger" (1975–)
American golfer who dominated world golf at the beginning of the 21st century.

Williams, Venus (1980–), and **Serena** (1981–)
American tennis players. In 2002 became the first sisters to hold the top two world rankings.

▶
Muhammad Ali stands over Sonny Liston after knocking him out in the first minute of their world heavyweight boxing title fight in 1965.

◀ *Polo is an expensive sport—players need to own a horse. It is now played mainly in Argentina, Britain, India, and the United States.*

Animal sports

Horses are the animals most commonly used in sports. Major horse races, such as the Kentucky Derby, can be worth a great deal of money to successful owners, trainers, and jockeys, as well as to the gamblers who bet on the winners.

Polo, a game that began in India, has players on horseback with long mallets that they use to hit a ball into a goal. Other animals used in racing sports include dogs, birds, and camels.

Mechanical and motor sports

The invention of the internal combustion engine soon led to races between cars. Today races involve cars in specific classes, with similar bodies and engines, so that like is pitted against like. These events include Indycar, Formula One, and drag racing. There are similar races for motorcycles. Success is often due as much to the expertise of the engineers and mechanics as to the skill of the drivers.

Bicycle races are also a form of mechanical sport, although cyclists require far more physical strength and stamina than motor racers. The Tour de France, a month-long annual bicycle race in Europe that always ends in Paris, was first held in 1903. It is now widely acknowledged as the toughest sporting event of its type in the world.

Disability sports

Disabled people now play more sports than ever before. Athletes with similar disabilities play against each other. Since 1960 the Paralympics, an international competition for disabled sportspeople, have been held every four years at the same place as the summer Olympic Games. Male and female Paralympic athletes compete in archery, track and field, table tennis, basketball, shooting, racquetball, tennis, swimming, and weight lifting (men only).

SEE ALSO: Olympic Games

✳ STANTON, ELIZABETH CADY (1815–1902)

American reformer Elizabeth Cady Stanton was one of the most radical thinkers of the early women's movement.

Born Elizabeth Cady on November 12, 1815, in Johnstown, New York, she grew up in a time when women faced routine discrimination. At age 24 she married Henry B. Stanton and began working on behalf of women.

In 1848 she helped organize the first women's rights convention in the United States. At the convention Cady Stanton unveiled her Declaration of Rights and Sentiments, based on the Declaration of Independence. It contained what were then revolutionary demands—that women be admitted into universities, trades, and professions, and most shockingly for the time, that women should be allowed to vote.

In 1854, while fighting for women's property rights with Susan B. Anthony,

Cady Stanton became the first woman to address the New York State legislature. She was also the first woman to try to run for Congress. In 1866, after the Civil War (1861–65) had ended, she was so bitterly disappointed that Congress was thinking of extending the vote to African American men but not to women that she ran for office in protest.

In 1869 Cady Stanton and Anthony founded the National Woman Suffrage Association, which in 1890 became the National American Woman Suffrage Association.

This photograph from 1856 shows Elizabeth Cady Stanton with her daughter.

SEE ALSO: Women's Rights Movement

✳ STAR

From Earth stars appear to be very faint, but they are really large, extremely bright balls of gas that give out enormous amounts of light and heat.

▶ *One of the densest clusters of stars in the Milky Way galaxy. It is located about 28,000 light-years away from Earth. All the stars are about 15 billion years old, and the bright red ones are nearing the ends of their lives.*

The Earth's sun is a star. Unlike other stars, it is relatively close to Earth—about 93 million miles (150 million km) away. Other stars are so far away that their distance from Earth is measured in light-years. One light-year is the distance that light travels in one year— nearly 6 trillion miles (9.6 trillion km).

Light from the sun takes about eight minutes to reach Earth. The nearest star to Earth after the sun is Alpha Centauri, which is about four light-years away. The brightest star in the sky is Sirius, which is about eight light-years away. Although Sirius is larger and hotter than the sun, it appears much smaller and dimmer because it is so far away. Many of the stars that we can see in the sky at night are hundreds of thousands of light-years away.

Stars are created in vast clouds of dust and gases that drift through space. Some of the gas in these clouds is made up of debris from old stars that have exploded, and some of it is gas from when the universe was first formed. When stars grow old, they explode and spread different elements throughout space. These elements become the building blocks of new stars.

Astronomers measure the physical characteristics of stars by attaching special instruments to a telescope. Brightness, for example, is measured by special electronic cameras. What the star is made from can be determined using a spectrometer. Temperature is measured using an instrument called a photometer.

AMAZING FACTS !

The chemical elements that make up stars are the same as those that make up humans and other objects on Earth. The elements in the stars exist in a different physical state than those found on Earth, however. The atoms of the different chemical elements on Earth combine to form water, carbon dioxide, and the complex molecules that make up the human body. In stars the temperatures are so hot that molecules such as these cannot exist. Instead, the atoms in stars form a hot gas called plasma.

SEE ALSO: Astronomy; Atom & Molecule; Constellation; Earth; Element, Chemical; Galaxy; Light; Sun

✳ SUN

The sun is a star. It is a huge ball of hot gases that give off intense light and heat. The sun's light and heat are necessary to all life on Earth.

At a distance of about 93 million miles (150 million km) the sun is the nearest star to the Earth. The next closest star, Alpha Centauri, is more than 250,000 times farther away. Light from the sun takes about eight minutes to reach the Earth, while light from Alpha Centauri takes four years.

Because the sun is so close to Earth, astronomers can study it more easily than other stars. That allows them to learn more about stars in general. Astronomers also study the sun with great interest because of its importance to Earth. Any changes in the amount of light and heat the sun produces could have tremendous consequences for everything on Earth.

Look carefully

Although it is possible to look directly at the stars at night because they are so far away, it is very dangerous to look directly at the sun. Its intense brightness can seriously injure people's eyes. This means that astronomers have to use special telescopes, called solar telescopes, that spread out the light from the sun instead of concentrating it.

Solar telescopes contain spectrographs, sensitive instruments that spread the sun's light into a band of colors called a spectrum. With the aid of spectrographs astronomers have been able to analyze the chemical elements in the sun. They now know that the sun is made up mostly of hydrogen and helium, and that it also contains traces of other elements found on Earth.

Scientists estimate that the sun is about 4.55 billion years old, almost the same age as the Earth and the other planets in the solar system. In comparison scientists think that the universe is more than 15 billion years old. By studying how stars are formed today, scientists now think that the sun and planets were formed from a swirling cloud of dust and gases.

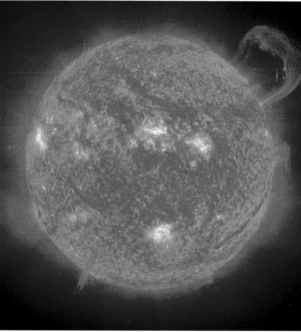

▲
This photograph of the surface of the sun was taken from a high-powered modern telescope. An immense cloud of glowing gas, called a prominence, extends outward at top right.

AMAZING FACTS !

The sun is 10 times wider than the largest planet, Jupiter. More than a million Earths would fit inside the sun.

SEE ALSO: Earth; Element, Chemical; Light; Solar System; Star

Switzerland's
national flag

Liechtenstein's
national flag

✳ SWITZERLAND AND LIECHTENSTEIN

Switzerland is a small nation in west central Europe. Liechtenstein is often called a miniature Switzerland because of its similar Alpine landscape.

SWITZERLAND &
LIECHTENSTEIN

GERMANY
FRANCE
Rhine River
Basel
Zurich
AUSTRIA
Bern
LIECHTEN-
STEIN
Jura Mountains
Lausanne
St. Moritz
Alps
Geneva
Rhone River
Brig
Locarno
Alps
Zermatt
Lugano
ITALY

Switzerland is known for the grandeur of its snowcapped Alps, which are among the highest mountain peaks in western Europe. Liechtenstein is on the right bank of the Rhine River, which separates it from Switzerland. It, too, is a land of high mountains, and part of the Alps forms its eastern and northern border with Austria.

The climates of both countries vary considerably depending on how mountainous the area is, and how much protection is provided to the valleys by the surrounding mountain ranges. In general, winters are cold, and summers are mild but not hot. The higher Alpine peaks are covered with snow year-around.

People, economy, and history
Swiss people come from three main cultural backgrounds: German, French, and Italian. Each group has its own language, traditions, and customs. Liechtensteiners come from a German background. Today

Switzerland has a high percentage of foreign workers—one person in five living in the country is a non-national.

Switzerland is one of the world's richest nations. It is a center of international banking and finance. It also imports raw materials from other countries and turns them into high-quality finished products, including watches and precision optical instruments, such as microscopes. Chemicals and pharmaceuticals are also among its chief manufactured goods. Millions of tourists come to enjoy the spectacular scenery and sports such as skiing and mountain climbing.

Switzerland is a confederation of states called cantons. It has strong armed forces but follows a policy of neutrality. It has not been involved in a war in two centuries.

In 1719 Liechtenstein became a principality (ruled by a prince). It was part of the Holy Roman Empire until 1806 and became independent in 1815. The country is ruled by a hereditary monarch and enjoys a high standard of living.

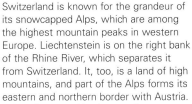

SEE ALSO: Austria

KEY FACTS

OFFICIAL NAME
Swiss Confederation

AREA
15,943 sq. mi.
(41,293 sq. km)

POPULATION
7,386,000

CAPITAL
Bern

LARGEST CITY
Zurich

OFFICIAL NAME
Principality of Liechtenstein

AREA
61 sq. mi. (157 sq. km)

POPULATION
33,000

CAPITAL
Vaduz

Like most major Swiss centers, the city of Brig lies in a valley between Alpine mountains.

✳ TASTE AND SMELL

Taste and smell are two senses that work closely together. The most important organs for taste and smell are the tongue and the nose.

The tongue has many small bumps, called papillae (singular papilla), on its surface. They contain taste buds that respond to chemical reactions. Food dissolves in the saliva in the mouth, and the taste buds detect levels of bitterness, salt, sourness, and sweetness. Nerve cells send these messages to the brain.

Taste helps people enjoy food. But it has a more important function. Many poisons and other dangerous substances have a strong, bitter taste. Food that is spoiled often tastes sour. If something tastes bad, we can spit it out before swallowing, and it is less likely to do harm.

The tastes that people enjoy can vary greatly. Some people like very sweet foods, while others prefer saltiness. Different cultures have different ideas about what tastes good.

Smell

Before food enters the mouth, a person can often smell it. Anything that has an odor gives off gas particles. There are receptor cells high up in the nose that are used to identify different odors. They send messages to the brain so that it can identify the smell.

Smell stimulates the appetite—if someone smells hot pizza or a baking cake, saliva flows faster into the mouth. Smell is also important because it can

◄ *In the storeroom of a cheese factory in Parma, Italy, a cheesemaker tests the quality of a piece of parmesan cheese by smelling it.*

protect against danger. Many harmful substances, such as natural gas, give off bad smells.

The sense of smell affects the sense of taste. That is because food in the mouth also gives off gases that reach the smell receptors. If something happens to restrict the sense of smell—for example, a cold—the sense of taste is also dulled.

As with taste, different people like different smells. That can be an individual or a cultural preference. The durian fruit, for example, is a great delicacy in Southeast Asia, but many people in the West find the smell unpleasant. Their brains interpret the smell differently.

AMAZING FACTS ❗

An adult human has about 10,000 taste buds in the tongue, palate, and cheeks.
A human has about 40 million receptor cells to identify odors, but a rabbit has 100 million, and a dog has 1 billion.

SEE ALSO: Brain & Nervous System; Human Body

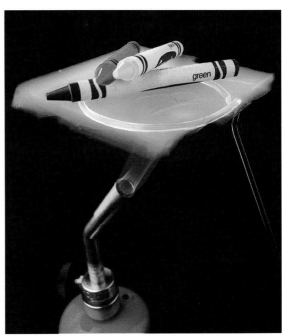

✳ TECHNOLOGY

Technology is the term for all the many different methods that people use to make products or perform tasks in order to make life better.

Almost every part of our lives is touched by technology, from the food we eat to the way we spend our leisure time. Technology is not the same as science, but the two subjects are connected. Scientists help us understand the technologies we use and develop new ideas. Technology gives scientists new tools and methods with which to make discoveries. Technology is concerned with ways of making and doing things.

Technological change

Technology is changing all the time. For example, humans learned long ago to build houses and sow crops, but research still continues in construction and agriculture. Today we can build energy-efficient homes and grow disease-resistant soybeans.

Sometimes a change in one area of technology leads to change in others. Radar, developed to spot enemy war planes, now helps control air traffic at airports. Materials developed for space travel have found many uses on Earth.

The pace of technological change was once much slower than it is today. The Chinese, for example, were making paper by about A.D. 100, but it took more than 1,000 years for the technology to reach western Europe. By contrast, only a century has passed since the Wright brothers first flew their powered airplane, and yet today jet airliners carry more than a billion passengers a year.

Technological change sped up after the Industrial Revolution, which began in Europe in the 1700s. Textiles and other goods began to be produced by machine rather than by hand. Plants were built to house the machines, and people began to produce goods faster and in greater quantities than ever before.

The 20th century saw great leaps in technology. Computers can now run entire plants and have become basic tools of research, education, communication, and business. Rockets have launched humans into space. Communications satellites circle the planet, watching the world, foretelling the weather, and sending on information. With nuclear technology people have developed new sources of energy—and powerful new weapons.

Effects of technology

Some societies are more technologically advanced than others. They have become richer, while less-developed societies remain poor. Also, technology may bring harmful as well as helpful effects. For example, mass production can perform

▲
This experiment demonstrates the insulating property of aerogel—despite the concentrated flame, aerogel prevents the wax crayons from melting. First developed in 1931, aerogel came into its own in the 1970s for use in space. Aerogel is the lightest solid material known. A block the size of a person weighs less than a pound and is only three times the density of air.

TECHNOLOGY TIMELINE

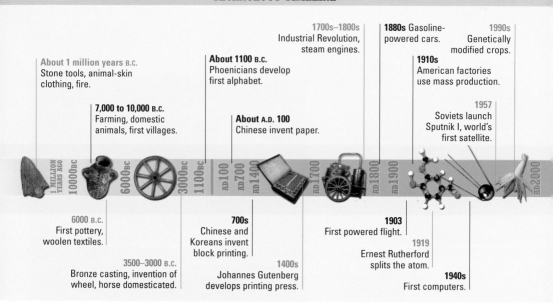

About 1 million years B.C.
Stone tools, animal-skin clothing, fire.

7,000 to 10,000 B.C.
Farming, domestic animals, first villages.

About 1100 B.C.
Phoenicians develop first alphabet.

1700s–1800s
Industrial Revolution, steam engines.

About A.D. 100
Chinese invent paper.

1880s Gasoline-powered cars.

1990s Genetically modified crops.

1910s
American factories use mass production.

1957
Soviets launch Sputnik I, world's first satellite.

6000 B.C.
First pottery, woolen textiles.

3500–3000 B.C.
Bronze casting, invention of wheel, horse domesticated.

700s
Chinese and Koreans invent block printing.

1400s
Johannes Gutenberg develops printing press.

1903
First powered flight.

1919
Ernest Rutherford splits the atom.

1940s
First computers.

tasks once performed by laborers. This means that the workers have more free time—but because they have less work, some have also become poorer.

Modern medical equipment and drugs mean that people can live longer and healthier lives. Diseases that once killed thousands of people are now under control. But the high cost of care means that often only wealthier individuals benefit. Modern airplanes and cars make transportation faster and easier, but also pollute the air and cause many deaths.

Technology can provide ways to solve these problems, however. Materials can be recycled, for example. New synthetic materials are being developed to replace natural materials that are in short supply. Technology can also provide better ways

to limit pollution. The challenge for the future is to make sure that the benefits of technological change outweigh the harmful effects.

SEE ALSO: Aircraft; Alphabet; Ancient Civilizations; Energy; Engine; Genetics; Industrial Revolution; Inventors & Inventions; Manufacturing; Matter; Medicine; Metals; Pollution; Printing; Radar & Sonar; Robot; Rocket; Satellite; Science; Ship & Boat; Space Exploration; Telecommunications; Tools; Transportation; Wright, Orville & Wilbur

✳ TELECOMMUNICATIONS
Technology that allows people to communicate, frequently over great distances, is called telecommunications.

The devices people use today to communicate include the telephone, fax machine, radio, television, and increasingly, computers. Many computers, telephones, and other machines are linked together in what are known as networks. They enable people to share large amounts of information.

Using electricity
The telegraph, invented by Samuel Morse in 1837, was an early device that used the flow of electricity to transmit messages from sender to receiver. Operators tapped on keys to spell out messages in combinations of short and long electrical pulses, called dots and dashes. They corresponded to letters and numbers in a system known as Morse code. The pulses traveled over wires to other telegraph machines, where operators translated the code back into the original message. Inventors figured out how to transmit the human voice over telegraph wires in the 1870s, and the long-distance telephone service was developed.

Facsimile, or fax, machines are able to send and receive documents. Early systems enabled newspapers to exchange photographs of events around the world. Faster and cheaper machines that used regular telephone lines became common during the 1980s. By the 1990s faxes could be sent and received using computers connected to telephone lines.

Using radio waves
In 1901 Guglielmo Marconi sent a message in dots and dashes across the Atlantic Ocean using radio waves. Radio broadcasts of voices and music became a source of entertainment, but radio also provided a vital link for vehicles such as ships and planes because it enabled them

▲
Optical fibers are threads of glass or plastic that transmit light. They are used in telephone, computer, and cable-television networks.

to communicate without wires. Pagers, which are pocket-sized devices that display word messages or alerts, are a newer application of radio. Cellular telephones, portable devices connected to telephone networks through a series of radio transmitter-receivers that cover small areas, or cells, are also very popular.

Inventors began to experiment with broadcasting moving pictures over radio waves in the early part of the 20th century. Television was widely available by the middle of the century: Today it is the leading source of news and entertainment. Even in the remotest parts of the world, beyond the reach of ordinary TV broadcast stations, people can receive television signals directly from satellites using dish-shaped antennas.

Two kinds of relay systems are used to transmit radio signals over long distances: microwaves and satellites. Microwaves are radio waves with very short wavelengths. They travel in narrow, straight lines (like a beam) and carry signals between towers spaced many miles apart. Satellites are positioned 22,300 miles (36,000km) above the Earth and circle the planet at the same rate as Earth rotates, remaining fixed over one spot. Ground stations send them microwave transmissions that are then relayed to other stations.

Using light waves to communicate
Fiber-optic technology uses pulses of light generated by a tiny laser. These pulses are transmitted over very thin strands of glass called optical fibers, which are able to carry much more information than cables or microwaves. A device detects the light and converts the signal back into electrical pulses.

Digital communications
The greatest recent change in telecommunications has been the move from analog to digital signals. Analog signals are electrical currents or electromagnetic waves that change smoothly in their amplitude (height) or frequency. Digital signals represent the original signals in strings of 1s and 0s, which are known as bits (short for "binary digits"). Bits correspond to "on" and "off" electrical pulses (similar to how the telegraph worked) and can represent a sound wave's changing amplitude and frequency or the letters and numbers of computer data. Development of methods of data compression, or reducing the number of bits needed to send a message, and of error correction means that messages can now be sent with great speed and accuracy.

Samuel Morse stands beside a telegraph machine. The alphabet system used to send messages was named Morse code after its inventor. ▼

AMAZING FACTS!

An optical fiber cable is less than ½ inch (1cm) in diameter. In 1988 the first undersea fiber-optic system to cross the Atlantic Ocean was laid. It could carry more than 40,000 telephone conversations at once.
Some advanced digital systems are able to transmit information at a rate of more than a gigabit (1 billion bits) or a terabit (1 trillion bits) per second. At this rate the entire text of the *Grolier Student Encyclopedia* could be transmitted in less than a millisecond.

The first computer network was developed in the 1960s in order for scientific researchers at a few universities in the United States to share information. It eventually grew to connect millions of computers across the world in what is now known as the Internet. One of the earliest uses of the Internet and other networks was electronic mail, or e-mail. An e-mail message is typed on a computer keyboard and travels from the sender's computer over the network to a central computer. The recipient uses his or her computer to retrieve the message.

A recent use of the Internet is the World Wide Web. It is a method of sharing information in computer files or pages that can be viewed on a computer monitor. Text, pictures, and videos can be displayed on the screen. Sounds can also be heard through a computer's speakers. Collections of such pages are called websites. Sites connect their pages to each other or to those of other sites using coded words or pictures called hyperlinks.

SEE ALSO: Communication; Electricity; Inventors & Inventions; Radio; Satellite

✴ THAILAND

The country of Siam changed its name to Thailand in 1939. The new name means "land of the free"— the country was never colonized by a western power.

Thailand is at the heart of Southeast Asia, bordering the Andaman Sea and the Gulf of Thailand. The country's most fertile regions are the plains of its two major river systems, where most Thais live. Northwestern Thailand is mountainous.

Thailand's climate is tropical, with three seasons: hot, rainy, and cool. Average temperatures range from 65 to 95 degrees Fahrenheit (18 to 35 degrees Celsius). Rainfall is highest in the south.

People, economy, and history

Most of Thailand's people are ethnic Thais. There are also many people of Chinese and Malay ancestry, and Cambodians and Vietnamese. Most people live in small villages along the coast or near rivers.

The economy is based on agriculture, but Thailand is also the world's largest exporter of seafood. From 1985 to 1995 the country had the world's most rapid economic growth thanks to exports of manufactured goods, such as computers.

The Thais may descend from people who moved from south-central China to establish a new kingdom by the 1200s.

The Gulf of Thailand is popular for fishing and diving. The beaches also attract many tourists. ▼

Thailand's national flag

In the 1800s Europeans began to build colonial empires in Asia. The Thai kingdom kept its independence but lost much of its territory. In 1932 a bloodless revolution replaced an absolute monarch with a constitutional monarch.

Since 1946, Thailand has been ruled by King Phumiphon Adunyadet. The head of government is Prime Minister Thaksin Shinawatra, whose Democrat Party's Apirak Kosayodhin became governor of Bangkok in August 2004, in an election that is seen by many as a measure of Shinawatra's popularity in the capital.

SEE ALSO: Government

KEY FACTS

OFFICIAL NAME
Kingdom of Thailand

AREA
198,457 sq. mi.
(514,000 sq. km)

POPULATION
64,865,523

CAPITAL & LARGEST CITY
Bangkok

MAJOR RELIGION
Buddhism

MAJOR LANGUAGE
Thai

CURRENCY
Baht

✳ THEATER

A theater is a place in which actors perform for an audience. The word "theater" also describes the whole process of producing and performing drama.

▶ *The Greek tragedy* Oedipus *by Sophocles (about 496–406 B.C.), performed with the actors wearing traditional masks to show their expressions of grief.*

A typical theater building has a stage, an auditorium, and a backstage area. The actors perform on the stage, and the audience sits in the auditorium. "Backstage" (behind the stage) are the actors' dressing rooms, as well as stored scenery and props—items used on stage.

Theater people

The playwright, or dramatist, writes the play. The producer selects the play, and the director is responsible for the whole process of presenting the play. The director works with the actors and the rest of the company to turn the playwright's words into drama. The stage manager helps the director and is in charge backstage during the performance.

▶ *The English playwright Aphra Behn (1640–89) wrote plays as well as poems and novels to pay off her debts. She was probably the first Englishwoman to earn a living from writing.*

Actors take on the roles of characters in the play. Theirs is an ancient tradition, dating back thousands of years to when the first actors danced, chanted, and sang in religious ceremonies. Actors need to be able to speak clearly, to take on the personality of their characters, and to show feelings with their facial expressions and body movements.

Before the mid-1900s many leading actors formed their own theater companies, choosing plays, playing leading roles, and handling business and financial arrangements. From 1594, for example, the English dramatist William Shakespeare (1564–1616) wrote all his plays for the King's Men—a group of actors who were also his business partners and personal friends.

392

Other members of the theater company include set designers, lighting and sound designers, costume designers, and makeup artists. They all play a role in bringing an atmosphere of make-believe to the stage. They are all assisted by electricians and the backstage crew, who carry props and operate equipment.

Theater around the world
Theater is a worldwide art form. In most countries the government helps pay for at least one major national theater. Universities and colleges also run their own theaters, staffed by students. In a commercial theater any profit from ticket sales is divided among the people who invest in the company. Annual theater festivals, held usually in the summer, bring many different companies together. They include Scotland's Edinburgh Festival, the Williamstown Theater Festival in Massachusetts, and the Shakespeare Festival in Stratford, Ontario, Canada.

New York City's theaters are clustered in a theater district called Broadway. In London, England, most of the theaters are located in a part of town called the West End. France's most famous theater, the Comédie-Française in Paris, began in 1680. Germany has no main

FAMOUS PLAYWRIGHTS
This is a small selection of the many famous writers who have written for the theater. There are many more.

Euripides (about 484–406 B.C.)
Ancient Greek writer whose tragedies (plays with sad endings) were known for their down-to-earth characters.

Molière (Poquelin, Jean-Baptiste) (1622–73)
French playwright whose comic plays mocked the church, the government, and social attitudes.

Chekhov, Anton (Pavlovich) (1860–1904)
Russian playwright and story writer who wrote about the social situation in Russia in the late 1800s and early 1900s.

Glaspell, Susan (1882–1948)
American who wrote both one-act and full-length plays for the Provincetown Players, the Massachusetts theater company she cofounded.

O'Neill, Eugene (Gladstone) (1888–1953)
American who wrote 45 plays and won the Nobel Prize in literature in 1936.

Hellman, Lillian (Florence) (1905–1984)
American playwright who was also a political activist. She based many characters on members of her own family.

Beckett, Samuel (Barclay) (1906–89)
Influential Irish writer who invented new styles of drama.

Williams, Tennessee (Thomas Lanier) (1911–83)
American who dramatized family conflicts. His plays are tragedies set mainly in the South.

Soyinka, Wole (Akinwande Oluwole) (1934–)
This Nigerian playwright was the first black African to win the Nobel Prize in Literature (1986).

modern plays. Russia's Moscow Art Theater was founded by Konstantin Stanislavsky in 1898. It is famed for its productions of plays by Anton Chekhov.

Traditional or classical theater in China blends song, gesture, and music performed in a time-honored style. Chinese shadow puppet plays are especially popular with children.

The two most famous forms of Japanese drama are Noh and Kabuki. The Noh plays use ancient Japanese language and are performed very slowly.

American Arthur Miller (1915–) has written many plays that criticize society's prejudices. Death of a Salesman, first performed in 1949, is considered by theater critics to be one of the greatest dramas of the 1900s. ◄

393

Kabuki plays, written in the 1500s and 1600s, have more action, and their language is more modern.

Dance is the most important kind of theater in India and Southeast Asian countries. Traditional drama in these countries combines dance with poetry, music, and storytelling.

In Africa theater is emerging as an important art form, particularly in Nigeria, Ghana, and South Africa.

SEE ALSO: Literature; Nobel Prize; Shakespeare, William; Writers, World

✳ TOOLS

A tool is a device used to carry out a task. The ability to use tools is one of the most important differences between human beings and animals.

Some animals use sticks and stones to carry out simple tasks, but that is the extent of their tool use. People have been using tools for such tasks for more than 100,000 years.

Anything from a paintbrush to a computer could be called a tool. Usually, however, the term describes hammers, drills, and other such implements that are used to make and mend objects. Tools can be divided into hand tools, hand power tools, and machine tools.

Some of the many hand tools include hammers and mallets (for pounding), axes, chisels, and saws (cutting), planes and files (shaping), drills (boring), wrenches (turning), pliers (holding), and rules (measuring).

Powered hand tools, driven by small electric motors, are light, fast, and powerful. An electric drill may be the most versatile power tool. It not only drills holes but can also screw, brush, polish, sand, rasp, and cut. Other useful power tools include routers

◄
Between about 10,000 and 4,000 B.C., a period known as the New Stone Age, people made tools like this blade from pieces of stone. They were used to scrape flesh from animal skins so that people could wear them.

The Building of Noah's Ark, painted in 1423 by an unknown artist. The workmen are using hammers, drills, planes, and axes.

create a sharp edge—were used to skin animals. Bone awls (spikes) were used to make holes in a skin in order to stitch it into clothing. The first drills were long stones shaped into sharp points, which were simply twisted back and forth.

During the Copper and Bronze Ages (about 4000 B.C. to 1000 B.C.) people discovered how to use fire to separate copper ore from rock. By pouring molten copper into clay molds, they created metal tools. Later they added tin to copper to make a stronger, harder metal— bronze. Metal tools were easier to handle and produced finer work.

During the Iron Age (about 1000 B.C. to A.D. 400s) iron replaced copper and bronze as the metal for tools. Tools made from iron had sharper edges and points that lasted longer. The Romans used many iron tools and introduced iron nails.

During the Middle Ages (about 500 to 1500) tools changed little, although planes became popular and were developed for specialized uses. During the 1600s and 1700s toolmaking became a separate trade, requiring years of training. Lathes for turning metal appeared and were first used by clockmakers. Steel, a stronger metal than iron, was widely used, greatly improving the effectiveness of tools.

Before the Industrial Revolution hand tools were used to produce goods. The invention of steam meant that goods were produced by power-driven machines that could only be manufactured by machine tools. Electricity also brought huge changes to tool use. Today factory production is largely automated— controlled by computers and robots.

(for cutting moldings and channels in wood) and saws (for cutting wood).

Machine tools include lathes (for turning wood and metal), drills, grinders, and power saws. Their size and power mean that they are far faster than a worker with hand tools, they can handle much larger pieces of work, and they can produce hundreds of identical parts. This makes them ideal for mass production.

History of tools

Humans probably picked up sticks and stones to use as simple tools about one million years ago. It was not, however, until about 10,000 B.C. that people began to make tools similar to those of today.

New Stone Age (10,000 B.C to 4000 B.C.) tools were made from wood, bone, ivory, and shell as well as stone. Hammers were simple hand-sized stones. Scrapers—stones chipped on one side to

SEE ALSO: Ancient Civilizations; Engine; Industrial Revolution; Manufacturing; Metals; Robot; Technology

✱ TRADE

Trade is the exchange of one product for another product or for money. For thousands of years trade has been the cornerstone of wealth and civilization.

◄ *Many cities on the coast of the Baltic Sea, such as Lübeck, Germany, prospered through international sea trade during the Middle Ages (about 500–1500).*

The exchange of goods and services to satisfy the needs of consumers is known as trade or commerce. "Trade" usually refers to the exchange of particular products. For example, people might say that a country's main trade is in coffee or tea or sugar. The word "commerce" covers all aspects of trading.

History

The earliest trading was barter—the exchange of one kind of goods for another, such as grain for cloth or cloth for knives, and so on. But traders could not always find other traders with the kind of goods they wanted. Gradually, people began to exchange their goods for money, with which they could buy anything.

For thousands of years traders traveled from place to place to exchange goods. Most international trade was in luxuries—

goods that people could not get at home. At the height of the Roman Empire the market stalls in Rome sold spices, silks, and precious stones from Egypt, marble from Greece, ivory from Africa, amber from Germany, and tin from Britain.

With the fall of the western Roman Empire in the fifth century A.D. trading declined. The people of Europe went back to bartering or growing their own produce until the wars called the Crusades in the 11th to 13th centuries revived the trade in Eastern luxuries.

Christopher Columbus's voyage to the Americas in 1492 and the discovery of a sea route to Asia brought new life to world trade. Different countries fought for control of the newly discovered lands, and many people left Europe for the New World and Asia to set up plantations (large farms) growing sugar, tea, tobacco, and

A spice seller at his shop in Aswan, Egypt.

DID YOU KNOW?

In ancient times the spices of Eastern lands, such as cinnamon, ginger, and cloves, were in great demand in the West. Merchants, in particular Arab traders, took spices from east to west across Asia, each charging a little extra as they passed them on. The cost of trade duties at wealthy ports such as Alexandria and Venice added to the price of the spices. By the time the spices reached the markets of western Europe, they had become very expensive.

It was to cut out the "middlemen" that 15th-century European explorers sailed west in search of the spice islands of the East. They discovered America instead, which opened a new chapter in trade. Eventually, in the late 1400s, explorers found a sea route around the tip of Africa that gave Europe's merchants the east–west shortcut they had long sought.

coffee. Traders also formed powerful associations, such as the Hanseatic League in Baltic Europe, to increase their share of the international market.

The 19th century brought railroads and steamships that could carry goods rapidly from one place to another. It also heralded the age of heavy machinery, which produced goods cheaply and quickly in large factories. Different regions came to specialize in different kinds of goods. The modern system of trade and commerce is based on this specialization.

Trade and commerce today

Specialization helps a nation make the best use of its natural resources (such as forests, farmland, or coalfields), capital goods (machines and factories), and labor (workers). Not every country has the same resources. Saudi Arabia, for example, is a largely desert nation in the Middle East with one-quarter of the

world's reserves of fuel oil. It specializes in exporting oil to countries who need more than they can produce. Meanwhile, it imports about 70 percent of its food needs to make up for its lack of farmland.

There are special organizations that help control trade. The World Trade Organization (WTO), founded in 1995, took over from the General Agreement on Tariffs and Trade (GATT), founded in 1947. Both were set up to encourage trade between nations. Many countries have a government department that tries to ensure smooth and profitable trading.

SEE ALSO: Ancient Civilizations; Columbus, Christopher; Crusades; Industrial Revolution; Manufacturing; Money; Natural Resources; Roman Empire; Transportation

* TRANSPORTATION

Modern transportation includes bicycles, cars, boats, trains, and airplanes. They save time and effort when traveling from one place to another.

A roadtrain, a truck towing trailers, carries road-building materials in Brisbane, Australia.

For thousands of years walking and running were the only means of transportation. Historians do not know when the first boats were built, but people probably started floating on logs many thousands of years ago. By 8,000 B.C. dugout canoes were being used in Europe and North America. Larger sailing boats have been in use since at least 4000 B.C.

The first land vehicles were probably sleds. They may have been pulled by people wearing skis. Archaeologists have found fragments of skis that are about 7,000 years old.

Russian steppes (grasslands) began to ride horses rather than eat them. Horse-drawn wagons then came into wider use.

However, long-distance travel with wheeled vehicles was not practical until the Romans began to build true roads in the 300s B.C. Roads made trade between cities and peoples much easier because merchants could carry large quantities of goods over long distances. When the western Roman Empire collapsed in the fifth century A.D., people stopped building roads, existing roads were no longer repaired, and trade dropped.

A detail from The Bayeux Tapestry, a famous piece of medieval needlework, shows a typical 11th-century northern European sailing ship. Its hull was made of overlapping wooden planks. Sailors steered with a special oar lashed to the right-hand side near the stern. There was a single mast with a large rectangular sail made of cloth.

The wheel

The earliest known wheels were made in Mesopotamia (modern Iraq) between about 3500 and 3000 B.C. At about the same time, people discovered that animals, especially cattle, could be used to pull heavy things, and warriors from the

The great explorers

For many years it was easier to travel long distances by sea than by land. The Phoenicians, Greeks, and Romans used ships with large sails and oars. Slaves often did the rowing. In about 1200 the compass, a Chinese invention, came to

One reason was the lack of good roads. As the number of vehicles grew, more and better roads were built. The improved roads, in turn, made it possible to build larger trucks. Today more than two-thirds of the communities in the United States rely on trucks to supply all their needs.

The air and beyond

The first air travelers were the French Montgolfier brothers, who built hot air balloons in the 1790s. But it was not until 1903 that the first powered flying machine took off. The American Wright brothers built a gasoline-powered airplane that flew a few yards at Kitty Hawk, North Carolina.

Airplane technology developed very quickly. In 1927 Captain Charles Lindbergh made the first solo nonstop flight across the Atlantic Ocean. The development of the jet engine in the 1950s made speeds of 300 mph (480km/h) and more standard.

Rocket technology made possible travel beyond the Earth's atmosphere. The space age began with the launch of the Soviet satellite Sputnik in 1957. The first people went into space in 1961.

Modern transportation

Developments in transportation have had many benefits. Travel around the world, for business or pleasure, gets less and less expensive. Companies can also transport goods for sale around the world.

However, modern transportation has also created problems. Roadbuilding and vehicle emissions cause environmental damage and pollution, and destroy animal habitats. Increased air transportation causes noise nuisance to people living under flightpaths. Increased car ownership causes gridlock in many cities.

Charles Lindbergh completed the first solo, nonstop flight across the Atlantic—from Long Island, New York, to Paris, France—in the Spirit of St. Louis *aircraft in May 1927.*

Europe. In 1450 the first three-masted ships set sail. Developments such as these helped explorers like Christopher Columbus explore and map the New World.

Mechanical transportation

The next great development in transportation came when people learned how to harness the power of steam. In 1769 a Frenchman called Nicolas Cugnot built a steam-powered automobile, but it was impossible to control and crashed into a wall on its first journey. In 1787 the American John Fitch built the first practical steamboat. The first crossing of the Atlantic entirely under steam power took place in 1838. An Englishman, Richard Trevithick, built the first steam locomotive to run on tracks in 1804. By the mid-1800s railroads were beginning to cross Europe and North America.

In the 1880s two Germans, Gottlieb Daimler and Karl Benz, developed the first engine to run on liquid fuel. The first automobiles to use the internal combustion engine were very expensive. However, in 1908 Henry Ford produced the first Model T in a Detroit, Michigan, factory. As prices dropped, ordinary people could afford to buy cars.

In time the automobile was adapted to carry goods and freight as well. At first trucks were used in limited numbers.

DID YOU KNOW?

The Chinese introduced the first speed limits and traffic regulations in the first century B.C. The roads were so crowded that the rulers of the Chou Dynasty (ruling family) had to make laws to prevent accidents.

SEE ALSO: Aircraft; Bicycle & Motorcycle; Car; Engine; Manufacturing; Road; Ship & Boat; Space Exploration; Train & Railroad; Wright, Orville & Wilbur

✳ TUBMAN, HARRIET (ABOUT 1821–1913)

Harriet Tubman was a former slave who helped more than 300 other fugitives reach freedom and safety. She was called "the Moses of her people."

Harriet Tubman led 19 groups of slaves to freedom. She used the North Star as a guide.

Tubman was born into slavery in Dorchester County, Maryland. She escaped in 1849 and reached Philadelphia, where she worked as a cook. It was there that she heard of the Underground Railroad, a network that helped fugitive slaves reach the North. Tubman led groups of slaves out of the South. They traveled by night and hid by day. In 1857 Tubman succeeded in freeing her own parents.

Slaveholders offered rewards for her capture, but she was never caught. During the Civil War (1861–65) she was a spy in the South and encouraged slaves to join the Union army. After the war she lived in Auburn, New York, where she set up a home for poor black people. After she died in 1913, the people of Auburn put up a monument in her honor.

✳ TUNNEL

Tunnels are underground passages that are used in many ways, from carrying water to a city to routes for trains and cars through mountains.

The first step in building a tunnel is to plan its exact route. Surveyors make maps showing how deep in the ground or how far below a body of water the tunnel must be dug. Geologists try to learn about the materials through which the tunnel will pass. They drill deep holes and bring up samples of what lies beneath the surface—hard rock, soft soil, wet soil, clay, or sand.

Rock tunnels

There are two main ways of building tunnels through rock. One is to blast the rock into pieces with explosives. Another is to use a machine called a mechanical mole. It has a number of wheels with

steel teeth that grind the rock into small pieces. In order to keep bits of rock from falling off the walls, tunnels may be lined with bricks, blocks of stone, or concrete, a mixture of cement and water.

Soft materials

When digging through soft material, such as soil, there is a danger of the tunnel collapsing. The soil can be hardened by pumping a mixture of cement and chemicals into it. In another technique the front of a steel shield is pressed against the tunnel's face where the workers dig out the soil. Powerful jacks push the shield forward so that the workers are always just within the shield's protection.

To help the workers breathe, large fans keep the tunnel ventilated. They force fresh air in and draw contaminated air out. Finished tunnels also need ventilation.

History
The first permanent tunnels were built about 3,000 years ago, not for the passage of people but to carry water to towns or dry areas. Tunnels through rock were made by building a fire close to the rock face and then throwing cold water on the heated rock until it cracked and could be broken up. Another method involved driving wooden wedges into holes or cracks in the rock. The wedges were kept wet until they swelled enough to put pressure on the rock and split it into bits.

These ancient tunneling methods were used until the 1700s, when factories first required large-scale transportation of goods and people. Tunnels through

mountains were built using powerful new explosives, new equipment, and new methods.The first underwater tunnel was dug under the Thames River in London, England, and opened in 1843.

Opened in 1994, the Channel Tunnel provides a rail link between the United Kingdom and the rest of Europe.

SEE ALSO: Explosive; Road; Train & Railroad; Transportation

✳ TURKEY AND THE CAUCASUS
Turkey lies on two continents—Europe and Asia. Armenia, Azerbaijan, and Georgia are south of the Caucasus Mountains, which divide Europe and Asia.

European Turkey is separated from Asian Turkey by a narrow waterway connecting the Aegean and Black seas. Turkey is a land of mountains, plateaus, and rugged coastlines. The Caucasus are a great mountain system that occupy the isthmus (a narrow strip of land) between the Black and Azov seas in the west and the Caspian Sea in the east. The region south of the range is called Transcaucasia.

People and economy
The land that is now Turkey has been seized by many different peoples. The Turks who came in the 11th century from Central Asia dominate the population. Armenia's residents now live on a tiny corner of their ancient homeland, most of which is now in Turkey. Eighty percent of Azerbaijan's people are Azeris,

descended from an ancient Central Asian people. Georgians trace their roots back over 3,000 years.

About 40 percent of Turkey's workforce is engaged in agriculture, with cotton and tobacco as the major crops. Cotton textiles are its most important industry. Mineral extraction and manufacturing are important in Turkey and the Caucasus. Azerbaijan is a leading oil producer.

History
In about the 1200s B.C. Greeks began to establish states along the coasts. In the 600s B.C. the Greek city of Byzantium was founded. In A.D. 330 it was renamed Constantinople (modern Istanbul) when it became the capital of the eastern Roman Empire, later the Byzantine Empire. The Byzantine Empire became a great world

KEY FACTS

TOTAL AREA
373,317 sq. mi.
(966,976 sq. km)

LARGEST COUNTRY
Turkey

SMALLEST COUNTRY
Armenia

POPULATION
82,813,000

NUMBER OF COUNTRIES
4

RELIGIONS
Islam, Christianity

LANGUAGES
Turkish, Kurdish, Azeri Turkish, Armenian

Turkey's national flag

Armenia's national flag

Azerbaijan's national flag

Georgia's national flag

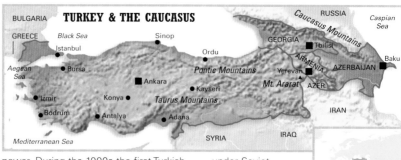

power. During the 1000s the first Turkish tribes, the Seljuks, came from western Central Asia. They attacked the Byzantine Empire and set up a Muslim state in what is now central and eastern Turkey. By 1360 the Ottomans, a group of Muslim tribes from Central Asia, had conquered most of what is now Turkey. At its peak in the 1500s the Ottoman Empire stretched from east–central Europe to southwest Asia and North Africa. The modern Republic of Turkey was founded in 1923 by Mustafa Kemal, known as Kemal Atatürk ("Father of the Turks").

Thousands of years ago Armenia, Azerbaijan, and Georgia were divided into numerous different kingdoms that later fell to the Ottoman Turkish, Persian, and Russian empires. In 1920 they came under Soviet control, but finally won independence in 1991 with the breakup of the Soviet Union. In Georgia independence was followed by civil war. The conflict was resolved by 1995. In 1991 Azerbaijan and Armenia began fighting over the territory of Nagorno-Karabakh, which lies in Azerbaijan but whose people are mostly Armenian. A ceasefire halted the fighting in 1995, but tensions continued, and Armenian troops remained in the area.

SEE ALSO: Asia; Greece, Ancient

The Goreme Valley near Kayseri in Cappadocia, Turkey. About 60 million years ago volcanic eruptions spread a thick layer of ash over the area. It hardened into a soft stone called tufa. Erosion from rain and wind created interesting formations called "fairy chimneys."

✳ UNITED KINGDOM

The United Kingdom is a small country in northwest Europe about the size of Oregon. England, Scotland, and Wales make up the island of Great Britain.

◄ *Tower Bridge in London is one of many bridges spanning the Thames River. The roadway parts and lifts to let tall ships and large craft pass through.*

The United Kingdom consists of four distinct parts: England, Scotland, Northern Ireland, and Wales. The island of Great Britain extends about 600 miles (966km) from north to south. Northern Ireland occupies a small area on the island of Ireland, the rest of which is made up of the Republic of Ireland.

Land and climate
Scotland has three major land regions. They are the Highlands in the north, the Central Lowlands, and the Uplands of Southern Scotland. Its highest peak is Ben Nevis, which rises to 4,406 ft. (1,343m).

The low mountains of the Pennine chain extend like a backbone from the Scottish border to central England. Yorkshire is to the east of the Pennines, and the Lake District is to the west. To the south lies the Midlands, the industrial heartland of England. London is in southeast England.

Wales occupies the land on the western edge of Great Britain. Most of its interior is hilly, with Snowdon, the highest peak, rising to 3,560 ft. (1,085m).

Northern Ireland makes up about one-sixth of the island of Ireland. It has a varied landscape with low mountains, rolling plains, and deep valleys.

The United Kingdom has a temperate climate. Temperatures rarely rise above 75°F (24°C) in summer or fall below 23°F (–5°C) in winter. Annual rainfall ranges from more than 100 in. (2,540mm) in some areas to about 26 in. (660mm).

People

Although small in area, the United Kingdom is one of the most densely populated countries in Europe. England is the largest and most populous of the four parts of the kingdom. The Welsh, Scots, and Northern Irish have maintained their individuality. Both Gaelic and Welsh, Celtic languages that were spoken by the early Britons, are still spoken. Many British cities are home to immigrants from Britain's former colonies in Africa, Asia, and the Caribbean, providing a rich mix of different cultures.

Economy

Britain was once the wealthiest nation in the world and is still one of the world's most important trading nations. In 1973 the United Kingdom was admitted to the European Economic Community, which became the European Union (EU) in 1993.

Service industries are now the largest part of the economy, employing more than two-thirds of the labor force. London, in particular, is an international center of finance and commerce. Tourism is also a major source of income.

History

Britain's island location, close to the European mainland but separated from it by water, has played an important role in its history. In the first century B.C. Britain became part of the Roman Empire. In the eighth and ninth centuries Vikings raided the coasts. In 1066 William of Normandy, France, conquered England.

Between the late 1700s and the mid-1900s Britain was the world's leading

UNITED KINGDOM

North Sea
SCOTLAND
Aberdeen
▲ Ben Nevis
Glasgow ● ● Edinburgh
NORTHERN
IRELAND ● Newcastle
● Belfast
Pennines
● York
Liverpool ● ● Leeds
REPUBLIC ● Manchester
OF IRELAND
● Birmingham
WALES
ENGLAND
● Cardiff
Swansea ● Thames River ■ London
ATLANTIC
OCEAN
English Channel
FRANCE

United Kingdom's national flag

naval power. British explorers, traders, and colonists sailed to most of the world. Many of the world's nations based their governments on the British parliament. English is the world's most widely used language, and English literature is one of the world's best known.

The Industrial Revolution began in Britain in the mid-1700s. Along with the growth of its industry Britain acquired a vast empire. In the early 1900s one-quarter of the world's land and about one-fifth of its people were governed by Britain or according to British laws. During the 25 years after World War II (1939–45) most of its colonies became independent.

SEE ALSO: Europe; Industrial Revolution; Vikings; World War I; World War II

✳ UNITED NATIONS

The United Nations was formed in 1945 to maintain international peace. Today it has 191 member countries. Its headquarters are in New York City.

In February 2003 the UN Security Council listens to a report on the search for weapons of mass destruction in Iraq. In March the United States and the United Kingdom attacked Iraq.

United Nations' flag

The first plans for the United Nations (UN) were made during World War II (1939–45). In 1944, at the Dumbarton Oaks conference in Washington, D.C., the Soviet Union, the United Kingdom, the Republic of China, and the United States agreed on proposals for an international organization to work for world peace and security. The UN Charter came into force on October 24, 1945.

The United Nations is made up of many specialized agencies, but there are six main bodies. The General Assembly is made up of one representative from each member nation. Each country casts one vote in every decision, so smaller nations have a great deal of influence.

The UN Security Council has five permanent members—the United States, the Russian Federation, France, the United Kingdom, and China—and 10 members that each serve two years. The council's chief role is to maintain world peace and security.

The UN Economic and Social Council has 54 nonpermanent members and deals with major concerns such as economic development. The UN Trusteeship Council oversaw the colonies of European nations before they became independent or self-governing. It rarely meets now.

The International Court of Justice settles disputes submitted by nations for final decision and advises UN agencies. It sits at The Hague in the Netherlands. The court has 15 judges.

The Secretariat is the administrative body of the United Nations. It is headed by the UN's chief executive, the secretary-general. Every member nation is represented on the Secretariat staff.

The United Nations has successfully negotiated cease-fires between warring nations and ended civil wars in, for example, Mozambique and Angola. UN peacekeepers have also been active in Bosnia and Somalia. However, the UN has not always been able to ensure the peaceful resolution of disputes.

Various UN programs work to improve economic and social conditions in developing countries. They include UNICEF, which fosters the well-being of children; UNESCO, which tries to seek better understanding between the peoples of the world; and the World Food Program, which provides food aid.

Human rights

One of the UN's main objectives is to safeguard human rights. They include freedom of speech, religion, and assembly; the right to fair and equal treatment under the law; the right to vote; and the rights to work and obtain an education. The Universal Declaration of Human Rights sets standards for human rights, but it is not legally enforceable. The UN seeks ways of ending abuses but violations continue all over the world.

SEE ALSO: Roosevelt, Eleanor; World War II

405

✻ UNITED STATES OF AMERICA

The United States is the fourth largest country in the world. It is also the world's wealthiest and most politically powerful nation.

UNITED STATES OF AMERICA

CANADA

PACIFIC OCEAN

MEXICO

CANADA

Washington, D.C.

Gulf of Mexico

United States of America's national flag

Forty-nine states are on the continent of North America. Hawaii is located far to the west in the Pacific Ocean. Three-quarters of all Americans are classified as white, while nearly one-eighth are black. The next largest group is Hispanics. Inuits, Aleuts, Native Americans, and Pacific Islanders complete the population.

Over 80 percent of Americans are Christians. English is the most widely spoken language, followed by Spanish. Four in five Americans live in urban areas. New York City is the banking and business center. The capital, Washington, D.C., is not part of any state but occupies its own federal district, the District of Columbia.

The map above shows all the American states.

1 Alabama	14 Indiana	27 Nebraska	40 South Carolina
2 Alaska	15 Iowa	28 Nevada	41 South Dakota
3 Arizona	16 Kansas	29 New Hampshire	42 Tennessee
Arkansas	17 Kentucky	30 New Jersey	43 Texas
5 California	18 Louisiana	31 New Mexico	44 Utah
6 Colorado	19 Maine	32 New York	45 Vermont
7 Connecticut	20 Maryland	33 North Carolina	46 Virginia
8 Delaware	21 Massachusetts	34 North Dakota	47 Washington
9 Florida	22 Michigan	35 Ohio	48 West Virginia
10 Georgia	23 Minnesota	36 Oklahoma	49 Wisconsin
11 Hawaii	24 Mississippi	37 Oregon	50 Wyoming
12 Idaho	25 Missouri	38 Pennsylvania	
13 Illinois	26 Montana	39 Rhode Island	

Government and economy

The nation is a constitutional democracy, led by a president who is elected to serve a four-year term of office. Individual states draw up their own body of laws, but all American citizens must also obey federal (central government) laws.

Since the collapse of the Soviet Union in the 1990s the United States is today the world's only superpower. It has an economic strength at least twice that of any other nation.

History

At least a million Native Americans, belonging to many different peoples, lived on the land that is now the United States many thousands of years ago.

European settlement of the Americas began in the 1490s with the voyages of Christopher Columbus. Spanish and French colonists were followed by English, Dutch, and Swedes. Many had fled wars or harsh religious laws for a freer, more peaceful life, although some just came to seek their fortune.

The first of England's 13 colonies was established at Jamestown, Virginia, in 1607. The colonies planted crops such as tea and tobacco to be sent back to Europe. The exports were especially important to the Southern colonies, where slaves grew crops such as cotton on large farms called plantations.

Relations between

colonists and Native Americans were uneasy. There were frequent fights, especially in New England in the 1670s. French and English settlers also fought. In the French and Indian Wars (1689–1763) Britain won most of Canada, plus the Ohio and Mississippi valleys.

By the mid-1700s life in the 13 colonies was relatively peaceful. But when Britain imposed a new set of taxes, many American colonists rebelled. The American Revolution broke out in 1775. With the Declaration of Independence in 1776 Americans hardened their resolve to throw off British rule. After heavy loss of life on both sides independence came in 1783. In 1789 George Washington was elected first president of the United States, and a new set of federal laws—the Constitution—was approved.

In 1803 the nation bought France's vast American territories, which stretched from present-day Louisiana to Canada, doubling the area of the United States. It is known as the Louisiana Purchase. Between 1804 and 1805 the Lewis and Clark expedition followed the Missouri River to the Rockies and then crossed to the Pacific Coast.

Britain was at war with France, and British warships stopped American merchant vessels, taking their crews. Because of this, in 1812 the United States declared war on Britain. Americans also hoped that they might conquer Canada. But victory escaped them, and Canada remained British.

British forces surrender after the Battle of Trenton, New Jersey, in December 1776. It was one of George Washington's great victories over the British in the American Revolution.

Immigration and expansion

The United States continued to grow, acquiring Florida from the Spanish in 1819. Newly invented machines for farming cotton, spinning textiles, and mass-producing other goods boosted the nation's industrial strength. Steamboats now plied inland waterways, and after 1830 railroads began to connect towns. Immigrants flocked from Europe to start new lives. To make room for them, during the 1830s over 60,000 Native Americans were forced to move to lands west of the Mississippi River. About 15,000 died on the journey.

Americans now looked to new lands in the West. From 1821 onward American settlers had moved to Texas, a Mexican province. In 1836 they won independence. The United States bought part of the Oregon Territory from Britain in 1846, but Mexico refused to sell California. War broke out between Mexico and the United States. Mexico's defeat in 1848 gave California to the United States, as well as present-day Utah and Nevada, and most of what is now Arizona and New Mexico.

Secession and Civil War

By now Americans were arguing bitterly over slavery. The Union was more or less evenly divided between the "free" states of the North (in which slavery was banned) and those states in the South in which the practice was permitted. New

laws threatened to allow slavery to spread in the recently acquired territories.

The split between North and South grew steadily wider. In 1860 Abraham Lincoln, who hated slavery, was elected president. This angered the Southern states. Many of them seceded from the Union and set up their own nation— the Confederate States of America.

Lincoln was determined to hold the Union together. In 1861, when civil war broke out between Confederate and Union states, he tried to recapture the South. After nearly five years of bloody combat, during which there were terrible casualties on both sides, the North finally emerged victorious in 1865.

A nation shattered by civil war turned to rebuilding itself in a period known as Reconstruction. Southern states were gradually allowed back into the Union.

Growth of the nation

As settlers continued to push west by wagon and railroad, Native Americans lost even more of their homelands, along with the vast herds of bison that had roamed the prairies. Alaska was bought from Russia in 1867. Meanwhile, the steady flow of immigrants from Europe saw huge growth in the industrial cities. By 1890 the nation had more than doubled its pre-Civil War population and had become one of the world's leading industrial nations.

In 1898 the United States took control of Hawaii. It also waged a brief war with Spain in order to free Cuba from Spanish rule. After the war Spain yielded Puerto Rico, the Philippines, and the Pacific island of Guam to the United States.

War and peace

The first years of the 20th century are known as the Progressive Era, a time when President Theodore Roosevelt responded to calls for sweeping changes in society and big business.

In 1914 World War I broke out in Europe. In 1917 the United States sent a force of some two million men and helped end the war in 1918. President Woodrow Wilson

◄ The development of heavy artillery meant that the Civil War became a war of sieges. The Union troops had larger guns, which helped them win the war.

KEY FACTS

OFFICIAL NAME
United States of America

AREA
3,717,796 sq. mi. (9,629,091 sq. km)

POPULATION
281,421,906 (2000 census)

CAPITAL
Washington, D.C.

LARGEST CITY
New York

MAJOR RELIGIONS
Christianity, Judaism, Islam

MAJOR LANGUAGE
English

CURRENCY
U.S. dollar

then set about rebuilding postwar Europe.

The 1920s were a time of prosperity—of jazz music, the rise of automobile production, and the start of a golden age for Hollywood's movie studios. But greed and excessive risk-taking in the business world led to the collapse of the stock market in 1929. Businesses folded, unemployment soared, and America entered the Great Depression. This downturn in the economy was also felt all across the world. President Franklin D. Roosevelt passed a batch of reforms known as the New Deal. He ordered huge construction programs, and Congress passed many laws to protect the poor.

Germany, defeated in the last war, started another war in 1939 that involved the world. The United States entered World War II when Japanese airplanes bombed the U.S. Pacific fleet base at Pearl Harbor in December 1941. American planes helped end the war in 1945 by dropping two atomic bombs on Japanese cities. By then the economic boost from the war effort had revived the United States so much that it was now the world's most powerful nation.

Cold War and civil rights

During World War II the Soviet Union extended its area of control into new parts of Europe and Asia. The communist nation's interests often clashed with those of the United States, and the next 45 years became known as the Cold War. Although there was never an actual war between them, there was constant tension as both sides built ever more

powerful nuclear missiles with which to threaten each other. American soldiers went to fight in Korea (1950–53) and Vietnam (1965–72) in attempts to contain the spread of communism. At home unjust laws in the South still denied African Americans their full rights as citizens. A growing protest movement overthrew these laws with the Civil Rights Acts of 1964 and 1968.

The modern era

President Lyndon B. Johnson spoke of creating a "Great Society," and much was done by later presidents to build that society despite wars in the Persian Gulf and Afghanistan and a continuing gap between rich and poor at home. Since the terrorist attacks on New York City and Washington, D.C., on September 11, 2001, the nation's foreign policy has concentrated on efforts to defeat terrorism throughout the world.

SEE ALSO: Frontier, The American; King, Martin Luther, Jr.; Korean War; Pilgrims; Russia & the Baltic States; Segregation & Integration; Vietnam War; World Trade Center; World War I; World War II

✳ URANUS

Four times the size of Earth, Uranus is the third largest planet in the solar system. Like Jupiter, Saturn, and Neptune, it is made mainly of gas.

In 1781 the British astronomer William Herschel surveyed the sky with a telescope he had built himself, examining every star and looking for something unusual. One night he found a tiny shining disk that was clearly not a star. At first he thought it was a comet, but other astronomers realized he had discovered a new planet. They named it Uranus for the Greek god of the heavens. It only looks tiny when viewed through a telescope because it is so far away from Earth.

Odd angle of orbit

The tilt of Uranus on its axis at 98° is unique in the solar system. Astronomers think that may be because the planet was struck by a large object at about the time it was formed.

Uranus appears different from the other gas giants, Jupiter, Saturn, and Neptune. Those three planets all have bands of clouds that can be seen clearly in their atmospheres. The surface of Uranus, however, is uniformly greenish-blue and almost featureless. The clouds lower down in the planet's atmosphere are hidden from view by a smoglike haze in the outermost layers. The temperature at the upper layers of Uranus's atmosphere is extremely cold, typically about −355°F (−215°C).

The atmosphere of Uranus is composed mainly of hydrogen and helium, with traces of methane and other gases.

Little is known about what lies beneath the planet's outer layers, but there may be a vast ocean of water, ammonia, and methane. At a distance of 1.8 billion miles (2.9 billion km) from the sun, Uranus revolves around it in a large, elliptical, or oval-shaped, orbit that is 19 times larger than that of Earth.

Ring system

Uranus is surrounded by a complex system of rings, which are much narrower and darker—and therefore harder to see—than those of Saturn. The rings of Uranus are made up of tiny particles of ice and rock.

This image of Uranus, taken by the Hubble Space Telescope, shows the planet and its elaborate ring system.

Many moons

Uranus has at least 20 moons, and there may be several more small natural satellites orbiting among the planet's rings. The five largest are Miranda, Ariel, Umbriel, Titania, and Oberon.

Miranda is unlike any other moon in the solar system. Giant cliffs, icy canyons, and ancient cratered regions are mixed with much younger ridges, dark and light patches, and strange, round features. Scientists think that Miranda must have been broken apart by a collision and then put together again by gravity—perhaps not once but several times.

SEE ALSO: Astronomy; Solar System

KEY FACTS

POSITION IN THE SOLAR SYSTEM
Seventh from the sun

AVERAGE DISTANCE FROM THE SUN
1,800,000,000 mi.
(2,900,000,000km)

SOLAR ORBIT
84 Earth years

DIAMETER
32,000 mi.
(51,500km)

MASS
87 sextillion tons

ATMOSPHERE
Hydrogen, helium, methane

AXIAL ROTATION
17 hours

✳ URUGUAY

Uruguay lies on the eastern coast of South America between Brazil to the north, Argentina to the west, and the Atlantic Ocean to the south.

Uruguay's national flag

KEY FACTS

OFFICIAL NAME
Oriental Republic of Uruguay

AREA
67,035 sq. mi.
(173,620 sq. km)

POPULATION
3,337,000

CAPITAL & LARGEST CITY
Montevideo

MAJOR RELIGION
Roman Catholicism

MAJOR LANGUAGE
Spanish

CURRENCY
Uruguayan peso

ARGENTINA
URUGUAY
BRAZIL
Uruguay River
● Salto
● Paysandú
Negro River
Lake Rincón del Bonete
● Fray Bentos
Río de la Plata
■ Montevideo
ATLANTIC OCEAN

Uruguay is the second smallest country in South America, after Suriname. It is the only South American country with no large uninhabited areas.

Summers in Uruguay are long but usually not extremely hot. Winters are short and not usually uncomfortably cold.

People
The early people of the region were Indians. Spanish explorers arrived in 1516, but Spanish settlement did not begin until the 1600s. At the beginning of the 19th century most people were of mixed Spanish and Indian ancestry. Today most Uruguayans are of European descent.

Economy
Most of Uruguay's agricultural land is devoted to raising livestock. Beef and meat products became leading exports in the 1870s, when refrigerated ships began to carry cargoes of frozen meat to Europe. The government has encouraged farmers to grow crops such as cereals and citrus fruits. It has also encouraged tourism, offshore fishing, and manufacturing.

Gauchos—or cowboys—drive cattle along a rough track near Salto in Uruguay.
▶

History
Uruguay fought hard for independence from Spain in the early 19th century. The army also had to fight the Portuguese, who wanted the territory to be part of Brazil, and the Argentinians, who wanted it to be part of Argentina.

Until the beginning of the 20th century the country was beset by civil wars, revolts, and foreign intervention. The election of José Batlle y Ordóñez (1856–1929) as president was a turning point in the nation's history. As president from 1903 to 1907 and from 1911 to 1915 he introduced many social reforms.

In the late 1960s and early 1970s Uruguay was faced with growing economic problems and antigovernment terrorism. The army was brought in to govern and in 1976 took full control of the country. A gradual return to constitutional rule under an elected president began in the 1980s. In 1999 Jorge Batlle, the grand nephew of José Batlle y Ordóñez, was elected president.

SEE ALSO: America, South

✳ VEGETABLES

Vegetables are herbaceous—nonwoody—plants with edible parts. People eat different parts of different vegetables, for example, leaves, flowers, and stems.

Historians believe that cabbages were grown in gardens over 4,000 years ago. The edible part of the plant is a bud formed of many leaves. Some varieties are green, and some are red.

Early people probably gathered wild pod-bearing plants such as beans and peas and root plants such as carrots. The ancient Egyptians grew lettuce, cabbage, melons, broad beans, radishes, onions, garlic, and artichokes by the Nile River. The Greeks and later the Romans were familiar with the vegetables grown by the Egyptians. In addition they raised cucumbers, asparagus, and celery. Farmers in the New World grew beans, squashes, potatoes, sweet potatoes, corn, and tomatoes. These vegetables were brought back to Europe by explorers, but many did not become popular until the 1800s.

In the 19th century farmers started using better farming methods. The invention of the train, and then the automobile, also meant that vegetables could be transported quickly from the farm to the market.

Cultivating vegetables

Climate and the nature of the soil are the two main factors that determine which vegetables farmers grow. The ideal temperature for cabbage and broccoli, for example, is between 60 and 65°F (15.5°C to 18°C).

As in other areas of agriculture, farmers use machinery to sow and harvest many of their vegetables. However, much of the work is still done by hand. Lettuces, for example, must be picked carefully so that their leaves do not bruise.

Most vegetables reach the stores within a few days of picking and need to be eaten while they are fresh. However, modern methods of freezing, canning, and packaging mean that vegetables can last months or even years.

Vegetables that are out of season in one part of the world can be grown in another and shipped in refrigerated containers or transported by air, enabling people to enjoy them all year around.

AMAZING FACTS !

The largest vegetable is the tropical yam. The edible tubers can grow to lengths of over 8 ft. (2.4m) and weigh over 130 lb. (59kg). These vegetables are not the same as sweet potatoes, which are sometimes called yams in North America.

SEE ALSO: Ancient Civilzations; Nutrition; Plant

✳ VENEZUELA

Venezuela is a nation on the northern coast of South America. It is the world's largest oil producer outside the Middle East.

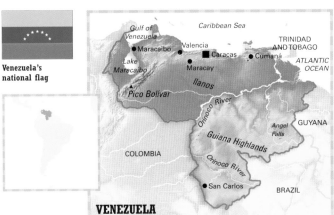

Venezuela's national flag

VENEZUELA

OFFICIAL NAME
Bolivarian Republic of Venezuela

AREA
352,143 sq. mi. (912,050 sq. km)

POPULATION
24,170,000

CAPITAL & LARGEST CITY
Caracas

MAJOR RELIGION
Roman Catholicism

MAJOR LANGUAGES
Spanish (official), Indian languages

CURRENCY
Bolívar

Venezuela has many plateaus and mountains in the north and south. The highest point is Pico Bolívar, at 16,427 ft. (5,007m). Other important areas include the lowlands around Lake Maracaibo and the huge, grassy plains called the llanos. Native animals include pumas, jaguars, sloths, monkeys, and many colorful birds.

The most important waterway is the Orinoco. Angel Falls, in the Guiana Highlands, is the world's highest waterfall.

Venezuela is evenly warm all year, with high rainfall in many regions. The lowlands are hot and humid, with cooler conditions on high ground.

People and economy
About 70 percent of Venezuelans are mestizos, or people of mixed European and native Indian descent. The

Crested oropendolas are found in Venezuela's tropical areas and also throughout South America. They are sociable birds, flocking together and nesting in small colonies.

rest of the population is mostly of European, African, or Indian descent.

Petroleum products make up more than 80 percent of Venezuela's export earnings. More than two-thirds of the work force are employed in service industries, such as retail and real estate. Coffee is the chief commercial crop.

History
The first inhabitants of Venezuela were Carib and Arawak Indians. Christopher Columbus landed in 1498, but the first European settlement was not until 1523. Venezuela was a Spanish colony for nearly 300 years. In the early 1800s there were two unsuccessful revolts against Spanish rule. In 1819 Simón Bolívar, known as the Liberator, invaded Venezuela and then defeated the Spanish. Venezuela joined a republic with Colombia and Ecuador, then became independent in 1830.

For many years political instability and dictatorship dominated the country. In the early 1900s President Juan Vicente Gómez arranged contracts with foreign oil companies, and Venezuela became one of the world's leading oil exporters. The election of Rómulo Betancourt, in 1959, ended the years of dictatorship. In 1998 President Hugo Chávez Frías took over an impoverished and divided country.

SEE ALSO: America, South; Columbus, Christopher

413

✳ VENUS

The closest planet to Earth, Venus can be seen
before sunrise, when it is called the morning star,
and after sunset, when it is called the evening star.

The light that appears to be coming from
Venus is really the light of the sun
reflecting off the tops of the planet's
clouds. Venus is always surrounded by a
thick, dense layer of gleaming white
clouds. The first space probes to fly
through them revealed that they are made
of carbon dioxide plus tiny droplets of
sulfuric acid.

The clouds end about 30 miles (48km)
above the surface of Venus. Strong winds
blow the cloud layers around the planet.
Moving at a speed of about 225 miles
(362km) per hour, the clouds circle Venus
in about four Earth days.

Underneath the clouds
Venus has a dry, desertlike surface. More
than 60 percent of it is covered with
low-lying plains. Above the plains are

two high, mountainous regions. Venus also
has several large volcanic regions covered
with hundreds of volcanoes, each over
12 miles (19km) in diameter, and tens
of thousands of smaller volcanoes.

The atmosphere of Venus consists of
about 97 percent carbon dioxide and 3
percent nitrogen, with small amounts of
other gases. The atmosphere is densest
near the surface of the planet, where the
temperature is about 900°F (480°C).

Venus has the most circular orbit (path
around the sun) of any planet in the solar
system. It turns very slowly on its axis. A
"day" on Venus is 243 Earth days. Venus
rotates from east to west; most other
planets revolve in the opposite direction.

Until the first space probes in the
1970s Venus was a mystery shrouded
by dense layers of clouds. Although
Earth and Venus are very different in
many ways, scientists hope that by
studying Venus they will add
to their understanding of
the Earth.

*Hundreds of radar
images taken by
the Magellan
spacecraft in
the early 1990s
have been used to
create a computer-
simulated view
of Venus.*

SEE ALSO:
Solar
System;
Space
Exploration

✳ VICTORIA, QUEEN (1819–1901)

During the reign of Queen Victoria the British Empire reached the height of its power. Her strong sense of duty won her the devotion of her subjects.

Victoria came to the throne in 1837, aged only 18, after the death of her uncle, William IV. At the time the British monarchy was unpopular with its people. The young Victoria was high-spirited and fun-loving, but her behavior was influenced by her marriage in 1840 to a distant cousin, Albert, a German prince. Albert taught Victoria that a queen should always act with dignity. They had a happy marriage, and by the time of Albert's death in 1861 they had raised nine children together. Victoria continued to maintain her interest in religion, morals, art, music, and fashion. Her reign is associated with a stern morality.

The prime ministers who served Victoria were men of great ability. They included Robert Peel, William Gladstone, and Benjamin Disraeli. In 1875 Britain gained control of the Suez Canal, Egypt, and in 1876 Victoria was proclaimed empress of India.

In 1897 Victoria celebrated her Diamond Jubilee—60 years of rule. People of all political beliefs showed her much affection. When she died four years later, she left behind an empire that seemed secure. Britain, however, would soon lose its place as leader of the world. Victoria was succeeded by her eldest son, who became Edward VII.

This photo of Queen Victoria was taken in 1887, the fiftieth year of her reign. She reigned longer than any other British monarch.

SEE ALSO:
United Kingdom

✳ VIETNAM WAR

War devastated the Southeast Asian country of Vietnam between about 1957 and 1975. The United States fought on the side of South Vietnam.

Helicopters fly over two American soldiers in 1967 during an attack in South Vietnam.

France ruled Vietnam, then called Indochina, from the late 1800s. Between 1946 and 1954 the French fought a long and brutal war with the communist Vietminh, led by Ho Chi Minh. In 1954, after discussions in Geneva, Switzerland, Vietnam was divided at the 17th parallel. The Communists dominated the northern zone. The United States supported the president of the southern zone, Ngo Dinh Diem.

Communist guerrillas, called the Vietcong, began to attack the government of the south in 1957. U.S.

troops secretly began to take part in the fighting. In 1963 and 1964 there were two military takeovers in the south. General Nguyen Khanh took power. The South Vietnamese government remained unstable during the war.

America joins the war

In 1964 U.S. aircraft began bombing North Vietnam, and in March 1965 President Lyndon Johnson sent ground troops into South Vietnam. By 1969 there were 554,000 U.S. troops in South Vietnam.

In early 1968 the Communists launched the Tet Offensive, a series of attacks on cities in the south. They were not successful, but the attacks showed that in three years of fighting U.S. troops had not defeated the Vietcong.

Peace talks began in Paris, France, in May 1968, but with little success. The war was becoming increasingly unpopular in the United States, which was spending nearly $30 billion a year on the conflict.

Richard M. Nixon became president in 1969. He announced that U.S. troops would withdraw from Vietnam. The last U.S. troops left the country in 1972. A peace treaty was agreed on in 1973, but neither side kept to its terms. In 1975 forces from North Vietnam invaded, and the South Vietnamese government surrendered. Vietnam was united under communist rule in 1976.

More than 58,000 Americans died or disappeared in the war. More than a million Vietnamese also lost their lives.

SEE ALSO: Nixon, Richard M.

✳ VIKINGS

Between the eighth and 11th centuries Scandinavian warriors traveled throughout Europe and sailed to Greenland and North America.

The Vikings originally lived in the lands that are now called Norway, Denmark, and Sweden. They were farmers and traders. They worshiped the Norse gods, including Odin and Thor. Their history and legends were recorded in long poems called sagas, which were not written down but passed by word of mouth from one generation to another. The Vikings were also expert sailors. By the late 700s they had built fast boats for war called longships or dragon-ships.

Exploration and invasion

In the late 700s Vikings began to raid England, taking away many rich treasures and kidnapping people to sell as slaves. Over the next 250 years they carried out similar raids on England, Scotland, Ireland, France, and the Netherlands, and as far south as Spain and Italy.

However, they were not simply violent robbers. Swedish Vikings under Rurik traveled eastward from 862, and began a dynasty (ruling family) that would eventually become the nation of Russia.

A fleet of Viking longships races across the North Sea toward England.

In 911 the Viking Hrolf, or Rollo, became the first Duke of Normandy, in northern France. Many of his followers settled in Normandy. Danish and Norwegian Vikings built settlements in northeastern England and in Ireland. The Danish King Canute ruled England between 1017 and 1035.

The Vikings also colonized Iceland. In 982 an Icelandic Viking named Eric the Red traveled farther west and settled in Greenland. His son, Leif Eriksson, explored even farther west and landed on the island now called Newfoundland, in Canada.

Christianity eventually replaced Viking beliefs and culture in Scandinavia and other areas of Viking influence. But Viking explorations and settlements had a lasting effect throughout Europe.

✳ VOLCANO

Melted rock and other hot substances inside the Earth sometimes erupt from beneath the surface. A place where this happens is called a volcano.

Heat in the Earth's interior continually escapes toward the surface. As it rises, it heats rock, which melts. This molten rock, called magma, usually cools within the Earth. Sometimes, however, the magma mixes with hot gases, such as steam. Gas-filled magma is lighter and can rise through a series of channels toward the surface. When it reaches a vent, or opening, in the surface, it spews out. Magma that comes out of a vent is called lava. During eruption it reaches temperatures of about 2,000°F (1,100°C). Cooled lava and other fragments build up to form the cone of a volcano. The hole at the top of the cone is called a crater.

Most volcanoes are located on the edges of continents. That is where the huge plates that form the Earth's crust rub against each other, creating faults.

Types of volcano
Volcanoes vary in height and shape. Volcanologists, the scientists who study volcanoes, divide them into four types.

Stratovolcanoes are formed from a number of layers of ash and lava. They usually have large, circular depressions at their summits. Mount Fuji, in Japan, is an example of a stratovolcano.

The largest examples are shield volcanoes. They form when large flows of lava spread out rapidly from central vents. Shield volcanoes have broad bases and gentle slopes. The large island of Hawaii is made of five overlapping shield volcanoes. The largest is Mauna Loa.

Small volcanoes, called cinder cones, dot the landscape in volcanic regions. There are more cinder cones than any other type of volcano. They form when small explosions of magma occur many times from one vent, leaving chunks of ash and lava on the surface.

The most powerful eruptions create ash-flow calderas. The magma and other material blow so far from the vent that there is almost no mountain. Instead, a wide crater, called a caldera, forms in a low hill of ash.

Types of eruption

Scientists use special terms for the different kinds of eruption. The gentlest are Hawaiian eruptions, which are nonexplosive. Strombolian eruptions, named for a volcano in Italy, have many weak eruptions. Vulcanian eruptions produce a lot of ash but little lava.

Peléan eruptions are named after Mount Pelée, on the Caribbean island of Martinique. They are violently explosive, with rapid flows of ash, rock, and gases. The most violent eruptions are Plinian ones, which hurl plumes of ash many miles into the sky. They are named for Pliny the Elder, a Roman scholar killed when Vesuvius erupted in A.D. 79.

Scientists also classify volcanoes by how often they erupt. Extinct volcanoes

have not erupted for many thousands of years. Dormant volcanoes have also been inactive for many years, but might erupt at some time in the future. Active volcanoes can erupt at any time.

There are special observatories around the world where volcanologists can monitor active volcanoes. Earthquakes, emission of gases, and rises in temperature can be signs that a volcano is about to erupt. A violent eruption can kill many thousands, but with warning, people can be evacuated from the area.

Mount St. Helens volcano in Washington erupts. The massive explosion on May 18, 1980, created a cloud of gas and ash over 15 miles (24km) high. Scientists monitor the volcano for further eruptions.

SEE ALSO: Earth; Earthquake; Geology

✳ WARFARE

As far back in history as we have evidence, humans have fought wars. Regardless of its rights and wrongs, warfare is an important human activity.

This mosaic is thought to show the Battle of Gaugamela in 331 B.C. The Greeks, led by Alexander the Great, won a great victory against the Persians, led by King Darius III (in the chariot). Alexander's army of foot soldiers armed with long spears and cavalry made up the finest fighting force of the age.

Early peoples fought with clubs or bows and later with axes, spears, and swords. Hand-to-hand fighting was very tiring, and battles probably lasted only a few hours. An important part of early warfare was attacking enemy villages and building fortifications to defend them. Ever since, defending and attacking fortified places have been key parts of war.

Nomads (wandering peoples) in Central Asia started riding horses in about 3500 B.C. In about 1850 B.C. they built chariots, two-wheeled carts that served as stable fighting platforms. Chariots were eventually replaced by cavalry—skilled riders who charged at the enemy.

Foot soldiers

Not every commander depended on cavalry. Although the ancient Greeks and Alexander the Great (356–323 B.C.) used cavalry, the core of their armies remained units of foot soldiers. The Roman army, the finest fighting force of its day, developed much larger units of foot soldiers called legions. Legionaries were foot soldiers armed with spears, javelins (throwing spears), and short swords. Superior tactics, discipline, and organization gave them an advantage even over a mounted enemy.

After the fall of the western Roman Empire in A.D. 476 cavalry dominated warfare in Europe and Asia. The cavalry armies of the Mongol Genghis Khan (about 1162–1227) conquered the largest empire the world has ever seen. In India armies fought each other mounted not only on horses but also on elephants.

By the mid-1300s in Europe English infantry armed with powerful longbows inflicted defeats on French cavalry. In the battles of Crécy (1346) and Agincourt (1415) English archers rained arrows down on heavily armored French knights, causing many casualties.

Firearms

By then, however, a revolutionary new substance—gunpowder—had reached Europe from the East. Large cannons named siege guns helped Turkish forces capture Constantinople in 1453. The use of firearms spread swiftly. The 1600s and 1700s saw the rise of professional, uniformed infantry armed with musket and bayonet. Battles were very precisely planned and executed. Armies drew up in lines facing one another so that each man could use his musket.

Dutch and English ships fight against and destroy the Spanish Armada in 1588. This painting dates from 1608.

New, lightweight cannons, named field guns, of the late 1700s arrived in time for the French Emperor Napoleon Bonaparte to make brilliant use of them. He broke with tradition, favoring flexible tactics and skirmishes, and concentrated his forces at the point where they would cause the most damage to the enemy.

By the time of the American Civil War (1861–65) firearms had developed to the point at which traditional tactics were no longer possible. Advancing lines of brightly uniformed troops would simply be cut down in a hail of gunshot. The need for infantry to seek cover and the arrival of railroads (a recent invention) greatly extended the scale of battles. Although Napoleon had been defeated in a day at Waterloo (1815), the Civil War battle of Gettysburg (1863) lasted three days.

At the front lines in World War I (1914–18) machine guns and artillery pinned troops in trenches and caused enormous casualties. Many soldiers died at Cambrai (1917), when tanks were first used on a large scale, at the gain of just a few miles of ground.

Aircraft
World War I saw the arrival of two new weapons of war—the tank and aircraft. Tanks could roll over defensive trenches and were impervious to bullets. Aircraft

were used to spy on enemy forces, to drop bombs, and to "dogfight" with enemy planes. Tanks and aircraft played an even more important part in World War II (1939–45), serving in every battle theater. Two atomic bombs dropped on Japan by U.S. airplanes in 1945 helped end the war—and heralded a new era.

The atomic age
From 1945 to 1990 the United States and the Soviet Union, the victors of World War II, faced each other in a tense stand off known as the Cold War. Neither side dared attack the other because both had atomic and then nuclear weapons of enormous destructive power.

Modern warfare
Today's armed forces use guided missiles, satellite surveillance, and jet fighters. The line between war and peace is not always clear. In some countries there are civil wars. Terrorist organizations form "invisible" worldwide armies.

Revolvers with cartridges and gunpowder used in the Civil War (1861–65). The invention of guns changed the nature of warfare. It meant that soldiers had to seek cover, and battles lasted longer.

A nuclear bomb can cause massive destruction and leaves a mushroom-shaped cloud in the sky. The explosion of the first nuclear bomb in 1945 changed the nature of warfare.

SEE ALSO: Aircraft; Ancient Civilizations; Caesar, Julius; Hitler, Adolf; Korean War; Mongols; Napoleon; Radar & Sonar; Roman Empire; Ship & Boat; Vietnam War; World War I; World War II

✷ WARHOL, ANDY (ABOUT 1930–87)

The American artist Andy Warhol was a leader in the style that came to be called pop art. He drew his subjects from American popular culture.

As well as being an influential artist, Andy Warhol also inspired musicians.

Warhol was born Andrew Warhola in Pittsburgh, Pennsylvania, the son of Czech immigrants. Warhol's exact birthdate is unknown, but he was probably born between 1928 and 1930. He studied art at the Carnegie Institute of Technology in Pittsburgh. After graduating in 1949, Warhol settled in New York City, where he became a successful commercial artist. By the 1960s he had won recognition as a painter.

Warhol's work aroused controversy at first because it disregarded traditional artistic standards. Among the images he depicted were consumer products, such as Coca-Cola bottles and Campbell's soup cans, and the faces of celebrities, such as the actress Marilyn Monroe and the Chinese leader Mao Zedong. Using a printmaking process called silk screening, he duplicated these images many times, varying only the colors.

Warhol became a celebrity. He was devoted to showmanship and art collecting. He also made experimental films, produced records, and wrote books such as *The Philosophy of Andy Warhol: From A to B and Back Again* (1975).

SEE ALSO: Art; Printing

✳ WATER

Water is the most common substance on Earth, covering almost three-quarters of the planet's surface. All living things depend on it for survival.

Water is composed of two chemical elements, hydrogen (H) and oxygen (O). Each molecule of water consists of two hydrogen atoms and one oxygen atom. Chemists write this formula as H_2O.

At normal temperatures water is a liquid. However, it also appears as a solid and as a gas. When its temperature falls below 32°F (0°C), it expands and becomes a solid called ice. When its temperature is raised above 212°F (100°C), water becomes a gas, called vapor or steam. These temperatures are, respectively, the freezing and boiling points of water.

The amount of water on Earth has remained about the same since the planet was formed. But its form is always changing—from solid to liquid, from liquid to gas, and back again. It moves in a pattern called the water cycle. Heat from the sun causes water in oceans, lakes, and rivers to evaporate into vapor. Further water vapor is given off by plants and animals. As the vapor rises, it cools and condenses into tiny droplets that form clouds. Water in the clouds gathers to form raindrops, snowflakes, or hailstones that fall back to Earth.

Water use

Only 3 percent of water is fresh (not salt water). Two-thirds of that fresh water is frozen in glaciers and ice caps.

People now use over half of the fresh water available in rivers, lakes, and underground supplies. If the world's population continues to grow at its current rate, people could be using over 90 percent of all available fresh water within 25 years, leaving just 10 percent for all other living things.

Almost three-quarters of the fresh water used by humans is for agriculture. It takes an enormous amount of water

▲
Children in Udaipur, India, draw water from a well. In the developing world such sources are not always clean and may cause disease.

to produce crops. For example, 1,000 tons of water are needed to produce just one ton of grain.

Water and health

During the 20th century the world's human population tripled, and water use increased sixfold. In the same period half the world's wetlands disappeared, and many freshwater fish became endangered. Agriculture uses more water every year to meet the food demands of a growing population. As a result, other users have less and less water. About 5 million people die every year from diseases caused by water pollution or lack of water.

In 1972 the Clean Water Act was passed in the United States. Before then only one-third of U.S. streams, lakes, and coastal waters were clean enough for fishing and swimming. Now two-thirds of our waters are safe.

SEE ALSO: Atom & Molecule; Fish; Human Body; Matter; Pollution; Wetlands

☀ WATERFALL
A waterfall is a stream of water that drops sharply from a higher to a lower level. In large falls thousands of gallons pour down every second.

The world's highest waterfall, Angel Falls on the Churún River in southeast Venezuela.

Waterfalls usually form when rivers flow over rock that is softer than the surrounding area. Soft rock wears away faster than the hard rock. This creates a ledge, over which the water pours. Waterfalls are also found where glaciers (rivers of ice) have dug valleys deeper than their tributaries or in places where a river channel was raised or lowered.

The amount of water going over a waterfall can vary enormously. If the volume of water is small, it is called a cascade; if large, it is called a cataract. The biggest discharge of water ever recorded was 470,000 cubic ft. (13,300 cu. m) in a second over the Guaíra Falls, between Brazil and Paraguay. However, the falls are now submerged by the Itaipu dam.

Harnessing the energy
For hundreds of years the fast-flowing water downstream from waterfalls has been used to turn the great stone wheels of mills to grind grain into flour for bread. Today the energy of fast-flowing water is converted into electricity by hydroelectric power plants.

Every year hundreds of thousands of people come to view the most famous falls, such as Niagara Falls on the border of Canada and the United States, Ribbon Fall and Yosemite Falls in California, and Victoria Falls on the border of the African nations of Zambia and Zimbabwe.

THE WORLD'S HIGHEST WATERFALLS

Angel, Venezuela	3,212 ft. (979m)
Tugela, South Africa	2,800 ft. (853m)
Utigord Falls, Norway	2,625 ft. (800m)
Monge Falls, Norway	2,540 ft. (774m)
Mutarazi, Zimbabwe	2,499 ft. (762m)
Yosemite, California	2,452 ft. (739m)
Ostre Mardalofoss, Norway	2,151 ft. (655m)
Tyssestrengene, Norway	2,123 ft. (647m)
Kukenan, Guyana–Venezuela	2,000 ft. (610m)
Sutherland Falls, New Zealand	1,904 ft. (580m)

Many waterfalls have several drops; the figures give the total fall.

SEE ALSO: Energy; River; Water

✷ WEIGHTS AND MEASURES

Sometimes it is not enough to say that something is
heavy or short or wide. Measurements give the
exact dimensions of objects and substances.

In Indonesia tea
pickers are paid
according to the
weight of leaves
that they have
harvested.

As human civilization developed, the need
for measurements began. Explorers and
soldiers needed to measure distances
between places, and traders needed to
measure quantities.

Customary measures
The first measurements were based on
the human body. The Romans counted the
number of times their right feet went
forward. A thousand paces was called
mille passus, which gives the English
word "mile." A cloth merchant measured
his goods by stretching them from his
nose to his fingertips. People compared
small objects with grains of wheat. Larger
objects were compared with stones.

The problem with these methods was
that the units were not consistent. A tall

cloth merchant with long arms would
measure more cloth than a short
merchant. Grains and stones are not
always the same size. A common
standard was needed. If two towns
were 50 miles apart, everyone had to
agree how long a mile was. Gradually
people began to develop fixed quantities
for measurement. According to legend,
the yard is based on the distance from
the nose to the fingertip of Henry I,
king of England in the 1100s. The
measurements of feet, miles, pounds,
pints, and so on formed the basis of
customary measures. This is the system
used today in the United States.

There were still disagreements between
different parts of the world. Some of them
continue today. For example, a gallon,

Usage des Nouvelles Mesures.

French workers in the 1790s trying to get used to the new metric system of measurement.

To convert from customary units of measurement to metric, multiply the number of customary units by the metric figure. For example, 2 in. equals 5cm.

used to measure quantities of liquid, is slightly larger in Britain than in the United States.

As commerce and communications advanced, many people found it hard to see the link between the systems and the objects being measured. It seemed to them unnecessarily complicated that 12 inches should make a foot, 3 feet a yard, 1,760 yards a mile, and so on. They began to look for new, simplified measurements.

The metric system

In the 1790s French scientists developed a new system. They wanted a set of measurements that would be easier to understand and the same around the world. They decided to make the units fit together in multiples of 10 to make calculations easier. The system they came up with is called the *Système International d'Unités*— International System of Units—or SI. The units they developed were based on specific measurements. A meter was defined as $\frac{1}{40,000,000}$ of the circumference of the Earth. Later calculations showed that their measurement of the Earth was wrong, but the meter remained the same.

Larger and smaller metric units were also based on factors of 10. A centimeter

A six-foot tape measure. The distance between each of the lines marked is $\frac{1}{32}$nd of an inch.

CONVERSIONS

Customary	Metric
1 inch	2.54cm
1 foot	30.48cm
1 yard	91.44cm
1 mile	1.609km
1 square inch	6.45 sq. cm
1 square foot	0.09 sq. m
1 square yard	0.83 sq. m
1 square mile	2.59 sq. km
1 acre	0.4 ha.
1 ounce	31.1g
1 pound	0.37kg
1 fluid ounce	29.57ml
1 pint	473.2ml
1 gallon	3.78l

is one hundredth of a meter. A kilometer is 1,000 meters (about 1,094 yards). The SI unit of weight, or mass, is a gram. It was originally defined as the mass of one cubic centimeter of water. Its name is derived from the Latin word *gramma*, meaning "little weight."

Over the next 200 years the metric system became standard in most of the world. The United States is one of the few countries that still prefers the old systems of weights and measures, although even here the metric system is increasingly used by sports authorities and scientists.

SEE ALSO: Math & Numbers

425

✳ WETLANDS

A wetland is an area where the soil is saturated (wet through) with water or covered by shallow pools of water for long periods of time.

Wetlands cover 6 percent of the Earth's land surface and are found in all countries and in all climates. They include swamps, bogs, and marshes.

Swamps

Swamps are forested wetlands. In shallow-water swamps the ground stays moist all year. Deep-water swamps form along rivers and often flood. Along the seacoasts of tropical areas saltwater swamps sometimes form. Some trees in swamps grow right out of the water. Others grow on small islands called hummocks. The animal and plant species that thrive in swamps vary. Hemlock and willow trees are both suited to wet ground. Mangrove trees can survive in both salty and freshwater environments.

Bogs

Bogs are usually found in northern regions in the depressions left by glaciers (rivers of ice). Water settles in the depressions, and plants take root. Because of poor drainage plant matter does not decay fully. Spongy moss grows on the surface of the water. A brown material called peat builds up below the surface. Wood frogs and some small mammals thrive in bogs.

Marshes

The main vegetation in marshes is soft-stemmed plants called emergents. Saw grass, wild rice, and rushes are examples. Emergents grow with part of their stems below the water and the tops above the

◄ *Cypress Creek National Wildlife Refuge provides a habitat for many animals that are in danger of becoming extinct (dying out).*

surface. Marshes are an important habitat for many kinds of fish, birds, such as herons, and otters and beavers.

The importance of wetlands

Most wetlands provide habitats for a wide variety of wildlife. Many species are only found in swamps, bogs, or marshes. Humans also benefit from these environments, raising fish and growing crops. Rice grows in marshes. Wetlands control flooding and also prevent erosion. Laws have maintained some wetlands as conservation areas, but people have already destroyed about half the world's natural wetlands. They have been drained and built over for roads, houses, and factories, for example.

SEE ALSO: Biome; Environment; Glacier; Habitat; Water

✳ WILDER, LAURA INGALLS (1867–1957)

Laura Ingalls Wilder was the author of the "Little House" series of books on American pioneer life. She received many awards and honors for her books.

The Ingalls family lived in a log cabin in Wisconsin. Laura was the second of four sisters. From 1869 to 1879 the family traveled by covered wagon throughout the Midwest in search of productive land. Wilder's first memories were of their move to Kansas. They finally settled on a homestead in South Dakota in 1880.

When she was in her forties, Wilder started writing for regional magazines and newspapers. At the age of 65 she published her first novel, *Little House in the Big Woods*. Popular demand led her to write eight more books based on the story of the family's adventures.

▲ *Laura Wilder wrote about her family's adventures on the American frontier.*

Wilder's books made her internationally famous. They were widely used in schools to teach about frontier life. During her lifetime she answered thousands of letters from admiring readers. She died at her Missouri farm at age 90.

A popular television series in the 1970s and 1980s, *Little House on the Prairie*, was loosely based on Wilder's stories. All her former homes have been restored to honor her life and work.

✳ WIND

Wind is the effect of air moving because of changes in air temperature or pressure. Wind can provide benefits, but it can also be very destructive.

Several factors cause air to move. One is temperature. Warm air is lighter than cold air, so it rises. A nearby area of cold air will move to replace the risen air. A region of air movement is called a circulation cell.

Air pressure also produces wind. When two places close together have different levels of air pressure, air moves from the high-pressure area to the low-pressure area. The greater the difference in pressure, the stronger the wind.

Types of wind

Scientists classify winds in various ways. The Beaufort scale measures wind speed based on how it affects the surface of the sea. On land an instrument called an anemometer converts wind into electrical current. A stronger current indicates a greater wind speed. Winds between 32

and 63 mph (51–101 km/h) are called gale force winds. At speeds of over 74 mph (119 km/h) a wind is at hurricane force.

Winds also blow in patterns called wind systems. The gentlest of them are called breezes. They are caused by circulation

▲ *A tornado strikes Phuket Island, Thailand.*

cells. In coastal areas breezes often come in from the ocean because the air is cooler above the sea than above the land.

Some winds are stronger. Thunder storms form when downdrafts strike the ground. Wind speeds of 50 mph (80km/h) or more can occur. Tornadoes, monsoons, and other large storms are accompanied by even stronger winds.

Strong winds and storms can cause massive destruction. Winds combined with cold weather can create an effect called wind chill, which can kill people.

However, winds can also make the Earth more habitable for people and other species. They reduce the heat of the tropical regions and warm the polar areas with air from the tropics. They also aid in the evaporation and movement of water.

In recent years people have harnessed winds to provide new sources of energy. Large groups of windmills produce electricity in California and other areas. This is a renewable energy source, since the Earth can never exhaust the supply.

SEE ALSO: Climate & Weather; Electricity; Energy; Hurricane, Tornado, & Typhoon; Natural Resources; Water

✳ WOMEN'S RIGHTS MOVEMENT

For most of history, and in most cultures, women have not enjoyed the same rights as men. The first campaigns for women's rights began in the 1800s.

▶ *Mary Wollstonecraft Godwin, a founder of the modern feminist movement. She argued that women should enjoy the same rights as men.*

Until the late 1800s western women were second-class citizens. They could not vote. It was very difficult for them to enter college or a profession. If they married, all their property belonged to their husbands.

One of the most important thinkers in the early women's movement was Mary Wollstonecraft Godwin (1759–97). In her book *Vindication of the Rights of Woman* she argued that women should have equal rights in marriage, politics, and education.

The first meeting for women's rights in the United States took place in 1848, at Seneca Falls, New York. The organizers presented a "Declaration of Rights and Sentiments." It was based on the Declaration of Independence but announced that "all men and women are created equal."

The early leaders of the American women's movement were Susan B. Anthony, Elizabeth Cady Stanton, and Lucy Stone. They pressured state legislatures to reform voting and property laws. Many campaigners for women's rights were also involved in the struggle to abolish slavery.

Gradually women began to win property rights and the right to attend college. They could also vote in some states. By the

Campaigners for women's right to vote, known as suffragists, march in front of the Capitol in Washington, D.C., in 1913.

early 1900s many other countries had overtaken the United States in the freedoms that women had won. The National Woman's Party, founded in 1913, took radical action in its campaigning for women's rights. The NWP called for a picket of the White House, and 168 women were imprisoned. But it was not until 1920 that the 19th Amendment was passed permitting women to vote in all elections.

The battle for equality

Alice Paul, one of the founders of the NWP, carried on the campaign for women's rights after the 19th Amendment was passed. In 1923 she drafted the first version of the Equal Rights Amendment. It stated simply: "Men and women shall have equal rights throughout the United States and every place subject to its jurisdiction." It was introduced to Congress but did not pass.

By the end of World War II, in 1945, women had the vote in most democratic countries. However, they were nowhere near equality with men. Employers were allowed to pay women less than men for

the same work. Some professions and organizations were still closed to women. Women were often expected to stop working when they became mothers.

The campaign for full equality between men and women became a major force throughout the world during the 1960s. The first female political leaders of countries took power in Sri Lanka and India. Writers such as Simone de Beauvoir, Germaine Greer, and Betty Friedan publicized the ideas of women's rights and led the campaign. People began to use a new word for these arguments—feminism.

DID YOU KNOW?

The United Nations Convention on the Elimination of All Forms of Discrimination Against Women became an international treaty in 1981. It calls for the abolition of women's slavery, equal access to education and employment opportunities, maternity leave, and the right to control the number and spacing of children.

President John F. Kennedy ordered federal agencies to treat men and women equally in employment. In 1963 he signed the Equal Pay Act, which meant that employers had to pay men and women the same amount for the same work.

The 1964 Civil Rights Act was intended to give rights to African Americans and other ethnic groups. But Alice Paul and other campaigners succeeded in also protecting equality for women. The Equal Employment Opportunity Commission was set up to enforce these laws.

In 1966 a new group, the National Organization for Women (NOW), was founded. It began a campaign to put Alice Paul's Equal Rights Amendment into law. The campaign failed but increased publicity for the argument that women and men should be treated equally.

Women's rights around the world
In North America, Europe, and other parts of the world women's rights are now guaranteed by law. But in many countries religious or economic restrictions mean that women are still second-class citizens. Campaigners disagree about whether the west should force these countries to accept women's rights—or whether this is forcing western ideals onto other cultures.

SEE ALSO: Stanton, Elizabeth Cady; United Nations; Women's Suffrage

✳ WOMEN'S SUFFRAGE

Suffrage is the right to vote. For many years men in democratic countries had the right to vote for leaders and governments, while women did not.

In some democracies at the start of the 1800s many men did not have the vote. In the United States slaves could not vote. In the United Kingdom and other countries people could be stopped from voting if they did not own land, or if they followed a particular religion. However, by the second half of the century all men were able to vote in most democratic countries. But women still did not have the vote. Some people thought that women were not intelligent enough to vote. Others thought that if women became involved in politics, they would not want to be wives or mothers.

Women's suffrage was one of the main demands of campaigners for women's rights in the 1800s and early 1900s. Women such as Emmeline Pankhurst in the United Kingdom were prepared to go to prison to support their struggle. New Zealand gave women the vote in 1893.

In 1912 Ohio suffragists tried to persuade people to vote for an amendment to Ohio's constitution proposing women's suffrage. However, their campaign failed.

World War I (1914–18) was a major turning point. Many women worked in factories and took over "male" jobs. They argued that if they could be equal with men in industry, they should have equal rights to vote. By 1919, 15 countries had given women the vote, including the United Kingdom, Canada, Germany, and Russia.

Campaigns in the United States
Women met at Seneca Falls, New York, in 1848 and made suffrage a core part of their campaign. Supporters of women's suffrage and the abolition of slavery often supported each other's claims. However, after the end of the Civil War in 1865 some abolitionists withdrew their support.

The National American Woman Suffrage Association formed in 1890. By 1900 four states—Colorado, Idaho, Utah, and Wyoming—had given the vote to women. But an amendment to the Constitution was needed to ensure that women in all states could vote. In 1917 President Woodrow Wilson gave his backing to an amendment ensuring votes for women. The 19th Amendment, giving the vote to women, was finally ratified in 1920.

SEE ALSO: Government; Women's Rights Movement

✳ WORLD TRADE CENTER

For many years the twin towers of the World Trade Center dominated the skyline of New York City. They were destroyed in the terrorist attacks of 2001.

The World Trade Center was built between 1966 and 1972. The architect was Minoru Yamasaki in cooperation with Emery Roth & Sons. Because of the great height of the towers the designers had to make them rigid to cope with the force of strong winds. Each floor was trussed to the walls at the corners, to prevent the buildings from bending and swaying.

When the 110 story-towers opened in 1973, they were 1,368 ft. (417m) and 1,362 (415m) tall and held 13 million sq. ft. (1.2 million sq. m) of office space. They cost an estimated $1.5 billion and were the tallest skycrapers in the world. However, the Sears Tower in Chicago, Illinois, broke the record the following year at 1,454 ft. (443m) tall. The Twin Towers remained the tallest structures in New York City.

The Twin Towers dominated the New York skyline before their destruction in September 2001.

431

Attacks on the towers

On February 26, 1993, a bomb exploded in an underground garage in the center. Six people died, and more than 1,000 were injured. Over the next four years six people were convicted of the attacks. They were linked to terrorist groups in the Middle East.

On September 11, 2001, terrorists hijacked four airliners. They flew two of them into the towers of the World Trade Center. Within hours both towers collapsed, and nearly 3,000 people lost their lives. Another airliner caused serious damage to the Pentagon in Arlington, Virginia. The last one was heading for the Capitol, in Washington, D.C., but was brought down by passenger action in a field in Pennsylvania. The chief suspect as mastermind of the attacks was Osama bin Laden, head of the Al Qaeda network, a group of Islamic extremists.

It was the most destructive terrorist act in history and an attack on the American way of life. The American people, and our friends around the world, were thrown into mourning. On September 20, 2001, President George W. Bush announced a War on Terrorism to bring the organizers of the attacks to justice.

SEE ALSO: Skyscraper

✳ WORLD WAR I

World War I (1914–18) involved more than 30 nations. It claimed more than 14 million lives, devastated Europe, and toppled kings and emperors.

▶ *An American soldier and his horse wear gas masks to protect them against poison gas.*

When war broke out in 1914, there had long been tension between France and Germany, which had fought a war in 1871. By the 1900s Europe formed two hostile camps—France, Russia, and Great Britain on one side, and Germany, Italy, and Austria-Hungary on the other. Germany's kaiser (emperor), Wilhelm II, wanted a great empire to rival that of Great Britain and was preparing to take it by force.

The spark for war came in the Balkans. On June 28, 1914 a Serbian student assassinated Archduke Franz Ferdinand, heir to the throne of Austria-Hungary. Austria attacked Serbia on July 28. Russia was allied to Serbia, and its ally France also prepared for war. Germany sided with Austria and declared war in early August. When German troops marched into neutral Belgium to attack France, Britain entered the war. Japan later joined the Allies (France, Britain, and Russia).

Western front, 1914

In the west the German plan was to sweep through tiny Belgium into France. The Belgians fought bravely, but the Germans pressed on and advanced almost to Paris, the French capital, by early September. They were stopped at the battle of the Marne. By Christmas the fighting was at stalemate. The front (the zone of fighting) was a shell-cratered maze of trenches and barbed wire stretching 475 miles (765km). Already more than 1.5 million soldiers had died.

The wider conflict

In the east the Germans had driven back Russian attacks in August and September 1914. In October the Ottoman (Turkish) Empire joined the Central Powers (headed by Germany and Austria-Hungary). The Turks prevented shipping from taking supplies to Russia via the Black Sea, and they defeated all Allied attempts to reopen the route. In 1915 Bulgaria joined the Central Powers and Italy joined the Allies, while in 1916 Romania and Greece also joined the Allied side. Fighting would later spread into the Middle East and Africa.

Western front, 1915–17

The fighting in the west during 1915 was marked by futile offensives by both sides. Men fell in their thousands, cut down by machine guns or choked by a deadly new German weapon—poison gas. But the front lines did not move as much as 3 miles (5km) in any direction. The British tried to draw pressure off the French by advancing along the Somme River in 1916. They brought a new weapon of their own: the tank. It was in vain, however: At the Battle of the Somme an estimated 1.2 million men died for 5 miles (8km) of land.

The year 1917 was another dark one for the Allies. Attempts to break through the German positions in northern France failed. At the Second Battle of the Aisne parts of the French Army mutinied (refused to obey orders). At the Battle of Passchendaele months of fighting cost the British some 300,000 dead.

The United States

In 1916 Russia launched a grand offensive against Austria, but after early successes the onslaught ground to a halt, with more than a million Russian soldiers killed. In March 1917 the Russian people overthrew their czar (emperor), Nicholas II, and in November the Communists swept to power. Their leader, Vladimir Lenin, took Russia out of the war in December, 1917.

So far the United States had kept out of the fighting. In 1917, however, German submarines began attacking American shipping. President Woodrow Wilson declared war on Germany, and in June the first American troops landed in France.

Final stages

By 1918, with Russia out of the war, Germany transferred more than a million troops from the eastern front to the west. On March 21 the Germans launched the enormous "Michael" offensive. Once again they were halted, after terrible loss of life on both sides. By May, however, American troops were at last tipping the balance in the Allies' favor, and bit by bit the German army weakened until it was decisively defeated in the fall.

On September 30 Bulgaria surrendered. Turkey followed on October 30, and Austria on November 3. Finally, on November 11, Germany signed a truce. The war was over.

British soldiers advance toward German trenches in 1918. The killing power of machine-guns changed the nature of warfare. The guns pinned their targets down in whatever cover could be found or made. This meant that the front lines of the two sides were often separated by only a short distance.

▶
German soldiers attack from a trench. Trenches were filthy ditches where soldiers ate, slept, and waited to be sent "over the top" in wave after wave of infantry attack, only to be shot down in a hail of enemy fire.

Aftermath

World War I changed the map of Europe and sowed the seeds for World War II. The Ottoman Empire broke up. The Austro-Hungarian Empire crumbled, giving rise to new states, including Czechoslovakia, Yugoslavia, and Poland. Finland, Estonia, Latvia, and Lithuania broke free from the Russian Empire. Through the Treaty of Versailles, signed in France in 1919, the Allied powers blamed Germany for the war, stripped it of land, and ordered it to pay billions of dollars.

SEE ALSO: Europe; Revolution; Warfare; World War II

✳ WORLD WAR II

World War II (1939–45) was the most destructive war in history. It involved all the world's great powers and many of the smaller nations.

After the bloodshed of World War I (1914–18) the world's most powerful countries signed treaties that they hoped would create a lasting peace. But economic problems and political tensions between the traditional ruling groups, the middle classes, and revolutionary communist parties ravaged much of central Europe. In 1933 an ambitious ex-soldier, Adolf Hitler, came to power in Germany. He blamed Germany's defeat in World War I on a Jewish plot. He ruled as a dictator (leader with total power) at the head of his National Socialist (or Nazi) Party and steadily built up Germany's armed forces.

Other brutal dictators also rose to power after World War I: Benito Mussolini in Italy and military leaders in Japan, including Tojo Hideki. Italy and Japan would fight alongside Germany as the major Axis powers.

War breaks out

Hitler, Mussolini, and Japan's leaders all wanted to build great empires. During the 1930s Japan invaded eastern China, and Italy invaded Ethiopia in East Africa. Germany swallowed up the Rhineland, its neighbor Austria, and Czechoslovakia. When Hitler invaded Poland in September 1939, Britain and France declared war on Germany. But Germany swiftly conquered Poland, helped by the Soviet Union.

Hitler's armies were the finest in Europe. Their fighting tactics were called Blitzkrieg ("lightning war"). In spring 1940 they overran Belgium, the Netherlands, Luxembourg, Norway, and Denmark. Winston Churchill became prime minister of Great Britain on May 10. Three days later the Germans invaded France. Only the British Royal Air Force and Royal Navy stopped Germany from crossing the English Channel and attacking England.

Mussolini, meanwhile, had invaded Albania in 1939. In 1940 he attacked British-held Egypt from his colony in Libya, but the Italians were fiercely opposed by British forces, and Hitler was forced to send German military support.

The eastern front

In spring 1941 Hitler attacked the Balkans, and then on June 22, 1941, he marched into the Soviet Union. German troops and armor rolled victoriously across the vast land until the fall, when rain made their progress slower. They reached the suburbs of Moscow in December 1941. Russian counterattack and the winter cold halted them. By the fall of 1942 German forces had reached the city of Stalingrad.

America and the Pacific

The United States had lent warships to Britain to help defeat the U-boats (German submarines) that were sinking Allied supply ships in the North Atlantic Ocean. Otherwise it had deliberately kept out of the conflict. Then, on December 7, 1941, Japanese aircraft attacked the U.S. Pacific fleet at its base in Pearl Harbor, Hawaii. Two days later the United States entered the war.

Japan mounted offensives in the Pacific and controlled much of southeastern Asia by May 1942. From that point, however,

U.S. naval forces began to hit back. The battles of the Coral Sea in May and Midway in early June severely damaged Japan's vital aircraft carrier fleet.

Europe and North Africa

By 1943 the tide had begun to turn against Hitler in Europe. Allied aircraft were pounding Axis factories and supply routes. Soviet troops had surrounded and destroyed the German Sixth Army at Stalingrad. Axis troops in North Africa were finally defeated in May 1943.

The Allies invade Europe

From July 1943 Allied troops invaded and fought their way up through Italy, finally taking Rome in June 1944. On June 6, "D-Day," American, British, and Canadian forces landed in Normandy, France. Weeks of bitter fighting followed. They freed Paris on August 25 and pressed on to reach the German border by October. The Soviet Red Army, which had been steadily advancing west, reached the

▲
British fighter planes, known as Spitfires, flying in formation at over 300 miles (480km) per hour.

Supplies arrive for U.S. Marines on the Japanese-held island of Iwo Jima. The island was of vital importance in the battle between the United States and Japan in 1945.
◄

outskirts of Berlin in April 1945. Hitler committed suicide on the 30th. Two days earlier Italian freedom fighters had shot Mussolini, and Italy's war was over. Germany surrendered on May 7.

After the fighting ended in Europe, war still raged in the Pacific between the Allies and the Japanese. To end the bloodshed as swiftly as possible, President Harry S. Truman gave the order to drop atomic bombs on the Japanese cities of Hiroshima and Nagasaki on August 6 and 9, 1945. The two explosions instantly killed over 150,000 people. Japan surrendered on September 2.

Aftermath

World War II has been called a "total war." Land, sea, and air forces all played their part. Civilians were deliberately killed.

Perhaps the worst aspect of the war on civilians was the attempt by followers of Hitler to wipe out Europe's Jews during the Holocaust. The use of atomic weapons took the political world into a dangerous new age. The United States, its economy boosted by the war, was now a superpower. Europe, which had once ruled the world, lay in ruins. In the years to come European colonies in Africa and Asia would rush to claim independence.

SEE ALSO: Germany; Hitler, Adolf; Holocaust; Italy; Japan; Roosevelt, Franklin D; Russia & the Baltic States; United Kingdom; United States of America; Warfare; World War I

✳ WORM

Worms are invertebrates—animals without backbones—with soft, long bodies. They can live on land, in water, and even in other animals.

The most familiar type of worm is the earthworm. It is an annelid, a word meaning "small rings." The body of an annelid is divided into small segments, or rings. An earthworm has no eyes or ears and spends most of its time underground. It burrows through the ground, taking soil into an inner digestive tube that runs the length of its body. It takes nutrition from plant and animal matter in the soil, and discards the rest. This process turns and aerates the soil, which is why earthworms are so important to farmers.

The largest group of annelids are bristle worms. Most bristle worms have tiny eyes and hard jaws. They often live in tubes made in sand or soil, or from a hard, limey substance made by the worm itself.

The brandling worm is an annelid with small rings, or segments. They are used by gardeners to make compost heaps and by fishermen as bait.

Ragworms and bloodworms are part of this group. Leeches are also annelids. They have smooth bodies with suckers at each end. They attach themselves to live animals, including humans, and suck out blood for food. This is called parasitism.

Roundworms

Roundworms, or nematodes, have digestive tubes inside an outer body tube, like annelids. However, the body is not segmented. Most roundworms are tiny, although some can grow to 3 ft. (1m) long. Many live in soil or water, but some, such as the hookworm, can enter the human body. Hookworms are parasites, entering the intestines and sucking blood.

Flatworms

Planarians, flukes, and tapeworms are all flatworms. Most flatworms are small and thin. Planarians usually live in shallow water, feeding on tiny animals. They can be found under stones in clear water or gliding over the sand in shallow salt water. Flukes and tapeworms are parasites. They feed on the body fluids and tissues of their hosts such as a sheep or a pig. Flukes and tapeworms can enter the human body and live on body fluids, causing damage to the internal organs.

SEE ALSO: Animal

✱ WRIGHT, FRANK LLOYD (1867–1959)

Some people believe Frank Lloyd Wright was the most important American architect in history. His buildings still influence modern designers.

Wright was born in Richland Center, Wisconsin, on June 8, 1867. His mother gave him wooden blocks and shaped cards to play with, and that gave him an early interest in building things.

Wright moved to Chicago, where he worked for the architect Louis Sullivan, whom he called "Master." In 1893 Wright opened his own office.

When designing buildings, Wright followed the rule that "form follows function." This means that the needs of a building's users should determine its structure, not rules laid down by architects in the past. Many of Wright's creations were shocking to people used to more conservative designs. They were often low and flat, and seemed to blend in with their natural surroundings. Wright was also one of the first architects to use concrete as the main material for construction without disguising it under other materials.

By the end of Wright's long life he had designed buildings in 36 states. His fame spread in Europe earlier than the United States. Colleagues did not always get on with him, finding him stubborn and arrogant. But even his enemies acknowledged his importance and influence as an architect.

◄

Frank Lloyd Wright designed more than 400 buildings during a career that lasted 70 years. He designed his own home and studio in Arizona.

✳ WRIGHT, ORVILLE AND WILBUR

The Wright brothers invented the first power-driven airplane. Other people had flown in balloons and gliders, but they were the first to build an airplane.

The Wright Brothers invented the first airplane. Wilbur Wright (left) flew about 120 feet (36.5m) on the beach at Kitty Hawk on the North Carolina coast.

Wilbur Wright was born in Milville, Indiana, on April 16, 1867. Orville was born in Dayton, Ohio, on August 19, 1871. From childhood the brothers were greatly interested in mechanics.

In 1889 Orville started a printing business using a press he had made. Wilbur joined the business, and it did very well. In 1893, when bicycling became popular, the brothers decided to open a bicycle repair shop. Eventually they built and sold bicycles as well as repairing them.

The brothers had long been fascinated by the idea of flight. After experimenting with box kites, they built a glider that looked like a big box kite with two wings. They took their glider to Kitty Hawk on the

North Carolina coast in the fall of 1900. It was a good place to conduct gliding experiments because of its strong, steady wind.

The brothers made about a dozen glides, but did not have complete control of the glider. Back home they built a series of wind tunnels and experimented with miniature wings of different sizes and shapes. Eventually they replaced the tail fins with a single movable rudder to make the glider easier to control.

First flight

Now all the brothers needed to make an airplane was an engine, but there were no engines light and powerful enough to put in an airplane. The brothers worked through most of the spring and summer of 1903 building their own engine. In September they went back to Kitty Hawk, but were delayed by engine breakdowns and bad weather.

It was not until December that the engine was in good repair and the weather was calm. On the morning of December 17, 1903, Wilbur Wright flew the plane a short distance. He was only airborne for 59 seconds, but he had made history. In 1909 the brothers formed the American Wright Company to manufacture airplanes.

Wilbur died on May 30, 1912. Orville continued to experiment and help advance the cause of aviation. He died on January 30, 1948, having lived long enough to know that a plane could fly faster than the speed of sound.

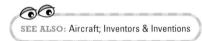

SEE ALSO: Aircraft; Inventors & Inventions

✴ WRITERS, AMERICAN

The stories and culture of Native Americans were passed down by word of mouth. This meant that the first American writers were Europeans.

Much of the earliest writing from America consists of diaries and sermons by colonists. These works revolve around the writers' relationship with God. The colonies' first printing press was set up at Harvard College, Massachusetts, in 1639.

The first American writer to achieve international fame was Benjamin Franklin. His *Poor Richard's Almanack* (1733–38) became hugely popular. In 1828 Noah Webster's *An American Dictionary of the English Language* identified a specifically American language that was developing apart from the English spoken in Britain.

American fiction

In the early 1800s novels and stories with a specifically American flavor began to appear. In the 1820s Washington Irving wrote stories about characters such as Ichabod Crane and Rip Van Winkle that are still read today. James Fenimore Cooper's novels, such as *The Last of the Mohicans* (1826), defined the popular idea of the American frontier. Nathaniel Hawthorne's most famous work, *The Scarlet Letter* (1850), is about the Puritan colonists of Salem, Massachusetts, in the 1600s.

Later novelists wrote about the social problems of the growing nation. Harriet Beecher Stowe attacked slavery in *Uncle Tom's Cabin* (1852). Stephen Crane's works focused on war and poverty. His best-known novel is *The Red Badge of Courage* (1895).

American poetry

Poets such as Henry Wadsworth Longfellow wrote verse about the history of America. They were popular in Europe as well as the United States. Two of the nation's greatest poets wrote in the late 1800s. Walt Whitman's work is full of passion for people working together

▲ *The novelist F. Scott Fitzgerald (1896–1940) wrote about the dark side of life in the jazz age of the 1920s.* **The Great Gatsby** *is his most famous novel.*

and appreciating nature. Emily Dickinson was much more concerned with the individual's inner thoughts, and her poems are often about death.

The 20th century

In the 1900s many novelists concentrated on the problems of society. Sinclair Lewis attacked the self-satisfied middle classes. John Dos Passos and John Steinbeck dealt sympathetically with the problems of the poor. Richard Wright, James Baldwin, Maya Angelou, and Ralph Ellison confronted racism and brought the African American perspective to a wide readership. But other writers did not deal with society in such a straightforward way. T. S. Eliot, Ezra Pound, and Gertrude Stein were all important figures in the Modernist movement. The language and structure of their writing was new and often difficult for readers.

The second half of the century saw the United States become one of the most important political, economic, and cultural

MAJOR AMERICAN WRITERS

These are just a few of the many writers who have shaped American literature. There are many more.

Irving, Washington (1783–1859)
Short story writer, influenced by New England folklore.

Longfellow, Henry Wadsworth (1807–1882)
Poet, wrote *The Song Of Hiawatha* and *Paul Revere's Ride*.

Poe, Edgar Allan (1809–49)
Short story writer and poet, wrote tales of suspense and horror.

Stowe, Harriet (Elizabeth) Beecher (1811–96)
Her powerful antislavery novel *Uncle Tom's Cabin* is often said to have been one of the causes of the Civil War.

Melville, Herman (1819–91)
Novelist, wrote tales of the sea, famously *Moby Dick*.

James, Henry (1843–1916)
Novelist, wrote about the relations between American and European cultures.

Wharton, Edith (Newbold) (1862–1937)
Novelist, wrote about women in high society.

Henry, O. (Porter, William Sidney) (1862–1910)
Short story writer, noted for a surprise twist at the end of his stories.

Frost, Robert (Lee) (1874–1963)
Based his poems on ordinary speech and set them in New England.

Williams, William Carlos (1883–1963)
Poet who wrote about the American landscape and people.

Eliot, T. S. (Thomas Stearns) (1888–1965)
Poet and critic, an important figure in the Modernist movement.

Hurston, Zora Neale (1891–1960)
Novelist influenced by Southern folklore.

Faulkner, William (Cuthbert) (1897–1962)
Novelist and short story writer, set most of his works in Mississippi.

Steinbeck, John (Ernst) (1902–68)
Novelist, wrote about migrant farm workers during the Depression.

Hughes, (James) Langston (1902–1967)
Poet and novelist of the Harlem Renaissance, wrote about the lives of ordinary black people.

Salinger, J. D. (Jerome David) (1919–)
Novelist and short story writer, author of *The Catcher In The Rye*.

Walker, Alice (1944–)
Novelist who won the Pulitzer Prize in 1983 for *The Color Purple*.

forces in the world. Authors such as Saul Bellow, Isaac Bashevis Singer, and Toni Morrison won the Nobel Prize in literature. In the past American writers looked to Europe for inspiration. Today the works of writers such as John Updike, Joan Didion, and Thomas Pynchon influence writers around the world. Although they usually deal with life in America, their style and themes are universal.

The poet Walt Whitman (1819–92) wrote about human relationships and nature.

Maya Angelou (1928–), novelist, critic, and autobiographer who writes about African American lives.

SEE ALSO: Hemingway, Ernest; Literature; Nobel Prize; Writers, World

✳ WRITERS, WORLD

People have recorded their thoughts in permanent form for over 5,000 years. But the word "writer" is usually applied to those with a skill for language.

People communicated and told stories well before the development of writing. Tales were passed down the generations by word of mouth. Many were myths that tried to explain the mysteries of creation or the weather.

The first examples of written language come from Sumeria (modern Iraq) in about 3500 B.C. *The Epic of Gilgamesh*, a Sumerian poem from about 2500 B.C., is one of the earliest known pieces of creative writing. Some of the stories that make up the Old Testament of the Bible also date from around this time.

The ancient Greeks and Romans wrote classical works that are still read today. The great poems of Homer and Virgil and the dramas of Sophocles and Plautus influenced many later writers. The Greek writer Aesop wrote short moral stories called fables that are still popular today. Lady Murasaki, in Japan, wrote about love and politics; Shi Nai-an, in China, wrote *The Water Margin*, tales of legendary heroes and warriors.

Printed books

From the 1200s poets, such as Dante, Boccaccio, and Chaucer, wrote long works about religion, love, and life that are still popular. However, most people still could not read. When Johannes Gutenberg invented the printing press in the 1400s, books became cheaper and easier to produce. Gradually, more people learned to read.

At the same time, people became more interested in the world around them and in how it worked. This period is called the Renaissance.

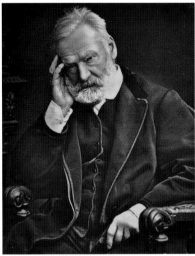

The French novelist and poet Victor Hugo (1802–85) wrote books such as Notre-Dame de Paris (The Hunchback of Notre Dame) that criticized social and political injustice.

Books of nonfiction—dealing with facts, not stories or poems—were important in communicating ideas.

Until the early 1800s poetry was the most popular form of imaginative writing. Even dramatists, such as Shakespeare and Moliére, usually wrote in verse. The first great European novel was Cervantes's *Don Quixote*, published in the early 1600s. In the 1700s the English writer Henry Fielding developed the form, with books such as *Tom Jones*. But the greatest novelists wrote in the 1800s. They included Charles Dickens, Jane Austen, and the Brontë sisters in England; Victor Hugo, Honoré de Balzac, and Emile Zola in France; and Leo Tolstoy and Fyodor Dostoyevsky in Russia. They used the novel to study emotions and society.

Charlotte Brontë and her sisters Emily and Anne in England wrote poems and short stories as well as novels. Charlotte's most famous novel, Jane Eyre, is based on her experiences as a governess in a large house.

441

GREAT WRITERS

These are just a few of the world's most famous writers. There are many, many more.

Homer (about 800s B.C.)
Ancient Greek poet, wrote the *Iliad* and the *Odyssey*, epic (heroic) poems about the Trojan War and Odysseus's travels afterward.

Lady Murasaki (Murasaki Shikibu) (about A.D. 978–1026)
Japanese author and diarist, wrote the six-part *Tale of Genji*, regarded by many as the first novel.

Dante (Alighieri) (1265–1321)
Italian poet, wrote *The Divine Comedy*, the tale of a journey from hell to heaven.

Chaucer, Geoffrey (about 1343–1400)
English poet (pictured below), wrote *The Canterbury Tales*, a collection of stories told by a group of pilgrims.

Cervantes, Miguel de (1547–1616)
Spanish author of *Don Quixote*, an important early novel about a deluded, romantic knight.

Milton, John (1608–1674)
English poet, wrote *Paradise Lost*, based on the biblical stories of Adam, Eve, and Satan.

Goethe, Johann Wolfgang von (1749–1832)
German poet, dramatist, and novelist, wrote *Faust*, the best-known version of a legend about a scholar who sells his soul to Satan.

Brontë, Charlotte (1816–55), **Emily (Jane)** (1818–48), and **Anne** (1820–49)
English sisters who wrote passionate novels with strong female characters. The best known are Charlotte's *Jane Eyre* and Emily's *Wuthering Heights*.

Eliot, George (Evans, Mary Ann) (1819–80)
English novelist who wrote under a man's name. Her most famous work is *Middlemarch*.

Tolstoy, Leo (1828–1910)
Russian novelist, wrote *War and Peace* and *Anna Karenina*. A major writer about people's place in history and society.

Woolf, (Adeline) Virginia (1882–1941)
English novelist and essayist. Developed new, nonrealistic styles of writing fiction, particularly stream of consciousness, which mimics the flow of thoughts by using words without punctuation.

García Márquez, Gabriel (1928–)
Colombian novelist, wrote *One Hundred Years of Solitude*, the magical tale of an imaginary South American community.

▶ *A 19th-century illustration from the Tale of Genji by Lady Murasaki. The novel describes Japanese court society. Lady Murasaki was a lady-in-waiting at the royal court at the beginning of the 11th century.*

Modern writers

In the 1900s some writers became dissatisfied with traditional forms of fiction and poetry. Writers such as James Joyce and Virginia Woolf were important figures in a movement called Modernism. At first many people did not understand their works because they did not always follow normal rules of grammar and sentence structure. Their books challenged traditional ideas and certainties about religion and society.

Other novelists experimented with new subjects. The French novelist Marcel Proust explored the workings of human memory and emotions in *Remembrance of Things Past*. Austrian writer Franz Kafka portrayed a frightening world of isolation and despair. German writer Thomas Mann described the conflicts between artists and society.

From the late 1900s movies, pop music and other new art forms influenced many writers. But the most popular writers remain those who can tell a story that holds the attention—just like the storytellers who passed their tales down even before writing was invented.

SEE ALSO: Ancient Civilizations; Literature; Printing; Renaissance; Shakespeare, William; Theater; Writers, American

✳ X-RAY

X-rays are similar to light in many ways. But there is one important difference—x-rays can penetrate many materials that will stop most forms of light.

X-rays are beamed through an object to a sheet of photographic film. The image of the inner structure of the object is recorded on the film. The material in one part of the object may be penetrated by many more x-rays than the material in another part. This difference will show on the film, revealing the inner structure of the object. One use of x-rays is to inspect machinery and metal parts for flaws.

Medical uses

Doctors use x-rays to show the inner parts of the body. X-rays can tell the difference between bone, soft tissues (muscles, blood vessels, and major organs), fat, and air (in the lungs). An x-ray picture of an arm shows the bones because the x-rays cannot move through them as easily as the muscles around them. A chest x-ray shows the heart surrounded by air in the lungs. The branch of medicine that uses x-rays is called radiology.

In the late 1960s scientists developed an x-ray machine called a computerized axial tomography (CAT) scanner. It is a combination of an x-ray machine and a computer. The CAT scanner produces cross-sectional views of the body and is particularly useful for examining the brain, chest, and stomach.

History

X-rays were discovered accidentally by the German scientist Wilhelm Conrad Roentgen in 1895, when he was experimenting with a special kind of lamp called a cathode-ray tube. Although Roentgen learned how to produce the new rays and became familiar with their characteristics, he never found out exactly what they were. For this reason he called them x-rays, "x" standing for unknown.

HOW X-RAYS WORK

x-rays

photographic plate

image on x-ray film

▷ *The best-known use of x-rays is in medicine. The beam of x-rays is sent through the patient's body onto a plate of photographic film. Bones absorb a large amount of the x-rays and show up as white shadows on the film. Other tissues absorb fewer x-rays, so they show up as gray areas.*

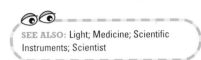

SEE ALSO: Light; Medicine; Scientific Instruments; Scientist

✳ YUKON TERRITORY

The Yukon Territory lies in the northwestern corner
of Canada's mainland. It borders British Columbia,
Alaska, Northwest Territories, and the Beaufort Sea.

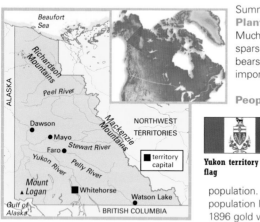

Most of the Yukon consists of a high
central plateau—about 3,940 ft. (1,200m)
above sea level—broken up by mountains
and deep valleys. Many of the Yukon's
mountains are covered by permanent
ice caps. They include Canada's tallest
peaks—Mount Logan is the highest
mountain in Canada.

Winters are mostly very cold. The
lowest temperature ever recorded
in Canada is –81°F (–63°C) at Snag.

Summers are warm and can be hot.

Plant and animal life

Much of the Yukon's forest is very
sparse and slow growing. Fish,
bears, and caribou are traditionally
important for food and clothing.

People, history, and economy

**Yukon territory
flag**

Native Americans and
Inuits have lived in the
area for centuries, and
Native Americans now
make up about 20
percent of the
population. Over 75 percent of the
population live in the Whitehorse area. In
1896 gold was discovered at Bonanza
Creek, starting the world's biggest gold
rush. In 1898 the Yukon became a
separate territory.

Although there are still gold, silver, zinc,
lead, and copper mines, the mining
industry began to decline in the late 20th
century. The population is also decreasing.
Today tourism and government provide
the majority of jobs.

SEE ALSO: Canada; Inuit

AREA
205,346 sq. mi.
(531,844 sq. km);
rank, 3rd territory

POPULATION
29,900 (2001
census); rank, 2nd
territory

ELEVATION
Highest—19,524 ft.
(5,951m) at Mt.
Logan; lowest—
sea level

CAPITAL
Whitehorse

**TERRITORY
ESTABLISHED**
1898

**TERRITORY
MOTTO**
No official motto

**TERRITORY
FLOWER**
Purple firewood

**TERRITORY
TREE**
Subalpine fir

**TERRITORY
BIRD**
Common raven

✳ ZOOLOGY

Zoology is the branch of science that deals with all aspects of animal life. The word comes from the Greek for "knowledge of animals."

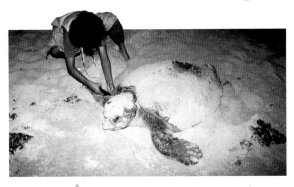

A zoologist tags a loggerhead turtle at the Archie Carr National Wildlife Refuge in Florida, where the habitat and nesting areas of the turtles are being protected.

Scientists studied animals thousands of years ago. Aristotle, in ancient Greece, and Pliny the Elder, in Rome, both tried to classify all animal species.

In the 1500s Leonardo da Vinci and Andreas Vesalius dissected (cut up) animals in order to discover more about the body. In the 1700s Carolus Linnaeus created the modern system of classifying animals. It uses a different Latin name for each kind of animal.

In the 1800s the English scientist Charles Darwin was the first to publish a theory of evolution—that animal species adapt to their environments over generations. The 1900s saw new discoveries about inheritance involving genes and DNA. These developments expanded scientific knowledge about all forms of life, including animals. In recent years zoologists have taken a more active role in protecting animal life, not just observing but campaigning against human activity that puts animals in danger.

Some zoologists concentrate on observing animals in their natural habitat. They may be researching animal behavior or seeking ways to protect endangered species. Others work in zoos or safari parks. Many species of animal would now be extinct (died out) if they had not been kept in captivity. Zoologists working in natural history museums also use their knowledge to inform the public.

Many zoologists work in universities or laboratories. They study live animals and cell samples. Their scientific discoveries benefit humans as well as animals.

SEE ALSO: Animal; Aristotle; Biology; Botany; DNA; Environment; Evolution; Genetics; Leonardo da Vinci; Science; Scientist

PICTURE CREDITS